CIVIL WAR BOOKS

A Priced Checklist

Second Edition

1983

by

Tom Broadfoot and Marianne Pair

Roger Hunt
Union Regimentals

1983

Broadfoot Publishing Co.

Wendell, N. C.

This volume is dedicated to my father
Winston Broadfoot,
who urged me to become a bookdealer
rather than get a job.

1st Edition 1978
Reprinted 1979
Second Edition October 1983

Additional copies are available
from Broadfoot's Bookmark
Route 3, Box 318
Wendell, N. C. 27591

PREFACE

The values given in this volume are our estimate of the retail value for good used copies in the market of late 1983. These values were determined almost entirely from the 18,000 plus entries we have catalogued since the first edition of this checklist in 1978.

We made no attempt to list all Civil War titles. Unless we knew the value of a particular title it was not listed.

There are also omissions of choice as follows:

1. Removed magazine and journal articles.

2. Removed government documents unless of particular value.

3. For titles published in many editions, in most cases we did not list all editions after 1970.

From all indications the interest in Civil War books is stronger than ever. There are more collectors; values, especially of rare material, are rapidly increasing and many new titles are being published and reprinted in the field.

I hope you will find this volume worthwhile. Suggestions, comments and corrections are solicited. Criticisms are especially welcome — those we find most valuable.

Tom Broadfoot
Wendell, NC
August 1983

HOW TO USE THIS GUIDE

A. Determine the category of the volume you wish to evaluate.

GENERAL BOOKS: This category contains most Civil War volumes.

REGIMENTALS: Material containing information relating to particular states or fighting units is contained within this section. In this category are most narratives by soldiers, memorials and funeral sermons for soldiers, and annual reunions and veterans' reports. Location of regimentals can best be determined by the title or the author's or subject's unit of service.

CONFEDERATE IMPRINTS: Material printed in the Confederate States during the War is considered to be of Confederate imprint. This designation also applies to material printed in other countries for the Confederacy and brought through the blockade. Official publications of the Confederate States Government in Richmond date from February 1861 through March 1865. In identifying imprints by place of publication, the dates of secession constitute a useful guideline.

 1. South Carolina — Dec. 20, 1860
 2. Mississippi — Jan. 9, 1861
 3. Florida — Jan. 10, 1861
 4. Alabama — Jan. 11, 1861
 5. Georgia — Jan. 19, 1861
 6. Louisiana — Jan. 26, 1861
 7. Texas — Feb. 1, 1861
 8. Virginia — Apr. 17, 1861
 9. Arkansas — May 6, 1861
 10. North Carolina — May 20, 1861
 11. Tennessee — June 8, 1861
 *12. Missouri — Aug. 19, 1861
 *13. Kentucky — Dec. 9, 1861

*Rump sessions of the Missouri and Kentucky legislatures passed ordinances of secession and these states were admitted into the Confederacy on Aug. 19 and Dec. 9, 1861. For this reason the Confederate flag contained thirteen stars. In reality both Kentucky and Missouri were divided states, and neither contributed much in the way of Confederate imprints. Thus far only two Confederate imprints have been assigned to Kentucky and four to Missouri.

B. Find the volume within the category.

Look under the author's last name.
If no author is given, look under name of editor or compiler.
If neither author nor editor is given, look under the title.

DETERMINING VALUE

Having found a listing for your title, match the editions. The price given will be for a good used copy. Titles after 1940 are assumed to have original dust-jackets.

Determining good used condition is akin to nailing down the exact definition of a pretty woman. However, the following points should be considered.

CONDITIONS NOT AFFECTING VALUE

1. Previous owners name or inscription on front fly
2. Tasteful bookplate verso front cover
3. Minor soiling or rubbing of cover — some wear is assumed
4. Minor fraying of dust jacket — some wear is assumed

CONDITIONS ADDING TO VALUE

1. Dust jacket for titles prior to 1940. These are difficult to evaluate as frequently the dust wrap is worth as much as the book.
2. Signature or presentation by author. Unless author is in the Lincoln or Lee category the additional value is probably $5 - $10.
3. Marginal notations by author or someone of knowledge adding or correcting information in the text.

DEFECTS
Common and Forgivable — But Detracting from Value

1. Former owners name elsewhere than front fly
2. Embossed seals
3. Library markings within the text — except on title page (see next category)
4. Lack of dust-jacket for books after 1940, or dust-jacket chipped or torn
5. Notations or underlining in pencil
6. More than minor wear to cover; tips of spine chipped, corners rubbed, hinges loose or cracked, fading
7. Pages folded, foxed (brown spots from age), unevenly separated at outer edges, soiled, torn without loss of text

DEFECTS
Major

1. Rebound or lacking original covers or wraps
2. Library markings on title page or spine
3. Extensive underlining — non-erasable
4. Cover or pages badly stained

THE DEFECT
FATAL TO ALL BUT THE RAREST OF BOOKS

Loss of text via missing pages, page or any portion of a page containing written matter.

CONTENTS

Page

HOW TO USE THIS GUIDE..vii

GENERAL BOOKS 1

U. S. GOVERNMENT PUBLICATIONS.......................................194

REGIMENTALS AND STATE INTEREST 197

CONFEDERATE IMPRINTS: OFFICIAL PUBLICATIONS.....................309

CONFEDERATE IMPRINTS: UNOFFICIAL PUBLICATIONS 324

GENERAL

BOOKS

AARON, Daniel   The Unwritten War, American Writers and the Civil War.
    1973   New York   20.
ABBOT, Willis J.   Battle Fields and Camp Fires.
    1889   New York   30.
    1890   New York   25.
ABBOT, Willis J.   Blue Jackets of '61 A History of the Navy in the War of Secession.
    1886   New York   30.
    1889   New York   25.
    1890   New York   25.
ABBOT, Willis J.   The Naval History of the United States. 2 vols.
    1896   New York   35.
ABBOTT, Henry L.   Course of Lectures Upon the Defence of the Seacoast of the United
    States. Wraps
    1888   New York   30.
ABBOTT, Henry L.   Siege Artillery in the Campaigns Against Richmond. Wraps
    1867   Washington   75.
ABBOTT, John S. C.   History of the Civil War in America. 2 vols.
    1863-66   New York   20.
    1863-66   Springfield   20.
ABBOTT, John S. C.   The Life of General Ulysses S. Grant
    1868   Boston   20.
    1872   Boston   15.
ABDILL, George B.   Civil War Railroads, Pictorial Story of the Iron Horse 1861-1865.
    1961   New York   25.
    1961   Seattle   25.
    n.d.   New York   20.
ABEL, Annie H.   The Slaveholding Indians. 3 vols.
    1915-1925   Cleveland   450.
    Vol. 1 — American Indians as Slaveholder & Secessionist   150.
    Vol. II - American Indians as Participant in Civil War   150.
    Vol III — American Indians Under Reconstruction   100.
ABEL, Parker   Uncle Tom in England or A Proof That Black's White. Wraps
    1852(?)   New York   35.
About the War, Plain Words to Plain People by a Plain Man. Wraps
    1863   Philadelphia   20.
Abraham Lincoln Der Wiederherfteller Der Nordamerifanifchen Union. Wraps
    1866   Leipzig   35.
Abraham Lincoln, His Efforts to Make America a White Nation. Wraps
    n.d.   (Circa 1930)   n.p.   20.
Abraham Lincoln Quarterly. Wraps
    1940-1952   125.
ABRAHAMS, Robert D.   Mr. Benjamin's Sword
    1948   Philadelphia   10.
ABRAHAMS, Robert D.   The Uncommon Soldier: Major Alfred Mordecai.
    1959   n.p.   10.
ABSHIRE, David M.   The South Rejects a Prophet, the Life of Senator D. M. Key
    1824-1900.
    1967   New York   15.
Acceptance and Unveiling of the Statue of Wade Hampton.
    1929   Washington   20.
Acceptance and Unveiling of the Statues of Jefferson Davis and James Z. George.
    1932   Washington   15.
**Acceptance of the Statues of George Washington and Robert E. Lee Presented by the State
    of Virginia.**
    1934   Washington   15.
**An Account of the Reception Given by the Citizens of N.Y. to the Survivors of the
    Officers and Crews of the U.S. Frigates Cumberland & Congress.**
    1862   New York   25.

Account of the Supplies Sent to Savannah. Wraps
    1865   Boston   25.
ACHESON, Sam and **O'CONNELL,** Julia (eds)   **George Washington Diamond's Account of the Great Hanging at Gainesville, 1862.**
    1963   Austin   10.
ADAM, G. Mercer   **The Life of General Robert E. Lee.**
    1905   New York   20.
ADAMS, Charles Francis   **Charles Frances Adams 1835-1915 An Autobiography.**
    1916   Boston   15.
ADAMS, Charles Francis   **The Confederacy and the Transvaal: A People's Obligation to Robert E. Lee.** Wraps
    1901   Boston   10.
ADAMS, Charles Francis   **A Cycle of Adams Letters 1861-1865** edited by Worthington C. Ford
    1920   Boston/New York   2 vols.   20.
    1921   London   2 vols.   15.
    1969   New York   2 vols. in one   15.
ADAMS, Charles Francis   **Lee at Appomattox.**
    1902   Boston & New York   15.
ADAMS, Charles Francis   **Lee's Centennial: An Address Delivered at Lexington, Virginia.**
    1948   Chicago   15.
ADAMS, Charles Francis   **Seward and the Declaration of Paris.** Wraps
    1912   Boston   25.
ADAMS, Charles Francis   **Some Phases of the Civil War.** Wraps
    1906   Cambridge   15.
ADAMS, Charles Francis   **Speech of _____ of Mass., Delivered in the House of Representatives, Jan. 31, 1861.** Wraps
    1861   Washington   10.
ADAMS, Charles Francis   **Studies; Military and Diplomatic**
    1911   New York   20.
ADAMS, Charles Francis   **"Tis Sixty Years Since," Address.**
    1913   New York   15.
ADAMS, Charles Francis   **Trans-Atlantic Historical Solidarity.**
    1913   Oxford   20.
ADAMS, Ephraim D.   **Great Britain and the American Civil War**
    1925   London   2 vols.   30.
    1957   New York   2 vols. in 1   15.
    1957   Gloucester   2 vols. in 1   15.
    1958   New York   2 vols. in 1   15.
    1960   New York   2 vols. in 1   15.
ADAMS, F. Colburn   **Siege of Washington, D.C.**
    1867   New York   20.
ADAMS, George Worthington   **Doctors in Blue.**
    1952   New York   30.
ADAMS, George Worthington (ed)   **Mary Logan — Reminiscence of the Civil War and Reconstruction**
    1970   Carbondale, Ill.   15.
ADAMS, Henry   **The Great Secession Winter of 1860-61.** edited by George Hochfield
    1958   New York   15.
ADAMS, James Truslow   **America's Tragedy.**
    1934   New York   15.
    1935   New York   15.
ADAMS, Julia Davis   **Stonewall.**
    1931   New York   30.
ADAMS, N.   **A South Side View of Slavery.**
    1855   Boston   30.

ADAMS, Nehemiah   **The Sable Cloud: A Southern Tale, with Northern Comments.**
  1861   Boston   25.
ADAMS, William F.   Blue and Gray series in matched bindings with decorated boards
  Brother Against Brother   1894   Boston   15.
  A Lieutenant At Eighteen   1896   Boston   15.
  On the Staff   1897   Boston   15.
  Our Standard Bearer   1868   Boston   15.
  Stand by the Union   1892   Boston   15.
  Taken by the Enemy   1888   Boston   15.
  A Victorious Union   1894   Boston   15.
  Within the Enemy's Lines   1890/1894   Boston   15.
  The Yankee Middy   1875   Boston   15.
ADDEY, Markinfield   **"Old Jack" and His Foot Cavalry.**
  1864   New York   65.
  1865   New York   60.
ADDEY, Markinfield   **"Stonewall Jackson," Life and Military Career of Thomas
Jonathan Jackson.**
  1863   New York   60.
The Address of Southern Delegates in Congress, to Their Constituents. Wraps
  n.d.   n.p.   50.
AFFLECK, C. J. & Douglas, B.M.   **Confederate Bonds and Certificates.** Wraps
  1960   Boyce, Va.   20.
AGEE, Rucker   **Forrest-Streight Campaign of 1863.** Wraps
  1958   Milwaukee (?)   25.
AGEE, Rucker   **Let's Keep the Record Straight!** Wraps
  1963   Birmingham (?)   10.
AGNEW, Daniel   **The Spirit and Poetry of Law.** Wraps
  1866   Philadelphia   10.
AGNUS, Felix   **A Woman of War and Other Stories.**
  1908   Baltimore   15.
AIMONE, Alan Conrad   **Official Records of the American Civil War.**
  1972   West Point   10.
AIKEN, Warren   **Letters of _____ , Confederate Congressman.** edited by Bell I. Wiley
  1959   Athens   15.
ALBAUGH, William A. III, and **SIMMONS,** Edward N.   **Confederate Arms.**
  1957   Harrisburg   30.
  1960   Harrisburg   25.
  n.d.   New York   Bonanza reprint   15.
ALBAUGH, William A., III   **The Confederate Brass-Framed Colt & Whitney.** Wraps
  1955   Falls Church, Va.   Ltd.   50.
ALBAUGH, William A., III   **Confederate Edged Weapons.**
  1960   New York   35.
  n.d.   New York   reprint   15.
ALBAUGH, William A., III   **Confederate Faces.**
  1970   Salona Beach, Cal.   125.
ALBAUGH, William A, **BENET,** Hugh, and **SIMMONS,** Edward   **Confederate
Handguns**
  1963   Philadelphia   40.
  1963   New York   40.
  1967   Philadelphia   25.
  1969   New York   25.
  n.d.   New York   Bonanza reprint   15.
ALBAUGH, William A., III and **STEUART,** Richard D.   **Handbook of Confederate
Swords.** Wraps
  1951   Harriman   20.
ALBAUGH, William A., III   **More Confederate Faces.**
  1972 (?)   Washington   50.

ALBAUGH, William A., III and **STEUART,** Richard D.   **The Original Confederate Colt**
    1953   New York   35.

ALBAUGH, William A., III   **A Photographic Supplement of Confederate Swords.**
    1979   Orange, Va.   20.

ALBAUGH, William A.   **Tyler, Texas, C.S.A.**
    1958   Harrisburg, Pa.   15.

ALCOTT, Louisa M.   **Hospital Sketches and Camp and Fireside Stories**
    1869   Boston   30.
    1890   Boston   25.
    1960   Cambridge   15.

ALDEN, Carroll Storrs   **George Hamilton Perkins Commodore, U.S.N., His Life and Letters.**
    1914   Boston   30.

ALDEN, James   **Official Memoir of Lieutenant Commander A. Boyd Cummings, U.S.N.** Wraps
    1862 (?)   n.p.   15.

ALDERMAN, Edwin Anderson & Gordon, Armistead C.   **J.L.M. Curry.**
    1911   New York   25.

ALEXANDER, Augustus W.   **Grant as a Soldier.**
    1887   St. Louis   15.

ALEXANDER, E. P.   **The American Civil War.**
    1908   London   75.

ALEXANDER, Edward P.   **Military Memoirs of a Confederate.**
    1907   New York   100.
    1908   New York   80.
    1910   New York   75.
    1912   New York   75.
    1914   n.p.   60.
    1962   Bloomington   30.
    1977   Dayton   30.

ALEXANDER, Edwin P.   **Civil War Railroads and Models.**
    1977   New York   15.

ALEXANDER, Frederick Warren   **Stratford and the Lees Connected with Its History.**
    1912   Oak Grove, Va.   20.

ALEXANDER, Holmes M.   **Washington and Lee.**
    1966   Belmont, Mass.   15.

ALEXANDER, John Brevard   **Reminiscences of the Past Sixty Years.**
    1908   Charlotte, N. C.   50.

ALEXANDER, Thomas B. and **BERINGER,** Richard E. (eds.)   **The Anatomy of the Confederate Congress.**
    1972   Nashville   15.

ALEXANDER, Thomas B.   **Thomas A. R. Nelson of East Tennessee.**
    1956   Nashville   10.

ALEXANDER, William   **Elements of Discord in Secessia.** Wraps
    1863   New York   10.

The "Alexandria" The Attorney-General versus Sillem and Others.
    1863   Liverpool   75.

ALFRIEND, Frank H.   **Life of Jefferson Davis.**
    1868   Cincinnati   30.

ALLABEN, Frank   **John Watts De Peyster.** 2 vols.
    1908   New York   20.

ALLAN, Elizabeth Preston   **The Life and Letters of Margaret Junkin Preston.**
    1903   Boston   50.

ALLAN, Elizabeth Randolph Preston   **A March Past, Reminiscences of** _____ edited by Janet A. Bryan
    1938   Richmond   40.

ALLAN, Lyman Whitney   **Abraham Lincoln. A Poem.**
    1909   New York   7.

ALLAN, William. **The Army of Northern Virginia in 1862.**
    1892   Boston   125.
ALLEN, William   **History of the Campaign of Gen. T. J. (Stonewall) Jackson in the Shenandoah Valley of Virginia.**
    1880   Philadelphia   175.
    1892   Boston   100.
    1912   London   entitled: **Stonewall Jackson's Campaign in the Shenandoah Valley**   100.
    1974   Dayton   15.
ALLEN, William   **Jackson's Valley Campaign, Address.** Wraps
    1878   Richmond   125.
ALLEMAN, Mrs. Tillie Pierce   **At Gettysburg, or, What a Girl Saw and Heard of the Battle.**
    1889   New York   45.
ALLEN, Hall   **Center of Conflict.** Wraps
    1961   Paducah   10.
ALLEN, Hervey   **Action at Aquila.**
    1938   New York   15.
ALLEN, Ivan   **Atlanta from the Ashes.**
    1928   Atlanta   Ltd.   20.
ALLEN, James S.   **Reconstruction — The Battle for Democracy.**
    1937   New York   20.
ALLEN, Walter   **"Public Duty Is My Only Master" Governor Chamberlain's Administration in South Carolina.**
    1888   New York   50.
ALLEN, Walter   **Ullysses S. Grant.**
    1901   Boston   10.
ALLEN, William H. (comp.)   **The American Civil War Book and Grant Album.**
    1894   Boston   40.
ALLSOP, Fred W.   **Albert Pike, A Biography.**
    1982   Little Rock   40.
ALOE, A.   **Twelfth U.S. Infantry: 1789-1919.**
    1919   New York   25.
Alphabetical Index to Places of Interment of Deceased Union Soldiers in the Various States and Territories. Wraps
    1868   Washington   20.
Alphabetical List of Graduates of the Virginia Military Institute from 1839 to 1910 with Post Office Address. Wraps
    1910   Lynchburg, Va.   20.
Alphabetical List of the Battles of the War of the Rebellion with Dates. Wraps
    n.d. (circa 1870)   Philadelphia   20.
ALSTON, J. Motte   **Rice Planter and Sportsman, the Recollections of _____ 1821-1909** edited by Arney R. Childs
    1953   Columbia, S. C.   25.
ALTSHELER, Joseph A.   **Before the Dawn, a Story of the Fall of Richmond.**
    1903   New York   25.
ALTSHELER, Joseph A.   **The Guns of Shiloh.**
    1942   New York   20.
ALTSHELER, Joseph A.   **The Sword of Antietam.**
    1942   New York   25.
ALTSHELER, Joseph A.   **The Tree of Appomattox: A Story of the Civil War's Close.**
    1916   New York   16.
ALVERSON, James Gibson & James Jr. (eds.)   **Memoirs of J. M. Gibson: Terrors of the Civil War and Reconstruction Days** by J. M. Gibson
    1929   Houston, Texas   20.
AMANN, William (ed.)   **Personnel of the Civil War.**
    1961   New York   30.
    1964   New York   25.
    1968   New York   25.

AMBROSE, Stephen E.   **Halleck: Lincoln's Chief of Staff.**
   1962   Baton Rouge   20.
AMBROSE, Stephen E.   **Struggle for Vicksburg.**
   1967   Harrisburg, Pa.   25.
AMBROSE, Stephen E.   **Upton and the Army.**
   1964   Baton Rouge   30.
American Almanac for 1861.
   1861   Boston   20.
American Annual Cyclopedia and Register of Important Events 1861-1865.
   5 vols.
   n.d.   n.p.   100.
American Caricatures Pertaining to the Civil War.
   1918   New York   30.
American Christian Commission Doc. 1. Wraps
   1867   New York   15.
The American Civil War: A Centennial Exhibition, Library of Congress. Wraps
   1961   Washington   20.
The American Jew in the Civil War, an Exhibit . . . Los Angeles, Dec. 10, 1962 To Jan. 11, 1963. Wraps
   n.d.   n.p.   10.
The American Soldier in the Civil War.
   1895   New York   60.
American War Songs.
   1925   Philadelphia   20.
AMES, Adelbert   **Capture of Fort Fisher, North Carolina Jan. 15, 1865.** Wraps
   1897   n.p.   35.
AMES, Blanche   **Adelbert Ames, General, Senator, Governor — 1835-1933**
   1964   London   25.
   1964   New York   20.
AMES, Blanche Butler (comp)   **Chronicles from the Nineteenth Century — Family Letters of Blanche Butler and Adelbert Ames.** 2 vols.
   1957   Clinton, Mass.   30.
AMES, Herman V.   **John C. Calhoun and Secession Movement of 1850.** Wraps
   1918   Worcester   15.
AMES, Mary   **From a New England Woman's Diary in Dixie in 1865.**
   1906   Springfield, Mass.   20.
AMMEN, Daniel   **The Atlantic Coast.**
   1883   New York   25.
   1885   New York   25.
AMMEN, Daniel   **The Old Navy and the New.**
   1891   Philadelphia   45.
ANDERS, Curt   **Fighting Confederates.**
   1968   New York   25.
ANDERSON, Archer   **Robert Edward Lee: An Address Delivered at The Dedication of the Monument to General Robert Edward Lee at Richmond, Va., May 29, 1890.**
   1890   Richmond   30.
ANDERSON, Bern   **By Sea and By River, the Naval History of the Civil War.**
   1962   New York   20.
ANDERSON, Betty Baxter   **Alabama Raider.**
   1957   Philadelphia   10.
ANDERSON, Charles   **The Cause of the War: Who Brought It On and for What Purpose? A Speech.** Wraps.
   1863   New York   15.
ANDERSON, Charles   **Letter Addressed to the Opera House Meeting, Cincinnati.** Wraps
   1863   New York   20.
ANDERSON, Charles C.   **Fighting By Southern Federals.**
   1912   New York   125.

ANDERSON, Edward C.　**Confederate Foreign Agent.** edited by Wm. Stanley Hoole.
　　1973　　Dayton　　12.50
ANDERSON, Frank Maloy　**The Mystery of "A Public Man."**
　　1948　　Minneapolis　　25.
ANDERSON, Galusha　**The Story of a Border City During the Civil War.**
　　1908　　Boston　　30.
　　1918　　Washington　　20.
ANDERSON, J. H.　**Grant's Campaign in Virginia May 1 — June 30, 1864.**
　　1908　　London　　75.
ANDERSON, J. C.　**Notes on the Life of Stonewall Jackson and His Campaigning in Virginia.**
　　1904　　London　　125.
　　1905　　London　　100.
ANDERSON, James H.　**Life and Letters of Judge Thomas J. Anderson and Wife.**
　　1904　　n.p.　　50.
ANDERSON, John Q.　**A Texas Surgeon in the C.S.A.** Wraps
　　1957　　Tuscaloosa　　Ltd.　　30.
ANDERSON, Mabel Washbourne　**The Life of General Stand Watie.**
　　1915　　Pryor, Okla.　　75.
　　1931　　Pryor, Okla.　　60.
ANDERSON, Nicholas Longworth　**The Letters and Journals of _____** edited by Isabel Anderson
　　1892　　New York　　25.
ANDERSON, Thomas M.　**The Political Conspiracies Preceding the Rebellion.**
　　1882　　New York　　20.
ANDREWS, C. C.　**History of the Campaign of Mobile.**
　　1867　　New York　　80.
ANDREWS, Eliza Frances　**The War Time Journal of a Georgia Girl.**
　　1908　　New York　　50.
　　1960　　Macon, Ga.　　edited by Spencer Bidwell King, Jr.　　20.
ANDREWS, J. Cutler　**The North Reports the Civil War.**
　　1955　　Pittsburgh　　Ltd. autographed edition　　30.
　　trade edition　　25.
ANDREWS, J. Cutler　**The South Reports the Civil War.**
　　1970　　Princeton　　25.
　　1971　　Princeton　　25.
ANDREWS, Marietta Minnigerode　**Memoirs of A Poor Relation.**
　　1927　　New York　　30.
ANDREWS, Marietta Minnegerode　**Scraps of Paper.**
　　1929　　New York　　30.
ANDREWS, Mary　**The Counsel Assigned.**
　　1920　　New York　　10.
ANDREWS, Mary Raymond Shipman　**The Perfect Tribute.**
　　1907　　New York　　10.
　　1910　　New York　　10.
ANDREWS, Matthew Page　**The Dixie Book of Days.**
　　1912　　Philadelphia　　15.
ANDREWS, Matthew Page　**Women of the South in War Times.**
　　1920　　Baltimore　　30.
　　1923　　Baltimore　　25.
　　1924　　Baltimore　　25.
ANDREWS, Sidney　**The South Since the War.**
　　1866　　Boston　　40.
ANGLE, Paul M.　**Abraham Lincoln His Autobiographical Writings.**
　　1948　　New Brunswick　　Ltd. & numbered　　20.
ANGLE, Paul M. and **MIERS**, Earl S.　**A Ballad of the North and South.**
　　1959　　Kingsport, Tenn.　　Ltd.　　Boxed　　25.
ANGLE, Paul M.　**"Created Equal" The Complete Lincoln Douglas Debates of 1858.**
　　1958　　Chicago　　20.

ANGLE, Paul M.   **Here I Have Lived. A History of Lincoln's Springfield 1821-1865.**
    1935   Springfield   20.
    1950   New Brunswick   15.
ANGLE, Paul M., et al.   **Lincoln Day by Day.** 4 vols.
    1933-41   Springfield   50.
ANGLE, Paul M. (ed)   **The Lincoln Reader.**
    1947   New Brunswick   10.
ANGLE, Paul and **MIERS,** Earl   **The Living Lincoln.**
    1955   New Brunswick   10.
ANGLE, Paul M.   **New Letters and Papers of Lincoln.**
    1930   Boston   20.
ANGLE, Paul M.   **A Pictorial History of the Civil War Years.**
    1967   New York   15.
ANGLE, Paul M.   **A Shelf of Lincoln Books, A Critical, Selective Bibliography of Lincolniana.**
    1946   New Brunswick   20.
ANGLE, Paul M., & **MIERS,** Earl S.   **The Tragic Years.**
    2 vols.
    1960   New York   20.
The Annals of Harper's Ferry with Sketches of Its Founder . . .by Josephus, Junior. Wraps
    1872   Martinsburg, WV   50.
Annals of the War. See: **MCCLURE,** Alexander K.
Annual Reports. See: Issuing organization
ANTRIM, Earl   **Civil War Prisons and Their Covers.**
    1961   New York   30.
A. O. W. See: **WHEELER,** A. O.
An Appeal for the Union. Wraps
    1860   n.p.   25.
APPELL, George C.   **The Man Who Shot Quantrill.**
    1957   New York   10.
APPLER, A. C.   **The Younger Brothers, Their Life and Character.**
    1955   New York   10.
APTHEKER, Herbert   **The Negro in the Civil War.** Wraps
    1938   New York   35.
ARCENEAUX, William   **Acadian General, Alfred Mouton and the Civil War.**
    1981   Lafayette, La.   20.
ARCHER, W.   **Through Afro-America; An English Reading of the Race Problem.**
    1910   New York   45.
AMES, Ethel   **Stratford Hall, The Great House of the Lee's.**
    1936   Richmond   Lts. & signed   125.
    trade edition   80.
Army and Navy Offical Gazette. Vols. 1 & 2, 1863-1865.   1864 & 1865
    Washington   150.
    Vol. 1   75.
    Vol. 2   75.
The Army Reunion.
    1869   Chicago   25.
The Army Songster.
    See: Confederate Imprints
ARNETT, Ethel Stephens   **Confederate Guns Were Stacked, Greensboro, N. C.**
    1965   Greensboro, N. C.   25.
ARNOLD, Edgar **The Young Refugees.**
    1912   Richmond   15.
ARNOLD, Edwin   **Land of Fadeless Stars.**
    1948   Boston   10.
ARNOLD, George   **Life and Adventures of Jefferson Davis.**
    1865   New Haven   30

ARNOLD, Isaac   **Abraham Lincoln: A Paper.** Wraps
   1881   Chicago   15.
ARNOLD, Isaac N.   **The Life of Abraham Lincoln.**
   1885   Chicago   10.
ARNOLD, Isaac N.   **Sketch of the Life of Abraham Lincoln.**
   1869   New York   15.
ARNOLD, Matthew   **General Grant** edited by John Y. Simon.
   1966   Illinois   10.
ARNOLD, Samuel Bland   **Defense and Prison Experiences of a Lincoln Conspirator, Statements and Autobiographical Notes.**
   1943   Hattiesburg   50.
ARNOLD, Thomas Jackson   **Early Life and Letters of General Thomas J. "Stonewall" Jackson.**
   1916   New York   75.
   1957   New York   25.
   1957   Richmond   25.
ARP, Bill (pseud.) See: **SMITH,** Charles H.
ASHBY, Thomas A.   **Life of Turner Ashby.**
   1914   New York   275.
ASHBY, Thomas A.   **The Valley Campaigns, Being the Reminiscences of a Non-Combatant.**
   1914   New York   125.
ASHE, S. W.   **The Trial and Death of Henry Wirz, With Other Matters Pertaining Thereto.** Wraps
   1908   Raleigh   35.
ASHE, Samuel A.   **Gen'l Robert E. Lee, The South's Peerless Soldier and Leader, Oration.** Wraps
   1906   Raleigh, N. C.   25.
ASHE, Samuel A.   **Hon. George Davis.** Wraps
   1916   Raleigh   20.
ASHE, Samuel A. and **TYLER,** Lyon G.   **Secession, Insurrection of the Negroes, and Northern Incendiarism.** Wraps.
   1933 (?)   n.p.   20.
ASHE, Samuel A.   **A Southern View of the Invasion of the Southern States and War of 1861-65,** Wraps
   1935   Raleigh, N. C.   75. **Assassination of Abraham Lincoln.**
   1867   Washington, D.C.   20.
The Assassination of Abraham Lincoln, Late President of the U.S.A. and the Attempted Assassination of William H. Seward and Frederick W. Seward.
   1866   Washington   40.
ATKINS, John Black   **The Life of Sir William Howard Russell, The First Special Correspondent.** 2 vols.
   1911   London   50.
ATKINSON, C. F.   **Grant's Campaigns of 1864 and 1865.**
   1908   London   35.
ATKINSON, Edward   **Cheap Cotton by Free Labor: By a Cotton Manufacturer.** Wraps
   1861   Boston   25.
ATKINSON, Eleanor   **The Boyhood of Lincoln.**
   1908   New York   10.
ATWATER, Dorence   **List of Union Soldiers Buried at Andersonville.**
   1866   New York   30.
AUCHAMPAUGH, Philip Gerald   **James Buchanan and His Cabinet on the Eve of Secession.** Wraps
   1926   Lancaster, Pa.   30.
   1966   Boston   10.
AUCHAMPAUGH, Philip Gerald   **Robert Tyler, Southern Rights Champion 1847-1866.**
   1934   Duluth, Minn.   40.
AUGHEY, John   **The Iron Furnace.**
   1863   Philadelphia   15.

AUGHEY, John H.   **Tupelo.**
   1888   Lincoln, Neb.   30.
AUSTIN, Anne L.   **The Woolsey Sisters of New York.** Wraps
   1971   Philadelphia   20.
**Autographs of Prominent Men of the Southern Confederacy and Historical
   Documents, E. M. Bruce Collection.** Wraps
   n.d. (circa 1900)   Houston, Texas   25.
AVARY, Myrta Lockett   **Dixie After the War.**
   1906   Richmond   40.
   1906   New York   35.
   1937   Boston   25.
   1937   New York   25.
   1946   New York   20.
AVARY, Myrta Lockett   **A Virginia Girl in the Civil War.**
   1903   New York   40.
AVERELL, William W.   **Report of _____ to Gen'l W. B. Franklin of an Inspection of
   State Homes for Disabled Soldiers and Sailors of the U.S. Made in Dec. 1888
   January 1889.**
   1889   Washington   35.
AVERILL, James P. (comp)   **Andersonville Prison Park   Report of Its Purchase and
   Improvement.** Wraps
   n.d. (circa 1900)   Atlanta   20.
AVERY, A. C.   **Memorial Address on the Life and Character of Lt. General D. H. Hill.**
   Wraps
   1893   Raleigh, N. C.   35.
AVERY, I. M.   **In Memory, Alexander Hamilton Stephens.** Wraps
   1883   Atlanta   20.
AVERY, William B. **Gunboat Service on the James River.** Wraps
   1884   Providence   Ltd.   25.
AVEY, Elijah   **Eye Witness. The Capture and Execution of John Brown.**
   1906   Chicago   40.
AVIRETT, James B.   **The Memoirs of General Turner Ashby and His Compeers.**
   1867   Baltimore   250.
AVIRETT, James B.   **An Oration . . . on the Occasion of Laying the Foundation Stone
   . . . in the North Carolina Plot in the Stonewall Cemetery, Winchester, Virginia,
   17th September, 1897.** Wraps
   1897 (?)   n.p.   50.
AYER, I. Winslow   **The Great North-Western Conspiracy.**
   1895   Chicago   20.
Ayer's American Almanac. Wraps
   1864   Lowell, Mass.   20.
BABCOCK, Bernie   **Booth and the Spirit of Lincoln.**
   1925   Philadelphia   10.
BABCOCK, Bernie   **The Soul of Ann Rutledge Abraham Lincoln's Romance.**
   1919   New York   10.
BACHE, Richard M.   **Life of General George Gordon Meade.**
   1897   Philadelphia   20.
BACHELDER, John B.   **Descriptive Key to the Painting of the Repulse of Longstreet's
   Assault at the Battle of Gettysburg (July 3, 1863) . . . painted by James Walker.**
   1870   New York   20.
BACHELDER, John B.   **Gettysburg: What to See and How to See It.**
   1889   Boston   15.
BACHELLER, Irving   **A Man for the Ages, A Story of the Builders of Democracy.**
   n.d.   New York   5.
BACON, Georgeanna Woolsey, and **HOWLAND,** Eliza Woolsey (eds)   **Letters of a
   Family During the War for the Union.** 2 vols.
   1899   n.p.   100.
BACON-FOSTER, Corra   **Clara Barton   Humanitarian.**
   1918   Washington   25.

BADEAU, Adam   **Grant in Peace. From Appomattox to Mt. McGregor.**
    1887   Hartford   35.
    1888   Philadelphia   30.
    1971   New York   15.
BADEAU, Adam   **Military History of Ulysses S. Grant.** 3 vols.
    1881   New York   75.
    1882   New York   50.
    1885   New York   50.
BADLAM, William H.   **Kearsarge and Alabama.** Wraps
    1894   Providence   Ltd.   30.
BAGBY, George W.   **The Old Virginia Gentleman and Other Sketches** edited by Ellen
Bagby.
    1938   Richmond   30.
BAGLEY, William Chandler   **Soil Exhaustion and the Civil War.** Wraps
    1942   Washington   20.
BAILEY, Hugh C.   **Hinton Rowan Helper: Abolitionist — Racist.**
    1967   University, Alabama   18.50
BAILEY, L. D.   **Quantrell's Raid on Lawrence.**
    1889   Lyndon, Kansas   Ltd.   100.
BAIN, William E. (ed)   **B & O in the Civil War from the Papers of Wm. Prescott Smith.**
    1966   Denver   20.
BAKELESS, John   **Spies of the Confederacy.**
    1970   Philadelphia   15.
BAKER, Lafayette C.   **History of the U. S. Secret Service in the Late War.**
    1867   Philadelphia   40.
    1868   Philadelphia   30.
    1869   Philadelphia   30.
BAKER, Lafayette C.   **Spies, Traitors and Conspirators of the Late Civil War.**
    1894   Philadelphia   25.
BAKER, LaFayette C.   **The United States Secret Service.**
    1889   Philadelphia   25.
    1900   Chicago   25.
BAKER, Nina Brown   **Cyclone in Calico.**
    1952   Boston   20.
BAKER, Nina Brown   **The Story of Abraham Lincoln.**
    1952   New York   10.
BAKER, W. W.   **Memoirs of Service with John Yates Beall, C.S.N.** edited by Douglas
Southall Freeman.
    1910   Richmond   200.
BAKER, William Mumford   **Inside: A Chronical of Secession** by George F. Harrington.
    1866   New York   60.
BALCH, Thomas W.   **The Alabama Arbitration.**
    1900   Philadelphia   30.
BALCH, W.   **Life and Public Services of Gen. Grant.**
    1855   n.p.   15.
BALCH, William Ralston   **The Battle of Gettysburg, An Historical Account.**
    1885   Philadelphia   25.
BALLARD, C. B.   **The Military Genius of Abraham Lincoln, An Essay.**
    1952   Cleveland   20.
    1965   New York   15.
BALTZ, John D.   **Colonel E. D. Baker's Defense in the Battle of Ball's Bluff.**
    1888   Lancaster, Pa.   65.
BANCROFT, A. C. (Ed)   **The Life and Death of Jefferson Davis, Ex-President of
the Southern Confederacy.** Wraps
    1889   New York   30.
    1890   New York   25.
BANCROFT, Frederic   **The Life of William H. Seward.** 2 vols.
    1900   New York   30.

BANCROFT, Frederic   **Slave-Trading in the Old South.**
1931   Baltimore   30.
BANCROFT, George   **Memorial Address on the Life and Character of Abraham Lincoln.**
1866   Washington   15.
BANKS, John   **A Short Biographical Sketch of the Undersigned by Himself.**
1936   Austell, Ga.   50.
BANKS, L. A.   **Immortal Songs of Camps and Fields.**
1898   Cleveland   30.
Bannerman's Military Goods Catalogues. Wraps
15. each
1945   Anniversary Catalogue   25.
BARBEE, Muriel Culp   **A Union Forever.**
1949   Philadelphia   15.
BARBER, Joseph   **War Letters of a Disabled Volunteer. Embracing His Experiences as Honest Abe's Bosom Friend and Unofficial Adviser.**
1864   New York   20.
BARINGER, William E.   **A House Dividing — Lincoln as President Elect.**
1945   Springfield, Ill.   10.
BARINGER, William E.   **Lincoln's Rise to Power.**
1937   Boston   15.
BARINGER, William E.   **Lincoln's Vandalia A Pioneer Portrait.**
1949   New Brunswick   15.
BARINGER, William E. (comp)   **The Philosophy of Abraham Lincoln in his Own Words.**
1959   Indian Hills, Co.   10.
BARKER, Alan   **The Civil War in America.**
1961   New York   15.
BARKER, Jacob   **The Rebellion: Its Consequences, and the Congressional Committee, Denominated the Reconstruction Committee, With Their Action.**
1866   New Orleans   75.
BARNARD, F.A.P.   **Letter to the President of the United States by a Refugee.** Wraps
1863   New York   20.
BARNARD, George N.   **Photographic Views of Sherman's Campaign.** Wraps
1977   New York   10.
BARNARD, J. G.   **The C.S.A and the Battle of Bull Run.**
1862   New York   100.
BARNARD, J. G.   **Eulogy on the Late Bvt. Maj. Gen. Joseph G. Totten, Chief Engineer United States Army.** Wraps
1866   Washington   15.
BARNARD, J. G.   **Notes on a Sea-Coast Defence.**
1861   New York   50.
BARNARD, J. G.   **The Peninsular Campaign and Its Antecedents.**
1864   New York   50.
1864   Washington   50.
BARNARD, J. G. and **BARRY,** W. F.   **Report of the Engineer and Artillery Operations of the Army of the Potomac.**
1863   New York   125.
1864   New York   100.
BARNARD, J. G.   **Report on the Defenses of Washington.**
1871   Washington   125.
BARNES, Albert   **The Condition of Peace, A Thanksgiving Discourse.** Wraps
1863   Philadelphia   20.
BARNES, David M.   **The Draft Riots in New York, July 1863.** Wraps
1863   New York   20.
BARNES, Gilbert Hobbs   **The Antislavery Impulse 1830-1844.**
1957   Gloucester, Mass.   15.
BARNEY, William L.   **The Secessionist Impulse, Alabama and Mississippi in 1860.**
1974   Princeton, N. J.   17.

BARNS, George C.   **Denver, the Man.**
   1949   Wilmington, Ohio   30.
BARNWELL, Robert W., Sr.   **The Lines and Nature of Lincoln's Greatness.** Wraps
   1931   Columbia, S. C.   10.
BARNWELL, Robert W., Sr.   **Sherman and Grant Contrasted (For Historians).** Wraps
   n.d.   n.p.   10.
BARONDESS, Benjamin   **Three Lincoln Masterpieces.**
   1954   W. Va.   15.
BARR, Alwyn (ed)   **Charles Porter's Account of the Confederate Attempt to Seize Arizona and New Mexico.**
   1964   Austin   15.
BARRETT, Don C.   **The Greenbacks and Resumption of Specie Payments 1862-1879.**
   1931   Cambridge   30.
BARRETT, Frank W. Z.   **Mourning for Lincoln.**
   1909   Philadelphia   20.
BARRETT, John G.   **Sherman's March Through the Carolinas.**
   1956   Chapel Hill   20.
BARRETT, Jos. H.   **Life of A. Lincoln.**
   1865   New York   20.
BARRETT, Thomas   **The Great Hanging at Gainesville, Cooke Co., Texas.**
   1961   Austin, Texas   15.
BARRIGER, John W.   **Railroads in the Civil War.** Wraps
   1966   n.p.   10.
BARRINGER, Paul B.   **The Natural Bent: The Memoirs of Dr. Paul B. Barringer.**
   1949   Chapel Hill   25.
BARROW, Willie Micajah   **The Civil War Diary of _____, Sept. 23, 1861 to July 13, 1862** edited by Wendell H. Stephenson & Edwin A. Davis. Wraps
   n.d.   n.p.   20.
BARTHELL, Edward E., Jr.   **Mystery of the Merrimack.**
   1959   Muskegon, Mich.   15.
BARTHOLOW, Roberts   **A Manual of Instructions for Enlisting and Discharging Soldiers.**
   1864   Philadelphia   125.
BARTLETT, Catherine Thom (ed)   **My Dear Brother, A Confederate Chronicle.**
   1952   Richmond   25.
BARTLETT, D. W.   **The Life and Public Services of Hon. Abraham Lincoln.**
   1860   New York   15.
BARTLETT, Irving H.   **Wendell Phillips, Brahmin Radical.**
   1961   Boston   20.
BARTLETT, W. C.   **An Idyl of War-Times.**
   1890   New York   25.
BARTON, George   **Angels of the Battlefield.**
   1897   Philadelphia   50.
   1898   Philadelphia   40.
BARTON, William E.   **Abraham Lincoln and His Books.**
   1920   Chicago   20.
BARTON, William E.   **Abraham Lincoln and the Hooker Letter, an Address Delivered Before the Pennell Club of Philadelphia.**
   1928   N.Y.   Ltd.   25.
BARTON, William E.   **Abraham Lincoln and Walt Whitman.**
   1928   Indianapolis   20.
BARTON, William E.   **Abraham Lincoln, Kentucky Mountaineer.** Wraps
   1923   Berea, Kentucky   Ltd.   25.
BARTON, William E.   **A Beautiful Blunder, the True Story of Lincoln's Letter to Mrs. Lydia A. Bixby.**
   1926   Indianapolis   Ltd.   25.
BARTON, William E.   **A Hero in Homespun.**
   1897   Boston   25.

BARTON, William E.   **The Influence of Chicago Upon Abraham Lincoln, An Address.**
Wraps
1923   Chicago   10.
BARTON, William E.   **The Life of Abraham Lincoln.**
1924   Indianapolis   2 vols.   20.
1925   Indianapolis   2 vols. in 1   15.
BARTON, William E.   **Lincoln at Gettysburg.**
1930   Indianapolis   20.
1950   New York   10.
BARTON, William E.   **The Lineage of Lincoln.**
1929   Indianapolis   20.
BARTON,William E.   **The Paternity of Abraham Lincoln.**
1920   New York   30.
BARTON, William E.   **President Lincoln.** 2 vols.
1933   Indianapolis   30.
BARTON, William E.   **The Soul of Abraham Lincoln.**
1920   New York   20.
BARTON,   William E.   **The Women Lincoln Loved.**
1927   London   30.
1927   Indianapolis   15.
BASLER, Roy P.   **Abraham Lincoln: His Speeches and Writings.**
1946   Cleveland, Ohio   15.
BASLER, Roy P.   **The Collected Works of Abraham Lincoln.** 8 vols. plus index plus
supplement.
1953   New Brunswick   120.
BASLER, Roy P. (ed)   **Walt Whitman's Memoranda During the War and Death of
Abraham Lincoln.**
1962   Bloomington, Indiana   15.
BASSETT, John S.   **Running the Blockade from Confederate Ports.** Wraps
1898   n.p.   25.
BASSO, Hamilton   **Beauregard, The Great Creole.**
1933   New York & London   35.
The Bastille in America; or Democratic Absolutism By an Eye-Witness. Wraps
1861   London   20.
BATES, David Homer   **Lincoln in the Telegraph Office.**
1907   New York   20.
1939   New York   10.
BATES, David Homer   **Lincoln Stories.**
1926   New York   15.
BATES, Edward   **The Diary of Edward Bates 1859-1866** edited by Howard K. Beale in:
Annual Report of the American Historical Association for 1930, Vol. IV.
1933   Washington   25.
BATES, Finis L.   **The Escape and Suicide of John Wilkes Booth.**
1907   Memphis   75.
BATES, Samuel P.   **The Battle of Chancellorsville.**
1882   Meadville, Pa.   40.
1883   Meadville, Pa.   40.
BATES, Samuel P.   **The Battle of Gettysburg.**
1875   Philadelphia   50.
BATES, William C. (ed)   **Stars and Stripes in Rebeldom.**
1862   Boston   40.
BATTEN, John M.   **Reminiscences of Two Years in the United States Navy.**
1881   Lancaster, Pa.   45.
BATTINE, Cecil   **The Crisis of the Confederacy.**
1905   London   100.
1905   New York   100.
BATTLE, Kemp P.   **History of the University of North Carolina.** 2 vols.
1912   Raleigh, N. C.   75.
n.d.   n.p.   Reprint   50.

BATTLE, Kemp P.   **Memories of an Old-Time Tar Heel.**
    1945   Chapel Hill   25.
Battle of Atlanta Short Sketch of the Battles Around, Siege, Evacuation and Destruction of Atlanta, Ga. in 1864. Wraps
    1895   Atlanta   20.
Battle of Belmont. Wraps
    1921   Camp Benning, Ga.   30.
The Battle of Chancellorsville and the 11th Army Corps. Wraps
    1863   New York   40.
Battle of Chicamauga, Ga., Sept. 19-20, 1863, Organization of the Army of the Chickamauga Cumberland and the Army of Tennessee. Wraps
    1893   Washington   20.
Battle of Mansfield, Mansfield, Louisiana, Fought April 8, 1864, Gen. Richard Taylor, Commander Confederate Forces, Gen. N. P. Banks, Commander Federal Forces. Wraps
    1949   Logansport, La.   20.
Battle of Wilson's Creek. Wraps
    1951   Springfield, Mo.   10.
BATTLE, William H.   **Report of Proceedings in Habeas Corpus Cases: Kerr, Moore, Also in Case of Lt. Burgen.** Wraps
    1870   Raleigh   35.
Battlefield Markers Association, Western Division. Wraps
    1929   Charlottesville, Va.   10.
Battlefields in Dixie Land and Chickamauga National Military Park. Wraps
    n.d. (1917)   Nashville, Tn.   15.
Battlefields of the South from Bull Run to Fredericksburg with Sketches of Confederate Commanders, and Gossip of the Camps by an English Combatant. 2 vols.
    1860   London   350.
    1863   London   300.
    1864   New York   300.
Battles About Chattanooga, Tennessee. Wraps
    1932   Washington   15.
Battles and Leaders of the Civil War. See: **JOHNSON,** Robert U. & **BUEL,** Clarence C.
Battles of Atlanta. Wraps
    1895   Atlanta, Ga.   25.
Battles of the Civil War 1861-1865, A Pictorial Presentation. Kurz and Allison Lithographs.
    1970   . Little Rock   75.
    1976   Birmingham   100.
BAXLEY, Henry Willis   **Republican Imperialism is Not American Liberty.** Wraps
    n.d. (circa 1862)   n.p.   25.
BAXTER, Charles N. & **DEARBORN,** James M.   **Confederate Literature, A List of Books and Newspapers, Maps, Music, and Miscellaneous Matter printed in the South During the Confederacy, Now in the Boston Athenaeum.**
    1917   Boston   100.
BAXTER, D.W.C.   **The Volunteer's Manual.** Wraps
    1861   Philadelphia   50.
BAXTER, J. H.   **Statistics, Medical and Anthropological, of the Provost-Marshal-General's Bureau.** 2 vols.
    1875   Washington   175.
BAXTER, William   **Pea Ridge and Prairie Grove, or Scenes and Incidents of the War in Arkansas.**
    1864   Cincinnati   150.
    1957   Van Buren   20.
BAYARD, Samuel J.   **The Life of George Dashiell Bayard.**
    1874   New York   60.

BEALE, Howard K.   **The Critical Year — A Study of Andrew Johnson and Reconstruction.**
1930   New York   15.
BEALE, James (comp)   **The Battle Flags of the Army of the Potomac at Gettysburg.**
1885   Philadelphia   Ltd.   1000.
BEALE, James   **Chancellorsville, A Paper Read Before the United Service Club Philadelphia, Penna on Wednesday, February 8, 1888.**
1892   Philadelphia   Ltd.   30.
BEALS, Charleton   **War Within a War — The Confederacy Against Itself.**
1965   Philadelphia   15.
BEAMAN, Charles C.   **The National and Private "Alabama Claims" and "Their Final and Amicable Settlement."**
1871   Washington   20.
BEAN, W. G.   **Stonewall's Man, Sandie Pendleton.**
1959   Chapel Hill   20.
BEARD, W. E.   **The Battle of Nashville.** Wraps
1913   Nashville   75.
BEARSS, Edwin C., and **Gibson,** A. M.   **Fort Smith, Little Gibraltar on the Arkansas.**
1969   Norman, Oklahoma   25.
BEARSS, Edwin C.   **Hardluck Ironclad.**
1966   Baton Rouge   20.
1968   Baton Rouge   20.
BEARSS, Edwin C.   **Protecting Sherman's Lifeline The Battles of Brices Cross Roads and Tupelo 1864.** Wraps
1971   Washington   10
BEARSS, Edwin C.   **Rebel Victory at Vicksburg.**
1963   Little Rock   30.
BEARSS, Edwin C.   **Steele's Retreat from Camden and the Battle of Jenkin's Ferry.**
1967   Little Rock   30.
n.d.   Little Rock   30.
BEATH, Robert B.   **History of the Grand Army of the Republic.**
1888   New York   30.
1889   New York   25.
BEATIE, R. H., Jr.   **Road to Manassas.**
1961   Cooper Square   25.
BEATY, John C.   **John Esten Cooke, Virginian.**
1922   New York   30.
1965   New York   10.
BEAUREGARD, G. T.   **A Commentary on the Campaign and Battle of Manassas of July 1861.**
1891   New York   80.
BEAUREGARD, G. T.   **General Order No. 14 to Fire on Fort Sumter, April 11, 1861.**
1906   Boston   Ltd.   20.
BEAUREGARD, G. T.   **July, 1861.**
1891   New York   75.
BEAUVOIR,   **Jefferson Davis Shrine.** Wraps
1945   Gulfport   10.
BECK, James B.   **Military Despotism to Supersede the Constitution. Speech.** Wraps
1871   Washington   15.
BECKER, Stephen   **When the War Is Over.**
1969   New York   15.
BEECHAM, R. K.   **Gettysburg, The Pivotal Battle of the Civil War.**
1911   Chicago   30.
BEECHER, Henry Ward   **American Rebellion, Report of the Speeches of** _____
1864   London   20.
BEERS, Fannie A.   **Memories: A Record of Personal Experience and Adventure During Four Years of War.**
1888   Philadelphia   25.
1889   Philadelphia   25.
1891   Philadelphia   25.

BEERS, Henry Putney   **Guide to the Archives of the Government of the Confederate States of America.**
    1968   Washington   25.
BEESON, Marvin F.   **Die Organization Der Negererziehung in Den Dereinigten Staaten Von America Seit 1860.** Wraps
    1915   Leipzig, Germany   25.
BEITZELL, Edwin W.   **Point Lookout, Prison Camp for Confederates.**
    1972   n.p.   15.
    1976   n.p.   15.
BELDEN, Bauman l.   **War Medals of the Confederacy.** Wraps
    1915   New York   75.
    1957   Rochester   Ltd.   20.
    1970   Glendale   10.
BELDEN, David   **Obsequies of President Lincoln, An Oration Delivered in Nevada City in 1865.** Wraps
    n.d.   Marysville, Ca.   20.
BELDEN, Thomas Graham, and **BELDEN,** Marva Robins   **So Fell the Angels.**
    1956   Boston   15.
BELL, John W.   **Memoirs of Governor William Smith of Virginia, His Political, Military and Personal History.**
    1891   New York   100.
BELL, Landson C.   **Robert E. Lee An Address.** Wraps
    1929   n.p.   20.
BELLAH, J.W.   **Soldier's Battle: Gettysburg.**
    1962   New York   15.
BELLOWS, H. W.   **Speech of the Rev. _____ President of U.S. Sanitary Commission . . . 1863.** Wraps
    1863   Philadelphia   20.
BELZ, Herman   **Reconstructing the Union — Theory and Policy During the Civil War.**
    1969   New York   15.
BEMIS, George   **Hasty Recognition of Rebel Belligerency and Our Right to Complain to It.**
    1865   Boston   25.
BEMIS, George   **Precedents of American Neutrality.** Wraps
    1864   Boston   25.
BENET, Stephen Vincent   **John Brown's Body.**
    1927   New York   30.
    1928   Garden City, N. Y.   25.
    1948   New York   20.
BENET, Stephen Vincent   **A Treatise of Military Law and the Practice of Courts Martial.**
    1862   New York   30.
BENHAM, Wm. Burton   **Life of Osborn H. Oldroyd Founder and Collector of Lincoln Mementos.**
    1927   Washington   20.
BENJAMIN, Judah P.   **The African Slave Trade, The Secret Purpose of the Insurgents to Revive It . . . Benjamin's Intercepted Instructions to L.Q.C. Lamar.** Wraps
    1863   Philadelphia   25.
BENJAMIN, Judah P.   **Defence of the National Democracy Against the Attack of Judge Douglas — Constitutional Rights of the States, Speech.** Wraps
    1860   Washington   20.
BENJAMIN, Judah P.   **Speech of _____ of Louisiana on the Right of Secession.** Wraps
    1860   Washington   25.
BENJAMIN, Marcus (ed.)   **Washington During War Time.** Wraps
    1902   Washington   20.
BENNER, Judith Ann   **Fradulent Finance: Counterfeiting and the Confederate States 1861-1865.** Wraps
    1970   Hillsboro   10.

BENNETT, Frank M.   **The Monitor and the Navy Under Steam.**
1900   Boston   60.
BENNETT, Frank M.   **The Steam Navy . . . of the . . . United States.**
1896   Pittsburgh   200.
BENNETT, Lorenzo T.   **Our Present Duties and Responsibilities as Christian Patriots, A Sermon. Wraps**
1861   New Haven   10.
BENSON, B. K.   **Bayard's Courier.**
1902   New York   25.
BENSON, B. K.   **Who Goes There?**
1902   New York   20.
BENSON, Berry   **Berry Benson's Civil War Book** edited by Susan Williams Benson.
1962   Athens, Ga.   40.
BENTON, Josiah Henry   **Voting in the Field: A Forgotten Chapter of Civil War.**
1915   Boston   25.
BENTON, Thomas H.   **Examination of the Dred Scott Case.**
1860   New York   30.
BENTON, Thomas H. **Thirty Years View.** 2 vols.
1856   New York   30.
BERKELEY, Henry Robinson **Four Years in the Confederate Artillery: The Diary of** _____ edited by William H. Runge.
1961   Richmond   40.
1961   Chapel Hill   40.
BERLIN, Ira   **Slaves Without Masters, the Free Negro in the Antebellum South.**
1974   New York   15.
BERNARD, George S.   **War Talks of Confederate Veterans.**
1892   Petersburg, Va.   50.
BERNARD, Mountague   **A Historical Account of the Neutrality of Great Britain During the American Civil War.**
1870   London   150.
BERNATH, Stuart L.   **Squall Across the Atlantic, American Civil War Prize Cases and Diplomacy.**
1970   Berkeley, Calif.   15.
BERRY, Thomas Franklin   **Four Years with Morgan and Forrest.**
1914   Oklahoma City   250.
BESSE, S. B.   **C. S. Ironclad Virginia.** Wraps
1937   Newport News, Va.   10.
BESSE, S. B.   **U. S. Ironclad Monitor.** Wraps
1936   Newport News, Va.   10.
BETHEL, Elizabeth (comp)   **War Department Collection of Confederate Records.** Wraps
1957   Washington   20.
BEVERIDGE, Albert J.   **Abraham Lincoln.**
1928   Cambridge, Mass.   2 vols.   35.
1928   Boston   4 vols.   manuscript ed.   100.
BEYER, Walter F. And **KEYDEL,** Oscar F.   **Deeds of Valor.** 2 Vols.
1905   Detroit   60.
1906   Detroit   40.
1907   Detroit   30.
BEYMER, William Gilmore   **On Hazardous Service, Scouts & Spies of the North and South.**
1912   New York   25.
Bibliography of State Participation in the Civil War 1861-1866.
1913   Washington   50.
1961   Charlottesville   30.
BICKHAM, W. D.   **Rosecrans' Campaign with the Fourteenth Army Corps by W.D.B.**
1863   Cincinnatti   50.
BIDWELL, Frederick David   **The Life of General Daniel Davidson Bidwell.**
n.d.   Albany   50.

BIGELOW, D.   **William C. Church and the Army and Navy Journal.**
    1952   New York   15.
BIGELOW, John, Jr.   **Campaign of Chancellorsville.**
    1910   New Haven, Conn.   Ltd.   500.
BIGELOW, John, Jr.   **France and the Confederate Navy.**
    1888   New York   30.
BIGELOW, John, Jr.   **The Principles of Strategy Illustrated Mainly from American Campaigns.**
    1891   London   75.
BIGHAM, R. W.   **Joe: A Boy in the War-Times.**
    1890   Nashville   20.
BILL, Alfred Hoyt   **The Beleagured City Richmond 1861-1865.**
    1946   New York   20.
BILL, Alfred Hoyt   **Rehearsal for Conflict The War with Mexico 1846-1848.**
    1947   New York   20.
BILL, Ledyard (comp)   **Lyrics, Incidents, and Sketches of the Rebellion.**
    1864   New York   30.
BINGHAM, John A.   **Reply of Judge Advocate _____ to the Defence of the Accused . . . for the Trial of Brig. Gen. William A. Hammond.** Wraps
    1864   Washington   15.
BINGHAM, John A.   **Trial of the Conspirators for the Assassination of President Lincoln.** Wraps
    1865   Washington   25.
BINNEY, Horace   **The Privilege of the Writ of Habeas Corpus Under the Constitution.** Wraps
    1862   Philadelphia   20.
A Biographical Sketch . . . John Sedgwick Major General.
    1899   New York   Ltd.   20.
BIRCHMORE, W. E.   **Chickamauga and Chattanooga National Military Park.** Wraps
    1895   Chattanooga   20.
BIRDSONG, George L. F.
    See: **Confederate Imprints**
BISHOP, Carter R.   **"The Cockade City of the Union" Petersburg, Virginia.** Wraps
    1907   n.p.   20.
BISHOP, Jim   **The Day Lincoln Was Shot.**
    1955   New York   10.
BISSET, Johnson   **The Mysteries of Chancellorsville, Who Killed Stonewall Jackson.** Wraps
    1945   New York   20.
BIVINS, Viola Cobb   **Echoes of the Confederacy.**
    1950   Longview, Texas   15.
BLACK, Robert C.   **The Railroads of the Confederacy.**
    1952   Chapel Hill, N. C.   15.
BLACKBURN, J. S. & **McDONALD**, W. N.   **A Grammar-School History of the United States.**
    1871   Baltimore   20.
BLACKFORD, Charles M.   **Campaign and Battle of Lynchburg, Va.** Wraps
    1901   Lynchburg, Va.   100.
BLACKFORD, Charles M.   **The Trials and Trial of Jefferson Davis.**
    1900   Richmond   20.
    1901   Lynchburg   20.
BLACKFORD, L. Minor   **The Great John B. Minor and His Cousin Mary Face the War.** Wraps
    1953   Virginia   10.
BLACKFORD, L. Minor   **Mine Eyes Have Seen the Glory.**
    1954   Cambridge   20.

BLACKWELL, Robert   **Original Acrostics on Some of the Southern States, Confederate Generals, and Various Other Persons and Things.**
1869   St. Louis   35.
1873   Baltimore   30.
BLACKWELL, Sarah Ellen   **A Military Genius Life of Anna Ella Carroll of Maryland.**
1891   Washington   45.
BLAINE, James G.   **Jefferson Davis-Amnesty, In the House of Representatives Monday, January 10, 1876.**
1876   Washington   15.
BLAINE, James G.   **Twenty Years of Congress.** 2 vols.
1884   Norwich   40.
1886   Norwich   30.
BLAIR, Carvel Hall   **Submarines of the Confederate Navy.** Wraps
1952   Annapolis   15.
BLAIR, Francis P.   **Confiscation of Rebel Property — Speech Delivered in the House of Representatives.** Wraps
1864   Washington   15.
BLAIR, Maria   **Matthew Fontaine Maury.** Wraps
1981   Richmond   20.
BLAKE, Michael   **American Civil War Cavalry.**
1973   London   15.
BLAKE, Nelson Morehouse   **William Mahone of Virginia.**
1935   Richmond   40.
BLAKE, Sarah Swan   **Diaries and Letters of Francis Minot Weld, M.D.**
1925   Boston   60.
BLAKE, W. O.   **The History of Slavery & the Slave Trade, Ancient & Modern.**
1859   Columbus   50.
BLAKE, W. O. (comp)   **Pictorial National Records.** Vol. 1.
1865   Columbus, Ohio   30.
BLAKE, Walter H.   **Hand Grips. The Story of the Great Gettysburg Reunion July 1913.**
1913   Vineland, N. J.   15.
BLAND, T. A.   **Life of Benjamin F. Butler.**
1879   Boston   15.
BLANDENBURG, Heinrich   **Die Innern Kampfe Der Nordamerifanifchen Union.**
1869   Leipzig   30.
BLANDING, Stephen F.   **Recollections of a Sailor Boy.**
1886   Providence   50.
BLAY, John S.   **The Civil War, A Pictorial Profile.**
1958   New York   30.
BLEASE, Cole L.   **Destruction of Property in Columbia, S. C. by Sherman's Army, Speech.** Wraps
1930   Washington   20.
BLEDSOE, Albert Taylor   **An Essay on Liberty and Slavery.**
1856   Philadelphia   20.
BLEDSOE, Albert Taylor   **Is Davis a Traitor; Or Was Secession a Constitutional Right Previous to the War of 1861?**
1866   Baltimore   25.
1879   Lynchburg   20.
1907   Richmond   20.
1915   Lynchburg   20.
BLEDSOE, Albert Taylor   **The War Between the States.**
1915   Lynchburg, Va.   20.
Blockade Runners Pictorial Supplement III, The American Neptune. Wraps
1961   Salem, Mass.   15.
Blue and Grey. Wraps
Monthly periodical of Civil War interest   20. per issue
BLYTHE, Vernon.   **A History of the Civil War in the United States.**
1914   New York   60.

BOATNER, Mark M.　**The Civil War Dictionary.**
1959　New York　25.
BOETHEL, Paul C.　**The Big Guns of Fayette.** Wraps
1965　Austin　20.
BOGGS, William R.　**Military Reminiscences of Gen. Wm. R. Boggs, C.S.A.**
1913　Durham, N. C.　50.
BOKER, George H.　**The Second Louisiana.**
1863　n.p.　Philadelphia (?)　50.
BOKUM, Hermann　**Testimony of a Refugee from East Tennessee.** Wraps
1863　Philadelphia　30.
BOKUM, Hermann　**Wanderings North and South.** Wraps
1864　Philadelphia　35.
BOLAND, M. D.　**Reinterpreting History.**
1947　Tacoma, Washington　20.
BOLLES, Albert S.　**The Financial History of the United States from 1861-1885.**
1894　New York　50.
BOLLINGER, James W.　**Lincoln Statesman and Logician.**
1944　Davenport, Iowa　Ltd.　20.
BOND, Christiana　**Memories of General Robert E. Lee.**
1926　Baltimore　20.
BOND, W. R.　**Pickett or Pettigrew? An Historical Review.** Wraps
1888　Weldon, N. C.　80.
1888 (?)　Scotland Neck, N. C.　80.
1900　Scotland Neck, N. C.　40.
BONEY, F. N.　**John Letcher of Virginia.**
1966　University, Ala.　20.
BONHAM, Milledge L.　**The British Consuls in the Confederacy.**
1911　New York　75.
BONNER, James C. (ed)　**The Journal of a Milledgeville Girl 1861-1867.** Wraps
1964　Athens, Ga.　15.
BOOKER, Richard　**Abraham Lincoln in Periodical Literature.**
1941　Chicago　30.
BOOTH, Mary L.　**The Uprising of a Great People.**
1861　New York　20.
BORCKE, Heros Von and **SCHEIBERT,** Justus　**The Great Cavalry Battle of Brandy Station** Translated by Stuart Wright and F. D. Bridgewater. Wraps
1976　Winston-Salem, N. C.　Ltd.　10.
BORCKE, Heros Von　**Memoirs of the Confederate War for Independence.** 2 vols.
1866　Edinburgh　300.
1867　Philadelphia　150.
1886　Berlin　300.
1938　New York　40.
BORRESON, Ralph　**When Lincoln Died.**
1965　New York　25.
The Boston Almanac for the Year 1862 No. XXVII.
1862　Boston (?)　35.
BOTKIN, B. A. (ed.)　**A Civil War Treasury of Tales, Legends, and Folklore.**
1960　New York　20.
BOTTS, John Minor　**The Great Rebellion.**
1866　New York　20.
BOTUME, Elizabeth Hyde　**First Days Amongst the Contrabands.**
1893　Boston　25.
BOURKE, John G.　**On the Border with Crook.**
1891　New York　60.
1892　New York　50.
BOWEN, John J.　**The Strategy of Robert E. Lee.**
1914　New York　50.
BOWERS, Claude G.　**The Tragic Era.**
1929　Cambridge　20.

BOWIE, Marshall L.   **A Time of Adversity and Courage, Story of Montgomery and West
Point Railroad.** Wraps
   1961 (?)   n.p.   10.
BOWMAN, S. M. and **IRWIN,** R. B.   **Sherman and His Campaigns.**
   1865   New York   30.
   1868   New York   30.
BOYD, Belle   See: **HARDINGE,** Belle B.
BOYD, David French   **General W. T. Sherman as College President.** Wraps
   1910   Baton Rouge   10.
BOYD, J. L. R.   **John Angus Campbell, C.S.A. 1840-1933.** Wraps
   n.d.   Atlanta   20.
BOYD, James   **Marching On.**
   1927   New York   20.
BOYD, James P.   **The Gallant Trooper, General Philip H. Sheridan.**
   1888   Philadelphia   15.
BOYD, James P.   **The Life of General William T. Sherman.**
   1891   n.p.   25.
BOYD, James P.   **Military and Civil Life of General U. S. Grant.**
   1887   Philadelphia   30.
   1892   Philadelphia   25.
BOYDEN, Anna   **War Reminiscences A Record of Mrs. Rebecca R. Pomroy's Experience in War-Times.**
   1884   Boston   20.
BOYER, Richard O.   **The Legend of John Brown.**
   1973   New York   20.
BOYER, Samuel P.   **Naval Surgeon.**
   1963   Bloomington   20.
BOYKIN, Edward   **Beefsteak Raid.**
   1960   New York   25.
BOYKIN, Edward   **Congress and the Civil War.**
   1955   New York   15.
BOYKIN, Edward   **Ghost Ship of the Confederacy: The Story of the Alabama and Her
Captain, Raphael Semmes.**
   1957   New York   25.
BOYKIN, Edward   **Sea Devil of the Confederacy, Story of the Florida.**
   1959   New York   25.
BOYNTON, Charles B.   **History of the Navy During the Rebellion.** 2 vols.
   1867-68   New York   75.
   1869-70   n.p.   75.
BOYNTON, Edward C.   **History of West Point . . . and the Origin and Progress of the
U.S. Military Academy.**
   1863   New York   75.
BOYNTON, H. V.   **Chattanooga and Chickamauga.** Wraps
   1888   Washington   25.
BOYNTON, H. V.   **Dedication of the Chickamauga and Chattanooga National Military
Park Sept. 18-20, 1895.**
   1896   Washington   20.
BOYNTON, H. V.   **The National Military Park, Chickamauga-Chattanooga, An
Historical Guide.**
   1895   Cincinnati   20.
BOYNTON, H. V.   **Organization of the Army of the Cumberland and of the Army of
Tennessee.** Wraps
   1893   Washington   25.
BOYNTON, H. V.   **Sherman's Historical Raid.**
   1875   Cincinnati   25.
BRACKETT, Albert G.   **History of the United States Cavalry.**
   1865   New York   50.
   1965   New York   Reprint   20.

BRADFORD, Gamaliel, Jr.   **Confederate Portraits.**
    1912   Boston   25.
    1914   Boston   25.
    1942   Boston   25.
    1968   Freeport   20.
BRADFORD, Gamaliel, Jr.   **Lee the American.**
    1912   Boston   25.
    1914   Boston   20.
    1927   Boston   20.
    1929   Boston   20.
BRADFORD, Gamaliel, Jr.   **Union Portraits.**
    1916   Boston   30.
BRADFORD, Ralph   **Reprieve, A Christmas Story of 1863.**
    1940   n.p.   20.
BRADLEE, Francis, B. C.   **Blockade Running During the Civil War.**
    1925   Salem, Ma.   150.
BRADLEE, Francis B. C.   **A Forgotten Chapter in Our Naval History, A Sketch of the Career of Duncan Nathaniel Ingraham.** Wraps
    1923   Salem, Mass.   50.
BRADLEE, Francis B. C.   **Kearsarge-Alabama Battle.** Wraps
    1921   Salem, Mass.   15.
BRADLEY, Erwin Stanley   **Simon Cameron Lincoln's Secretary of War.**
    1968   Philadelphia   20.
BRADLEY, James   **The Confederate Mail Carrier.**
    1894   Mexico, Mo.   200.
BRADLOW, Edna & Frank   **Here Comes the Alabama.**
    1958   Cape Town   25.
BRADY, Cyrus Townsend   **A Little Traitor to the South.**
    1907   New York   10.
BRADY, Cyrus Townsend   **On the Old Kearsarge: A Story of the Civil War.**
    1910   New York   15.
BRADY, Cyrus Townsend   **The Southerners.**
    1903   New York   15.
BRAGG, Edward S.   **Address of Gen. _____ Before the Society of the Army of the Potomac at Detroit, Michigan June 14, 1882.** Wraps
    1882   Washington   25.
BRAGG, Junius Newport   **Letters of A Confederate Surgeon, 1861-1865.** edited by Mrs. T. J. Faughan.
    1960   Camden, Ark.   Ltd.   25.
BRAGUE, S. B.   **Notes on Colored Troops and Military Colonies on Southern Soil, By An Officer of the 9th Army Corps.** Wraps
    1863   New York   15.
BRANCH, Mary Polk   **Memoirs of a Southern Woman "Within the Lines" and a Genealogical Record.**
    1912   Chicago   40.
BRANDT, J. D.   **Gunnery Catechism as Applied to the Service of Naval Ordnance.**
    1864   New York   40.
BRANSCOM, Alexander C.   **Mystic Romances of the Blue and the Grey.**
    1883   New York   100.
BRANSON, H. C.   **Salisbury Plain, A Novel of the Civil War.**
    1965   New York   10.
BRECKINRIDGE, Lucy   **Lucy Breckinridge of Grove Hill, the Journal of a Virginia Girl 1862-1864** edited by Mary D. Robertson.
    1979   Kent, Ohio   15.
BRECKINRIDGE, Robert J.   **Our Country: Its Peril and Its Deliverance.** Wraps
    1861   Cincinnati   15.
BREEDEN, James O.   **Joseph Jones, M.D. Scientist of the Old South.**
    1975   Lexington, Ky.   20.

BREIHAN, Carl W.   **The Killer Legions of Quantrill.**
1971   Seattle   15.
BREIHAN, Carl W.   **Life of Jesse James.**
n.d.   New York   10.
BREIHAN, Carl W.   **Quantrill and His Civil War Guerillas.**
1959   New York   10.
1959   Denver   10.
BREMNER, Robert H.   **The Public Good.**
1980   New York   15.
BRENT, Joseph   **Memoirs of the War Between the States.**
1940   n.p.   Ltd.   250.
BRENT, Joseph L.   **Capture of the Ironclad "Indianola."**
1926   New Orleans   20.
BRENT, Joseph L.   **Mobilizable Fortifications, and Their Controlling Influence in War.**
1885   Boston   100.
BRESLIN, Howard   **A Hundred Hills.**
1960   New York   15.
BREWER, J. H. F.   **History of the 175th Infantry.**
1955   Baltimore   15.
BREWER, James H.   **The Confederate Negro: Virginia's Craftsmen and Military Laborers 1861-1865.**
1969   Durham, N. C.   15.
BRICE, Marshall M.   **Conquest of a Valley.**
1965   Charlottesville   15.
1967   Verona, Va.   10.
1974   Verona, Va.   10.
BRICE, Marshall M.   **The Stonewall Brigade Band.**
1967   Verona, Va.   20.
BRICK, John   **Jubilee.**
1956   Garden City   8.
BRICK, John   **The Richmond Raid.**
1963   New York   8.
BRIDGES, Hal (ed)   **A Lee Letter on the "Lost Dispatch" and the Maryland Campaign of 1862.** Wraps
1958   Virginia   10.
BRIDGES, Hal   **Lee's Maverick General, Daniel Harvey Hill.**
1961   New York   25.
BRIDGES, Mrs. Soule Jones   **A Story Founded on Fact and Verses.**
1903   Memphis   40.
BRIGANCE, William Norwood   **Jeremiah Sullivan Black, A Defender of the Constitution and the Ten Commandments.**
1934   Philadelphia   25.
BRIGHT, Leslie S.   **The Blockade Runner Modern Greece and Her Cargo.** Wraps
1977   Raleigh, N. C.   25.
BRINKERHOFF, Roeliff   **Recollections of a Lifetime.**
1900   Cincinnati   40.
1901   Cincinnati   30.
BRINTON, John H.   **Personal Memoirs of _____ Major and Surgeon U.S.V.**
1914   New York   70.
BRISBIN, James S.   **The Lives of Ulysses S. Grant and Schuyler Colfax.**
1869   Cincinnati   15.
BRISBIN, James S.   **Winfield Scott Hancock, Major-General U.S.A., His Life.** Wraps
1880   Philadelphia   20.
BRISTOL, Frank Milton   **The Life of Chaplain McCabe, Bishop of the Methodist Episcopal Church.**
1908   New York   25.
BRISTOW, B. W.   **Oration . . . Decoration of Soldiers' Graves at Cave Hill Cemetery.** Wraps
1875   Washington   20.

BRISTOW, J. Q.   **Tales of Old Fort Gibson.**
    1961   New York   10.
BRITTON, Wiley   **The Aftermath of the Civil War.**
    1924   Kansas City   15.
BRITTON, Wiley   **A Traveling Court Based on Investigation of War Claims.**
    1926   Kansas City   30.
BROCK, R. A. (ed)   **Gen. Robert Edward Lee — Soldier, Citizen and Christian Patriot.**
    1897   Richmond   75.
BROCK, R. A.   **Paroles of the Army of Northern Virginia, SHSP, Vol. 15.**
    1887   Richmond   Wraps   40.
    1962   New York   entitled **The Appomattox Roster.**   Ltd.   40.
BROCK, Sallie A.
    See: **PUTNAM**, Sallie A.
BROCK, W. R.   **An American Crisis — Congress and Reconstruction 1865-1867.**
    1963   London   15.
BROCKETT, Linus L. P.   **Battle-Field and Hospital.**
    n.d. (circa 1870)   New York   20.
BROCKETT, Linus P.   **Philanthropic Results of the War.**
    1864   New York   20.
BROCKETT, Linus P.   **Scouts, Spies and Heroes of the Great Civil War.**
    1892   Cleveland   20.
    1892   Jersey City   20.
    1899   Washington   20.
    1911   n.p.   15.
BROCKETT, Linus P. and **VAUGHAN**, Mary C.   **Woman's Work in the Civil War.**
    1867   Philadelphia   30.
    1867   Boston   30.
BROCKWAY, Beaman   **Fifty Years in Journalism Embracing Recollections and Personal Experiences with an Autobiography.**
    1891   Watertown, New York   20.
BRODIE, Fawn M.   **Thaddeus Stevens.**
    1959   New York   15.
BRONAUGH, W. C.   **The Youngers' Fight for Freedom.**
    1906   Columbia   45.
BROOKE, John M.   **The Virginia or Merrimac, Her Real Projector.** Wraps
    1891   Richmond   25.
BROOKES, Iveson L.   **A Defense of Southern Slavery Against the Attacks of Henry Clay and Alexander Campbell by a Southern Clergyman.** Wraps
    1851   Hamburg, S. C.   35.
BROOKS, Aubrey Lee & **LEFLER**, Hugh Talmage   **The Papers of Walter Clark.** 2 vols.
    1950   Chapel Hill   25.
BROOKS, Aubrey Lee   **Walter Clark, Fighting Judge.**
    1944   Chapel Hill, N. C.   20.
BROOKS, Fred Emerson   **Picketts Charge and Other Poems.**
    1903   Boston   20.
BROOKS, Noah   **Abraham Lincoln.**
    1900   New York   10.
    1909   New York   10.
BROOKS, Noah   **Mr. Lincoln's Washington The Civil War Dispatches of _____ edited by P. J. Straudenraus.**
    1967   New York   15.
    1967   South Brunswick   15.
BROOKS, Noah   **Washington in Lincoln's Time.**
    1895   New York   15.
    1958   New York   10.
BROOKS, R. P.   **Conscription in the Confederate States of America 1862-1865.** Wraps
    1917   Georgia   25.
BROOKS, Stewart   **Civil War Medicine.**
    1966   Springfield   30.

BROOKS, U. R.   **Butler and His Cavalry in the War of Secession 1861-1865.**
    1909   Columbia, S. C.   80.
BROOKS, U. R. (ed.)   **Stories of the Confederacy.**
    1912   Columbia, S. C.   75.
BROOKS, William E.   **Grant of Appomattox.**
    1942   Indianapolis   15.
BROOKS, William E.   **Lee of Virginia.**
    1932   Indianapolis   20.
    1932   Garden City   20.
BROSS, William   **Biographical Sketch of the Late Gen. B. J. Sweet.**
    History of Camp Douglas. Wraps.
    1878   Chicago   35.
BROUN, Thomas L. (comp)   **Dr. William Leroy Broun.**
    1912   New York   35.
BROWN, D. Alexander   **The Galvanized Yankees.**
    1963   Urbana   25.
BROWN, D. Alexander   **Grierson's Raid.**
    1954   Urbana, Ill.   25.
BROWN, George W.   **Reminiscences of Gov. R. J. Walker, with the True Story of the**
    Rescue of Kansas from Slavery.
    1902   Rockford, Ill.   30.
BROWN, George William   **Baltimore and the 19th of April, 1861.**
    1887   Baltimore   20.
BROWN, Willard   **The Signal Corps, U.S.A. in the War of the Rebellion.**
    1896   Boston   125.
BROWN, Joseph M.   **Kennesaw's Bombardment How the Sharpshooters Woke up the**
    Batteries. Wraps
    1890   Atlanta   100.
BROWN, Joseph M.   **The Mountain Campaign in Georgia.**
    1886   Buffalo, N. Y.   30.
    1889   New York   25.
BROWN, Leonard   **American Patriotism.**
    1869   Des Moines   35.
BROWN, Louis A.   **The Salisbury Prison, A Case Study of Confederate Military Prisons**
    1861-1865.
    1980   Wendell, N. C.   15.
BROWN, Norman D.   **Edward Stanly: Whiggery's Tar Heel Conqueror.**
    1974   University, Alabama   20.
BROWN, Spencer Kellogg   **Spencer Kellogg Brown as Disclosed By His Diary** edited by
    George G. Smith.
    1903   New York   30.
BROWN, Stuart E., Jr.   **The Guns of Harpers Ferry.**
    1968   Berryville, Va.   20.
BROWN, Wilbur F.   **A Tribute of Respect by Lafayette Post No. 140 . . . in Memory of**
    Commander Richard Worsam Meade.
    1898   New York   25.
BROWNE, A.   **Sketch of the Official Life of John A. Andrew, as Governor of**
    Massachusetts.
    1868   New York   10.
BROWNE, Francis F. (ed)   **Bugle-Echoes.**
    1886   New York   15.
BROWNE, Junius Henri   **Four Years in Secessia.**
    1865   Hartford   20.
BROWNE, Samuel T.   **First Cruise of the Montauk.** Wraps
    1880   Providence   20.
BROWNING, Orville Hickman   **The Diary of** _____ edited by Theodore C. Pease &
    James G. Randall. 2 vols.
    1925   Springfield   45.

BROWNLEE, Richard S.   **Gray Ghosts of the Confederacy.**
   1958   Baton Rouge   25.
   1968   Baton Rouge   20.
BROWNLOW, W. G.   **Sketches of the Rise, Progress and Decline of Secession.**
   1862   Philadelphia   30.
BROWNSON, O. A.   **The American Republic: Its Constitution, Tendencies, and Destiny.**
   1866   New York   40.
BRUCE, Phillip A.   **Brave Deeds of Confederate Soldiers.**
   1916   Philadelphia   30.
BRUCE, Philip A.   **Robert E. Lee.**
   1907   Philadelphia   20.
BRUCE, Robert V.   **Lincoln and the Tools of War.**
   1956   Indianapolis   20.
BRUNK, H. A.   **Life of Peter S. Hartman.**
   1937   n.p.   25.
BRUNKER, H. M. E.   **Story of the Campaign in Eastern Virginia, April, 1861 to May 1863.**
   1910   London   50.
BRYAN, Emma Lyon   **A Romance of the Valley of Virginia.**
   1892   Harrisonburg, Va.   30.
BRYAN, George S.   **The Great American Myth The True Story of Lincoln's Murder.**
   1940   New York   25.
BRYAN, J., III   **The Sword Over the Mantel — The Civil War and I.**
   1960   New York   10.
BUCHANAN, James   **Mr. Buchanan's Administration on the Eve of Rebellion.**
   1866   New York   25.
BUCHANAN, Lamont   **A Pictorial History of the Confederacy.**
   1951   New York   25.
   1959   New York   25.
   1963   New York   25.
BUCK, Charles W.   **Colonel Bob and A Double Love.**
   1922   Louisville, Kentucky   15.
BUCK, Irving A.   **Cleburne and His Command.**
   1908   New York & Washington   50.
   1959   Jackson   edited by Thomas R. Hay   35.
BUCK, Lucy Rebecca   **Sad Earth, Sweet Heaven.**
   1940   n.p.   Wraps   125.
   1973   n.p.   15.
BUCK, Paul H.   **The Road to Reunion 1865-1900.**
   1938   Boston   10.
   1947   Boston   10.
BUCKE, Richard M. (ed)   **Walt Whitman — The Wound Dresser Letters Written to His Mother from the Hospitals in Washington During the Civil War.**
   1949   New York   20.
BUCKERIDGE, Justin O.   **Lincoln's Choice.**
   1956   Harrisburg   20.
BUCKINGHAM, J. E.   **Reminiscences and Souvenirs of the Assassination of Abraham Lincoln.**
   1894   Washington   40.
BUCKINGHAM, Samuel G.   **The Life of William A. Buckingham The War Governor of Connecticut.**
   1894   Springfield, Mass.   15.
BUCKLEY, William   **Buckley's History of the Great Reunion of the North and South.**
   1923   Staunton, Va.   30.
BUCKLIN, Sophronia E.   **In Hospital and Camp: A Woman's Record of Thrilling Incidents Among the Wounded in the Late War.**
   1869   Philadelphia   30.
BUCKNER, W. P.   **Calculated Tables and Ranges for Navy and Army Guns.**
   1865   New York   20.

BUEL, J. W.   **The Authorized Pictorial Lives of James Gillespie Blaine and John Alexander Logan.**
    1884   Cincinnati   15.
BUELL, Augustus C.   **The Cannoneer, Recollections of Service in the Army of the Potomac.**
    1890   Washington   75.
    1897   n.p.   Wraps   40.
BULLARD, F. Lauriston   **Abraham Lincoln and the Widow Bixby.**
    1946   New Brunswick   10.
BULLARD, F. Lauriston   **Famous War Correspondents.**
    1914   Boston   25.
BULLARD, F. Lauriston   **A Few Appropriate Remarks Lincoln's Gettysburg Address.**
    1944   Harrogate, Tenn.   Ltd.   20.
BULLITT, J. C.   **A Review of Mr. Binney's Pamphlet on "The Privilege of the Writ of Habeas Corpus Under the Constituion."** Wraps
    1862   Philadelphia   20.
BULLOCH, James D.   **The Secret Service of the Confederate States in Europe.** 2 vols.
    1883   London   300.
    1884   New York   75.
    1959   New York   Boxed   50.
The Bummer Boy, A "Spoony" Biography. Wraps
    1868   Washington   20.
BURCH, John P.   **Charles W. Quantrell.**
    1923   Vega, Texas   25.
BURCHARD, Peter   **One Gallant Rush, Robert Gould Shaw and His Brave Black Regiment.**
    1965   New York   10.
BURCKMYER, Cornelius L.   **The Burckmyer Letters — March 1863 — June 1865.**
    1926   Columbia, S. C.   35.
BURGE, Dolly Sumner L.   **The Diary of Dolly Lunt Burge** edited by James I. Robertson.
    1962   Athens   25.
BURGE, Dolly Sumner L.   **A Woman's Wartime Journal.**
    1918   Macon, Ga.   45.
    1927   Macon, Ga.   40.
BURGER, Nash K.   **Confederate Spy: Rose O'Neale Greenhow.**
    1967   New York   10.
BURGER, Nash K. and **BETTERSWORTH,** John K.   **South of Appomattox.**
    1959   New York   20.
BURGESS, John W.   **The Civil War and the Constitution.** 2 vols.
    1903   New York   15.
BURGESS, John W.   **Reconstruction and the Constitution.**
    1902   New York   10.
BURKE, Robert   **Escape from a Southern Prison, a Brief History of the Prison Life and Escape . . . From Camp Ford Prison.** Wraps
    n.d. (circa 1880)   Indianapolis   100.
BURN, James Dawson   **Three Years Among the Working-Classes in the United States During the War.**
    1865   London   125.
BURNE, Alfred H.   **Lee, Grant and Sherman.**
    1938   Aldershot, Eng.   30.
    1939   New York   20.
BURNETT, C.   **Captain John Ericsson, Father of the "Monitor."**
    1960   New York   12.
BURNS, Zed H.   **Confederate Forts.**
    1977   Natchez   25.
BURNSIDE, Ambrose E.   **The Burnside Expedition.** Wraps
    1882   Providence   Ltd.   30.

BURR, Frank A.   **The Life of Gen. Philip H. Sheridan.**
1886   Providence   20.
1888   Providence   20.
1890   New York   20.
BURRAGE, Henry Sweetser   **Gettysburg and Lincoln.**
1906   New York   15.
BURT, Richard W.   **War Songs, Poems and Odes, Dedicated to My Comrades of the Mexican and Civil Wars.**
1906   Peoria, Ill.   50.
BURTON, E. Milby   **The Siege of Charleston 1861-1865.**
1907   Columbia   20.
BURTSCHI, Mary   **James Hall of Lincoln's Frontier World.**
1977   Vandalia, Ill.   10.
BURTSCHI, Mary   **Vandalia: Wilderness Capital of Lincoln's Land.**
1977   Vandalia, Ill.   15.
BUSEY, John W. & **MARTIN,** David G.   **Regimental Strengths at Gettysburg.**
1982   Baltimore   15.
BUSHNELL, Samuel C.   **The Story of the Monitor and the Merrimac.** Wraps
n.d. (circa 1920)   n.p.   20.
BUSHONG, Millard Kessler   **Old Jube, A Biography of Jubal A. Early.**
1955   Boyce, Virginia   30.
1961   Boyce, Virginia   20.
BUTLER, Benjamin F.   **Autobiography and Personal Reminiscences.**
1892   Boston   25.
BUTLER, Benjamin F.   **Character and Results of the War.** Wraps
1863   Philadelphia   10.
1863   New York   10.
1863   New York   10.
BUTLER, Benjamin F.   **Private and Official Correspondence of _____ During the Period of the Civil War.** 5 vols.
1917   Norwood   300.
BUTLER, Lorine Letcher   **John Morgan and His Men.**
1960   Philadelphia   30.
BUTLER, M. C.   **Address on the Life, Character and Services of General Wade Hampton.** Wraps
1903   Washington, D. C.   50.
BUTLER, Pierce   **Judah P. Benjamin.**
1906   Philadelphia   15.
1907   Washington   15.
BUTTERFIELD, Daniel   **Camp and Outpost Duty for Infantry.**
1862   New York   50.
BUTTERFIELD, Daniel   **Major General Joseph Hooker and the Troops from the Army of the Potomac.** Wraps
1896   New York   15.
BUTTS, Frank B.   **The Monitor and the Merrimac.** Wraps
1890   Providence   Ltd.   25.
BYRD, Ethel Maddox & **CASSEY,** Zelda Haas   **Memoirs of the War Between the States.**
1961   Richmond   25.
BYRNE, Frank L., and **WEAVER,** Andrew T. (eds)   **Haskell of Gettysburg, His Life and Civil War Papers.**
1970   Madison   20.
The "C" Letters as Published in "The North State." Wraps
1878   Greensboro, N. C.   45.
CABELL, Sears Wilson   **The "Bulldog" Longstreet at Gettysburg and Chickamauga.** Wraps
1938   Atlanta   10.
CABLE, George W.   **The Cavalier.**
1901   New York   15.

CABLE, George W.   **Kincaid's Battery.**
    1908   New York   15.
CADWALLADER, Sylvanus   **Three Years with Grant, as Recalled by War Correspondent Sylvanus Cadwallader.** edited by Benjamin P. Thomas.
    1955   New York   20.
    1967   New York   15.
CAIN, James M.   **Mignon.**
    1962   New York   15.
CAIN, Marvin R.   **Edward Bates of Missouri, Lincoln's Attorney General.**
    1965   Columbia, Mo.   15.
CAIRNES, John E.   **The Slave Power: Its Character, Career and Probable Designs.**
    1863   New York   30.
CALDWELL, J. F. J.   **The Stranger.**
    1907   New York   20.
CALHOUN, John C.   **Mr. Calhoun's Reply to Col. Benton.** Wraps
    n.d. (circa 1850)   n.p.   40.
CALIFF, Joseph M.   **Record of the Services of the 7th Regiment US Colored Troops, from Sept. 1863 to Nov. 1866.** Wraps.
    1878   Providence, R.I.   50.
CALLAHAN, John Morton   **The Diplomatic History of the Southern Confederacy.**
    1901   Baltimore   50.
    1964   New York   15.
Campaigns in Kentucky and Tennessee Including the Battle of Chickamauga 1862-4, Vol. 7 of MHSM.
    1908   Boston   50.
Campaigns of the Civil War. 13 vols. **Navy in the Civil War,** 3 vols. Together, 16 vols.
    1881-1905   New York   175.
    1963   New York   8 vols.   80.
    For individual titles, see author.
CAMPBELL, Andrew Jackson   **The Civil War Diary of** _____ edited by Jill K. Garrett. Wraps
    1965   Columbia, Tenn.   30.
CAMPBELL, Helen Jones   **The Case for Mrs. Surratt.**
    1943   New York   15.
CAMPBELL, Helen Jones   **Confederate Courier, the Historic Trial of Johnny Surratt For the Murder of Abraham Lincoln.**
    1964   New York   15.
CAMPBELL, James H.   **McClellan: A Vindication of the Military Career of General George B. McClellan.**
    1916   New York   50.
CAMPBELL, John A.   **Reminiscences and Documents Relating to the Civil War During the Year 1865.** Wraps
    1887   Baltimore   75.
CANBY, Courtlandt   **Lincoln and the Civil War.**
    1960   New York   12.
CANFIELD, Cass   **The Iron Will of Jefferson Davis.**
    1978   New York   15.
CANFIELD, Eugene B.   **Notes on Naval Ordnance of the American Civil War.** Wraps
    1960   Washington, D.C.   20.
CANNON, LeGrand B.   **Personal Reminiscences of the Rebellion.**
    1895   New York   40.
CAPERS, Ellison   **An Address on Memorial Day, May 20, 1890 Greenville, S.C..** Wraps
    1890   Greenville, S. C.   20.
CAPERS, Gerald M.   **Occupied City New Orleans Under the Federals 1862-1865.**
    1965   University, Kentucky   15.
CAPERS, Gerald M.   ·**Stephen A. Douglas Defender of the Union.**
    1959   Boston   10.
CAPERS, Henry D.   **The Life and Times of C. G. Memminger.**
    1893   Richmond   60.

CAPERS, Walter B.   **The Soldier-Bishop, Ellison Capers.**
     1912   New York   80.
CAPPS, Claudius Meade   **The Blue and the Gray, Best Poems of the Civil War.**
     1943   Boston   20.
Captain Walter Mason Dickinson.
     1898   Amherst, Maine   25.
Carleton   See: **COFFIN,** Charles Carleton
CARMAN, Harry J. & **LUTHIN,** Reihard H.   **Lincoln and the Patronage.**
     1964   Gloucester, Mass.   15.
CARNAHAN, J. W.   **Manual of the Civil War and Key to the Grand Army of the Republic.**
     1899   Washington   20.
CARNAHAN, James R.   **Camp Morton.** Wraps
     1892   Indianapolis   40.
CARNEGIE, D.   **Lincoln the Unknown.**
     1938   New York   5.
CARPENTER, F. B.   **Six Months at the White House with Abraham Lincoln.**
     1866   New York   20.
CARPENTER, Jesse T.   **The South as a Conscious Minority 1789-1861.**
     1963   Gloucester, Mass.   15.
CARPENTER, John A.   **Sword and Olive Branch Oliver Otis Howard.**
     1964   Pittsburgh   20.
CARPENTER, Louis H.   **Record of the Military Service of Brig.-Gen. Louis Henry Carpenter . . . 1861 to 1899.**
     1903   Philadelphia   Ltd.   50.
CARPENTER, Stephen D.   **Logic of History . . . Results of Slavery Agitation.**
     1864   Madison, Wisconsin   100.
CARR, Clark E.   **Lincoln at Gettysburg, An Address.**
     1906   Chicago   15.
CARROLL, Anna Ella   **The Union of the States.** Wraps
     1856   Boston   20.
CARROLL, Daniel B.   **Henri Mercier and the American Civil War.**
     1971   Princeton, New Jersey   20.
CARROLL, Gordon (ed)   **The Post Reader of Civil War Stories.**
     1958   New York   10.
CARROLL, J. E.   **An Autobiography.**
     189   Greenville, Pa.   45.
CARRUTHERS, Olive   **Lincoln's Other Mary.**
     1946   New York   5.
CARSE, Robert   **Blockade, The Civil War at Sea.**
     1958   New York   20.
CARSE, Robert   **Department of the South: Hilton Head Island in the Civil War.**
     1961   Columbia   25.
CARSON, James Petigru   **Life, Letters & Speeches of James Louis Petigru.**
     1920   Washington   35.
CARTER, Hodding   **The Angry Scar, The Story of Reconstruction.**
     1959   New York   20.
CARTER, Hodding   **Their Words Were Bullets, The Southern Press in War, Reconstruction, and Peace.**
     1969   Athens, Ga.   10.
CARTER, Samuel III   **The Final Fortress: The Campaign for Vicksburg 1862-1863.**
     1980   New York   20.
CARTER, Samuel, III   **The Last Cavaliers, Confederate and Union Cavalry in the Civil War.**   1979   New York   15.
CARTER, Samuel, III   **The Riddle of Dr. Mudd.**
     1974   New York   10.
CARTER, Samuel, III   **The Siege of Atlanta 1864.**
     1973   New York   25.
CARTER, W. H.   **Old Army Sketches.**
     1906   Baltimore   30.

CARTER, William H.   **The 6th Regiment of Cavalry U.S.A.**
   n.d. (circa 1890)   n.p.   40.
CARTER, William Harding   **Life of Lieutenant General Chaffee.**
   1917   Chicago   30.
CARTLAND, Fernando G.   **Southern Heroes or the Friends in War time.**
   1895   Cambridge   35.
   1897   Poughkeepsie   30.
CARTNELL, Thomas Kemp   **Shenandoah Valley Pioneers and Their Descendants.**
   n.d.   n.p.   30.
CASE, Lynn M. (comp)   **French Opinion on the United States and Mexico 1860-1867.**
   1936   New York & London   20.
CASE, Lynn M., and **SPENCER,** Warren F.   **The United States and France: Civil War Diplomacy.**
   1970   Philadelphia   25.
CASEY, Silas   **U.S. Infantry Tactics for the Instruction Exercise and Maneuvres of the United States Infantry.** 3 vols.
   1862   Philadelphia   150.
   1863   New York   150.
CASKIE, J.   **Life and Letters of Matthew Fontaine Maury . . . The Pathfinder of the Seas.**
   1928   Richmond   30.
CASSIDY, Vincent H. and **SIMPSON,** Amos E.   **Henry Watkins Allen of Louisiana.**
   1964   Baton Rouge   8.
CASSON, Henry   **"Uncle Jerry." Life of Gen. Jeremiah M. Rush.**
   1895   Madison, Wisconsin   25.
CASTEL, Albert   **General Sterling Price and the Civil War in the West.**
   1968   Baton Rouge   25.
CASTLEMON, Harry   **Frank Before Vicksburg.**
   n.d. (circa 1920)   Chicago   15.
CASTLEMON, Harry   **Frank on the Lower Mississippi.**
   1868   Philadelphia   15.
CASTLEMON, Harry   **Marcy the Blockade-Runner.**
   1891   Philadelphia   25.
A Catalogue of Brady's Photographic Views of the Civil War. Wraps
   n.d.   Watkins Glen, New York   12.
A Catalogue of Lincolniana with an Essay on Lincoln. Wraps
   n.d.   New York   25.
Catalogue of Rebel Flags Captured by Union Troops Since April 19, 1861. Wraps
   n.d.   n.p.   30.
Catalogue of Valuable Miscellaneous Books & Pamphlets Relating to American History, Southern Confederacy, Scarce Trials, etc. Wraps
   1876   Philadelphia   20.
CATE, Wirt Armistead   **Lucius Q. C. Lamar: Secession and Reunion.**
   1935   Chapel Hill, N. C.   25.
CATHEY, James H.   **Truth is Stranger than Fiction.**
   1899   n.p.   40.
   1939   Canton, N.C.   entitled **The Genesis of Lincoln**   35.
CATTON, Bruce   **America Goes to War.**
   1958   Middletown, Conn.   20.
CATTON, Bruce & **KETCHUM,** Richard (eds)   **American Heritage Picture History of the Civil War.**
   1960   New York   2 vols.   Boxed   25.
   1960   New York   1 vol.   ed.   15.
CATTON, Bruce   **The Army of the Potomac.**
   Vol. 1 — **Mr. Lincoln's Army.**
   Vol. 2 — **Glory Road.**
   Vol 3 — **A Stillness at Appomattox.**
   1962   New York   3 vols.   30.
   v.d.   Odd volumes   10. each

CATTON, Bruce   **Banners at Shenandoah.**
   1955   New York   15.
CATTON, Bruce   **A Bibliography of the American Civil War.** Wraps
   1962   New York   10.
CATTON, Bruce   **The Centennial History of the Civil War.**
   Vol. 1 — **The Coming Fury.**
   Vol. 2 — **Terrible Swift Sword.**
   Vol. 3 — **Never Call Retreat.**
   1961-65   Garden City, New York   3 vols. 30.
   v.d.   odd volumes   10. each
CATTON, Bruce   **Gettysburg: The Final Fury.**
   1974   Garden City   Boxed   10.
CATTON, Bruce   **Grant Moves South.**
   1960   Boston   10.
CATTON, Bruce   **Grant Takes Command.**
   1969   Boston   10
CATTON, Bruce   **The Meaning of the Civil War.** Wraps
   1961   Chicago   15.
CATTON, Bruce   **Prefaces to History.**
   1970   Garden City, New York   10.
CATTON, Bruce   **Reflections on the Civil War.**
   1981   Garden City   16.
CATTON, Bruce   **This Hallowed Ground.**
   1956   Garden City, New York   10.
CATTON, Bruce   **U. S. Grant and the American Military Tradition.**
   1954   Boston   15.
CATTON, Bruce   **Waiting for the Morning Train An American Boyhood.**
   1972   Garden City, New York   15.
CATTON, Bruce   **War Lords of Washington.**
   1969   New York   10.
CATTON, William & Bruce   **Two Roads to Sumter.**
   1963   New York   10.
CAUTHEN, Charles E. (ed)   **Family Letters of Three Wade Hamptons 1782-1901.**
   1953   Columbia, S. C.   30.
CAVE, Robert Catlett   **The Men in Gray.**
   1911   Nashville, Tenn.   50.
CAVELYN, Edward   **Memories of Some Courageous Southerners Before and After the Civil War.**
   1940   Boston   50.
Celebration of the 100th Anniversary of the Birth of Admiral Raphael Semmes C.S.N. Montgomery, Alabama Sept. 27, 1898. Wraps
   n.d.   n.p.   15.
The Century War Book.
   1894   New York   60.
   1978   New York   25.
Ceremonies and Reenactment of the One Hundredth Anniversary of the Second Inauguration of Abraham Lincoln.
   1967   Washington   15.
Ceremonies connected with the Inauguration of the Mausoleum and the Unveiling of the Recumbent Figure of General Robert Edward Lee, at Washington and Lee University. Wraps
   1833   Richmond   20.
CHACE, Elizabeth Buffum and LOVELL, Lucy Buffum   **Two Quaker Sisters From the Original Diaries.**
   1937   New York   30.
CHADWICK, French Ensor   **Causes of the Civil War.**
   1906   New York   10.
CHAMBERLAYNE, John Hampden   **Ham Chamberlayne: Virginian Letters & Papers**

of an Artillery Officer in the War . . . 1861-1865 — introduction and notes by his son.
   1932   Richmond   Ltd.   75.
CHAMBERS, Lenoir   **"Stonewall" Jackson.** 2 vols.
   1959   New York   Boxed   40.
CHAMBERS, Robert W.   **Smith's Battery.**
   1898   New York   15.
CHAMBRUN, the Marquis Adolphe de   **Impressions of Lincoln and the Civil War.**
Translated from the French by General Adelbert de Chambrun.
   1952   New York   10.
De CHANAL, V.   **L'Armee Americaine.**
   1872   Paris   40.
CHANNING, W. E.   **Slavery.**
   1835   Boston   50.
CHAPMAN, John Jay   **William Lloyd Garrison.**
   1913   New York   10.
CHAPMAN, Thomas   **False Reconstruction: or, The Slavery That Is Not Abolished.**
Wraps
   1876   Saxonville, Mass.   20.
CHARNWOOD, Lord   **Abraham Lincoln.**
   1917   New York   25.
CHASE, Edward   **Memorial Life of General William Tecumseh Sherman.**
   1891   Chicago   15.
CHASE, Philip H.   **Basic Classification and Listing, Confederate States of America Paper Money 1861-1865.** Wraps
   1936   n.p.   35.
CHASE, Philip H.   **Confederate Treasury Notes.**
   1947   Philadelphia   20.
CHASE, Salmon P.   **Diary and Correspondence . . .** In: **American Historical Society Annual Report for 1902,** Vol. 2.
   1903   Washington   40.
CHASE, Salmon P.   **Inside Lincoln's Cabinet, Civil War Diaries of** _____ edited by David Donald.
   1954   New York   20.
CHASE, William C.   **Story of Stonewall Jackson.**
   1901   Atlanta   250.
A Checkered Life Being a Brief History of the Countess Portales Formerly Miss Marie Boozer. Wraps
   1915   Columbia   25.
CHESHIRE, Joseph B.   **The Church in the Confederate States.**
   1912   New York   35.
   1914   New York   30.
CHESNEY, C. C.   **A Military View of Recent Campaigns in Virginia and Maryland.**
   1863   London   200.
   1864-65   London   2 vols.   200.
CHESNUT, Mary Boykin   **A Diary From Dixie** edited by Isabelle D. Martin & Myrta Lockett Avary.
   1905   New York   30.
   1905   London   35.
   1906   New York   25.
   1949   Boston   edited by Ben Ames Williams   20.
CHESTERMAN, W. D.   **Guide to Richmond and the Battle-Fields.** Wraps
   1881   Richmond   15.
   1890   Richmond   15.
   1891   Richmond   15.
CHILDE, Edward Lee   **Le General Lee. Sa Vie Et Ses Campagnes.** Wraps
   1874   Paris   35.
CHILDS, George W.   **Recollections of General Grant.**
   1890   Philadelphia   20.

CHIPMAN, N. P.   **The Tragedy of Andersonville Trial of Capt. Henry Wirz.**
    1911   Sacramento, Cal.   50.
    1911   San Francisco   50.
CHITTENDEN, L. E.   **Lincoln and the Sleeping Sentinel.**
    1909   New York   10.
CHITTENDEN, L. E.   **Personal Reminiscences 1840-1890.**
    1893   New York   25.
CHITTENDEN, L. E.   **Recollections of President Lincoln and His Administration.**
    1891   New York   15.
CHITTENDEN, L. E.   **A Report of the Debates and Proceedings in the Secret Sessions of the Conference Convention . . . 1861.**
    1864   New York   45.
CHRISTIAN, George L.   **The Confederate Cause and Its Defenders: An Address.** Wraps
    1898   Richmond   20.
CHRISTIAN, George L.   **Sketch of the Origin and Erection of the Confederate Memorial Institute at Richmond, Virginia.** Wraps
    n.d. (circa 1925)   n.p.   30.
CHURCH, William C.   **Life of John Ericsson.** 2 vols.
    1890   New York   30.
    1891   New York   30.
    1906   New York   25.
    1911   n.p.   1 vol/ed   15.
CHURCH, William C.   **Ulysses S. Grant and the Period of Preservation and Reconstruction.**
    1897   New York   10.
    1926   Garden City   10.
CHURCHILL, Franklin Hunter   **Sketch of the Life of Bvt. Gen. Sylvester Churchill Inspector General U. S. Army.**
    1888   New York   25.
CHURCHILL, Sir Winston   **The American Civil War.**
    1961   New York   10.
CIST, Henry M.   **The Army of the Cumberland.**
    1882   New York   20.
    1894   New York   20.
Civil and Mexican Wars, Vol. 13 of MHSM.
    1913   Boston   50.
Civil War and Miscellaneous Papers, Vol. 14 of MHSM.
    1918   Boston   40.
Civil War Centennial Commission May 1958, Vol. 1, No. 1 — June 1965, Vol. 8, no. 6 — 86 numbers.
    1965   Washington, D. C.   100.
Civil War Naval Chronology 1861-1865.
    1961-66   Washington   6 parts   wraps   25.
    1971   Washington   20.
CLACK, Louise   **Our Refugee Household.**
    1866   New York   40.
CLAIBORNE, John Herbert,   **Seventy-Five Years in Old Virginia.**
    1904   New York   100.
CLARE, Virginia   **Thunder and Stars: The Life of Mildred Rutherford.**
    1941   Oglethorpe, Ga.   20.
CLARK, Allen C.   **Abraham Lincoln, the Merciful President, the Pardon of the Sleeping Sentinel.**
    1927   Washington   20.
CLARK, Douglas   **Rhythmic Ramblings in Battle-Scarred Manassas.** Wraps
    1905   Philadelphia   15.
CLARK, Thomas D. (ed)   **Travels in the New South.** 2 vols.
    1962   Norman, Oklahoma   35.
CLARKE, Asia Booth   **The Unlocked Book.**
    1938   New York   25.

CLARKE, George Herbert   **Some Reminiscences and Early Letters of Sidney Lanier.** Wraps
1907   Macon, Georgia   25.
CLARKE, H. C.   See: **Confederate Imprints**
CLARKE, O. P.   **The Colonel of the 10th Cavalry A Story of the War.** Wraps
1891   Utica, New York   30.
CLARKSON, Charles Ervine   **"A Rose of Old Virginia."**
1927   Ft. Smith, Arkansas   15.
CLAVREUL, H.   **Diary of Reverend H. Clavreul.** Wraps
1910   Waterbury   15.
CLAY, Mrs.   See: **CLAY-CLOPTON,** Virginia
CLAY-CLOPTON, Virginia   **A Belle of the Fifties, Memoirs of Mrs. Clay of Alabama**
ed. by Ada Sterling.
1904   New York   30.
1905   New York   30.
CLAYTON, Victoria V.   **White and Black Under the Old Regime.**
1899   Milwaukee   30.
CLAYTON, W. F.   **A Narrative of the Confederate States Navy.**
1910   Weldon, N. C.   500.
CLEAVES, Freeman   **Meade of Gettysburg.**
1960   Norman, Oklahoma   30.
CLEAVES, Freeman   **Rock of Chickamauga: Life of Gen. George H. Thomas.**
1948   Norman, Oklahoma   35.
CLEMENCEAU, Georges   **American Reconstruction.**
1928   New York   20.
CLEMENTS, Bennett A.   **Memoir of Jonathan Letterman, M.D., Surgeon United States Army and Medical Director of the Army of the Potomac.** Wraps
1909   Washington   20.
CLEMMER, Mary   **Ten Years in Washington or Inside Life and Scenes in Our National Capital As a Woman Sees Them.**
1882   Hartford, Conn.   **15.**
CLEVELAND, Henry   **Alexander H. Stephens, In Public and Private.**
1866   Philadelphia   40.
1866   v.p.   40.
n.d.   Philadelphia   30.
CLIFFORD, Philip Greely   **Nathan Clifford, Democrat (1803-1881).**
1922   New York   25.
CLIFT, G. Glenn (ed)   **The Private War of Lizzie Hardin.**
1963   Frankfort, Kentucky   25.
COATSWORTH, S. S.   **The Loyal People of the Northwest.**
1869   Chicago   50.
COCHIN, Augustin   **The Results of Emancipation.**
1863   Boston   20.
COCHRAN, Hamilton   **Blockade Runners of the Confederacy.**
1958   Indianapolis   25.
1958   New York   25.
COCHRANE, John   **The War for the Union, Memoir of _____.** Wraps
n.d. (circa 1886)   n.p.   35.
COCKRELL, Monroe F. (ed)   **The Lost Account of the Battle of Corinth and the Court Martial of Gen. Van Dorn.** Wraps
1955   Jackson   10.
COCKRELL, Monroe F.   **Stonewall Jackson.** Wraps
1955   Evanston, Ill.   Ltd.   50.
CODDINGTON, Edwin B.   **The Gettysburg Campaign.**
1968   New York   25.
COFFIN, C. C.   **Abraham Lincoln.**
1892   New York   15.
COFFIN, Charles Carleton   **Drum Beat of the Nation.**
1888   New York   15.

COFFIN, Charles Carleton   **Following the Flag.**
1892   Boston   15.
COFFIN, Charles Carleton   **Four Years of Fighting.**
1866   Boston   30.
1881   Boston   entitled **The Boys of '61 or Four Years of Fighting**   25.
v.d.   Boston   30.
COFFIN, Charles Carleton   **Freedom Triumphant.**
1891   New York   15.
COFFIN, Charles Carleton   **Marching to Victory.**
1889   New York   20.
COFFIN, Charles Carleton. **My Days and Nights on the Battlefield.**
1864   Boston   20.
COFFIN, Charles Carleton   **Redeeming the Republic The Third Period of the War of the Rebellion in the Year 1864.**
1898   New York   20.
COFFIN, Charles Carleton   **Stories of Our Soldiers. War Reminiscences by "Carleton" and by Soldiers of New England. 2 Vols.**
1893   Boston   40.
COGGIN, J. C.   **Abraham Lincoln An North Carolinian With Proof.**
1927   Gastonia, N. C.   35.
COGGINS, Jack   **Arms and Equipment of the Civil War.**
1962   Garden City, New York   20.
COKER, Elizabeth B.   **La Belle.**
1959   New York   15.
COLE, Arthur Charles   **The Irrepressible Conflict 1850-1865.**
1934   New York   15.
COLE, J. R.   **The Life and Public Services of Winfield Scott Hancock Major General U.S.A.**
1880   Cincinnati   25.
COLEMAN, S. B.   **A July Morning with the Rebel Ram Arkansas.** Wraps
1890   Detroit   20.
COLLINS, Loren Warren   **The Story of a Minnesotan.**
n.d.   n.p.   40.
COLLINS, William H.   **Second Address to the People of Maryland.** Wraps
1861   Baltimore   25.
COLTON, Ray C.   **The Civil War in the Western Territories.**
1959   Norman, Oklahoma   20.
COLVER, A.   **Mr. Lincoln's Wife.**
1943   New York   15.
COMMAGER, Henry Steele (ed)   **The Blue and the Gray. 2 vols.**
1950   Indianapolis   Boxed   35.
1950   Indianapolis   2 vols. in 1   15.
COMMAGER, Henry Steele (ed)   **Illustrated History of the Civil War.**
1976   New York   30.
Compilation of Official Documents Illustrative of the Organization of the Army of the United States from 1789 to 1876.
1876   Washington   60.
Comprehensive Sketch of the Battle of Manassas. Wraps
1887   Washington   40.
Comprehensive Sketch of the Merrimac and Monitor Naval Battle. Wraps
1886   New York   25.
CONDON, William H.   **Life of Major-General James Shields.**
1900   Chicago   35.
Confederate Centennial Studies. Wraps
27 numbers   Ltd. to 450 copies   complete set   750.
For individual number, see author.
Confederate Historical Society, Journal of. Wraps
10. per number

Confederate Leaders and Other Citizens Request the House of Delegates to Repeal the Resolution of Respect to Abraham Lincoln, the Barbarian. Wraps
1928 (?)   n.p.   20.
Confederate Memorial Addresses, Monday, May 11, 1885, New Bern, N. C. Ladies Memorial Association. Wraps
1886   Richmond   30.
The Confederate Memorial Literary Society Yearbook 1908-9.
1909   Richmond   15.
Confederate Receipt Book.
1960   Athens, Georgia   20.
Confederate Soldiers, Sailors and Civilians Who Died as Prisoners of War at Camp Douglas, Chicago, Ill. 1862-1865. Wraps
n.d. (circa 1962)   Kalamazoo, Michigan   20.
Confederate States of America, Journal of the Congress 1861-1865. 7 vols.
1904   Washington   350.
n.d.   n.p.   (reprint   250.
Confederate Victories in the Southwest: Prelude to Defeat.
1961   Albuquerque   20.
Confederate War Journal. Wraps
Monthly Journal   15. per issue
CONGDON, Charles T.   **Tribune Essays, Leading Articles Contributed to NY Tribune from 1857 to 1863.**
1869   New York   20.
CONGDON, Don (ed)   **Combat: The Civil War.**
1967   New York   30.
1967   New York   20.
CONGER, Arthur L.   **The Rise of U. S. Grant.**
1931   New York   25.
The Congressional Globe: Debates and Proceedings of the Second Session of the Thirty-Sixth Congress Also of the Special Session of the Senate Dec. 6, 1860 — Feb. 19, 1861.
1861   Washington   40.
The Congressional Globe: Debates and Proceedings of the Second Session of the 37th Congress.
1862   Washington   35.
CONNELLEY, William E.   **Quantrill and the Border Wars.**
1910   Cedar Rapids, Iowa   150.
1956   New York   CWBC ed.   30.
1956   New York   Trade ed.   20.
CONNELLY, Thomas L.   **The Marble Man.**
1977   New York   15.
CONNELLY, Thomas Lawrence   **Army of the Heartland, The Army of Tennessee 1861-1862.**
1967   Baton Rouge   25.
1972   Baton Rouge   20.
CONNELLY, Thomas Lawrence   **Autumn of Glory, The Army of Tennessee.**
1971   Baton Rouge   25.
1974   Baton Rouge   20.
CONNELLY, Thomas Lawrence   **The Politics of Command, Factions and Ideas in Confederate Strategy.**
1973   Baton Rouge   20.
CONNELLY, Thomas Lawrence   **Will Success Spoil Jeff Davis? The Last Book About the Civil War.**
1963   New York   10.
CONNER, James   **Letters of General James Conner, C.S.A.** edited by Mary Conner Moffett.
1950   Columbia   Ltd.   500.
CONNOR, Daniel Ellis   **A Confederate in the Colorado Gold Fields** edited by Donald J. Berthrong & Odessa Davenport.
1970   Norman, Oklahoma   15.

CONNOR, George C.   **Guide to Chattanooga and Lookout Mountain.** Wraps
    n.d. (circa 1885)   Chattanooga   30.
CONNOR, Henry G.   **John Archibald Campbell Associate Justice of the U. S. Supreme**
    Court 1853-1861.
    1920   Boston   30.
CONRAD, Mary Lynn   **Confederate Banners.** Wraps
    n.d.   Harrisonburg, Va.   25.
CONRAD, Thomas N.   **A Confederate Spy — A Story of the Civil War.** Wraps
    1892   New York   125.
    n.d.   n.p.   Reprint   10.
CONRAD, Thomas N.   **The Rebel Scout.**
    1904   Washington   150.
CONSTELLANO, Illion   **The Hunted Unionist . . . A Record of Late Occurrences in**
    Georgia. Wraps
    1864   New York   75.
CONWAY, Moncure D.   **The Golden Hour.**
    1862   Boston   25.
CONWAY, Moncure D.   **The Rejected Stone: or, Insurrection Vs. Resurrection in**
    America by a Native of Virginia.
    1862   Boston   20.
CONWELL, Russell H.   **Magnolia Journey.**
    1974   University, Alabama   12.
CONYNGHAM, David P.   **Sherman's March Through the South.**
    1865   New York   75.
COOK, Adrian   **The Armies of the Streets: The New York City Draft Riots of 1863.**
    1974   Lexington   20.
COOK, Harvey T.   **Sherman's March Through South Carolina in 1865.** Wraps
    1938   Greenville, S. C.   12.
COOK, Joel   **The Siege of Richmond: A Narrative of the Military Operations of Major-**
    General George B. McClellan During the Months of May and June 1862.
    1862   Philadelphia   35.
COOK, Roy Bird   **The Family and Early Life of Stonewall Jackson.**
    1924   Richmond   75.
    1925   Richmond   50.
    1948   Charleston, W. Va.   35.
    1967   Charleston, W. Va.   Wraps   20.
COOK, Roy Bird   **Thomas J. Jackson, A God-Fearing Soldier of the C.S.A.**
    1961   Cincinnati   25.
COOK, Walter Henry   **Secret Political Societies in the South During the Period of Recon-**
    struction, an Address. Wraps
    n.d. (circa 1900)   Cleveland, Ohio   40.
COOKE, Giles. B.   **Just Before and After Lee Surrendered to Grant.** Wraps
    n.d. (circa 1922)   n.p.   20.
COOKE, John Esten   **Hammer and Rapier.**
    1807   New York   60.
    1898   New York   35.
COOKE, John Esten   **Hilt to Hilt.**
    1869   New York   40.
    1890   New York   30.
    1893   Charleston   30.
COOKE, John Esten   **Leather and Silk.**
    1893   Charleston, S. C.   35.
COOKE, John Esten   **A Life of Gen. Robert E. Lee.**
    1871   New York   100.
    1883   New York   75.
    1887   New York   50.

COOKE, John Esten. **The Life of Stonewall Jackson. By a Virginian.**
    1863   New York   75.
    1864   New York   50.
    1866   New York   40.
COOKE, John Esten.   **Mohun or the Last Days of Lee and His Paladins.**
    1869   New York   50.
    1893   Charleston   30.
    1936   Charlottesville, Va.   30.
COOKE, John Esten   **Outlines from the Outpost** edited by Richard Harwell.
    1961   Chicago   25.
COOKE, John Esten   **Stonewall Jackson: A Military Biography.**
    1866   New York   150.
    1876   New York   75.
COOKE, John Esten   **Stonewall Jackson and the Old Stonewall Brigade** edited by Richard B. Harwell.
    1954   Charlottesville, Va.   35.
COOKE, John Esten.   **Surry of Eagle's Nest.**
    1866   New York   75.
    1889   New York   40.
    1894   New York   30.
    1894   Chicago   30.
COOKE, John Esten   **Wearing of the Gray.**
    1867   New York   125.
    1959   Bloomington, Indiana   edited by Philip Van Doren Stern   25.
COOKE, Phillip St. George   **Cavalry Tactics.** 2 vols.
    1861   Washington   60.
COOLIDGE, Louis   **Ulysses S. Grant.**
    1917   Boston   15.
    1922   Boston   15.
COOLING, Benjamin Franklin   **Symbol, Sword, and Shield.**
    1975   Hamden, Conn.   20.
COOPER, Charles R.   **Chronological and Alphabetical Record of the Engagements of the Great Civil War.**
    1904   Milwaukee   25.
COOPER, Peter   **Reconstruction, Letter from Peter Cooper to President Johnson.** Wraps
    n.d.   n.p.   25.
COPPEE, Henry   **Field Manual of Courts-Martial.**
    1863   Philadelphia   35.
COPPEE, Henry   **General Thomas.**
    1883   New York   30.
    1893   New York   25.
    1897   New York   20.
COPPEE, Henry   **Grant and His Campaigns: A Military Biography.**
    1866   New York   20.
COPPEE, Henry   **Life and Services of Gen. U. S. Grant.**
    1868   New York   15.
Copperhead Conspiracy in the North-West An Espose of the Treasonable Order of the "Sons of Liberty." Wraps
    n.d. (circa 1863)   New York   20.
CORBIN, Diana Fontaine Maury   **A Life of Matthew Fontaine Maury, USN and CSN.**
    1888   London   75.
CORBIN, Richard W.   **Letters of a Confederate Officer to His Family in Europe, During the Last Year of the War of Secession.** Wraps
    1967   Ann Arbor, Michigan   20.
CORNISH, Dudley Taylor   **The Sable Arm, Negro Troops in the Union Army, 1861-1865.**
    1956   New York   25.
    1966   New York   15.

CORNISH, Joseph Jenkins, III **The Air Arm of the Confederacy.** Wraps
1963 Richmond 15.

A Correspondence Between General Early and Mahone in Regard to a Military Memoir of the Latter. Wraps
1871 n.p. 40.

Correspondence on the Present Relations Between Great Britain and the United States of America. Wraps
1862 Boston 30.

Correspondence Relating to the Insurrection at Harper's Ferry, Oct. 17, 1859. Wraps
1860 Annapolis 50.

Correspondence Relative to the Case of Messrs. Mason and Slidell. Wraps
1861 Washington 30.

CORRINGTON, John William **And Wait for the Night.**
1964 New York 15.

CORSAN, W. C. **Two Months in the Confederate States.**
1863 London 200.

CORT, Charles Edwin **"Dear Friends" The Civil War Letters and Diary of _____** edited by Helen W. Tomlinson.
1962 n.p. 15.

COSTON, Martha **Signal Success, The Work and Travels of Mrs. Martha Coston, An Autobiography.**
1866 Philadelphia 75.

COTTERILL, R. S. **The Old South.**
1939 Glendale 25.

COTTON, John W. **Yours Till Death, Civil War Letters of John W. Cotton** edited by Lucille Griffith.
1951 University, Alabama 35.

COULTER, E. Merton **The Confederate States of America, Vol 7 of A History of the South.**
1950 Baton Rouge, La. 25.
1968 Baton Rouge, La. 20.

COULTER, E. Merton **Planters' Wants in the Days of the Confederacy.** Wraps
1928 Savannah, Georgia 20.

COULTER, E. Merton **The South During Reconstruction, 1865-1877.**
1947 Baton Rouge 30.
1962 Baton Rouge 20.
1965 Baton Rouge 20.

COULTER, E. Merton **Travels in the Confederate States.**
1948 Norman, Oklahoma 50.
1961 Norman, Oklahoma 35.
1890 Wendell, N. C. 25.

COULTER, E. Merton. **William G. Brownlow.**
1937 Chapel Hill, N. C. 20.
1971 Knoxville 15.

COULTER, E. Merton **William Montague Browne.**
1967 Athens, Georgia 15.

COUPER, William **Claudius Crozet, Soldier, Scholar, Educator, Engineer.** Wraps
1936 Charlottesville, Va. 35.

COUPER, William **One Hundred Years at Virginia Military Institute.** 4 vols.
1939 Richmond 100.

COUPER, William **The V.M.I. New Market Cadets.**
1933 Charlottesville 50.

COURTNEY, Patrick C. **The Seven Days Battles Around Richmond, The Civil War Round Table of London, England.** Wraps
1960 London 15.

COWARD, Asbury **The South Carolinians Colonel Asbury Coward's Memoirs** edited by Natalie Jenkins Bond & Osmun L. Coward.
1968 New York 25.

COWELL, A. T.   **Tactics at Gettysburg.** Wraps
        1910   Gettysburg   20.
COWLES, William H. H.   **The Life and Services of Gen'l James B. Gordon, An Address.**
Wraps
        1887   Raleigh, N. C.   40.
COWLEY, Charles   **Leaves From a Lawyer's Life: Afloat and Ashore.**
        1879   Lowell, Mass.   30.
COX, Earnest Sevier   **Lincoln's Negro Policy.**
        1972   Richmond   15.
COX, Jacob D.   **Atlanta.**
        1882   New York   20.
        1895   New York   20.
COX, Jacob D.   **The Battle of Franklin, Tennessee, November 30, 1864.**
        1897   New York   Ltd.   100.
COX, Jacob D.   **The March to the Sea: Franklin and Nashville.**
        1882   New York   20.
        1898   New York   20.
COX, Jacob D.   **Military Reminiscences of the Civil War.** 2 vols.
        1900   New York   100.
COX, Jacob D.   **The Second Battle of Bull Run as Connected with the Fitz-John Porter
Case, A Paper.** Wraps
        1882   Cincinnati   50.
COX, Lawanda, and COX, John H.   **Politics, Principle, and Prejudice 1865-1866.**
        1963   London   20.
COX, Lawanda & COX, John H. (eds.)   **Reconstruction, the Negro, and the New South.**
        1973   Columbia   20.
COX, Samuel S.   **Amnesty and the Jefferson Davis Amendment, Speech.** Wraps
        1876   Washington   25.
COX, Samuel S.   **Punishment or Pardon; Force or Freedom, for the Wasted Land,
Speech.** Wraps
        1875   Washington   20.
COX, Samuel S.   **Three Decades of Federal Legislation, 1855 to 1885.**
        1885   Providence   15.
COX, William Ruffin   **Address on the Life and Services of Gen. James H. Lane.** Wraps
        1908   Richmond   50.
COX, William Ruffin   **Address on the Life and Services of General Marcus J. Wright.**
Wraps
        1915   Richmond   75.
COX, William V.   **The Defenses of Washington. General Early's Advance
on the Capital and the Battle of Fort Stevens, July 11 and 12, 1864.** Wraps
        1901   Washington   30.
COXE, Elizabeth Allen   **Memories of a South Carolina Plantation During the War.**
        1912   n.p.   Ltd.   150.
CRABB, Alfred Leland   **Home to Tennessee, A Tale of Soldiers Returning.**
        1952   Indianapolis   25.
CRAFTS, W. A.   **The Southern Rebellion.** 2 vols.
        1862   Boston   75.
CRAIG, Hugh   **Grand Army Picture Book   From April 12, 1861 to April 26, 1865.**
        n.d.   New York   70.
CRAIG, Reginald S.   **The Fighting Parson   The Biography of Colonel John M.
Chivington.**
        1959   Los Angeles   35.
CRAMER, John H.   **Lincoln Under Enemy Fire.**
        1948   Baton Rouge   20.
CRANDALL, Marjorie Lyle   **Confederate Imprints.** 2 vols.
        1955   Boston   125.

CRANDALL, Warren D. and **NEWELL**, Isaac D.   **History of the Ram Fleet and the Mississippi Marine Brigade.**
  1907   St. Louis   300.
CRANE, Stephen   **The Red Badge of Courage.**
  1930   New York   10.
CRAVEN, Avery   **Civil War in the Making 1815-1860.**
  1959   Baton Rouge   15.
  1968   Baton Rouge   10.
CRAVEN, Avery   **The Coming of the Civil War.**
  1942   New York   15.
CRAVEN, Avery   **Edmund Ruffin, Southerner.**
  1932   New York   20.
  1972   Baton Rouge   15.
CRAVEN, Avery   **The Growth of Southern Nationalism 1848-1861.**
  1964   Baton Rouge   15.
CRAVEN, Avery   **An Historian and the Civil War.**
  1964   Chicago   20.
CRAVEN, Avery   **The Repressible Conflict 1830-1861.**
  1939   University, Louisiana   20.
CRAVEN, John J.   **Prison Life of Jefferson Davis.**
  1866   New York   25.
  1866   London   30.
  1905   New York   15.
CRAWFORD, Samuel Wylie   **The Genesis of the Civil War.**
  1887   New York   40.
  1896   New York   Entitled: **The History of the Fall of Fort Sumter.** Wraps   30.
  1898   New York   20.
CREELMAN, James   **Why We Love Lincoln.**
  1909   New York   15.
CREIGHTON, Wilbur Foster   **The Life of Major Wilbur Fisk Foster.**
  1961 (?)   Nashville, Tenn. (?)   50.
CRENSHAW, Ollinger   **The Slave States in the Presidential Election of 1860.**
  1945   Baltimore   25.
CRISSEY, Elwell   **Lincoln's Lost Speech The Pivot of His Career.**
  1967   New York   20.

CRIST, Nelson   **Battle of Atlanta, Story of the Cyclorama.** Wraps
  1919   n.p.   25.
CRISWELL, Grover C. & Clarence L.   **Confederate and Southern State Bands.**
  1961   St. Petersburg   25.
CRISWELL, Grover C. and Clarence L.   **Confederate and Southern State Currency.**
  1957   Pass-A-Grille Beach, Florida   plus supplement   25.
CRITTENDEN, H. H.   **The Battle of Westport.**
  1938   Kansas City   20.
CRITTENDEN, H. H.   **The Crittenden Memoirs.**
  1936   New York   50.
  1938   Kansas City   40.
CROCKER, James F.   **Gettysburg Pickett's Charge and Other War Addresses.**
  1915   Portsmouth   125.
CROLY, David G.   **Seymour and Blair Their Lives and Services.**
  1868   New York   30.
CROMIE, Alice Hamilton   **A Tour Guide to the Civil War.**
  1975   New York   20.
CROOK, D. P.   **The North, the South and the Powers 1861-1865.**
  1974   New York   20.
CROOK, George   **General George Crook, His Autobiography** edited by Martin F. Schmitt.
  1946   Norman, Oklahoma   30.

CROOK, William H.   **Through Five Administrations: Reminiscences Col. Wm. H. Crook, Body Guard to Lincoln.**
1910   New York   15.
CROSBY, Alpheus   **The Present Position of the Seceded States, etc., An Address.** Wraps
1865   Boston   20.
CROSBY, Frank   **Life of Abraham Lincoln.**
1866   Philadelphia   25.
CROSS, Andrew B.   **The War, Battle of Gettysburg and the Christian Commission.** Wraps
1865   Baltimore   40.
CROWN, Francis J., Jr.   **Confederate Postal History.**
1976   Lawrence, Mass.   30.
CROZIER, Emmet   **Yankee Reporters 1861-65.**
1956   New York   20.
CROZIER, R. H.   **The Confederate Spy.**
1885   Louisville   45.
CRUMPTON, Washington Bryan   **A Book of Memories 1842-1920.**
1921   Montgomery, Alabama   25.
CRUSE, Mary A.   **Cameron Hall: A Story of the Civil War.**
1867   Philadelphia   25.
CULBRETH, David M. R.   **The University of Virginia.**
1908   New York   75.
CULLEN, Andrews Battle   _____, **Patriot, Orator, Soldier, Christian.** Wraps
n.d. (circa 1905)   n.p.   75.
CULLEN, Joseph P.   **The Peninsula Campaign 1862.**
1973   Harrisburg   15.
CULLON, Shelby M.   **Fifty Years of Public Service.**
1911   Chicago   25.
CULLOP, Charles P.   **Confederate Propaganda in Europe 1861-1865.**
1969   Coral Gables, Florida   15.
CULLUM, George W.   **Biographical Register of the Officers and Graduates of the U.S. Military Academy.** 2 Vols.
1868   New York   60.
1891   Boston and New York   75.
CULLUM, George W.   **Biographical Sketch of Brigadier General Joseph G. Swift, Chief Engineer of the U.S. Army.** Wraps
1877   New York   25.
CULLUM, George W.   **Register of the Officers and Graduates of the U.S. Military Academy.**
1850   New York   30.
CUMMING, Kate   **Gleanings from Southland.**
1892   Birmingham   40.
CUMMINGS, Kate   **A Journal of Hospital Life in the Confederate Army of Tennessee.**
1866   Louisville   200.
1959   Baton Rouge, La.   entitled **The Journal of a Confederate Nurse** edited by Richard B. Harwell   25.
CUMMINGS, A. Boyd   **Official Memoir of Lieutenant Commander A. Boyd Cummings.** edited by James Alden. Wraps
n.d.   n.p.   30.
CUMMINGS, Charles M.   **Yankee Quaker, Confederate General, the Curious Career of Bushrod Rust Johnson.**
1971   Rutherford, N. J.   35.
CUMMINGS, Edward   **Marmaduke of Tennessee.**
1914   Chicago   15.
CUMMINS, A. B.   **The Wilson-Kautz Raid.** Wraps
1961   Blackstone, Virginia   10.
CUNNINGHAM, Edward   **The Port Hudson Campaign   1862-1863**
1963   Baton Rouge   20.

CUNNINGHAM, Frank   **General Stand Watie's Confederate Indians.**
  1959   San Antonio, Texas   1959   Signed Ltd. Edition   60.
  Trade edition   40.
  1960   San Antonio   40.
CUNNINGHAM,Frank   **Knight of the Confederacy   Gen. Turner Ashby.**
  1960   San Antonio, Texas   35.
CUNNINGHAM, Horace H.   **Doctors in Gray.**
  1958   Baton Rouge   40.
  1960   Baton Rouge   35.
  1970   Gloucester, Mass.   15.
CUNNINGHAM, Horace H.   **Field Medical Services at the Battles of Manassas.** Wraps
  1968   Athens   10.
CURRENT, Richard N.   **Lincoln and the First Shot.**
  1963   Philadelphia   15.
CURRENT, Richard N.   **The Lincoln Nobody Knows.**
  1958   New York   20.
CURRENT, Richard N.   **Old Thad Stevens, A Story of Ambition.**
  1942   Madison, Wisconsin   15.
CURRENT, Richard N. (editor)   **Reconstruction in Retrospect.**
  1969   Baton Rouge   15.
CURRIE, George E.   **Warfare Along the Mississippi. The Letters of** _____ edited by
  Norman E. Clarke.
  1961   Mt. Pleasant, Michigan   20.
CURRY, Charles   **John Brown Baldwin — Lawyer, Soldier, Statesman.** Wraps
  1928   Staunton, Virginia   25.
CURRY, J. L. M.   **Civil History of the Confederate States with some Personal
  Reminiscences.**
  1900   Richmond   20
  1901   Richmond   20.
CURRY, J. L. M.   **The Southern States of the American Union.**
  1895   Richmond   15.
CURRY, Leonard P.   **Blueprint for Modern American, Non-Military Legislation of the
  First Civil War Congress.**
  1968   Nashville   15.
CURRY, Richard Orr   **A House Divided.**
  1964   Pittsburgh   15.
CURTIS, Newton Martin   **The Capture of Fort Fisher.** Wraps
  1900   Boston   30.
CUSHING, Caleb   **The Treaty of Washington.**
  1873   New York   25.
CUSSONS, John   **Jack Sterry, The Jessie Scout.** Wraps
  1907   Harrisonburg   30.
CUSSONS, John   **United States "History" as the Yankee Makes and Takes It, By a
  Confederate Soldier.** Wraps
  1900   Glen Allen, Va.   40.
CUSTER, Elizabeth B.   **"Boots and Saddles" or Life in Dakota with General Custer.**
  1885   New York   35.
CUSTER, Elizabeth B.   **Tenting on the Plains.**
  1887   New York   40.
  1889   New York   30.
CUTHBERT, N. B. (editor)   **Lincoln and the Baltimore Plot 1861.**
  1949   Los Angeles   15.
CUTTING, Elizabeth   **Jefferson Davis, Political Soldier.**
  1930   New York   20.
  1939   New York   20.
DABNEY, Robert   **A Defence of Virginia.**
  1867   New York   25.

DABNEY, Robert L.   **Life and Campaigns of Lieut. Gen. Thomas J. Jackson.**
    1866   New York   50.
    1976   Harrisonburg, Virginia   17.
DABNEY, Robert L.   **Life of Lieut. Gen. Thomas J. Jackson (Stonewall Jackson)**
    1864-66   London   2 vols.   125.
DAGNALL, John M.   **Daisy Swain, The Flower of Shenandoah, A Tale of the Rebellion.**
    1865   Brooklyn, N. Y.   35.
DAHLGREN, John A. B.   **Memoir of Ulric Dahlgren.**
    1872   Philadelphia   40.
DAINGERFIELD, Foxhall, Jr.   **The Southern Cross A Play in Four Acts.** Wraps
    1909   Lexington, Kentucky   15.
DAINGERFIELD, N. G.   **Frescati A Page from Virginia History.**
    1909   New York   50.
DALE, Edward Everett, and **LITTON**, Gaston   **Cherokee Cavaliers.**
    1940   Norman, Oklahoma   40.
    1969   Norman, Oklahoma   20.
DALL, Caroline H.   **Barbara Fritchie, A Study.**
    1892   Boston   15.
DALTON, Kit   **Under the Black Flag.** Wraps
    n.d.   Memphis   60.
DALY, Maria L.   **Diary of a Union Lady 1861-1865** edited by Harold Earl Hammond.
    1962   New York   20.
DALY, R. W.   **How the Merrimac Won . . . The Strategic Story of C.S.S. Virginia.**
    1957   New York   20.
DALZELL, George W.   **The Flight from the Flag.**
    1940   Chapel Hill, N. C.   15.
DAMER, Eyre   **When the Ku Klux Rode.**
    1912   New York   40.
DANA, Charles A., and **WILSON**, J. H.   **The Life of Ulysses S. Grant.**
    1868   Springfield, Mass.   30.
    1868   Portland   30.
DANA, Charles A.   **Recollections of the Civil War.**
    1898   New York   20.
    1899   New York   20.
    1902   New York   15.
DANIEL, Edward M.   **The Speeches and Orations of John Warwick Daniel.**
    1911   Lynchburg   50.
DANIEL, F. E.   **Recollections of a Rebel Surgeon.**
    1899   Austin   60.
    1901   Chicago   40.
DANIEL, J. W.   **A Maid of the Foot-Hills.**
    1905   New York   20.
DANIEL, John W.   **Campaign and Battles of Gettysburg. Address.** Wraps
    1875   Lynchburg   50.
DANIEL, John W.   **Character of Stonewall Jackson.** Wraps
    1868   Lynchburg   50.
DANIEL, John W.   **Life and Reminiscences of Jefferson Davis by Distinguished Men of His Time.**
    1890   Baltimore   50.
DANIEL, John W.   **Oration: Ceremonies Connected with the Inauguration of the Mausoleum and the unveiling of the Recumbent Figure of General Robert Edward Lee, at Washington and Lee University, Lexington, Va. June 28 1883.**
    1883   Lexington, Virginia   25.
    1883   Lynchburg   Wraps   15.
    1883   Richmond   20.
DANIEL, John W.   **Oration on the Life, Services and Character of Jefferson Davis.**
    Wraps
    1890   Richmond   10.
    1890   Baltimore   10.

DANIEL, John W. and **WILLIAMS,** Robert G.   **Robert Edward Lee — An Oration and an address.**
1931   Strasburg, Virginia   20.
DANIEL, Lizzie Carrie   **Confederate Scrap-Book.**
1893   Richmond   30.
DANIEL, Raleigh T.   **The Unveiling of the Monument to the Confederate Dead of Alexandria, Va.** Wraps
1889   Alexandria   40.
DANIELS, Jonathan   **Mosby, Gray Ghost of the Confederacy.**
1959   Philadelphia   10.
DANIELS, Jonathan   **Prince of Carpetbaggers.**
1958   Philadelphia   15.
DANIELS, Larry J., and **GUNTER,** Riley W.   **Confederate Cannon Foundries.**
1977   Union City   20.
Danner's Pocket Guide Book of the Battlefield of Gettysburg. Wraps
n.d.   Gettysburg   25.
DANNETT, Sylvia G. L. and **BURKART,** Rosamond H.   **Confederate Surgeon: Aristides Monteiro.**
1969   New York   20.
DANNETT, Sylvia G. L. (comp)   **Noble Women of the North.**
1959   New York   20.
DANNETT, Sylvia G. L. and **JONES,** Katharine M.   **Our Women of the Sixties.** Wraps
1963   Washington   10.
DANNETT, Sylvia G. L.   **A Treasury of Civil War Humor.**
1963   New York   25.
DARLING, Henry   **Slavery and the War: A Historical Essay.** Wraps
1863   Philadelphia   20.   1863   Philadelphia   20.
DARSEY, E. W.   **A War Story of a Yankee Prison.** Wraps
1959   Statesboro, Georgia   20.
DAUGHERTY, James   **Lincoln's Gettysburg Address.**
1947   Chicago   10.
DAVIDSON, Donald   **Lee in the Mountains and Other Poems.**
1938   Boston   75.
DAVIDSON, Homer K.   **Black Jack Davidson A Cavalry Commander on the Western Frontier.**
1974   Glendale, California   15.
DAVIDSON, Nora Fontaine M.   **Cullings from the Confederacy   1862-1866.** Wraps
1903   Washington   25.
DAVIDSON, William H. (ed.)   **War Was the Place A Centennial Collection of Confederate Soldier Letters.** Wraps
1961   n.p.   20.
1962   Oakbowery   20.
DAVIES, Henry E.   **General Sheridan.**
1895   New York   20.
1897   New York   15.
DAVIS, Archie K.   **Colonel Harry Burgwyn of the 26th North Carolina Regiment.** Wraps
1961   Jackson, N. C.   30.
DAVIS, Burke   **Gray Fox, Robert E. Lee and the Civil War.**
1956   New York   20.
DAVIS, Burke   **Jeb Stuart: The Last Cavalier.**
1956   New York   25.
DAVIS, Burke   **Our Incredible Civil War.**
1960   New York   20.
DAVIS, Burke   **Sherman's March.**
1980   New York   15.
DAVIS, Burke   **They Called Him Stonewall.**
1954   New York   20.
DAVIS, Burke   **To Appomattox: Nine April Days, 1865.**
1959   New York   20.

DAVIS, Carl L. **Arming the Union, Small Arms in the Civil War.**
1973 Port Washington, N. Y. 20.
DAVIS, Charles H. **Life of Charles Henry Davis, Rear Admiral.**
1899 Boston 35.
DAVIS, Charles S. **Colin J. McRae: Confederate Financial Agent.** Wraps
1961 Tuscaloosa, Alabama Ltd. 20.
DAVIS, Edwin Adams **Fallen Guidon The Forgotten Saga off General Jo Shelby's Confederate Command.**
1962 Santa Fe 40
DAVIS, Evangeline and Burke **Rebel Raider: A Biography of Admiral Semmes.**
1966 Philadelphia 10.
DAVIS, H. **General Sheridan.**
1895 New York 15.
DAVIS, J. C. Bancroft **Mr. Fish and the Alabama Claims A Chapter in Diplomatic History.**
1893 Boston 25.
DAVIS, J. C. Bancroft **Mr. Sumner, the Alabama Claims, and Their Settlement, a Letter to the "New York Herald."** Wraps
1878 New York 30.
DAVIS, Jefferson **Jefferson Davis, Constitutionalist: His Letters, Papers and Speeches.**
edited by Dunbar Rowland. 10 vols. and index
1923 Jackson, Miss. 300.
DAVIS, Jefferson **Private Letters 1823-1889,** edited by Hudson Strode
1966 New York 20.
DAVIS, Jefferson **The Rise and Fall of the Confederate Government.** 2 vols.
1881 New York 75.
1938 Richmond 50.
1958 New York Boxed 30.
DAVIS, Jefferson **Robert E. Lee** edited by Harold B. Simpson.
1966 Hillsboro 20.
DAVIS, Jefferson **A Short History of the Confederate States of America.**
1890 New York 65.
DAVIS, Julia **The Shenandoah.**
1945 New York 20.
DAVIS, Maggie **The Far Side of Home.**
1963 New York 15.
DAVIS, Margaret B. **The Woman Who Battled for the Boys in Blue: Mother Bickerdyke.**
1886 San Francisco 30.
DAVIS, Michael **The Image of Lincoln in the South.**
1971 Knoxville 20.
DAVIS, Nora M. (comp.) **Military and Naval Operations in South Carolina 1860-1865.** Wraps
1959 Columbia 15.
DAVIS, Paxton **The Battle of New Market. A Story of V.M.I.**
1963 Boston 20.
DAVIS, Robert S. **History of the Rebel Steam Ram "Atlanta," . . . for the Benefit of the Union Volunteer Refreshment Saloon, Philadelphia.** Wraps
1863 Philadelphia 25.
DAVIS, Rollin V. **U. S. Sword Bayonets 1847-1865.** Wraps
1963 Pittsburgh 15.
DAVIS, Varina Howell. **Jefferson Davis Ex-President of the Confederate States of America. A Memoir By His Wife.** 2 vols.
1890 New York 75.
DAVIS, Washington **Camp-Fire Chats of the Civil War.**
1886 Chicago 25.
DAVIS, William C. **Battle at Bull Run.**
1977 New York 10.

DAVIS, William C. **The Battle of New Market.**
    1975   Garden City, N. Y.   15.
DAVIS, William C. **Breckinridge, Statesman, Soldier, Symbol.**
    1974   Baton Rouge   30.
DAVIS, William C. **Duel Between the First Ironclads.**
    1975   Garden City   20.
DAVIS, William C. (ed) **The Image of War 1861-65.** 2 vols.
    1981   New York   60.
    Additional volumes in process
DAWSON, George F. **Life and Services of Gen. John A. Logan.**
    1884   Washington   20.
    1887   New York   20.
DAWSON, Sarah Morgan **A Confederate Girl's Diary.**
    1913   Boston & New York   45.
    1960   Bloomington, Indiana   edited by James Robertson, Jr.   25.
DAWSON, William Forrest (ed) **A Civil War Artist at the Front Edwin Forbes' Life Studies of the Great Army.**
    1957   New York   20.
DEADERICK, Barron **Campaigns and Battles of America 1755-1865.**
    1959   Boston   10.
DEADERICK, Barron **Shiloh, Memphis and Vicksburg.** Wraps
    1960   Memphis   10.
DEADERICK, Barron **Strategy in the Civil War.**
    1946   Harrisburg   20.
DEADERICK, J. B. **The Truth About Shiloh.** Wraps
    1942   Memphis   20.
DEAN, Henry C. **Crimes of the Civil War and Curse of the Funding System.**
    1868   Baltimore   45.
    1869   Baltimore   30.
DEBOW, J. D. **Statistical View of the United States, Embracing Its Territory, Population, White, Free Colored, and Slave.**
    1854   Washington   30.
Dedication of Confederate Soldiers' and Sailors' Monument, Richmond May 30, 1894. Wraps
    1894   Richmond   20.
Dedication of Double Equestrian Statue: General Robert E. Lee and General Thomas J. (Stonewall) Jackson. Wraps
    1948   Baltimore   15.
Dedication of the Equestrian Statue of Major-General John Sedgwick. Erected on the Battlefield of Gettysburg by the State of Connecticut June 19, 1913.
    1913   Hartford   15.
Dedication of Monument . . . To Commemorate the Charge of General Humphries' Division . . . On Marye's Heights, Fredericksburg. Wraps
    1908   Philadelphia   20.
Dedication of the Statue of . . . Lieut. Gen. Stephen Dill Lee, C.S.A. Wraps
    1909   Vicksburg   15.
Defence of Commodore W. D. Porter Before the Naval Retiring Board. Wraps
    1863   New York   30.
A Defense of Southern Slavery.   See: **BROOKES,** Iveson L.
DE FONTAINE, F. G. **Army Letters of "Personne," 1861-1865.** Nos. 1-2 (all issued) Wraps
    1896   Columbia, S. C.   125.
DeFOREST, John William **Miss Ravenel's Conversion From Secession to Loyalty.**
    1939   New York/London   30.
DeFOREST, John William **A Union Officer in the Reconstruction.**
    1948   New Haven, Conn.   20
DEGLER, Carl **The Other South.**
    1974   v.p.   10.

De GRUMMOND, Lena Y & **De GRUMMOND** Delaune, Lynn   **Jeb Stuart.**
1962   New York   15.
DELANEY, Norman C.   **John McIntosh Kell of the Raider Alabama.**
1973   University, Alabama   20.
DE LEON, T. C.   **Belles, Beaux and Brains of the 60's.**
1909   New York   50.
DE LEON, T. C.   **Four Years in Rebel Capitals.**
1890   Mobile   100.
1892   Mobile   75.
DE LEON, T. C.   **John Holden, Unionist.**
1893   St. Paul   20.
DE LEON   T. C.   **Joseph Wheeler, The Man, the Statesman, the Soldier.** Wraps
1899   Atlanta   150.
1960   Kennesaw, Georgia   20.
DE LEON, T. C.   **South Songs: From the Lays of Later Days.**
1866   New York   75.
DEMING, Henry C.   **The Life of Ulysses S. Grant.**
1868   Hartford   20.
The Democratic Almanac for 1866. Wraps
1866   New York   25.
Democratic National Convention, Official Proceedings of, Held in 1860 — at Charleston. Wraps
1860   Cleveland   30.
The Demon of Andersonville; Or, the Trial of Wirz. Wraps
1865   Philadelphia   75.
DENISON, Charles W.   **Hancock the Superb.**
1880   Philadelphia   30.
DENISON, C. W.   **Illustrated Life Campaigns and Public Services of Philip H. Sheridan (Major-General Sheridan).**
1865   Philadelphia   35. **DENISON,** Charles W.   **Winfield, The Lawyer's Son and How He Became a Major-General.**
1865   Philadelphia   30.
DENISON, George T.   **A History of Cavalry.**
1913   London   50.
DENNETT, John Richard   **The South as it is 1865-1866.**
1965   New York   20.
DENNETT, Tyler (ed)   **Lincoln and the Civil War in the Diaries and Letters of John Hay.**
1939   New York   15.
DENSON, Claude B.   **An Address Delivered in Raleigh, N. C. on Memorial Day May 10, 1895. . .Memoir. . . Wm. H. C. Whiting.** Wraps
1895   Raleigh   40.
DE PEYSTER, John Watts   **The Decisive Conflicts of the Late Civil War or Slaveholders Rebellion.** Wraps
1867   New York   20.
DE PEYSTER, John Watts.   **Personal and Military History of Philip Kearny.**
1869   New York   50.
1870   New York   40.
1870   Elizabeth, N. J.   40.
DE PEYSTER, John Watts   **Sketch of Gen. George H. Thomas A Biographical Work.** Wraps
n.d.   New York   75.
DeROSIER, Arthur H., Jr. (ed)   **Through the South with a Union Soldier.**
1969   Johnson City, Tenn.   20.
DERRY, Joseph T.   **Story of the Confederate States.**
1895   Richmond   60.
1896   Richmond   50.
1898   Richmond   40.

DERRY, Joseph T.   **The Strife of Brothers A Poem.**
   1903   Atlanta   40.
   1904   Atlanta   30.
DeSAUSSURE, Mrs. N. B.   **Old Plantation Days Being Recollections of Southern Life Before the Civil War.**
   1909   New York   30.
A Descriptive List of the Burial Places of the Remains of Confederate Soldiers, Who Fell in the Battles of Antietam, South Mountain, Monocacy, and other Points in Washington and Frederick Counties, In the State of Maryland. Wraps
   1868(?)   Hagerstown, MD   75.
DEVENS, Charles, Jr.   **General Meade & The Battle of Gettysburg.** Wraps
   1873   Morrisania, New York   20.
DEVEREUX, Margasret   **Plantation Sketches.**
   1906   Cambridge   75.
DEVLIN, B.   **St. Albans Raid, Speech.** Wraps
   1865   Montreal   35.
DEW, Charles B.   **Ironmaker to the Confederacy, Joseph R. Anderson and the Tredegar Iron Works.**
   1966   Binghamton, New York   50.
DEWITT, David Miller   **The Assassination of Abraham Lincoln and Its Expiation.**
   1909   New York   60.
DEWITT, David Miller   **The Impeachment and Trial of Andrew Johnson.**
   1903   New York   45.
   1967   Madison   15.
DEXTER, Henry Martyn   **What Ought to be Done with the Freedmen and With the Rebels? A Sermon.** Wraps
   1865   Boston   25.
DIAL, Marshall   **The Boothell Swamp Struggle.** Wraps
   1961   Lilbourn, Mo.   20.
The Diary of a Public Man.
   1945   Chicago   15.
DICEY, Edward   **Spectator of America.**
   1972   London   20.
DICEY, Edward J.   **Six Months in the Federal States.** 2 vols.
   1863   London   125.
DICKINSON, Sally Bruce   **Confederate Leaders.**
   1937   Staunton   75.
DICKSON, Capers   **John Ashton: A Story of the War Between the States.**
   1896   Atlanta   35.
DIETZ, August, Sr.   **The Confederate States Post-Office Department.** Wraps
   1948   Richmond   15.
   1950   Richmond   10.
DIETZ, August, Sr. (ed.)   **Dietz Confederate States Catalog and Hand-Book of the Postage Stamps and Envelopes of the Confederate States.**
   1945   Richmond   30.
DIETZ, August, Sr. (ed.)   **The Postal Service of the Confederate States of   America.**
   1929   Richmond   250.
DIMITRY, Adelaide Stuart   **War-Time Sketches Historical and Otherwise.**
   n.d.   New Orleans   250.
DINKINS, James   **Personal Recollections and Experiences in the Confederate Army 1861 to 1865.**
   1897   Cincinnati   300.
The Dismissal of Major Granville Haller of the Regular Army. Wraps
   1863   Paterson, N. J.   20.
DIX, Morgan   **Memoirs of John Adams Dix.** 2 vols.
   1883   New York   30.
DIXON, Samuel H.   **Robert Warren, The Texan Refugee.**
   n.d.   New York   50.

DIXON, Thomas Jr.   **The Clansman.**
   1905   New York   20.
DIXON, Thomas, Jr.   **The Leopard's Spots.**
   1903   New York   20.
DIXON, Thomas, Jr.   **The Man in Gray.**
   1921   New York   20.
DIXON, Thomas, Jr.   **The Traitor, A Story of the Fall of the Invisible Empire.**
   1907   New York   20.
DODD, William E.   **Expansion and Conflict.**
   1915   New York   15.
DODD, William E.   **Jefferson Davis.**
   1907   Philadelphia   25.
DODD, William E.   **Lincoln or Lee.**
   1928   New York   25.
DODGE, Grenville M.   **The Battle of Atlanta, and Other Campaigns.**
   1910   Council Bluffs, Iowa   40.
   1911   Council Bluffs, Iowa   30.
   1965   Denver   15.
DODGE, Grenville M.   **Personal Recollections of President Abraham Lincoln, General Ulysses S. Grant, and General William T. Sherman.**
   1914   Iowa   30.
DODGE, Grenville M.   **Sketch of the Military Service of Major General Wager Swayne.** Wraps
   1903   New York   30.
DODGE, Theodore Ayrault   **A Birds-Eye View of our Civil War.**
   1883   Boston   25.
   1884   Boston   25.
   1897   Boston   20.
DODGE, Theodore Ayrault   **The Campaign of Chancellorsville.**
   1881   Boston   35.
DODGE, William Sumner   **History of the Old Second Division Army of the Cumberland.**
   1864   Chicago   100.
DODSON, W. C. (ed.)   **Campaigns of Wheeler and His Cavalry.**
   1899   Atlanta   75.
Does the Country Require a National Armory and Foundry West of the Allegheny Mountains. Wraps
   1862   Pittsburg   30.
DONALD, David   **Charles Sumner and the Coming of the Civil War.**
   1961   New York   20.
DONALD, David   **Charles Sumner and the Rights of Man.**
   1907   New York   20.
DONALD, David, et al. (eds.)   **Divided We Fought. A Pictorial History of the Civil War.**
   1952   New York   25.
   1953   New York   20.
   1956   New York   20.
DONALD, David   **Lincoln Reconsidered.**
   1956   New York   10.
DONALD, David   **Lincoln's Herndon.**
   1948   New York   20.
DONALD, David   **The Politics of Reconstruction 1863-1867,**
   1965   Baton Rouge   20.
DONALD, David (ed)   **Why the North Won the Civil War.**
   1960   Baton Rouge   15.
DONNELLY, Ralph W.   **The History of the Confederate States Marine Corps.** Wraps
   1976   Washington   Ltd.   25.
DONNELLY, Ralph W.   **Service Records of Confederate Enlisted Marines.** Wraps
   1979   New Bern, N. C.   10.

DONOVAN, Frank and **CATTON,** Bruce   **Ironclads of the Civil War.**
1961   New York   15.
DONOVAN, Frank   **Mr. Lincoln's Proclamation: The Story of the Emancipation Proclamation.**
1964   New York   10.
DORNBUSCH, Charles E. (comp)   **Military Bibliography of the Civil War.** 3 vols.
1971-72   New York   125.
various parts in wraps — 5. each
DORRIS, Jonathan Truman   **Pardon and Amnesty Under Lincoln and Johnson.**
1953   Chapel Hill   30.
DOUBLEDAY, Abner   **Chancellorsville and Gettysburg.**
1882   New York   25.
1887   New York   15.
DOUBLEDAY, Abner   **Gettysburg Made Plain.** Wraps
1888   New York   20.
DOUBLEDAY, Abner   **Reminiscences of Forts Sumter and Moultrie in 1860-'61.**
1876   New York   30.
DOUGLAS, Henry Kyd   **The Douglas Diary: Student Days at Franklin-Marshall College 1856-1858.**
1973   Lancaster   20.
DOUGLASS, Frederick   **Life and Times of _____ Written By Himself.**
1882   Hartford   25.
1962   New York   15.
DOUGLASS, Frederick   **Narrative of the Life of _____ An American Slave Written by Himself** edited by Benjamin Quarles.
1960   Cambridge, Mass.   15.
DOUGLASS, H. Paul   **Christian Reconstruction in the South.**
1909   Boston   35.
DOW, Neal   **The Reminiscences of Neal Dow, Recollections of Eighty Years.**
1898   Portland, Maine   35.
DOWD, Clement   **Life of Zebulon B. Vance.**
1897   Charlotte, N. C.   25.
DOWDEY, Clifford   **Bugles Blow No More.**
1937   Boston   15.
1937   New York   15.
1946   Boston   15.
DOWDEY, Clifford   **Death of a Nation.**
1958   New York   15.
DOWDEY, Clifford   **Experiment in Rebellion.**
1946   New York   20.
1947   New York   20.
DOWDEY, Clifford   **The Land They Fought For.**
1955   Garden City, New York   20.
DOWDEY, Clifford   **Last Night the Nightingale.**
1962   New York   15.
DOWDEY, Clifford   **Lee.**
1965   Boston/Toronto   20.
DOWDEY, Clifford   **Lee's Last Campaign.**
1960   Boston   25.
DOWDEY, Clifford   **The Proud Retreat.**
1953   Garden City, New York   35.
DOWDEY, Clifford   **The Seven Days: The Emergence of Lee.**
1964   Boston   15.
1964   New York   15.
DOWDEY, Clifford and **MANARIN,** Louis (eds)   **The Wartime Papers of R. E. Lee**
1961   Boston   30.
1961   New York   30.
DOWNER, Edward T.   **Stonewall Jackson's Shenandoah Valley Campaign 1862.** Wraps
1959   Lexington, Va.   10.

DOWNEY, Fairfax   **Clash of Cavalry: The Battle of Brandy Station June 9, 1863.**
    1959   New York   30.
DOWNEY, Fairfax   **The Guns at Gettysburg.**
    1958   New York   40.
DOWNEY, Fairfax   **Sound of the Guns.**
    1956   New York   20.
    1955   New York   20.
DOWNEY, Fairfax   **Storming of the Gateway.**
    1960   New York   30.
DRAKE, Edwin L. (ed)   **The Annals of the Army of Tennessee and Early Western History Vol I, Apr-Dec 1878.** (all published)
    1878   Nashville   500.
DRAKE, James Vaulx   **Life of General Robert Hatton.**
    1867   Nashville   200.
DRAKE, Samuel Adams   **The Battle of Gettysburg.**
    1892   Boston   30.
DRAPER, John William   **History of the American Civil War.** 3 vols.
    1867-70   New York   60.
DREW, Benjamin   **The Refugee: Or the Narratives of Fugitive Slaves in Canada.**
    1856   Boston   80.
DRINKWATER, John   **Abraham Lincoln: A Play.**
    1919   Boston   5.
DRINKWATER, John   **American Vignettes 1860-1865.**
    1931   Boston   20.
DRINKWATER, John   **Robert E. Lee, A Play.**
    1923   London   10.
    1923   Boston   10.
DRINKWATER, John   **The World's Lincoln.**
    1928   New York   Ltd.   20.
DUBAY, Robert W.   **John Jones Pettus, Mississippi Fire-Eater: His Life and Times 1813-1867.**
    1975   Jackson   15.
DUBERMAN, M.   **The Antislavery Vanguard.**
    1965   Princeton   25.
DUBERMAN, Martin B.   **Charles Francis Adams 1807-1886.**
    1961   Boston   20.
DUBOSE, John W.   **General Joseph Wheeler and the Army of Tennessee.**
    1912   New York   275.
DUBOSE, John W.   **Life and Times of William Lowndes Yancey.**
    1892   Birmingham   175.
    1942   New York   2 vols.   50.
DUDLEY, Dean (ed)   **Officers of Our Union Army and Navy: Their Lives, Their Portraits.**   Vol. 1 (all published).
    1862   Boston   35.
DUFOUR, Charles L.   **The Night the War Was Lost.**
    1960   Garden City, N. Y.   25.
DUFOUR, Charles L.   **Nine Men in Gray.**
    1963   Garden City   30.
DUGAN, M. C. (comp)   **Outline History of Annapolis and the Naval Academy.** Wraps
    1902   Baltimore   25.
DUKE, Basil W.   **The Great Indiana-Ohio Raid by Brig. Gen. John Hunt Morgan and His Men July 1863.** Wraps
    1955   Louisville   20.
DUKE, Basil W.   **History of Morgan's Cavalry.**
    1867   Cincinnati   75.
    1906   New York/Washington   80.
    1960   Bloomington   edited by L. M. Holland   25.
DUKE, Basil W.   **Reminiscences of General Basil W. Duke, C.S.A.**
    1911   New York   75.

DUMOND, Dwight L. **Anti-Slavery. The Crusade for Freedom in America.**
1939   Ann Arbor   25.
DUMOND, Dwight L. **Antislavery Origins of the Civil War in the United States.**
1959   Ann Arbor   15.
DUMOND, Dwight L. **The Secession Movement 1860-1861.**
1931   New York   25.
DUMOND, Dwight L. (ed) **Southern Editorials on Secession.**
1931   New York   30.
DUNCAN, George W. **John Archibald Campbell.** Wraps
1905   Montgomery, Alabama   20.
DUNCAN, Louis C. **The Medical Department of the United States Army in the Civil War.** Wraps
1910 (?)   Washington   40.
DUNCAN, Robert Lipscomb **Reluctant General: The Life and Times of Albert Pike.**
1961   New York   30.
DUNCAN, Thomas D. **Recollections of _____, A Confederate Soldier.** Wraps
1922   Nashville   150.
DUNHAM, Chester Forrester **The Attitude of the Northern Clergy Toward the South 1860-1865.** Wraps
1942   Chicago   15.
DUNKLE, John J. **Prison Life During the Rebellion. By Fritz Fuzzlebug.** Wraps
1869   Singer's Glen, Va.   50.
DUNLOP, W. S. **Lee's Sharpshooters.**
1899   Little Rock   175.
DUNN, Byron A. **On General Thomas's Staff.**
1899   Chicago   20.
DUNNING, William A. **The British Empire and the United States.**
1969   New York   20.
DUNNING, William Archibald **Essays on the Civil War.**
1898   New York   25.
1931   New York   15.
DU PONT, H. A. **The Campaign of 1864 in the Valley of Virginia and the Expedition to Lunchburg.**
1925   New York   50.
DU PONT, H. A. **Rear Admiral Samuel Francis Du Pont.**
1926   New York   50.
DU PONT, Samuel Francis **Official Dispatches and Letters of Rear Admiral DuPont, U.S. Navy 1846-48 1861-63.**
1883   Wilmington, Del.   350.
DUPRE, Louis J. **Fagots from the Camp Fire.**
1881   Washington   25.
DUPUY, Ernest and Trevor N. **The Compact History of the Civil War.**
1960   New York   20.
DURDEN, Robert F. **The Gray and the Black.**
1972   Baton Rouge   20.
DURKIN, Joseph T. **Stephen R. Mallory, Confederate Navy Chief.**
1954   Chapel Hill, N. C.   30.
DUVERGIER DE HAURANNE, Ernest **A Frenchman in Lincoln's America.** 2 vols.
1974   Chicago   35.
DUYCKINCK, Evert A. **A National History of the War for the Union, Civil, Military and Naval.** 3 vols.
3 vols.
1861   New York   75.
1868   New York   75.
DWIGHT, Allan **Linn Dickson Confederate.**
1934   New York   20.
DWIGHT, Charles Stevens **A South Carolina Rebel's Recollections.** Wraps
1919   Columbia   Ltd.   200.

DWIGHT, Theo F. (ed)   **Campaigns in Virginia 1861-1862. Vol. 1 of MHSM.**
       1895   Boston   40.
DWIGHT, Theo. F. (ed)   **Campaigns in Virginia, Maryland and Pennsylvania 1862-1863, Vol. 3 of MHSM.**
       1903   Boston   35.
DWIGHT, Theo. F. (ed.)   **Critical Sketches of Some of the Federal and Confederate Commanders. Vol. 10 of MHSM.**
       1895   Boston   50.
DWIGHT, Theo. F. (ed.)   **The Virginia Campaign of 1862 Under Pope. Vol. 2 of MHSM.**
       1895   Boston   35.
DWIGHT, Theo. F. (ed.)   **The Wilderness Campaign May-June 1864. Vol. 4 of MHSM.**
       1905   Boston   35.
DYE, John S.   **History of the Plots and Crimes of the Great Conspiracy to Overthrow Liberty in America.**
       1866   New York   25.
DYER, Frederick H.   **A Compendium of the War of the Rebellion.**
       1908   Des Moines   1 vol. ed.   150.
       1959   New York   3 vols.   75.
       1959   New York   3 vols.   Ltd. ed. of 50 sets in leather   250.
DYER, John P.   **From Shiloh to San Juan, The Life of "Fightin' Joe" Wheeler.**
       1941   Baton Rouge   40.
       1961   Baton Rouge   25.
DYER, John P.   **The Gallant Hood.**
       1950   Indianapolis   30.
EARLE, Peter   **Robert E. Lee.**
       1973   New York   15.
EARLE, Pliny   **Memoirs of _____, M.D. with Extracts from his Diary and Letters** edited by F. B. Sanborn.
       1898   Boston   30.
EARLY, Jubal A.   **Address Contained in Proceedings of the Third Annual Meeting of the Survivor's Association of the State of South Carolina.** Wraps
       1872   Charleston   35.
EARLY, Jubal A.   **Campaigns of Gen. Robert E. Lee.** Wraps
       1872   Baltimore   100.
EARLY, Jubal A.   **The Heritage of the South.**
       1915   Lynchburg   30.
EARLY, Jubal A.   **Jackson's Campaign Against Pope in August, 1862, An Address . . .Before the First Annual Meeting of Assoc. of Maryland Line.** Wraps
       1883 (?)   n.p.   75.
EARLY, Jubal A.   **Lieutenant General Jubal Anderson Early, C.S.A Autobiographical Sketch and Narrative of the War Between the States.**
       1912   Philadelphia   150.
       1960   Bloomington   entitled **War Memoirs**   35.
EARLY, Jubal A.   **A Memoir of the Last Year of the War for Independence in the Confederate States of America.** Wraps
       1866   Toronto   200.
       1867   Lynchburg   100.
       1867   Augusta, Ga.   75.
       1867   New Orleans   100.
EARLY, Jubal A.   **The Relative Strength of the Armies of Generals Lee and Grant.** Wraps
       1870   n.p.   50.
The Early Life, Campaigns, & Public Services of Robert E. Lee.
       1871   New York   50.
EASBY-SMITH, Anne   **William Russell Smith of Alabama: His Life and Works.**
       1931   Philadelphia   25.

EATON, Clement **A History of the Southern Confederacy.**
   1954   New York   20.
   1959   New York   20.
EATON, Clement **Jefferson Davis.**
   1977   New York   15.
EATON, Clement **The Mind of the Old South.**
   1969   Baton Rouge   20.
EATON, J. H. **Army Paymaster's Manual.**
   1864   Washington   75.
EATON, John **Grant, Lincoln and the Freedmen.**
   1907   New York   40.
EBY, Cecil D., Jr. **Porte Crayon, The Life of David Hunter Strother.**
   1960   Chapel Hill   15.
Echoes from the South. See: **ESTVAN,** B.
ECKENRODE, H. J. & **CONRAD,** Bryan **George B. McClellan.**
   1941   Chapel Hill   25.
ECKENRODE, H. J. & **CONRAD,** Bryan **James Longstreet, Lee's War Horse.**
   1936   Chapel Hill   60.
ECKENRODE, H. J. **Jefferson Davis.**
   1923   New York   25.
   1930   New York   15.
ECKENRODE, H. J. **Life of Nathan B. Forrest.**
   1918   Richmond   30.
EDGE, Frederick M. **Major General McClellan and the Campaign on the Yorktown Peninsula.**
   1865   London   75.
EDMONDS, David C. **Yankee Autumn in Acadiana.**
   1979   Lafayette, La.   20.
EDMONDS, Franklin Spencer **Ulysses S. Grant.**
   1915   Philadelphia   20.
EDMONDS, George (Pseud.)
   See: **MERIWETHER,** Elizabeth A.
EDMONSTON, Catherine Devereux **The Journal of _____ 1860-1866** edited by Margaret Mackay Jones.
   1954   Mebane, N. C.   Ltd.   60.
EDMONDSTON, Catherine Ann Devereux **Journal of a Secesh Lady: The Diary of _____ 1860-1866** edited by Beth Crabtree and James W. Patton.
   1979   Raleigh   28.
EDWARDS, E. M. H. **Commander W. B. Cushing of the U. S. Navy.**
   1898   New York   50.
EDWARDS, Mrs. J. Griff & **ANDREWS,** Matthew P. (comp & ed) **Echoes From Dixie, Old Time Southern Songs**
   1918   New York   40.
EDWARDS, John N. **Biography, Memoirs, Reminiscences and Recollections,** compiled by Jennie Edwards.
   1889   Kansas City   125.
EDWARDS, John N. **Noted Guerrillas, or Warfare of the Border.**
   1877   St. Louis   150.
EDWARDS, John N. **Shelby and His Men.**
   1867   Cincinnati   125.
   1897   Kansas City   75.
EDWARDS, John **Shelby's Expedition to Mexico.**
   1964   Austin   Boxed   50.
EDWARDS, Ward **Lion-Hearted Luke; or, The Plan to Capture Mosby, War Library Vol. 7, No. 235.** Wraps
   1887   New York   50.
EDWARDS, William B. **Civil War Guns: The Complete Story of Federal and Confederate Small Arms.**
   1962   Harrisburg   30.

EFLOR, Oram   **Chain-Shot; or Mosby and His Men, War Library Vol. 2, No. 35.** Wraps
    1883   New York   50.
EGAN, J. B. and **DESMOND,** A. W.   **The Civil War. Its Photographic History.**
    1941   Wellesley Hills   25.
EGGLESTON, George Cary   **The History of the Confederate War — Its Causes and Its
    Conduct.** 2 vols.
    1910   New York   90.
EGGLESTON, George Gary   **Southern Soldier Stories.**
    1898   New York   40.
EGLE, William H.   **Life and Times of Andrew Gregg Curtin.**
    1896   Philadelphia   20.
EHLE, John   **Time of Drums.**
    1970   New York   10.
EHRMANN, Bess V.   **The Missing Chapter in the Life of Abraham Lincoln.**
    1938   Chicago   Ltd.   30.
EISENSCHIML, Otto & **NEWMAN,** Ralph   **The American Iliad — The Epic Story of
    the Civil War as Narrated by Eyewitnesses and Contemporaries.**
    1947   Indianapolis   15.
    1947   Indianapolis   Ltd., signed & boxed   50.
    1956   New York   entitled **The Civil War**   2 vols.   25.
EISENSCHIML, Otto, and **LONG,** E. B.   **As Luck Would Have It.**
    1958   Indianapolis   20.
    1948   Indianapolis   25.
EISENSCHIML, Otto   **The Celebrated Case of Fitz John Porter.**
    1950   Indianapolis   25.
EISENSCHIML, Otto   **The Hidden Face of the Civil War.**
    1961   Indianapolis   20.
EISENSCHIML, Otto   **Historian Without an Armchair.**
    1962   Indianapolis   20.
EISENSCHIML, Otto   **In the Shadow of Lincoln's Death.**
    1940   New York   30.
EISENSCHIML, Otto   **Reviewers Reviewed.** Wraps
    1940   Ann Arbor   15.
EISENSCHIML, Otto   **The Story of Shiloh.**
    1946   Chicago   30.
EISENSCHIML, Otto   **Why the Civil War?**
    1958   Indianapolis   25.
EISENSCHIML, Otto   **Why Was Lincoln Murdered?**
    1937   Boston   25.
EISENSCHIML, Otto   **Without Fame The Romance of a Profession.**
    1942   Chicago   25.
Elements of Discord in Secessia.   See: **ALEXANDER,** William
ELIOT, Ellsworth, Jr.   **Theodore Winthrop.**
    1938   New Haven   25.
ELIOT, Ellsworth, Jr.   **West Point in the Confederacy.**
    1941   New York   30.
ELIOT, Ellsworth, Jr.   **Yale in the Civil War.**
    1932   New Haven, Conn.   40.
ELIOT, George Fielding   **Caleb Pettengill, U.S.N.**
    1956   New York   10.
ELLICOTT, John M.   **The Life of John Ancrum Winslow, Rear Admiral, USN.**
    1905   New York   30.
ELLIOTT, Charles Winslow   **Winfield Scott, The Soldier and the Man.**
    1937   New York   30.
ELLIOTT, James W.   **Transport to Disaster (The Sultana).**
    1962   New York   15.
ELLIS, Daniel   **Thrilling Adventures of Daniel Ellis.**
    1867   New York   35.
    1974   Kingsport, Tenn.   Ltd.   15.

ELLIS, Edward S.   **The Campfires of General Lee.**
  1886   Philadelphia   40.
ELLIS, Thomas T.   **Leaves from the Diary of an Army Surgeon.**
  1863   New York   40.
ELSON, H. W.   **Civil War Through the Camera.**
  1912   New York   50.
  1912   New York   16 parts, each in wraps   75.
ELY, Alfred   **Journal of** _____ edited by Charles Lanman.
  1862   New York   30.
EMBICK, Milton A.   **Military History of the Third Division, Ninth Corps Army of the Potomac.**
  1913   Harrisburg   25.
EMERSON, Bettie Alder Calhoun   **Historic Southern Monuments.**
  1911   New York   100.
EMPSON, W. H.   **Let Us Forgive, But Not Forget, or What I Saw and Suffered.** Wraps
  n.d.   New York   125.
EMURIAN, Ernest K.   **The Sweetheart of the Civil War.**
  1962   Natick, Mass.   15.
EMURIAN, Ernest K.   **Stories of Civil War Songs.**
  1960   Natick, Mass.   15.
Encounter at Hanover: Prelude to Gettysburg.
  1963   Hanover   35.
ENGEL, L.   **Panorama Views of Chattanooga and all the Battlefields.** Wraps
  1914   Chattanooga   25.
EPPES, Susan Bradford   **Through Some Eventful Years.**
  1926   Macon, Georgia   75.
  1968   Gainesville   15.
The Equestrian Statue of Major General Joseph Hooker, Erected and Dedicated by the Commonwealth of Massachusetts.
  1903   Boston   25.
ERVING, Annie Priscilla   **Reminiscences of the Life of a Nurse in Field, Hospital and Camp During the Civil War.** Wraps
  1904   New York   40.
ESPOSITO, Vincent J. (ed.)   **West Point Atlas of American Wars, 1689-1953.** 2 vols.
  1959   New York   50.
  1962   New York   50.
ESTES, Claud (comp)   **List of Field Officers, Regiments and Battalions in the Confederate States Army 1861-1865.**
  1912   Macon, Georgia   150.
ESTVAN, B.   **Echoes From the South.**
  1866   New York   25.
ESTVAN, B.   **War Pictures From the South.**
  1863   New York   50.
EVANS, Augusta, J.   **Macaria.**
  1896   New York   50.
  n.d. (circa 1910)   New York   30.
EVANS, Robley D.   **A Sailor's Log.**
  1901   New York   35.
  1902   New York   30.
EVANS, W. A.   **Mrs. Abraham Lincoln A Study of Her Personality & Her Influence on Lincoln.**
  1932   New York   25.
EVANS, W. McKee   **Ballots and Fence Rails.**
  1967   Chapel Hill   15.
EVANS, W. McKee   **To Die Game, The Story of the Lowry Band, Indian Guerillas of Reconstruction.**
  1971   Baton Rouge   20.

EVE, F. Edgeworth   **Address Delivered Before the Confederate Survivors' Association . . . on Memorial Day, April 27th, 1896.** Wraps
    1896   Augusta, Georgia   30.
EVERETT, Edward   **Address of _____, at the Consecration of the National Cemetery at Gettysburg.**
    1864   Boston   30.
EVERETT, Edward   **The Great Issues Now Before the Country, An Oration.** Wraps
    1861   New York   25.
EVERETT, Lloyd T.   **For Maryland's Honor   A Story of the War for Southern Independence.**
    1922   Boston   25.
EWELL, R. S.   **The Making of a Soldier, Letters of General R. S. Ewell** edited by Percy G. Hamlin.
    1935   Richmond   30
EWING, E. W. R.   **Northern Rebellion and Southern Secession.**
    1904   Richmond   60.
An Excursion in Southern History Briefly Set Forth in the Correspondence Between Senator A. J. Beveridge and David Rankin Barbee. Wraps
    1928   Asheville   15.
Executive and Congressional Directory of the Confederate States 1861-1865. Wraps
    1899   Washington   20.
An Extraordinary Collection of Engraved Portraits and Views Relating to the Civil War in America Belonging to the Hon. James T. Mitchell. Wraps
    1910   Philadelphia   25.
FAGAN, W. D. (ed)   **Southern War Songs.**
    1890   New York   40.
FALLON, John T.   **List of Synonyms of Organizations in the Volunteer Service of the United States.**
    1885   Washington   40.
FALLOWS, Alice Katharine   **Everybody's Bishop: Being the Life and Times of the Right Reverend Samuel Fallows.**
    1927   New York   25.
False Reconstruction; Or, The Slavery That is Not Abolished. Wraps
    1876   Saxonville, Mass.   20.
Famous Adventures and Prison Escapes of the Civil War.
    1893   New York   45.
    1898   New York   30.
FARLEY, Joseph P.   **West Point in the Early Sixties.** Wraps
    1902   Troy, N. Y.   25.
FARLEY, Joseph Pearson   **Three Rivers   The James, The Potomac, The Hudson.**
    1910   New York/Washington   65.
FARR, Finis   **Margaret Mitchell of Atlanta, The Author of Gone With The Wind.**
    1965   New York   20.
FARRAGUT, Loyall   **The Life of David Glasgow Farragut, First Admiral of the U.S. Navy.**
    1879   New York   15.
    1882   New York   15.
FARRAR, C.C.S.   **The War   Its Causes and Consequences.**
    1864   Cairo   35.
FARROW, Edward   **Farrow's Military Encyclopedia.** 3 vols.
    1895   New York   200.
FAULKNER, William   **The Unvanquished.**
    1965   New York   20.
FAUST, Drew Gilpin   **A Sacred Circle, the Dilemma of the Intellectual in the Old South, 1840-1860.**
    1977   Baltimore   12.
FAY, Frank B.   **War Papers of Frank B. Fay.** edited by William H. Reed.
    1911   Boston   30.

FEARN, Frances (ed.)   **Diary of a Refugee.**
    1910   New York   50.
FEATHERSTON, John C.   **Battle of the Crater, Address.** Wraps
    1906   n.p.   30.
FEATHERSTONHAUGH, G. W.   **Excursion Through the Slave States.**
    1844   New York   1 vol. ed.   50.
    1844   London   2 vols.   150.
FEHRENBACHER, Don E.   **The Dred Scott Case, Its Significance in American Law and Politics.**
    1978   New York   20.
FEHRENBACHER, Don E.   **Prelude to Greatness, Lincoln in the 1850's.**
    1962   Stanford, California   12.
FERGUSON, Robert   **American During and After the War.**
    1866   London   60.
FERGUSON, W. J.   **I Saw Booth Shoot Lincoln.**
    1930   Boston   20.
FERRI-PISANI, Camille   **Prince Napoleon in America, 1861.**
    1959   Bloomington, Indiana   25.
FERRIS, Norman B.   **Desperate Diplomacy.**
    1976   Knoxville   20.
FERRIS, Norman B.   **The Trent Affair, A Diplomatic Crisis.**
    1977   Knoxville   20.
FEUERLICHT, Roberta Strauss   **Andrews' Raiders.**
    1967   New York   15.
FIEBEGER, G. J.   **The Campaign and Battle of Gettysburg.**
    n.d. (circa 1915)   n.p.   25.
FIEBEGER, G. J.   **Campaigns of the American Civil War.**
    1910   West Point   25.
    1914   West Point   20.
FIELD, Henry M.   **Bright Skies and Dark Shadows.**
    1890   New York   25.
FIELDER, Herbert   **A Sketch of the Life and Times and Speeches of Joseph E. Brown.**
    1883   Springfield, Mass.   30.
FIELDS, Joseph E.   **Robert E. Lee's Farewell Order.** Wraps
    1949   New York   20.
FILLER, Louis   **The Crusade Against Slavery 1830-1860** edited by Henry S. Commager, & Richard B. Morris.
    1960   London   20.
The First Manassas, Correspondence Between Generals R. S. Ewell and G. T. Beauregard, etc. Wraps
    1885   Nashville   75.
    1907   n.p.   Ltd.   15.
FISCHER, L. H. and **GILL,** J.   **Confederate Indian Forces Outside of Indian Territory.** Wraps
    1969   Oklahoma City   7.
FISCHER, L. H. and **RAMPP,** L. C.   **Quantrill's Civil War Operations in Indian Territory.** Wraps
    1968   Oklahoma City   5.
FISCHER, Leroy H.   **Lincoln's Gadfly, Adam Gurowski.**
    1964   Norman   15.
FISH, Carl Russell   **The American Civil War.**
    1937   London   20.
FISHER, George Adams   **The Yankee Conscript.**
    1864   Philadelphia   25.
FISHER, Horace   **A Staff Officer's Story.**
    1960   Boston   35.
FISHER, Richard Swainson   **A Chronological History of the Civil War in America.**
    1863   New York   75.

FISHWICK, Marshall   **Lee After the War.**
    1963   New York   15.
FISHWICK, Marshall   **The Life and Work of Michael Miley, Gen. Lee's Photographer.**
    1954   Chapel Hill, N. C.   15.
FISKE, Ethel F.   **Letters of John Fiske.**
    1940   New York   20.
FISKE, John   **The Mississippi Valley in the Civil War.**
    1900   Boston   25.
    1901   Cambridge   20.
    1902   Boston   20.
FITCH, John   **Annals of the Army of the Cumberland.**
    1864   Philadelphia   60.
FITE, David   **Social and Industrial Conditions in the North During the Civil War.**
    1910   New York   35.
    1930   New York   20.
FITE, Emerson David   **The Presidential Campaign of 1860.**
    1911   New York   20.
FITZGERALD, O. P.   **John B. McFerrin, A Biography.**
    1888   Nashville   25.
Flags of the Army of the United States Carried During the War of the Rebellion.
    1887   Philadelphia   350.
Flags of the Confederate Armies Returned to the Men Who Bore Them by the   U.S. Govt. Wraps
    1905   St. Louis   35.
The Flags of the Confederate States of America. Wraps
    1907   n.p.   20.
FLEET, Betsy, and **FULLER,** John (eds)   **Green Mount, A Virginia Plantation Family During the Civil War.**
    1962   Lexington   25.
FLEMING, A. M.   **A Soldier of the Confederacy.**
    1934   Boston   35.
FLEMING, Vivian Minor   **Battles of Fredericksburg and Chancellorsville, Virginia.**
    1921   Richmond   55.
FLEMING, Vivian Minor   **Campaigns of the Army of Northern Virginia Including the Jackson Valley Campaign, 1861-1865.**
    1928   Richmond   100.
FLEMING, Vivian Minor   **The Wilderness Campaign.** Wraps
    1922   Richmond   35.
FLEMING, Walter L.   **Documentary History of Reconstruction.**
    1906-07   Cleveland   2 vols.   100.
    1950   New York   2 vols. in 1   35.
FLEMING, Walter L. (ed)   **General W. T. Sherman as College President.**
    1912   Cleveland   25.
FLEMING, Walter L.   **Louisiana State University 1860-1863.**
    1936   Baton Rouge   30.
FLEMING, Walter L.   **The Sequel of Appomattox.**
    1921   New Haven   20.
FLIPPIN, Percy Scott   **Herschel V. Johnson of Georgia.**
    1931   Richmond   40.
FLOAN, Howard R.   **The South in Northern Eyes 1831-1861.**
    1958   Austin, Texas   15.
FLOURNOY, Mary H.   **Side Lights on Southern History.**
    1939   Richmond   20.
FLOWER, Frank Abial   **Edwin McMasters Stanton.**
    1905   Boston   30.
    1905   Akron   30.
FLUKER, Anne and Winifred   **Confed'ric Gol!**
    1926   Macon, Georgia   30.

FOLTZ, Charles S.   **Surgeon of the Seas.**
    1931   Indianapolis   30.
FONER, Eric   **Politics and Ideology in the Age of the Civil War.**
    1980   New York   15.
FONTAINE, Francis   **Etowah . A Romance of the Confederacy.**
    1887   Atlanta   30.
FOOTE, Caleb and **WILDER,** Mary   **Reminiscences and Letters** edited by Mary Wilder
    Tileston.
    1918   Boston   20.
FOOTE, Henry S.   **Casket of Reminiscences.**
    1874   Washington   150.
FOOTE, Henry S.   **War of the Rebellion.**
    1866   New York   40.
FOOTE, Kate   **Harriet Ward Foote Hawley.**
    n.d. (circa 1890)   n.p.   30.
FOOTE, Shelby   **The Civil War: A Narrative.** 3 vols.
    1958-1974   New York   40.
FOOTE, Shelby   **Shiloh.**
    1952   New York   10.
FORAKER, Joseph Benson   **Notes of a Busy Life.**
    1916   Cincinnati   40.
    1917   Cincinnati   30.
FORBES, Edwin   **An Artist's Story of the Great War.**
    1890   New York   4 vols.   100.
    1890   New York   20 parts in wrappers.   450.
FORBES, Edwin   **Life Studies of the Great Army.** 40 copper plate etchings.
    1876   New York   1000.
FORBES, Mrs. Ida B.   **General Wm. T. Sherman, His Life and Battles.**
    1886   New York   20.
FORBES, John Murray   **Letters and Recollections** edited by Sarah Forbes Hughes.
    2 vols.
    1899   Boston   30.
    1900   Boston   20.
FORBES, Robert B.   **Personal Reminiscences.**
    1878   Boston   40.
FORCE, M. F.   **From Fort Henry to Corinth.**
    1881   New York   20.
    1882   New York   20.
FORD, Jesse Hill   **The Raider.**
    1975   Boston/Toronto   20.
FORD, Sally Rochester   **Raids and Romance of Morgan and His Men.**
    1864   New York   75.
FORD, Worthington C. (ed)   **A Cycle of Adams Letters 1861-1865.** 2 vols.
    1920   Boston   20.
FORMBY, John   **The American Civil War.** 2 vols.
    1910   London   50.
    1910   New York   40.
FORNEY, John W.   **Anecdotes of Public Men.** 2 vols.
    1881   New York   30.
FORNEY, John W.   **Life and Military Career of Winfield Scott Hancock.**
    1880   Philadelphia   15.
FORRESTER, Izola   **This One Mad Act ... The Unknown Story of John Wilkes Booth
    and His Family.**
    1937   Boston   25.
"Fort LaFayette Life." 1863-4 **In Extracts from a "Right Flanker."**
    1865   London   200.
Fort Sumter Memorial. The Fall of Fort Sumter. edited by Frank Moore.
    Replacing the Flag Upon Sumter. Adapted by F. Milton Willis and General Robert

Anderson. By Ed. S. Cornell.
    1915   New York   Ltd.   60.
FORTEN, Charlotte L.   **The Journal of Charlotte L. Forten.** edited by Ray Allen
    Billington.
    1953   New York   15.
FOSTER, John   **Rebel Sea Raider, The Story of Raphael Semmes.**
    1965   New York   15.
FOSTER, Lillian   **President Johnson.**
    1866   New York   20.
FOSTER, Stephen   **A Treasury of Stephen Foster.**
    1946   New York   20.
FOSTER, William Lovelace   **Vicksburg: Southern City Under Siege, William Lovelace
Foster's Letter Describing the Defense and Surrender of the Confederate Fortress on
the Mississippi.** edited by Kenneth T. Urquhart.
    1980   New Orleans   15.
FOULKE, William Dudley   **Lucas B. Swift, A Biography.**
    1930   Indianapolis   20.
FOWLER, William Chauncey   **The Sectional Controversy.**
    1862   New York   25.
    1863   New York   25.
FOX, Charles K. (ed)   **Gettysburg.**
    1969   New York   10.
FOX, Gustavus Vasa   **Confidential Correspondence of** _____ edited by Robt M.
Thompson and Richard Wainwright. 2 vols.
    1918   New York   Ltd.   Boxed   75.
FOX, John A.   **The Capture of Jefferson Davis.** Wraps
    1964   New York   15.
FOX, William F.   **Regimental Losses in the American Civil War 1861-1865.**
    1889   Albany   100.
    1893   Albany   75.
FRANK, John P.   **Lincoln as a Lawyer.**
    1961   Urbana, Illinois   10.
Frank Leslie's Illustrated Famous Leaders and Battle Scenes of the Civil War
    edited by Louis S. Moat.
    1896   New York   125.
Frank Leslie's Illustrated History of the Civil War edited by Louis S. Moat.
    1895   New York   150.
Frank Leslie's Illustrated Newspaper 1861-65.
    5 vols.   bound   1000.
    individual volumes   150.
Frank Leslie's Pictorial History of the Civil War edited by Ephraim Squire. 2 vols.
    1861-62   New York   100.
Frank Leslie's Scenes and Portraits of the Civil War. 10 parts in 1 vol.
    1894   New York   100.
FRANKLIN, Charles H.   **Study on Project of Publication, The War of the
Rebellion.**
    1931   Washington   25.
FRANKLIN, John Hope   **The Militant South 1800-1861.**
    1956   Cambridge   10.
FRANKLIN, John Hope   **Reconstruction: After the Civil War.**
    1961   Chicago   10.
FRANKLIN, Samuel R.   **Memories of a Rear-Admiral.**
    1898   New York   30.
FRANKLIN, William B.   **Reply to the Report of the Joint Committee of
Congress on the Conduct of the War.** Wraps
    1863   New York   50.
FRANTZ, Mabel Goode   **Full Many a Name, The Story of Sam Davis, Scout
and Spy, C.S.A.**
    1961   Jackson   20.

FRASSANITO, William A.   Antietam, the Photographic Legacy of America's
Bloodiest Day.
1978   New York   16.
FRASSANITO, William A.   Gettysburg, A Journey in Time.
1975   New York   16.
FREDERIC, Harold   Marsena and Other Stories of the Wartime.
1894   New York   20.
FREDERICKSON, George M.   The Inner Civil War.
1965   New York   15.
FREEHLING, William W.   Prelude to Civil War: The Nullification Controversy in
South Carolina 1816-1836.
1966   New York   15.
FREEMAN, Benjamin H.   The Confederate Letters of _____ edited by Stuart E. Wright.
1974   New York   15.
FREEMAN, Douglas Southall   A Calendar of Confederate Papers.
1908   Richmond   Ltd.   50.
FREEMAN, Douglas Southall   The Cornerstones of Stratford, An Address. Wraps
1935(?)   n.p.   49.
FREEMAN, Douglas Southall   The Last Parade.
1932   Richmond   Ltd.   125.
FREEMAN, Douglas Southall   Lee of Virginia.
1958   New York   20.
FREEMAN, Douglas Southall & McWHINEY, G.   Lee's Dispatches, Unpublished
Letters of Gen. Robert E. Lee to Jefferson Davis 1862-1865.
1915   New York   50.
1957   New York   25.
FREEMAN, Douglas Southall   Lee's Lieutenants. 3 vols.
1942-44   New York   60.
1946   New York   Arlington Edition   75.
FREEMAN, Douglas Southall   R. E. Lee. 4 vols.
1934-35   New York   75.
1936   New York   Pulitzer Prize Edition   100.
Issued hereafter about once a year in New York   60.
FREEMAN, Douglas Southall   The South to Posterity.
1939   New York   50.
1951   New York   40.
FREESE, Jacob R.   Secrets of the Late Rebellion.
1882   Philadelphia   10.
FREIDEL, Frank (ed)   Union Pamphlets of the Civil War. 2 vols.
1957   Cambridge   30.
FREMANTLE, Arthur J. L.   Three Months in the Southern States.
1863   Edinburgh   200.
1863   London   200.
1864   New York   100.
1904   Boston   40.
1954   Boston   entitled The Fremantle Diary edited by Walter Lord   20.
FREMANTLE, Arthur J. L. & HASKELL, Frank   Two Views of Gettysburg edited
by Richard Harwell.
1964   Chicago   30.
FRENCH, "Chester" S. Bassett   Centennial Tales, Memoirs of _____ compiled by Glenn
C. Oldaker.
1962   New York   15.
FRENCH, Samuel G.   Two Wars: An Autobiography.
1901   Nashville   125.
FRENCH, Samuel L.   The Army of the Potomac from 1861 to 1863.
1905   New York   60.
1906   New York   50.

FRENCH, William H. et al   **Instruction for Field Artillery.**
    1860   Philadelphia   75.
    1861   n.p.   75.
    1863   Philadelphia   50.
    1968   New York   25.
FROHMAN, Charles   **Rebels on Lake Erie.**
    1956   Columbus   15.
FROST, Holloway H.   **Union Joint Operations Along the Confederate Coast in the Civil War.** Wraps
    1932   Washington   Ltd.   75.
FROST, Lawrence A.   **The Custer Album, A Pictorial Biography of General George A. Custer.**
    1964   Seattle   15.
FROST, Lawrence A.   **The Phil Sheridan Album.**
    1968   Seattle   15.
FROST, Lawrence   **U. S. Grant Album, A Pictorial Biography.**
    1966   New York   20.
    1966   Seattle   15.
FRY, James B.   **The Conkling and Blaine-Fry Controversy in 1866.**
    1893   New York   15.
FRY, James B.   **McDowell and Tyler in the Campaign of Bull Run 1861.** Wraps
    1884   New York   35.
FRY, James B.   **Operations of the Army Under Buell from June 10th to October 30th, 1862.**
    1884   New York   50.
FRY, Smith D.   **Lincoln and Lee A Patriotic Story.** Wraps
    1922   Washington   5.
FULKERSON, H. S.   **A Civilian's Recollections of the War Between the States.** edited by P. O. Rainwater.
    1939   Baton Rouge   Ltd.   150.
FULLAM, George Townley   **The Journal of** _____ edited by Charles G. Summersell.
    1973   University, Alabama   15.
FULLER, Claud E.   **Confederate Currency and Stamps 1861-1865.**
    1949   Nashville   50.
FULLER, Claud E. and **STEUART,** R. D.   **Firearms of the Confederacy.**
    1944   Huntington, Va.   75.
FULLER, Claud E.   **The Rifled Musket.**
    1958   Harrisburg   30.
FULLER, Claud E. (comp)   **Springfield Muzzle-Loading Shoulder Arms.**
    1930   New York   50.
FULLER, J. F. C.   **Decisive Battles of the U.S.A.**
    1942   New York   20.
    1953   New York   15.
FULLER, J. F. C.   **The Generalship of Ulysses S. Grant.**
    1929   New York   30.
    1929   London   35.
    1958   Bloomington, Indiana   25.
FULLER, J. F. C.   **Grant and Lee.**
    1933   New York   20.
    1933   London   25.
    1957   Bloomington   20.
FURBISH, J.   **The Flower of Liberty.**
    1869   Boston   75.
FURNAS, J. C.   **Goodbye to Uncle Tom.**
    1956   New York   10.
FURNAS, J. C.   **The Road to Harpers Ferry.**
    1959   New York   10.
FUTCH, Ovid L.   **History of Andersonville Prison.**
    1968   Gainesville, Florida   15.

FUZZLEBUG, Fritz (pseud.) See: **DUNKLE,** John J.
GAINES, Francis Pendleton **Lee, The Final Achievement.**
 1933 New York Ltd. Signed 35.
 1933 n.p. Wraps 20.
GANNON, Michael V. **Rebel Bishop, The Life and Era of Augustin Verot.**
 1964 Milwaukee 25.
GANTT, E. W. **Address: Brigadier General E. W. Gantt, C.S.A.**
 1860 Little Rock 150.
 n.d. (1863) n.p. (Philadelphia) 75.
GARBER, Mrs. A. W. (ed) **In Memoriam Sempiternam, Confederate Memorial Literary Society.**
 1896 Richmond 15.
GARD, R. Max **Morgan's Raid into Ohio.**
 1963 Lisbon, Ohio 20.
GARDNER, Alexander **Gardner's Photographic Sketchbook of the Civil War.** Wraps
 1959 New York 15.
GARDNER, Alexander **Original Photographs Taken on the Battlefields During the Civil War.**
 1907 Hartford 100.
GARDINER, Asa Bird **Argument on Behalf of Lieut. Gen. Philip H. Sheridan . . . Before the Court of Inquiry: The Battles of "Gravelly Run," "Dinwiddie Court House," and "Five Forks," Va. 1865.** Wraps
 1881 Washington 50.
 1881 Chicago 45.
GARDNER, W. **Life of Stephen A. Douglas.**
 1905 Boston 20.
GARESCHE, Louis **Biography of Lieut. Col. Julius P. Garesche.**
 1887 Philadelphia 30.
GARFIELD, James A. **The Wild Life of the Army: Civil War Letters of _____** edited by Frederick D. Williams.
 1964 Chapel Hill 15.
GARLAND, Hamlin **Ulysses S. Grant His Life and Character.**
 1898 New York 35.
 1920 New York 15.
GARNETT, John J. **Gettysburg, A Complete Historical Narrative of the Battle.** Wraps
 1888 New York 30.
GARNETT, Theodore S. **J. E. B. Stuart . . . An Address.**
 1907 New York 50.
GARRISON, Fielding H. **John Shaw Billings, A Memoir.**
 1915 New York 35.
GARTH, David **Gray Canaan.**
 1947 New York 15.
GASPARIN, Agenor de **America Before Europe Principles and Interests.**
 1862 New York 30.
GASPARIN, Agenor de **The Uprising of a Great People.**
 1861 New York 25.
 1861 Paris entitled: **Les Etats-Unis En 1861 Un Grande Peuple Qui Se Releve.** wraps 30.
GASTON, Paul M. **The New South Creed.**
 1970 New York 15.
GATES, Paul W. **Agriculture and the Civil War.**
 1965 New York 25.
GAVIN, William G. **Accoutrement Plates, North and South 1861-1865.**
 1863 Philadelphia 25.
 1975 New York 20.
GAVRONSKY, Serge **The French Liberal Opposition and the American Civil War.**
 1968 New York 15.
GAY, George H. **A Few Remarks on the Primary Treatment of Wounds.** Wraps
 1862 Boston 30.

GAY, Mary A. H.   **Life in Dixie During the War.**
 1892 Atlanta 100.
 1894 Atlanta 100.
 1897 Atlanta 75.
 1901 Atlanta 40.
GAY, Mary A. H.   **The Transplanted, A Story of Dixie Before the War.**
 1907 New York/Washington 50.
GEER, Walter   **Campaigns of the Civil War.**
 1926 New York 75.
GELMAN, Barbara (ed)   **The Wood Engravings of Winslow Homer.**
 1969 New York 20.
General Grant's Tour Around the World.
 1879 Chicago 10.
General Washington and General Jackson on Negro Soldiers. Wraps
 1863 Philadelphia 25.
Generals and Battles of the Civil War.
 1891 Canton, Ohio 100.
GENOVESE, Eugene D.   **Roll, Jordan, Roll, the World the Slaves Made.**
 1974 New York 20.
GENTRY, Claude   **The Battle of Brice's Crossroads.** Wraps
 1968 Baldwyn, Mississippi 10.
GENTRY, Claude   **Private John Allen.**
 1951 Decatur 30.
GEORGE, James Z.   **Political History of Slavery in the United States.**
 1915 New York 50.
GERNON, Blaine Brooks   **The Lincolns in Chicago.**
 1934 Chicago 10.
GERRISH, T.   **Will Newton   The Young Volunteer.**
 1884 Maine 15.
GERSON, Noel B.   **The Trial of Andrew Johnson.**
 1977 New York 10.
Gettysburg Blue Book of the Geological Field Excursion from New York to Gettysburg. Wraps
 1926 New York 15.
Gettysburg. A Comprehensive Description of the Greatest Work of the Celebrated French Artist Paul Philippoteaux   Battle of Gettysburg. Wraps
 n.d. (1933?) n.p. (Chicago?) 20.
Gettysburg Memorial Commission, Report of.
 1887 Columbus Wraps 15.
 1914 Harrisburg 20.
Gettysburg National Military Park, Annual Reports to the Secretary of War.
 1900 Washington 1893-1899 15.
 1902 Washington 1893-1901 15.
 1905 Washington 1893-1904 30.
GIBBES, James G.   **Who Burnt Columbia?**
 1902 Newberry, S. C. 100.
GIBBON, John   **An Address on the Unveiling of the Statue of Maj. Gen. George G. Meade in Philadelphia.** Wraps
 1887 Philadelphia 25.
GIBBON, John   **The Artillerist's Manual.**
 1863 New York 75.
 1970 Glendale 20.
 1971 West Port, Connecticut 20.
GIBBON, John   **Personal Recollections of the Civil War.**
 1928 New York 75.
GIBSON, J. M.   **Memoirs of J. M. Gibson: Terrors of the Civil War and Reconstruction Days** edited by James G. Alverson & James, Jr.
 1929 Houston, Texas 50.
 1966 n.p. 10.

GIBSON, John M. **Those 163 Days.**
1961   New York   15.
GIBSON, Randall Lee   **Shiloh, Equestrian Monument Erected by the Veterans of the Army of Tennessee.** Wraps
1887   New Orleans   15.
GIBSON, Ronald (ed)   **Jefferson Davis and the Confederacy.**
1977   Dobbs Ferry, New York   12.
GILBERT, C. E.   **Two Presidents: Abraham Lincoln, Jefferson Davis.** Wraps
1927   Houston, Texas   25.
GILBERT, J. Warren   **Battle of Gettysburg Made Plain, Historical Guide-Book.** Wraps
n.d. (circa 1890)   Gettysburg   20.
GILBERT, J. Warren   **The Blue and Gray.** Wraps
1922   n.p.   20.
GILCHRIST, Robert C.   **The Confederate Defence of Morris Island.** Wraps
1884   Charleston, S. C.   40.
GILDERSLEEVE, Basil L.   **The Creed of the Old South 1865-1915.**
1915   Baltimore   35.
GILHAM, William   **Manual of Instruction for the Volunteers and Militia of the United States.**
1861   Philadelphia   75.
GILLMORE, Q. A.   **Engineer and Artillery Operations Against the Defenses of Charleston Harbor in 1863.**
1862   New York   100.
1865   New York   80.
1868   New York   80
GILLMORE, Q. A.   **Official Report of the Siege and Reduction of Fort Pulaski, Georgia Feburary, March and April 1862.**
1862   New York   50.
GILLS, Mary Louise   **It Happened at Appomattox.** Wraps
1948   Richmond   10.
GILMAN, Bradley   **Robert E. Lee.**
1915   New York   10.
GILMORE, James   **Among the Pines; or, South in Secession-Time.**
1862   New York   25.
1865   New York   25.
GILMORE, James   **Down in Tennessee.**
1864   New York   35.
GILMORE, James   **Life in Dixie's Land; Or, South in Secession-Time.**
1863   London   75.
GILMORE, James   **My Southern Friends.**
1863   New York   25.
GILMORE, James   **On the Border.**
1867   Boston   20.
GILMORE, James   **Patriot Boys and Prison Pictures.**
1866   Boston   25.
GILMORE, James   **Personal Recollections of Abraham Lincoln and the Civil War.**
1898   Boston   20.
1899   London   20.
GIRARD, Charles   **Les Etats Confederes d'Amerique Visites en 1863.**
1864   Paris   75.
GIRARD, Charles   **A Visit to the Confederate States of America in 1863.** Wraps
1962   Tuscaloosa   Ltd.   25.
GLASS, Paul, and **SINGER,** Louis C.   **Singing Soldiers: A History of the Civil War in Song.**
1968   New York   20.
GLENN, William Wilkins   **Between North and South: A Maryland Journalist Views the Civil War, the Narrative of _____ 1861-1869** edited by B. E. Marks and M. N. Schatz.
1976   Rutherford, New Jersey   20.

GLICKSBERG, Charles I.(ed)   **Walt Whitman and the Civil War, A Collection of Original Articles and Manuscripts.**
   1933   Philadelphia   25.
GLOVER, W.   **Abraham Lincoln and the Sleeping Sentinel of Vermont.**
   1936   Montpelier   15.
GLYNDON, Howard (pseud.)   See: **SEARING,** Laura C. R.
GODDARD, Joseph A.   **A Brief Autobiography of Joseph A. Goddard.**
   1929   Muncie   50.
GODDARD, Samuel A.   **Letters on the American Rebellion.**
   1870   London   60.
GOEBEL, Dorothy Burne, and **GOEBEL,** Jr. Julius   **Generals in the White House.**
   1945   New York   15.
GOFF, Richard D.   **Confederate Supply.**
   1969   Durham   15.
GOLTZ, Carlos W.   **Incidents in the Life of Mary Todd Lincoln.** Wraps
   1928   Sioux City   15.
GOODE, John   **Recollections of a Lifetime.**
   1906   New York & Washington   40.
GOODMAN, Thos. M.   **A Thrilling Record** edited by Thomas R. Hooper. Wraps
   1960   Maryville, Missouri   Ltd.   20.
GOODRICH, Frank B.   **The Tribute Book.**
   1865   New York   30.
GOODRICH, Frederick E.   **The Life and Public Services of Winfield Scott Hancock.**
   1880   Indianapolis   20.
   1880   Boston   20.
   1886   Boston   16.
GOODWIN, Thomas S.   **The Natural History of Secession.**
   1864   New York   40.
GORDON, Armistead C.   **Figures from American History; Jefferson Davis.**
   1918   New York   30.
GORDON, Armistead C.   **In the Picturesque Shenandoah Valley.**
   1930   Richmond   40.
GORDON, Armistead C.   **William Fitzhugh Gordon, A Virginian of the Old School.**
   1909   New York   40.
GORDON, Armistead C.   **William Gordon McCabe A Brief Memoir.**
   1920   Richmond   25.
GORDON, Caroline   **None Shall Look Back.**
   1937   New York   20.
GORDON, George H.   **A War Diary of Events of the War of the Great Rebellion.**
   1882   Boston   50.
GORDON, John B.   **Reminiscences of the Civil War.**
   1903   New York   75.
   1904   New York   50.
   1905   New York   30.
GORE, James Howard   **My Mother's Story.**
   1923   Philadelphia   35.
GORGAS, Josiah   **The Civil War Diary of** _____ edited by Frank E. Vandiver.
   1947   University, Alabama   60.
GORHAM, George G.   **Life and Public Services of Edwin M. Stanton.** 2 vols.
   1899   Boston   25.
GOSNELL, H. Allen   **Guns on the Western Waters.**
   1949   Baton Rouge   25.
GOSS, Warren Lee   **Jed. A Boy's Adventures in the Army of '61-'65.**
   1889   New York   20.
GOUGH, J. E.   **Fredericksburg and Chancellorsville.**
   1913   London   150.
GOULD, Alta Isadore   **The Veteran's Bride and Other Poems.**
   1894   Grand Rapids   15.

GOVAN, Gilbert E., and **LIVINGOOD,** James W.   **A Different Valor: The Story of General Joseph E. Johnston, C.S.A.**
   1956   New York   30.
   1973   Westport   20.
GRACIE, Archibald.   **The Truth About Chickamauga.**
   1911   Boston   85.
GRAEBNER, Norman A. (ed)   **Politics and the Crisis of 1860.**
   1961   Urbana, Illinois   15.
GRAHAM, C. R.   **Under Both Flags.**
   1896   Philadelphia   20.
Grand Army of the Republic (G.A.R.), Proceedings at Encampments.
   1st-10th   20. each   thereafter 10. each
GRANGER, J. T.   **A Brief Biographical Sketch of the Life of Major-General Grenville M. Dodge.** Wraps
   1893   New York   35.
GRANT, A. F.   **Sharpshooter and Spy; or, The Terrible Panic at Bull Run. War Liberty Vol. 7, No. 242.** Wraps
   n.d.   n.p.   20.
GRANT, A. F.   **The War Detective; or Secret Service in the Rebellion. The War Library, Vol. 7, No. 232.**
   Wraps
   n.d.   n.p.   20.
GRANT, Jesse R.   **In the Days of My Father, General Grant.**
   1925   New York   15.
The Grant Memorial in Washington.
   1924   Washington   20.
GRANT, Ulysses S.   **The Papers of Ulysses S. Grant** edited by John Y. Simon. 10 vols. (still being issued)
   1967-82   Carbondale, Illinois
   Vols. 1-4   22.50 each
   Vols. 5-6   30. each
   Vols. 7-8   35. each
   Vols. 9-10   40. each
GRANT, Ulysses S.   **Personal Memoirs of U. S. Grant.** 2 Vols.
   1885-86   New York   30.
   Many later editions   25.
GRANT, Ulysses S.   **Report of Lieut. Gen. U. S. Grant, of the Armies of the United States, 1864-65.** Wraps
   1865   Washington   25.
GRANT, Ulysses S., III   **Ulysses S. Grant: Warrior and Statesman.**
   1969   New York   20.
GRAY, Amy   **The Lily of the Valley.**
   1868   Baltimore   20.
GRAY, John Chipman & **ROPES,** John Codman   **War Letters 1862-1865.**
   1927   New York   30.
   1927   Boston   30.
   1927   Cambridge   30.
GRAY, Wood   **The Hidden Civil War.**
   1942   New York   25.
GRAYDON, Nell S.   **Another Jezebel.**
   1958   Columbia, S. C.   15.
The Grayjackets.   See: **McCABE,** James D., Jr.
GRAYSON, William   **James Louis Petigru.**
   1866   New York   50.
The Great Impeachment and Trial of Andrew Johnson, President of the U.S.
   1868   Philadelphia   20.
GREELEY, Horace   **The American Conflict.** 2 vols.
   1864   Hartford   40.
   Many later editions   30.

GREELEY, Horace, and **CLEVELAND,** John (comp)   **A Political Text-Book for 1860.**
    1860   New York   25.
GREELEY, Horace   **Recollections of a Busy Life.**
    1868   New York   15.
    1869   New York   15.
GREELY, A. W.   **Reminiscences of Adventure and Service.**
    1927   New York   35.
GREEN, Anna Maria   **The Journal of a Milledgeville Girl 1861-1867** edited by James
    A. Bonner. Wraps
    1964   Athens, Georgia   15.
GREEN, Horace   **General Grant's Last Stand A Biography.**
    1936   New York   25.
GREEN, Horace   **Triumph, General Grant's Final Victory.**
    1941   New York   10.
GREEN, Thomas W.   **The Artillery of the Civil War, Civil War Round Table of London,
    England.** Wraps
    1959   London   20.
GREEN, Thomas W.   **Ironclads of the Sixties.** Wraps
    1959   London   15.
GREEN, Thomas W.   **Major Caleb Huse, C.S.A. A Memoir.** Wraps
    1966   London   25.
GREENBIE, Marjorie Barstow   **Lincoln's Daughters of Mercy.**
    1944   New York   10.
GREENBIE, Marjorie Barstow   **My Dear Lady The Story of Anna Ella Carroll.**
    1940   New York   25.
GREENBIE, Sydney & **GREENBIE,** Marjorie Barstow   **Anna Ella Carroll and
    Abraham Lincoln A Biography.**
    1952   Manchester, Maine   25.
GREENE, Francis Vinton   **The Mississippi.**
    1882   New York   20.
    Many later editions   15.
GREENE, Jacob L.   **General William B. Franklin and the Operations of the Left Wing
    at the Battle of Fredericksburg Dec, 13, 1862.**
    1900   Hartford   40.
GREENE, John W.   **Camp Ford Prison and How I Escaped.**
    1893   Toledo   200.
GREENE, Laurence   **The Raid, A Biography of Harper's Ferry.**
    1953   New York   15.
GREENHOW, Rose   **My Imprisonment & the First Year of the Abolition Rule at
    Washington.**
    1863   London   100.
GREENLEAF, Margery   **Letters to Eliza from a Union Soldier 1862-1865.**
    1970   New York   25.
GREGG, David McM.   **The Second Cavalry Division of the Army of the Potomac in the
    Gettysburg Campaign.** Wraps
    1907   Philadelphia   25.
GRESHAM, Otto   **The Greenbacks, or, The Money that Won the Civil War.**
    1927   Chicago   60.
GRIERSON, Francis   **The Valley of Shadows.**
    1948   Boston   15.
GRIMES, Messr.   **The Navy in Congress.** Wraps
    1865   Washington   25.
GRIMM, Herbert L. and **ROY,** Paul L.   **Human Interest Stories of the Three Days'
    Battles at Gettysburg.** Wraps
    1927   Gettysburg   15.
GRISWOLD, B. Howell, Jr.   **The Spirit of Lee and Jackson.**
    1927   Baltimore   40.

GROSE, Parlee C.   **The Case of Private Smith & the Remaining Mysteries of the Andrews Raid.** Wraps
    1963   McComb, Ohio   10.
GUNDERSON, Robert G.   **Old Gentleman's Convention: The Washington Peace Conference of 1861.**
    1961   Madison, Wisconsin   10.
GUROWSKI, Adam   **Diary from March 4, 1861 to Nov. 12, 1862.**
    1862   Boston   25.
GUROWSKI, Adam   **Diary from Nov. 18, 1862 to Oct. 18, 1863.**
    1864   New York   25.
GUROWSKI, Adam   **Diary: 1863-'64-'65.**
    1866   Washington   25.

HABERSHAM, Josephine Clay   **Ebb Tide As Seen Through the Diary of** _____ **edited by Spencer Bidwell King, Jr.**
    1958   Athens, Georgia   20.
HACKETT, Horatio B.   **Christian Memorials of the War.**
    1864   Boston   15.
HAGOOD, Johnson.   **Memoirs of the War of Secession.**
    1910   Columbia, S.C.   100.
HAGUE, Parthenia Antoinette   **A Blockaded Family.**
    1888   Boston   50.
    1889   Boston   40.
    1894   Boston   30.
HAIGHT, Theron Wilbur   **Three Wisconsin Cushings A Sketch of the Lives of Howard B., Alonzo H., & William B. Cushing, Children of a Pioneer Family of Waukesha County.**
    1910   n.p. (Madison)   20.
HALDERMAN, Cyrus S.   **A True Romance of the Rebellion.**
    1886   Boston   20.
HALE, Donald   **They Called Him Bloody Bill, The Missouri Badman Who Taught Jesse James Outlawry.** Wraps
    1975   Clinton, Missouri   7.
HALE, Donald R.   **We Rode with Quantrill.** Wraps
    1975   Independence, Missouri   7.
HALE, Edward E. (ed)   **Stories of War Told by Soldiers.**
    1879   Boston   15.
HALE, John P.   **Report on Abandonment of Pensacola and Norfolk Navy Yards.**
    1861   Washington   25.
HALE, Laura Virginia   **Belle Boyd, Southern Spy of the Shenandoah.** Wraps
    n.d.   Front Royal, Virginia   10.
HALE, Laura Virginia   **Four Valiant Years in Lower Shenandoah Valley 1861-1865.**
    1968   Strasburg, Virginia   40.
    1973   Strasburg, Virginia   35.
HALE, Laura Virginia   **Memories in Marble: The Story of the Four Confederate Monuments at Front Royal, Va.** Wraps
    1956   n.p.   10.
HALL, Charles B.   **Military Records of General Officers of the Confederate States of America.**
    1898   New York   Ltd.   2500.
    1963   Austin   Boxed   100.
HALL, Clifton R.   **Andrew Johnson — Military Governor of Tennessee.**
    1916   Princeton   20.
HALL, Courtney Robert   **Confederate Medicine, Medical Life, Sept 1935.** Wraps
    1935   n.p.   25.
HALL, Florence Howe   **Memories Grave and Gay.**
    1918   New York   20.
HALL, Florence Howe   **The Story of the Battle Hymn of the Republic.**
    1916   New York   10.

HALL, Granville Davisson   **Lee's Invasion of Northwest Virginia in 1861.**
    1911   Chicago   35.
HALL, John Leslie   **Half-Hours in Southern History.**
    1907   Richmond   20.
HALL, Martin Hall   **Sibley's New Mexico Campaign.**
    1960   Austin   45.
HALL, Newman   **The American War A Lecture to Working Men Delivered in London Oct 20, 1862.** Wraps
    1863   New York   30.
HALL, Sam S.   **Wild Bill, The Union Scout of Missouri,** War Library Vol. 6, No. 282. Wraps
    1888   New York   50.
HALL, W. W.   **Soldier-Health.**
    1863   New York   65.
HALL, Wade H.   **Reflections of the Civil War in Southern Humor.** Wraps
    1962   Gainesville, Florida   10.
HALLUM, John   **Reminiscences of the Civil War. Vol. 1.** (all pub.)
    1903   Little Rock   75.
HALSEY, Ashley, Jr.   **Who Fired the First Shot?**
    1963   New York   15.
HALSEY, Don P., Jr.   **A Sketch of the Life of Capt. Don P. Halsey of the Confederate States Army.** Wraps
    1904   Richmond   25.
HALSTEAD, Murat   **Caucuses of 1860. A History of the National Political Conventions of the Current Presidential Campaign.**
    1860   Columbus   75.
HAMERSLY, Lewis R.   **Records of Living Officers of the U.S. Navy & Marine Corps.**
    1870   Philadelphia   75.
    1884   Philadelphia   75.
    1890   Philadelphia   75.
HAMIL, H. M.   **Sam Davis, A True Story of a Young Confederate Soldier.** Wraps
    1912   Griffin, Georgia   75.
    1959   Kennesaw   9.
HAMILTON, A. G.   **The Story of the Libby Prison Tunnel Escape.** Wraps
    1893   Chicago   65.
HAMILTON, Charles, and **OSTENDORF**, Lloyd   **Lincoln in Photographs.**
    1963   Norman, Oklahoma   30.
HAMILTON, H. S.   **The Dixie Jacket.** Wraps
    1935   n.p.   20.
HAMILTON, Holman   **Prologue to Conflict — The Crisis and Compromise of 1850.**
    1964   Kentucky   15.
HAMILTON, J. G. de R. and **HAMILTON**, Mary T.   **The Life of Robert E. Lee, For Boys and Girls.**
    1917   Boston   10.
HAMILTON, J. G. de R.   **The Papers of Thomas Ruffin.** 4 vols.
    1918   Raleigh   125.
HAMILTON, James   **The Battle of Fort Donelson.**
    1968   South Brunswick   15.
    1968   New York   15.
HAMILTON, Peter Joseph   **A Little Boy in Confederate Mobile.**
    1947   Mobile, Alabama   Ltd.   40.
HAMLIN, Augustus C.   **Battle of Chancellorsville.**
    1896   Bangor, Maine   40.
HAMLIN, Augustus C.   **Martyria: or, Andersonville Prison.**
    1866   Boston   20.
HAMLIN, Charles   **Brief Sketch of the Battle of Gettysburg.** Wraps
    1898   Portland   50.
HAMLIN, Percy Gatling.   **Old Bald Head (General R. S. Ewell).**
    1940   Strasburg, Virginia   60.

HAMMER, Jefferson J. (ed)   **Frederic Augustus James' Civil War Diary.**
  1973   Rutherford, New Jersey   10.
HAMMETT, Hugh B.   **Hilary Abner Herbert: A Southerner Returns to the Union.**
  Wraps
  1976   Philadelphia   15.
HAMMOND, Bray   **Sovereignty and an Empty Purse, Banks and Politics in the Civil War.**
  1970   Princeton, New Jersey   20.
HAMMOND, William A.   **A Treatise on Hygiene with Special Reference to the Military Service.**
  1863   Philadelphia   25.
HAMPTON, Wade   **Address on the Life and Character of Gen. Robert E. Lee.** Wraps
  1872   Baltimore   40.
HANCHETT, William   **Irish, Charles G. Halpine in Civil War America.**
  1970   New York   20.
HANCOCK, Cornelia   **The South After Gettysburg: Letters of Cornelia Hancock** edited
  by Henrietta S. Jaquette.
  1937   Philadelphia   25.
  1956   New York   15.
HANCOCK, Mrs. W. S.   **Reminiscences of Winfield S. Hancock.**
  1887   New York   40.
HANDLIN, Oscar & Lilian   **Abraham Lincoln and the Union.**
  1980   Boston   10.
HANDY, Isaac W. K.   **United States Bonds.**
  1874   Baltimore   100.
HANLY, Frank J.   **Andersonville.**
  1912   Cincinnati   25.
HANNA, A. J. and **HANNA,** Kathryn Abbey   **Confederate Exiles in Venezuela.** Wraps
  1960   Tuscaloosa, Alabama   Ltd.   25.
HANNA, A. J.   **Flight into Oblivion.**
  1938   Richmond   25.
  1959   Bloomington   20.
HANSON, Joseph Mills   **Bull Run Remembers.** Wraps
  1952   Manassas   10
  1953   Manassas   10.
HAPGOOD, Norman   **Abraham Lincoln.**
  1900   New York   20.
HARCOURT, William   **Letters by Historicus on Some Questions of International Law.**
  1863   London   50.
HARDEE, W. J.   **Rifle and Light Infantry Tactics.**
  1861   Philadelphia   2 vols.   50.
  1861   New York   1 vol. ed.   Wraps   50.
  1907   Glendale   20.
HARDEN, Samuel   **Those I Have Met.**
  1888   Anderson, Indiana   35.
HARDESTY, Jesse   **Killed and Died of Wounds, In the Union Army During the Civil War.** Wraps
  1915   San Jose   35.
HARDIN, Bayless   **Brigadier General John Hunt Morgan of Kentucky "Thunderbolt of the Confederacy."** Wraps
  1938 (?)   Frankfort, Kentucky   25.
HARDINGE, Belle B.   **Belle Boyd in Camp and Prison.**
  1865   London   2 vols.   100.
  1865   New York   2 vols. in 1   50.
  1867   New York   2 vols. in 1   50.
  1968   New York   edited by C. C. Davis   15.
HARLOW, Alvin F.   **Brass-Pounders, Young Telegraphers of the Civil War.**
  1962   Denver   15.

HARMON, George D.   **Confederate Migrations to Mexico.** Wraps
    1938   Bethlehem, Pennsylvania   20.
HARMON, George D.   **Political Aspects of Slavery and the Civil War.** Wraps
    1952   Bethlehem, Pennsylvania   25.
HARNSBERGER, Caroline Thomas   **The Lincoln Treasury.**
    1950   New York   20.
HARPER, HAMMOND, SIMMS, and **DEW**   **The Pro-Slavery Argument as Maintained by the Most Distinguished Writers of the Southern States.**
    1853   Philadelphia   40.
Harper's Pictorial History of the Great Rebellion.
    1866   New York   2 vols.   150.
    1866   New York   2 vols. in 1   125.
    1894   Chicago   2 vols.   125.
    1896   Chicago   2 vols.   125.
    n.d.   New York   Reprint   2 vols. 75.
Harper's Weekly 1861-1865.
    Bound in 5 vols.   1800.
    Same in individual issues   2000.
HARRINGTON, Fred Harvey   **Fighting Politician Major General N. P. Banks.**
    1948   Philadelphia   30.
    1973   n.p.   15.
HARRINGTON, George F. (pseud.)   See: **BAKER,** William Mumford
HARRIS, Cicero W.   **The Sectional Struggle.**
    1902   Philadelphia   30.
HARRIS, Gertrude   **A Tale of Men Who Knew Not Fear.** Wraps
    1935   San Antonio   30.
HARRIS, Joel Chandler   **On the Wings of Occasions.**
    1900   New York   20.
HARRIS, Leon, and **BEALS,** Frank   **Look Away Dixieland.**
    1937   New York   15.
HARRIS, N. E.   **The Civil War, Its Results and Lessons: An Address.** Wraps
    1906   Macon   15.
HARRIS, Thomas L.   **The Trent Affair.**
    1896   Indianapolis   30.
HARRIS, William C.   **Leroy Pope Walker.** Wraps
    1962   Tuscaloosa   Ltd.   25.
HARRISON, Mrs. Burton   **Recollections Grave and Gay.**
    1911   New York   35.
    1912   London   35.
HARRISON, Ida Withers   **Beyond the Battle's Rim.**
    1918   New York   50.
HARRISON, Ida Withers   **Memoirs of William Temple Withers.**
    1924   Boston   40.
HARRISON, Walter   **Pickett's Men: A Fragment of War History.**
    1870   New York   80.
HART, Albert Bushnell   **Salmon Portland Chase.**
    1899   Boston   20.
HARTJE, Robert G.   **Van Dorn, The Life and Times of a Confederate General.**
    1967   Nashville   30.
Harvard Memorial Biographies. 2 vols.
    1866   Cambridge   25.
    1867   Cambridge   25.
HARVEY, Paul, Jr.   **Old Tige: General William L. Cabell, C.S.A.**
    1970   Hillsboro   20.
HARWELL, Richard Barksdale   **A Confederate Diary of the Retreat from Petersburg.** Wraps
    1953   Atlanta   20.

HARWELL, Richard Barksdale (ed) **A Confederate Marine: A Sketch of Lt. Henry Lea Graves with Excerpts from the Graves Family Correspondence.** Wraps
1963 Tuscaloosa Ltd. 25.
HARWELL, Richard Barksdale. **Confederate Music.**
1950 Chapel Hill, North Carolina 25.
HARWELL, Richard Barksdale, (ed) **The Confederate Reader.**
1957 New York 25.
HARWELL, Richard Barksdale **Cornerstones of Confederate Collecting.**
1952 Charlottesville, Virginia Wraps 40.
1953 Charlottesville, Virginia 50.
HARWELL, Richard Barksdale **Lee, An Abridgement** of the set by Douglas Southall Freeman.
1961 New York 25.
HARWELL, Richard Barksdale (ed) **Louisiana Burge: The Diary of a Confederate College Girl.** Wraps
1952 Georgia 15.
HARWELL, Richard Barksdale **More Confederate Imprints.** 2 vols. Wraps
1957 Richmond 25.
HARWELL, Richard Barksdale (ed.) **Songs of the Confederacy.**
1951 New York 40.
HARWELL, Richard Barksdale **The Union Reader.**
1958 New York 25.
HARWELL, Richard Barksdale **The War They Fought.** Confederate Reader & Union Reader in 1 vol.
1960 New York 30.
HASKELL, John Cheves **The Haskell Memoirs** edited by G. Govan & J. Livingood.
1960 New York 20.
HASKIN, William L. **The History of the First Regiment of Artillery, from its Organization in 1821 to January 1st 1876.**
1879 Portland, Me. 125.
HASSLER, Warren W., Jr. **Commanders of the Army of the Potomac.**
1962 Baton Rouge 25.
HASSLER, Warren W., Jr. **Crisis at the Crossroads.**
1970 University, Alabama 10.
HASSLER, Warren W., Jr. **General George B. McClellan.**
1957 Baton Rouge 20.
HASSLER, William Woods **A. P. Hill, Lee's Forgotten General.**
1957 Richmond 25.
1962 Chapel Hill 20.
1962 Richmond 20.
HASSLER, William Woods **Colonel John Pelham, Lee's Boy Artillerist.**
1960 Richmond 20.
HATCH, Carl E. (ed.) **Dearest Susie: A Civil War Infantryman's Letters to His Sweetheart.**
1971 New York 10.
HATCHER, Edmund N. **The Last Four Weeks of the War.**
1891 Columbus 40.
1892 Columbus 35.
HATCHER, William E. **Along the Trail of the Friendly Years.**
1910 New York 15.
HATHAWAY, John L. **General Philip H. Sheridan — US Army.** Wraps
1891 Milwaukee 20.
HATTAWAY, Herman **General Stephen D. Lee.**
1976 Jackson 12.
HAUPT, Hermann **Military Bridges.**
1864 New York 100.
HAUPT, Hermann **Reminiscences of General Herman Haupt.**
1901 Milwaukee Ltd., numbered, signed. 125.

HAWK, Emory Q.   **Economic History of the South.**
    1934   New York   20.
HAWKINS, John Parker   **Memoranda Concerning Some Branches of the Hawkins**
    Family and Connections
    1913   Indianapolis   75.
HAY, David & Joan   **The Last of the Confederate Privateers.**
    1977   n.p.   20.
HAY, John   **Letters of John Hay and Extracts from Diary.** 3 vols.
    1908   Washington   300.
HAY, Thomas Robson   **Braxton Bragg and the Southern Confederacy.** Wraps
    1925   Savannah   25.
HAY, Thomas Robson   **Hood's Tennessee Campaign.**
    1929   New York   100.
    1976   Dayton   20.
HAYDON, F. Stansbury   **Aeronautics in the Union and Confederate Armies.** Vol. 1
    (all pub.)
    1941   Baltimore   100.
HAYES, John D. (ed)   **Samuel Francis DuPont, A Selection from His Civil War Letters.**
    3 vols.
    1969   Ithaca, New York   50.
HAYES, M.   **Mr. Lincoln Runs for President.**
    1960   New York   10.
HAYNES, George H.   **Charles Sumner.**
    1909   Philadelphia   20.
HAYWARD, J. Henry   **Poetical Pen-Pictures of the War; Selected from Our Union**
    Poets.
    1863   New York   25.
HAZELTON, Joseph P. (pseud.)   See: **BROCKETT,** Linus P.
HEADLEY, J. T.   **Farragut and Our Naval Commanders.**
    1867   New York   25.
HEADLEY, J. T.   **Grant and Sherman.**
    1865   New York   20.
    1866   New York   20.
HEADLEY, J. T.   **The Great Rebellion.**
    1863   Hartford   2 vols. in 1   20.
    1864   Hartford   2 vols.   30.
    1866   Hartford   2 vols.   30.
    1898   Washington   2 vols.   30.
HEADLEY, J. T.   **The Great Riots of New York 1712 to 1873.**
    1873   New York   30.
HEADLEY, J. T.   **The Life and Travels of General Grant.**
    1897   Philadelphia   10.
    1881   Philadelphia   10.
HEADLEY, J. T.   **The Life of U. S. Grant.**
    1868   New York   15.
    1885   New York   10.
HEADLEY, John W.   **Confederate Operations in Canada and New York.**
    1906   New York   125.
HEADLEY, P. C.   **The Life and Campaigns of Lieut.-Gen. U. S. Grant.**
    1866   New York   25.
HEADLEY, P. C.   **Life and Military Career of Major-General Philip Henry Sheridan.**
    1865   New York   10.
    1889   Boston   10.
HEADLEY, P. C.   **Life and Naval Career of Vice-Admiral David Glasgow Farragut.**
    1865   New York   15.
HEADSPETH, W. Carroll   **The Battle of Staunton River Bridge.** Wraps
    1949   South Boston, Virginia   25.
HEAGNEY, H. J.   **Blockade Runner: A Tale of Adventure Aboard the Robt. E. Lee.**
    Wraps   1952   Chicago   20.

HEALY, Laurin Hall & **KUTNER,** Luis **The Admiral.**
 1944 Chicago 15.
HEAPS, Willard A., and **PORTER,** W. **The Singing Sixties.**
 1960 Norman, Oklahoma 20.
HEARTMAN, Charles F. **What Constitutes a Confederate Imprint? Preliminary Suggestions for Bibliographers and Catalogers.** Wraps
 1939 Hattiesburg, Mississippi Ltd. 50.
HEBERT, Walter H. **Fighting Joe Hooker.**
 1944 Indianapolis 30.
HECK, Frank H. **Proud Kentuckian, John C. Breckinridge 1821-1875.**
 1976 Lexington, Kentucky 10.
HEDRICK, Mary A. **Incidents of the Civil War.**
 1888 Lowell, Massachusetts 25.
HEGARTY, Lela Whitton **Father Wore Gray.**
 1963 San Antonio 20.
HEIN, O. L. **Memories of Long Ago.**
 1925 New York 60.
HEITMAN, Francis B. **Historical Register and Dictionary of the United States Army**
 1890 **Washington** **1 vol. edition** **50.**
 1903 **Washington** **2 vols.** **100.**
 1965 **Urbana** **40.**
HELM, Katherine **The True Story of Mary, Wife of Lincoln.**
 1928 New York 10.
HELPER, Hinton Rowan **Compendium of the Impending Crisis of the South.** Wraps
 1859 New York 50.
 1860 New York 50.
HELPER, Hinton Rowan **The Impending Crisis of the South.**
 1857 New York 35.
 1859 New York 30.
 1860 New York 25.
HELPER, Hinton Rowan **Nojoque: A Question for a Continent.**
 1867 New York 25.
HEMMERLEIN, Richard F. **Prisons and Prisoners of the Civil War.**
 1934 Boston 30.
HENDERSON, G. F. R. **The Campaign of Fredericksburg, Nov. — Dec., 1862.**
 1886 London 150.
 1888 London 150.
 1908 London 150.
HENDERSON, G. F. R. **The Civil War. A Soldier's View.** edited by Jay Luvaas.
 1958 Chicago 25.
 1959 Chicago 20.
HENDERSON, G. F. R. **The Science of War.**
 1905 London 125.
 1912 New York 30.
 1916 London 30.
HENDERSON, G. F. R. **Stonewall Jackson and the American Civil War.** 2 vols.
 1898 London 75.
 1898 New York 60.
 Many later editions 1899 — 50.
 1949 New York 2 vols. in 1 25.
HENDRICK , Burton J. **The Lees of Virginia.**
 1935 Boston 35.
HENDRICK, Burton J. **Lincoln's War Cabinet.**
 1946 Boston 25.
HENDRICK, Burton J. **Statesmen of the Lost Cause.**
 1939 New York 20.
HENKELS, Stan V. (comp) **Valuable Collection of Engraved Portraits Belonging to the Hon. James T. Mitchell Embracing the Portion Relating to the Civil War.** Wraps
 1910 Philadelphia 20.

HENNESSY, Dorothy (ed)   **Civil War The Years Asunder.**
    1973   Waukesha, Wisconsin   25.
HENRY, Guy V.   **Military Record of Civilian Appointments in the US Army.** 2 vols.
    1869-1873   New York   75.
HENRY, H. F.   **Souvenir of the Battlefield of Bull Run.** Wraps
    1900   Manassas   25.
HENRY, Robert Selph   **As They Saw Forrest.**
    1956   Jackson, Tennessee   35.
HENRY, Robert Selph   **First with the Most Forrest.**
    1944   Indianapolis   40.
    1969   Jackson, Tennessee   30.
HENRY, Robert Selph   **The Story of the Confederacy.**
    1931   Indianapolis   20.
    1931   Garden City   20.
    1931   New York   20.
HENRY, Robert Selph   **The Story of Reconstruction.**
    1938   New York   20.
    1963   Gloucester   10.
HENRY, Will   **Journey to Shiloh.**
    1960   New York   10.
HENSEL, W. U.   **Robert E. Lee — As a Citizen, Soldier & Statesman.** Wraps
    1909   Lancaster   15.
HENSHAW, Sarah Edwards   **Our Branch and Its Tributaries, Being a History of the Work of the Northwestern Sanitary Commission and Its Auxiliaries.**
    1868   Chicago   30.
HENTY, G. A.   **With Lee in Virginia.**
    n.d.   London   10
    n.d.   New York   10.
HEPWORTH, George H.   **The Whip, Hoe & Sword.**
    1864   Boston   25.
HERBERT, George B. (comp)   **Anecdotes of the Rebellion.** Wraps
    1894   Springfield, Ohio   20.
HERBERT, George B.   **The Popular History of the Civil War in America.**
    1884   n.p.   15.
HERBERT, Hilary A., et. al.   **Why the Solid South?** or, **Reconstruction and Its Results.**
    Wraps
    1890   Baltimore   30.
HERBST, Frank   **The Lone Sentinel of Fort Fisher.** Wraps
    n.d. (circa 1920)   n.p.   20.
HERGESHEIMER, Joseph   **Sheridan: A Military Narrative.**
    1931   New York   30.
HERGESHEIMER, Joseph   **Swords and Roses.**
    1929   New York   20.
HERNDON, Dallas T.   **Letters of David O. Dodd with Biographical Sketch.** Wraps
    n.d. (circa 1920)   n.p.   30.
HERNDON, William H. and **WEIK,** Jesse W.   **Abraham Lincoln.** 2 vols.
    1893   New York   25.
HERNDON, William H., and **WEIK,** Jesse W.   **Herndon's Life of Lincoln.**
    1942   Cleveland   15.
HERNDON, William H. & **WEIK,** Jesse W.   **Herndon's Lincoln: The True Story of a Great Life, The History and Personal Recollections of Abraham Lincoln.** 3 vols.
    1889   Chicago   100.
HERNON, Joseph M., Jr.   **Celts, Catholics and Copperheads: Ireland Views the American Civil War.**
    1968   Ohio State   15.
HERTZ, Emanuel   **Abraham Lincoln, A New Portrait.** 2 vols.
    1931   New York   15.
HERTZ, Emanuel (ed)   **Abraham Lincoln, the Tribute of the Synagogue.**
    1927   New York   25.

HERTZ, Emanuel **The Hidden Lincoln.**
    1938   New York   10.
HESS, George **The Maryland Campaign from Sept. 1st to Sept. 20th, 1862.** Wraps
    1890   Hagerstown, Maryland   35.
HESSELTINE, William B. and **WOLF**, Hazel C. **The Blue and the Gray on the Nile.**
    1861   Chicago   20.
HESSELTINE, William B. **Civil War Prisons.**
    1930   Columbus, Ohio   35.
    1962   Kent, Ohio   10.
    1964   New York   15.
HESSELTINE, William B. **Confederate Leaders in the New South.**
    1950   Baton Rouge   25.
HESSELTINE, William B. **Lincoln and the War Governors.**
    1948   New York   20.
    1955   New York   15.
HESSELTINE, William B. **Lincoln's Plan of Reconstruction.**
    1963   Gloucester   6.
HESSELTINE, William B. (ed.) **Three Against Lincoln, Murat Halstead Reports the Caucuses of 1860.**
    1960   Baton Rouge   20.
HESSELTINE, William B. **The Tragic Conflict — The Civil War and Reconstruction.**
    1962   New York   15.
HESSELTINE, William B. **Ulysses S. Grant, Politician.**
    1935   New York   20.
    1948   New York   15.
    1957   New York   15.
HETH, Henry **The Memoirs of Harry Heth** edited by James L. Morrison.
    1974   Westport   25.
HEYMAN, Max **The Prudent Soldier.**
    1959   Glendale   30.
HEYWARD, Dubose, and **SASS**, Herbert Ravenel **Fort Sumter.**
    1938   New York   30.
HEYWARD, Dubose **Peter Ashley.**
    1932   New York   20.
HICKERSON, Thomas Felix , **Echoes of Happy Valley.**
    1962   Durham   20.
HIGDON, Hal **The Union Vs. Dr. Mudd.**
    1964   Chicago   10.
HIGGINSON, Thomas Wentworth **Army Life in a Black Regiment.**
    1870   Boston   75.
    1960   Lansing   20.
HIGGINSON, Thomas Wentworth **Letters and Journals of Thomas Wentworth Higginson, 1846-1906.**
    1921   Boston   30.
HILDEBRAND, Samuel S. **Autobiography of** _____ edited by James W. Evans & A Wendell Keith.
    1870   Jefferson City   125.
HILL, A. F. **John Smith's Funny Adventures on a Crutch.**
    1869   Philadelphia   15.
HILL, Benjamin H., Jr. **Senator Benjamin H. Hill of Georgia.**
    1893   Atlanta   30.
HILL, D. H. **The Old South, An Address . . . at Ford's Grand Opera House . . .June 6, 1887, etc.** Wraps
    1887   Baltimore   50.
HILL, Frederick **Lincoln the Lawyer.**
    1906   New York   10.
HILL, Jim Dan **Sea Dogs of the Sixties.**
    1935   Minneapolis   35.

HILL, John Wesley   **If Lincoln Were Here.**
    1925   New York   10.
HILL, Louise B.   **Governor Brown and the Confederacy.** Wraps
    1938   Nashville   10.
HILL, Louise B.   **Joseph E. Brown and the Confederacy.**
    1939   Chapel Hill, North Carolina   35.
HILL, Louise B.   **State Socialism in the Confederate States of America.** Wraps
    1936   Charlottesville, Virginia   10.
HILL, Richard Taylor & **ANTHONY,** William Edward   **Confederate Longarms & Pistols.**
    1978   Charlotte   30.
HILL, Sarah Jane Full   **Mrs. Hill's Journal — Civil War Reminiscences** edited by Mark M. Krug.
    1980   Chicago   25.
HILLARD, G. S.   **Life and Campaigns of George B. McClellan.**
    1864   Philadelphia   10.
HILLS, Alfred C.   **MacPherson, The Confederate Philosopher.**
    1864   New York   40.
HINSDALE, Harriet   **Confederate Gray: The Story of Traveler.**
    1963   Peterborough, New Hampshire   10.
HINTON, Richard J.   **John Brown and His Men.**
    1894   New York   20.
HINTON, Richard J.   **Rebel Invasion of Missouri and Kansas.**
    1865   Chicago   75.
HIRSHON, Stanley P.   **Grenville M. Dodge, Soldier, Politician, Railroad Pioneer.**
    1967   Bloomington   25.
Historic Views of America's Greatest Battlefield Gettysburg. Wraps
    n.d.   n.p.   15.
Historical Data on Major General John H. Forney, CSA, Vol. 1. Wraps
    1961   n.p.   40.
Historicus.   See: **HARCOURT,** Sir William
History of General Leonidas Polk.
    1888   Park Place, New York   35.
History of the Confederated Memorial Associations of the South.
    1903   New Orleans   30.
    1904   New Orleans   30.
    1904   Washington   30.
History of the Great Western Sanitary Fair.
    1864   Cincinnati   25.
History of the Life of Rev. Wm. Mack Lee Body Servant of General Robert E. Lee. Wraps
    1918   Norfolk, Virginia   35.
History of the North-Western Soldiers' Fair.
    1864   Chicago   20.
History ofthe Third Division, Ninth Corps, Army of the Potomac.
    1892   Harrisburg   25.
A History of the U. S. Signal Corps.
    1961   New York   20.
HITCHCOCK, Benjamin   **Hitchcock's Chronological Record of the American Civil War.** Wraps
    1868   New York   25.
HITCHCOCK, Caroline Hanks   **Nancy Hanks The Story of Abraham Lincoln's Mother.**
    1900   New York   40.
HITCHCOCK, Ethan Allen   **Fifty Years in Camp and Field.** edited by W. A. Croffut.
    1909   New York   55.
HITCHCOCK, Henry   **Marching with Sherman, Passages from the Letters and Campaign Diaries.**
    1927   New Haven, Connecticut   40.

HOBART-HAMPDEN, Augustus C.   **Hobart Pasha: Blockade-Running, Slaver Hunting, and War Sports in Turkey.** edited by Horace Kephart.
 1915   New York   50.
HOBART-HAMPDEN, Augustus C.   **Never Caught.**
 1867   London   250.
 1967   Carolina Beach   Wraps   10.
HOBART-HAMPDEN, Augustus C.   **Sketches From My Life.**
 1886   London   175.
 1887   New York   100.
HOBBS, Thomas Hubbard   **The Journals of** _____ edited by Faye Acton Axford.
 1976   University, Alabama   10.
HOBEIKA, John E.   **Lee, The Soul of Honor.**
 1932   Boston   10.
HOBEIKA, John E.   **A Tribute to the Confederate Soldier   An Address.** Wraps
 1930   n.p.   10.
HOBSON, Charles and **SHANKMAN,** Arnold   **Colonel of the Bucktails: Civil War Letters of Charles Frederick Taylor.** Wraps
 1973   n.p.   20.
HODGMAN, Stephen A.   **The Nation's Sin and Punishment.**
 1864   New York   20.
HODGSON, Joseph   **The Cradle of the Confederacy.**
 1876   Mobile   100.
 1975   Spartanburg   21.
HOEHLING, A. A.   **Last Train From Atlanta.**
 1958   New York   15.
HOEHLING, A. A.   **Thunder at Hampton Roads.**
 1976   Englewood Cliffs, New Jersey   15.
HOEHLING, A. A.   **Vicksburg, 47 Days of Siege, May 18-July 4, 1863.**
 1969   Englewood Cliffs, New Jersey   25.
HOEHLING, Mary   **Girl Soldier and Spy — Sarah Emma Edmundson.**
 1959   New York   25.
HOFFMAN, Wickham   **Camp, Court and Siege.**
 1877   New York   30.
HOGAN, John Joseph   **On the Mission in Missouri   1857-1888.**
 1892   Kansas City, Missouri   90.
HOGE, Mrs. A. H.   **The Boys in Blue.**
 1867   New York   25.
HOKE, J.   **Reminiscences of the War or Incidents Which Transpired in and About Chambersburg, During the War of the Rebellion.**
 1884   Chambersburg, Pennsylvania   40.
HOKE, Jacob   **The Great Invasion of 1863.**
 1887   Dayton   40.
 1913   Dayton   35.
 1959   New York   25.
HOLCOMBE, R. I. and **ADAMS**   **An Account of the Battle of Wilson's Creek.**
 1883   Springfield   100.
 1961   Springfield   25.
HOLDEN, W. W.   **Memoirs of W. W. Holden.**
 1911   Durham   40.
HOLLAND, Cecil Fletcher   **Morgan and His Raiders.**
 1942   New York   30.
HOLLAND, J. G.   **Das Leben Abraham Lincoln's.**
 1866   Springfield, Massachusetts (?)   15.
HOLLAND, J. G.   **The Life of Abraham Lincoln.**
 1866   Springfield   10.
HOLLAND, Lynwood M.   **Pierce M. B. Young, The Warwick of the South.**
 1964   Athens, Georgia   20.

HOLLAND, Mary H.   **Our Army Nurses.**
  1895   Boston   40.
  1897   Boston   40.
HOLLIDAY, F. W. M.   **In Memoriam — General Robert E. Lee, Oration.** Wraps
  1871   Winchester   40.
HOLLINGSWORTH, Alan M. and **COX,** James M.   **The Third Day at Gettysburg: Pickett's Charge.** Wraps
  1959   New York   10.
HOLLOWAY, Laura C.   **Howard: The Christian Hero.**
  1885   New York   15.
HOLLYDAY, Frederic B. M. (ed)   **Running the Blockade: Henry Hollyday Joins the Confederacy.** Wraps
  n.d. (circa 1947)   n.p.   15.
HOLMES, Anne Middleton   **Southern Relief Association of New York City 1866-67.** Wraps
  1928   New York   15.
HOLMES, Clay W.   **The Elmira Prison Camp.**
  1912   New York   80.
HOLMES, Fred L.   **Abraham Lincoln Traveled This Way.**
  1930   Boston   10.
HOLMES, John Haynes   **The Life and Letters of Robert Collyer 1823-1912.** 2 vols.
  1917   New York   25.
HOLSTEIN, Mrs. W. H.   **Three Years in Field Hospitals of the Army of the Potomac.**
  1867   Philadelphia   45.
HOLT, Joseph   **An Address to the People of Kentucky.** Wraps
  1861   New York   25.
HOLZMAN, Robert S.   **Stormy Ben Butler.**
  1954   New York   15.
HOOD, J. B.   **Advance and Retreat.**
  1880   New Orleans   80.
  1880   Philadelphia   60.
  1959   Bloomington, Indiana   edited by Richard N. Current   25.
HOOLE, Wm. Stanley   **Four Years in the Confederate Navy: The Career of Captain John Low on the C.S.S. Fingal, Florida, Alabama, Tuscaloosa and Ajax.**
  1964   Athens   25.
HOOLE, Wm. Stanley   **Lawley Covers the Confederacy.** Wraps
  1964   Tuscaloosa   Ltd.   20.
HOOLE, Wm. Stanley   **Vizetelly Covers the Confederacy.** Wraps
  1957   Tuscaloosa, Alabama   Ltd.   20.
HOPE, A. J. B. Beresford   **A Popular View of the American Civil War.** Wraps
  1861   London   25.
HOPKINS, Garland Evans   **The First Battle of Modern Naval History.**
  1943   Richmond   Ltd. and signed edition   100.
HOPKIN, J. H.   **Scriptural, Ecclesiastical and Historical View of Slavery.**
  1864   New York   50.
HOPLEY, Catherine Cooper   **Life in the South, From the Commencement of the War . . . to August, 1862, By a Blockaded British Subject.** 2 vols.
  1863   London   250.
HOPPIN, James Mason   **Life of Andrew Hull Foote.**
  1874   New York   35.
HOPSON, Ella Lord   **Memoirs of Dr. Winthrop Hopson.**
  1887   Cincinnati   40.
HORAN, James D.   **Confederate Agent.**
  1954   New York   20.
  1960   New York   15.
HORAN, James D.   **Desperate Women.**
  1952   New York   25.

HORAN, James D.   **Mathew Brady, Historian With a Camera.**
  1955   New York   25.
  1959   New York   20.
HORAN, James D.   **The Pinkertons: The Detective Dynasty That Made History.**
  1969   New York   20.
HORAN, James D.   **Timothy O'Sullivan, America's Forgotten Photographer.**
  1966   New York   30.
HORGAN, Paul   **Citizen of New Salem.**
  1961   New York   12.
HORN and **WALLACE** (comps)   **Union Army Operations in the Southwest.**
  1961   Albuquerque   35.
HORN, Stanley F.   **The Army of Tennessee.**
  1941   Indianapolis   50.
  1952   Norman   30.
  1953   Norman   30.
  1953   Indianapolis   30.
HORN, Stanley F.   **The Battle of Stone's River.** Wraps
  1972   Harrisburg   10.
HORN, Stanley F.   **The Boy's Life of Robert E. Lee.**
  1935   New York   15.
HORN, Stanley F.   **The Decisive Battle of Nashville.**
  1956   Baton Rouge   25.
  1957   Baton Rouge   20.
  1968   Knoxville   15.
HORN, Stanley F.   **Gallant Rebel. The Fabulous Cruise of the C.S.S. Shenandoah.**
  1947   New Brunswick, N. J.   25.
HORN, Stanley F.   **Invisible Empire, The Story of the Ku Klux Klan.**
  1939   Boston   40.
  1969   Cos Cob, Conn.   30.
HORN, Stanley F.   **The Robert E. Lee Reader.**
  1949   Indianapolis   30.
HORNBECK, Betty   **Upshur Brothers of the Blue and Gray.**
  1967   Parsons, W. Va.   30.
HORNER, Dan   **The Blockade-Runners.**
  1968   New York   25.
HORNER, Harlan H.   **Lincoln and Greeley.**
  1953   Urbana, Ill.   10.
HORSFORD, E. N.   **The Army Ration.** Wraps
  1864   New York   30.
  1961   n.p.   10.
HORST, Samuel   **Mennonites in the Confederacy.**
  1967   Scottdale   25.
HORTON, Louise   **Samuel Bell Maxey: A Biography.**
  1974   Austin, Texas   20.
HORTON, R. G.   **A Youth's History of the War of 1861.**
  1867   New York   15.
HOSMER, G. W.   **As We Went Marching On: A Story of the War.**
  1885   New York   20.
  1900   New York   25.
HOSMER, James Kendall   **The American Civil War.** 2 vols.
  1913   New York   25.
HOSMER, James Kendall   **The Appeal to Arms 1861-1863.**
  1907   New York   25.
HOSMER, James Kendall   **Outcome of the Civil War   1863-1865.**
  1935   New York   15.
HOSPITAL TRANSPORTS.   See: **OLMSTED,** Frederick Law
HOTCHKISS, Jed & **ALLEN,** William   **The Battle Fields of Virginia. . . Chancellorsville.**
  1867   New York   200.

HOTCHKISS, Jed   **Make Me A Map of the Valley: The Civil War Journal of Jackson's Topographer** edited by Archie P. McDonald.
   1973   Dallas   30.
HOUGH, Albert L.   **Soldier in the West, The Civil War Letters of** _____ edited by Robert G. Athearn.
   1957   Philadelphia   20.
HOUK, Eliza P. T.   **A Tribute to General Gates Phillips Thruston.**
   1914   Nashville   40.
HOUSER, M. L.   **The Books That Lincoln Read.** Wraps
   1929   Peoria, Illinois   15.
HOVEY, Carl   **Stonewall Jackson.**
   1900   Boston   40.
HOWARD, Charles Wallace   **An Address: The Women of the Late War.** Wraps
   1875   Charleston   20.
HOWARD, F. K.   **Fourteen Months in American Bastiles.** Wraps
   1863   Baltimore   40.
HOWARD, Frances Thomas   **In and Out of the Lines.**
   1905   New York/Washington   125.
HOWARD, Jas. H. W.   **Bond and Free.**
   1886   Harrisburg   30.
HOWARD, Oliver Otis.   **Autobiography.** 2 vols.
   1907   New York   100.
HOWARD, Oliver Otis   **General Taylor**
   1892   New York   Trade Edition   25.
   L.P. Edition   Ltd.   50.
HOWARD, Philip E.   **The Life Story of Henry Clay Trumbull.**
   1905   Philadelphia   20.
HOWARD, Robert M.   **Reminiscences.**
   1912   Columbus, Georgia   50.
HOWE, Daniel Wait   **Political History of Secession.**
   1914   New York   25.
HOWE, W. W.   **Kinston, Whitehall and Goldsboro Expedition.**
   1890   New York   100.
HOWELLS, W. D.   **Life of Abraham Lincoln.**
   1960   Bloomington, Indiana   7.
HOWLAND, Edward   **Grant as a Soldier and Statesman.**
   1868   Hartford   15.
HUBBELL, Raynor   **Confederate Stamps, Old Letters and History.**
   n.d.   n.p.   50.
HUBNER, Charles W. (comp)   **War Poets of the South and Confederate Camp-Fire Songs.**
   n.d.   Atlanta (?)   75.
HUDSON, E. M.   **The Second War of Independence in America.** Wraps
   1863   London   50.
HUEBNER, Henry Richard   **Civil War Artillery Manual.** Wraps
   1962   Indianapolis   15.
HUGHES, Nathaniel Cheairs, Jr.   **General William J. Hardee, Old Reliable.**
   1965   Baton Rouge   40.
HUGHES, Robert M.   **General Johnston.**
   1893   New York   L.P. Edition   Ltd.   60.
   1893   New York   Trade Edition   40.
HUGHES, W. J.   **Rebellious Ranger, Rip Ford & The Old Southwest.** Wraps
   1964   Norman   15.
HULL, Augustus.   **The Campaigns of the Confederate Army.**
   1901   Atlanta   100.
HULL, Susan R.   **Boy Soldiers of the Confederacy.**
   1905   New York   125.
HUME, Edgar Erskine   **Colonel Heros Von Borcke.** Wraps
   1935   Charlottesville, Virginia   25.

HUME, Edgar Erskine   **Colonel Theodore O'Hara, Author of the Bivouac of the Dead.** Wraps
1936   Charlottesville   15.
HUMPHREYS, Andrew A.   **From Gettysburg to the Rapidan.**
1883   New York   35.
HUMPHREYS, Andrew A.   **The Virginia Campaign of 1864 and 1865.**
1883   New York   25.
1885   New York   20.
HUMPHREYS, David   **Heroes and Spies of the Civil War.**
1903   New York   75.
HUMPHREYS, Henry H.   **Andrew Atkinson Humphreys; A Biography.**
1924   Philadelphia   60.
HUMPHREYS, Henry S. (ed)   **Songs of the Confederacy, Civil War Song-Anthology.** Wraps
1966   Cincinnati, Ohio   10.
HUNT, Aurora   **The Army of the Pacific.**
1951   Glendale   85.
HUNT, Cornelius R.   **The Shenandoah: or The Last Confederate Cruiser.**
1867   New York   50.
HUNT, Gaillard (comp)   **Israel, Elihu and Cadwallader Washburn: A Chapter in American Biography.**
1925   New York   25.
HUNT, Grace Lea   **Some Old Southern Letters.** Wraps
1924   n.p.   15.
HUNTER, Alexander   **The Women of the Debatable Land.**
1912   Washington   100.
HUNTER, David   **Report of the Military Services of _____ During the War of the Rebellion.** Wraps
1892   New York   25.
HUNTER, Martha T.   **A Memoir of Robert M. T. Hunter.**
1903   Washington   100.
HUNTER, R. M. T.   **Correspondence of R. M. T. Hunter** edited by Charles H. Ambler In: **Annual Report of the American Historical Association 1916** Vol. II.
1918   Washington   20.
HUNTON, Eppa   **Autobiography of Eppa Hunton.**
1933   Richmond   Ltd.   2500.
HULBERT, W.   **Gen. McClellan and the Conduct of the War.**
1864   New York   25.
HUSE, Caleb   **The Supplies for the Confederate Army.** Wraps
1904   Boston   75.
1907   Houston   75.
HUTCHINS, E. R. (comp)   **The War of the Sixties.**
1912   New York   125.
HUTCHINSON, William F.   **The Bay Fight A Sketch of the Battle of Mobile Bay.** Wraps
1879   Providence   Ltd.   25.
HYDE, Thomas W.   **Following the Greek Cross.**
1894   Boston   50.
HYLTON, J. D.   **The Bride of Gettysburg, An Episode of 1863.**
1878   Palmyra, New Jersey   30.
HYMAN, Harold (ed)   **Heard Around the World, The Impact Abroad of the Civil War.**
1969   New York   20.
HYMAN, Harold M.   **Era of the Oath.**
1954   Philadelphia   10.
HYMAN, Harold M.   **A More Perfect Union, the Impact of the Civil War and Reconstruction on the Constitution.**
1973   New York   15.

HYMAN, Harold M. (ed)   **New Frontiers of the American Reconstruction.**
    1966   Urbana, Illinois   20.
ICKIS, Alonzo Ferdinand   **Bloody Trails Along the Rio Grande: The Diary of** _____
    edited by Nolie Mumey.
    1958   Denver   Ltd.   75.
Illustrated Catalogue of Arms and Military Goods: Regulations for the Uniform of the Army, Navy, Marine and Revenue Corps of the United States, Wraps
    1864   New York   40.
Illustrated Life, Services, Martyrdom, and Funeral of Abraham Lincoln.
    1865   Philadelphia   25.
Illustrated London News.   Jan. 1861 — Dec. 1866
    Bound   1000.
    Unbound   1200.
The Immortal Autograph Letters, Documents, Manuscripts, Portraits, Personal Relics and Other Lincolniana.
    1952   New York   40.
In Memoriam. Abner Doubleday 1819-1893 and John Cleveland Robinson 1817-1897.
    1918   Albany   20.
In Memoriam: Charles Ewing By His Youngest Corporal.
    1888   Philadelphia   20.
In Memoriam Francis Channing Barlow 1834-96.
    1923   Albany   25.
In Memoriam. George Sears Greene, Brevet Major-General United States Volunteers 1801-1899
    1909   Albany   30.
In Memoriam, Henry W. Slocum   (Title on cover **Slocum and His Men**).
    1904   Albany   35.
In Memoriam James Samuel Wadsworth 1807-1864.
    1916   Albany   25.
In Memoriam. Major-General Winfield Scott Hancock, United States Army.
    n.d.   n.p.   15.
In Memoriam. William T. Sherman Proceedings of the Senate and Assembly of the State of N. Y.
    1892   Albany   10.
Inauguration of the Jackson Statue. Address of Gov. Kemper and . . .Rev. Hoge. . .Oct. 26, 1875. Wraps
    1875   Richmond   20.
INGERSOLL, Charles   **A Letter to a Friend in a Slave State by a Citizen of Pennsylvania.** Wraps
    1862   Philadelphia   45.
INGERSOLL, Charles   **An Undelivered Speech on Executive Arrests.** Wraps
    1862   Philadelphia   25.
INGERSOLL, L. D.   **A History of the War Department of the United States.**
    1879   Washington   25.
INGRAHAM, Prentiss   **The Two Flags; or, Love for the Blue, Duty for the Gray.**
    1897   New York   50.
Instruction for Field Artillery.
    1968   New York   20.
Instruction for Heavy Artillery.
    1863   New York   75.
IRWIN, Richard B.   **History of the Nineteenth Army Corps.**
    1892   New York   75.
    1893   New York   70.
ISHAM, A. Chapman   **Autobiography of Asa Brainerd Isham, M.D. 1844-1912.** Wraps
    1957   Michigan   20.
ISHAM, Asa B. and **DAVIDSON,** Henry M. and **FURNESS,** Henry B.   **Prisoners of War and Military Prisons.**
    1890   Cincinnati, Ohio   125.

JACKSON, Alto Loftin (ed)   **So Mourns the Dove, Letters of a Confederate Infrantryman.**
　　1965　New York　20.
JACKSON, Harry F. and **O'DONNELL,** Thomas F. (eds.)   **Herman Clark and His Letters.**
　　1965　Syracuse　15.
JACKSON, Henry R.   **Letter from _____ of Georgia to Ex-Senator Allen G. Thurman.** Wraps
　　1887　Atlanta　20.
JACKSON, J. C.   **Grant's Strategy and Other Addresses.**
　　1910　Ohio　15.
JACKSON, Mary Anna.   **Julia Jackson Christian.**
　　1910　Charlotte, N. C.　30.
JACKSON, Mary Anna   **Life and Letters of General Thomas J. Jackson by His Wife.**
　　1892　New York　50.
　　1895　Louisville　Enl. Ed. entitled **Memoirs of Stonewall Jackson**　100.
　　1976　Dayton　35.
JACOBS, Michael.   **Notes on the Rebel Invasion of Maryland and Pennsylvania and the Battle of Gettysburg.**
　　1864　Philadelphia　40.
　　1884　Gettysburg　Wraps　35.
　　1909　Gettysburg　Wraps　20.
JACOBS, Thornwell   **When For the Truth.**
　　1950　Charleston　15.
JAFFA, Harry V.   **Crisis of the House Divided: An Interpretation of the Issues in the Lincoln-Douglas Debates.**
　　1959　New York　10.
JAHNS, Patricia   **Mathew Fontaine Maury and Joseph Henry: Scientists of the Civil War.**
　　1961　New York　20.
JAMES, Bushrod Washington   **Echoes of Battle.**
　　1895　Philadelphia　30.
JAMES, Frederick Augustus   **Civil War Diary** edited by Jefferson Hammer.
　　1973　Rutherford　20.
JARRELL, Hampton M.   **Wade Hampton and the Negro.**
　　1949　Columbia, S. C.　35.
Jefferson Davis and "Stonewall" Jackson.
　　1866　Philadelphia　30.
　　1885　Philadelphia　20.
JEFFREY, William H.   **Richmond Prisons, 1861-1862.**
　　1893　St. Johnsbury, Vermont　25.
JENKINS, Brian   **Fenians and Anglo-American Relations During Reconstruction.**
　　1969　London　20.
JENKINS, Paul B.   **The Battle of Westport.**
　　1906　Kansas City　60.
JENNINGS, Janet   **The Blue & The Gray.**
　　1910　Madison, Wisconsin　20.
JENNINGS, N. A.   **A Texas Ranger.**
　　1959　Austin, Texas　Boxed　25.
JENNISON, Keith W.   **The Humorous Mr. Lincoln.**
　　1965　New York　10.
JEROME, Edward S.   **Edwin McMasters Stanton: The Great War Secretary.** Wraps
　　1909　n.p.　10.
JERVEY, Theodore D.   **The Elder Brother.**
　　1905　New York　35.
JERVEY, Theodore D.   **The Railroad the Conquerer.** Wraps
　　1913　Columbia　35.
JERVEY, Theodore D.   **The Slave Trade.**
　　1925　Columbia, S. C.　35.

JEWELL, Jacob   **Heroic Deeds of Noble Master Masons During the Civil War.**
    1916   Colorado   20.
JILLSON, Willard Rouse   **Lincoln Back Home.**
    1932   Lexington   10.
JOEL, Joseph A., and **STEGMAN,** Lewis R.   **Rifle Shots and Bugle Notes.**
    1884   New York   25.
JOHANNSEN, Robert W.   **Stephen A. Douglas.**
    1973   New York   20.
JOHN, Evan   **Atlantic Impact 1861.**
    1952   Kingswood, England   20.
    1952   New York   15.
JOHNS, George S.   **Philip Henson, The Southern Union Spy.** Wraps
    1887   St. Louis   75.
JOHNS, Rev. J.   See: **Confederate Imprints.**
JOHNS, Jane Martin   **Personal Recollections of Early Decatur, Abraham Lincoln, Richard J. Oglesby.**
    1912   Decatur   25.
JOHNSON, Andrew   **The Papers of _____** edited by Leroy Graf and Ralph W. Haskins. 3 vols.
    1967   Knoxville, Tenn.   45.
JOHNSON, Bradley T.   **The First Maryland Campaign, An Address . . . 4th Annual Re-Union of the Assoc. of the Maryland Line.** Wraps
    1886   Baltimore   25.
JOHNSON, Bradley T. (ed)   **A Memoir of the Life and Public Service of Joseph E. Johnston.**
    1891   Baltimore   50.
    1894   Baltimore   40.
JOHNSON, Byron Berkeley   **Abraham Lincoln and Boston Corbett with Personal Recollections of Each.**
    1914   Waltham, Mass.   20.
JOHNSON, Clifton   **Battleground Adventures.**
    1915   Boston and New York   15.
JOHNSON, Gerald W.   **The Secession of the Southern States.**
    1933   New York   30.
JOHNSON, Gerald W.   **The Undefeated.**
    1927   New York   10.
JOHNSON, John   **The Defense of Charleston Harbor.**
    1890   Charleston, S. C.   150.
    1970   Freeport   30.
JOHNSON, John   **Fort Sumter.** Wraps
    1899   Charleston   20.
JOHNSON, John Lipscomb   **Autobiographical Notes.**
    1958   n.p.   Ltd.   35.
JOHNSON, John Lipscomb.   **The University Memorial Biographical Sketches of Alumni of the University of Virginia Who Fell in the Confederate War.**
    1871   Baltimore   5 vols. in 1   50.
JOHNSON, Ludwell H.   **Red River Campaign.**
    1958   Baltimore   30.
JOHNSON, Richard W   **Memoir of Maj. Gen. George H. Thomas.**
    1881   Philadelphia   50.
JOHNSON, Richard W.   **A Soldier's Reminiscences in Peace and War.**
    1886   Philadelphia   40.
    1961   Chapel Hill   20.
JOHNSON, Robert Erwin   **Rear Admiral John Rodgers 1812-1882.**
    1967   Annapolis   25.
JOHNSON, Robert U. and **BUEL,** Clarence C.   **Battles and Leaders of the Civil War.**
    1884-1888   New York   4 vols.   175.
    1887   New York   Vols. 1-4 in 32 parts   Wraps   100.

1887-1888   4 vols.   125.

1894   New York   **Century War Book People's Pictorial
  Edition.**   Wraps   20 parts   150.

1956   New York   4 vols.   Boxed   80.

1956   New York   Bound in full morrocco   175.

1956   New York   edited by Ned Bradford   1 vol. condensed edition   15.

JOHNSON, Rossiter   **Campfire and Battlefield.**

1894   Boston   100.

1894   New York   100.

1896   New York   75.

1960   New York   25.

JOHNSON, Rossiter   **The Fight for the Republic.**

1917   New York   35.

JOHNSON, Rossiter   **A Short History of the War of Secession.**

1888   Boston   20.

1910   New York   15.

JOHNSON, Thomas Cary   **The Life and Letters of Benjamin Morgan Palmer.**

1903   Richmond   50.

1906   Richmond   40.

JOHNSON, Virginia Weisel   **The Unregimented General   A Biography of Nelson A.
  Miles.**

1962   Boston   20.

JOHNSON, W. Fletcher   **Life of William Tecumseh Sherman.**

1891   Philadelphia   25.

JOHNSON, William J.   **Abraham Lincoln, the Christian.**

1913   New York   10.

JOHNSON, Zachary T.   **The Political Policies of Howell Cobb.**

1929   Nashville   25.

JOHNSTON, Angus James   **Virginia Railroads in the Civil War.**

1961   Chapel Hill   25.

JOHNSTON, Gertrude K.   **Dear Pa — And So It Goes.**

1971   Harrisburg   20.

JOHNSTON, Joseph E.   **Narrative of Military Operations Directed During the War
  Between the States.**

1874   New York   75.

1959   Bloomington   30.

1969   New York   25.

JOHNSTON, Mary   **Cease Firing.**

1912   Boston   15.

1912   Boston   Ltd. signed edition   40.

JOHNSTON, Mary   **The Long Roll.**

1911   Boston   15.

1911   Boston   Ltd. signed edition   40.

JOHNSTON, Mary   **To Have and to Hold.**

1900   Boston   15.

JOHNSTON, Mary Tabb & **LIPSCOMB,** Elizabeth Johnston   **Amelia Gayle Gorgas
  A Biography.**

1978   University, Alabama   12.

JOHNSTON, Richard Malcolm   **Autobiography.**

1900   Washington   35.

JOHNSTON, Richard Malcolm, and **BROWNE,** William H.   **Life of Alexander H.
  Stephens.**

1878   Philadelphia   30.

JOHNSTON, Robert M.   **Bull-Run, Its Strategy and Tactics.**

1913   Boston   45.

JOHNSTON, William Preston   **The Life of Gen. Albert Sidney Johnston.**

1878   New York   60.

1879   New York   60.

JOHNSTONE, H. W.   **Truth of the War Conspiracy of 1861.** Wraps
     1921   Curryville, Georgia   20.
JOINVILLE, Prince Francois F.P.L.M. de   **Album of Paintings by the Prince de Joinville 1861-1862.**
     1964   New York   In Slipcase   35.
JOINVILLE, Prince Francois F.P.L.M. de   **The Army of the Potomac.** Wraps
     1862   New York   35.
JOINVILLE, Prince Francois F.P.L.M. de   **Campagne de L'Armee Du Potomac.** Wraps
     1862   New York   30.
JOLLY, Ellen Ryan   **Nuns of the Battlefield.**
     1927   Providence   20.
JOMINI, Baron de   **The Art of War.**
     1854   New York   35.
     1862   Philadelphia   25.
     1965   Harrisburg   entitled **Jomini and His Summary of the Art of War**
        (condensed version) edited by J. D. Hittle.   5.
     1854   New York   35.
JONES, Archer   **Confederate Strategy, From Shiloh to Vicksburg.**
     1961   Baton Rouge   20.
JONES, Archer   **Tennessee and Mississippi: Joe Johnston's Strategic Problem.** Wraps
     1959   Tennessee   10.
JONES, Beuhring H.   **The Sunny Land; or Prison Prose and Poetry.**
     1868   Baltimore   20.
JONES, Charles C., Jr.   **An Address Delivered Before the Confederate Survivor's Association, In Augusta, Georgia.** Wraps
     1881   Augusta, Georgia   25.
JONES, Charles C., Jr.   **Battle of Honey Hill: An Address.** Wraps
     1885   Augusta, Georgia   35.
JONES, Charles C., Jr.   **Brigadier General Robert Toombs. An Address . . .April 26, 1886.** Wraps
     1886   Augusta   15.
JONES, Charles C., Jr.   **The Evacuation of Battery Wagner, and the Battle of Green Pond. . . .An Address.** Wraps
     1888   Augusta, Georgia   25.
JONES, Charles C., Jr.   **Funeral Oration Pronounced . . . In Honor of President Jefferson Davis.** Wraps
     1889   Augusta, Georgia   30.
JONES, Charles C. Jr.   **General Sherman's March from Atlanta to the Coast . . . An Address.** Wraps
     1884   Augusta, Georgia   25.
JONES, Charles C., Jr.   **The Life and Services of Commodore Josiah Tattnall.**
     1878   Savannah   100.
JONES, Charles C., Jr.   **Military Lessons Inculcated on the Coast of Georgia During the Confederate War: An Address.** Wraps
     1883   Augusta   30.
JONES, Charles C., Jr.   **Military Operations in Georgia During the War Between the States, An Address.** Wraps
     1893   Augusta   30.
JONES, Charles C., Jr.   **The Old South, An Address.** Wraps
     1887   Augusta   15.
JONES, Charles C., Jr.   **Post-Bellum Mortality Among Confederates, Address Delivered Before the Confederate Survivors' Association.** Wraps
     1887   Augusta, Georgia   30.
JONES, Charles C., Jr.   **The Siege of Savannah in December, 1864.** Wraps
     1874   Albany, New York   60.
JONES, Charles C., Jr.   **The Siege and Evacuation of Savannah, Ga. Dec. 1864, An Address.** Wraps
     1890   Augusta   40.

JONES, Charles C. Jr.   **Sons of Confederate Veterans. An Address.** Wraps
   1891   Augusta, Georgia   20.
JONES, Charles Edgeworth   **In Memoriam Col. Charles C. Jones, Jr.** Wraps
   1893   Augusta   15.
JONES, Edgar DeWitt   **Lincoln and the Preachers.**
   1948   New York   10.
JONES, Edward Smyth   **The Sylvan Cabin, A Centenary Ode on the Birth of Lincoln.**
   1911   Boston   15.
JONES, Evan Rowland   **Lincoln, Stanton and Grant Historical Sketches.**
   1875   London   35.
JONES, J. Wm.   **Army of Northern Virginia Memorial Volume.**
   1880   Richmond   100.
   1976   Dayton   17.50
JONES, J. Wm.   **Christ in the Camp.**
   1887   Richmond   50.
   1888   Richmond   40.
   1904   Atlanta   30.
JONES, J. Wm.   **The Davis Memorial Volume.**
   1890   Richmond   20.
   1890   Atlanta   20.
JONES, J. Wm.   **Life and Letters of Robert Edward Lee.**
   1906   New York/Washington   50.
JONES, J. Wm.   **Personal Reminiscences, Anecdotes & Letters of Gen. Robert E. Lee.**
   1875   New York   40.
   1875   New York   40.
JONES, James P.   **Black Jack, John A. Logan & Southern Illinois in the Civil War Era.**
   1967   Tallahassee   20.
JONES, James P. and **KEUCHEL,** Edward F.   **Civil War Marine, A Diary of the Red River Expedition, 1864.** Wraps
   1975   Washington   10.
JONES, James Pickett   **Yankee Blitzkrieg: Wilson's Raid Through Alabama and Georgia.**
   1976   Athens   20.
JONES, John B.   **A Rebel War Clerk's Diary.**
   1866   Philadelphia   2 vols.   200
   1866   Philadelphia   2 vols. in 1   200.
   1935   New York   2 vols. edited by Howard Swiggett   40.
   1958   New York   edited by Earl Schenck Miers   1 vol. edition   20.
JONES, Katharine M. (comp.)   **Heroines of Dixie.**
   1955   Indianapolis   10.
JONES, Katharine M.   **Ladies of Richmond.**
   1962   Indianapolis   15.
JONES, Katharine M.   **The Plantation South.**
   1957   Indianapolis   15.
JONES, Katharine M.   **When Sherman Came: Southern Women and the "Great" March.**
   1964   New York   25.
JONES, Mabel Cronise   **Gettysburg.** Wraps
   1902   Syracuse, New York   3.
JONES, Mary Sharpe, and **MALLARD,** Mary Jones   **Yankees A'Coming.** edited by Haskell Monroe.
   1959   Tuscaloosa, Alabama   Ltd.   20.
JONES, Robert H.   **The Civil War in the Northwest.**
   1960   Norman   20.
   1961   Norman   15.
JONES, Robert H.   **Disrupted Decades. The Civil War & Reconstruction.**
   1973   New York   25.
JONES, S. B. (comp)   **Twenty Favorite Songs for the Grand Army of the Republic.** Wraps
   1882   Omaha   20.

JONES, Samuel   **The Siege of Charleston & The Operations on the South Atlantic Coast in the War Among the States.**
  1911   New York   175.
JONES, Sarah L. (pseud.)   See: **HOPLEY,** Catherine Cooper
JONES, Thomas A.   **J. Wilkes Booth.**
  1893   Chicago   200.
  n.d.   n.p.   Wraps   10.
JONES, Thomas G.   **Last Days of the Army of Northern Virginia An Address.** Wraps
  1893   Richmond, Virginia   125.
JONES, Virgil Carrington   **The Civil War at Sea.**
  Vol I — **The Blockaders**
  Vol II — **The River War**
  Vol. III —**The Final Effort**
  1960-62   New York   3 vols.   75.
  Odd Volumes   25. each
JONES, Virgil Carrington   **Eight Hours Before Richmond.**
  1957   New York   20.
JONES, Virgil Carrington   **Gray Ghosts and Rebel Raiders.**
  1956   New York   25.
JONES, Walter B.   **War Poems of the Southern Confederacy, An Address.** Wraps
  1946   n.p.   15.
JONES, Walter Burgwyn (ed)   **Confederate War Poems.**
  1959   Montgomery, Alabama   5.
JONES, Walter Burgwyn   **The South Faces History Unafraid, An Address.** Wraps
  1945 (?)   Montgomery, Alabama   10.
JONES, Wilbur D.   **The Confederate Rams at Birkenhead.** Wraps
  1961   Tuscaloosa   Ltd.   20.
JONES, Mrs. Wilbur Moore (ed)   **Historic Beauvoir, Souvenir Booklet of Beauvoir-on-the-Gulf, Harrison County, Mississippi.** Wraps
  1921   Hattiesburg   10.
JONES, Winfield   **Knights of the Ku Klux Klan.**
  1941   New York   75.
JORDAN, Donaldson and **PRATT,** Edwin J.   **Europe and the American Civil War.**
  1931   Boston   35.
JORDAN, Jan   **Dim the Flaring Lamps, A Novel of the Life of John Wilkes Booth.**
  1972   Englewood Cliffs, New Jersey   12.
JORDAN, Robert Paul   **The Civil War.**
  1969   New York   15.
JORDAN, Thomas and **PRYOR,** J. P.   **The Campaigns of Lieut. Gen. N. B. Forrest and of Forrest's Cavalry.**
  1868   New Orleans   200.
  1868   St. Louis/Cincinnati   150.
  1869   New Orleans   150.
  1973   Dayton   27.
JORDAN, Weymouth T.   **Rebels in the Making.** Wraps
  1958   Tuscaloosa, Alabama   Ltd.   25.
Joseph Bryan His Times His Family His Friends.
  n.d.   n.p.   30.
JOSEPHUS, Junior   See: **Annals of Harper's Ferry.**
Journal of the Congress of the Confederate States of America 1861-1865. 7 vols.
  1904-05   Washington   300.
JUNKIN, D. X., and **NORTON,** Frank H.   **Life of Winfield Scott Hancock.**
  1880   New York   30.
JUNKIN, G.   **Political Fallacies.**
  1863   New York   20.
KANE, Harnett T.   **Bride of Fortune.**
  1948   New York   10.
KANE, Harnett T.   **The Gallant Mrs. Stonewall.**
  1957   New York   10.

KANE, Harnett T.   **Gone Are the Days.**
  1960   New York   20.
KANE, Harnett T.   **The Lady of Arlington.**
  1953   Garden City   5.
KANE, Harnett T.   **The Romantic South.**
  1961   New York   5.
KANE, Harnett T.   **The Smiling Rebel.**
  1955   Garden City, New York   10.
KANE, Harnett T.   **Spies for the Blue and Gray.**
  1954   Garden City, New York   20.
  1954   Garden City   Southern Edition signed by author   25.
KANTOR, MacKinlay   **Andersonville.**
  1955   New York   15.
KANTOR, MacKinlay   **Gettysburg.**
  1952   New York   15.
KANTOR, MacKinlay   **The Jaybird.**
  1932   New York   15.
KANTOR, MacKinlay   **Long Remember.**
  1934   New York   15.
KAUTZ, August V.   **The Company Clerk.**
  1863   Philadelphia   25.
KEAN, Robert G. H.   **Inside the Confederate Government the Diary of** _____ edited by Edward Younger.
  1957   New York   25.
  1957   New York   Autographed edition.   35.
KEARNY, Thomas   **General Philip Kearny.**
  1937   New York   40.
KEELER, William Frederick   **Aboard the USS Florida: 1863-65, the Letters of Paymaster to His Wife** edited by Robert W. Daly.
  1968   Annapolis   14.
KEELER, William Frederick   **Aboard the USS Monitor 1862 The Letters of** _____ edited by Robert W. Daly.
  1964   Annapolis   16.
KEENE, Jesse L.   **The Peace Convention of 1861.** Wraps
  1961   Tuscaloosa, Alabama   Ltd.   20.
KEIFER, J. Warren   **A Forgotten Battle: Sailor's Creek April 6, 1865.** Wraps
  1888   Cincinnati   35.
KEILEY, A. M.   **In Vinculis, or, the Prisoner of War.**
  1866   New York   50.
  1866   Petersburg, Virginia   60.
KEIM, Deb. Randolph   **William T. Sherman: A Memorial in Art, Oratory and Literature by the Society of the Army of Tennessee.**
  1904   Washington   20.
KELL, John McIntosh   **Recollections of a Naval Life.**
  1900   Washington   100.
KELLER, Allan.   **Morgan's Raid.**
  1961   Indianapolis   25.
KELLER, Allan   **Thunder at Harper's Ferry.**
  1958   Englewood Cliffs, New Jersey   20.
KELLER, Morton   **The Art and Politics of Thomas Nast.**
  1968   New York   25.
KELLEY, Dayton   **General Lee & Hood's Texas Brigade at the Battle of the Wilderness.** Wraps
  1969   Waco, Texas   15.
KELLEY, Duren F.   **The War Letters of** _____ **1862-1865** edited by R. S. Offenberg and R. R. Parsonage.
  1967   New York   10.
KELLEY, Evelyn O.   **Seeded Furrows.**
  1957   Daytona Beach   10.

KELLEY, William D.　　**Lincoln & Stanton.**
　　1885　　New York　　15.
KELLOGG, Sanford C.　　**The Shenandoah Valley and Virginia 1861 to 1865.**
　　1903　　New York　　75.
KELSEY, Albert Warren　　**Autobiographical Notes and Memoranda.**
　　1911　　Baltimore　　Ltd.　　100.
KELSEY, D. M.　　**Deeds of Daring by Both Blue and Gray.**
　　1883　　Philadelphia　　20.
　　1899　　Chicago　　15.
KELSO, Isaac　　**The Stars and Bars.**
　　1863　　Boston　　50.
　　1864　　Boston　　35.
KEMPF, Edward J.　　**Abraham Lincoln's Philosophy of Common Sense.** 3 vols.
　　1965　　New York　　Boxed　　45.
KENDRICK, Benj. B.　　**The Journal of the Joint Committee of Fifteen on Reconstruction, 39th Cong 1865-1867.** Wraps
　　1914　　New York　　20.
KENDRICKEN, Paul Henry　　**Memoirs.**
　　1910　　Boston　　60.
KENNARD, Martin P.　　**Address ... On Presentation to the Town of a Memorial Portrait of the Late Brig. Gen. Edward Augustus Wild.**
　　1894　　Brookline, Massachusetts　　10.
KENNAWAY, John H.　　**On Sherman's Track or the South After the War.**
　　1867　　London　　80.
KENNY, Thomas Moore　　**Two Graves.**
　　1902　　Baltimore　　10.
KERBEY, J. O.　　**The Boy Spy.**
　　1889　　Chicago　　25.
　　1890　　Chicago　　15.
　　1898　　Washington　　Wraps　　15.
KERBEY, J. O.　　**On the War Path. A Journey Over the Historic Grounds of the Late Civil War.**
　　1890　　Chicago　　20.
KERBY, Robert L.　　**Confederate Invasion of New Mexico and Arizona.**
　　1958　　Los Angeles, California　　Ltd.　　35.
KERBY, Robert L.　　**Kirby-Smith's Confederacy: The Trans-Mississippi South 1863-1865.**
　　1972　　New York　　20.
KERCHEVAL, Samuel　　**A History of the Valley of Virginia.**
　　1925　　Strasburg　　40.
KERKSIS, Sydney C. (comp)　　**The Atlanta Papers.**
　　1980　　Dayton　　35.
KERKSIS, Sydney C. and **DICKEY,** Thomas S.　　**Field Artillery Projectiles of the Civil War 1861-1865.**
　　1968　　Atlanta　　30.
KERKSIS, Sydney C.　　**Heavy Artillery Projectiles of the Civil War.**
　　1972　　Kennessaw, Georgia　　17.50
KERKSIS, Sydney C.　　**Plates and Buckles of the American Military 1795-1874.**
　　1974　　Kennesaw　　25.
KERR, John Leeds　　**The Story of a Southern Carrier, The Louisville and Nashville R.R.**
　　1933　　New York　　25.
KERR, William S. R.　　**The Confederate Secession.**
　　1864　　Edinburgh　　75.
KERSHAW, John　　**Address Delivered Before the Ladies' Memorial Association and Citizens of Charleston.** Wraps
　　1893　　Charleston, S. C.　　20.
KETCHUM, Hiram　　**General McClellan's Peninsula Campaign. Review of the Report of the Committee on the Conduct of the War Relative to the Peninsula Campaign.** Wraps
　　1864　　n.p.　　16.

KETTELL, Thomas P.   **History of the Great Rebellion.**
  1865   Hartford   25.
KETTELL, Thomas P.   **Southern Wealth and Northern Profits.**
  1860   New York   40.
  1965   University, Alabama   15.
KEY, William   **The Battle of Atlanta and the Georgia Campaign.**
  1958   New York   15.
KEYES, E. D.   **Fifty Year's Observations of Men and Events, Civil and Military.**
  1884   New York   20.
KEYES, Edward L.   **Lewis Atterbury Stimson, M.D.**
  1918   New York   30.
KIBLER, Lillian Adel   **Benjamin F. Perry, South Carolina Unionist.**
  1946   Durham   25.
KIDD, Reuben Vaughan   **Soldier of the Confederacy.**
  1947   Petersburg   35.
KIELL, Norman (ed)   **Psychological Studies of Famous Americans, The Civil War Era.**
  1964   New York   10.
KIMBALL, William J.   **Richmond in Time of War.** Wraps
  1960   Boston   10.
KIMMEL, Stanley   **The Mad Booths of Maryland.**
  1940   Indianapolis   30.
KIMMEL, Stanley   **Mr. Davis's Richmond.**
  1958   New York   25.
KIMMEL, Stanley   **Mr. Lincoln's Washington.**
  1957   New York   15.
KINCHEN, Oscar A.   **Confederate Operations in Canada and the North.**
  1970   N. Quincy, Massachusetts   20.
KINCHEN, Oscar A.   **Daredevils of the Confederate Army.**
  1959   Boston   20.
KING, Alvy   **Louis T. Wigfall, Southern Fire-Eater.**
  1970   Baton Rouge   17.
KING, Charles   **Between the Lines.**
  1889   New York   15.
KING, Charles   **Campaigning with Crook.**
  1890   New York   45.
KING, Charles   **The General's Double: A Story of the Army of the Potomac.**
  1898   Philadelphia   15.
KING, Charles   **In Spite of Foes or Ten Years Trial.**
  1901   Philadelphia   20.
KING, Charles   **Norman Holt A Story of the Army of the Cumberland.**
  1901   New York   15.
KING, Charles   **The Rock of Chickamauga.**
  1907   New York   15.
KING, Charles   **A War-Time Wooing.**
  1888   New York   10.
KING, Grace   **Memories of a Southern Woman of Letters.**
  1932   New York   30.
KING, Horatio C.   **The Army of the Potomac, Sketch and the Phantom Column, Poem.**
  Wraps
  1898 (?)   New York   15.
KING, Horatio   **Turning on the Light.**
  1895   Philadelphia   20.
KING, W. C. and **DERBY,** W. P. (comps.)   **Camp-Fire Sketches and Battle-Field Echoes of the Rebellion.**
  1887   Springfield   35.
  1888   Cleveland   30.
  1889   Springfield   30.
KING, Willard L.   **Lincoln's Manager David Davis.**
  1960   Cambridge, Massachusetts   10.

KINSLEY, D. A.   **Favor the Bold, Custer: The Civil War Years.**
1967   New York   10.
KIRKE, Edmund (pseud.)   See: **GILMORE,** James
KIRKLAND, Charles P.   **The Destiny of our Country.** Wraps
1864   New York   20.
KIRKLAND, Charles P.   **A Letter to Peter Cooper, On "The Treatment to be Extended to the Rebels Individually," and the Mode of Restoring the Rebel States to the Union.** Wraps
1865   New York   25.
KIRKLAND, Charles P.   **Liability of the Government of Great Britain for the Depredations of Rebel Privateers on the Commerce of the United States Considered.** Wraps
1863   New York   35.
KIRKLAND, Edward Chase   **The Peacemakers of 1864.**
1927   New York   15.
KIRKLAND, Frazar   **The Pictorial Book of Anecdotes and Incidents of the War of the Rebellion.**
1866   Hartford   20.
1887   St. Louis   15.
KIRKLAND, Frazar   **Reminiscences of the Blue and Gray, '61-'65.**
1866   Hartford   30.
1895   Chicago   30.
KIRWAN, Albert D. (ed)   **The Confederacy.**
1959   New York   15.
KIRWAN, Albert D.   **John J. Crittenden, The Struggle for the Union.**
1962   Lexington   15.
KITTREDGE, Walter   **Tenting on the Old Camp Ground.**
1891   Troy, New York   40.
KLEIN, Maury   **Edward Porter Alexander.**
1971   Athens   30.
KLEMENT, Frank L.   **The Copperheads in the Middle West.**
1960   Chicago   20.
KLEMENT, Frank L.   **The Limits of Dissent.**
1970   Lexington, Kentucky   22.
KNAPP, David   **The Confederate Horseman.**
1966   New York   35.
KNAPP, David   **The Magnificent Rebels.** Wraps
1967   Mobile   15.
Knapsack & Rifle or Life in the Grand Army.
1888   Philadelphia   15.
KNAUSS, William H.   **The Story of Camp Chase.**
1906   Nashville   60.
KNIFFIN, Gilbert C.   **Assault and Capture of Lookout Mountain.**
1895   Washington   125.
1898   Chattanooga   25.
KNIGHT, Josephine Augusta Clarke   **Symbols of the South.**
1941   Richmond   25.
KNIGHT, Lucian Lamar   **Alexander H. Stephens.** Wraps
1930   n.p.   10.
KNIGHT, Lucian Lamar   **Stone Mountain.**
1923   Atlanta   10.
KNOLES, George Harmon (ed)   **The Crisis of the Union 1860-1861.**
1965   Baton Rouge   15.
KNOWLES, David   **The American Civil War — A Brief Sketch.**
1926   Oxford   20.
KNOX, Rose B.   **Gray Caps.**
1933   Garden City, New York   15.
KNOX, Thomas W.   **Boy's Life of General Grant.**
1899   Akron   10.

KNOX, Thomas W.   **Camp-Fire & Cotton-Field.**
    1865   New York   50.
KNOX, Thomas W.   **The Lost Army.**
    1894   New York   20.
    1899   New York   20.
KORN, Bertram Wallace   **American Jewry and the Civil War.**
    1951   Philadelphia   25.
    1957   Philadelphia   20.
KORNGOLD, Ralph   **Thaddeus Stevens.**
    1955   New York   25.
KOUNTZ, John S.   **Record of the Organizations Engaged in the Campaign, Siege and Defense of Vicksburg.** Wraps
    1901   Washington   30.
KRANZ, Henry B.   **Abraham Lincoln A New Portrait.**
    1959   New York   7.
KREMER, W. P.   **100 Great Battles of the Rebellion.**
    1906   Hoboken, New Jersey   30.
KRICK, Robert K.   **Lee's Colonels, A Biographical Register of the Field Officers of the Army of Northern Virginia.**
    1979   Dayton   30.
KRICK, Robert K.   **Neale Books, An Annotated Bibliography.**
    1977   Dayton   17.50
KUNHARDT, Dorothy M., and **KUNHARDT,** Phillip   **Twenty Days.**
    1965   New York   20.
KUNTZ, Wilbur G.   **The Atlanta Cyclorama, the Story of the Famed Battle of Atlanta.** Wraps
    1954   Atlanta   10.
KURTZ, Lucy F. & **RITTER,** Benny   **A Roster of Confederate Soldiers Buried in Stonewall Cemetery, Winchester, Virginia.** Wraps
    1962   n.p.   15.
LABOULAYE, Edouard R. L. de   **Les 'Estats-Unis Et La France.** Wraps
    1862   Paris   45.
LABOULAYE, Edouard R. L. de   **Upon Whom Rests the Guilt of the War?** Wraps
    1863   New York   15.
LaBREE, Ben (ed)   **Camp Fires of the Confederacy.**
    1898   Louisville, Ky.   100.
    1899   Louisville   80.
LaBREE, Ben (ed)   **The Confederate Soldier in the Civil War.**
    1895   Louisville   100.
    1897   Louisville   90.
    1959   New York   40.
    1977   New York   25.
LAIR, John   **Songs Lincoln Loved.** Wraps
    1954   New York   5.
LAMAR, Joseph R.   **The Private Soldier of the Confederacy. Address.** Wraps
    1902   New York   75.
LAMB, Sarah Anne Chaffee   **Letters from the Colonel's Lady: Correspondence of Mrs. (Col.) William Lamb written from Fort Fisher, N. C., C.S.A. . . . Dec. 1861 to Jan. 1865** edited by Cornelius M.D. Thomas, Clarendon Imprint No. 7.
    1965   Wilmington   30.
LAMB, William   **The Battle of Fort Fisher, North Carolina 1861-1865.** Wraps
    n.d.   n.p.   10.
LAMB, William   **Colonel Lamb's Story of Fort Fisher: The Battles Fought Here in 1864 and 1865.** Wraps
    1966   Carolina Beach, N. C.   10.
LAMBERT, William H.   **George Henry Thomas, Oration Before the Society of the Army of the Cumberland . . . 1884.**
    1884   Philadelphia   35.

LAMBERT, William H.   **Major General Winfield Scott Hancock, Oration at the National Cemetery, Gettysburg May 29, 1886.** Wraps
 1886   Philadelphia   Ltd.   25.

LAMERS, William M.   **The Edge of Glory, A Biography of General William S. Rosecrans.**
 1961   New York   25.

LAMON, Ward H.   **The Life of Abraham Lincoln from His Birth to His Inauguration as President.**
 1872   Boston   50.

LAMON, Ward H.   **Recollections of Abraham Lincoln 1847-1865.**
 1895   Chicago   15.

LAMPREY, L.   **Days of the Leaders.**
 1925   New York   20.

LANCASTER, Bruce   Night March.
 1958   Boston   10.

LANCASTER, Bruce   Roll Shenandoah.
 1956   Boston   15.

LANCASTER, Bruce   The Scarlet Patch.
 1947   Boston   15.

The Land We Love.
 Vols. 1-6, May 1866 — March 1869   Charlotte, N.C.
  Complete set bound   600.
  Complete set wraps   750.

LANDIS, Robert W.   **The Duty and Obligations of American Citizens in Relations to the Union, An Oration.** Wraps
 1860   Somerset   30.

LANG, H. Jack   **Lincoln's Fireside Reading.**
 1965   Cleveland   8.

LANGHEIN, Eric,   **Jefferson Davis Patriot.**
 1962   New York   15.

LANGSDORF, Edgar   **Price's Raid and the Battle of Mine Creek.** Wraps
 1964   Topeka   10.

LANIER, Sidney   **Poems of Sidney Lanier** edited by His Wife.
 1884   New York   30.
 1892   New York   20.
 1893   New York   20.
 Various Later Editions   15.

LANMAN, C.   **Dictionary of the U. S. Congress.**
 1864   Washington   30.

LANUX, Pierre De   **Sud.** Wraps
 1932   Paris   30.

LANZA, Conrad H.   **Fort Henry and Fort Donelson Campaigns, February 1862.**
 1923   Ft. Leavenworth   75.

LARKE, Julian K.   **General Grant and His Campaigns.**
 1864   New York   10.

LARSEN, Arthur J. (ed)   **Crusader and Feminist Letters of Jane Grey Swisshelm 1858-1865.**
 1934   Saint Paul, Minnesota   30.

LATANE, Lucy Temple   **A Short Sketch of James Allen Latane.**
 1949   Richmond   25.

LATHROP, George Parsons   **History of the Union League of Philadelphia.**
 1884   Philadelphia   30.

LATHROP, H. W.   **The Life and Times of Samuel J. Kirkwood.**
 1893   Iowa City   20.

LATIMER, E.   **Idyls of Gettysburg.**
 1872   Philadelphia   10.

LATTA, James W.   **Was Secession Taught at West Point?** Wraps
 1909   n.p.   25.

LATTIMORE, Ralston B. (ed)   The Story of Robert E. Lee.
    1964   Philadelphia   25.
    1964   Philadelphia   Wraps   20.
LAUGEL, Auguste   Les Etats-Unis Pendant La Guere 1861-1865. Wraps
    1866   Paris   30.
LAUGEL, Auguste   The United States During the War.
    1866   New York   25.
    1961   Bloomington, Indiana   entitled: The United States During the Civil War
    edited by Allen Nevins   25.
    1969   New York   15.
LAUGHLIN, Clara   The Death of Lincoln.
    1909   New York   35.
LAURENCE, Robert   The George Walcott Collection of Used Civil War Patriotic
    Covers.
    1893   n.p.   100.
    1934   New York   35.
LAW, Tom   Citadel Cadets, The Journal of Cadet Tom Law.
    1942   Clinton, S. C.   30.
LAWRENCE, Alexander A.   James Moore Wayne. Southern Unionist.
    1943   Chapel Hill   25.
LAWRENCE, Alexander A.   Johnny Leber and the Confederate Major.
    1962   Darien, Georgia   Ltd.   30.
LAWRENCE, Alexander A.   Present for Mr. Lincoln — The Story of Savannah From
    Secession to Sherman.
    1961   Macon   20.
LAWRENCE, George Alfred   Border and Bastille.
    n.d.   New York   35.
LAWRENCE, William   Life of Amos A. Lawrence.
    1888   Boston   15.
Laws of War, and Martial Law. Wraps
    1863   Boston   40.
LAWTON, Eba Anderson   Major Robert Anderson and Fort Sumter, 1861.
    1911   New York   30.
The Lay of John Haroldson. Wraps
    1866   Philadelphia   Ltd.   100.
LEARNED, Marion Dexter   Abraham Lincoln.
    1909   Philadelphia   Ltd.   50.
L'ECLAIR   Lenare: A Story of the Southern Revolution and Other Poems.
    1866   New Orleans   60.
LeCONTE, Emma   When the World Ended: The Diary of Emma LeConte edited by
    Earl Schenck Miers.
    1957   New York   25.
LeCONTE, Joseph   The Autobiography of _____ edited by William Dallam Armes.
    1903   New York   75.
LeCONTE, Joseph   'Ware Sherman, A Journal of Three Months' Personal Experience
    in the Last Days of the Confederacy.
    1937   Berkeley   25.
    1938   Berkeley   30.
LeDUC, William G.   Recollections of a Civil War Quartermaster: Autobiography
    of LeDuc.
    1963   St. Paul   15.
LEE, Baker P.   Confederate Memorial Address, Delivered at Elmwood Cemetery,
    Norfolk, Va. May 19, 1887. Wraps
    1887   Richmond   25.
    1888   Richmond   20.
LEE, Brother Basil Leo   Discontent in New York City 1861-1865 A Dissertation. Wraps
    1943   Washington   20.

LEE, Cazenove Gardner   **Lee Chronicle Studies of the Early Generations of the Lees of Virginia.**
    1957   New York   25.
LEE, Charles Robert, Jr.   **The Confederate Constitutions.**
    1963   Chapel Hill   25.
LEE, Edmund Jennings   **Lee of Virginia 1642-1892.**
    1895   Philadelphia   100.
    1974   Baltimore   25.
LEE, Fitzhugh   **Chancellorsville: Address Before Virginia Division of the Army of Northern Virginia.**
    1879   Richmond   100.
LEE, Fitzhugh   **General Lee.**
    1894   New York   30.
    1894   New York   L.P. Edition   Ltd.   75.
    1895   New York   30.
    1905   New York   15.
LEE, Guy Carleton   **The True History of the Civil War.**
    1903   Philadelphia   15.
LEE, Robert E.   **Glimpses of the Past, Letters of Robert E. Lee to Henry Kayser 1838-1846.** Wraps
    1936   St. Louis   15.
LEE, Robert E., Jr.   **My Father, General Lee.**
    1960   Garden City, New York   15.
LEE, Robert E.   **Recollections and Letters of General Robert E. Lee.**
    1904   New York   30.
    1905   New York   25.
    1924   New York   20.
LEE, Robert E.   **"To Markie": The Letters of Robert E. Lee to Martha Custis Williams** edited by Avery Craven.
    1933   Cambridge   40.
LEE, Susan P.   **Memoirs of William Nelson Pendleton.**
    1893   Philadelphia   175.
LEECH, Margaret   **The Garfield Orbit.**
    1978   New York   15.
LEECH, Margaret. **Reveille in Washington.**
    1941   New York   15.
    1945   New York   15.
LEECH, Samuel Vanderlip   **The Raid of John Brown at Harper's Ferry as I Saw It.**
    1909   Washington   30.
LEFLER, Hugh Talmage   **Hinton Rowan Helper, Advocate of "White America."** Wraps
    1935   Charlottesville, Virginia   15.
A Legal View of the Seizure of Messrs. Mason and Slidell. Wraps
    1861   New York   25.
Legends of the Operations of the Army of the Cumberland. Wraps.
    1869   Washington   50.
LeGRAND, Julia   **The Journal of** _____ edited by Kate Mason Rowland and Mrs. Morris L. Croxall.
    1911   Richmond   60.
LEIB. Charles   **Nine Months in the Quartermaster's Department.**
    1862   Cincinnati   60.
LELAND, Charles Godfrey   **Memoirs.**
    1893   New York   25.
LELAND, John A.   **A Voice from South Carolina.**
    1879   Charleston, S. C.   100.
LENTZ, Perry   **The Falling Hills.**
    1967   New York   15.
LESTER, C. Edwards   **Life and Public Services of Charles Sumner.**
    1874   New York   25.

LESTER, John C. & **WILSON,** D. L.   **Ku Klux Klan, Its Origin, Growth and Disbandment.**
   1905   New York   175.
LESTER, Richard I.   **Confederate Finance and Purchasing in Great Britain.**
   1975   Charlottesville   16.
Letter to the President by a Refugee.   See: **BARNARD,** F. A. P.
LETTERMAN, Jonathan   **Medical Recollections of the Army of the Potomac.**
   1866   New York   75.
LEWIS, Berkeley R.   **Notes on Ammunition of the American Civil War 1861-1865.** Wraps
   1959   Washington   20.
LEWIS, Berkeley R.   **Notes on Cavalry Weapons of the American Civil War.** Wraps
   1961   Washington   20.
LEWIS, Berkeley R.   **Small Arms and Ammunition in the U.S. Service 1776-1865.**
   1956   Washington   35.
LEWIS, Charles Bertrand   **Field, Fort and Fleet.**
   1885   Detroit   70.
LEWIS, Charles Lee   **Admiral Franklin Buchanan.**
   1929   Baltimore   35.
LEWIS, Charles Lee   **David Glasgow Farragut, Our First Admiral.**
   1943   Annapolis   20.
LEWIS, Charles Lee   **Matthew Fontaine Maury, Pathfinder of the Seas.**
   1927   Annapolis   15.
LEWIS, Lloyd   **Captain Sam Grant.**
   1950   Boston   20.
LEWIS, Lloyd   **Letters from Lloyd Lewis Showing Steps in the Research for His Biography of U.S. Grant.**
   1950   Boston   10.
LEWIS, Lloyd   **Myths After Lincoln.**
   1929   New York   10.
   1941   New York   10.
LEWIS, Lloyd   **Sherman, Fighting Prophet.**
   1932   New York   25.
   1958   New York   15.
LEWIS, Montgomery S.   **Legends That Libel Lincoln.**
   1946   New York   10.
LEWIS, Oscar   **The War in the Far West: 1861-1865.**
   1961   New York   12.
LEWIS, Paul   **Yankee Admiral A Biography of David Dixon Porter.**
   1968   New York   15.
LEWIS, Samuel E.   **Surgeon General Samuel Preston Moore and the Officers of the Medical Depts. of the Confederate States.** Wraps
   1911   n.p.   40.
LEWIS, Samuel E.   **The Treatment of Prisoners-of-War 1861-65.** Wraps
   1910   Richmond   15.
The Libby Chronicle Devoted to Facts and Fun.
   1889   Albany, New York   50.
LIDDELL HART, Basil H.   **Sherman: The Genius of the Civil War.**
   1930   London   30.
LIDDELL HART, Basil H.   **Sherman: Soldier, Realist, American.**
   1929   New York   20.
   1930   New York   20.
   1958   New York   15.
LIEBER, Francis   **Guerrilla Parties Considered with Reference to the Laws and Usages of War.** Wraps
   1862   New York   50.
LIEBER, Francis   **Instructions for the Government of Armies of the United States in the Field.** Wraps
   1863   New York   25.

LIEBER, Francis   **No Party Now, But All For Our Country: An Address.** Wraps
  1863   Philadelphia   5.
  1863   Philadelphia   5.
  1864   New York   5.
Life and Character of William Allan Late Principal of McDonogh School. Wraps
  1889   McDonogh   20.
The Life and Public Services of Major-General Benjamin F. Butler. Wraps
  1864   Philadelphia   35.
Life and Reminiscences of General William T. Sherman by Distinguished Men of His Time.
  1891   n.p.   30.
The Life, Campaigns and Battles of General Ulysses S. Grant.
  1868   New York   7.
The Life, Campaigns, and Public Services of General McClellan.
  1864   Philadelphia   15.
Life in the South   See: **HOPLEY,** Catherine C.
Life of Stephen A. Douglas.
  1860   New York   10.
The Life, Trial and Execution of Capt. John Brown.
  1859   New York   50.
The Light and Dark of the Rebellion.
  1863   Pennsylvania   30.
LIGHTFOOT, Robert M., Jr. (comp)   **The Lincoln Collections of Bradley University.**
  Wraps
  1962   Peoria, Illinois   15.
LINCOLN, Abraham   **Addresses and Letters of** _____ edited by Charles W. Moore.
  1914   New York   8.
LINCOLN, Abraham   **Complete Works of Abraham Lincoln** edited by John Nicolay
  and John Hay. 12 Vols.
  1905   New York   100.
LINCOLN, Abraham   **Complete Works** edited by John Nicolay and John Hay. 2 vols.
  1907   New York   15.
LINCOLN, Abraham   **. . . His Autobiographical Writings** prefaced . . .by Paul M. Angle.
  1947   Kingsport, Tennessee   Ltd.   10.
LINCOLN, Abraham   **. . . His Speeches and Writings** edited by Roy P. Basler.
  1946   Cleveland   10.
LINCOLN, Abraham   **"A House Divided Against Itself Cannot Stand".**
  1936   Chicago   Ltd.   15.
LINCOLN, Abraham   **Uncollected Letters of . . .** edited by Gilbert A. Tracy.
  1916   Boston   Ltd.   15.
  1917   Boston   Ltd.   15.
LINCOLN, Abraham   **The Writings of Abraham Lincoln** edited by Arthur Brooks
  Lapsley. 8 vols.
  1905   New York   30.
Lincoln and His America with the Words of Abraham Lincoln arranged by David Plowden.
  1970   New York   20.
Lincoln-Douglas Debates.   See: **Political Debates . . .**
Lincoln Letters (The Bibliophile Society).
  1913   n.p.   10.
Lincoln's Ellsworth Letter.
  1916   New York   Ltd.   30.
Lincoln's Last Speech in Springfield in the Campaign of 1858.
  1925   Chicago   25.
LINDEMAN, Jack (ed)   **The Conflict of Convictions, American Writers Report the Civil
  War.**
  1968   Philadelphia   15.
LINDQUIST, Orville A.   **Common Fallacies Regarding United States History.** Wraps
  1953   Richmond   5.
LINK, Arthur S. and **REMBERT,** W. Patrick (eds)   **Writing Southern History, Essays
  in Historiography in Honor of Fletcher M. Green.**
  1967   Baton Rouge   10.

A List of the Awards of the Congressional Medal of Honor . . . Under the Authority of the Congress of the United States 1862-1926. Wraps
    1927   Washington   20.
List of Staff Officers of the Confederate States Army. Wraps
    1891   Washington   75.
LITTLETON, William G.   **The Battle Between the Alabama and the Kearsarge, Off Cherbourg, France, Sunday June 19, 1864 An Address.** Wraps
    1932   n.p.   20.
LITWACK, Leon F.   **Been in the Storm So Long, the Aftermath of Slavery.**
    1979   New York   20.
LIVELY, Robert A.   **Fiction Fights the Civil War.**
    1957   Chapel Hill, N. C.   20.
LIVERMORE, Mary A.   **My Story of the War: A Woman's Narrative.**
    1888   Hartford   25.
    1889   Hartford   25.
    1890   Hartford   20.
    1891   Hartford   20.
LIVERMORE, Mary A.   **The Story of My Life.**
    1897   Hartford   25.
    1898   Hartford   25.
LIVERMORE, Thomas L.   **Numbers and Losses in the Civil War — 1861-1865.**
    1901   Boston   25.
    1957   Bloomington   15.
    1969   New York   15.
Lives of Jefferson Davis and Stonewall Jackson.
    1890   New York   20.
Lloyd's Battle History of the Great Rebellion Complete in One Volume.
    1866   New York   30.
LOCKE, David R.   **Divers Views, Opinions and Prophecies of Petroleum V. Nasby.**
    1867   Cincinnati   15.
LOCKE, E. W.   **Three Years in Camp and Hospital.**
    1870   Boston   30.
    1871   Boston   30.
    1872   Boston   25.
LOCKRIDGE, Ross, Jr.   **Raintree County.**
    1948   Boston   10.
LOGAN, India W. P.   **Kelion Franklin Peddicord of Quirk's Scouts, Morgan's Kentucky Cavalry, C.S.A.**
    1908   New York   250.
LOGAN, John A.   **The Great Conspiracy.**
    1886   New York   20.
LOGAN, John A.   **Speech on the Fitz-John Porter Case Dec. 29, 1882 and Jan. 2-3 1883.**
    1883   Washington   30.
LOGAN, John A.   **The Volunteer Soldier of America.**
    1887   Chicago   25.
LOGAN, Mrs. John A.   **Reminiscences of a Soldier's Wife.**
    1913   New York   25.
LOGAN, Kate Virginia Cox   **My Confederate Girlhood, Memoirs** edited by Lily L. Morrill.
    1932   Richmond   25.
LOGAN, T.M.   **Oration Delivered at the Reunion of the Hampton Legion in Columbia, S. C. July 21, 1875.** Wraps
    1875   Charleston   20.
LOMASK, Milton   **Andrew Johnson: President on Trial.**
    1960   New York   12.
LOMAX, Elizabeth Lindsay   **Leaves From an Old Washington Diary, 1854-1863** edited by Lindsay Lomax Wood.
    1943   New York   20.

LONDON, H. A.   **Memorial Address on the Life and Services of General Bryan Grimes, etc.** Wraps
    1886   Raleigh   75.
LONG, A. L. & **WRIGHT,** Marcus J. (eds)   **Memoirs of Robert E. Lee.**
    1877   New York   40.
    1886   New York   40.
    1887   New York   40.
LONG, E. B. and **LONG,** Barbara   **The Civil War Day By Day, An Almanac 1861-1865.**
    1971   Garden City, New York   20.
LONG, H. W.   **The Story of the Battle as the Field is Marked Today, Gettysburg, as the Battle was Fought.** Wraps
    1927   n.p.   15.
LONG, J. T.   **The Sixteenth Decisive Battle of the World . . . Gettysburg.** Wraps
    1906   Gettysburg   15.
    1911   Gettysburg
LONG, James T.   **Gettysburg: How the Battle Was Fought.** Wraps
    1890   Harrisburg   25.
    1890   Harrisburg   25.
LONG, James T. (comp)   **. . . Gettysburg Souvenir . . .Compliments of . . .Hotel Gettysburg.** Wraps
    n.d. (circa 1890)   Gettysburg   15.
LONGACRE, Edward G.   **From Union Stars to Top Hat: Biography of General James Harrison Wilson.**
    1972   Harrisburg   25.
LONGACRE, Edward G.   **The Man Behind the Guns, a Biography of General Henry Jackson Hunt.**
    1977   South Brunswick   15.
LONGACRE, Edward G.   **Mounted Raids of the Civil War.**
    1975   South Brunswick   20.
LONGMORE, T. A.   **Treatise on Gunshot Wounds, Authorized and Adopted by Surgeon General of U.S. Army., etc.**
    1863   Philadelphia   50.
LONGSTREET, Helen D.   **Lee and Longstreet at High Tide.**
    1904   Gainesville, Georgia   100.
    1905   Gainesville, Georgia   75.
    1969   New York   20.
LONGSTREET, James   **From Manassas to Appomattox.**
    1896   Philadelphia   175.
    1903   Philadelphia   100.
    1960   Bloomington   edited by James I. Robertson   35.
    1976   Millwood, New York   30.
LONN, Ella   **Desertion During the Civil War.**
    1928   New York   50.
    1966   Gloucester   15.
LONN, Ella   **Foreigners in the Confederacy.**
    1940   Chapel Hill   65.
    1965   Glouster   15.
LONN, Ella   **Foreigners in the Union Army and Navy.**
    1951   Baton Rouge   40.
    1965   Gloucester   15.
LONN, Ella   **Salt as a Factor in the Confederacy.**
    1933   New York   65.
    1965   University   20.
LOOMIS, John S.   **Report of . . . Expedition of Surgeons and Nurses . . . to Vicksburg and Memphis for Relief of Sick and Wounded Soldiers.** Wraps
    1863   Springfield, Illinois   20.
LORANT, Stefan   **Lincoln, His Life in Photographs.**
    1941   New York   15.

LORANT, Stefan   **Lincoln, A Picture Story of His Life.**
   1952   New York   15.
   1957   New York   10.
LORD, Francis A., and **WISE,** Arthur   **Bands and Drummer Boys of the Civil War.**
   1966   New York   25.
LORD, Francis A.   **Civil War Collector's Encyclopedia, Arms, Uniforms, and Equipment of the Union and Confederacy.**
   1963   Harrisburg   25.
   Various later printings   20.
LORD, Francis A.   **Civil War Collectors Encyclopedia.** Vol. 2.
   1975   n.p.   19.50
LORD, Francis A.   **Civil War Collector's Encyclopedia.** Vol. 3.
   1979   West Columbia, S. C.   17.50
LORD, Francis A.   **Civil War Sutlers and Their Wares.**
   1969   New York   15.
LORD, Francis A.   **Lincoln's Railroad Man: Herman Haupt.**
   1969   Rutherford   20.
LORD, Francis A.   **They Fought For the Union.**
   1960   Harrisburg   25.
   1969   New York   20.
LORD, Francis A., and **WISE,** Arthur   **Uniforms of the Civil War.**
   1970   New York   20.
LORD, Theodore A.   **A Summary of the Case of General Fitz-John Porter.** Wraps
   1883   San Francisco   35.
LORING, Charles G. et al.   **Correspondence on the Present Relations Between Great Britain and the United States.**
   1862   Boston   30.
LORING, Charles G.   **England's Liability for Indemnity: Remarks on the Letter of "Historicus" Dated Nov. 4, 1863.** Wraps
   1864   Boston   20.
LORING, Charles G.   **Neutral Relations of England and the United States.** Wraps
   1863   New York   15.
   1863   Boston   15.
LORING, W. W.   **A Confederate Soldier in Egypt.**
   1884   New York   40.
LOSSING, Benson J.   **A History of the Civil War.**
   1912   New York   16 parts   Wraps   80.
   1912   New York   1 vol. edition   75.
LOSSING, Benson J.   **The League of States.**
   1863   New York   15.
LOSSING, Benson J.   **The Life, Campaigns and Battles of General Ulysses S. Grant.**
   1868   New York   10.
LOSSING, Benson J.   **Memoir of Lieut.-Col. John T. Greble.**
   1870   Philadelphia   30.
LOSSING, Benson J.   **The Pictorial Field Book of the Civil War.** 3 vols.
   1878   New Haven   60.
   Many Other Editions   60.
LOSSING, Benson J.   **Pictorial History of the Civil War.** 3 vols.
   1866-68   Philadelphia   75.
   1876   Hartford   75.
   Many Later Editions   40.
LOTHROP, Thornton K.   **William Henry Seward.**
   1899   Boston   10.
LOUGHBOROUGH, Mrs. James   **My Cave Life in Vicksburg . . . By a Lady.**
   1864   New York   50.
   1882   Little Rock   40.
   1882   St. Louis   40.

The Love-Life of Brig. Gen Henry M. Naglee Consisting of a Correspondence on Love, War and Politics.
    1867   n.p.   15.

LOW, John   **The Logs of the CSS Alabama and the CSS Tuscaloosa 1862-1863.** edited by W. Stanley Hoole. Wraps
    1972   University, Alabama   25.

LOWELL, Charles Russell   **Memoirs of the War of '61 and Cousins . . .**
    1920   Boston   30.

LOWENFELS, Walter (comp. and ed.)   **Walt Whitman's Civil War.**
    1960   New York   12.

LOWREY, Grosvenor P.   **English Neutrality. Is the Alabama a British Pirate?** Wraps
    1863   Philadelphia   60.
    1863   New York   60.

Loyalist's Ammunition. Wraps
    1863   Philadelphia   10.

LUBBOCK, Francis R.   **Six Decades in Texas** or, **Memoirs of Francis Richard Lubbock, Governor of Texas in War Time 1861-1863** edited by C. W. Raines.
    1900   Austin   150.

LUCAS, Daniel B.   **Memoir of John Yates Beall: His Life, Trial; Correspondence; Diary.**
    1865   Montreal   300.

LUCAS, Marion B.   **Sherman and the Burning of Columbia.**
    1976   College Station, Texas   12.

LUDLOW, William   **The Battle of Allatoona October 5, 1864.** Wraps
    n.d.   Michigan   15.

LUDWIG, Emil   **Lincoln.**
    1930   Boston   7.

LUNT, Dolly Sumner   See: **BURGE,** Dolly S. L.

LUNT, George   **The Origin of the Late War.**
    1866   New York   35.
    1867   New York   25.

LUSK, William Thompson   **War Letters of _____ Captain, Assistant Adjutant-General U.S. Vols 1861-1863.**
    1911   New York   50.

LUTHIN, R.   **The First Lincoln Campaign.**
    1944   Cambridge   7.

LUTHIN, Reinhard H.   **The Real Abraham Lincoln.**
    1960   Englewood Cliffs, New Jersey   20.

LUVAAS, Jay   **The Military Legacy of the Civil War: The European Inheritance.**
    1959   Chicago   30.

LYMAN, Theodore   **Meade's Headquarters 1863-65 Letters of Col. Theodore Lyman from the Wilderness to Appomattox,** edited by George R. Agassiz.
    1922   Boston   40.
    1970   Freeport   20.

LYNCH, John R.   **The Facts of Reconstruction.**
    1913   New York   40.

LYON, Mattie Harris   **My Memoirs of the War Between the States.** Wraps
    1960   n.p.   25.

LYONS, W. F.   **Brigadier-General Thomas Francis Meagher.**
    1870   New York   15.
    1886   New York   15.

Lyrics, Incidents, and Sketches of the Rebellion.
    See: **BILL,** Ledyard

LYTLE, Andrew Nelson   **Bedford Forrest and His Critter Company.**
    1931   New York   35.
    1938   London   30.
    1960   New York   20.

McCALLISTER, Anna   **Ellen Ewing, Wife of General Sherman.**
    1936   New York   30.

McCALLISTER, Robert   **Civil War Letters of General Robert McAllister** edited by
James I. Robertson.
1965   New Brunswick   30.
MacBRIDE, Robert   **Civil War Ironclads.**
1962   Philadelphia   15.
MacBRIDE, Van Dyk   **Confederate Patriotic Covers.** Wraps
1943   Federalsburg, Maryland   15.
McBRYDE, Randell W.   **The Historic "General" A Thrilling Episode of the Civil War.**
1904   Chattanooga   35.
1967   n.p.   Wraps   7.
McCABE, James D., Jr.   **The Grayjackets . . . By a Confederate.**
1867   Richmond   150.
McCABE, James D., Jr.   **The Great Republic.**
1871   Toledo   20.
McCABE, James D., Jr.   **Life and Campaigns of General Robert E. Lee.**
1866   St. Louis   50.
1867   New York   50.
McCABE, W. Gordon   **Brief Sketch of Andrew Reid Venable, Jr.** Wraps
1909   Richmond   20.
McCABE, W. Gordon   **Col. John Barry Purcell 1849-1916.** Wraps
1971   n.p.   20.
McCABE, W. Gordon   **George Ben Johnston, M.D. of Richmond 1853-1916.** Wraps
1918   n.p.   20.
McCABE, W. Gordon   **Joseph Bryan. A Brief Memoir.**
1909   Richmond   60.
McCABE, W. Gordon   **Major-General George Washington Custis Lee.** Wraps
1914   Washington   50.
McCAGUE, James   **The Second Rebellion: The Story of the New York City Draft Riots
of 1863.**
1968   New York   12.
McCALL, Samuel M.   **Thaddeus Stevens.**
1899   Boston   10.
McCANTS, E. C.   **One of the Grayjackets and Other Stories.**
1908   Columbia   60.
McCARTHY, Charles H.   **Lincoln's Plan of Reconstruction.**
1901   New York   200.
McCLELLAN, Carswell   **General Andrew A. Humphreys at Malvern Hill.** Wraps
1888   St. Paul   25.
McCLELLAN, Carswell   **The Personal Memoirs and Military History of U.S. Grant
Versus the Record of the Army of the Potomac.**
1887   Boston   15.
McCLELLAN, George B.   **McClellan's Own Story.**
1887   New York   25.
McCLELLAN, George B.   **Manual of Bayonet Exercise.**
1862   Philadelphia   35.
McCLELLAN, George B.   **Report on the Organization and Campaigns of the Army of
the Potomac.**
1864   New York   30.
1864   New York   30.
1864   Boston   30.
McCLELLAN, H. B.   **The Life and Campaigns of Major General J. E. B. Stuart.**
1885   Boston   150.
1958   Bloomington   entitled **I Rode with Jeb Stuart** edited by Burke Davis   35.
1969   New York   30.
McCLURE, A. K.   **Abraham Lincoln and Men of War-Times.**
1892   Philadelphia   20.
McCLURE, Alexander K. (comp)   **Annals of the War Written by Leading Participants
North and South.**
1879   Philadelphia   60.

McCLURE, Alexander K.   **Recollections of a Half a Century.**
   1902   Salem, Mass.   15.
McCLURE, J. B.   **Stories and Sketches of General Grant at Home and Abroad.**
   1879   Chicago   7.
McCLURE, John R.   **Hoosier Farm Boy in Lincoln's Army, the Civil War Letters**
   _____ edited by Nancy N. Baxter.
   1971   n.p.   20.
McCOLL, Nellie Thomas   **Old Folks at Home.**
   1921   n.p.   40.
McCONKEY, Harriet E. B.   **Dakota War Whoop: or Indian Massacres and War in Minnesota, of 1862-3.**
   1864   St. Paul   50.
   1965   Chicago   20.
McCORDOCK, Robert Stanley   **The Yankee Cheese Box.**
   1938   Philadelphia   20.
McCORKLE, John   **Three Years with Quantrill: A True Story by O. S. Barton.**
   n.d. (circa 1914)   Armstrong, Missouri   175.
   1967   New York   20.
McCORMICK, Robert R.   **Ulysses S. Grant.**
   1934   New York   25.
McCORMICK, Robert R.   **The War Without Grant.**
   1950   New York   20.
McCRADY, Louis DeB.   **General Edward McCrady.** Wraps
   1905   Charleston   30.
McCREA, Tully   **Dear Belle, Letters from a Cadet and Officer to His Sweetheart 1858-1865** edited by Catherine S. Crary.
   1965   Middletown, Conn.   10.
McCULLOUGH, Hugh   **Men and Measures of Half a Century.**
   1888   New York   25.
McCURDY, Charles M.   **Gettysburg, A Memoir.** Wraps
   1929   Pittsburgh   30.
McDANIEL, H. Pleasants   **War Poems 1861-1865.**
   1901   New York   25.
McDONALD, Cornelia.   **A Diary with Reminiscences of the War and Refugee Life in the Shenandoah Valley.**
   1934   Nashville   75.
MacDONALD, Helen G.   **Canadian Public Opinion on the American Civil War.** Wraps
   1926   New York   30.
McDONALD, John W.   **A Soldier of Fortune.**
   1888   New York   35.
MacDONALD, Rose Mortimer Ellzey   **Mrs. Robert E. Lee.**
   1939   Boston   12.
McDONOUGH, James L.   **Schofield: Union General in the Civil War and Reconstruction.**
   1972   Tallahassee   10.
McDONOUGH, James L.   **Shiloh — In Hell Before Night.**
   1977   Knoxville   12.50
McDONOUGH, James L.   **Stones River — Bloody Winter in Tennessee.**
   1980   Knoxville   14.50
McDOWELL, Amanda and **BLANKENSHIP,** Lela McDowell   **Fiddles in the Cumberlands.**
   1943   New York   30.
MacDUFF, J. R.   **The Soldier's Text-Book: or, Confidence in Time of War.** Wraps
   n.d. (circa 1861)   New York   30.
McELROY, J. C.   **The Battle of Chickamauga Historical Map and Guide Book.** Wraps
   n.d. (circa 1900)   Chattanooga, Tenn.   15.
McELROY, J. C.   **Chickamauga, Record of the Ohio Chickamauga and Chattanooga National Park Commission.**
   1896   Cincinnati   18.

McELROY, John   **Further Haps and Mishaps to Si Klegg and Shorty.** Wraps
  1898   Washington   15.
McELROY, John   **The Red Acorn A Romance of the War.** Wraps
  1883   Washington   20.
McELROY, John   **Si, "Shorty" and Boys on "the March to the Sea."** Wraps
  1902   Washington   20.
McELROY, John   **The Struggle for Missouri.**
  1909   Washington   12.
  1913   Washington   10.
McELROY, Robert   **Jefferson Davis, The Unreal and the Real.**
  1937   New York   2 vols.   Boxed   30.
  1969   New York   2 vols. in 1   25.
McFEELY, William S.   **Grant A Biography.**
  1981   New York   19.95
McFEELY, William S.   **Yankee Stepfather. Gen. O. O. Howard and the Freedmen.**
  1968   New Haven   20.
McGAVOCK, Randal W.   **Pen and Sword, The Life and Journals of Randal W.
  McGavock, Colonel CSA** edited by Hershel Gower and Jack Allen.
  1959   Nashville   35.
  1960   Nashville   30.
McGEHEE, J. O.   **Causes That Led to the War Between the States.**
  1915   Atlanta   15.
McGIFFIN, Lee   **Swords, Stars and Bars.**
  1959   New York   20.
McGOODWIN, Bessie Ware   **War-Time Memories of the Southland.**
  n.d.   n.p.   25.
McGREGOR, James C.   **The Disruption of Virginia.**
  1921   New York   15.
McGUIRE, Hunter   **Address by _____ Medical Director 2nd Army Corps
  (Stonewall Jackson's), Army of Northern Virginia.** Wraps
  1897   Lynchburg   25.
McGUIRE, Hunter   **An Address on Stonewall Jackson.** Wraps
  1897   Richmond   50.
  1899   Richmond   40.
McGUIRE, Hunter, and **CHRISTIAN**, Geo. L.   **The Confederate Cause and the Conduct of the War Between the States.**
  1907   Richmond   35.
  1911   Richmond   30.
McGUIRE, Judith W.   **Diary of a Southern Refugee During the War By a Lady of
  Virginia.**
  1867   New York   60.
  1867   Richmond   60.
  1868   New York   40.
  1889   Richmond   40.
McGUIRE, Ruth Robertson   **Stuart McGuire: An Autobiographical Sketch.**
  1956   Richmond   10.
McGUIRE, Stuart   **Hunter Holmes McGuire, M.D.** Wraps
  1938   New York   25.
McHENRY, George   **The Cotton Trace . . . in Connection with . . . Negro Slavery in the
  Confederate States.**
  1863   London   75.
McILWAINE, Richard   **Memories of Three Score Years and Ten.**
  1908   New York and Washington   75.
McINTIRE, John Jackson   **As I Saw It.**
  1902   San Francisco   50.
McINTOSH, David Gregg   **The Campaign of Chancellorsville.** Wraps
  1915   Richmond   75.
McINTYRE, B. F.   **Federals on the Frontier: Diary of _____ 1862-1864** edited by
  Nannie M. Tilley.
  1963   Austin   25.

McINVALE, Morton R.   **The Battle of Pickett's Mill, "Foredoomed to Oblivion."** Wraps
  1977   Atlanta   10.
McKAY, Mrs. C. W.   **Stories of Hospital and Camp.**
  1876   Philadelphia   40.
McKEE, Irving   **"Ben-Hur" Wallace.**
  1947   Berkeley, California   20.
McKEE, James Cooper   **Narrative of the Surrender of a Command of U. S. Forces at Fort Fillmore.**
  1960   Houston   Ltd.   20.
McKEE, W. Reid & Mason, M. E., Jr.   **Civil War Projectiles II   Small Arms & Field Artillery.**
  1980   n.p.   22.
MacKENZIE, Robert   **America and Her Army.**
  1865   London   35.
McKIM, Randolph H.   **The Motives and Aims of the Soldiers of the South in the Civil War.** Wraps
  1904 (?)   n.p.   50.
McKIM, Randolph H.   **The Numerical Strength of the Confederate Army.**
  1912   New York   100.
McKIM, Randolph H.   **The Soul of Lee.**
  1918   New York   35.
McKINNEY, Francis F.   **Education in Violence. The Life of George H. Thomas and the Army of the Cumberland.**
  1961   Detroit   45.
McKITRICK, Eric L.   **Andrew Johnson and Reconstruction.**
  1960   Chicago   15.
McLAUGHLIN, Jack   **Gettysburg, the Long Encampment.**
  1963   New York   10.
McLAUGHLIN, James Fairfax   **The American Cyclops, the Hero of New Orleans and Spoiler of Silver Spoons.**
  1868   Baltimore   30.
McLAUGHLIN, William   **Ceremonies Connected with the Unveiling of the Bronze Statue of Gen. Thomas J. (Stonewall) Jackson at Lexington, VA July 21, 1891.** Wraps
  1891   Baltimore   30.
McLEOD, Martha N.   **Brother Warriors, The Reminiscences of Union and Confederate Veterans.**
  1940   Washington   40.
McMAHON, Martin T.   **General John Sedgwick, An Address.** Wraps
  1880   Rutland   12.
McMASTER, John B.   **History of the People of the United States During Lincoln's Administration.**
  1927   New York   30.
McMEEKIN, Isabel McLennan   **Robert E. Lee: Knight of the South.**
  1950   New York   20.
McMURTY, R. Gerald   **Ben Hardin Helm: "Rebel" Brother-in-Law of Abraham Lincoln.**
  1943   Chicago   Ltd.   60.
McPHERSON, Edward   **Political History of the United States During the Great Rebellion.**
  1865   Washington   20.
  1876   Washington   entitled: **The Political History of the U.S.A. During the Civil War.**   15.
McPHERSON, Edward   **The Political History of the United States of America During the Period of Reconstruction.**
  1876   Washington   20.
  1880   Washington   15.
McPHERSON, Edward   **A Political Manual for 1866.**
  1866   Washington   25.

McPHERSON, James M. **The Negro's Civil War.**
1965 New York 15.
McPHERSON, James M. **The Struggle for Equality.**
1964 Princeton, N. J. 20.
McSWAIN, J. J. **The Causes of Secession: An Essay.** Wraps
1917 Greenville, S. C. 15.
McWHINEY, Grady and **JAMIESON,** Perry D. **Attack and Die, Civil War Military Tactics and the Southern Heritage.**
1982 University, Alabama 15.
McWHINEY, Grady **Braxton Bragg and Confederate Defeat, Vol. 1 Field Command.**
1969 New York 20.
McWHINEY, Grady (ed) **Grant, Lee, Lincoln and the Radicals — Essays on Civil War Leadership.**
1964 n.p. 15.
McWHINEY, Grady **Southerners and Other Americans.**
1973 New York 15.
McWILLIAMS, Carey **Ambrose Bierce: A Biography.**
1929 New York 35.
MACARTNEY, Clarence Edward **Grant and His Generals.**
1953 New York 20.
MACARTNEY, Clarence Edward **Highways and Byways of the Civil War.**
1926 Philadelphia 30.
1938 Pittsburgh 20.
MACARTNEY, Clarence Edward **Lincoln and His Cabinet.**
1931 New York 10.
MACARTNEY, Clarence Edward **Lincoln and His Generals.**
1925 Philadelphia 10.
1926 Philadelphia 10.
MACARTNEY, Clarence Edward **Mr. Lincoln's Admirals.**
1956 New York 15.
MACHEN, Arthur W. **Letters of _____ with Biographical Sketch** compiled by Arthur W. Machen, Jr.
1917 Baltimore 15.
MACLAY, Edgar Stanton **A History of the United States Navy from 1775 to 1902.** 3 vols.
1894-1901 New York 75.
MACLAY, Edgar Stanton **Reminiscences of the Old Navy (1800-1875).**
1898 New York Ltd. 75.
MACON, Nathaniel **Letters to Charles O'Connor — The Destruction of the Union Is Emancipation.** Wraps
1862 Philadelphia 20.
MADDEX, Jack P., Jr. **The Virginia Conservatives 1867-1879.**
1970 Chapel, N. C. 10.
MADISON, Lucy Foster **Lincoln.** 2 vols.
1928 New York Boxed 30.
MAFFITT, Emma Martin The Life and Services of John Newland Maffitt.
1906 New York 250.
MAGEE, Harvey White **The Story of My Life.**
1926 Albany 25.
MAGILL, Mary Tucker **Women or Chronicles of the Late War.**
1871 Baltimore 20.
MAHAN, A. T. **Admiral Farragut.**
1892 New York 15.
1893 New York 15.
1897 New York 15.
MAHAN, A. T. **From Sail to Steam.**
1907 New York 30.
MAHAN, A. T. **The Gulf and Inland Waters.**
1883 New York 25.

MAHAN, A. T.   The Navy in the Civil War.
    1898   New York   25.
MAHAN, Asa   A Critical History of the Late American War.
    1877   New York   75.
MAHAN, D. H.   An Elementary Treatise on Advanced Guard, Outpost and Detachment
    Service of Troops.
    1861   New York   20.
MAHAN, D. H.   A Treatise on Field Fortifications.
    1846   New York   25.
    1861   New York   25.
MAHONE, William   The Battle of the Crater. Wraps
    n.d.   Petersburg   100.
MAHONY, D. A.   The Prisoner of State.
    1863   New York   20.
MAIN, Ed. M.   The Story of the Marches, Battles, and Incidents of The Third United
    States Colored Cavalry.
    1970   New York   25.
MAJOR, Duncan K., and FITCH, Roger S.   Supply of Sherman's Army During the
    Atlanta Campaign.
    1911   Ft. Leavenworth   45.
Major General Henry W. Lawton of Fort Wayne, Indiana. Wraps
    1954   Fort Wayne   5.
MALET, William Wyndham   An Errand to the South in the Summer of 1862.
    1863   London   175.
MALKUS, Alida Sims   We Were There at the Battle of Gettysburg.
    1955   New York   12.
MALLARD, R. Q.   Plantation Life Before Emancipation.
    1892   Richmond   25.
MALTBY, Charles   The Life and Public Services of Abraham Lincoln.
    1884   Stockton, California   40.
MANARIN, Louis H. (ed)   Richmond at War.
    1966   Chapel Hill   30.
MANIGAULT, G.   The United States Unmasked.
    1879   London   20.
MANLY, Marline   The Old Knapsack; or, Longstreet's Mad Charge at Knoxville. Wraps
    n.d.   n.p.   20.
MANN, A. Dudley   "My Ever Dearest Friend" The Letters of A. Dudley Mann to
    Jefferson Davis edited by John P. Moore. Wraps
    1960   Tuscaloosa   Ltd.   25.
MANNING, J. F.   Epitome of the Geneva Award Contest in the Congress of the U.S.
    1882   New York   25.
MANNIX, D. P. and COWLEY, M.   Black Cargoes: A History of the Atlantic Slave
    Trade 1518 to 1865.
    1963   New York   14.
MANSFIELD, Edward D.   The Life and Military Services of Lieut.-General Winfield
    Scott.
    1861   New York   15.
MANSFIELD, Edward D.   A Popular and Authentic Life of Ulysses S. Grant.
    1868   Cincinnati   15.
MANTELL, Martin E.   Johnson, Grant, and Reconstruction Politics.
    1973   New York   15.
Manual of the Panorama of the Battle of Shiloh.
    1885   Chicago   20.
MAPP, Alf J., Jr.   Frock Coats and Epaulets.
    1963   New York   25.
MARBURG, Theodore   In the Hills.
    1895   n.p.   20.
Margaret Mitchell and Her Novel, Gone With the Wind.
    1936   New York   15.

MARKEY, Morris   **The Band Plays Dixie.**
   1927   New York   12.
MARSHAL, Francis   **The Battle of Gettysburg.**
   1914   New York   75.
MARSHALL, Charles   **Address Delivered Before the Lee Monument Association at Richmond, Virginia.** Wraps
   1888   Baltimore   15.
MARSHALL, H. Snowden   **Address Delivered at the Opening of the Building of the Confederate Memorial Institute at Richmond, Va. on May 3, 1921.** Wraps
   1921   Richmond   25.
   1925   Richmond   15.
MARSHALL, John A.   **American Bastile.**
   1871   Philadelphia   35.
   1875   Philadelphia   30.
   1876   Philadelphia   30.
   1885   Philadelphia   25.
MARSHALL, Park   **A Life of William B. Bate.**
   1908   Nashville   75.
MARSHALL-CORNWALL, James   **Grant as Military Commander.**
   1970   London   20.
MARTIN, Robert Hugh   **A Boy of Old Shenandoah.**
   1977   Parsons, West Virginia   7.50
MARTIN, Thomas Ricaud   **The Great Parliamentary Battle and Farewell Addresses of the Southern Senators on the Eve of the Great Civil War.**
   1905   New York   45.
The Martyr's Monument Being the Patriotism and Political Wisdom of Abraham Lincoln as Exhibited in Speeches, etc.
   1865   New York   15.
MARX, Karl, and **ENGLES,** Frederick   **The Civil War in the United States, Works of Marxism-Leninism.**
   1937   New York   35.
   1940   New York   25.
MASON, Amos Lawrence (ed)   **Memoir and Correspondence of Charles Steedman, Rear-Admiral United States Navy with His Autobiography and Private Journals 1811-1890.**
   1912   Harvard   Ltd.   60.
MASON, Emily V.   **Popular Life of Gen. Robert E. Lee.**
   1874   Baltimore   30.
MASON, Emily V. (comp)   **The Southern Poems of the War.**
   1867   Baltimore   40.
   1878   Baltimore   40.
MASON, Virginia   **The Public Life and Diplomatic Correspondence of James M. Mason with Some Personal History.**
   1906   New York   50.
MASSEY, John E.   **Autobiography of _____** edited by Elizabeth H. Hancock.
   1909   New York   60.
MASSEY, Mary Elizabeth   **Bonnet Brigades, American Women & The Civil War.**
   1966   New York   25.
MASSEY, Mary Elizabeth   **Ersatz in the Confederacy.**
   1952   Columbia, S. C.   35.
MASSEY, Mary Elizabeth   **Refugee Life in the Confederacy.**
   1964   Baton Rouge   35.
MASSIE, James William   **America: The Origin of Her Present Conflict.**
   1864   London   75.
MASTERS, Edgar Lee   **Lee, A Dramatic Poem.**
   1926   New York   10.
MASTERS, Edgar Lee   **Lincoln the Man.**
   1931   New York   15.
   1931   London   15.

MATHENY, H. E.   **Major General Thomas M. Harris.**
1963   Parsons   25.
MATHES, J. Harvey   **General Forrest.**
1902   New York   75.
1976   Memphis   22.50
MATHEWS, W. H.   **Harry: Being the Recollections of an English Boy Who Served in the Union Army.**
1927   Iowa City   60.
MATHIAS, Frank F. (ed)   **Incidents and Experiences in the Life of Thomas W. Parsons from 1826 to 1900.**
MATTHEWS, Joseph J. (ed)   **The Capture and Wonderful Escape of General John H. Morgan.** Wraps
1947   Atlanta   10.
MATTHEWS, Byron H., Jr.   **The McCook-Stoneman Raid.**
1976   Philadelphia   10.
MAULL, D. W.   **The Life and Military Services of the Late Brigadier General Thomas A. Smyth.**
1870   Wilmington, Delaware   25.
MAURICE, Frederick   **An Aide-De-Camp of Lee.**
1927   Boston   20.
MAURICE, Frederick   **Robert E. Lee, The Soldier.**
1925   Boston   25.
1925   London   25.
1925   New York   20.
MAURICE, Frederick   **Statesmen and Soldiers of the Civil War.**
1926   Boston   15.
MAURY, Dabney Herndon   **Recollections of a Virginian in the Mexican, Indian, and Civil Wars.**
1894   New York   40.
1897   New York   25.
MAURY, Richard L.   **A Brief Sketch of the Work of Matthew Fontaine Maury During the War 1861-1865.** Wraps
1915   Richmond   100.
MAXWELL, William Quentin   **Lincoln's Fifth Wheel: The Political History of the U.S. Sanitary Commission.**
1956   New York   20.
MAY, Samuel J.   **Some Recollections of our Antislavery Conflict.**
1869   Boston   17.
MEAD, F.   **Heroic Statues in Bronze of Abraham Lincoln.**
1932   Fort Wayne   Ltd.   30.
MEADE, George   **Battle of Gettysburg.** Wraps
1924   Ambler, Pennsylvania   15.
MEADE, George   **Did General Meade Desire to Retreat at the Battle of Gettysburg?** Wraps
1883   Philadelphia   30.
MEADE, George   **General Meade's Letter on Gettysburg.** Wraps
1886   Philadelphia   25.
MEADE, George   **The Life and Letters of George Gordon Meade.** 2 vols.
1913   New York   75.
MEADE, George   **With Meade at Gettysburg.**
1930   Philadelphia   35.
MEADE, Richard W.   **Forty-five Years of Active Service.** Wraps
1896   New York   15.
MEADE, Robert Douthat   **Judah P. Benjamin Confederate Statesman.**
1943   New York   35.
MEARNS, David C.   **Largely Lincoln.**
1961   New York   10.

MEARNS, David C.   **The Lincoln Papers.**
    1948   Garden City   2 vols.   Boxed   20.
    1969   New York   2 vols. in 1   15.
MEBANE, John   **Books Relating to the Civil War.**
    1963   New York   25.
The Medal of Honor of the United States Army.
    1948   Washington   15.
Medal of Honor 1863-1968 "In the Name of the Congress of the United States."
    1968   Washington   10.
Medical and Surgical History of the War of the Rebellion. 6 vols.
    1870-1888   Washington   1000.
    Individual Vols.   125. each
    For Prospectus See: **Reports of the Extent . . .**
Meeting of the Pilot Knob Memorial Association on the 40th Anniversary of the Battle of Pilot Knob, Sept. 27, 1904. Wraps
    1904   St. Louis   50.
MEIER, Heinz K. (ed)   **Memoirs of a Swiss Officer in the American Civil War.**
    1972   Switzerland   30.
MELIGAKES, N. A.   **The Spirit of Gettysburg.**
    1950   Gettysburg   10.
    1950   n.p.   10.
MELLON, James (comp & ed)   **The Face of Lincoln.**
    1979   New York   60.
MELTON, Maurice   **The Confederate Iron Clads.**
    1968   New York   20.
MELVILLE, Herman   **Battle-Pieces and Aspects of the War.**
    1866   New York   20.
    1963   New York   entitled: **The Battlepieces of Herman Melville** edited by
        Hennig Cohen.   10.
    1964   New York   10.
MEMMINGER, Christopher G.   **Address of _____, Special Commissioner from the State of South Carolina before . . . State of Virginia Jan 19, 1860.** Wraps
    1860   Richmond   30.
MEMMINGER, Christopher G.   **The Mission of South Carolina to Virginia.** Wraps
    n.d.   n.p.   50.
Memoir of George Boardman Boomer.
    1864   Boston   20.
Memoir of James Allen Hardie, Inspector-General, United States Army.
    1877   Washington   35.
Memoir of Lieut. Edward Lewis Mitchell Who Fell at the Battle of Shiloh, Aged Twenty-two Years.
    1864   New York   15.
A Memoir Rufus R. Dawes Born July 4, 1838 Died August 1, 1899.
    n.d.   n.p.   Ltd.   35.
Memorandum Relative to the General Officers Appointed by the President in the Armies of the Confederate States 1861-1865. Wraps
    1905   Washington   Ltd.   50.
    1908   Washington   25.
Memorial Addresses on the Life and Character of Ambrose Burnside.
    1882   Washington   10.
Memorial Addresses on the Life and Character of Andrew Johnson.
    1876   Washington   10.
Memorial Addresses on the Life and Character of John Warwick Daniel.
    1911   Washington   20.
Memorial Addresses on the Life and Character of William H. F. Lee Delivered in the House of Representatives.
    1892   Washington   20.

Memorial Day Annual 1912 The Causes and Outbreak of the War Between the States 1861-1865. Wraps
   1912   Richmond   10.
Memorial of Capt. Jacob V. Marshall.
   n.d.   Staunton, Virginia   25.
A Memorial of Charles Sumner.
   1874   Boston   12.
Memorial of Gen. J.K.F. Mansfield, Who Fell in Battle at Sharpsburg.
   1862   Boston   15.
Memorial of Joel Parker.
   1889   Freehold, New Jersey   15.
Memorial of Margaret E. Breckinridge.
   1865   Philadelphia   35.
A Memorial of Philip Henry Sheridan from the City of Boston.
   1889   Boston   20.
Memorial to Brevet Major General Galusha Pennypacker.
   1934   Philadelphia   10.
The Memorial to Major General George Gordon Meade in Washington, D.C.
   1927   n.p.   10.
Memorial to Samuel K. Zook, Brevet Major-General.
   1889   Philadelphia   25.
MENCKEN, August (ed)   **By the Neck A Book of Hangings.**
   1942   New York   15.
MENDE, Elsie and **PEARSON,** Henry   **An American Soldier and Diplomat, Horace Porter.**
   1927   New York   20.
MERCER, Philip   **The Life of the Gallant Pelham.**
   1929   Macon, Georgia   150.
   1958   Kennesaw, Georgia   25.
MEREDITH, Roy   **The American Wars. A Pictorial History from Quebec to Korea.**
   1955   New York   20.
MEREDITH, Roy   **The Face of Robert E. Lee in Life and Legend.**
   1947   New York   30.
MEREDITH, Roy   **Mr. Lincoln's Camera Man, Mathew B. Brady.**
   1946   New York   30.
MEREDITH, Roy   **Mr. Lincoln's Contemporaries: An Album of Portraits by Mathew B. Brady.**
   1951   New York   20.
MEREDITH, Roy   **Mr. Lincoln's General: Ulysses S. Grant.**
   1959   New York   20.
MEREDITH, Roy   **Storm Over Sumter.**
   1957   New York   20.
MEREDITH, Roy   **The World of Mathew Brady Portraits of the Civil War Period.**
   1976   Los Angeles   20.
MERIWETHER, Colyer   **Raphael Semmes.**
   1913   Philadelphia   35.
MERIWETHER, Elizabeth A.   **Facts and Falsehoods Concerning the War on the South.** Wraps
   1904   Memphis, Tenn.   30.
MERIWETHER, Elizabeth Avery   **Recollections of 92 Years 1824-1916.**
   1958   Nashville   25.
MERLI, Frank J.   **Great Britain and the Confederate Navy 1861-1865.**
   1970   Bloomington   15.
MERRICK, Caroline E.   **Old Times in Dixie Land.**
   1901   New York   35.
MERRILL, James M.   **Battle Flags South.**
   1970   Cranbury, New Jersey   20.
MERRILL, James M.   **The Rebel Shore.**
   1957   Boston   20.

MERRILL, James M.   **Spurs to Glory, The Story of the U.S. Cavalry.**
  1966   Chicago   15.
MERRILL, James M.   **William Tecumseh Sherman.**
  1971   Chicago   15.
The Merrimac and Monitor Naval Engagement. Wraps
  n.d.   Baltimore   20.
MERRITT, Elizabeth   **James Henry Hammond 1806-1864.** Wraps
  1923   Baltimore   20.
MESERVE, Frederick Hill   **Grant in the Wilderness.** Wraps
  1914   New York   Ltd.   40.
MESERVE, F. H. and **SANDBURG,** Carl   **The Photographs of Abraham Lincoln.**
  1944   New York   30.
MEYER, H. N.   **Colonel of the Black Regiment.**
  1967   New York   15.
MEYER, Howard N.   **Let Us Have Peace, The Story of Ulysses S. Grant.**
  1966   New York   7.
MICHIE, Peter S.   **General McClellan.**
  1901   New York   25.
MICHIE, Peter S.   **The Life and Letters of Emory Upton.**
  1885   New York   35.
MIERS, Earl Schenck   **The American Civil War.**
  1961   New York   20.
MIERS, Earl Schenck   **Billy Yank and Johnny Reb.**
  1961   New York   15.
MIERS, Earl Schenck   **The General Who Marched to Hell, William Tecumseh Sherman.**
  1951   New York   20.
MIERS, Earl Schenck and **BROWN,** Richard A. (eds)   **Gettysburg.**
  1948   New Brunswick   25.
MIERS, Earl Schenck   **The Great Rebellion.**
  1958   Cleveland   20.
MIERS, Earl Schenck   **The Last Campaign . . . Grant Saves the Union.**
  1972   Philadelphia   10.
MIERS, Earl Schenck (ed)   **Lincoln Day by Day.** 3 vols.
  1960   Washington   40.
MIERS, Earl Schenck   **Robert E. Lee, A Great Life in Brief.**
  1956   New York   10.
  1967   New York   7.
MIERS, Earl Schenck   **The Web of Victory.**
  1955   New York   25.
MILES, Nelson A.   **Personal Recollections and Observations.**
  1896   Chicago   75.
  1897   Chicago   60.
MILES, Nelson A.   **Serving the Republic.**
  1911   New York   30.
MILHAM, Charles G.   **Gallant Pelham: American Extraordinary.**
  1959   Washington, D.C.   50.
MILHOLLEN, Hirst D. and **JOHNSON,** J. R.   **Best Photos of the Civil War.**
  1961   New York   20.
  1969   New York   15.
MILHOLLEN, Hirst D. & **MUGRIDGE,** Donald H. (comps)   **Civil War Photographs
1861-1865.** Wraps
  1961   Washington   10.
MILHOLLEN, Hirst D., **JOHNSON,** Jas. and **BILL,** Alfred   **Horsemen Blue and Gray.**
  1960   New York   30.
Military Despotism: Suspension of the Habeas Corpus: Curses Coming Home to Roost!
  Wraps
  1863   New York   15.
Military Historical Society of Massachusetts (MHSM)   See: Individual Titles.

MILLER, Delavan S.   **A Drum's Story & Other Tales.**
  1909   Watertown, New York   20.
MILLER, Emily Van Dorn (ed)   **A Soldier's Honor with Reminiscences of Major-General Earl Van Dorn.**
  1902   New York   200.
MILLER, Francis T. (ed)   **The Photographic History of the Civil War.** 10 vols.
  1911-1912   New York   250.
  1957   New York   10 vols. in 5   Boxed   100.
MILLER, Francis T.   **Portrait Life of Lincoln.**
  1910   Chicago   25.
  1910   Springfield   25.
MILLIGAN, John D. (ed)   **From the Fresh-Water Navy: 1861-64.**
  1975   Annapolis   15.
MILLIGAN, John D.   **Gunboats Down the Mississippi.**
  1965   Annapolis   15.
MILLS, Anson   **My Story.**
  1918   Washington   30.
MILLS, Lewis E.   **General Pope's Virginia Campaign of 1862.** Wraps
  1870   Cincinnati   30.
MILTON, George Fort   **Abraham Lincoln and the Fifth Column.**
  1942   New York   20.
MILTON, George Fort   **The Age of Hate. Andrew Johnson and the Radicals.**
  1930   New York   20.
MILTON, George Fort   **Conflict. The American Civil War.**
  1941   New York   15.
MILTON, George Fort   **The Eve of Conflict.**
  1934   Boston   15.
MIMS, Edwin   **Sidney Lanier.**
  1905   Boston   20.
MINNIGH, Luther W.   **Gettysburg.** Wraps
  1892   n.p.   20.
  1917   Gettysburg   20.
  1920   n.p.   20.
  1924   n.p.   15.
MINOR, Benjamin Blake   **The Southern Literary Messenger 1834-1864.**
  1905   New York   80.
MINOR, Charles L. C.   **The Real Lincoln.** edited by Kate Mason Rowland. Wraps
  1901   Richmond   15.
MINOR, Kate P.   **Subject Index to the Southern Historical Society Papers.**
  1970   Dayton   20.
MINOR, Kate Pleasants (comp)   **From Dixie.**
  1893   Richmond   30.
The Mississippi Valley, Tennessee, Georgia, Alabama 1861-1864, Vol. 8 of MHSM.
  1910   Boston   40.
Mr. Buchanan's Administration on the Eve of Rebellion.
  1866   New York   20.
MITCHEL, Cora   **Reminiscences of the Civil War.**
  n.d.   Providence   15.
MITCHEL, F. A.   **Ormsby MacKnight Mitchel, Astronomer and General.**
  1887   Boston   30.
MITCHELL, Mrs. A. L. (comp)   **Songs of the Confederacy and Plantation Melodies.** Wraps
  1901   Cincinnnati, Ohio   30.
MITCHELL, D. W.   **Ten Years in the United States.**
  1862   London   60.
MITCHELL, Joseph B.   **The Badge of Gallantry.**
  1968   New York   10.
MITCHELL, Joseph B.   **Decisive Battles of the Civil War.**
  1955   New York   15.

MITCHELL, Joseph B. and **HART**, Scott (eds)   **1st Manassas (Bull Run) and the War Around it.** Wraps
    1961   Manassas   10.
MITCHELL, Joseph B.   **Military Leaders in the Civil War.**
    1972   New York   15.
MITCHELL, Margaret   **Gone With the Wind.**
    1936   New York   1st Edition   1st Issue (May)   125.
    1968   New York   2 vols.   Limited Editions Club   80.
MITCHELL, S. Weir   **In War Time.**
    1885   Boston   15.
MITCHELL, Stewart   **Horatio Seymour of New York.**
    1938   Cambridge   20.
MITCHELL, T. K.   **Autobiography of Dr. T. K. Mitchell, Sr.** Wraps
    1914   Atlanta   35.
MITCHELL, William   **General Greeley, The Story of a Great American.**
    1936   New York   30.
MITGANG, Herbert (ed)   **Lincoln As They Saw Him.**
    1956   New York   7.
MITGANG, Herbert (ed)   **Washington in Lincoln's Time.**
    1958   New York   10.
MOAT, Louis Shepheard   See: **LESLIE**, Frank
MOEHRING, E., and **KAYLIN**, Arleen (eds)   **The Civil War Extra.**
    1975   New York   25.
MOGELEVER, Jacob   **Death to Traitors.**
    1960   New York   20.
MONAGHAN, Jay   **Civil War on the Western Border 1854-65.**
    1955   New York   20.
    1955   Boston   20.
MONAGHAN, Jay   **Custer — The Life of General George Armstrong Custer.**
    1959   Boston   40.
MONAGHAN, Jay   **Diplomat in Carpet Slippers Abraham Lincoln Deals with Foreign Affairs.**
    1945   Indianapolis   15.
MONAGHAN, Jay   **Lincoln Bibliography 1839-1939.** 2 vols.
    1943   Springfield   40.
MONAGHAN, Jay   **The Man Who Elected Lincoln.**
    1956   Indianapolis   5.
MONAGHAN, Jay   **Swamp Fox of the Confederacy.** Wraps
    1956   Tuscaloosa, Alabama   Ltd.   35.
MONNETT, Howard N.   **Action Before Westport 1864.**
    1964   Kansas City   Ltd.   30.
Monograph on the Monitor, The First Monitor and Its Builders. Wraps
    1884   Poughkeepsie, New York   30
MONROE, Haskell M., Jr. and **McINTOSH**, James T. (eds)   **The Papers of Jefferson Davis.** Vols. 1-3.
    1971-81   Baton Rouge   Still in Publication   35. each
MONROE, J.   **The Company Drill of the Infantry of the Line.**
    1862   New York   40.
MONSELL, Helen A.   **Boy of Old Virginia: Robert E. Lee.**
    1937   Indianapolis   7.
MONTGOMERY, Horace   **Johnny Cobb Confederate Aristocrat.** Wraps
    1964   Athens, Georgia   15.
MONTGOMERY, Horace   **A Union Officer's Recollections of the Negro as a Soldier.** Wraps
    1961   Pennsylvania   25.
MONTGOMERY, James Stuart   **The Shaping of a Battle: Gettysburg.**
    1959   Philadelphia   25.
MOODY, Claire N.   **Battle of Pea Ridge or Elkhorn Tavern March 7-8, 1862.** Wraps
    1956   Little Rock   10.

MOODY, Granville   **A Life's Retrospect, Autobiography of Rev. Granville Moody**
edited by Rev. Sylvester Weeks.
1890   Cincinnati   35.
MOODY, Loring   **The Destruction of Republicanism the Object of the Rebellion.**
1863   Boston   15.
MOON, H. L.   Balance of Power: The Negro Vote.
1948   New York   15.
MOORE, Albert B.   **Conscription and Conflict in the Confederacy.**
1924   New York   40.
1963   New York   25.
MOORE, Alison   **Old Bob Wheat, High Private.** Wraps
1957   Baton Rouge   20.
MOORE, Avery C.   **Destiny's Soldier (Gen. Albert Sidney Johnston).** Wraps
1958   San Francisco   20.
MOORE, Charles (comp)   **Lincoln's Gettysburg Address & Second Inaugural.**
1927   Boston   Ltd.   20.
MOORE, Claude Hunter   **Thomas Overton Moore: A Confederate Governor.**
1960   Clinton, N. C.   15.
MOORE, Frank   **Anecdotes, Poetry and Incidents of the War: North & South 1860-1865.**
1867   New York   25.
MOORE, Frank   **The Civil War in Song and Story.**
1882   New York   25.
1889   New York   25.
MOORE, Frank   **Rebel Rhymes and Rhapsodies.**
1864   New York   30.
MOORE, Frank (ed)   **The Rebellion Record.** 12 vols.
1862-69   New York   350.
MOORE, Frank   **Women of the War.**
1866   Hartford   20.
1867   Hartford   20.
MOORE, Glover   **William Jemison Mims, Soldier and Squire.**
1966   Birmingham   25.
MOORE, Guy W.   **The Case of Mrs. Surratt.**
1954   Norman, Oklahoma   20.
MOORE, James   **A Complete History of the Great Rebellion: or The Civil War in the United States, 1861-1865.**
1866   New York   10.
MORAN, Benjamin   **The Journal of _____ 1857-1865** edited by Sarah A.
Wallace & Frances E. Gillespie. 2 vols.
1948-49   Chicago   30.
MORAN, Frank E.   **Bastiles of the Confederacy A Reply to Jefferson Davis.**
1890   Baltimore   25.
MORDECAI, Samuel   **Virginia Especially Richmond, in By-Gone Days.**
1946   Richmond   15.
MORFORD, Henry   **The Days of Shoddy.**
1863   Philadelphia   30.
MORFORD, Henry   **Red-Tape and Pigeon-Hole Generals. By a Citizen-Soldier.**
1864   New York   35.
MORGAN, James Morris   **Recollections of a Rebel Reefer.**
1917   Boston   75.
1918   London   75.
MORGAN, John Hunt   **The Great Indiana-Ohio Raid.** Wraps
n.d.   Louisville, Kentucky   15.
MORGAN, Julia   **How it Was: Four Years Among the Rebels.**
1892   Nashville   100.
MORGAN, Murray   **Dixie Raider: The Saga of the C.S.S. Shenandoah.**
1948   New York   20.
MORLEY, Christopher (ed)   **The Blue and the Gray or War is Hell.**
1930   Garden City   12.

MORRILL, Lily Logan   **A Builder of the New South.**
1940   Boston   30.
MORROW, Honore   **Great Captain.**
n.d.   New York   10.
MORROW, Honore   **Mary Todd Lincoln.**
1928   New York   10.
MORROW, Josiah   **Life and Speeches of Thomas Corwin.**
1896   Cincinnati   20.
MORROW, Maude E.   **Recollections of the Civil War.** Wraps
1901   Lockland, Ohio   25.
MORSE, John T.   **Abraham Lincoln.** 2 vols.
1893   Boston   20.
MORTON, John Watson   **The Artillery of Nathan Bedford Forrest's Cavalry.**
1909   Nashville   175.
1962   Kennesaw   35.
MORTON, Joseph W., Jr. (ed)   **Sparks from the Campfire, or Tales of the Old Veterans.**
1890   Philadelphia   30.
1899   Philadelphia   30.
MORTON, Oliver T.   **The Southern Empire.**
1892   Boston   20.
MOSES, Belle   **The Gray Knight, The Story of Robert E. Lee.**
1936   New York   15.
MOSS, Lemuel   **Annals of the United States Christian Commission.**
1868   Philadelphia   35.
MOTLEY, John Lathrop   **The Causes of the American Civil War.** Wraps
1861   New York   15.
MOTTELAY, Paul F. and **CAMPBELL-COPELAND,** T. (eds)   **The Soldier in our Civil War.** 2 vols.
1884-1885   New York   100.
MUDD, Nettie (ed)   **The Life of Dr. Samuel A. Mudd.**
1906   New York   150.
1955   Marietta, Georgia   20
MUFFLY, J. W.   **Fort Sumter, A Paper.** Wraps
1897   Des Moines   30.
MULHOLLAND, St. Clair   **A Military Order Congress Medal of Honor Legion of the United States.**
1905   Philadelphia   75.
MULLER, William F.   **War Papers of the Confederacy.** Wraps
1961   Charlottesville, Virginia   15.
MULVIHILL, M. J.   **Vicksburg, Fort St Peter, Fort Snyder.** Wraps.
1931   Vicksburg   10.
MUNDEN, Kenneth W. and **BEERS,** Henry Putney   **Guide to Federal Archives Relating to the Civil War.**
1962   Washington   20.
MUNFORD, George Wythe   **The Jewels of Virginia: A Lecture, etc.** Wraps
1867   Richmond   20.
MUNROE, James P.   **A Life of Francis Amasa Walker.**
1923   New York   15.
1934   New York   15.
MURDOCK, Eugene C.   **One Million Men: The Civil War Draft in the North.**
1971   Madison   20.
MURDOCK, Eugene C.   **Patriotism Limited 1862-1865 The Civil War Draft and the Bounty System.**
1967   n.p.   20.
MURFIN, James V.   **The Gleam of Bayonets.**
1965   New York   30.
1968   New York   20.
MURPHY, James B.   **L.Q.C. Lamar Pragmatic Patriot.**
1973   Baton Rouge   15.

MURRAY, Elizabeth Dunbar   **My Mother Used to Say.**
    1959   Boston   25.
MURRAY, George W.   **A History of George W. Murray and His Long Confinement at Andersonville, Ga.** Wraps
    186?   Hartford   30.
My Cafe Life in Vicksburg.   See: **LOUGHBOROUGH,** Mrs. James
MYERS, Raymond E.   **The Zollie Tree.**
    1964   Louisville, Kentucky   20.
MYERS, Robert Manson (ed)   **The Children of Pride, A True Story of Georgia and the Civil War.**
    1972   New Haven   35.
MYERS, William   **General George Brinton McClellan.**
    1934   New York   25.
NAGEL, Charles   **A Boy's Civil War Story.**
    1934   St. Louis   40.
    1937   Philadelphia   30.
NAGLEE, H. M.   **The Secret History of the Peninsular Campaign Letter of _____ About General McClellan. A Message from Old Soldiers to the Army . . . by the McClellan Legion.** Wraps
    n.d. (circa 1864)   n.p.   25.
NAISAWALD, L. Van Loan   **Grape and Canister.**
    1960   New York   45.
NALTY, Bernard C.   **The US Marines in the Civil War.** Wraps
    1958   Washington   20.
Narrative of Privations and Sufferings of United States Officers and Soldiers While Prisoners of War in the Hands of the Rebel Authorities. Wraps
    1864   Philadelphia   25.
    1864   Boston   25.
    1865   Boston   20.
NASBY, Petroleum (pseud)   See: **LOCKE,** David R.
NASH, Charles Edward   **Biographical Sketches of Gen. Pat Cleburne and General T. C. Hindman.**
    1898   Little Rock   450.
    1977   Dayton   15.
NASH, Howard P.   **A Naval History of the Civil War.**
    1973   New York   20.
NASH, Howard P.   **Stormy Petrel: The Life and Times of General Benjamin F. Butler 1818-1893.**
    1969   Rutherford   20.
NASON, Elias   **The Life and Public Services of Henry Wilson.**
    1876   Boston   15. **NASON,** Elias   **The Life and Times of Charles Sumner.**
    1874   Boston   15.
The National Tribune Scrap Book. Stories of the Camp, March, Battle, Hospital & Prison Told by Comrades. Wraps. 3 Vols.
    n.d.   Washington   75.
The National Tribune Soldier's Handbook, Pensions, Increase. Plus supplement. Wraps
    1898   Washington   15.
National Union Convention, Proceedings Held in Phila, Pa. . . . 1966. Wraps
    1866   Washington   30.
Naval Actions and History 1799-1898, Vol. 12 of MHSM.
    1902   Boston   40.
NEILSON, Eliza Lucy Irion   **Lucy's Journal.**
    1967   Greenwood, Mississippi   30.
NEIMAN, S. E.   **Judah Benjamin.**
    1963   New York   25.
NELSON, Larry E.   **Bullets, Ballots, and Rhetoric, Confederate Policy for the United States Presidential Contest of 1864.**
    1980   University, Alabama   15.50

NEMO, Remarks on the Policy of Recognizing the Independence of Southern States of North America, and the Struggle in that Continent. Wraps
1863 London 35.
NEPVEUX, Ethel S. George Alfred Trenholm and Company that Went to War 1861-1865.
1973 Charleston 25.
NEVILLE, Edmund Rebellion & Witchcraft — A Thanksgiving Sermon. Wraps
1861 Newark, New Jersey 15.
NEVINS, Allan, and **ROBERTSON,** James I., Jr., and **WILEY,** Bell I. (eds)
Civil War Books: A Critical Bibliography. 2 vols.
1967 Baton Rouge 45.
NEVINS, Allan The Emergence of Lincoln. 2 vols.
1950 New York Boxed 20.
NEVINS, Allan (ed) Lincoln and the Gettysburg Address Commemorative Papers.
1964 Urbana, Illinois 10.
NEVINS, Allan Ordeal of the Union. 2 vols.
1947 New York Boxed 25.
NEVINS, Allan The Statesmanship of the Civil War.
1953 New York 20.
NEVINS, Allan The War for the Union. 4 vols.
Vol. 1 — The Improvised War.
Vol. 2 — War Becomes Revolution
Vol. 3 — The Organized War 1863-1864
Vol. 4 — The Organized War to Victory 1864-1865
1959-1971 New York 35.
New Light on Lincoln's Character. Wraps
n.d. n.p. 15.
New Market Day at V.M.I. Wraps
1903 n.p. 25.
The New Reign of Terror in the Slaveholding States for 1859-1860.
1860 New York 35.
New York Times.
Complete run 1861-65 1500.
150. per year
NEWBERRY, J. S. The U. S. Sanitary Commission in the Valley of the Mississippi During the War of the Rebellion.
1871 Cleveland 50.
NEWCOMB, M. A. Four Years of Personal Reminiscences of the War.
1893 Chicago 30.
NEWCOMB, Rexford In the Lincoln Country Journeys to the Lincoln Shrines.
1928 Philadelphia 5.
NEWCOMB, Simon A Critical Examination of our Financial Policy During the Southern Rebellion.
1865 New York 30.
NEWHALL, F. C. How Lee Lost the Use of His Cavalry Before the Battle of Gettysburg. Wraps
1878 Philadelphia 40.
NEWMAN, Ralph G. (ed) Abraham Lincoln, His Story in His Own Words.
1975 New York 10.
NEWMAN, Ralph G. and **LONG,** E. B. The Civil War Digest.
1960 New York 10.
NEWMAN, Ralph G. (ed) Lincoln for the Ages.
1960 New York 10.
1960 New York Ltd. 25.
NEWTON, Joseph Fort Lincoln and Herndon.
1910 Cedar Rapids, Iowa 20.
NEWTON, Virginius The Confederate States Ram Merrimac or Virginia. Wraps
1892 Richmond 20.
1907 Richmond 20.

NEY, James W.   **The Issues Raised by the Rebellion, the Status of the Seceded States . . . Speech.** Wraps
   1866   Washington   20.
NICHOLS, Alice   **Bleeding Kansas.**
   1954   New York   15.
NICHOLS, Edward J.   **Toward Gettysburg.**
   1958   State College, Pennsylvania   30.
NICHOLS, George W.   **The Sanctuary: A Story of the Civil War.**
   1866   New York   25.
NICHOLS, George W.   **The Story of the Great March.**
   1865   New York   35.
   1866   New York   35.
NICHOLS, James L.   **Confederate Engineers.** Wraps
   1957   Tuscaloosa, Alabama   Ltd.   40.
NICHOLS, James L.   **The Confederate Quartermaster in the Trans-Mississippi.**
   1964   Austin, Texas   15.
NICHOLS, Roy F.   **The Disruption of American Democracy.**
   1948   New York   15.
NICKELSON, B. C.   **Brief Sketch of the Life of a Confederate Soldier.** Wraps
   1928   Dallas   30.
NICOLAY, Helen   **Lincoln's Secretary: A Biography of John G. Nicolay.**
   1949   New York   10.
NICOLAY, Helen   **Personal Traits of Abraham Lincoln.**
   1912   New York   10.
NICOLAY, John G. and **HAY,** John   **Abraham Lincoln A History.** 10 vols.
   1890   New York   75.
   1914   New York   50.
NICOLAY, John G.   **The Outbreak of Rebellion.**
   1881   New York   30.
   1901   New York   20.
NIVEN, John   **Gideon Welles, Lincoln's Secretary of the Navy.**
   1973   New York   20.
NIXDORFF, Henry M.   **Life of Whittier's Heroine Barbara Fritchie.**
   1906   Frederick, Maryland   15.
NOBLE, Glenn   **John Brown and the Jim Lane Trail.**
   1977   Nebraska   10.
NOBLE, Hollister   **Woman with a Sword, Biographical Novel of Anna Ella Carroll of Maryland.**
   1948   New York   10.
NOBLIN, Stuart   **Leonidas LaFayette Polk, Agrarian Crusader.**
   1949   Chapel Hill   35.
NOEL, Baptist Wriothesley   **The Rebellion in America.**
   1863   London   50.
NOLL, Arthur Howard   **General Kirby-Smith.**
   1907   Sewanee, Tennessee   Ltd.   225.
The North & South (or) Slavery & Its Contrasts.
   1852   Philadelphia   30.
NORTH, S.N.D. & **NORTH,** Ralph H.   **Simeon North, First Official Pistol Maker of the United States.**
   1913   Concord, New Hampshire   60.
NORTHROP, Henry Davenport   **Life and Deeds of General Sherman.**
   n.d. (circa 1880)   Brooklyn   20.
   1891   Waukesha, Wisconsin   20.
NORTON, Andre   **Ride Proud, Rebel!**
   1961   Cleveland   10.
NORTON, Herman   **Rebel Religion.**
   1961   St. Louis   30.
NORWOOD, Thomas Manson   **A True Vindication of the South.**
   1917   Savannah, Georgia   20.

NOYES, Geo. F.   **The Bivouac & the Battle-Field.**
    1863   New York   25.
    1864   New York   20.
NUNN, W. C.   **Escape from Reconstruction.**
    1956   Fort Worth, Texas   30.
NUNN, W. C. (ed)   **Ten More Texans in Gray — Ford, Green, Johnston, Maxey,**
  McCulloch, Roberts, Ross, Sibley, Terry, Throckmorton.
    1980   Hillsboro, Texas   10.50
NUNN, W. C. (ed)   **Ten Texans in Gray.**
    1968   Hillsboro, Texas   20.
NYE, Wilbur Sturtevant   **Here Comes the Rebels!**
    1965   Baton Rouge   40.
OATES, Stephen B.   **Confederate Cavalry West of the River.**
    1961   Austin, Texas   35.
OATES, Stephen B.   **Our Fiery Trial, Abraham Lincoln, John Brown, and the Civil War**
  Era.
    1979   Amherst, Massachusetts   15.
OATES, Stephen B.   **With Malice Toward None, the Life of Abraham Lincoln.**
    1977   New York   15.
OATES, William C.   **Speech . . . On the Battles of Chickamauga and Chattanooga.**
  Wraps
    1895   Montgomery, Alabama   20.
OATS, Sergeant (pseud)   See: **VAUGHTER,** John B.
OBERHOLTZER, E. P.   **Abraham Lincoln.**
    1904   Philadelphia   7.
OBERHOLTZER, Ellis P.   **Jay Cooke, Financier of the Civil War.** 2 vols.
    1907   Philadelphia   50.
O'BRIEN, John Emmet   **Telegraphing in Battle.**
    1910   Scranton, Pennsylvania   75.
Obsequies of Abraham Lincoln in the City of New York.
    1866   New York   20.
O'CONNOR, Richard   **Hood: Cavalier General.**
    1949   New York   30.
O'CONNOR, Richard   **Sheridan the Inevitable.**
    1953   Indianapolis   30.
    1954   New York   25.
O'CONNOR, Richard   **Thomas: Rock of Chickamauga.**
    1948   New York   30.
O'CONNOR, Mrs. T. P.   **My Beloved South.**
    1914   New York   30.
O'CONNOR, Thomas H.   **Lords of the Loom.**
    1968   New York   15.
OEMLER, Marie Conway   **Johnny Reb.**
    1929   New York   20.
Officers in the Confederate States Navy, 1861-65. Wraps
    1898   Washington   50.
Officers of the Army and Navy (Regular and Volunteer) Who Served in the Civil War.
    1894   Philadelphia   150.
Official Army Register of the Volunteer Force of the U. S. Army for the Years 1861, '62, '63,
  '64, '65. 8 parts. Wraps
    1865   Washington   350.
    Individual parts   40. each
Official Documents of the Post Office Department of the Confederate States of America. 2
vols.
    1979   Holland, Michigan   50.
Official Documents Relating to a "Chaplain's Campaign (Not) with General Butler," but in
  New York. Wraps
    1865   Lowell   15.

Official Records — Atlas.   178 plates in 35 parts
    1891-1895   Washington   700.
       Bound   700.
    1958   New York   1 vol.   125.
    1978   New York   1 vol.   125.
Official Records of the Union and Confederate Armies, War of the Rebellion. 127 vols. & index (See appendix for checklist.)
    1880-1901   Washington   1700.
       Leather Bound Edition   3000.
       Vols. 54 & 55 (Serial Nos. 112 & 113) were never published
    1972   reprint   1500.
Official Records of the Union and Confederate Navies, War of the Rebellion. 30 vols & index.
    1894-1922   Washington   750.
Official Register of the Officers and Cadets of the U. S. Military Academy, West Point, NY.
    Wraps
    1864   New York
    1865   New York   15.
O'FLAHERTY, Daniel   **General Jo Shelby: Undefeated Rebel.**
    1954   Chapel Hill   30.
OGLESBY, T. K.   **The Britannica Answered and the South Vindicated.** Wraps
    1891   Montgomery   25.
Ohio Boys in Dixie: The Adventures of 22 Scouts Sent By Gen. O. M. Mitchell to Destroy a Railroad. Wraps
    1863   New York   35.
OLBRICH, Emil   **The Development of Sentiment on Negro Suffrange to 1860.**
    1912   Wisconsin   20.
The Old Flag and the New Nation or Paul Wyman's Experience . . . Wraps
    1901   n.p.   50.
The Old Flag Camp Ford, Tyler, Smith Co., Texas Feb. 17, Mar. 1, Mar. 13, 1864.
    1864   n.p.   200.
The Old Guard. Wraps
    Monthly periodical   5. per issue
Old Johnie   See: **DINKINS,** James
OLDROYD, Osborn H.   **The Assassination of Abraham Lincoln.**
    1901   Washington   25.
    1907   Washington   20.
    1917   Washington   20.
OLDROYD, Osborn H.   **The Lincoln Memorial: Album-Immortelles.**
    1882   Boston   25.
OLDROYD, Osborn H. (ed)   **The Poets' Lincoln.**
    1915   Washington   15.
OLDROYD, Osborn H.   **The Words of Lincoln.**
    1895   Washington   5.
OLMSTED, Frederick Law   **The Cotton Kingdom.** 2 vols.
    1861   London   250.
OLMSTED, Frederick Law   **Hospital Transports, a Memoir of the Embarkation of the Sick and Wounded from the Peninsula of Virginia in the Summer of 1862.**
    1863   Boston   30.
OLMSTED, Frederick Law   **A Journey in the Seaboard Slave States.**
    1856   New York   60.
    1859   New York   50.
OLSEN, Otto H.   **Carpetbagger's Crusade: The Life of Albion Winegar Tourgee.**
    1965   Baltimore   20.
O'NEILL, Charles   **Wild Train.**
    1956   New York   30.
Operations on the Atlantic Coast 1861-1865, Virginia 1862, 1864, Vicksburg, Vol. IX of MHSM.
    1912   Boston   50.
OPTIC, Oliver (pseud)   See: **ADAMS,** William F.

Ordnance Manual for the Use of Officers of the United States Army.
　1862　Philadelphia　50.
　1958　Bangor, Maine　Wraps　10.
　1976　Dayton　25.
Organization of the Lee Monument Association & the Association of the Army of Northern Virignia. Wraps
　1871　Richmond　15.
ORVIN, Maxwell Clayton　**In South Carolina Waters 1861-1865.**
　1961　Charleston, S. C.　30.
OSBORNE, Arthur D.　**The Capture of Fort Fisher by Maj. Gen. Alfred H. Terry.** Wraps
　1911　New Haven　40.
OSOFSKY, Gilbert (ed)　**Puttin' on Ole Massa, the Slave Narratives of Henry Bibb, William Wells Brown, and Solomon Northup.**
　1969　New York　15.
OSTENDORF, Lloyd　**Mr. Lincoln Came to Dayton.** Wraps
　1959　Dayton　10.
OSTERWEIS, Rollin　**Judah P. Benjamin, Statesman of the Lost Cause.**
　1933　New York　30.
OSTRANDER, Alson B.　**An Army Boy of the Sixties.**
　1926　New York　25.
OULD, Robert　**The Argument of Robert Ould in the "Salt Cases" in the Court of Appeals in Virginia.** Wraps
　n.d.　n.p.　15.
Our Acre and Its Harvest, Historical Sketch of the Soldiers' Aid Society of Northern Ohio.
　1869　Cleveland　25.
Our Confederate Dead, Souvenir, Ladies' Hollywood Memorial Assoc., Richmond, Va. Wraps
　1896　Richmond　20.
Our Living and Our Dead, Vol. 1 through Vol. 4, No. 1, Sept. 1874 — Mar. 1876. (all published). Wraps
　Raleigh, N. C.　500.
　Individual issues　5. each
Our Village in War-Time.
　1864　New York　25.
Our War Songs North and South.
　1887　Cleveland, Ohio　30.
Our Women in the War.
　1885　Charleston, S. C.　45.
OWEN, Narcissa　**Memoirs of _____ 1831-1907.**
　1907　Washington　60.
OWSLEY, Frank Lawrence　**King Cotton Diplomacy: Foreign Relations of the Confederate States.**
　1931　Chicago　35.
　1959　Chicago　20.
OWSLEY, Frank Lawrence　**The South: Old and New Frontiers,** Selected Essays edited by Harriet Chappell Owsley.
　1969　Athens, Georgia　15.
OWSLEY, Frank Lawrence　**State Rights in the Confederacy.**
　1925　Chicago　40.
　1931　Chicago　30.
OWSLEY, Frank Lawrence, Jr.　**The C.S.S. Florida Her Building and Operations.**
　1965　Philadelphia　20.
OXLEY, J. MacDonald　**Baffling the Blockade.**
　1896　London　30.
PADOVER, Saul K.　**Karl Marx on America and the Civil War.** Wraps
　n.d.　New York　30.

PAGE, Charles A.   **Letters of a War Correspondent.**Edited by James R. Gilmore.
    1899   Boston   50.
PAGE, Elwin L.   **Cameron for Lincoln's Cabinet.** Wraps
    1954   Boston   20.
PAGE, Rosewell   **The Iliads of the South.**
    1932   Richmond   20.
PAGE, Rosewell   **Thomas Nelson Page A Memoir of a Virginia Gentleman.**
    1923   New York   30.
    1923   New York   Ltd. Numbered Edition   40.
PAGE, Thomas Nelson   **Among the Camps.**
    1899   New York   15.
PAGE, Thomas Nelson   **The Burial of the Guns and Other Stories.**
    1894   London   25.
PAGE, Thomas Nelson   **Meh Lady, a Story of the War.**
    1909   New York   20.
PAGE, Thomas Nelson   **Red Rock, A Chronicle of Reconstruction.**
    1900   New York   15.
PAGE, Thomas Nelson   **Robert E. Lee, Man and Soldier.**
    1909   London   25.
    1911   New York   20.
PAGE, Thomas Nelson   **Robert E. Lee, The Southerner.**
    1908   New York   20.
    1909   New York   20.
PAGE, Thomas Nelson   **Two Little Confederates.**
    1908   New York   20.
    1909   New York   20.
    1924   New York   15.
PAKULA, Marvin H.   **Centennial Album of the Civil War.**
    1960   New York   35.
PALFREY, Francis W.   **The Antietam and Fredericksburg.**
    1882   New York   20.
    1885   New York   20.
    1893   New York   15.
PALMER, B. M.   **The Present Crisis and Its Issues.** Wraps
    1872   Lexington, Virginia   15.
PALMER, Bruce   **Chancellorsville, Disaster in Victory.**
    1967   New York   15.
PALMER, Bruce   **First Bull Run, the Nation Wakes to War.**
    1965   New York   12.
PALMER, George Thomas   **A Conscientious Turncoat: The Story of John M. Palmer, 1817-1900.**
    1941   New Haven   40.
PALMER, H. R. (ed)   **In Dixie Land, Stories of the Reconstruction Era.**
    1926   New York   20.
PALMER, Loomis T.   **The Life of General U. S. Grant.**
    1885   Chicago   10.
    1885   New Haven   10.
PALUDAN, Phillip Shaw   **Victims, a True Story of the Civil War.**
    1981   Knoxville   12.
Panorama of the Battle of Gettysburg on Exhibition . . . Chicago.
    1884   Chicago   15.
PARIS, Comte de   **The Battle of Gettysburg.**
    1886   Philadelphia   40.
PARIS, Comte de   **History of the Civil War in America.** 4 vols.
    1875-1888   Philadelphia   100.
PARISH, Peter J.   **The American Civil War.**
    1975   New York   15.
PARK, Clyde W.   **Morgan the Unpredictable.**
    1959   n.p.   40.

PARKER, Foxhall A.   **The Battle of Mobile Bay.**
   1878   Boston   100.
PARKER, Joel   **The Character of the Rebellion, and the Conflict of the War.** Wraps
   1862   Cambridge   10.
PARKER, Joel   **Habeas Corpus, and Martial Law   A Review.** Wraps
   1861   Cambridge   20.
PARKER, Joel   **The Right of Secession. A Review of the Message . . .of Jefferson Davis.**
   Wraps
   1861   Cambridge   15.
PARKER, John A.   **What Led to the War or the Secret History of the Kansas-Nebraska**
   Bill. Wraps
   1886   Washington   25.
PARKER, William H.   **Instruction for Naval Light Artillery, Afloat or Ashore.** Wraps
   1861   Annapolis   40.
PARKER, William H.   **Recollections of a Naval Officer, 1861-1865.**
   1883   New York   30.
   1885   New York   30.
PARKS, Joseph H.   **Gen. Edmund Kirby Smith, C.S.A.**
   1954   Baton Rouge   45.
   1962   Baton Rouge   40.
PARKS, Joseph II.   **General Leonidas Polk, C.S.A. The Fighting Bishop.**
   1962   Baton Rouge   50.
PARKS, Joseph H.   **Joseph E. Brown of Georgia.**
   1977   Baton Rouge   35.
PARRISH, Randall   **My Lady of the South   A Story of the Civil War.**
   1909   Chicago   15.
Partial Chronology of the Rebellion, War Department, Adjutant General's Office
   December 1860-65.
   1866   Washington   25.
PARTON, James   **General Butler in New Orleans.**
   1864   Boston   30.
   1864   New York   30.
   1892   Boston   20.
PASHA, Admiral Hobart   See: **HOBART-HAMPDEN,** Augustus Charles
PASQUINO (pseud)   See: **McLAUGHLIN,** James Fairfax
PATCH, Joseph Dorst   **The Battle of Ball's Bluff.** edited by Fitzhugh Turner.
   1958   Leesburg   20.
   1958   Leesburg   Wraps   10.
PATRICK, Marsena Rudolph   **Inside Lincoln's Army, the Diary of** _____ edited by
   David S. Sparks
   1964   New York   20.
PATRICK, Rembert W.   **The Fall of Richmond.**
   1960   Baton Rouge   15.
PATRICK, Rembert W.   **Jefferson Davis and His Cabinet.**
   1944   Baton Rouge   30.
   1961   Baton Rouge   25.
PATRICK, Rembert W.   **The Reconstruction of the Nation.**
   1967   New York   7.
PATRICK, Robert W.   **Knapsack and Rifle.**
   1887   Chicago   15.
The Patriotic Glee Book.
   1863   Chicago   40.
The Patriot's Offering: or the Life Services, Military Career of the Noble Trio, Ellsworth,
   Lyon and Baker.
   1862   New York   15.
PATTEN, George   **Patten's Army Manual.**
   1862   New York   40.
PATTEN, George   **Patten's Infantry Tactics, Bayonet Drill, etc.** Wraps
   1862   New York   60.

PATTERSON, Robert   **A Narrative of the Campaign in the Valley of the Shenandoah in 1861.**
1865   Philadelphia   50.

PATTON, James Welch (ed)   **Minutes of the Proceedings of the Greenville Ladies Association in Aid of Volunteers of the Confederate Army.** Wraps
1937   Durham   15.

PATTON, John S.   **Jefferson, Cabell and the University of Virginia.**
1906   New York   50.

PAXSON, Frederic L.   **The Civil War.**
1911   New York   10.

PAXTON, Elisha Franklin   **Memoir and Memorials Elisha Franklin Paxton** arranged by his son, John G. Paxton.
1905   n.p.   300.
1907   New York   325.

PEABODY, Andrew P.   **Lessons from our Late Rebellion. An Address.** Wraps
1867   Boston   10.

PEARCE, Haywood J.   **Benjamin H. Hill.**
1928   Chicago   25.

PEARL, Cyril   **Rebel Down Under.**
1970   Melbourne   20.

PEARSON, Elizabeth W.   **Letters from Port Royal Written at the Time of the Civil War.**
1906   Boston   35.

PEARSON, Henry Greenleaf   **James S. Wadsworth of Geneseo.**
1913   New York   35.

PECK, Geo. W.   **How Private Geo. W. Peck Put Down the Rebellion.**
1887   Chicago   25.
1900   Chicago   15.

PECK, Taylor   **Round-Shot to Rockets, A History of the Washington Navy Yard and U.S. Naval Gun Factory.**
1949   Annapolis   20.

PECKHAM, James   **Gen. Nathaniel Lyon, and Missouri in 1861.**
1866   New York   30.

PECQUET DU BELLET, Paul   **The Diplomacy of the Confederate Cabinet of Richmond and Its Agents Abroad** edited by Wm. Stanley Hoole. Wraps
1963   Tuscaloosa   Ltd.   20.

PEGRAM, John C.   **Recollections of the U.S. Naval Academy.** Wraps
1891   Providence   Ltd.   20.

PELLETAN, Eugene   **Adresse Au Roi Coton.** Wraps
1863   New York   20.

PEMBER, Phoebe Yates   **A Southern Woman's Story.**
1897   New York   175.
1959   Jackson   edited by Bell I. Wiley   30.

PEMBERTON, John C.   **Pemberton, Defender of Vicksburg.**
1942   Chapel Hill   35.

PENDER, William Dorsey   **The General to His Lady . . . The Civil War Letters of . . . to Fanny Pender** edited by Wm. W. Hassler.
1965   Chapel Hill   30.

PENDLETON, Louis   **Alexander H. Stephens.**
1908   Philadelphia   35.

PENICK, Charles Clifton   **Our Dead: Our Memories: Our Lessons: Our Duties: An Oration.** Wraps
1888   Louisville   15.

The Peninsular Campaign of Gen. McClellan in 1862. Vol. I of MHSM.
1881   Boston   40.

PENNELL, Orrin Henry (comp)   **Religious View of Abraham Lincoln.** Wraps
1899   Alliance, Ohio   20.

PENNYPACKER, Isaac R.   **General Meade.**
1901   New York   35.

PEREYRA, Lillian A.   **James Lusk Alcorn, Persistent WHIG.**
    1966   Baton Rouge   15.
PERKINS, Fred B. (comp)   **The Picture and the Men: Being Biographical Sketches of President Lincoln and His Cabinet.**
    1867   New York   10.
PERKINS, George H.   **Letters of Capt. George H. Perkins, USN 1856-1880** edited by George E. Belknap.
    1886   Concord, New Hampshire   40.
    1908   Concord, New Hampshire   25.
PERKINS, Howard Cecil (ed)   **Northern Editorials on Secession.** 2 vols.
    1942   New York   50.
PERKINS, J. R.   **Trails, Rails, and War.**
    1929   Indianapolis   30.
PERRY, Benjamin Franklin   **Reminiscences of Public Men.**
    1889   Greenville, S. C.   25.
PERRY, Bliss   **Life and Letters of Henry Lee Higginson.**
    1921   Boston   20.
PERRY, Milton F.   **Infernal Machines: The Story of Confederate Submarine and Mine Warfare.**
    1965   Baton Rouge   35.
PERSICO, Joseph E.   **My Enemy, My Brother   Men and Days of Gettysburg.**
    1977   New York   15.
Personal Narratives of the Rebellion   Rhode Island Soldiers and Sailors Historical Society. Wraps
    1st-7th Series 1878-1915   Ltd.   100 numbers   2000.
    See Author, Title Listing for Individual Numbers.
PERSONNE   See: **De FONTAINE,** F. G.
Petersburg, Chancellorsville, Gettysburg, Vol. 5 of MHSM.
    1906   Boston   30.
PETERSEN, Frederick A.   **Military Review of the Campaign in Virginia and Maryland.** Parts 1 & 2. Wraps
    1862-63   New York   125.
    Individually   35. each
PETERSEN, Svend   **The Gettysburg Address, the Story of Two Orations.**
    1963   New York   10.
PETERSON, C. Stewart   **Admiral John A. Dahlgren; Father of U.S. Naval Ordnance.** Wraps
    1945   New York   10.
PETERSON, C. Stewart   **Last Civil War Veteran in Each State.** Wraps
    1951   Baltimore   10.
PETERSON, Cyrus A. and **HANSON,** Joseph M.   **Pilot Knob.**
    1914   New York   100.
    1964   Cape Girardeau   20.
PETERSON, Harold L.   **Notes on Ordnance of the American Civil War.** Wraps
    1959   Washington   20.
PETERSON, Harold L.   **Round Shot and Rammers.**
    1969   Harrisburg, Pennsylvania   20.
PETERSON, Mendel L.   **The Journals of Daniel Noble Johnson 1822-1863 United States Navy.** Wraps
    1959   Washington   10.
PETROFF, Peter   **Ante-Mortem Depositions of Peter Petroff.**
    1895   San Francisco   20.
PETTIT, Ira S.   **The Diary of a Dead Man: Letters and Diary of _____** edited by J. P. Ray.
    1972   n.p.   15.
    1976   n.p.   10.
PEYTON, John Lewis   **The American Crisis; or Pages from the Note-Book of a State Agent During the Civil War.** 2 vols. in 1.
    1867   London   75.

PHELPS, Charles A.   **Life and Public Services of General Ulysses S. Grant.**
 1868   Boston   15.
PHELPS, Mrs. Lincoln (ed)   **Our Country, In Its Relations to the Past, Present and Future.**
 1864   Baltimore   20.
PHILIPPOTEAUX, Paul   **Battle of Gettysburg.** Wraps
 1866   Boston   15.
 1889   Boston   15.
PHILLIPS, Isaac N. (ed)   **Abraham Lincoln By Some Men Who Knew Him.**
 1910   Bloomington   10.
PHILLIPS, S. K.   **Immortelles and Other Memorial Poems.**
 1890   Chattanooga   25.
PHILLIPS, Stanley S.   **Excavated Artifacts from Battlefields and Campsites of the Civil War.**
 1975   n.p.   20.
 1977   n.p.   20.
PHILLIPS, Ulrich B. (ed)   **The Correspondence of Robert Toombs, Alexander H. Stephens and Howell Cobb, AHA Report 1911.**
 1913   Washington   25.
 1970   New York   15.
PHILLIPS, Ulrich B.   **The Course of the South to Secession.** edited by E. Merton Coulter.
 1958   Gloucester, Massachusetts   15.
PHILLIPS, Ulrich B.   **Life and Labor in the Old South.**
 1929   Boston   15.
 1929   New York   15.
 1941   n.p.   15.
PHILLIPS, Ulrich B.   **The Life of Robert Toombs.**
 1913   New York   40.
PHILLIPS, Wendell   **Speeches, Lectures and Letters.**
 1863   Boston   10.
 1880   Boston   10.
 1905   Boston   10.
PHILLIPS, William   **The Conquest of Kansas, Missouri and Her Allies.**
 1856   Boston   25.
PHILPOTT, William Bledsoe   **The Sponsor Souvenir Album and History of the United Confederate Veterans.**
 1895   Houston   125.
PHISTERER, Frederick   **Assoc. of Survivors, Regular Brigade 14th Corps, Army of the Cumberland.**
 1898   Columbus   50.
PHISTERER, Frederick   **Statistical Record.**
 1883   New York   25.
 1885   New York   25.
 1886   New York   25.
 1895   New York   25.
PIATT, Donn   **General George H. Thomas, A Critical Biography.**
 1893   Cincinnati   40.
PIATT, Donn   **Memories of the Men Who Saved the Union.**
 1887   New York   20.
The Picket.
 1862   Philadelphia   20.
The Picket Line and Camp Fire Stories.
 n.d. (circa 1880)   New York   15.
PICKETT, George E.   **The Heart of a Soldier.**
 1913   New York   30.
 A copy that is not signed by Mrs. Pickett is unusual; not rare, just unusual.

PICKETT, George E.   **Soldier of the South, Gen. Pickett's War Letters to His Wife** edited
  by Arthur C. Inman.
  1928   Boston   30.
PICKETT, LaSalle Corbell   **Across My Path: Memories of People I Have Known.**
  1916   New York   20.
PICKETT, LaSalle Corbell   **The Bugles of Gettysburg.**
  1913   Chicago   15.
PICKETT, LaSalle Corbell   **Pickett & His Men.**
  1899   Atlanta   45.
  1900   Atlanta   40.
  1909   Atlanta   40.
  1913   Philadelphia   40.
PICKETT, LaSalle Corbell   **What Happened to Me.**
  1917   New York   30.
PICKETT, Thomas E.   **A Soldier of the Civil War by a Member of the Virginia
  Hist. Society.**
  1900   Cleveland   Ltd.   100.
PICKETT, W.   **The Negro Problem A. Lincoln's Solution.**
  1909   New York   12.
PIERCE, Edward L.   **Memoirs and Letters of Charles Sumner.** 4 vols.
  1893   Boston   50.
PIERCE, Wendell E.   **The Acadia A Blockade Runner 1865.** Wraps
  1973   n.p.   25.
PIKE, Albert   **State or Province? Bond or Free?** Wraps
  1861   Little Rock   100.
PIKE, James S.   **First Blows of the Civil War.**
  1879   New York   50.
**The Pilgrim's Book Containing the Articles of Constitution of the Pilgrims to the Battlefields
  of the Rebellion.**
  1911   Philadelphia   60.
PILLSBURY, Parker   **Acts of the Anti-Slavery Apostles.**
  1883   Concord, New Hampshire   25.
PILSEN, John   **Reply to Emil Schalk's Criticisms of the Campaign in the Mountain
  Department Under Maj-Gen. Fremont.** Wraps
  1863   New York   25.
PINCHON, Edgcumb   **Dan Sickles.**
  1945   Garden City, New York   15.
PINKERTON, Allan   **History and Evidence of the Passage of Abraham Lincoln from
  Harrisburg, Pa. to Washington, D.C. on . . . 1861.**
  1906   New York   30.
PINKERTON, Allan   **The Spy of the Rebellion.**
  1883   Hartford   40.
  1884   Boston   40.
  1885   Cincinnati   40.
  1886   Hartford   40.
  1886   New York   30.
  1888   New York & Philadelphia   30.
PINKOWSKI, Edward   **Pills, Pen & Politics.**
  1974   Wilmington, Delaware   10.
PITMAN, Ben   **The Assassination of President Lincoln and the Trial of the Conspirators.**
  1865   New York   75.
  1954   New York   25.
PITMAN, Benn   **The Trials for Treason at Indianapolis.**
  1865   Cincinnati   100.
  1865   Salem, Indiana   75.
PITTENGER, William   **Capturing a Locomotive.**
  1882   Philadelphia   25.
  1883   Philadelphia   20.
  1885   Washington   20.
  1905   Washington   Wraps   15.

PITTENGER, William   **Daring and Suffering: A History of the Andrews Railroad Raid Into Georgia . . .**
    1863   Philadelphia   25.
    1864   Philadelphia   25.
    1887   New York   Wraps   20.
    1929   Philadelphia   entitled **The Great Locomotive Chase.**   20.
PITTENGER, William   **In Pursuit of the General, A History of the Civil War Railroad Raid.**
    1965   San Marino, California   15.
PITTS, Charles F.   **Chaplains in Gray.**
    1957   Nashville, Tennessee   30.
PIVANY, Eugene   **Hungarians in the American Civil War.** Wraps
    1913   Cleveland   30.
PLAKE, Kate   **The Husband Outwitted by His Wife.**
    1868   Philadelphia   50.
PLOWDEN, John Covert   **The Letters of** _____ edited by Henry B. Rollins. Wraps
    1970   Sumter, S. C.   15.
PLUM, William R.   **The Military Telegraph During the Civil War in the U.S.** 2 vols.
    1882   Chicago   100.
    1974   New York   2 vols. in 1   40.
POAGUE, William Thomas   **Gunner with Stonewall. Reminiscences of** _____ edited by Monroe F. Cockrell.
    1957   Jackson, Tennessee   40.
POE, Clarence   **True Tales of the South at War.**
    1961   Chapel Hill   15.
    1961   Chapel Hill Confederate Descendants Edition   25.
POE, Orlando Metcalf   **Personal Recollections of the Occupation of East Tennessee and the Defense of Knoxville.** Wraps
    1889   Detroit   25.
POINDEXTER, James E.   **Address on the Life and Services of Gen. Lewis A. Armistead.** Wraps
    1909   Richmond   50.
POLE, J. R.   **Abraham Lincoln.**
    1964   London   10.
Political Debates Between Hon. Abraham Lincoln and Hon. Stephen A. Douglas, in the Celebrated Campaign of 1858.
    1860   Columbus   50.
    1908   Springfield, Illinois entitled **The Lincoln-Douglas Debates of 1858** edited by Edwin Erle Sparks   20.
POLK, James K.   **Correspondence of** _____ edited by Herbert Weaver & Paul H. Bergeron. 2 vols.
    1969   Nashville   15. each
POLK, William M.   **Leonidas Polk, Bishop and General.** 2 vols.
    1893   New York   150.
    1894   New York   150.
    1915   New York   60.
POLLARD, Edward A.   **The First Year of the War.**
    1863   New York   30.
    1863   London   30.
    1863   Toronto   40.
    1864   New York   30.
POLLARD, Edward A.   **The Second Year of the War.**
    1864   New York   30.
POLLARD, Edward A.   **The Third Year of the War.**
    1865   New York   30.
POLLARD, Edward A.   **The Last Year of the War.**
    1866   New York   30.

POLLARD, Edward A.   **Lee and His Lieutenants.**
     1867   New York   125.
     1870   New York   entitled **The Early Life, Campaigns, and Public Services of**
       R. E. Lee   75.
     1871   New York   75.
POLLARD, Edward A.   **Letters of the Southern Spy in Washington and Elsewhere.**
Wraps
     1861   Baltimore   100.
POLLARD, Edward A.   **Life of Jefferson Davis, With a Secret History of the Southern**
Confederacy.
     1869   Philadelphia   30.
POLLARD, Edward A.   **The Lost Cause.**
     1866   New York   50.
     1867   New York   40.
POLLARD, Edward A.   **La Cause Perdue, Histoire de la Guerre des Confederes.**
     1867   Nouvelle-Orleans   50.
POLLARD, Edward A.   **The Lost Cause Regained.**
     1868   New York   35.
POLLARD, Edward A.   **Southern History of the War.** 2 vols.
     1866   New York   50.
POLLARD, Henry Robinson   **Memoirs and Sketches of the Life of** _____ **An**
Autobiography.
     1923   Richmond   25.
POLLARD, Josephine   **Our Hero — General U. S. Grant.**
     1885   New York   15.
POND, Cornelia Jones   **Life on a Liberty County Plantation, The Journal of** _____
edited by Josephine Bacon Martin.
     1974   Darien, Georgia   Ltd.   25.
POND, George E.   **The Shenandoah Valley in 1864.**
     1883   New York   20.
     1884   New York   20.
     1885   New York   20.
     1892   New York   15.
POOL, John   **Admission of Georgia, Speech . . .in the Senate . . . April 15, 1870.** Wraps
     1870   Washington   20.
POORE, Ben Perley   **The Life and Public Services of Ambrose E. Burnside.**
     1882   Providence   25.
POORE, Ben Perley and **TIFFANY,** O. H.   **Life of U. S. Grant.**
     1892   New York   15.
POORE, Ben Perley   **Perley's Reminiscences of Sixty Years in the National Metropolis.**
2 vols.
     1886   Philadelphia   30.
POPE, John   **The Campaign in Virginia, of July and August, 1862.** Wraps
     1863   Milwaukee   45.
POPPENHEIM, Mary B. Merchant; **McKINNEY,** Maude; **FARIS,** May M., et al.
The History of the United Daughters of the Confederacy. 2 vols. in 1.
     1938   Richmond   30.
     1956   Raleigh   30.
PORCHER, Francis Peyre   See: **Confederate Imprints.**
PORTER, David D.   **Incidents and Anecdotes of the Civil War.**
     1885   New York   25.
     1886   New York   25.
PORTER, David D.   **Memoir of Commodore David Porter.**
     1875   Albany   40.
PORTER, David D.   **The Naval History of the Civil War.**
     1886   New York   125.
     1890   New York   50.
     1970   Glendale   20.

PORTER, Duval   **Lyrics of the Lost Cause.**
   1914   Danville, Virginia   40.
PORTER, Fitz-John   **Appeal to President of U.S. for Re-Examination of Proceedings of General Court Martial in His Case.** Wraps
   1869   Morristown, New Jersey   40.
PORTER, Fitz-John   **General Fitz John Porter's Statement of the Services of the Fifth Army Corps, in 1862, in North Carolina.** Wraps
   1878   New York   25.
PORTER, Horace   **Campaigning with Grant.**
   1897   New York   20.
   1906   New York   20.
   1907   New York   20.
   1961   Bloomington   25.
PORTER, Mary W.   **The Surgeon in Charge.**
   1949   Concord, New Hampshire   20.
PORTER, William D.   **State Sovereignty and the Doctrine of Coercion . . . Together with a Letter from Hon. J. K. Paulding.**
   n.d. (circa 1860)   Charleston, S. C.   50.
POST, Marie Caroline   **The Life and Memoirs of Comte Regis de Trobriand Major-General in the Army of the United States.**
   1910   New York   50.
POTTER, David M.   **The Impending Crisis 1848-1861.**
   1976   New York   16.
POTTER, David M.   **Lincoln and His Party in the Secession Crisis.**
   1942   New Haven   25.
POTTER, David M.   **The South and the Sectional Conflict.**
   1968   Baton Rouge   15.
POTTS, Frank   **The Death of the Confederacy: The Last Week of the Army of Northern Virginia as Set Forth in a Letter of April 1865.** Wraps
   1928   Richmond   150.
POWELL, Edward   **Nullification and Secession in the United States.**
   1898   New York   30.
POWELL, Lawrence N.   **New Masters   Northern Planters During the Civil War and Reconstruction.**
   1980   New Haven   15.
POWELL, W. H.   **List of Officers of the Army of the U. S. from 1779-1900.**
   1900   New York   40.
   1967   Detroit   25.
POWELL, William H.   **The Fifth Army Corps.**
   1896   New York   Ltd.   90.
POWELL, William H. and **SHIPPEN,** Edward (eds)   **Officers of the Army and Navy (Regular) Who Served in the Civil War.**
   1892   Philadelphia   75.
POWELL, William H. (ed.)   **Officers of the Army and Navy (Volunteer) Who Served in the Civil War.**
   1893   Philadelphia   75.
POWELL, William H.   **Records of Living Officers of the U. S. Army.**
   1890   Philadelphia   40.
POWER, John Hatch   **Anatomy of the Arteries of the Human Body.**
   1863   Philadelphia   200.
POWERS, Elvira J.   **Hospital Pencillings, Being a Diary While in Jefferson Gen. Hospital.**
   1866   Boston   35.
PRATT, Fletcher   **The Civil War.**
   1955   Garden City   10.
PRATT, Fletcher   **Civil War in Pictures.**
   1955   New York   10.
   1957   Garden City, New York   10.

PRATT, Fletcher   **Civil War on Western Waters.**
   1956   New York   20.
PRATT, Fletcher   **Ordeal By Fire.**
   1935   New York   20.
   1948   New York   15.
PRATT, Fletcher   **Stanton — Lincoln's Secretary of War.**
   1953   New York   20.
PRATT, Harry E. (comp)   **Concerning Mr. Lincoln.**
   1944   Springfield   6.
PRATT, Harry E.   **The Personal Finances of Abraham Lincoln.**
   1943   Springfield, Illinois   8.
PRAY, Mrs. R. F.   **Dick Dowling's Battle.**
   1936   San Antonio   20.
PREBLE, George H.   **The Chase of the Rebel Steamer of War Oreto, Commander J. N. Maffit, C.S.N. . . Sept 4 1862.** Wraps
   1862   Cambridge   150.
PREBLE, George H.   **Henry Knox Thatcher Rear Admiral U.S. Navy.** Wraps
   1882   Boston   20.
Presidents, Soldiers, Statesmen. 2 vols.
   1894   New York   60.
PRESTON, Margaret J.   **Beechenbrook.**
   1866   Baltimore   30.
   1867   Baltimore   30.
PRESTON, Margaret J.   **Semi-Centennial Ode for the Virginia Military Institute, Lexington, Virginia 1839-1889.** Wraps
   1889   New York   25.
PRESTON, Randolph   **Lee at Lexington, An Address.** Wraps
   1935   n.p.   5.
   1936   n.p.   5.
PRESTON, Walter C.   **Lee, West Point and Lexington.**
   1934   Yellowsprings, Ohio   35.
PRICE, George F.   **Across the Continent with the Fifth Cavalry.**
   1883   New York   150.
   1959   New York   Ltd.   50.
PRICE, William   **Memorials of Edward Herndon Scott, M.D.** Wraps
   1974   Wytheville, Virginia   10.
PRICE, William H.   **The Civil War Centennial Handbook.** Wraps
   1961   Arlington   5.
PRINGLE, Elizabeth W.   **The Chronicles of Chicora Wood.**
   1922   New York   35.
   1923   New York   35.
   1940   New York   25.
Proceedings at the Dedication of the Monumental Shaft . . . Erected Upon the Field of the Cavalry Engagement . . . Battle of Gettysburg. Wraps
   1885   Philadelphia   20.
Proceedings in Congress on the Occasion of the Reception and Acceptance of the Statue of General Ulysses S. Grant.
   1901   Washington   20.
PROCTER, Ben H.   **Not Without Honor — The Life of John H. Reagan.**
   1962   Austin, Texas   25.
PRUCHA, Francis Paul   **A Guide to the Military Posts of the United States 1789-1895.**
   1964   Madison, Wisconsin   15.
PRYOR, Mrs. Roger A.   **My Day. Reminiscences of a Long Life.**
   1909   New York   25.
   1924   New York   20.
PRYOR, Mrs. Roger A.   **Reminiscences of Peace and War.**
   1904   New York   25.
   1905   New York   25.
   1908   New York   20.

PURDUE, Howell and Elizabeth   **Pat Cleburne. Confederate General A Definitive Biography.**
1973   Hillsboro   40.

PUTNAM, Elizabeth C.   **Memoirs of the War of '61.**
1920   Boston   20.

PUTNAM, G.   **Address Spoken at the Funeral of Brig. Gen. Charles Russell Lowell.**
Wraps   1865   Cambridge, Massachusetts   8.

PUTNAM, George Haven   **Abraham Lincoln, the Great Captain Personal Reminiscences by a Veteran of the Civil War.**
1928   Oxford   12.

PUTNAM, George Haven   **Some Memories of the Civil War.**
1924   New York   25.
1928   New York   20.

PUTNAM, Sallie A.   **Richmond During the War.**
1867   New York   45.
1961   New York   entitled: **In Richmond During the Confederacy**   25.

QUAD, M. (pseud)   See: **LEWIS,** Charles Bertrand

QUAIFE, Milo M. (ed)   **Absalom Grimes: Confederate Mail Runner.**
1926   New Haven   30.

QUARLES, Benjamin   **Lincoln and the Negro.**
1962   New York   15.

QUARLES, Benjamin   **The Negro in the Civil War.**
1953   Boston   15.
1968   New York   10.

RADCLIFFE, George L.   **Governor Thomas H. Hicks of Maryland and the Civil War.**
1901   Baltimore   25.
1965   Baltimore   10.

RAINS, George W.   **History of the Confederate Powder Works.** Wraps
1882   Newburgh, New York   50.

RAMEY, Sanford W.   **Kings of the Battlefield.**
1885   Philadelphia   15.

RAMPP, Larry C., and **RAMPP,** Donald L.   **The Civil War in the Indian Territory.**
1975   Austin   15.

RAMSDELL, Charles W.   **Behind the Lines in the Southern Confederacy** edited by Wendell H. Stephenson.
1944   Baton Rouge   25.
1973   Greenwood   12.

RAMSDELL, Charles W. (ed)   **Laws and Joint Resolutions of the Last Session of the Confederate Congress (Nov. 7, 1964 — March 1865).**
1941   Durham, N. C.   45.

RANCK, James Byrne   **Albert Gallatin Brown — Radical Southern Nationalist.**
1937   New York   20.

RAND, Clayton   **Sons of the South.**
1961   New York   16.

RANDALL, J. G. and **DONALD,** David   **The Civil War and Reconstruction.**
1937   Boston   20.
1953   Boston   15.
1966   Boston   15.

RANDALL, J. G.   **Constitutional Problems Under Lincoln.**
1926   New York   20.
1951   Urbana, Illinois   15.

RANDALL, J. G. and **DONALD,** David   **The Divided Union.**
1961   Boston   15.

RANDALL, J. G.   **Lincoln and the South.**
1946   Baton Rouge   10.

RANDALL, J. G.   **Lincoln — The Liberal Statesman.**
1947   New York   10.

RANDALL, J. G.   **Lincoln the President.** 4 vols.
   1945-55   New York   35.
   1953   New York   1 vol   5.
RANDALL, J. G.   **Living with Lincoln and Other Essays.**
   1949   Decatur, Illinois   10.
RANDALL, J. G.   **Mr. Lincoln.** edited by R. Current.
   1957   New York   8.
RANDALL, Ruth Painter   **Lincoln's Sons.**
   1955   Boston   10.
RANDALL, Ruth Painter   **Mary Lincoln: Biography of a Marriage.**
   1953   Boston   15.
RANDEL, William P.   **The Ku Klux Klan.**
   1965   Philadelphia   15.
RANDOLPH, Hollins N.   **Address Delivered at the Annual Convention UDC,**
   Savannah, Ga., Nov. 19, 1924. Wraps
   1924 (?)   Savannah, Georgia (?)   20.
RANDOLPH, Isham   **Gleanings from a Harvest of Memories.**
   1937   Columbia, Missouri   50.
RANDOLPH, Sarah Nicholas   **Life of Gen. Thomas J. Jackson.**
   1876   Philadelphia   100.
RANKIN, Henry B.   **Personal Recollections of Abraham Lincoln.**
   1916   New York   8.
RANKINS, Walter   **Morgan's Cavalry and the Home Guard at Augusta, Kentucky**
   An Account of the Attack . . . Sept. 27, 1862. Wraps
   1953   Louisville   20.
RAPHAEL, Morris   **The Battle in the Bayou Country.**
   1975   Detroit   15.
Rare Autograph Letters and Manuscripts Collected by the Late Charles M. Wallace of
   Richmond, Virginia to be Sold at Auction Jan. 18, 1911. Wraps
   n.d.   n.p.   25.
Rare Confederate Books and Pamphlets. Wraps
   n.d. (1913?)   n.p.   35.
RATCHFORD, J. W.   **Some Reminiscences of Persons and Incidents of the Civil War.**
   n.d.   Austin   Boxed   40.
RAUM, Green B.   **The Existing Conflict Between Republican Government and Southern**
   Oligarchy.
   1884   Washington   35.
RAVENEL, Henry William   **The Private Journal of _____ 1859-1887** edited by
   Arney Robinson Childs.
   1947   Columbia, S. C.   25.
RAWLEY, James A.   **Race & Politic — "Bleeding Kansas" and the Coming of the Civil**
   War.
   1969   Philadelphia   8.
RAWLEY, James A.   **Turning Points of the Civil War.**
   1966   Lincoln   15.
RAY, Frederick E.   **Alfred R. Waud Civil War Artist.**
   1974   New York   15.
RAYMOND, Henry J.   **History of the Administration of President Lincoln.**
   1864   New York   15.
RAYMOND, Henry J.   **The Life and Public Services of Abraham Lincoln.**
   1865   New York   20.
RAYMOND, Henry J., and **SAVAGE,** John   **The Life of Abraham Lincoln, and of**
   Andrew Johnson.
   n.d.   New York   20.
REA, Ralph R.   **Sterling Price.**
   1959   Little Rock   35.
READ, Opie, and **PIXLEY,** Frank   **The Carpet-Bagger.**
   1899   Chicago   7.

READ, Thomas Buchanan   **Sheridan's Ride A Poem.**
   n.d.   n.p.   5.
READ, Thomas Buchanan.   **A Summer Story.**
   1865   Philadelphia   10.
REAGAN, John H.   **Memoirs, With Special Reference to Secession and the Civil War.**
   1906   New York   150.
   1958   Austin   15.
The Rebellion in Tennessee, Observations on Bishop Otey's Letter to the Hon. William H. Seward by a Native of Virginia. Wraps
   1862   Washington   30.
Rebellion Record: The Battle of Bull Run, or Stone Bridge, Wraps
   1861   New York   20.
The Rebuke of Secession Doctrines by Southern Statesmen. Wraps
   1863   Philadelphia   20.
Recognition of the Southern Confederacy. Wraps
   1863   London   55.
The Record of Hon. C. L. Vallandigham on Abolition, the Union and the Civil War. Wraps
   1863   Columbus, Ohio   20.
A Record of the Dedication of the Statue of Major General William Francis Bartlett: A Tribute of the Commonwealth of Massachusetts May 27, 1904.
   1905   Boston   20.
The Record of the Democratic Party, 1860-1865. Wraps
   n.d. (circa 1870)   n.p.   20.
Red-Tape and Pigeon-Hole Generals.   See: **MORFORD,** Henry
REDDEN, Laura C.   See: **SEARING,** Laura C. R.
REDPATH, James   **Public Life of Capt. John Brown.**
   1860   Boston   20.
REDWAY, G. W.   **Fredericksburg, A Study in War.**
   1906   New York   30.
REDWAY, G. W.   **The War of Secession.**
   1910   London   35.
REDWAY, Maurine Whorton   **Marks of Lee on our Land.**
   1972   San Antonio   15.
REDWAY, Maurine Whorton and **BRACKEN,** Dorothy Kendall   **Marks of Lincoln on Our Land.**
   1957   New York   15.
REDWING, Morris   **Mosby's Trail, or Guerrillas of the Potomac,** War Library, Vol. 3, No. 55. Wraps
   1883   New York   50.
REED, Charles W. and **HARLOW,** Louis K.   **Bits of Camp Life.**
   1886   Munich & New York   35.
REED, D. W.   **The Battle of Shiloh and the Organizations Engaged.**
   1903   Washington   30.
   1920   Washington   25.
REED, Emily   **Life of A. P. Dostie.**
   1868   New York   25.
REED, John C.   **The Brothers' War.**
   1905   Boston   25.
   1906   Boston   20.
REED, Rowena   **Combined Operations in the Civil War.**
   1978   Annapolis   16.95
REED, Samuel R.   **The Vicksburg Campaign.**
   1882   Cincinnati   30.
REED, W. B.   **A Paper Containing a Statement and Vindication of Certain Political Opinions.** Wraps
   1862   Philadelphia   20.
REED, William B.   **A Northern Plea for Peace, An Address.** Wraps
   1863   London   15.
REED, William Howell   **Hospital Life in the Army of the Potomac.**
   1866   Boston   30.

Register of Graduates and Former Cadets of U.S. Military Academy 1802-1965 Civil War Centennial Edition — II.
    1965   n.p.   25.
Register of the Commissioned and Warrant Officers of the Navy of the Confederate States, to January 2, 1863. Wraps
    1863 (?)   n.p.   35.
Register of the Confederate Dead. . . Hollywood Cemetery, Richmond, Virginia. Wraps
    1869   Richmond   45.
Register of the Officers & Cadets of the Virginia Military Institute — Lexington, Va. Wraps
    1857   Richmond   30.
Regulations for the Instruction, Formations & Movements of the Cavalry.
    1865   London   65.
REID, Samuel C., Jr.   See: **Confederate Imprints.**
REID, Whitelaw   **After the War: A Southern Tour.**
    1866   London   100.
    1866   Cincinnati   75.
    1965   New York   Wraps   10.
REINFIELD, Fred   **The Story of Civil War Money.**
    1959   New York   25.
The Rejected Stone.   See: **CONWAY,** Moncure D.
Reminiscences of an Army Surgeon 1860-1863. Wraps
    n.d.   n.p.   75.
REMLAP, L. T. (pseud)   See: **PALMER,** Loomis T.
Report of the Military Services of Gen. David Hunter During the War of the Rebellion. Wraps
    1892   New York   20.
Reports to the Contributors to the Pennsylvania Relief Association for East Tennessee. Wraps
    1864   Philadelphia   25.
Reports of the Extent and Nature of the Materials Available for the Preparation of a Medical and Surgical History of the Rebellion.
    1866   Philadelphia   250.
    See: **Medical and Surgical History . . .**
Representative Men of the South.
    1880   Philadelphia   65.
Republican Imperialism is Not American Liberty. Wraps
    n.d. (circa 1863)   n.p.   30.
The Returned Battle Flags, Presented to the Confederate Veterans at their Reunion, Louisville, Kentucky June 14, 1905. Wraps
    n.d.   n.p   30.
Reunion of Col. Dan McCook's Third Brigade, Second Division, Fourteenth A.C.
    1900   Chicago   75.

Reviews of Jefferson Davis, Constitutionalist; His Letters, Papers and Speeches.
    1924   Jackson, Mississippi   15.
Revised Regulations for the Army of the United States 1861.
    1861   Philadelphia   40.
    1861   New York   40.
    1862   Philadelphia   30.
    1863   Washington   30.
REYNOLDS, Donald E.   **Editors Make War.**
    1970   Nashville   20.
REYNOLDS, E. W.   **The True Story of the Barons of the South.**
    1862   Boston   35.
RHODES, Charles Dudley   **History of the Cavalry of the Army of the Potomac.**
    1900   Kansas City   75.
RHODES, Charles Dudley   **The Lineage of Robert E. Lee: Robert E. Lee, The Westpointer.**
    1932   Richmond   40.

RHODES, James A. and **JAUCHIUS,** Dean   The Trial of Mary Todd Lincoln.
    1959   Indianapolis   10.
RHODES, James Ford   **History of the Civil War.**
    1917   New York   25.
    1919   New York   25.
RHODES, James Ford   **Lectures on the American Civil War Delivered Before the Univ.
of Oxford . . . 1912.**
    1913   London   40.
    1913   New York   25.
RICE, Allen (ed)   **Reminiscences of Abraham Lincoln by Distinguished Men of His Time.**
    1886   New York   15.
    1886   Edinborough   15.
    1888   New York   10.
    1909   New York   10.
RICE, Arnold S.   **The Ku Klux Klan in American Politics.**
    1962   Washington   25.
RICE, Harvey Mitchell   **The Life of Jonathan M. Bennett.**
    1943   Chapel Hill   25.
RICE, Jessie Pearl   **J. L. M. Curry.**
    1949   New York   20.
RICH, Doris   **Fort Morgan and the Battle of Mobile Bay.** Wraps
    1973   n.p.   10.
RICHARD, J. Fraise (comp)   **The Florence Nightingale of the Southern Army
Experiences of Mrs. Ella K. Newsom Confederate Nurse in the Great War.**
    1915   New York   125.
RICHARDS, John T.   **Abraham Lincoln the Lawyer-Statesman.**
    1916   Boston & New York   10.
RICHARDSON, Albert D.   **A Personal History of Ulysses S. Grant.**
    1868   Hartford   15.
RICHARDSON, Albert D.   **The Secret Service, the Field, the Dungeon and the Escape.**
    1865   Hartford   35.
    1866   Hartford   25.
RICHARDSON, Charles   **The Chancellorsville Campaign.**
    1907   New York   125.
RICHARDSON, E. Ramsey   **"Little Aleck."**
    1932   Indianapolis   25.
RICHARDSON, Elmo R. and **FARLEY,** Alan W.   **John Palmer Usher   Lincoln's
Secretary of the Interior.**
    1960   Lawrence, Kansas   15.
RICHARDSON, James D.   **A Compilation of the Messages and Papers of the
Confederacy.** 2 vols.
    1906   Nashville   65.
    1896-99   Washington   75.
    1905   Nashville   65.
    1906   Nashville   65.
Richmond During the War.   See: **PUTNAM,** Sally Brock
RIDDLE, Albert Gallatin   **Recollections of War Times.**
    1895   New York   30.
RIDDLE, Donald W.   **Lincoln Runs for Congress.**
    1948   New Brunswick   7.
RIDLEY, Bromfield L.   **Battles and Sketches of the Army of Tennessee.**
    1906   Mexico, Missouri   125.
RILEY, Franklin L. (ed)   **General Robert E. Lee After Appomattox.**
    1922   New York   30.
    1930   n.p.   25.
RINGOLD, May Spencer   **The Role of the State Legislatures in the Confederacy.**
    1966   Athens, Georgia   20.
RIPLEY, Eliza McHatton   **From Flag to Flag: A Woman's Adventures.**
    1889   New York   50.

RIPLEY, Warren   **Artillery and Ammunition of the Civil War.**
1970   New York   25.
RISTER, Carl Coke   **Robert E. Lee in Texas.**
1946   Norman   25.
RITCHIE, George Thomas   **A List of Lincolniana in the Library of Congress.**
1903   Washington   35.
RITTENHOUSE, Benjamin F.   **Battle of Gettysburg as Seen from Little Round Top.**
Wraps
1887   Washington   40.
RIVES, John C.   **The Congressional Globe.**
1861   Washington   25.
ROARK, James L.   **Masters Without Slaves, Southern Planters in the Civil War and Reconstruction.**
1977   New York   12.95
ROBBINS, E. Y.   **The Soldier's Foe.**
1861   Cincinnati   40.
ROBBINS, Lois Brown   **The South's Finest Hour Essays on the War Between the States.**
1965   New York   10.
Robert E. Lee in Memoriam.
1870   Louisville   20.
Robert E. Lee: Soldier, Patriot, Educator, with Special Reference to His Life and Services at Washington and Lee University, Lexington, Va. Wraps
1921 (?)   n.p.   20.
Robert Edward Lee   Ceremonies at the Unveiling of the Statue of General Lee. Wraps
1932   Richmond   10.
Robert Warren, The Texan Refugee.   See: **DIXON,** Samuel H.
ROBERTS, Allen E.   **House Undivided The Story of Freemasonry & The Civil War.**
1964   New York   20.
ROBERTS, Captain (pseud)   See: **HOBART**-Hampden, Augustus Charles
ROBERTS, Derrell C.   **Joseph E. Brown and the Politics of Reconstruction.**
1973   University, Alabama   10.
ROBERTS, Joseph   **The Hand Book of Artillery for the Service of the U.S. (Army and Militia) with the Manual of Heavy Artillery.**
1861   New York   30.
1863   New York   35.
1865   New York   35.
ROBERTS, Octavia   **Lincoln in Illinois.**
1918   Boston   20.
ROBERTS, W. Adolphe   **Brave Mardi Gras.**
1946   Indianapolis   15.
ROBERTS, W. Adolphe   **Semmes of the "Alabama."**
1938   Indianapolis   40.
ROBERTS, William R.   **The Alabama Claims! England's Last Attempt to Destroy the American Republic.** Wraps
1872   Washington   15.
ROBERTSON, Alexander F.   **Alexander Hugh Holmes Stuart 1807-1891.**
1925   Richmond   30.
ROBERTSON, Archibald Thomas   **Life and Letters of John Albert Broadus.**
1901   Philadelphia   40.
ROBERTSON, Don   **By Antietam Creek.**
1960   Englewood Cliffs, New Jersey   15.
ROBERTSON, George F.   **A Small Boy's Recollection of the Civil War.**
1932   Clover, S. C.   35.
n.d.   n.p.   30.
ROBERTSON, James I., Jr.   **The Civil War.** Wraps
1963   Washington   5.
ROBERTSON, James I, Jr.   **Concise Illustrated History of the Civil War.**
1961   Harrisburg   5.
1971   Harrisburg   5.

ROBERTSON, James I., Jr. and **McMURRY,** Richard M. (eds)   **Rank and File, Civil War Essays in Honor of Bell Irwin Wiley.**
   1976   San Rafael, California   10.
ROBINS, Edward   **William T. Sherman.**
   1905   Philadelphia   15.
ROBINSON, Benjamin   **Delores: A Tale of Disappointment and Distress.**
   1868   New York   80.
ROBINSON, Charles   **The Kansas Conflict.**
   1892   New York   25.
ROBINSON, Mrs. J. Enders (ed)   **The Restoration of the Name of Jefferson Davis to the Cabin John Bridge, Washington, District of Columbia.** Wraps
   1909   New Orleans   10.
ROBINSON, Leigh   **Address Delivered Before R. E. Lee Camp Confederate Veterans. . . Acceptance of Portrait of Gen. William H. Payne.** Wraps
   1909   Richmond   25.
ROBINSON, Leigh   **Joseph E. Johnston, An Address.** Wraps
   1891   Washington   30.
ROBINSON, Leigh   **The South Before and at the Battle of the Wilderness, Address.** Wraps
   1878   Richmond   40.
ROBINSON, Luther Emerson   **Abraham Lincoln as a Man of Letters.**
   1918   Chicago   10.
ROBINSON, William J.   **Civil War Diary of Capt. William J. Robinson.** Wraps
   1975   n.p.   25.
ROBINSON, William M., Jr.   **The Alabama — Kearsarge Battle.** Wraps
   1924   Salem, Massachusetts   35.
ROBINSON, William M., Jr.   **The Confederate Privateers.**
   1928   New Haven, Connecticut   40.
ROBINSON, William M., Jr.   **Justice in Grey A History of the Judicial System of the Confederate States of America.**
   1941   Cambridge, Massachusetts   100.
   1968   New York   25.
ROBINTON, Madeline Russell   **An Introduction to the Papers of the New York Prize Court, 1861-1865.**
   1945   New York   20.
ROBLES, Philip K.   **U. S. Military Medals and Ribbons.**
   1971   Rutland, Vermont   12.
RODENBOUGH, Theo. F. and **HASKIN,** William L.   **The Army of the United States.**
   1896   New York   30.
RODENBOUGH, Theo. F.   **The Bravest 500 of '61.**
   1891   New York   35.
RODENBOUGH, Theo. F.   **From Everglade to Canon with Second Dragoons.**
   1875   New York   250.
RODENBOUGH, Theo. F.   **Photographic History of the Union & Confederate Cavalry.**
   1970   Glendale   25.
RODENBOUGH, Theo. F.   **Uncle Sam's Medal of Honor.**
   1886   New York   20.
RODGERS, Robert L.   **An Historical Sketch of the Georgia Military Institute, Marietta, Georgia.** Wraps
   1956   Atlanta   10.
RODGERS, Robert L.   **"Jeff" Davis and the Pope.** Wraps
   1925   Aurora, Missouri   40.
RODICK, Burleigh Cushing   **Appomattox: The Last Campaign.**
   1965   New York   15.
ROE, E. P.   **The Gray and the Blue.**
   1884   New York   15.
ROE, Mary   **E. P. Roe, Reminiscences of His Life.**
   1899   New York   20.

ROEMER, J.   **Cavalry: Its History, Management & Uses in War.**
   1863   New York   80.
ROGAN, Lafayette   **A Confederate Prisoner at Rock Island. The Diary of Lafayette Rogan.** edited by John H. Hauberg. Wraps
   1941   Springfield, Illinois   20.
ROGERS, A.   **Abraham Lincoln A Biography in Pictures with Text.**
   1939   Boston   15.
ROGERS, Cameron   **Colonel Bob Ingersoll.**
   1927   New York   30.
ROGERS, H. C. B.   **The Confederates and Federals at War.**
   1974   n.p.   12.
ROGERS, Henry Munroe   **Memories of Ninety Years.**
   1928   Boston/New York   25.
ROGERS, J. L.   **The Civil War Battles of Chickamauga and Chattanooga.**
   1942   Chattanooga   5.
ROGERS, J. W.   **Madame Surratt A Drama in Five Acts.**
   n.d.   Washington, D. C.   20.
ROLAND, Charles P.   **Albert Sidney Johnston — Soldier of Three Republics.**
   1964   Austin, Texas   50.
ROLAND, Charles P.   **The Confederacy.**
   1960   Chicago   15.
ROLL, Charles   **Colonel Dick Thompson, The Persistent Whig.**
   1948   Indianapolis   20.
Roll of Honor. Wraps
   1868   Washington   40.
Roll of Survivors of the Mississippi River Ram Fleet and Marine Brigade and Reported Deaths Since Formation of Society in 1887. Wraps
   1899   Belvedere, Illinois   75.
ROLLE, Andrew F.   **The Lost Cause, The Confederate Exodus to Mexico.**
   1965   Norman, Oklahoma   25.
   1966   Norman, Oklahoma   15.
ROLLER, John E.   **Address: Our Heroes, The Leaders of a New Reformation.** Wraps
   n.d. (circa 1907)   n.p.   20.
ROMAN, Alfred   **The Military Operations of General Beauregard.** 2 vols.
   1883   New York   150.
   1884   New York   125.
ROMINE, W. B.   **The Story of Sam Davis.** Wraps
   1928   Pulaski, Tennessee   30.
ROMINE, Mr. and Mrs. W. B.   **A Story of the Original Ku Klux Klan.** Wraps
   1924   Pulaski, Tennessee   35.
ROOD, Hosea Whitford   **Camp Randall Memorial Arch Dedicated in June 18-19, 1912.** Wraps
   n.d.   n.p.   20.
ROPER, Laura Wood   **FLO, A Biography of Frederick Law Olmsted.**
   1974   Baltimore   15.
ROPES, Hannah   **Civil War Nurse, The Diary and Letters of Hannah Ropes** edited by John R. Brumgardt.
   1980   Knoxville   15.
ROPES, John C.   **The Army Under Pope.**
   1881   New York   15.
   1882   n.p.   15.
   1885   New York   15.
ROPES, John C.   **The Story of the Civil War.**
   1894-1913   New York/London   3 vols. in 4   100.
   1933   New York   3 vols. in 4   75.
ROSCOE, Theodore   **Picture History of U.S. Navy.**
   1956   New York   10.
ROSCOE, Theodore   **The Web of Conspiracy.**
   1959   Englewood Cliffs   25.

ROSE, Mrs. S. E. F.   **The Ku Klux Klan.**
    1914   New Orleans   60.
ROSE, Victor M.   **The Life and Services of Gen. Ben McCulloch.**
    1888   Philadelphia   200.
    1958   Austin, Texas   Ltd.   Boxed   30.
ROSE, Willie Lee   **Rehearsal for Reconstruction, the Port Royal Experiment.**
    1964   Indianapolis   20.
ROSECRANS, W. S.   **Report on the Battle of Murfreesboro, Tennessee.**
    1863   Washington   40.
ROSENBERG, W. von (comp)   **Confederate Land Certificates, Legislative, Executive, and Judicial Action.** Wraps
    1969(?)   Austin, Texas   15.
ROSENBERGER, Francis Coleman   **The Cumberland Valley of Pennsylvania in the 1860's.** Wraps
    1963   Gettysburg   8.
ROSKE, Ralph J. and **VAN DOREN,** Charles   **Lincoln's Commando; The Biography of Commander W. B. Cushing.**
    1957   New York   25.
ROSS, Fitzgerald   **Cities and Camps of the Confederate States** edited by Richard Barksdale Harwell.
    1958   Urbana, Illinois   25.
ROSS, George   **Gathered Leaves   A Book of Verse Made from a Physician's Pad Leaflets.**
    1910   New York   25.
ROSS, Ishbel   **Angel of the Battlefield   The Life of Clara Barton.**
    1956   New York   15.
ROSS, Ishbel   **First Lady of the South.**
    1954   New York   20.
    1958   New York   15.
ROSS, Ishbel   **The General's Wife: The Life of Mrs. Ulysses S. Grant.**
    1959   New York   15.
ROSS, Ishbel   **The President's Wife   Mary Todd Lincoln.**
    1973   New York   15.
ROSS, Ishbel   **Proud Kate.**
    1953   New York   15.
ROSS, Ishbel   **Rebel Rose   Life of Rose O'Neal Greenhow.**
    1954   New York   20.
ROSSER, Thomas Lafayette   **The Cavalry, A.N.V. Address . . . at the Seventh Annual Reunion of the Association of the Maryland Line. . . February 22, 1889.** Wraps
    1889   Baltimore   200.
ROTHSCHILD, Alonzo   **Lincoln Master of Men.**
    1906   Boston   8.
ROWAN, Richard Wilmer   **The Story of Secret Service.**
    1937   New York   15.
ROWELL, Adelaide   **On Jordan's Stormy Banks.**
    1948   Indianapolis   10.
ROWLAND, Dunbar   **Jefferson Davis, Constitutionalist,** 10 vols + index
    1923   Jackson, MS   200.
ROWLAND, Dunbar   **Jefferson Davis' Place in History as Revealed in his Letters, Papers and Speeches.** Wraps
    1923   Jackson, Miss.   16.
ROWLAND, Eron   **Varina Howell: Wife of Jefferson Davis.** 2 vols.
    1927-31   New York   50.
ROY, Paul L.   **The Last Reunion of the Blue and Gray.** Wraps
    1950   Gettysburg   10.
ROYALL, William L.   **A Reply to "A Fool's Errand, By One of the Fools."** Wraps
    1880   New York   60.
ROZWENC, Edwin C. (ed.)   **The Causes of the American Civil War.** Wraps
    1961   Boston   5.

RUBY, James S. (ed.)   **Blue and Gray. Georgetown University and the Civil War.**
1961   Washington   10.
RUFFIN, Edmund   **The Diary of** _____ edited by William K. Scarborough. 2 vols.
1972-76   Baton Rouge   60.
RUGGLES, A. G.   **A National System of Finance.** Wraps
1862   Fond Du Lac, WI   20.
RUNYAN, N. P.   **A Quaker Scout.**
1900   New York   20.
RUSH, Benjamin   **Letter on the Rebellion, To a Citizen of Washington, From a Citizen of Philadelphia.** Wraps
1862   Philadelphia   20.
RUSLING, James Fowler   **Men and Things I Saw in the Civil War Days.**
1899   New York   45.
1914   New York   35.
RUSSELL, Don   **One Hundred and Three Fights and Scrimmages, The Story of General Reuben F. Bernard.**
1936   Washington   60.
RUSSELL, L. B.   **Granddad's Autobiography.** Wraps
1930   Comanche, TX   Ltd.   50.
RUSSELL, L. E.   **Abraham Lincoln: A Contribution Toward A Bibliography.** Wraps
1910   Cedar Rapids, Iowa   15.
RUSSELL, Phillips   **The Woman Who Rang the Bell, The Story of Cornelia Phillips Spencer.**
1949   Chapel Hill   20.
RUSSELL, William H.   **The Battle of Bull Run.** Wraps
1861   New York   35.
RUSSELL, William H.   **The Civil War in America.** Wraps
1861   Boston   75.
RUSSELL, William H.   **My Diary North and South,** 2 vols.
1863   New York   75.
1863   London   100.
1863   Boston   75.
1954   New York   ed. by Fletcher Pratt   25.
1954   Boston   25.
RUTHERFORD, Mildred Lewis   **Battles and Leaders. The Surrender and Results.** Wraps
1923   Athens, Georgia   10.
RUTHERFORD, Mildred Lewis   **Contrasted Lives of Jefferson Davis and Abraham Lincoln.** Wraps
1927   Athens, Georgia   10.
RUTHERFORD, Mildred Lewis   **Facts and Figures vs. Myths and Misrepresentations.** Wraps
1921   Athens, Georgia   10.
RUTHERFORD, Mildred Lewis   **Four Addresses.** Wraps
1916 (?)   Birmingham   10.
RUTHERFORD, Mildred Lewis   **Henry Wirz & Andersonville Prison.** Wraps
1921   Athens, Georgia   10.
RUTHERFORD, Mildred Lewis   **Henry Wirz, The True History of Andersonville Prison.** Wraps
1924   Athens, Georgia   10.
RUTHERFORD, Mildred Lewis   **History of the Ladies Memorial Associations: Monuments to the Confederate Soldiers.** Wraps
1924   Athens, Georgia   10.
RUTHERFORD, Mildred Lewis   **Jefferson Davis & Abraham Lincoln 1861-1865.** Wraps
1916   Athens, Georgia   10.
RUTHERFORD, Mildred Lewis   **Secession was Not Rebellion.** Wraps
1923   Athens, Georgia   10.

RUTHERFORD, Mildred Lewis   **The South Must Have Her Rightful Place In History.**
   Wraps
   1923   Athens, Georgia   10.
RUTHERFORD, Mildred Lewis   **The South's Greatest Vindication. Stone Mountain
   Memorial.** Wraps
   1924   Athens, Georgia   10.
RUTHERFORD, Mildred Lewis   **Text Books — The South's Responsibility.** Wraps
   1924   Athens, Georgia   10.
RUTHERFORD, Mildred Lewis   **Truths of History.** Wraps
   n.d.   n.p.   10.
RYAN, Abram J.   **Father Ryan's Poems.**
   1879   Mobile, Alabama   25.
RYAN, Abram J.   **Poems: Patriotic, Religious, Miscellaneous.**
   1880   Baltimore   10.
   1896   New York   10.
   1903   New York   10.
RYAN, Andrew   **News From Fort Craig.**
   1966   Santa Fe   Ltd.   30.
RYWELL, Martin   **Confederate Guns and Their Current Prices.** Wraps
   1952   Harriman, Tennessee   25.
   1958   Harriman, Tennessee   25.
RYWELL, Martin   **The Gun That Shaped American Destiny.**
   1957   Harriman, Tennessee   30.
RYWELL, Martin   **Judah Benjamin, Unsung Rebel Prince.**
   1948   Asheville, NC   30.
RYWELL, Martin   **United States Military Muskets, Rifles, Carbines and Their
   Current Prices.** Wraps
   1959   Harriman, Tennessee   15.
SACKETT, Frances Robertson   **Dick Dowling.**
   1927   Houston   25.
SAGE, William   **The Claybornes: A Romance of the Civil War.**
   1902   Boston   10.
St. Valentine, Planting the Guns on Kennesaw, A Poem. Wraps
   n.d.   n.p.   10.
SALA, George Augustus. **My Diary in America.** 2 vols.
   1865   London   150.
SALTER, William.   **The Life of James W. Grimes, Governor of Iowa.**
   1876   New York   20.
SAMUEL, Bunford   **Secession and Constitutional Liberty.** 2 vols.
   1920   New York   75.
SANBORN, Alvan F.   **Reminiscences of Richard Lathers.**
   1907   New York   Ltd.   40.
SANBORN, F. B. (ed.)   **Life and Letters of John Brown, Liberator of Kansas and
   Martyr of Virginia.**
   1885   Boston   30.
   1891   Boston   25.
SANBORN, Margaret   **Robert E. Lee.** 2 vols.
   1966-67   Philadelphia   30.
SANDBURG, Carl   **Abraham Lincoln. The Prairie Years.** 2 vols.
   1926   New York   30.
SANDBURG, Carl   **Abraham Lincoln: The War Years.** 4 vols.
   1939   New York   40.
SANDBURG, Carl   **Lincoln Collector. The Story of Oliver R. Barrett's Great
   Private Collection.**
   1950   New York   15.
SANDBURG, Carl and **ANGLE,** Paul   **Mary Lincoln. Wife and Widow.**
   1932   New York   15.
SANDBURG, Carl   **Storm Over the Land.**
   1942   New York   15.

SANDERSON, James Monroe   **My Record in Rebeldom.**
    1865   New York   100.
SANDS, Benjamin F.   **From Reefer to Rear-Admiral.**
    1899   New York   30.
SANFORD, George B.   **Fighting Rebels and Redskins, Experiences in Army Life of Colonel _____ 1861-1892.** edited by E. R. Hagemann.
    1969   Norman, Oklahoma   25.
SANGER, Donald Bridgman and **HAY,** Thomas Robson   **James Longstreet: I, Soldier II. Politician, Officeholder and Writer.**
    1952   Baton Rouge   40.
The Sanitary Commission of the United States Army . . . Its Works and Purposes.
    1864   New York   50.
SANTOVENIA, Emeterio S.   **Lincoln in Marti — A Cuban View of Abraham Lincoln.**
    1953   Chapel Hill   6.
SARGENT, F. W.   **England, The United States, and The Southern Confederacy.**
    1864   London   60.
SARMIENTO, F. L.   **Life of Pauline Cushman, The Celebrated Union Spy and Scout.**
    1865   Philadelphia   25.
    1878   Philadelphia   20.
    n.d.   (circa 1890)   New York   20.
SASS, Herbert Ravenel   **Look Back to Glory.**
    1933   Indianapolis   15.
SAVAGE, John   **The Life and Public Services of Andrew Johnson.**
    1866   New York   30.
A Savoury Dish for Loyal Men. Wraps
    1863   Philadelphia   15.
SCALES, Cordella Lewis   **"Dear Darling Loulic" Letters of Cordelia Lewis Scales to Loulie W. Irby During the War Between the States** edited by Martha Neville Lumpkin.
    1955   Boulder   30.
SCHAFF, Morris   **The Battle of the Wilderness.**
    1910   Boston   30.
SCHAFF, Morris.   **Jefferson Davis.**
    1922   Boston   20.
SCHAFF, Morris   **The Spirit of Old West Point.**
    1907   Boston   35.
    1908   Boston   30.
    1912   Boston   20.
SCHAFF, Morris.   **The Sunset of the Confederacy.**
    1912   Boston   25.
SCHALK, Emil   **Campaigns of 1862 & 1863.**
    1862   Philadelphia   35.
    1863   Philadelphia   30.
SCHARF, J. Thomas   **History of the Confederate States Navy.**
    1887   New York   175.
    1977   New York   25.
SCHEIBERT, Justus.   **Seven Months in the Rebel States During the North American War.**
    1874   Berlin (In German)   250.
    1876   Paris (In French)   250.
    1958   Tuscaloosa, Alabama   Ltd.   Wraps   25.
SCHELIHA, Viktor E. K. R. Von   **A Treatise on Coast-Defence.**
    1868   London   250.
    1971   Westport, Connecticut   30.
SCHELL, Herbert S.   **Dakota Territory During the Eighteen Sixties.** Wraps
    1954   Vermillion, SC   10.
SCHENCK, Martin   **Up Came Hill.**
    1958   Harrisburg, Pennsylvania   30.
SCHILDT, John W.   **Drums Along the Antietam.**
    1972   Parsons, West Virginia   20.

SCHILDT, John W.   **Roads from Gettysburg.**
    n.p.   1979   15.
SCHILDT, John W.   **Roads to Gettysburg.**
    Parsons, W. Va.
    1978   25.
    1982   20.
SCHILDT, John W.   **September Echoes — The Maryland Campaign of 1862.** Wraps
    1960   Middletown, Maryland   20.
SCHLEY, Winfield Scott.   **Forty-Five Years Under the Flag.**
    1904   New York   25.
SCHLUETER, Herman   **Lincoln, Labor and Slavery.**
    1913   New York   10.
SCHMITT, William A.   **The Last Days of the Lost Cause.** Wraps
    1949   Clarksdale   20.
SCHMUCKER, Samuel M.   **The History of the Civil War in the United States.**
    1865   Philadelphia   30.
SCHNECK, B. S.   **The Burning of Chambersburg, Pennsylvania.**
    1864   Philadelphia   35.
    1865   Philadelphia   35.
SCHOFIELD, John M.   **Forty-Six Years in the Army.**
    1897   New York   30.
SCHOULER, James   **Eighty Years of Union.**
    1903   New York   15.
SCHUCKERS, J. W.   **The Life and Public Services of Salmon Portland Chase.**
    1874   New York   30.
SCHULTZ, John A.   **One Year at War: The Diary of Private John A. Schultz** edited by
    Hobard Lewis Morris, Jr.
    1968   New York   20.
SCHURZ, Carl   **Abraham Lincoln, and The Gettysburg Address and Other Papers by
    Abraham Lincoln.**
    1891   Cleveland   15.
    1899   Cleveland   10.
SCHURZ, Carl   **The Autobiography of** _____.
    1961   New York   15.
SCHURZ, Carl   **Eulogy on Charles Sumner.** Wraps
    1874   New York   15.
SCHURZ, Carl   **The Reminiscences of** _____. 3 vols.
    1907-09   New York   50.
SCHURZ, Carl   **Speech of** _____. Wraps
    1864   Philadelphia   15.
SCHWAB, John Christopher   **The Confederate States of America.**
    1901   New York   35.
SCOTT, Allan M.   **Chronicles of the Great Rebellion.**
    1864   Cincinnati   25.
    1868   Cincinnati   25.
SCOTT, Eben Greenough   **Reconstruction During the Civil War in the United States
    of America.**
    1895   Boston   25.
SCOTT, Edwin J.   **Random Recollections of a Long Life.**
    1884   Columbia, SC   50.
SCOTT, Florence Johnson   **Old Rough and Ready on the Rio Grande.** Wraps
    1935   San Antonio   20.
SCOTT, H. L.   Military Dictionary.
    1862   New York   30.
    1863   New York   30.
    1956   Harriman, Tennessee   entitled **Civil War Military Dictionary,** edited by
    Martin Rywell   Wraps   6.
SCOTT, John   **The Lost Principle; or the Sectional Equilibrium by "Barbarossa."**
    1860   Richmond   50.

SCOTT, Winfield   **The Infantry Tactics.** 3 vols.
   1861   New York   75.
SCOTT, Winfield   **Memoirs, Written by Himself.** 2 vols.
   1864   New York   40.
SCOVILLE, Samuel, Jr.   **Brave Deeds of Union Soldiers.**
   1915   Philadelphia   10.
SCRIPPS, John L.   **The First Published Life of Abraham Lincoln.**
   1900   Detroit   Ltd.   50.
SCULLY, Everett G.   **The Story of Robert E. Lee.**
   1905   Portland, Maine   15.
SEABURY, Samuel D.   **The Union Volunteer.** Wraps
   1878   Portland, Maine   10.
SEAGER, Robert   **And Tyler Too, A Biography of John & Julia Gardiner Tyler.**
   1963   New York   10.
SEARING, Laura C. R.   **Idyls of Battle and Poems of the Rebellion.**
   1864   New York   10.
SEARS, Louis M.   **John Slidell.**
   1925   Durham, N. C.   50.
SEARS, Stephen (ed)   **The American Heritage Century Collection of Civil War Art.**
   1974   New York   25.
Secession and East Tennessee: A Poem.
   1864   Philadelphia   30.
Secret Correspondence Illustrating the Condition of Affairs in Maryland. Wraps
   1863   Baltimore   150.
SEDGWICK, John   **Correspondence of.** 2 vols.
   1902-1903   New York   Ltd.   125.
SEFTON, James E.   **The United States Army and Reconstruction 1865-1877.**
   1967   Baton Rouge   10.
SEITZ, Don C.   **Braxton Bragg, General of the Confederacy.**
   1924   Columbia, S. C.   100.
   1971   Freeport, New York   20.
SEITZ, Don C.   **The Dreadful Decade.**
   1926   Indianapolis   10.
SEITZ, Don C.   **Lincoln, The Politician.**
   1931   New York   7.
SELBY, John   **Stonewall Jackson as Military Commander.**
   1968   Princeton   25.
   1968   London   25.
SELBY, Julian A.   **Memorabilia and Anecdotal Reminiscences of Columbia, South Carolina.**
   1905   Columbia, S. C.   50.
   1970   n.p.   15.
A Selection from the Addresses, Lectures and Papers, with a Biographical Sketch of Arthur A. Putnam of Uxbridge, Mass.
   1910   Cambridge   20.
Selection of War Lyrics.
   1864   New York   20.
SELFRIDGE, Thomas O., Jr.   **Memoirs of _____**
   1924   New York   30.
SELPH, Fannie Eoline   **The South in American Life and History.**
   1928   Nashivlle   50.
SELPH, Fannie Eoline   **Texas (or) The Broken Link in the Chain of Family Honors.**
   1905   W. Nashville, Tennessee   20.
SEMMES, Raphael   **My Adventures Afloat . . . Cruises and Services in the "Sumter" and "Alabama".**
   1869   London   2 vols. in 1   200.
   1869   Baltimore   entitled: **Memoirs of Service Afloat During the War Between the States.**   100.

1877   Baltimore   entitled : **Service Afloat . . .**   100.
1887   London   100.
n.d.   New York   80.
SEMMES, Raphael   **The Confederate Raider Alabama** edited by Philip Van Doren Stern.
1962   Bloomington   35.
SEMMES, Raphael   **The Cruise of the Alabama and the Sumter.** 2 vols.
1864   London   275.
1864   London   entitled: **The Log of the Alabama and Sumter.**   175.
1864   New York   2 vols. in 1   100.
1864   Paris   2 vols. in 1   75.
SEMMES, Raphael   **Rebel Raider: Being an Account of Semmes Cruise in the C.S.S. Sumter** edited by Harper A. Gosnell.
1948   Chapel Hill   25.
SENOUR, Faunt   **Major General William T. Sherman and His Campaigns.**
1865   Chicago   35.
SENOUR, Faunt   **Morgan and His Captors.**
1864   Cincinnati   40.
1865   Cincinnati   40.
1865   Chicago   40.
SENSING, Thurman   **Champ Ferguson, Confederate Guerrilla.**
1942   Nashville   100.
Sequel to General M'call's Report of the Pennsylvania Reserves in the Peninsula. Wraps
n.d.   n.p.   15.
SEWARD, Frederick W.   **Reminiscences of War-Time Statesman and Diplomat 1830-1915.**
1916   New York   20.
SEWARD, William H.   **The Diplomatic History of the War from the Union, Being the Fifth Volume of the Works of** _____ edited by George F. Baker.
1884   Boston   25.
SEWARD, William H.   **Issues of the Conflict. Terms of Peace, Speech.** Wraps
1864   Washington   10.
SEWARD, William H.   **Speech for the Immediate Admission of Kansas into the Union.** Wraps
1856   Washington   10.
SEYMOUR, Digby   **The Divided Loyalties Fort Sanders and the Civil War in East Tennessee.**
1963   Knoxville   30.
SHAARA, Michael   **The Killer Angels.**
1974   New York   15.
SHACKLETON, Robert   **Strange Stories of the Civil War.**
1907   New York   15.
SHAFFNER, Tal. P.   **The War in America.**
1862   London   150
SHALHOPE, Robert E.   **Sterling Price, Portrait of a Southerner.**
1971   Columbia   20.
SHANKS, William F. G.   **Personal Recollections of Distinguished Generals.**
1866   New York   40.
SHANNON, Fred Albert   **The Organization and Administration of the Union Army 1861-65.** 2 vols.
1928   Cleveland   50.
1965   Gloucester   20.
SHAW, Albert   **Abraham Lincoln A Cartoon History.** 2 vols.
1929   New York   Boxed   40.
SHAW, Arthur Marvin   **William Preston Johnston.**
1943   Baton Rouge   40.
SHAW, Elton Raymond   **The Love Affairs of Washington and Lincoln.**
1923   Berwyn, Illinois   7.

SHAW, Frederick B.   **One Hundred and Forty Years of Service in Peace and War, History of the 2nd Infantry United States Army.**
1930   Detroit   30.
SHAW, James   **Our Last Campaign & Subsequent Service in Texas.** Wraps
1905   Providence   Ltd.   35.
SHEA, George   **Jefferson Davis.** Wraps
1877   London   20.
SHEA, John C.   **The Only True History of Quantrell's Raid Ever Published.** Wraps
1879   Kansas City   250.
SHEA, John Gilmary (ed)   **The Lincoln Memorial: A Record of the Life, Assassination, and Obsequies of the Martyred President.**
1865   New York   15.
SHELLABARGER, Samuel   **Disfranchisement of Rebels, Speech.** Wraps
1866   Washington   15.
SHELLABARGER, Samuel   **Reconstruction, Speech.** Wraps
1866   Washington   10.
SHELLABARGER, Samuel   **Speech, The Relations of the Constitution and of Public Law to Rebellion.** Wraps
1862   Washington   10.
SHELTON, Vaughan   **Mask for Treason: The Lincoln Murder Trial.**
1965   Harrisburg, Pennsylvania   30.
The Shenandoah Campaigns of 1862 and 1864 and The Appomattox Campaign 1865, Vol. 6 of MHSM.
1906   Boston   40.
SHENTON, James P.   **Robert John Walker, A Politician from Jackson to Lincoln.**
1961   New York   15.
SHEPARD, I. F.   **Memorial Day, May 30, 1870, Oration at Jefferson Barracks St. Louis, Missouri.** Wraps
1915   n.p.   10.
SHEPHERD, Henry E.   **Life of Robert Edward Lee.**
1906   New York and Washington   80.
SHEPPARD, Eric William   **The American Civil War 1864-1865.**
n.d. (circa 1938)   Aldershot   100.
SHEPPARD, Eric William   **Bedford Forrest, The Confederacy's Greatest Cavalry-Man.**
1930   New York   125.
SHEPPARD, William Arthur   **Red Shirts Remembered.**
1940   Atlanta   45.
SHEPPARD, William Arthur   **Some Reasons Why Red Shirts Remembered.** Wraps
1940   Greer   20.
SHERIDAN, Philip Henry   **Personal Memoirs.**
1888   New York   2 vols.   40.
1891   1 vol. ed.   20.
1902   New York   2 vols.   35.
SHERIDAN, Philip Henry   **Report of Operations of the Army of the Shenandoah from Aug. 4, 1864 to Feb. 27, 1865.** Wraps
n.d.   n.p.   20.
SHERIDAN, Philip Henry   **Report of Operations of the Cavalry Corps Army of the Potomac from April 6 to August 4, 1864.** Wraps
n.d.   n.p.   20.
Sheridan's Veterans, A Souvenir of Their Two Campaigns in the Shenandoah Valley. Wraps
1883   Boston   40.
SHERMAN, Henry   **The Centennial of the Confederacy, The United States of America, the Situation.**
1875   Washington   15.
SHERMAN, Henry   **Slavery in the United States of America.**
1860   Hartford   25.

SHERMAN, John   **Recollections of Forty Years in the House, Senate and Cabinet.**
2 vols.
    1895   Chicago   50.
    1895   n.p.   50.
SHERMAN, John   **Speech of Hon. _____ on Emancipation as a Compensation
for Military Service Rendered by Slaves.** Wraps
    1864   Washington   25.
SHERMAN, William T.   **From Atlanta to the Sea.**
    1961   London   15.
SHERMAN, William T.   **Home Letters of General Sherman.** edited by M. A.
DeWolfe Howe.
    1909   New York   25.
SHERMAN, William T.   **Marching Through Georgia, William T. Sherman's
Personal Narratives . . .**
    1978   New York   15.
SHERMAN, William T.   **Memoirs of General William T. Sherman by Himself.**
2 vols.
    1875   New York   40.
    1886   New York   35.
    1887   New York   35.
    1891   New York   2 vols. in 1   30.
    1957   Bloomington, Indiana   2 vols. in 1   25.
SHERMAN, William T.   **Official Account of His Great March.** Wraps
    1865   New York   75.
SHERMAN, William T.   **The Sherman Letters**   edited by Rachel Sherman
Thorndike.
    1894   New York   30.
    1969   New York   15.
SHERMAN, William T.   **Story of the Grand March.   Beadle's Dime Series.**
Wraps
    n.d.   New York   25.
SHERMAN, William T.   **"War Is Hell!" William T. Sherman's Personal Narrative
of His March through Georgia** edited by Mills Lane.
    1974   Savannah   25.
SHERRILL, Clarence O.   **The Grant Memorial in Washington.**
    1924   Washington   15.
SHERRILL, Samuel W.   **Heroes in Gray.** Wraps
    1909   Nashville   40.
SHERWIN, Oscar   **Prophet of Liberty — The Life and Times of Wendell Phillips.**
    1958   New York   20.
SHIELDS, S. J.   **A Chevalier of Dixie.**
    1907   New York   35.
SHINGLETON, Royce Gordon   **John Taylor Wood   Sea Ghost of the Confederacy.**
    1979   Athens   20.
SHORT, Dewey   **Address . . . Battle of Wilson's Creek.** Wraps
    1959   Washington   10.
SHOTWELL, Walter Gaston   **The Civil War in America.** 2 vols.
    1923   London   175.
SHOTWELL, Walter Gaston   **Life of Charles Sumner.**
    1910   New York   15.
SHREVE, William P.   **The Story of the Third Army Corps Union.**
    1910   Boston   40.
SHUMATE, Madge Bocock and **MANN,** Anne V.   **Thomas S. Bocock — Only
Speaker of the Confederate Congress.** Wraps
    1940   Richmond   15.
SHURTER, Edwin DuBois   **Oratory of the South.**
    1908   New York   50.
Sickness & Mortality of the Army During the First Year of the War. Wraps
    1863   Washington   25.

SIDEMAN, Belle Becker and **FRIEDMAN,** Lillian (eds) **Europe Looks at the Civil War, An Anthology.**
1960 New York 20.

SIEBERT, Wilbur Henry **The Mysteries of Ohio's Underground Railroads.**
1951 Columbus 20.

SIEVERS, Harry J. **Benjamin Harrison, Hoosier Warrior, 1833-1865.**
1952 Chicago 25.

SIGAUD, Louis A. **Belle Boyd, Confederate Spy.**
1944 Richmond 25.
1945 Richmond 20.

SIGELSCHIFFER, Saul **The American Conscience, The Drama of the Lincoln-Douglas Debates.**
1973 New York 15.

SIGILLOGIA **Being Some Account of the Great or Broad Seal of the Confederate States of America.** Wraps
1873 Washington 20.

SILBER, Irwin (comp) **Songs of the Civil War.**
1960 New York 20.

SILBEY, Joel H. **A Respectable Minority, The Democratic Party in the Civil War Era, 1860-1868.**
1977 New York 10.

SILVER, David M. **Lincoln's Supreme Court.**
1957 Urbana, Illinois 30.

SIMKINS, Francis B., and **PATTON,** James Welch **The Women of the Confederacy.**
1936 Richmond 35.

SIMMONS, Henry E. (comp) **A Concise Encyclopedia of the Civil War.**
1965 New York 15.

SIMMONS, William Joseph **The Klan Unmasked.**
1924 Atlanta, Georgia 35.

SIMMS, Henry H. **A Decade of Sectional Controversy 1851-1861.**
1942 Chapel Hill 20.

SIMMS, Henry H. **Life of Robert M. T. Hunter.**
1935 Richmond 30.

SIMMS, William Gilmore **Sack and Destruction of the City of Columbia, SC** edited by A. S. Salley.
1937 n.p. 30.
1971 Freeport, New York 20.

SIMMS, William Gilmore **War Poetry of the South.**
1867 New York 30.

SIMON, John Y. **The Personal Memoirs of Julia Dent Grant (Mrs. Ulysses S. Grant).**
1975 New York 20.

SIMONHOFF, Harry **Jewish Participants in the Civil War.**
1963 New York 30.

SIMPSON, Edward **A Treatise on Ordnance and Naval Gunnery.**
1862 New York 40.

SIMPSON, Harold B. **Brawling Brass, North and South.** Wraps
1960 Waco Ltd. 15.

SINCLAIR, Arthur **Two Years on the Alabama.**
1895 Boston 100.
1896 Boston 75.

SINCLAIR, Harold **The Cavalryman.**
1958 New York 15.

SINCLAIR Harold **The Horse Soldiers.**
1956 New York 15.

SINCLAIR, Peter **Freedom of Slavery in the United States.** Wraps
n.d. London 40.

SINCLAIR, Upton **Manassas.**
1904 New York 12.

SINGMASTER, Elsie   **A Boy at Gettysburg.**
    1924   Boston   10.
SINGMASTER, Elsie   **Gettysburg. Stories of the Red Harvest and the Aftermath.**
    1913   New York   25.
SKELLY, Daniel A.   **A Boy's Experiences During the Battles of Gettysburg.** Wraps.
    1932   Gettysburg   25.
Sketch of Life and Labors of Miss Catherine S. Lawrence.
    1893   Albany   25.
A Sketch of the Life and Service of General William Ruffin Cox.
    1921   Richmond   50.
SLATTERY, Charles Lewis   **Felix Reville Brunot 1820-1898.**
    1901   New York   15.
SLOAN, Benjamin   **The Merrimac and the Monitor.** Wraps
    1926   Columbia   20.
SLOAN, Edward W.   **Benjamin Franklin Isherwood: Naval Engineer, The Years as Engineer in Chief 1861-69.**
    1965   Annapolis   20.
SLOCUM, Charles E.   **The Life and Services of Major General Henry Warner Slocum.**
    1913   Toledo, Ohio   40.
SLONAKER, John   **The U. S. Army and the Negro.** Wraps
    1971   Carlisle Barracks, Pennsylvania   10.
SMALL, Cassandra Morris   **Letters of 1863.**
    n.d.   Detroit   30.
SMALL, William   **Camp-Fire Talk on the Life and Military Services of Maj. Gen. Judson Kilpatrick.** Wraps
    1887   Washington   75.
SMALLEY, George   **Anglo-American Memoirs.**
    1911   New York   15.
SMEDES, Susan Dabney   **Memorials of a Southern Planter.**
    1887   Baltimore   40.
    1889   London   50.
    1890   New York   entitled: **A Southern Planter.**   25.
    1956   New York   25.
SMITH, A. J.   **The Light of Other Days.** edited by J. P. Watson.
    1878   Dayton   15.
SMITH, Adelaide W.   **Reminiscences of an Army Nurse During the Civil War.**
    1911   New York   40.
SMITH, Arthur D. Howden   **Old Fuss & Feathers.**
    1937   New York   15.
SMITH, C. Carter, Jr. (ed)   **Two Naval Journals: 1864, The Journal of Mr. John C. O'Connell, CSN on the C.S.S. Tennessee, and The Journal of Pvt. Charles Brother, SUMC on the U.S.S. Hartford at the Battle of Mobile Bay.** Wraps
    1964   Chicago   10.
SMITH, Charles H.   **Bill Arp from the Uncivil War to Date 1861-1903.**
    1903   Atlanta   30.
SMITH, Charles H.   **Bill Arp, So Called   A Side Show of the Southern Side of the War.**
    1866   New York   20.
SMITH, Charles W.   **Life and Military Services of Brevet Major Gen. Robert S. Foster.** Wraps
    1915   Indianapolis   15.
SMITH, Daniel E. Huger, et al. (eds)   **Mason Smith Family Letters, 1860-68.**
    1950   Columbia, S. C.   35.
SMITH, Donald   **Chase and Civil War Politics.**
    1931   Columbus   25.
SMITH, E. Delafield   **The Peterhoff, Argument of _____ . . . in the Case of the Prize Steamer Peterhoff, July 10, 1863.** Wraps
    1863   New York   60.

SMITH, Edward C.   **Thomas Jonathan Jackson 1824-1863.**
  1920   Weston, West Virginia   75.
SMITH, Edward Conrad   **The Borderland in the Civil War.**
  1927   New York   25.
SMITH, Edward P.   **Incidents Among Shot and Shell.**
  1868   New York   20.
  1869   Philadelphia   entitled: **Incidents of the United States . . .Christian
Commission.**   30.
  1888   Philadelphia   9.50   20.
SMITH, Ernest A.   **The History of the Confederate Treasury.**
  1901   n.p.   30.
SMITH, Francis H.   **Introductory Address to the Corps of Cadets of the Virginia
Military Institute . . . on the Resumption of Academic Exercises.** Wraps
  1866   Baltimore   25.
SMITH, Frances H.   **Special Report of the Superintendent of the Virginia Military
Institute.** Wraps
  1859   Richmond   60.
SMITH, Francis H.   **The Virginia Military Institute.**
  1912   Lynchburg, Virginia   60.
SMITH, Gene   **High Crimes and Misdemeanors The Impeachment and Trial of
Andrew Johnson.**
  1977   New York   15.
SMITH, George B.   **Official Army List of the Western States for August 1862.**
Wraps
  1862   Chicago   75.
SMITH, George G.   **The Boy in Gray.**
  1894   Macon   35.
  1903   Nashville   25.
SMITH, George G.   **Leaves from a Soldier's Diary.** Wraps
  1906   Putnam, Connecticut   40.
SMITH, George Winston, and **JUDAH,** Charles   **Life in the North During the
Civil War, A Source History.**
  1966   Albuquerque   20.
SMITH, George Winston   **Medicines for the Union Army.** Wraps
  1962   Madison, Wisconsin   10.
SMITH, Goldwin   **The Civil War in America.**
  1866   London   30.
SMITH, Goldwin   **A Letter to a Whig Member of the Southern Independence
Association.** Wraps
  1864   Boston   25.
SMITH, Gustavus W.   **The Battle of Seven Pines.**
  1891   New York   Wraps   100.
  1974   Dayton, Ohio   15.
SMITH, Gustavus W.   **Confederate War Papers.**
  1884   New York   50.
SMITH, Gustavus W.   **Generals J. E. Johnston and G. T. Beauregard at the Battle
of Manassas.** Wraps
  1892   New York   40.
SMITH, H.   **Lincoln and the Lincolns.**
  1931   New York   15.
SMITH, H. Allen   **The Rebel Yell.**
  1954   Garden City, New York   10.
SMITH, H. H.   **J.E.B. Stuart, A Character Sketch.** Wraps
  n.d. (circa 1933)   Ashland, Virginia   20.
SMITH, H. H.   **Robert E. Lee — A Character Sketch.** Wraps
  n.d. (circa 1900)   n.p.   20.
SMITH, H. H.   **Stonewall Jackson — A Character Sketch.** Wraps
  n.d. (circa 1920)   Blackstone, Virginia   25.

SMITH, H. K., Jr.   **Some Encounters with General Forrest.** Wraps
   n.d. (circa 1956)   n.p.   15.
SMITH, James Power   **The Religious Character of Stonewall Jackson: An Address.**
   Wraps
   n.d.   Lexington, Virginia   15.
SMITH, Joseph A.   **An Address Delivered Before the Union League of Philadel-**
   phia. Wraps
   1906   Philadelphia   25.
SMITH, Myron J., Jr.   **American Civil War Navies: A Bibliography.**
   1972   Metuchen   20.
SMITH, Mrs. S. E. D.   **The Soldier's Friend.**
   1867   Memphis, Tennessee   75.
SMITH, Tunstall   **James McHenry Howard A Memoir.**
   1915   Baltimore   175.
SMITH, W.   **A Political History of Slavery.** 2 vols.
   1903   New York   50.
SMITH, William Ernest   **The Francis Preston Blair Family in Politics.** 2 vols.
   1969   New York   60.
SMITH, William F.   **From Chattanooga to Petersburg.**
   1893   Boston   30.
SMYTHE, Augustine T., Jr.   **Torpedo and Submarine Attacks on the Federal**
   Blockading Fleet off Charleston During the War of Secession. Wraps
   1907   Virginia   25.
SNEAD, Thomas L.   **The Fight for Missouri.**
   1886   New York   30.
SNIDER, Denton   **The American Ten Years War 1855-1865.**
   1906   St. Louis   20.
SNIDER, Denton   **Lincoln and Ann Rutledge.**
   1912   St. Louis   10.
SNOW, William P.   **Southern Generals.**
   1865   New York   50.
   1866   New York   50.
   1867   New York   entitled: **Lee and His Generals.**   50.
SNOWDEN, Yates   **Confederate Books.**
   1903   Charleston   60.
SNOWDEN, Yates   **Marching with Sherman.** Wraps
   1929   Columbia, S. C.   35.
SNOWDEN, Yates   **War-Time Publications (1861-1865) from the Press of Walker,**
   Evans & Cogswell Co., Charleston, SC.   Wraps
   1922   Charleston   50.
SNYDER, Anne E.   **The Civil War from a Southern Stand-Point.**
   1893   Nashville   35.
SNYDER, Anne E.   **A Narrative of the Civil War.**
   1899   Nashville   30.
SOBIESKI, John   **Life Story and Personal Reminiscences of Col. John Sobieski.**
   1900   Shelbyville, Illinois   50.
   n.d.   Los Angeles   50.
SOBOL, Donald J.   **Two Flags Flying.**
   1960   New York   25.
Society of the Army of the Cumberland, Reunions.
   v.d.   v.p.   15. each
Society of the Army of the Potomac, Annual Reunions.
   v.d.   v.p.   10. each
Society of the Army of the Tennessee, Reunions.
   v.d.   v.p.   20. each
Society of the Army of West Virginia, Proceedings of Meetings.
   v.d.   v.p.   30. each
SOKOLOFF, Alice Hunt   **Kate Chase for the Defense.**
   1971   New York   12.

Soldier's Aid Society of Northern Ohio, Annual Reports.
v.d.   v.p.   15. each
The Soldier's Casket. Vol. 1 (all pub) Jan-Dec 1865.
1865   Philadelphia   125.
Soldier's Hymns and Psalms.
n.s. (circa 1862)   New York   35.
Soldiers' National Cemetery (Gettysburg), Report of.
1864   Harrisburg   20.
Soldiers' National Cemetery (Gettysburg), Revised Report.
1867   Harrisburg   25.
The Soldier's Pocket Manual of Devotions.
1861   Philadelphia   30.
SOLEY, James R.   **Admiral Porter.**
1903   New York   30.
SOLEY, James R.   **The Blockade and the Cruisers.**
1883   New York   25.
1890   New York   25.
SOLEY, James R.   **The Sailor Boys of '61.**
1888   Boston   20.
SOLOMON, Eric (ed)   **Faded Banners.**
1960   New York   25.
SOMMERS, Richard J.   **Richmond Redeemed, The Siege at Petersburg.**
1981   Garden City   20.
SORRELL, G. Moxley   **Recollections of a Confederate Staff Officer.**
1905   New York   150.
1917   New York   75.
1958   Jackson, Tennessee   edited by Bell I. Wiley   35.
SOSEY, Frank H.   **Robert Devoy: A Tale of the Palmyra Massacre.**
1903   Palmyra, Missouri   50.
SOUDER, Mrs. Edmund A.   **Leaves from the Battlefield of Gettysburg.**
1864   Philadelphia   35.
"Southern Battlefields" A List of Battlefields on and Near the Lines of the Nashville, Chattanooga and St. Louis Railway and Western & Atlantic Railroad. Wraps
n.d. (circa 1890)   Atlanta   25.
Southern Bivouac, A Monthly Literary and Historical Magazine.
10. per issue
Southern Famine Relief Fund of Philadelphia. Wraps
1867   Philadelphia   20.
Southern Historical Society Papers. Vols. 1-52. Wraps
1876-1959   Bound w/wraps bound in   1200.
1977   reprint   bound   1000.
Individual issues 10.-20. depending on content
Southern Historical Society, Proceedings of the 2nd Annual Meeting Held in Richmond. Wraps
1874   Richmond   25.
Southern History of the War. Official Reports of Battles. See: Confederate Imprints.
SOUTHWOOD, Marion   **"Beauty and Booty" The Watchword of New Orleans.**
1867   New York   35.
Souvenir Memorial   Col. James C. Carmichael   157th Regiment   N.Y.S.V.
n.d.   n.p.   35.
Souvenir Views of Gettysburg, Pa. Wraps
n.d. (circa 1900)   Gettysburg, Pennsylvania (?)   15.
SPAULDING, E. G.   **History of the Legal Tender Paper Money Issued During the Great Rebellion.**
1869   Buffalo   45.
SPEAR, William E.   **The North and South at Antietam and Gettysburg.**
1908   Boston   25.
SPEARS, Zarel C. and **BARTON,** Robert S.   **Berry and Lincoln Frontier Merchants.**
1947   New York   10.

SPEED, James   **James Speed a Personality.**
  1914   Louisville   30.
  n.d.   n.p.   20.
SPEED, James   **Opinion on the Constitutional Power of the Military to Try and Execute the Assassins of the President.** Wraps
  1865   Washington   30.
SPEER, Emory   **Lincoln, Lee, Grant and Other Biographical Addresses.**
  1909   New York   50.
SPEER, John   **Life of Gen. James H. Lane.**
  1896   Garden City   40.
SPENCE, James   **The American Union.**
  1861   London   45.
  1862   London   35.
SPENCER, Ambrose   **A Narrative of Andersonville.**
  1866   New York   40.
SPENCER, Bella Z.   **Tried and True.**
  1868   Springfield   20.
SPENCER, Cornelia Phillips   **The Last Ninety Days of the War in North Carolina.**
  1866   New York   100.
SPICER, William A.   **The Flag Replaced on Sumter.** Wraps
  1885   Providence   25.
SPRAGUE, Dean   **Freedom Under Lincoln.**
  1965   Boston   7.
SPRAGUE, J. T.   **The Treachery in Texas. The Secession of Texas.** Wraps
  1862   New York   40.
SPRING, Leverett W.   **Kansas: The Prelude to the War for the Union.**
  1885   Boston   30.
SPRUILL, F. S.   **A Sketch of the Life and Service of General William R. Cox.**
  1921   Richmond   50.
SPRUNT, James   **Chronicles of the Cape Fear River 1660-1916.**
  1914   Raleigh   175.
  1916   Raleigh   225.
SPRUNT, James   **Derelicts, An Account of Ships Lost at Sea . . . and a Brief History of Blockade Runners Stranded Along the North Carolina Coast 1861-1865.**
  1920   Wilmington, N. C.   250.
SPRUNT, James   **Tales and Traditions of the Lower Cape Fear 1661-1896.** Wraps
  1896   Wilmington, N. C.   100.
  1960   Wilmington, N. C.   Ltd.   45.
SQUIRER, Ephraim   See: **Leslie,** Frank
STACKPOLE, Edward J.   **Chancellorsville.**
  1958   Harrisburg   25.
STACKPOLE, Edward J.   **Drama on the Rappahannock, The Fredericksburg Campaign.**
  1957   Harrisburg   25.
STACKPOLE, Edward J.   **From Cedar Mountain to Antietam.**
  1959   Harrisburg, Pennysylvania   25.
STACKPOLE, Edward J.   **Sheridan in the Shenandoah.**
  1961   Harrisburg   25.
STACKPOLE, Edward J.   **They Met at Gettysburg.**
  1956   Harrisburg   25.
STAFFORD, Frederick H.   **Medals of Honor Awarded for Distinguished Service During the War of the Rebellion.** Wraps
  1886   Washington   20.
STAMPP, Kenneth M.   **And the War Came The North and the Secession Crisis 1860-1861.**
  1950   Baton Rouge   20.
  1967   Baton Rouge   20.

STAMPP, Kenneth M.　**The Era of Reconstruction 1865-1877.**
1965　New York　20.
STAMPP, Kenneth M.　**The Peculiar Institution Slavery in the Anti-Bellum South.**
1956　New York　20.
STAMPP, Kenneth M.　**The Southern Road to Appomattox.** Wraps
1969　El Paso, Texas　10.
STANARD, Beverly　**Letters of a New Market Cadet** edited by John G. Barrett
and Robert K. Turner, Jr.
1961　Chapel Hill, N. C.　20.
STANARD, Mary Newton　**John Brockenbrough Newton.** Wraps
1924　Richmond　40.
STANARD, Mary Newton　**Richmond, Its People and Its Story.**
1923　Philadelphia　30.
STANLEY, F.　**E. V. Sumner Major General U. S. Army.**
1969　n.p.　20.
STANTON, Henry T.　**Poems of the Confederacy.**
1900　Louisville, Kentucky　30.
STANTON, R. L.　**The Church and the Rebellion.**
1864　New York　50.
STARK, Richard B. and Janet C.　**Surgical Care of the Confederate States Army.**
Wraps
1958　n.p.　15.
STARR, Darius　**From Spotsylvania Courthouse to Andersonville: A Diary of ____**
edited by E. Merton Coulter. Wraps
1957　Savannah, Georgia　10.
STARR, John W., Jr.　**Lincoln and the Railroads.**
1927　New York　25.
STARR, Thomas I. (ed)　**Lincoln's Kalamazoo Address Against Extending Slavery.**
1941　Detroit　Ltd.　15.
STARR, Louis M.　**Bohemian Brigade, Civil War Newsmen in Action.**
1954　New York　25.
STARR, Stephen Z.　**Colonel Grenfell's Wars — The Life of a Soldier of For-**
tune.
1971　Baton Rouge　20.
STARR, Stephen Z.　**The Union Cavalry in the Civil War.** 2 vols.
1979-81　Baton Rouge　60.
A Statement of the Case of Brigadier Gen. Joseph W. Revere. Wraps
1863　New York　35.
A Statement of the Causes Which Led to the Dismissal of Surgeon-General William
A. Hammond from the Army. Wraps
n.d. (circa 1870)　n.p.　40.
Statistical Pocket Manual of the Army, Navy and Census of the United States of
America.
1862　Boston　20.
STATON, Kate E. (comp)　**Old Southern Songs of the Period of the Confederacy;**
the Dixie Trophy Collection: Tarboro, N. C. Wraps
1926　New York　75.
STAUDENRAUS, P. J.　**Mr. Lincoln's Washington.**
1967　S. Brunswick　10.
STAUDENRAUS, P. J. (ed)　**The Secession Crisis, 1860-1861.** Wraps
1963　Chicago　10.
STEARNS, Charles　**The Black Man of the South and the Rebels.**
1872　New York　50.
STEARNS, Frank Preston　**The Life and Public Services of George Luther Stearns.**
1907　Philadelphia　15.
STEDMAN, Charles Ellery　**The Civil War Sketchbook of _____, Surgeon U.S.**
Navy.
1976　San Rafael, California　25.

STEEL, Edward M., Jr.	**T. Butler King of Georgia.**
	1964	Athens, Georgia	15.
STEEL, S. A.	**Explaining of Objection to "Rebel".** Wraps
	1913	Richmnond	20.
STEEL, S. A.	**The Sunny Road: Home Life in Dixie During the War.** Wraps
	n.d.	n.p.	60.
STEELE, Matthew Forney	**American Campaigns.** 2 vols.
	1909	Washington	50.
	1935	Washington	50.
	1951	Washington	50.
STEELE, Matthew Forney	**Atlas to Accompany Steele's American Campaigns.**
	edited by V. J. Esposito.
	1945	n.p.	30.
	1953	West Point	50.
STEERE, Edward	**The Wilderness Campaign.**
	1960	Harrisburg, Pennsylvania	25.
STEINER, Paul E.	**Disease in the Civil War: Natural Biological Warfare.**
	1968	Springfield	40.
STEINER, Paul E.	**Medical-Military Portraits of Union and Confederate Generals.**
	1968	Philadelphia	40.
STEINER, Paul E.	**Physician-Generals in the Civil War.**
	1966	Springfield	45.
STEINMETZ, Lee (ed)	**The Poetry of the American Civil War.**
	1960	East Lansing	12.
STEPHENS, Alexander H.	**A Constitutional View of the Late War Between the States.**
	1868-70	Philadelphia	2 vols.	75.
	1868	Philadelphia	2 vols. in 1	50.
STEPHENS, Alexander H.	**A Letter for Posterity: Alex Stephens to His Brother Linton June 3, 1864.** Wraps
	1954	Atlanta	6.
STEPHENS, Alexander H.	**Recollections of Alexander H. Stephens.** edited by Myrta Lockett Avary.
	1910	New York	30.
STEPHENS, Alexander H.	**The Reviewers Reviewed. A Supplement to the War Between the States.**
	1872	New York	50.
STEPHENSON, Mary Harriet	**Dr. B. F. Stephenson — Founder of the Grand Army of the Republic.**
	1894	Springfield	20.
STEPHENSON, N. W.	**The Question of Arming the Slaves.** Wraps
	1913	n.p.	15.
STEPHENSON, Nathaniel W.	**Abraham Lincoln and the Union.**
	1918	New Haven	15.
STEPHENSON, Nathaniel W.	**The Day of the Confederacy.**
	1919	New Haven	15.
STEPHENSON, Nathaniel W.	**Lincoln.**
	1922	Indianapolis	10.
	1924	Indianapolis	10.
STEPHENSON, Richard W.	**Civil War Maps An Annotated List of Maps & Atlases in Map Collections of the Library of Congress.** Wraps
	1961	Washington	10.
STEPHENSON, Wendell Holmes	**The Political Career of General James H. Lane. Contained in Kansas State Hist. Society Pubs. Vol. III, 1930.**
	1930	Topeka, Kansas	20.
STEPHENSON, Wendell Holmes	**The South Lives in History.**
	1955	Baton Rouge	20.
STEPP, John W. and **HILL,** I. William (comps & eds)	**Mirror of War.**
	1961	Englewood Cliffs, New Jersey	15.

STERLING, Ada   See: CLAY-CLOPTON, Virginia
STERN, Philip Van Doren (ed)   The Civil War Christmas Album.
   1961   New York   25.
STERN, Philip Van Doren   The Confederate Navy: A Pictorial History.
   1962   New York   30.
STERN, Philip Van Doren   An End to Valor.
   1958   Boston   25.
STERN, Philip Van Doren   The Man Who Killed Lincoln.
   1939   New York   20.
STERN, Philip Van Doren   Prologue to Sumter.
   1961   Bloomington, Indiana   15.
STERN, Philip Van Doren   Robert E. Lee, The Man and the Soldier.
   1963   New York   10.
STERN, Philip Van Doren   Secret Missions of the Civil War.
   1959   Chicago   20.
STERN, Philip Van Doren   Soldier Life in the Union and Confederate Armies.
   1961   Bloomington, Indiana   25.
   1961   New York   25.
STERN, Philip Van Doren   They Were There, The Civil War in Action as Seen by Its Combat Artists.
   1959   New York   30.
STERN, Philip Van Doren   When the Guns Roared — World Aspects of the American Civil War.
   1965   New York   15.
STEVENS, C. A.   Berdan's United States Sharpshooters in the Army of the Potomac.
   1892   St. Paul, Minnesota   150.
   1972   Dayton   25.
STEVENS, Hazard,   The Life of Isaac Ingalls Stevens. 2 vols.
   1900   Boston   40.
STEVENS, Hazard   The Storming of the Lines of Petersburg by the Sixth Corps, April 2, 1865. Wraps
   1904   Providence   Ltd.   25.
STEVENS, John Austin   Union Defense Committee of City of New York.
   1885   New York   20.
STEVENSON, R. Randolph   The Southern Side: or, Andersonville Prison.
   1876   Baltimore   80.
STEVENSON, William G.   Thirteen Months in the Rebel Army . . . By An Impressed New Yorker.
   1862   London   50.
   1862   New York   40.
   1863   New York   40.
STEWART, George R.   Pickett's Charge.
   1959   Boston   30.
STEWART, Lucy Shelton   The Reward of Patriotism.
   1930   New York   40.
STEWART, William H.   The Spirit of the South.
   1908   New York and Washington   65.
STICKLES, Arndt M.   Simon Bolivar Buckner Borderland Knight.
   1940   Chapel Hill   75.
STIDGER, Felix G. (ed)   Treason History of the Order of Sons of Liberty.
   1903   Chicago   100.
STILL, William   Still's Underground Rail Road Records with a Life of the Author.
   1886   Philadelphia   50.
STILL, William N., Jr.   Confederate Shipbuilding. Wraps
   1969   Athens, Georgia   10.
STILL, William N., Jr.   Iron Afloat.
   1971   Nashville   20.

STILLE, Charles J.   **How a Free People Conduct a Long War.** Wraps
    1862   Philadelphia   25.
STILLE, Charles J.   **Northern Interests and Southern Independence: A Plea for United Action.** Wraps
    1863   Philadelphia   30.
STILLWELL, Lucille   **Born to be a Statesman, John Cabell Breckenridge.**
    1936   Caldwell, Idaho   30.
STIMMEL, Smith   **Personal Reminiscences of Abraham Lincoln.**
    1928   Minneapolis   Ltd.   30.
STINE, J. H.   **History of the Army of the Potomac.**
    1892   Philadelphia   50.
    1893   Washington   45.
STOCKARD, Henry Jerome   **A Study in Southern Poetry.**
    1911   New York/Washington   40.
STODDARD, William O.   **Abraham Lincoln: The True Story of a Great Life.**
    1885   New York   30.
STODDARD, William O.   **Inside the White House in War Times.**
    1890   New York   15.
STODDARD, William O., Jr. (ed)   **Lincoln's Third Secretary . . . The Memoirs of William O. Stoddard.**
    1955   New York   15.
STONE, Irving   **Love Is Eternal A Novel About Mary Todd and Abraham Lincoln.**
    1954   New York   7.
STONE, Kate   **Brokenburn, The Journal of _____** edited by John Q. Anderson.
    1955   Baton Rouge   25.
    1956   Baton Rouge   25.
    1972   Baton Rouge   20.
STONE, William A.   **The Tale of a Plain Man.**
    n.d.   n.p.   40.
STONEBRAKER, J. Clarence   **The Unwritten South.**
    1903   Hagerstown   30.
    1908   n.p.   25.
STOREY, Moorfield   **Charles Sumner.**
    1900   Boston   10.
Stories of the Civil War. Wraps
    1965   Falls Church   10.
STORMONT, John W.   **The Economics of Secession and Coercion 1861.**
    1957   Victoria, Texas   20.
STORRICK, W. C.   **The Battle of Gettysburg.** Wraps
    1938   Harrisburg, Pennsylvania   10.
    1959   Harrisburg   5.
STORRICK, W. C.   **Gettysburg.**
    1932   Harrisburg   20.
The Story of the Confederate States' Ship "Virginia (Once Merrimac) Her Victory Over the Monitor. Wraps
    1879   Baltimore   25.
The Story of the "General". Wraps
    n.d. (circa 1900)   Nashville, Tennessee   15.
    n.d.   n.p.   10.
STOUT, L. H.   **Reminiscences of General Braxton Bragg.** Wraps
    1942   Hattiesburg, Mississippi   Ltd.   50.
STOVALL, Pleasant A.   **Robert Toombs.**
    1892   New York   50.
STOWE, Harriet Beecher   **Autographs for Freedom.**
    1853   Boston   25.
STOWE, Harriet Beecher   **Men of Our Times.**
    1868   Hartford   25.

STOWE, Harriet Beecher   **A Reply to "The Affectionate and Christian Address of Many Thousands of Women of Great Britain and Ireland, to Their Sisters, the Women of the United States of America.**
    1863   London   35.

STOWE, Harriet Beecher   **Uncle Tom's Cabin.** 2 vols.
    1852   Boston   1st ed.   1st printing   400.
    Later printings   40.

STRAIT, Newton A.   **Alphabetical List of Battles, 1754-1900.** Wraps
    1882   Washington   30.

STREET, James   **The Civil War.**
    1953   New York   7.

STRIBLING, R. M.   **Gettysburg Campaign and Campaigns of 1864 in Virginia.**
    1905   Petersburg, Virginia   50.

STRICKLER, Theodore D.   **When and Where We Met Each Other on Shore and Afloat.** Wraps
    1899   Washington   25.

STRIDER, Robert Edward Lee   **The Life and Work of George William Peterkin.**
    1929   Philadelphia   25.

STRODE, Hudson   **Jefferson Davis.**
    Vol. 1 — **American Patriot.**
    Vol. 2 — **Confederate President.**
    Vol. 3 — **Tragic Hero.**
    1955-1964   New York   75.   Individual Volumes   25. each

STRODE, Hudson (ed)   **Jefferson Davis, Private Letters 1823-1889.**
    1966   New York   25.

STRONG, George Templeton   **The Diary of _____.** edited by Allan Nevins.
    4 vols.
    1952   New York   75.

STRONG, George Templeton   **Diary of the Civil War 1860-1865** edited by Allan Nevins.
    1962   New York   30.

STROTHER, David Hunter   **A Virginia Yankee in the Civil War: The Diaries of _____** edited by Cecil D. Eby, Jr.
    1961   Chapel Hill, N. C.   20.

STROYER, Jacob   **My Life in the South.**
    1898   Salem, Massachusetts   60.

STRUNSKY, Rose   **Abraham Lincoln.**
    1914   New York   20.

STRYKER, Lloyd Paul   **Andrew Johnson.**
    1930   New York   25.

STUART, J. E. B.   **Letters of _____ to His Wife 1861.** edited by Bingham Duncan. Wraps
    1943   Atlanta   Ltd.   30.

STUART, Meriwether   **Colonel Ulric Dahlgren and Richmond's Union Underground, April 1864.** Wraps
    1964   Virginia   8.

STUART, Meriwether   **Samuel Ruth and General R. E. Lee Disloyalty and the Line of Supply to Fredericksburg 1862-63.** Wraps
    1963   Virginia   10.

STUTLER, Boyd B.   **Captain John Brown and Harper's Ferry.** Wraps
    1926   Harpers Ferry   25.

STUTLER, Boyd B.   **Glory, Glory, Hallelujah! The Story of "John Brown's Body" and "Battle Hymn of the Republic".**
    n.d.   Cincinnati   40.

STYRON, William   **The Confessions of Nat Turner.**
    1967   New York   15.

Subdued Southern Nobility by One of the Nobility.
    1882   New York   25.

SULLY, Langdon   **No Tears for the General, The Life of Alfred Sully, 1821-1879.**
1974   Palo Alto, California   15.
SUMMERS, Festus P.   **Johnson Newlon Camden.**
1937   New York   15.
SUMMERSELL, Charles G.   **The Cruise of the C.S.S. Sumter.** Wraps
1965   Tuscaloosa   Ltd.   30.
SUMNER, Charles   **Slavery and the Rebellion, One and Inseparable, Speech.** Wraps
1864   Boston   15.
SUMNER, Charles   **Speech of . . . Treatment of Prisoners of War.** Wraps
New York   1865   20.
SUMNER, Charles   **Speech . . ., on the Johnson-Clarendon Treaty for the Settlement of Claims.** Wraps
1870   Boston   20.
SUMNER, G. Lynn   **Meet Abraham Lincoln Profiles of the Prairie President.**
1946   New York   8.
SWANBERG, W. A.   **First Blood.**
1957   New York   15.
1957   New York   Special edition signed by author   25.
SWANBERG, W. A.   **Sickles, The Incredible.**
1956   New York   25.
1956   New York   CWBC edition signed by author   35.
SWANN, Leonard A.   **John Roach: Maritime Entrepreneur — The Years as Naval Contractor 1862-1886.**
1965   Annapolis   20.
SWASEY, Charles A. G.   **American Caricatures Pertaining to the Civil War.**
n.d. (circa 1875)   n.p.   60.
SWEENY, William M.   **A Biographical Memoir of Thomas William Sweeny, Brigadier General United States Army.**
n.d.   n.p.   40.
SWEET, William Warren   **The Methodist Episcopal Church and the Civil War.**
n.d.   Cincinnati   30.
SWIERENGA, Robert P. (ed)   **Beyond the Civil War Synthesis, Political Essays of The Civil War Era.**
1975   Westport, Connecticut   20.
SWIFT, Charles Jewett   **The Last Battle of the Civil War. A Paper.** Wraps
1915   Columbus, Georgia   75.
SWIGGETT, Howard   **The Rebel Raider.**
1934   Indianapolis   35.
1937   Garden City, New York   25.
SWINT, Henry L. (ed)   **Dear Ones at Home: Letters from Contraband Camps.**
1966   Nashville   15.
SWINTON, William   **Campaigns of the Army of the Potomac.**
1866   New York   35.
1867   New York   35.
1871   New York   30.
1882   New York   30.
SWINTON, William   **The Twelve Decisive Battles of the War.**
1867   New York   25.
SWINTON, William   **The War for the Union From Fort Sumter to Atlanta.** Wraps
n.d. (circa 1865)   n.p.   20.
SWISHER, James   **How I Know, or Sixteen Years Eventful Experiences.**
1880   Cincinnati   40.
SWISSHELM, Jane Grey   **Crusader and Feminist, Letters of _____** edited by Arthur J. Larsen.
1934   St. Paul, Minnesota   30.
SWORD, Wiley   **Shiloh: Bloody April.**
1974   New York   40.

SYLVIA, Stephen W. and **O'DONNELL,** Michael J.   **The Illustrated History of American Civil War Relics.**
1978   Orange, Virginia   35.
SYMONDS, H. C.   **Report of a Commissary of Subsistence 1861-5.**
1888   Sing Sing   30.
TAFFT, Henry S.   **Reminiscences of the Signal Service in the Civil War.** Wraps
1899   Providence   Ltd.   35.
1903   Providence   Ltd.   25.
TALBOT, Edith Armstrong   **Samuel Chapman Armstrong a Biographical Study.**
1904   New York   25.
TALCOTT, T. M. R.   **Stuart's Cavalry in the Gettysburg Campaign   A Reply to the Letter of Col. John S. Mosby, Published in the "Times'Dispatch" of January 30, 1910.** Wraps
1911   Richmond   75.
TANCIG, W. J.   **Confederate Military Land Units.**
1967   Brunswick   15.
TANKERSLEY, Allen P.   **John B. Gordon.**
1955   Atlanta   50.
TANNER, Robert B.   **Stonewall in the Valley.**
1976   Garden City, New York   20.
TARBELL, Ida and **DAVIS,** J. McCan.   **The Early Life of Abraham Lincoln.**
1896   New York   10.
TARBELL, Ida   **He Knew Lincoln.**
1909   New York   10.
TARBELL, Ida M.   **He Knew Lincoln and Other Billy Brown Stories.**
1922   New York   10.
TARBELL, Ida   **In the Footsteps of Lincoln.**
1924   New York   15.
TARBELL, Ida   **The Life of Abraham Lincoln.** 4 vols.
1901   New York   25.
1909   New York   25.
1924   New York   25.
TATE, Allen   **Jefferson Davis, His Rise and Fall.**
1929   New York   30.
TATE, Allen   **Stonewall Jackson, The Good Soldier.**
1928   New York   40.
1965   Ann Arbor   15.
TATUM, Edith   **When the Bugle Called.**
1908   New York   30.
TATUM, Georgia L.   **Disloyalty in the Confederacy.**
1934   Chapel Hill, N. C.   40.
1970   New York   15.
TAYLOR, A. Reed   **The War History of Two Soldiers: A Two-Sided View of the Civil War.** Wraps
1970   Alabama   15.
TAYLOR, Benj. F.   **Mission Ridge and Lookout Mountain, With Pictures of Life in Camp and Field.**
1872   New York   45.
1875   Chicago   entitled: **Pictures of Life in Camp and Field.**   35.
TAYLOR, Emerson Gifford   **Gouverneur Kemble Warren, The Life and Letters of an American Soldier 1830-1882.**
1932   Boston   50.
TAYLOR, George Rogers   **The American Railroad Network.**
1956   Cambridge   20.
TAYLOR, N. G.   **Relief for East Tennessee, Address . . . Meeting Cooper Institute.** Wraps
1864   New York   15.

TAYLOR, Richard   **Destruction and Reconstruction: Personal Experiences of the Late War.**
    1879   New York   60.
    1879   London   150.
    1903   New York   35.
    1955   New York   edited by Richard Harwell   25.
TAYLOR, Susie King   **Reminiscences of My Life in Camp with the 33rd United States Colored Troops.**
    1902   Boston   65.
TAYLOR, Thomas E.   **Running the Blockade.**
    1896   New York   100.
    1897   London   100.
    1912   London   60.
TAYLOR, Walter H.   **Four Years with General Lee.**
    1877   New York   100.
    1878   New York   75.
    1962   Bloomington   edited by James I. Robertson   20.
TAYLOR, Walter H.   **General Lee: His Campaigns in Virginia.**
    1906   Norfolk, Virginia   100.
    1975   Dayton   22.
TAYLOR, William   **Cause and Probable Results of the Civil War in America.**
    Wraps
    1862   London   40.
TENNEY, W. J.   **The Military and Naval History of the Rebellion in the United States.**
    1865   New York   30.
    1866   New York   25.
THANE, Elswyth   **Yankee Stranger.**
    1944   New York   15.
THARIN, Robert S.   **Arbitrary Arrests in the South.**
    1863   New York   40.
That Dashing Cavalry Commander and Brilliant Orator: Gen'l Judson Kilpatrick.
    Wraps
    n.d.   n.p.   20.
THAYER, Eli   **History of the Kansas Crusade.**
    1889   New York   25.
THAYER, M. Russell   **A Reply to Mr. Charles Ingersoll's "Letter to a Friend in a Slave State."** Wraps
    1862   Philadelphia   30.
THAYER, William M.   **A Youth's History of the Rebellion.** 4 vols.
    1864-65   40.
    per volume   10. each
THAYER, William Roscoe   **The Life and Letters of John Hay.** 2 Vols.
    1915   Boston   25.
This Discursive Biographical Sketch 1841-1902 of Richard Lathers.
    1902   Philadelphia   40.
THOMAS, Benjamin P.   **Abraham Lincoln.**
    1952   New York   15.
THOMAS, Benjamin P.   **Lincoln's New Salem.**
    1954   New York   7.
THOMAS, Benjamin P.   **Portrait for Posterity.**
    1947   New Brunswick   7.
THOMAS, Benjamin P. and **HYMAN,** Harold M.   **Stanton — The Life and Times of Lincoln's Secretary of War.**
    1962   New York   20.
THOMAS, Clarence   **General Turner Ashby The Centaur of the South.**
    1907   Winchester, Virginia   150.
THOMAS, Edison H.   **John Hunt Morgan and His Raiders.**
    1975   Lexington   10.

THOMAS, Edward J.   **Memoirs of a Southerner.**
1923   Savannah   40.
THOMAS, Emory M.   **The American War and Peace, 1860-1877.**
1973   Englewood Cliffs, New Jersey   15.
THOMAS, Emory M.   **The Confederacy as a Revolutionary Experience.**
1971   Englewood Cliffs   20.
THOMAS, Emory M.   **The Confederate Nation 1861-1865.**
1979   New York   20.
THOMAS, Emory M.   **The Confederate State of Richmond.**
1971   Austin   20.
THOMAS, George H.   **The Military Correspondence of Maj.-Gen. _____.** Wraps
1925   n.p.   20.
THOMAS, John P.   **Career and Character of General Micah Jenkins.** Wraps
1903 Columbus   Ltd.   75.
THOMAS, John P.   **The History of the South Carolina Military Academy.**
1893   Charleston   75.
THOMAS, Wilbur   **General George H. Thomas, The Indomitable Warrier.**
1964   New York   30.
THOMASON, John W., Jr.   **Jeb Stuart.**
1930   New York   30.
1934   New York   25.
1958   New York   20.
THOMASON, John W., Jr.   **Lone Star Preacher.**
1941   New York   35.
THOMES, W. H.   **Running the Blockade.**
1888   Chicago   25.
THOMPSON, Charles Willis   **The Fiery Epoch 1830-77.**
1931   Indianapolis   15.
THOMPSON, Gilbert   **The Engineer Battalion in the Civil War.** Wraps
1910   Washington   40.
THOMPSON, Henry Yates   **An Englishman in the American Civil War, The Diary
of _____** edited by Christopher Chancellor.
1971   New York   25.
THOMPSON, Jerry Don   **Colonel John Robert Baylor: Texas Indian Fighter and
Confederate Soldier.** Wraps
1971   Waco, Texas   20.
THOMPSON, Joseph P.   **Revolution Against Free Government.** Wraps
1864   Philadelphia   25.
THOMPSON, Magnus S.   **From the Ranks to Brigadier-General The Service Record of
Col. Elijah V. White 1861-1865.** Wraps
1923   n.p.   110.
THOMPSON, Samuel Bernard   **Confederate Purchasing Operations Abroad.**
1935   Chapel Hill   40.
1973   Gloucester   20.
THOMPSON, W. Fletcher, Jr.   **The Image of War.**
1960   New York   20.
THOMPSON, Wesley S.   **Tories of the Hills.**
1953   Boston   15.
THOMPSON, William Y.   **Robert Toombs of Georgia.**
1966   Baton Rouge   25.
THORNWELL, J. H.   **Hear the South The State of the Country.**
1861   New York   30.
Thrilling Stories of the Great Rebellion by a Disabled Officer.
1865   Philadelphia   20.
TICKNOR, Francis Orray   **The Poems of Francis Orray Ticknor** edited by Michelle
Cutliff Ticknor.
1911   New York   25.

TIEBOUT, Samuel   **The Civil War Diary of** _____ edited by Bruce T. McCully.
Wraps
1943   Cooperstown, NY   15.
TILLEY, John S.   **Facts the Historians Leave Out A Youth's Confederate Primer.** Wraps
1951   Montgomery, Alabama   10.
TILLEY, John S.   **Lincoln Takes Command.**
1941   Chapel Hill   20.
TILY, James   **The Uniforms of the United States Navy.**
1968   New York   15.
TINKCOM, Harry Marlin   **John White Geary, Soldier-Statesman   1819-1873.**
1940   Philadelphia   20.
TIPTON and BLOCKER   **Gettysburg, The Pictures and the Story.** Wraps
1913   Gettysburg   20.
**To the Memory of William M. Stanley Whose Soldier's Grave is Unmarked by Shaft
or Stone.**
1965   Tyler, Texas   Ltd.   25.
To the People of the South, Senator Hammond and the Tribune by Troup. Wraps
1860   Charleston   40.
TOBITT, John H.   **What I Heard in Europe During the "American Excitement."**
1865   New York   20.
TODD, Albert   **The Campaigns of the Rebellion.**
1884   Manhattan, Kansas   30.
TODD, Frederick P.   **Soldiers of the American Army 1775-1954.**
1954   Chicago   30.
TODD, Helen.   **A Man Named Grant.**
1940   Boston   15.
TODD, Richard C.   **Confederate Finance.**
1954   Athens   25.
TOEPPERWEIN, Herman   **Rebel in Blue, A Novel of the Southwest Frontier 1861-1865.**
1972   Fredericksburg, Texas   10.
TOLBERT, Frank X.   **Dick Dowling at Sabine Pass.**
1962   New York   25.
TOLBERT, Noble J. (ed)   **The Papers of John Willis Ellis.** 2 vols.
1964   Raleigh, NC   30.
TOMES, Robert   **The War With The South.** 3 vols.
1862-66   New York   100.
1865   New York   entitled **The Great Civil War**   100.
TOURGEE, Albion W.   **An Appeal to Caesar.**
1884   New York   20.
TOURGEE, Albion   **An Appeal to Pharaoh, the Negro Problem and Its
Radical Solution.**
1889   New York   20.
TOURGEE, Albion W.   **Bricks Without Straw.**
1880   n.p.   25.
1969   Baton Rouge   edited by Otto H. Olsen   10.
TOURGEE, Albion W.   **A Fool's Errand, And the Invisible Empire.**
1880   New York   20.
TOURGEE, Albion W.   **The Veteran & His Pipe.**
1888   Chicago   12.
TOUSARD, Louis De   **American Artillerist's Companion.** 3 vols.
1969   New York   100.
TOWNSEND, Cyrus Brady   **Three Daughters of the Confederacy.**
1905   New York   15.
TOWNSEND, E. D.   **Anecdotes of the Civil War in the United States.**
1884   New York   15.
TOWNSEND, George Alfred   **Campaigns of a Non-Combatant.**
1866   New York   25.
1950   Chapel Hill   entitled: **Rustics in Rebellion**   20.

TOWNSEND, George Alfred   **Katy of Catoctin Or the Chain-Breakers.**
1959   Cambridge, Maryland   8.
TOWNSEND, John   **The South Alone Should Govern the South.** Wraps
1860   Charleston, SC   100.
TOWNSEND, William H.   **Lincoln and His Wife's Home Town.**
1929   Indianapolis   20.
TOWNSEND, William H.   **Lincoln and Liquor.**
1934   New York   15.
TOWNSEND, William H.   **Lincoln, The Litigant.**
1925   Boston   20.
TRACY, J. Perkins   **The Blockade Runner.** Wraps
1896   New York   50.
TRAIN, Geo. Francis   **Great Speech on the Withdrawal of McClellan and the Impeachment of Lincoln.** Wraps
1865   New York   40.
TRAVER, Lorenzo   **The Battles of Roanoke Island and Elizabeth City.** Wraps
1880   Providence   Ltd.   30.
TREFOUSSE, Hans Louis   **Ben Butler. The South Called Him Beast!**
1957   New York   25.
TRELEASE, Allen W.   **Reconstruction, The Great Experiment.**
1971   New York   15.
TRELEASE, Allen W.   **White Terror, The Ku Klux Klan Conspiracy and Southern Reconstruction.**
1971   New York   20.
TREMAIN, Henry Edwin   **The Closing Days About Richmond.** Wraps
1884   Edinburgh   150.
TREMAIN, Henry Edwin   **Last Hours of Sheridan's Cavalry.**
1904   New York   35.
TREMAIN, Henry Edwin   **Sailors' Creek to Appomattox Court House.** edited by John Watts DePeyster. Wraps
1885   New York   50.
TREMAIN, Henry Edwin   **Two Days of War: A Gettysburg Narrative and Other Excursions.**
1905   New York   30.
TRENT, William P.   **Robert E. Lee.**
1899   Boston   25.
TRESCOTT, William Henry   **Memorial of the Life of J. Johnston Pettigrew.**
1870   Charleston, SC   100.
TREXLER, Harrison A.   **The Confederate Ironclad "Virginia" ("Merrimac").**
1938   Chicago   35.
TREZEVANT, D. H.   **The Burning of Columbia, SC.** Wraps
1866   Columbia   90.
n.d.   Columbia   5.
The Trial and Death of Henry Wirz. Wraps
1908   Raleigh   35.
The Trial of Hon. Clement L. Vallandigham.
1863   Cincinnati   75.
Trial of John Y. Beall, As a Spy and Guerrillero. Wraps
1865   New York   125.
The Trial of the Assassins and Conspirators at Washington City, D.C., May and June 1865, For the Murder of President Abraham Lincoln.
1865   Philadelphia   100.
Trial of the Officers and Crew of the Privateer Savannah, On the Charge of Piracy.
1862   New York   100.
Tribune Almanac and Political Register 1860-65. Wraps
10. each
The Trip of the Steamer Oceanus to Fort Sumter and Charleston . . . By A Committee.
1865   Brooklyn   75.

TROLLOPE, Anthony   **North America.**
    1862   Philadelphia   2 vols.   35.
    1951   New York   2 vols. in one   15.
Troop Movements at the Battle of Cold Harbor. Wraps
    1964   Richmond   25.
TROWBRIDGE, John T.   **Cudjo's Cave.**
    1864   Boston   20.
TROWBRIDGE, John T.   **My Own Story, With Recollections of Noted Persons.**
    1903   Boston   25.
TROWBRIDGE, John T.   **A Picture of the Desolated States and the Work
of Restoration.**
    1868   Hartford   35.
    1956   New York   entitled: **The Desolate South 1865-66** edited by Gordon
Carroll   20.
TROWBRIDGE, John T.   **The South: A Tour of its Battle Fields and Ruined Cities.**
    1866   Hartford   50.
    1867   Hartford   40.
TROWBRIDGE, John T.   **The Three Scouts.**
    1865   Boston   20.
TROWBRIDGE, Luther S.   **The Operations of the Cavalry in the Gettysburg Campaign.**
    1888   Detroit   30.
TRUESDALE, John.   **The Blue Coats, And How They Lived, Fought and Died
for the Union.**
    1867   Philadelphia   25.
TRUMBULL, H. Clay   **The Knightly Soldier, A Biography of Major Henry Ward Camp.**
    1865   Boston   30.
    1892   Philadelphia   25.
Trumpet of Freedom. Wraps
    1864   Boston   35.
TUCKER, Beverley   **Address of** _____ **To the People of the United States 1865.** edited
by James Harvey Young. Wraps
    1948   Atlanta   15.
TUCKER, Beverley   **The Partisan Leader.**
    1861   New York   25.
TUCKER, G. W.   **Lee and the Gettysburg Campaign.**
    1933   n.p.   25.
TUCKER, Glenn   **Chickaamauga.**
    1961   Indianapolis   30.
    1972   Dayton   20.
TUCKER, Glenn   **Hancock the Superb.**
    1960   Indianapolis   30.
    1980   Dayton   15.
TUCKER, Glenn   **High Tide at Gettysburg.**
    1958   Indianapolis   25.
TUCKER, Glenn   **Lee and Longstreet at Gettysburg.**
    1968   Indianapolis   25.
TUCKER, Glenn   **Zeb Vance — Champion of Personal Freedom.**
    1965   Indianapolis   20.
TUCKER, St. George   **A Dissertation on Slavery: With a Proposal for the Gradual
Abolition of It in the State of Virginia.** Wraps
    1861   New York   35.
TUCKERMAN, Henry T.   **The Rebellion: Its Latent Causes and True Significance.**
Wraps
    1861   New York   10.
TUNSTALL, Nannie Whitmell   **"No. 40" A Romance of Fortress Monroe and the
Hygeia.** Wraps
    1890   Richmond   35.
TURCHIN, John B.   **Noted Battles for the Union During the Civil War in the
United States of American 1861-65 — Chickamauga.**
    1888   Chicago   75.

TURNER, Edward Raymond   **The New Market Campaign   May 1864.**
    1912   Richmond   40.

TURNER, George Edgar   **Victory Rode the Rails.**
    1953   Indianapolis   30.

TURNER, Joseph Addison   **Autobiography of "The Countryman."** edited by
    Thomas H. English. Wraps
    1943   Atlanta   12.

TURNER, Justin G. and **LEVITT,** Linda   **Mary Todd Lincoln — Her Life and
Letters.**
    1972   New York   15.

**Two Diaries from Middle St. Johns Berkeley, S. C. Feb-May 1865   Journals Kept by
Susan R. Jervey and Charlotte S. J. Ravenel and Reminiscences of Mrs. Waring
Henagan.** Wraps
    1921   n.p.   Ltd.   35.

TYLER, C. W.   **The Scout: A Tale of the Civil War.**
    1911   Nashville   50.

TYLER, Lyon G.   **A Confederate Catechism.** Wraps
    1935   n.p.   5.

TYLER, Lyon G.   **Confederate Leaders and Other Citizens Request the House of
Delegates to Repeal the Resolution of Respect to Abraham Lincoln the Barbarian.**
Wraps
    1928   Richmond   20.

TYLER, Lyon G.   **General Lee's Birthday.** Wraps
    1929   n.p.   5.

TYLER, Lyon G.   **John Tyler and Abraham Lincoln   Who Was the Dwarf?**
    1929   Richmond   20.

TYLER, Lyon G.   **Virginia Principles Address.** Wraps
    1928   Richmond   20.

TYLER, Ronnie C.   **Santiago Vidaurri and the Southern Confederacy.**
    1973   Austin   20.

TYLER, Samuel   **Memoir of Roger Brooke Taney.**
    1872   Baltimore   15.

A Typical American, or Incidents in Life of Dr. John Swinburne of Albany.
    1888   Albany   15.

TYRNER-TYRNAUER, A. R.   **Lincoln and the Emperors.**
    1962   New York   15.

The Un-Civil War, Some Maps & Views of the South During 1861-1865. Wraps
    1974   Tiger Cave, Pennsylvania   Ltd.   15.

**Uncle Daniel's Story of Tom Anderson and Twenty Great Battles   By an Officer of
the Union Army.**
    1886   New York   20.

UNDERWOOD, J. L.   **The Women of the Confederacy.**
    1906   New York & Washington   150.

UNDERWOOD, Jno. C.   **Monument to the Confederate Dead at Chicago.**
    1896   Chicago   25.
    1897   Chicago   25.

Uniform and Dress of the Army and Navy of the Confederate States . . .   See
Confederate Imprints.

Uniform Regulations for the Army of the United States. Wraps
    1961   Washington   7.

The Union League of Philadelphia.
    1902   Philadelphia   10.

United Confederate Veterans, Reunions. Wraps
    15. each

United Daughters of the Confederacy, Programs at Conventions. Wraps
    1915-1956   10. each

The United Service, A Quarterly Review of Military and Naval Affairs, Philadelphia.
    Vols. 1-XVI, 1879-1896.
    25. each

The United States Army and Navy Journal, and Gazette of the Regular and Volunteer Forces. 52 issues per volume. Wraps
    Vol I   125.   Bound   100.
    Vol. II   125.   Bound   100.

United States Christian Commission for the Army and Navy, Annual Reports, 1863-65. Wraps
    20. each

U. S. Christian Commission, Record of the Federal Dead. Wraps
    50. per volume

U.S. Infantry Tactics.
    1861   Philadelphia   35.
    1862   Philadelphia   35.
    1863   Philadelphia   35.

U.S. Infantry Tactics . . . for the Use of Colored Troops.
    1863   Washington   150.

U.S. Sanitary Commission, Bulletins of.
    1863-1865   12 issues per year   1. per issue

U. S. Sanitary Commission Publication, Our Daily Fare Nos. 1-12 June 8, 1864 — June 21, 1864.
    Complete as issued   125.

U.S. Sanitary Commission A Sketch of Its Purposes and Its Work.
    1863   Boston   20.

U.S. Sanitary Commission, Statement of the Object and Methods.
    1863   New York   15.

United States Service Magazine.
    per volume   30.

Unveiling of the Equestrian Statue of Philip H. Sheridan.
    1961 (?)   Albany   15.

UPSHUR, Abel P.   **A Brief Enquiry into the True Nature and Character of our Federal Goverment.** Wraps
    1863   Philadelphia   25.

UPTON, E.   **A New System of Infantry Tactics.**
    1867   New York   30.
    1868   New York   25.

UPTON, Emory   **The Military Policy of the United States.**
    1904   Washington   35.
    1917   Washington   30.

URQUHART, David   **The Right of Search — Two Speeches.**
    1862   London   45.

UTLEY, Robert M.   **Frontiersmen in Blue — The U. S. Army & the Indian.**
    1967   New York   15.

VAIL, I. E.   **Three Years on the Blockade.**
    1902   New York   50.

VALLANDIGHAM, James L.   **Life of Clement L. Vallandigham.**
    1872   Baltimore   25.
    1872   New York   25.

Valuable American Historical Library of the Late Major Edward Willis of Charleston, SC. Wraps
    1914   Wraps   25.

The Valuable Papers of the Late Hon. Gideon Welles., Auction Catalog Jan. 4th, 1924. Wraps
    1924   n.p.   30.

VAN ALSTYNE, Lawrence   **Diary of an Enlisted Man.**
    1910   New Haven   50.

VANCE, Wilson J.   **Stone's River, The Turning-Point of the Civil War.**
    1914   New York   100.

VANCE, Zebulon B.   **The Last Days of the War in North Carolina, An Address.** Wraps
    1885   Baltimore   75.

VANCE, Zebulon B.   **The Papers of Zebulon Baird Vance,** Vol. 1 1843-1862. edited
by Frontis W. Johnston.
    1963   Raleigh, N. C.   10.
VANDERSLICE, John M.   **Gettysburg, Where and How the Regiments Fought and
Troops They Encountered.**
    1897   Philadelphia   25.
    1899   New York   35.
    1899   Chicago   25.
VANDER VELDE, Lewis G.   **The Presbyterian Churches and the Federal Union
1861-1868.**
    1932   Cambridge   30.
    1932   London   30.
VAN DEUSEN, Glyndon G.   **William Henry Seward.**
    1967   New York   25.
VAN deWATER, Frederic F.   **Glory-Hunter, A Life of Gen. Custer.**
    1934   Indianapolis   40.
VANDIVER, Frank E. (ed)   **Confederate Blockade Running Through Bermuda
1861-1865.**
    1946   Austin, Texas   50.
VANDIVER, Frank E. et al.   **Essays on the American Civil War.**
    1968   Austin, Texas   20.
VANDIVER, Frank E.   **Jefferson Davis and the Confederate States.** Wraps
    1964   Oxford   10.
VANDIVER, Frank E.   **Jubal's Raid.**
    1960   New York   25.
    1974   Westport   15.
VANDIVER, Frank E.   **Mighty Stonewall.**
    1957   New York   30.
    1957   New York   Ltd.   signed edition   40.
VANDIVER, Frank E.   **Ploughshares into Swords.**
    1952   Austin, Texas   60.
VANDIVER, Frank E.   **Rebel Brass.**
    1956   Baton Rouge   30.
    1971   Westport   20.
    1979   New York   15.
VANDIVER, Frank E.   **Their Tattered Flags.**
    1970   New York   25.
VAN HORNE, John Douglass   **Jefferson Davis and Repudiation in Mississippi.**
Wraps
    1915   n.p.   15.

VAN HORNE, Thomas B.   **History of the Army of the Cumberland.** 3 vols. (2 vols.
— Text, 1 vol. — Atlas)
    1875   Cincinnati   200.
VAN HORNE, Thomas B.   **The Life of Maj. Gen. George H. Thomas.**
    1882   New York   40.
VAN NESS, W. W.   **The National School for the Soldier.**
    1862   New York   20.
VAN NOPPEN, Ina Woestemeyer   **Stoneman's Last Raid.**
    1961   Raleigh   15.
VAN ZANDT, K. M.   **Force With Fanfare: The Autobiography of** _____
    1968   Fort Worth   10.
VASVARY, Edmund   **Lincoln's Hungarian Heroes, The Participation of Hungarians
in the Civil War 1861-1865.** Wraps
    1939   Washington   30.
VAUGHTER, John B.   **Prison Life in Dixie.**
    1880   Chicago   40.
VELAZQUEZ, Loreta Janeta   **The Woman in Battle.**
    1876   Richmond   50.
    1876   Hartford   40.
    1890   New York   entitled: **The Famous Female Spy.**   30.

VERNE, Ilian   **Phil, The Scout — The War Library Vol. 7, #233.** Wraps
    1887   New York   50.
VICKERS, George Edward   **Last Charge at Gettysburg.** Wraps
    1899   Philadelphia   20.
VICKERS, George Morley   **Under Both Flags.**
    1896   Boston   30.
    1896   Chicago   30.
    1896   Philadelphia   30.
VICTOR, Orville J.   **The History, Civil, Political and Military of the Southern Rebellion.** 4 vols.
    1861-68   New York   80.
VICTOR, Orville J.   **Incidents and Anecdotes of the War.**
    1862   New York   15.
    1866   New York   15.
VIELE, Egbert   **Hand-Book for Active Service.**
    1861   New York   30.
    1968   New York   15.
VILLARD, Henry   **Lincoln on the Eve of '61.**
    1941   New York   15.
VILLARD, Henry   **Memoirs of Henry Villard, Journalist & Financier 1835-1900.** 2 vols.
    1904   Boston   30.
VILLARD, Oswald G.   **John Brown . . . A Biography Fifty Years After.**
    1910   New York   30.
    1911   Boston   25.
VILLIERS, Brougham   **Anglo-American Relations 1861-1865.**
    1920   New York   30.
VINCENT, Thomas M.   **Abraham Lincoln and Edwin M. Stanton.** Wraps
    1890   Washington   20.
    1892   Washington   15.
The Virginia Campaign of Gen. Pope in 1862, Vol. 2 of MHSM.
    1886   Boston   40.
Virginia Historical Society, Collections of.
    Vols. I-VI   35. each
VLOCK, Laurel F. and **LEVITCH,** Joel A.   **Contraband of War, William Henry Singleton.**
    1970   New York   10.
VOEGELI, V. Jacque   **Free But Not Equal, the Midwest and the Negro During the Civil War.**
    1969   Chicago   15.
A Voice from Rebel Prisons Giving an Account of Some of the Horrors of the Stockades at Andersonville, Milan, and Other Prisons by a Returned Prisoner of War. Wraps
    1865   Boston   40.
VOLCK, Adelbert J.   **Confederate War Etchings.**
    1880 (?) 1890 (?)   Philadelphia (?)   Ltd.   29 plates   Loose in Binder 400.
The Volunteers' Roll of Honor. Wraps
    1864   Philadelphia   25.
VON ABELE, Rudolph   **Alexander H. Stephens, A Biography.**
    1946   New York   25.
VON HOLST, Hermann   **John Brown** edited by Frank P. Stearns.
    1888   Boston   30.
W. D. B.   See: **BICKHAM,** W. D.
WADDELL, Alfred Moore   **Some Memories of My Life.**
    1908   Raleigh   40.
WADDELL, James D. (ed)   **Biographical Sketch of Linton Stephens.**
    1877   Atlanta   25.

WADDELL, James I.   **C.S.S. Shenandoah: The Memoirs of Lieutenant Commander James I. Waddell** edited by James D. Horan.
1960   New York   30.
WAGENKNECHT, Edward   **Abraham Lincoln His Life, Work & Character.**
1947   New York   10.
WAINWRIGHT, Charles S.   **A Diary of Battle, The Personal Journals of** _____ edited by Allan Nevins.
1862   New York   30.
WALKER, C. Irvine   **The Life of Lieut. Gen. Richard Heron Anderson.**
1917   Charleston, S. C.   125.
WALKER, Charles D.   **Memorial V.M.I. Biographical Sketches of the Graduates . . . Who Fell During the War.**
1875   Philadelphia   125.
WALKER, Charles M.   **Sketch of the Life . . . of Oliver P. Morton.**
1878   Indianapolis   20.
WALKER, Francis A.   **General Hancock.**
1894   New York   20.
1894   New York   L.P. edition   50.
1897   New York   20.
WALKER, Francis A.   **A History of the Second Army Corps in the Army of the Potomac.**
1886   New York   60.
1891   New York   50.
WALKER, Georgiana Gholson   **Private Journal of** _____ **1862-65.** edited by Dwight F. Henderson. Wraps
1963   Tuscaloosa   Ltd.   25.
WALKER, Jeanie Mort   **Life of Capt. Joseph Fry, the Cuban Martyr.**
1875   Hartford   45.
WALKER, Margaret Walker   **Jubilee.**
1966   Boston   10.
WALKER, Peter F.   **Building a Tennessee Army: Autumn 1861.** Wraps
1957   Tennessee   10.
WALL, Alexander J.   **A Sketch of the Life of Horatio Seymour 1810-1886.**
1929   New York   Ltd.   40.
WALL, Bernhardt   **Following Abraham Lincoln 1809-1865.**
1943   Lime Rock, Connecticut   20.
WALL, Joseph Frazier   **Henry Watterson Reconstructed Rebel.**
1956   New York   15.
WALLACE, Elizabeth Curtis   **Glencoe Diary: The War-Time Journal of . . .** edited by Eleanor and Charles Cross. Wraps
1968   Virginia   20.
WALLACE, Isabel   **Life and Letters of Gen. W. H. L. Wallace.**
1909   Chicago   40.
WALLACE, Lewis   **Lew Wallace An Autobiography.** 2 vols.
1906   New York   50.
WALLIS, S. Teakle   **Address . . . Delivered at the Academy of Music, in Baltimore, April 20th, 1874, on Behalf of the Lee Memorial Assoc.** Wraps
1875   Baltimore   10.
WALSH, William S. (ed)   **Abraham Lincoln and the London Punch.**
1909   New York   15.
WALTER, R. S.   **A Ride for Life at Gettysburg.**
1896   Front Royal, Virginia   30.
WALTERS, John B.   **Merchant of Terror General Sherman and Total War.**
1973   Indianapolis   15.
WALTHALL, Ernest Taylor   **Hidden Things Brought to Light.**
1933   Richmond   Ltd.   30.
WALTON, William   **Army and Navy of the United States: From the Period of the Revolution to the Present day.**
1889-1895   Philadelphia   Green Wrappers in Cloth Portfolios   1000.

Same on Japanese vellum   2000.
1900   Philadelphia   (usually bound in 2 vols.)   1200.
The War 1861-1865 As Depicted in Prints by Currier & Ives. Wraps
1960   n.p.   6.
War Letters of a Disbanded Volunteer.
See: **BARBER**, J.
War Lyrics and Songs of the South.
1866   London   45.
War Papers of the Confederacy. Wraps
1961   Charlottesville, Virginia   15.
War Record, General I. F. Shepard 1861-1864. Wraps
1889 (?)   n.p.   20.
War Records. Wraps
1907   Columbia   20.
1908   Columbia   20.
WARD, Dallas T.   **War Songs of the Blue and Gray As Sung By the Brave Soldiers of the Union and Confederate Armies.**
n.d.   New York   25.
WARD, Dallas T.   **The Last Railroad Flag of Truce During the Civil War.** Wraps
n.d.   Raleigh   10.
WARD, James A.   **That Man Haupt, A Biography.**
1973   Baton Rouge   25.
WARD, Margaret Ketcham   **Testimony Before U.S. Senate Committee on Relations Between Labor and Capital.** Wraps
1936   Birmingham   75.
1965   Birmingham   25.
1977   Birmingham   10.
WARDEN, Robert   **An Account of the Private Life and Public Services of Salmon P. Chase.**
1874   Cincinnati   20.
WARING, Malvina Sarah   **One Old Reb.**
1929   Columbia, S. C.   40.
WARING, Mary   **Miss Waring's Journal 1863 and 1865** edited by Thad Holt, Jr. Wraps
1964   Chicago   15.
WARNER, Ezra J. and **YEARNS**, W. Buck   **Biographical Register of the Confederate Congress.**
1975   Baton Rouge   22.
WARNER, Ezra J.   **Generals in Blue.**
1964   Baton Rouge   25.
WARNER, Ezra J.   **Generals in Gray.**
1959   Baton Rouge   20.
1965   Baton Rouge   20.
Warren and Danner's Pocket Guide Book of Gettysburg and the Battlefield with Map.
n.d.   n.p.   10.
Warren County Civil War Centennial Commemoration, The Battle of Front Royal, May 19-20, 1862. Wraps
n.d.   n.p.   10.
WARREN, Edward   **A Doctor's Experiences in Three Continents.**
1885   Baltimore   75.
WARREN, G. K.   **An Account of the Operations of the 5th Army Corps Commanded by Maj.-Gen. G. K. Warren, at the Battle of Five Forks, April 1, 1865.** Wraps
1866   New York   30.
WARREN, Kittrell J.   See: **Confederate Imprints.**
WARREN, Louis A.   **Lincoln's Gettyburg Declaration.**
1964   Fort Wayne   Ltd.   10.
WARREN, Louis A.   **Lincoln's Youth Indiana Years Seven to Twenty-One 1816-1830.**
1959   New York   13.

WARREN, R.   **The Prairie President: Living Through the Years with Lincoln.**
n.d.   Chicago   10.
WARREN, Robert Penn   **John Brown — The Making of a Martyr.**
1929   New York   125.
WARREN, Robert Penn   **The Legacy of the Civil War.**
1961   New York   10.
WARREN, Robert Penn   **Wilderness, A Tale of the Civil War.**
1961   New York   10.
WARREN, Rose Harlow   **A Southern Home in War Times.**
1914   Broadway, New York   30.
WASHBURN, Emory   **Can a State Secede?** Wraps
1865   Cambridge   20.
WASHBURN, William D., Jr.   **Gettysburg.** Wraps
1908   Minneapolis   15.
WASHINGTON, Mrs. James Madison   **How Beauty Was Saved and Other
Memories of the Sixties.**
1907   New York   40.
WASHINGTON, John   **They Knew Lincoln.**
1942   New York   20.
WASON, Robert Alexander   **Babe Randolph's Turning Point, An Episode of the
Civil War.**
1904   Chicago   Ltd.   125.
WASSON, R. Gordon   **The Hall Carbine Affair.**
1948   New York   50.
WATERS, Willard O.   **Confederate Imprints in the Henry E. Huntington Library
Unrecorded in Previously Published Biographies of Such Material.** Wraps
1929   n.p.   25.
1930   n.p.   25.
WATKINS, Lizzie Stringfellow   **The Life of Horace Stringfellow.**
1931   Montgomery, Alabama   40.
WATSON, Thomas E.   **Bethany   A Story of the Old South.**
1929   Washington, D. C.   30.
WATSON, Thomas Shelby   **The Silent Riders.** Wraps
1971   Louisville   6.
WATSON, Virginia   **The Featherlys.**
1936   New York   15.
WATSON, William   **The Adventures of a Blockade Runner.**
1892   London   65.
1893   London   60.
1898   London   60.
WATSON, William   **Letters of a Civil War Surgeon** edited by Paul Fatout. Wraps
1961   W. Lafayette, Indiana   15.
WATTERSON, Henry   **Abraham Lincoln, An Oration.** Wraps
1899   Louisville   10.
WATTERSON, Henry   **"Marse Henry," an Autobiography.** 2 vols.
1919   New York   30.
WAUCHOPE, George Armstrong   **Henry Timrod: Man and Poet.** Wraps
1915   Columbia   20.
WAYDE, Bernard   **Along the Potomac, the War Library Vol 2, #256.** Wraps
1887   New York   50.
WAYLAND, John W.   **Battle of New Market   Memorial Address.** Wraps
1926   New Market, Virginia   30.
WAYLAND, John W.   **John Kagi and John Brown.**
1961   Strasburg, Virginia   20.
WAYLAND, John W.   **The Pathfinder of the Seas.**
1930   Richmond   35.
WAYLAND, John W.   **Robert E. Lee & His Family.**
1951   Staunton, Virginia   30.

WAYLAND, John W.   **Stonewall Jackson's Way.**
   1940   Staunton, Virginia   150.
   1969   Verona, Virginia   40.
WEAVER, Ward   **Hang My Wreath.**
   1941   New York   10.
WEBB, Alexander S.   **The Peninsula McClellan's Campaign of 1862.**
   1881   New York   25.
   1882   n.p.   20.
   1885   New York   20.
Webb and His Brigade at the Angle, Gettysburg.
   1916   Albany   25.
WEBB, Richard D. (ed)   **The Life and Letters of Captain John Brown.**
   1861   London   30.
WEBB, Willard   **Crucial Moments of the Civil War.**
   1961   New York   15.
WEBBER, Richard H.   **Monitors of the US Navy 1861-1937.** Wraps
   n.d.   Washington, D. C.   7.
WEBER, John B.   **Autobiography of John B. Weber.**
   1924   Buffalo   25.
WEBER, Thomas   **The Northern Railroads in the Civil War.**
   1952   New York   25.
   1953   New York   25.
WEEDEN, William B.   **War Government, Federal and State in Massachusetts, New York, Pennsylvania and Indiana 1861-1865.**
   1906   Boston   30.
WEEKS, Della Jerman   **Legends of the War.**
   1868   Boston   25.
WEICHMAN, Louis   **A True History of the Assassination of Abraham Lincoln and the Conspiracy of 1865.**
   1975   New York   15.
WEIGLEY, Russell F.   **Quartermaster General of the Union Army — A Biography of M. C. Meigs.**
   1959   New York   20.
WEIK, James W.   **The Real Lincoln A Portrait.**
   1922   Boston   15.
WEISBERGER, Bernard A.   **Reporters for the Union.**
   1953   Boston   20.
WELLES, Gideon   **Civil War and Reconstruction.** edited by Albert Mordell.
   1959   New York   7.
WELLES, Gideon   **Diary of _____, Lincoln's Secretary of the Navy.** 3 vols.
   1911   Boston   75.
   1960   New York   edited by Howard K. Beale   Boxed   60.
WELLES, Gideon   **Lincoln and Seward.**
   1874   New York   25.
   1969   New York   10.
WELLMAN, Manly Wade   **Giant in Gray. Wade Hampton.**
   1949   New York   35.
WELLMAN, Manly Wade   **Harpers Ferry Prize of War.**
   1960   Charlotte, N. C.   15.
WELLMAN, Manly Wade   **They Took Their Stand.**
   1959   New York   25.
WELLMAN, Paul I.   **The House Divides, the Age of Jackson and Lincoln from the War of 1812 to the Civil War.**
   1966   Garden City, New York   20.
WELLS, Damon   **Stephen Douglas The Last Years, 1857-1861.**
   1971   Austin, Texas   10.
WELLS, David A.   **Our Burden and Our Strength.** Wraps
   1864   Boston   10.

WELLS, Edward L.   **Hampton and His Cavalry in '64.**
1899   Richmond   75.
WELLS, Edward L.   **Hampton and Reconstruction.**
1907   Columbia, S. C.   125.
WELLS, J. W. and **STRAIT**, N. A.   **An Alphabetical List of the Battles of the War of the Rebellion.** Wraps
1883   Washington   25.
WELLS, James M.   **The Chisolm Massacre: A Picture of "Home Rule" in Mississippi.**
1878   Washington   50.
WELLS, Rosa Lee   **General Lee, A Great Friend of Youth.**
1950   New York   10.
WELLS, Tom H.   **The Confederate Navy.**
1971   University, Alabama   25.
WELLS, William (comp)   **The Original United States Warship "Monitor."**
1899   New Haven, Connecticut   35.
WENTZ, Henry   **The Autobiography of a Soldier Boy and Business Man.** Wraps
1924   Shelby, Ohio   125.
WERLICH, Robert   **"Beast Butler" The Incredible Career of Major General Benjamin Franklin Butler.**
1962   Washington   20.
WERNER, Edgar A. (comp)   **Historical Sketch of the War of the Rebellion from 1861 to 1865.**
1890   Albany, New York   30.
WERSTEIN, Irving   **Abraham Lincoln Vs. Jefferson Davis.**
1959   New York   10.
WERSTEIN, Irving   **1861-1865: The Adventure of the Civil War Told with Pictures.** Wraps
1960   Paterson, New Jersey   4.
WERSTEIN, Irving   **July 1863 — The Incredible Story of the Bloody New York City Draft Riots.**
1957   New York   10.
WERSTEIN, Irving   **Kearny the Magnificent.**
1962   New York   30.
WERSTEIN, Irving   **The Many Faces of the Civil War.**
1961   New York   10.
WESLEY, Charles H.   **The Collapse of the Confederacy.**
1937   Washington   40.
WESSELS, William L.   **Born to Be a Soldier . . . William Wing Loring.** Wraps
1971   Fort Worth   10.
WEST, G. M.   **St. Andrews, Florida** plus appendix containing the official record of the vessels employed on the Blockading Fleet of St. Andrews Bay.
1922   St. Andrews   50.
WEST, Nathaniel   **Ancestry, Life and Times of Henry Hastings Sibley.**
1889   St. Paul   45.
West Point and the War. Wraps
1863   St. Louis   20.
WEST, Richard S., Jr.   **Gideon Welles, Lincoln's Navy Department.**
1943   New York   30.
1974   Westport   15.
WEST, Richard S., Jr.   **Lincoln's Scapegoat General — A Life of Benjamin F. Butler 1818-1893.**
1965   Boston   25.
WEST, Richard S., Jr.   **Mr. Lincoln's Navy.**
1957   New York   25.
WEST, Richard S., Jr.   **The Second Admiral: Life of David Dixon Porter, 1813-1891.**
1937   New York   30.
WEST, W. Reed   **Contemporary French Opinion of the American Civil War.** Wraps
1924   Baltimore   20.

WESTCOTT, Allan   **Mahan on Naval Warfare.**
    1918   Boston   40.
WESTON, David   **Among the Wounded.** Wraps
    1864   Philadelphia   30.
WESTON, George M.   **The Progress of Slavery in the United States.**
    1857   Washington, D. C.   40.
WESTON, James A.   **Services Held in the Chapel of Rest, Yadkin Valley, NC at
the Funeral of the Late Capt. Walter Waightstill Lenoir.** Wraps
    1890   New York   100.
WESTRATE, E. V.   **Those Fatal Generals.**
    1936   New York   25.
WHALEY, Elizabeth J.   **Forgotten Hero: General James B. McPherson.**
    1955   New York   30.
WHAN, Vorin E., Jr.   **Fiasco at Fredericksburg.**
    1961   State College, Pennsylvania   30.
WHARTON, H. M.   **War Songs and Poems of the Southern Confederacy
1861-1865.**
    1904   Philadelphia   60.
WHEARE, K. D.   **Abraham Lincoln and the United States.**
    1964   London   10.
WHEELER, Francis B.   **Monograph on the Monitor.** Wraps
    1884   Poughkeepsie, New York   30.
WHEELER, Richard   **The Siege of Vicksburg.**
    1978   New York   15.
WHEELER, Richard   **Voices of the Civil War.**
    1976   New York   20.
WHEELER, Richard   **We Knew Stonewall: An Eyewitness Biography.**
    1977   New York   10.
WHEELER, Richard   **We Knew William Tecumseh Sherman.**
    1977   New York   20.
WHEELOCK, Julia S.   **The Boys in White.**
    1870   New York   40.
WHEELWRIGHT, Jere   **The Gray Captain.**
    1954   New York   15.
WHELAN, Charles E.   **Bascom Clarke. The Story of a Southern Refugee.**
    1913   Madison, Wisconsin   25.
WHIPPLE, J. Raynor, and **STORER,** Malcom   **Shinplasters of the Civil War.**
    Wraps
    1942   n.p.   10.
WHIPPLE, Wayne   **The Heart of Lee.**
    1918   Philadelphia   15.
WHIPPLE, Wayne   **The Story Life of Lincoln.**
    1908   n.p.   8.
WHIPPLE, Wayne   **Tad Lincoln: A True Story.**
    1926   New York   7.
WHISNER, Will. C.   **Mark Ellis, or Unsolved Problems.**
    1899   Morgantown, West Virginia   25.
WHITE, A. R.   **The Blue and the Gray.**
    1898   n.p.   30.
WHITE, Andrew Dickson   **A Letter to William Howard Russell.** Wraps
    1863   London   25.
WHITE, E. V.   **The First Ironclad Naval Engagement of the World.** Wraps
    1906   New York   35.
WHITE, E. V.   **History of the Battle of Ball's Bluff.** Wraps
    n.d. (circa 1900)   Leesburg, Virginia   100.
WHITE, Henry Alexander   **Robert E. Lee and the Southern Confederacy.**
    1897   New York   125.
    1910   New York   100.

WHITE, Henry Alexander   **Stonewall Jackson.**
1909   Philadelphia   60.
WHITE, Horace   **The Life of Lyman Trumbull.**
1913   Boston   20.
WHITE, Horace   **The Lincoln and Douglas Debates, An Address.** Wraps
1914   Chicago   10.
WHITE, John E.   **My Old Confederate, An Address.** Wraps
1908   Atlanta   15.
WHITE, Laura   **Robert Barnwell Rhett: Father of Secession.**
1931   New York   40.
WHITE, Leslie Turner   **Look Away.**
1943   Philadelphia   15.
WHITE, Mary Virginia Saunders   **Robert E. Lee.** Wraps
1935   Cleveland, Ohio   15.
WHITE, Melvin Johnson   **The Secession Movement in the United States 1847-1852.**
Wraps
1910   n.p.   25.
WHITE, Richard Grant (ed)   **Poetry of the Civil War.**
1866   New York   20.
WHITE, William and Ruth   **Tin Can on a Shingle: The Full Story of the Monitor
and the Merrimac.**
1957   New York   10.
WHITE, William W.   **The Confederate Veteran.** Wraps
1962   Tuscaloosa   Ltd.   25.
WHITEHEAD, A. C.   **Two Great Southerners, Jefferson Davis and Robert E. Lee.**
1912   New York   20.
WHITEMAN, Maxwell   **While Lincoln Lay Dying.**
1968   Philadelphia   Ltd.   25.
WHITING, William   **Military Arrests in Time of War.** Wraps
1863   Washington   20.
WHITING, William   **The War Powers of the President, and the Legislative Powers
of Congress in Relation to Rebellion, Treason and Slavery.** Wraps
1863   Boston   30.
WHITLEY, Edythe Johns Rucker   **Sam Davis, Confederate Hero.**
1947   n.p.   30.
1971   Nashville   12.
WHITMAN, Walt   **Specimen Days & Collect.**
1882-'83   Philadelphia   40.
WHITNEY, A. H.   **War Ballads, The Brave Days of Old.**
1884   Chicago   15.
WHITNEY, Henry Clay   **Life on the Circuit with Lincoln.**
1892   Boston   30.
1940   Caldwell, Idaho   15.
1950   Caldwell, Idaho   15.
WHITNEY, Louisa M.   **Goldie's Inheritance, A Story of the Siege of Atlanta.**
1903   Burlington, Vermont   25.
WHITRIDGE, Arnold   **No Compromise: The Story of the Fanatics Who Paved the
Way to the Civil War.**
1960   New York   15.
WHITSITT, William H.   **Genealogy of Jefferson Davis and of Samuel Davis.**
1910   New York   75.
WHITTAKER, Frederick A.   **A Complete Life of General George A. Custer.**
1876   New York   60.
WHITTIER, John Greenleaf   **In War Time and Other Poems.**
1864   Boston   15.
**Who Burnt Columbia? Official Depositions of Wm. Tecumseh Sherman and Gen.
O. O. Howard.** Wraps
1873   Charleston   60.

WIARD, Norman   **Marine Artillery as Adapted for Service on the Coast and Inland Waters.** Wraps
    1863   New York   50.
WIARD, Norman   **Wiard's System of Field Artillery.** Wraps
    1863   New York   35.
WIECZERZAK, Joseph W.   **A Polish Chapter in Civil War America.**
    1967   New York   16.
WIGHT, Willard E.   **Some Wartime Letters of Bishop Lynch.** Wraps
    1957   n.p.   10.
The Wilderness Campaign May — June 1864. Vol. 4 of MHSM.
    1905   Boston   35.
The Wilderness Campaign Organization of the Army of the Potomac. Wraps
    1864   n.p.   20.
WILEY, Bell I.   **The Common Soldier of the Civil War, The Life of Billy Yank, The Life of Johnny Reb.**
    1952 and 1942   2 vols.   boxed   60.
    1958   New York   2 vols. in 1   25.
WILEY, Bell I.   **Confederate Women.**
    1975   Westport   15.
WILEY, Bell I.   **Embattled Confederates.**
    1964   New York   25.
    1969   New York   15.
WILEY, Bell I.   **Kingdom Coming, The Emancipation Proclamation of Sept 22 1862, An Address Delivered at the Chicago Historical Society Sept 21, 1962.** Wraps
    1963   Chicago   25.
WILEY, Bell I.   **The Life of Billy Yank.**
    1952   Indianapolis   25.
    1971   New York   10.
WILEY, Bell I.   **The Life of Johnny Reb.**
    1943   Indianapolis   30.
    1971   New York   10.
WILEY, Bell I.   **Plain People of the Confederacy.**
    1944   Baton Rouge   35.
    1971   Gloucester, Massachusetts   15.
WILEY, Bell I.   **The Road to Appomattox.**
    1956   Memphis   25.
WILEY, Bell I.   **The Role of the Archivist in the Civil War Centennial.** Wraps
    1960   Georgia   10.
WILEY, Bell I.   **They Fought for the Union.**
    1949   New York   30.
WILEY, Bell I and **MILHOLLEN,** Hirst D.   **They Who Fought Here.**
    1959   New York   25.
WILKES, Charles   **Autobiography of _____, U.S. Navy 1798-1877** edited by William J. Morgan, et al.
    1978   Washington   20.
WILKES, George   **McClellan: From Ball's Bluff to Antietam.** Wraps
    1863   New York   25.
WILKES, George   **McClellan: Who He Is and What He Has Done.**
    1863   New York   25.
WILKIE, Franc B.   **Pen and Powder.**
    1888   Boston   100.
WILKINSON, Herbert A.   **The American Doctrine of State Secession.** Wraps
    1934   Baltimore   20.
WILKINSON, John   **The Narrative of a Blockade-Runner.**
    1877   New York   175.
WILLARD, Benjamin J.   **A Record of the Things Which Happened to Capt. Benjamin J. Willard, Pilot and Stevedore.**
    1895   Portland, Maine   40.

WILLETT, James R.   **Rambling Recollections of a Military Engineer.**   Wraps
   1888   Chicago   80.
WILLIAMS, Alfred B.   **Hampton and His Red Shirts.**
   1935   Charleston, SC   35.
WILLIAMS, Alpheus S.   **From the Cannon's Mouth The Civil War Letters of . . .**
   edited by Milo M. Quaife.
   1959   Detroit   25.
WILLIAMS, Ben Ames   **House Divided.**
   1947   Boston   10.
WILLIAMS, Charles   **The Life of Rutherford Birchard Hayes.** 2 vols. **Diary and Letters.**
   5 vols.
   1928   Columbus   7 vols.   75.
WILLIAMS, E. F., and **HUMPHREYS**, H. D. (eds)   **Gunboats and Cavalry as Told to**
   J. P. Pryor and Thomas Jordan by Nathan Bedford Forrest.   Wraps
   1965   Memphis   15.
WILLIAMS, Edward F., III   **Fustest with the Mostest — The Military Career of**
   Tennessee's Greatest Confederate Lt. Gen. Nathan Bedford Forrest.   Wraps
   1969   Tennessee   15.
WILLIAMS, F.   **The Burden Bearer An Epic of Lincoln.**
   1908   Philadelphia   Ltd.   10.
WILLIAMS, Flora McDonald   **Who's the Patriot? A Story of the Southern**
   Confederacy.
   1886   Louisville, Kentucky   20.
WILLIAMS, Frances L.   **Matthew Fontaine Maury.**
   1963   New Brunswick, New Jersey   20.
WILLIAMS, George W.   **A History of the Negro Troops in the War of the Rebellion.**
   1888   New York   75.
   1969   New York   15.
WILLIAMS, Hermann Warner, Jr.   **The Civil War: The Artists' Record.**   Wraps
   1961   Boston   15.
WILLIAMS, James.   **The Rise and Fall of the Model Republic.**
   1863   London   80.
WILLIAMS, John Sharp   **Address to Company "A" Confederate Veterans.**   Wraps
   1904   Memphis   30.
WILLIAMS, John Skelton   **Our Advance from Appomattox, An Address.**   Wraps
   1907 (?)   n.p.   30.
WILLIAMS, Kenneth P.   **Lincoln Finds a General.** 5 vols.
   1949-59   75.   Individual volumes   10. each
WILLIAMS, Noble C.   **Echoes from the Battlefield.**
   1902   Atlanta   30.
WILLIAMS, Samuel   **The Lincolns and Tennessee.**
   1942   Harrogate   10.
WILLIAMS, T. Harry   **Beauregard, Napoleon in Gray.**
   1954   Baton Route   35.
   1955   Baton Rouge   30.
   1960   Baton Rouge   25.
WILLIAMS, T. Harry   **General Ewell to the High Private in the Rear.**   Wraps
   n.d.   n.p.   20.
WILLIAMS, T. Harry   **Lincoln and His Generals.**
   1952   New York   15.
WILLIAMS, T. Harry   **Lincoln and the Radicals.**
   1941   Wisconsin   15.
WILLIAMS, T. Harry   **McClellan, Sherman and Grant.**
   1962   New Brunswick   20.
WILLIAMS, T. Harry   **The Military Leadership of the North and the South.**
   1960   Colorado   7.
WILLIAMS, T. Harry   **With Beauregard to Mexico.**
   1956   Baton Rouge   Ltd.   30.

WILLIAMSON, Mary L.   **The Life of Gen. Robert E. Lee for Children in Easy Words.**
    1893   Richmond   10.
    1895   Richmond   10.
WILLIAMSON, Mary L.   **The Life of Gen. Thomas J. Jackson.**
    1899   Richmond   15.
    1914   Richmond   15.
WILLS, Mary Alice   **The Confederate Blockade of Washington, D. C. 1861-62.**
    1975   Parsons, W. Va.   15.
WILLSON, Beckles   **John Slidell and the Confederates in Paris.**
    1932   New York   30.
WILMER, Richard H.   **The Recent Past From a Southern Standpoint.**
    1887   New York   30.
WILSON, Edmund   **Patriotic Gore — Studies in the Literature of the American Civil War.**
    1962   New York   30.
WILSON, Francis   **John Wilkes Booth.**
    1929   Boston-New York   30.
    1929   Boston-New York   Ltd.   50.
WILSON, H. W.   **Ironclads in Action.** 2 vols.
    1896   Boston   40.
WILSON, Henry.   **History of the Anti-Slavery Measures of the Thirty-Seventh and Thirty-Eighth United States Congresses.**
    1864   Boston   25.
WILSON, Henry   **History of the Reconstruction Measures.**
    1868   Hartford   30.
WILSON, Henry.   **History of the Rise and Fall of the Slave Power in America.** 3 vols.
    1872   Boston   75.
    1879   Boston   60.
WILSON, Hill.   **John Brown, Soldier of Fortune.**
    1913   Lawrence, Kansas   12.
WILSON, James   **General Grant.**
    1897   New York   15.
WILSON, James Grant   **The Life and Public Services of Ulysses Simpson Grant.** Wraps
    1885   New York   15.
WILSON, James H.   **General Edward Francis Winslow, A Leader of Cavalry in the Great Rebellion.** Wraps
    1915   New York   30.
WILSON, James Harrison   **The Life and Services of Brevet Brigadier-General Andrew Jonathan Alexander.**
    1887   New York   40.
WILSON, James Harrison   **Life and Services of William Farrar Smith.**
    1904   Wilmington, Delaware   30.
WILSON, James Harrison   **The Life of Charles A. Dana.**
    1907   New York   15.
WILSON, James Harrison   **The Life of John A. Rawlins.**
    1916   New York   60.
WILSON, James Harrison   **The Life of Ulysses S. Grant.**
    1868   Springfield, Mass.   10.
WILSON, James Harrison.   **Under the Old Flag.** 2 vols.
    1912   New York   60.
    1971   Westport   36.
WILSON, John A.   **Adventures of Alf Wilson.**
    1880   Toledo   100.
    1897   Washington   40.
    1972   Marietta   Wraps   10.
WILSON, John Laird   **Battles of the Civil War in the United States.** 2 vols.
    1878   New York   65.
WILSON, John Laird.   **Story of the War: Pictorial History of the Great Civil War.**
    1881   Chicago   50.

WILSON, Joseph   **Naval Hygiene.**
1870   Washington   40.
WILSON, Joseph T.   **The Black Phalanx.**
1888   Hartford   100.
1890   Hartford   75.
1891   Hartford   75.
WILSON, Rufus Rockwell (comp.)   **Lincoln Among His Friends.**
1942   Caldwell, Idaho   10.
WILSON, Rufus Rockwell (ed)   **Lincoln in Caricature.**
1945   Elmira, New York   35.
1953   New York   20.
WILSON, Rufus Rockwell   **Uncollected Works of Abraham Lincoln.** 2 vols.
1947   Elmira, New York   25.
WILSON, Sarah   **Life of _____, Experiences during the War of the Rebellion.** Wraps
n.d.   n.p.   75.
WILSON, William B.   **A Few Acts and Actors in the Tragedy of the Civil War.**
1892   Philadelphia   30.
WILSON, Woodrow   **Robert E. Lee, An Interpretation.**
1924   Chapel Hill   12.
WILTON, Mark   **Fremont, the Pathfinder, The War Library Vol. 7 #252.** Wraps
1887   New York   50.
WILTSE, Charles M.   **John C. Calhoun, Nullifier 1829-1839.**
1949   Ind.   15.
WILTSE, Charles M.   **John C. Calhoun, Sectionalist 1840-1850.**
1951   Ind.   20.
WIMSATT, Josephine Cleary   **Recollections.**
1926   Tientsin, China   75.
WINDER, William H.   **Secrets of the American Bastile.** Wraps
1863   Philadelphia   40.
WINDROW, John E.   **John Berrien Lindsley.**
1938   Chapel Hill   30.
WINGFIELD, Marshall   **General A. P. Stewart, His Life and Letters.**
1954   Memphis   50.
WINKLEY, J. W.   **John Brown, The Hero.**
1905   Boston   20.
WINKS, Robin W.   **Canada and the United States: The Civil War Years.**
1960   Baltimore   20.
WINSLOW, Arthur   **Francis Winslow: His Forebears and Life.**
1935   Norwood, Mass.   Ltd.   45.
WINSLOW, Hattie Lou and **MOORE,** Joseph R. H.   **Camp Morton 1861-1865.** Wraps
1940   Indianapolis   20.
WINSLOW, Richard Elliott   **General John Sedgwick, the Story of a Union Corps Commander.**
1982   Novato, California   20.
WINSLOW, William Henry   **Southern Buds and Sons of War.**
1907   Boston   15.
WINSTON, Robert W.   **Andrew Johnson, Plebian and Patriot.**
1928   New York   25.
WINSTON, Robert W.   **High Stakes and Hair Trigger.**
1930   New York   25.
WINSTON, Robert W.   **Robert E. Lee.**
1934   New York   20.
WISE, Barton H.   **The Life of Henry A. Wise of Virginia.**
1899   New York   60.
WISE, George   **Campaigns and Battles of the Army of Northern Virginia.**
1916   New York   125.
WISE, George M.   **Marching Through South Carolina: Another Civil War Letter of _____ edited by Wilfred W. Black.**
1957   n.p.   10.

WISE, Henry A.   **Seven Decades of the Union.**
    1872   Philadelphia   25.
WISE, Jennings C.   **The Long Arm of Lee.**
    1915   Lynchburg, Virginia   2 vols.   75.
    1959   New York   2 vols. in 1   35.
WISE, Jennings C.   **The Military History of the Virginia Military Institute.**
    1915   Lynchburg, Virginia   75.
WISE, Jennings C.   **Sunrise of the Virginia Military Institute as a School of Arms, Spawn of the Cincinnati.** Wraps
    1958   Lexington   40.
WISE, John S.   **The End of an Era.**
    1899   Boston   30.
    1901   Boston   25.
    1902   Boston   25.
WISE, John S.   **Memorial Address, Delivered . . . May 15, 1864.** Wraps
    n.d.   n.p.   30.
WISTER, Francis   **Recollections of the 12th U.S. Infantry and Regular Division 1861-1865.** Wraps
    1887   Philadelphia   25.
WISTER, Owen   **Ulysses S. Grant and the Seven Ages of Washington.**
    1928   New York   12.
With Sheridan in Lee's Last Campaign by a Staff Officer. (F. C. Newhall)
    1866   Philadelphia   50.
WITHERS, Robert Enoch   **Autobiography of an Octogenarian.**
    1907   Roanoke   125.
WITTENMYER, Annie   **Under the Guns.**
    1895   Boston   40.
WOLDMAN, Albert A.   **Lincoln and the Russians.**
    1952   Cleveland   15.
WOLF, Hazel Catherine   **On Freedom's Altar, the Martyr Complex in the Abolition Movement.**
    1952   Madison   15.
WOLF, Simon   **The American Jew as Patriot, Soldier and Citizen.**
    1895   Philadelphia   40.
WOLFE, Samuel M.   **Helper's Impending Crisis Dissected.** Wraps
    1860   Philadelphia   60.
WOLSELEY, Garnet Joseph (Viscount)   **The American Civil War: An English View** edited by James A. Rawley
    1964   Charlottesville   25.
WOLSELEY, Garnet Joseph (Viscount)   **The Story of a Soldier's Life,** 2 vols.
    1903   Westminster   100.
WOOD, Edward A., II   **Dr. Eugene V. H. Hall, Veteran of the Civil War.** Wraps
    1956   Chicago   10.
WOOD, Forrest G.   **Black Scare.**
    1970   Berkeley, California   15.
WOOD, John Sumner   **The Virginia Bishop: A Yankee Hero of the Confederacy.**
    1961   Richmond   20.
WOOD, Leonora A.   **Abraham Lincoln.**
    1942   Piedmont, W. Va.   8.
WOOD, Robert C.   **Confederate Hand-Book, A Compilation of Important Data . . . Relating to the War Between the States.**
    1900   New Orleans   75.
WOOD, W. B., and **EDMONDS,** J. E.   **A History of the Civil War in the United States 1861-1865.**
    1905   New York   40.
    1910   New York   40.
    1959   New York   entitled: **Military History of the Civil War.**   25.
WOOD, William   **Captains of the Civil War, Vol. 31 of Chronicle of America.**
    1921   New Haven   15.

WOODBURN, James Albert. **The Life of Thaddeus Stevens.**
1913   Indianapolis   15.
WOODLEY, T. Thaddeus Stevens.
1934   Harrisburg   60.
WOODMAN, Harold D. (ed) **The Legacy of the American Civil War.**
1973   New York   10.
WOODRUFF, William E. **With the Light Guns in '61-'65. Reminiscences of Eleven Arkansas, Missouri, and Texas Light Batteries, in the Civil War.**
1903   Little Rock   200.
WOODWARD, Ashbel. **Life of General Nathaniel Lyon.**
1862   Hartford   25.
WOODWARD, Ashbel **Memoir of General Nathaniel Lyon of the 1st Brigade Missouri Vols.**
1866   Boston   20.
WOODWARD, C. Vann **The Burden of Southern History.**
1960   Baton Rouge   20.
WOODWARD, C. Vann **Reunion and Reaction, The Compromise of 1877 and the End of Reconstruction.**
1951   Boston   15.
WOODWARD, Joseph J. **The Hospital Steward's Manual.**
1862   Philadelphia   50.
WOODWARD, Joseph J. **Outlines of Chief Camp Diseases of U. S. Armies.**
1863   Philadelphia   75.
WOODWARD, W. E. **Meet General Grant.**
1928   New York   15.
1939   New York   15.
WOODWARD, W. E. **Years of Madness.**
1951   New York   10.
WOOLFOLK, George Ruble **The Cotton Regency.**
1958   New York   15.
WOOLSEY, Jane Stuart **Hospital Days.** Wraps
1870   New York   150.
WOOLSEY, Theodore D. **Remarks on the Alabama Claims from the New Englander for July, 1869.** Wraps
1869   New Haven   30.
WORDEN, J. L., **GREENE,** S. D., and **RAMSEY,** H. A. **The Monitor and the Merrimac.**
1912   New York   25.
WORK, Henry C. **Marching Through Georgia.**
1889   Boston   20.
WORMELEY, Katherine P. **The Other Side of the War with the Army of the Potomac.**
1889   Boston   40.
WORMSER, Richard **The Yellowlegs. Story of the U. S. Cavalry.**
1966   New York   10.
WORTH, Jonathan. **Correspondence.** edited by J. G. De R. Hamilton   2 vols.
1909   Raleigh, NC   40.
WORTHINGTON, Glenn H. **Fighting for Time . . . Or, the Battle That Saved Washington.**
1932   Baltimore   75.
WRIGHT, Arthur A. **The Civil War in the Southwest.**
1964   Denver   25.
WRIGHT, Mrs. D. Giraud. **A Southern Girl in '61.**
1905   New York   35.
WRIGHT, E. N. **Conscientious Objectors in the Civil War.**
1931   Philadelphia   30.
1961   New York   15.
WRIGHT, Howard C. **Port Hudson, Its History from an Interior Point of View.** Wraps
1961   Baton Rouge   6.
WRIGHT, John S. **Citizenship Sovereignty.** Wraps
1863   Chicago   40.

WRIGHT, John S.   **Reply to Hon. Charles G. Loring Upon "Reconstruction".** Wraps
    1867   Chicago   15.
WRIGHT, Marcus J. (comp.)   **General Officers of the Confederate Army.**
    1911   New York   125.
WRIGHT, Marcus J.   **General Scott.**
    1894   New York   25.
WRIGHT, Marcus J. (comp.)   **List of Field Officers in the Confederate States Service plus List of Regiments and Battalions in the Confederate States Army 1861-1865.**
    1897   Washington   200.
WRIGHT, William C.   **The Secession Movement in the Middle Atlantic States.**
    1973   Rutherford   20.
WYETH, John Allan   **Life of General Nathan Bedford Forrest.**
    1899   New York   125.
    1900   New York   100.
    1959   New York   entitled: **That Devil Forrest: Life of General Nathan Bedford Forrest**   25.
WYNES, Charles E. (ed)   **The Negro in the South Since 1865.**
    1965   University, Alabama   15.
YATES, Bowling C.   **Historical Guide for Kennesaw Mountain National Battlefield Park and Marietta, Georgia.** Wraps
    1976   Marietta   8.
YATES, Bowling C.   **History of the Georgia Military Institute, Marietta, Georgia.**
    1968   Marietta   10.
YATES, Richard E.   **The Confederacy and Zeb Vance.**
    1958   Tuscaloosa, Alabama   Ltd.   25.   Wraps
Ye Book of Copperheads. Wraps
    1863   Philadelphia   40.
YEARNS, Wilfred Buck   **The Confederate Congress.**
    1960   Athens   25.
YEATMAN, James   **Report to the Western Sanitary Commission, St. Louis, Dec. 17, 1863.** Wraps
    1863 (?)   St. Louis (?)   20.
YORK, Brantley   **The Autobiography of** _____.
    1910   Durham   40.
YOUNG, Agatha   **The Women and the Crisis.**
    1959   New York   20.
YOUNG, Bennett H.   **Confederate Wizards of the Saddle.**
    1914   Boston   200.
    1958   Kennesaw, Georgia   50.
YOUNG, Bennett H.   **The South in History.** Wraps
    1910 (?)   Nashville, Tennessee   35.
YOUNG, James C.   **Marse Robert, Knight of the Confederacy.**
    1929   New York   25.
    1931   New York   20.
YOUNG, James Harvey   **Anna Elizabeth Dickinson and the Civil War.** Wraps
    1944   Mississippi   15.
YOUNG, Jesse Bowman   **The Battle of Gettysburg.**
    1913   New York   50.
YOUNG, John Russell.   **Around the World with General Grant.** 2 vols.
    1879   New York   35.
YOUNG, John Russell   **Men and Memories.** edited by May D. Russell Young.
    1901   New York   30.
YOUNG, Stark   **So Red the Rose.**
    1934   New York   15.
ZABRISKIE, George A.   **John Brown: Saint or Sinner?**
    1949   Ormond Beach, Florida   15.
ZINCKE, F. Barham   **Last Winter in the United States.**
    1868   London   60.

ZINN, Jack   **The Battle of Rich Mountain.** Wraps
    1971   Parsons, W. Va.   5.
    1972   parsons, W. Va.   5.
ZINN, Jack   **R. E. Lee's Cheat Mountain Campaign.**
    1974   parsons, W. Va.   20.
ZORNOW, William Frank   **Lincoln and the Party Divided.**
    1954   Norman   15.
ZUBER, Richard L.   **Jonathan Worth, A Biography of a Southern Unionist.**
    1965   Chapel Hill   20.
ZUBER, William P.   **My Eighty Years in Texas** edited by Janis B. Mayfield.
    1971   Austin   20.

U. S. GOVERNMENT PUBLICATIONS

During the war the U. S. Government issued tens of thousands of documents. With few exceptions these were issued in great quantity, are still commonly available, are hard to sell, and have little value. Most documents were issued individually and later printed and bound with similar documents in Annual Reports, Senate Documents, Senate Miscellaneous, Executive Documents, and in Annual Reports of the Secretaries.

However, per usual, there are exceptions to the rule, some of which are as follows:

A. CONGRESS

Ku Klux Conspiracy. Testimony Taken by the Joint Select Committee to Inquire into the Condition of Affairs in the Late Insurrectionary States. 13 vols
        1872   Washington   350.
        Individual volumes: Alabama   3 vols.   75.
                            Florida   1 vol.   30.
                            Georgia   2 vols.   50.
                            Mississippi   2 vols.   50.
                            North Carolina 1 vol.   30.
                            South Carolina 3 vols.   75.
                            Report of the Committee   1 vol.   25.

Permanent Fortifications and Sea-Coast Defenses. Report 86, 37th Congress, 2nd Session, Ho. of Reps.
        1862   Washington   40.

Report in the Senate, Committee on the Conduct of the War . . . Inquire into and Report the Facts Concerning Attack on Petersburg. Report 114, 38th Congress, 2nd Session, Senate.
        1864   Washington   30.

Report of the Joint Committee on the Conduct of the War.
        37th Congress, Third Session, Washington   1863
        Part I — Army of the Potomac
        Part II — Bull Run, Ball's Bluff
        Part III — Department of the West
        38th Congress, Second Session, Washington   1865
        Vol. I — Reports on Army of Potomac and Battle of Petersburg
        Vol II — Reports on Red River Expedition, Fort Fisher Expedition,
            Heavy Ordnance
        Vol. III — Reports on Sherman-Johnston, Light Draught Monitors, Massacre of
            Cheyenne Indians, Ice Contracts, Rosecrans' Campaigns & Misc.
        38th Congress, Second Session, Washington   1866   Supplemental Report
        Part I — Reports of Sherman, Thomas
        Part II — Reports of Pope, Foster, Pleasanton, Hitchcock, Sheridan, Ricketts,
            Communication & Memorial of Norman Wiard
        Set of 8 vols.   250.
        Individual vols.   25. each

Report of the Special Committee Appointed to Investigate the Troubles in Kansas. Report 200, 34th Congress, 1st Session, Ho. of Reps.
        1856   Washington   50.
Supplement to the Congressional Globe Containing the Proceedings of the Senate Sitting for the Trial of Andrew Johnson, President of the U.S. 40th Congress, 2nd Session.
        1868   Washington   75.

Trial of Andrew Johnson . . . Before the Senate of the U.S. on Impeachment by the House of Representatives for High Crimes and Misdemeanors. 3 vols.
    1868   Washington   45.

B. WAR DEPARTMENT

(McClellan, George B.) Letter of the Secretary of War Transmitting Report on the Organization of the Army of the Potomac.
    1864   Washington   30.

(Pope, John) Letter from the Secretary of War . . . Transmitting Copy of Report of Major General John Pope. 37th Congress, 3d Session, Ho. of Reps. Doc. 81.
    1863   Washington   30.

(Porter, Fitz John) Letter from the Secretary of War . . . Transmitting Copy of Proceedings of Court-Martial in the Trial of General Fitz John Porter. 37th Congress, 3d Session, Ho. of Reps. Doc. 71.
    1863   Washington   35.

Special Orders of the Adjutant and Inspector General's Office, Confederate States. Printed by Record & Pension Office of US War Dept. 2 vols. (Never compiled by the Confederacy)
    1889-1904   Washington   225.

C. ARMY — General Orders — Washington.
General Orders, issued by the Adjutant General's Office, Washington, were released individually and later reprinted in bound volumes at the year's end. With the exception of the Emancipation Proclamation, they are of little individual value. The individually issued orders were often bound later but can be distinguished from the government bound volumes by the following: handwritten corrections and annotations, creasing, soiling and other signs of use, perforations at the inner margin where tied together, no title page.

General Orders, War Department, Adjutant General's Office
Individual orders as issued unbound or in field binding
    1861   250.
    1862-65 per year   125.
    Same as printed & bound in one vol. at end of year   40. per volume

Emancipation Proclamation.   1862
    1862 General Order #139.   75.
    Reissued as General Order #1 for 1863.   25.

D. ARMY — General Orders — Elsewhere.
General Orders, Circulars and Memoranda were also issued by the Headquarters of the various Army departments — Department of the Missouri, Department of the South, Department of the Gulf, Department of Louisiana, etc. These were printed in lesser quantities and many are unlocated. Regretfully limits of space and knowledge preclude a detailed analysis of the orders for the various commands. However should anyone have questions about such material, we will be glad to help identify and evaluate.

E. NAVY

(Wilkes, Charles) Letter from the Secretary of the Navy . . . Proceedings of the Court-Martial Which Tried Commodore Charles Wilkes 38th Congress, 1st Session, Ho. of Reps. Doc. 102.
    1864   Washington   35.

Letter of the Secretary of the Navy . . . Connected with the Recent Engagements on the Mississippi River, Which Resulted in the Capture of Forts Jackson, St. Philip, and the City of New Orleans, the Destruction of the Rebel Flotilla, etc. 37th Congress, 2d Session, Senate Doc. 56.
    1862   Washington   40.

Ordinance Instructions for the United States Navy.
   1866   Washington   100.

Report of the Secretary of the Navy . . . Reports from Officers, Dec. 1863.
   1863   Washington   100.

Report of the Secretary of the Navy with an Appendix Containing Reports from Officers Dec. 1864.
   1864   Washington   100.

Report of the Secretary of the Navy in Relation to Armored Vessels.
   1864   Washington   40.

REGIMENTALS AND STATE INTEREST

ALABAMA
GENERAL REFERENCES

BREWER, Willis   **Alabama: Her History, . . . 1540-1872.**
  1872   Montgomery   80.
  1864   Tuscaloosa   20.
DELANEY, Caldwell   **Confederate Mobile: A Pictorial History.**
  1971   Mobile   25.
DORMAN, Lewy   **Party Politics in Alabama from 1850 through 1860.** Wraps
  1935   Wetumpka, Alabama   20.
DUBOSE, John W.   **Alabama's Tragic Decade.**
  1940   Birmingham   35.
EVANS, Clement A. (ed)   **Confederate Military History, Vol. VII. -
Alabama and Mississippi.**
  1899   Atlanta   40.
FLEMING, Walter L.   **Civil War and Reconstruction in Alabama.**
  1905   New York   100.
  1911   Cleveland   50.
  1949   New York   50.
  1978   Spartanburg   30.
HUNNICUTT, John L.   **Reconstruction in West Alabama, The Memoirs of**
  _____ edited by Wm. Stanley Hoole. Wraps
  1959   Tuscaloosa   Ltd.   25.
McMILLAN, Malcolm C.   **The Alabama Confederate Reader.**
  1963   University   30.
MARTIN, Bessie   **Desertion of Alabama Troops from the Confederate Army.**
  1932   New York   50.
  1966   New York   20.
RILEY, B. F.   **Makers and Romance of Alabama History.**
  n.d.   n.p.   60.
SMITH, S. A. and **SMITH,** C. C., Jr. (eds)   **Mobile: 1861-1865 Notes & Bibliography.** Wraps
  1964   Chicago/Mobile   5.
SMITH, William   **The History and Debates of the Convention of the People of Alabama.**
  1975   Spartanburg, S. C.   21.
STERKX, H. E.   **Partners in Rebellion: Alabama Women in the Civil War.**
  1970   Rutherford, New Jersey   20.
STERKX, H. E.   **Some Notable Alabama Women During the Civil War.** Wraps
  1962   University, Alabama   15.

REGIMENTALS

BARBIERE, Joseph   **Scraps from the Prison Table at Camp Chase and Johnson's Island.**
  1868   Doyleston   225.
BARNARD, Henry V.   **Tattered Volunteers, The Twenty-Seventh Alabama Infantry Regiment C.S.A.**
  1965   Northport   20.
CANNON, J. P.   **Inside of Rebeldom: The Daily Life of a Private in the Confederate Army.** Wraps
  1900   Washington   75.
CLARK, George   **A Glance Backward.**
  1914 (?)   Houston   50.
GOODLOE, Albert T.   **Confederate Echoes, A Voice from the South in the Days of Secession and of the Southern Confederacy.**
  1907   Nashville   200.

GOODLOE, Albert T.   **Some Relics from the Seat of War.**
 1893   Nashville   250.
HOOLE, William S.   **Alabama Tories: The Story of the First Alabama Cavalry USA.** Wraps
 1930   Tuscaloosa   Ltd.   30.
HOTZE, Henry   **Three Months in the Confederate Army.** edited by Richard Harwell. Wraps
 1952   University, Alabama   25.
HOUGHTON, William Robert   **Two Boys in the Civil War and After.**
 1912   Montgomery   150.
LITTLE, George and **MAXWELL**, James R.   **History of Lumsden's Battery, C.S.A.** Wraps
 n.d. (circa 1905)   Tuscaloosa   100.
LITTLE, R. H.   **A Year of Starvation and Plenty.**
 1966   Belton, Texas   20.
McCLENDON, W. A.   **Recollections of War Times.**
 1973   San Bernardino, California   30.
McMORRIES, Edward Young   **History of the First Regiment Volunteer Infantry C.S.A.**
 1904   Montgomery, Alabama   150.
MIMS, Wilbur F.   **War History of the Prattville Dragoons.** Wraps
 n.d.   Thurber, Texas   100.
 n.d.   n.p.   25.
OATES, William C.   **The War Between the Union and the Confederacy.**
 1905   New York/Washington   250.
 1974   Dayton   25.
PARK, Robert Emory   **Sketch of the 12th Alabama Infantry of Battle's Brigade, Rhodes' Division, Early's Corps, of the Army of Northern Virginia.** Wraps
 1906   Richmond   175.
PATTERSON, Edmund DeWitt   **Yankee Rebel Civil War Journal of _____ 9th Alabama Infantry.** edited by John G. Barrett
 1966   Chapel Hill   30.
PIERREPONT, Alice V. D.   **Reuben Vaughan Kidd: Soldier of the Confederacy.**
 1947   Petersburg   100.
SHAVER, Lewellyn A.   **A History of the 60th Alabama Regiment, Gracie's Alabama Brigade.**
 1867   Montgomery   400.
WILLETT, Elbert D.   **History of Company B** (originally Pickens Planters) **40th Alabama Regiment C.S.A. 1862-1865.**
 1902   Anniston   375.
 1963   n.p.   25.
WYETH, John Allan   **With Sabre and Scalpel.**
 1914   New York   75.

ARKANSAS

GENERAL REFERENCES

Report of the Adjutant General of State of Arkansas for the Period of the Late Rebellion and to November 1, 1866.
 1867   Washington   75.
CLAYTON, Powell   **The Aftermath of the Civil War in Arkansas.**
 1915   New York   100.
 1969   New York   25.
Confederate Women of Arkansas in the Civil War 1861-1865 Memorial Reminiscences.
 1907   Little Rock   60.

EVANS, Clement A. (ed)   **Confederate Military History, Vol. X — Louisiana and Arkansas.**
1899   Atlanta   40.

FERGUSON, John L. (comp & ed)   **Arkansas and the Civil War.**
1964   Little Rock   30.

FLETCHER, John Gould   **Arkansas.**
1947   Chapel Hill   30.

HARRELL, John M.   **The Brooks and Baxter War, A History of the Reconstruction Period in Arkansas.**
1893   St. Louis   100.

STAPLES, Thomas S.   **Reconstruction in Arkansas 1862-1874.**
1923   New York   50.

THOMAS, David Y.   **Arkansas in War and Reconstruction 1861-1874.**
1926   Little Rock   60.

WATSON, Lady Elizabeth   **Fight and Survive: A History of Jackson County, Arkansas in the Civil War.**
1973   Newport   20.

WORLEY, Ted R. (ed)   **At Home in Confederate Arkansas, Letters to and from Pulaski Countians 1861-1865.** Wraps
1955   Pulaski, Arkansas   25.

WRIGHT, Marcus J.   **Arkansas in the War 1861-1865.**
1963   Batesville   20.

REGIMENTALS

Union

BISHOP, Albert Webb   **Loyalty on the Frontier; or, Sketches of Union Men in the South West, With Incidents and Adventures in Rebellion on the Border.**
1863   St. Louis   125.

Confederate

BEVENS, W. E.   **Reminiscences of a Private Company "G" First Arkansas Regiment Infantry.** Wraps
1977   Newport, Arkansas   25.

CATE, Wirt Armistead (ed)   **Two Soldiers: The Campaign Diaries of Thomas J. Key, CSA Dec 7, 1863-May 7, 1865 and Robert J. Campbell, USA, Jan 1, 1864-July 21, 1864.**
1938   Chapel Hill   50.

COLLIER, Calvin L.   **First In — Last Out, The Capitol Guards, Arkansas Brigade in the Civil War.**
1961   Little Rock   35.

COLLIER, Calvin L.   **"They'll Do to Tie To!" The Story of the Third Regiment, Arkansas Infantry, C.S.A.**
1959   Little Rock, Arkansas   35.

COLLIER, Calvin L.   **The War Child's Children, The Story of the 3rd Regiment Arkansas Cavalry, Confederate States Army.**
1965   Little Rock   30.

DACUS, Robert H.   **Reminiscences of Co. "H" 1st Arkansas Mounted Rifles.** Wraps
1972   Dayton   7.50

FLETCHER, Elliott H.   **A Civil War Letter of** _____ edited by J. H. Atkinson. Wraps
1963   Little Rock   30.

GAMMAGE, W. L.   **The Camp, The Bivouac, and the Battle Field. Being a History of the 4th Arkansas Regiment.**
1958   Little Rock   40.

HAMMOCK, John C.   **With Honor Untarnished: The Story of the First Arkansas Infantry Regiment, C.S.A.**
1961   Little Rock   25.

LAVENDER, John W.   **The War Memoirs of . . . C.S.A.** edited by Ted R. Worley.
1956   Pine Bluff, Arkansas   30.

LEEPER, Wesley Thurman   **Rebels Valiant: Second Arkansas Mounted Rifles (Dismounted).**
1964   Little Rock   30.

McCOLLOM, Albert O.   **The War Time Letters of _____ Confederate Soldier.** edited by Walter J. Lemke. Wraps
1961   Fayetteville, Arkansas   35.

CALIFORNIA

GENERAL REFERENCES

Annual Report of the Adjutant General for the Years 1861, 1862, 1863, 1864/65.
1862-65   Sacramento   50. per volume

MOORE, Avery C.   **Confederate California.** Wraps
1956   Sonora, California   20.

ORTON, Richard H. (comp)   **Records of California Men in the War of the Rebellion.**
1890   Sacramento   125.
1979   Detroit   45.

REGIMENTALS

BENSELL, Royal A.   **All Quiet on the Yamhill, The Civil War in Oregon, The Journal of Corporal _____** edited by Gunter Barth.
1959   Eugene, Oregon   30.

HUNT, Aurora   **Major General James H. Carleton.**
1958   Glendale   30.

PETTIS, George H.   **The California Column. Its Campaign and Services in New Mexico, Arizona and Texas, During the Civil War.** Wraps
1908   Santa Fe   275.

PETTIS, George H.   **Frontier Service During the Rebellion, or a History of Company K, 1st Infantry Calif Volunteers.** Wraps
1885   Providence   Ltd.   150.

PETTIS, George H.   **Kit Carson's Fight with the Comanche and Kiowa Indians.** Wraps
1878   Providence   Ltd.   175.
1908   Santa Fe   175.

ROGERS, Fred B.   **Soldiers of the Overland . . . Services of General Patrick E. Conner & His Volunteers.**
1938   San Francisco   100.

KELEHER, William A.   **Turmoil in New Mexico 1846-1868.**
1952   Sante Fe, New Mexico   35.

COLORADO

GENERAL REFERENCES

NANKIVELL, John H.   History of the Military Organizations of the State of
Colorado.
1935   Denver   75.
WHITFORD, William Clarke   Colorado Volunteers in the Civil War; The New
Mexico Campaign in 1862. Wraps
1906   Denver   125.
1962   Chicago   30.

REGIMENTALS

HOLLISTER, Ovando J.   Boldly They Rode: History of 1st Colorado Regiment of
Volunteers.
1949   Lakewood   35.
HOLLISTER, Ovando J.   Colorado Volunteers in New Mexico 1862. edited by
Richard Harwell.
1962   Chicago   30.
MUMEY, Nolie   Bloody Trails Along the Rio Grande a Day by Day Diary of
Alonzo Ferdinand Ickis (1836-1917) A Soldier.
1958   Denver   Ltd.   100.
WILLIAMS, Ellen   Three Years and a Half in the Army, or History of the Second
Colorados.
1885   New York   250.

CONNECTICUT

GENERAL REFERENCES

Annual Report of the Adjutant General of the State of Connecticut 1862-65.
v.d.   Hartford   25. each
ANDERSON, Joseph   History of the Soldiers' Monument in Waterbury, Conn.
1886   n.p.   15.
Catalogue of Connecticut Volunteer Organizations, Infantry, Cavalry, and Artillery.
1869   Hartford   50.
Catalog of the 6th, 7th, 8th, 9th, 10th, and 11th Regiments of Infantry, 1st Light
Battery and 1st Battalion Cavalry, Connecticut Vols. 1861. Wraps
1862   Hartford   25.
Catalogue of the 12th and 13th Regiments Connecticut Volunteers. Wraps
1862   Hartford   20.
CROFFUT, W. A. and MORRIS, John M.   The Military and Civil History of
Connecticut . . . 1861-65.
1868   New York   30.
1869   New York   30.
DANA, Malcolm McG.   The Annals of Norwich in the Great Rebellion.
1873   Norwich   25.
Dedication of the Monument at Andersonville . . . in Memory of the Men of
Connecticut Who Suffered in Southern Military Prisons.
1908   Hartford   15.
History of Battle-Flag Day, September 17, 1879.
1879   Hartford   20.
LANE, J. Robert   A Political History of Connecticut During the Civil War. Wraps
1941   Washington   20.

NIVEN, John   **Connecticut for the Union.**
   1965   New Haven   20.
Record of Service of the Connecticut Men in the Army and Navy of the War of the Rebellion.
   1889   Hartford   75.

REGIMENTALS

ABBOT, Henry L.   **Siege Artillery in the Campaigns Against Richmond.** Wraps
   1867   Washington   150.
   1868   New York   125.
ANDREWS, E. Benjamin   **A Private's Reminiscences of the First Year of the War.** Wraps
   1886   Providence   Ltd.   25.
BEECHER, Herbert W.   **History of the 1st Light Battery Connecticut Volunteers.** 2 vols.
   1901   New York   150.
BLAKESLEE, B. F.   **History of the 16th Connecticut Volunteers.**
   1875   Hartford   75.
CADWELL, Charles K.   **The Old 6th Regiment.**
   1875   New Haven   75.
CHAPMAN, Horatio Dana   **Civil War Diary.**
   1929   Hartford   50.
DeFOREST, John William   **A Volunteer's Adventures.**
   1946   New Haven   20.
   1956   New Haven   15.
The 18th (Eighteenth) Regiment Connecticut Volunteer Infantry in the War of the Rebellion 1862-1865. Wraps
   1889   Hartford   30.
FENTON, E. B.   **From the Rapidan to Atlanta Leaves from the Diary of _____** Wraps
   1893   Detroit   25.
FISKE, Samuel Wheelock   **Mr. Dunn Browne's Experiences in the Army.**
   1866   Boston   30.
GODDARD, Henry P.   **14th Connecticut Volunteers, Regimental Reminiscences of the War.** Wraps
   1877   Middletown   35.
GODDARD, Henry P.   **Memorial of Deceased Officers of the 14th Regiment Connecticut Vols.** Wraps
   1872   Hartford   20.
HART, E. Marvin   **The 15th Regiment Connecticut Volunteers A History.**
   1889   Hartford   50.
A Journal of Incidents Connected with the Travels of the 22nd Regiment Connecticut Volunteers for Nine Months, in Verse by an Orderly Sergeant.
   1863   Hartford   20.
KELLOGG, Robert H.   **Life and Death in Rebel Prisons.**
   1865   Hartford   20.
   1866   Hartford   20.
   1867   Hartford   20.
LUCKE, James B.   **History of the New Haven Grays.**
   1876   New Haven   30.
LYNCH, Charles H.   **The Civil War Diary 1862-1865 of _____ 18th Conn. Volunteers.**
   1915   Hartford   40.
McNAMAR, J. B.   **Official Souvenir & Program of Monument, 1st Conn. Heavy Artillery.** Wraps
   1902   Hartford   25.
MARVIN, Edwin E.   **The Fifth Regiment, Connecticut Volunteers, A History.**
   1889   Hartford   55.

A Memorial of Lt. Daniel Perkins Dewey of the Twenty-Fifth Regiment Connecticut Volunteers.
1864   Hartford   20.
MURRAY, Thomas H.   **History of the 9th Regiment, Connecticut Volunteer Infantry, "The Irish Regiment."**
1903   New Haven   85.
NEWTON, A. H.   **Out of the Briars: An Autobiography and Sketch of the 29th Conn. Regiment of Volunteers.**
1910   Philadelphia   75.
1969   Miami   20.
OLCOTT, Mark   **The Civil War Letters of Lewis Bissell.** Wraps
1981   Washington   10.
OVIATT, George A.   **Memorial Address Delivered at the Funeral of Capt. Samuel B. Hayden at Windsor Locks.** Wraps
1863   Hartford   20.
QUIEN, George   **Reminiscences of the Service and Experience of Lieut. _____ Co. K, 23rd Conn. Vols.**
1906   Waterbury   40.
PAGE, Charles D.   **History of the 14th Regiment, Connecticut Volunteer Infantry.**
1906   Meriden, Connecticut   100.
PRESTON, Francis W.   **Port Hudson: A History of the Investment, Siege and Capture.** Wraps
1892   Brooklyn   60.
RATHBURN, Julius G.   **Trip of the First Regiment C.N.G. to Yorktown, Va. and Charleston, S. C.**
1882   Hartford   30.
Seventeenth Annual Reunion of the 17th Regiment C.V.I. Wraps
1884   Bridgeport   20.

SHELDON, Winthrop D.   **The "27th", A Regimental History.**
1866   New Haven   60.
SHERMAN, Andrew M.   **In the Lowlands of Louisiana in 1863, An Address.** Wraps
1908   Morristown, New Jersey   50.
Sixteenth Regiment Connecticut Volunteers, Excursion and Reunion at Antietam Battlefield, Sept 17, 1889.
1889   Hartford   20.
Sixteenth Regiment Connecticut Volunteers, Report of the 23rd Annual Reunion.
1890   Hartford   20.
SPRAGUE, Homer B.   **History of the 13th Infantry Regiment of Connecticut Volunteers.**
1867   Hartford   110.
SPRAGUE, Homer B.   **Lights and Shadows in Confederate Prisons, A Personal Experience 1864-1865.**
1915   New York   50.
STEVENS, Henry S.   **Souvenir of Excursion of Battlefields by Society of Fourteenth Connecticut Regiment . . . 1891.**
1893   Washington   40.
STORRS, John W.   **The "Twentieth Connecticut."**
1886   Naugatuck   80.
Story of the 21st Connecticut Volunteer Infantry During the Civil War.
1900   Middletown   75.
TAYLOR, Jeremiah   **The Sacrifice Consumed. Life of Edward Hamilton Brewer.**
1863   Boston   25.
TAYLOR, John C.   **History of the First Connecticut Artillery and of the Siege Trains of the Armies Operating Against Richmond 1862-1865.**
1893   Hartford   150.
THORPE, Sheldon B.   **History of the Fifteenth Connecticut Volunteers.**
1893   New Haven   90.

TRUMBULL, Henry Clay   **The Knightly Soldier, A Biography of Major Henry Ward Camp, Tenth Conn. Volunteers.**
    1865   Boston   25.
    1892   Philadelphia   20.
TRUMBULL, Henry Clay   **War Memories of an Army Chaplain.**
    1898   New York   30.
    1906   New York   30.
The 25th Regiment Connecticut Volunteers in the War of the Rebellion.
    1913   Rockville, Conn.   75.
VAILL, Dudley Landon   **The County Regiment A Sketch of the 2nd Regiment of Connecticut Volunteer Heavy Artillery.**
    1908   Litchfield   45.
VAILL, Theodore F.   **History of the Second Connecticut Volunteer Heavy Artillery Originally the Nineteenth Connecticut Vols.**
    1868   Winsted, Conn.   75.
WALKER, Edward A.   **Our First Year of Army Life, An Anniversary Address Delivered to First Regiment of Connecticut Volunteer Heavy Artillery.** Wraps
    1862   New Haven   45.
WALKER, William C.   **History of the Eighteenth Regiment Conn. Volunteers.**
    1885   Norwich   75.
WALKLEY, Stephen   **History of the 7th Connecticut Volunteer Infantry.**
    1905   Southington, Conn.   80.

DELAWARE

GENERAL REFERENCES

HANCOCK, Harold Bell   **Delaware During the Civil War, A Political History.**
    1961   Wilmington   30.
SPRUANCE, John S.   **Delaware Stays in the Union: The Civil War Period: 1860-1865.** Wraps
    1955   Newark   10.
WILKINSON, Norman B.   **The Brandywine Home Front During the Civil War.**
    1966   Wilmington   20.

REGIMENTALS

MAULL, D. W.   **The Life and Military Services of the Late Brigadier General Thomas A. Smyth.**
    1870   Wilmington   25.
MURPHEY, Thomas G.   **Four Years in the War. The History of the First Regiment of Delaware Veteran Volunteers.**
    1866   Philadelphia   100.
SEVILLE, William P.   **History of the First Regiment, Delaware Volunteers.** Wraps
    1884   Wilmington   45.
SMITH, Robert G.   **Brief Account of the Services Rendered by the Second Regiment Delaware Volunteers in the War.** Wraps
    1909   Wilmington   40.

DISTRICT OF COLUMBIA

War History of the National Rifles, Company A, Third Battalion District of Columbia Volunteers of 1861.
1887   Wilmington, Del.   150.

FLORIDA

GENERAL REFERENCES

DAVIS, William Watson   **The Civil War and Reconstruction in Florida.**
    1913   New York   175.
    1964   Gainesville   30.
JOHNS, John E.   **Florida During the Civil War.**
    1963   Gainesville   25.
LONG, Ellen Call   **Florida Breezes; or, Florida, New and Old.**
    1962   Gainesville   20.
PATRICK, Rembert W.   **Florida Under Five Flags.**
    1945   Gainesville   25.
SHOFNER, Jerrell H.   **Nor Is It Over Yet, Florida in the Era of Reconstruction 1863-1877.**
    1974   Gainesville   20.
WALLACE, John   **Carpet-Bag Rule in Florida.**
    1888   Jacksonville   Wraps   300.
    1959   Kennesaw, Georgia   25.

REGIMENTALS

DICKISON, Mary Elizabeth   **Dickison and His Men.**
    1890   Louisville, Kentucky   300.
    1962   Gainesville   35.

GEORGIA

GENERAL REFERENCES

AUSTIN, Aurelia   **Georgia Boys with "Stonewall" Jackson.** Wraps
    1967   Athens   15.
BATTEY, George Magruder, Jr.   **A History of Rome and Floyd County** (Ga.) **Vol. 1** (all pub).
    1922   Atlanta   75.
BRANTLEY, Rabun Lee   **Georgia Journalism of the Civil War Period.** Wraps
    1929   Nashville   30.
BRYAN, T. Conn   **Confederate Georgia.**
    1953   Athens   30.
    1964   Athens   25.
CANDLER, Allen D.   **The Confederate Records of the State of Georgia 1860-1868.**
    6 vols.
    1909-1911   Atlanta   750.
COLEMAN, Kenneth (ed)   **Athens, 1861-65, As Seen Through Letters in the University of Georgia Libraries.** Wraps
    1969   Athens   10.
COLEMAN, Kenneth   **Confederate Athens.**
    1967   Athens   20.

Confederate Soldiers Home of Georgia in Memory of the Heroes in Gray 1861-1928. Wraps
    1928 (?)   n.p.   50.
CONWAY, Alan   **The Reconstruction of Georgia.**
    1966   Minneapolis   25.
CORLEY, Florence Fleming   **Confederate City, Augusta, Georgia.**
    1960   Columbia, S. C.   25.
d'ANTIGNAC, Munroe   **Georgia's Navy 1861.** Wraps
    1945   Griffin, Georgia   50.
DUNCAN, Alexander Mc.   **Roll of Officers and Members of the Georgia Hussars and of the Cavalry Companies.**
    1906   Savannah   400.
FLANDERS, Ralph Betts   **Plantation Slavery in Georgia.**
    1967   CosCob, Connecticut   30.
HENDERSON, Lillian (comp)   **Roster of the Confederate Soldiers of Georgia 1861-1865.** 6 vols.
    1959-64   Hapeville, Georgia   125.
JONES, Charles C., Jr.   **Georgians During the War . . . An Address.** Wraps
    1889   Augusta   40.
JONES, Charles E.   **Georgia in the War 1861-1865.** Wraps
    1909   Atlanta   75.
MEANS, Alexander   **Diary for 1861.** Wraps
    1949   Atlanta   20.
Memoirs of Georgia. 2 vols.
    1895   Atlanta   150.
MONTGOMERY, Horace   **Johnny Cobb: Confederate Aristocrat.**
    1964   Athens   20.
NATHANS, Elizabeth S.   **Losing the Peace. Georgia Republicans and Reconstruction 1865-1871.**
    1968   Baton Rouge   20.
PHILLIPS, Ulrich B.   **Georgia and State Rights. (Annual Report of American Historical Assoc. . . . 1901)**
    1902   Washington   30.
ROGERS, William Warren   **Thomas County** (Georgia) **During the Civil War.**
    1964   Tallahassee   20.
SARTAIN, James Alfred   **History of Walker County, Georgia.** Vol. 1 (all pub)
    1932   Dalton   75.
STANDARD, Diffee William   **Columbus, Georgia, in the Confederacy.**
    1954   New York   20.
STEGEMAN, John F.   **These Men She Gave: The Civil War Diary of Athens, Georgia.**
    1964   Athens   25.
A Stenographic Report of the Proceedings of the Constitutional Convention Held in Atlanta, Ga., 1877.
    1877   Atlanta   40.
THOMAS, Henry W.   **History of the Doles-Cook Brigade, Army of Northern Virginia, C.S.A.**
    1903   Atlanta   175.
THOMPSON, C. Mildred   **Reconstruction in Georgia.**
    1915   New York   Wraps   50.
    1964   Gloucester   20.
WILLINGHAM, Robert M., Jr.   **No Jubilee, The Story of Confederate Wilkes.**
    1976   Washington, Georgia   15.
WOOLLEY, Edwin C.   **The Reconstruction of Georgia.** Wraps
    1901   New York   30.

REGIMENTALS

ADAMSON, Augustus Pitt   **Brief History of the Thirtieth Georgia Regiment.** Wraps
    1912   Griffin, Georgia   750.

CALHOUN, William L.   **History of the 42nd Regiment, Georgia Volunteers, C.S.A. Infantry.** Wraps
    1900   Atlanta   125.

CALLAWAY, Felix Richard   **The Bloody Links.**
    1907   Shreveport, Louisiana   250.

CLARK, Walter A.   **Under the Stars and Bars or Memories of Four Years Service with the Oglethorpes.**
    1900   Augusta   500.

EDWARDS, John Frank   **Army Life of Frank Edwards, Confederate Veteran.**
    1911   La Grange   350.

FITZPATRICK, Marion Hill   **Letters to Amanda . . . 1862-1865.** Wraps
    1976   Culloden, Georgia   25.

GIBBONS, A. R.   **The Recollections of an Old Confederate Soldier: A. R. Gibbons.** Wraps
    n.d.   Shelbyville, Missouri   25.

HAGAN, John W.   **Confederate Letters of _____** edited by Bell I. Wiley. Wraps
    1954   Athens   25.

HAYNES, Draughton Stith   **The Field Diary of a Confederate Soldier.**
    1963   Darien, Georgia   Ltd.   30.

HENDERSON, Lindsey P., Jr.   **The Oglethorpe Light Infantry.** Wraps
    1961   Savannah   35.

HERMANN, Isaac   **Memoirs of a Veteran.**
    1911   Atlanta   250.
    1974   Lakemont, Georgia   Ltd.   25.

HOWARD, Wiley C.   **Sketch of Cobb Legion Cavalry and Some Incidents and Scenes Remembered.** Wraps
    n.d. (circa 1949)   Marietta, Georgia   15.

JONES, Charles C., Jr.   **Historical Sketch of the Chatham Artillery During the Confederate Struggle for Independence.**
    1867   Albany   200.

KING, John H.   **Three Hundred Days in a Yankee Prison.**
    1904   Atlanta   200.
    1959   Kennesaw, Georgia   20.

MAGILL, Robert M.   **Co. "F", 39th Georgia Infantry.**
    1907   Richmond   125.

MONTFORT, Theodorick W.   **Rebel Lawyer: Letters of _____ 1861-1862** edited by Spencer B. King, Jr. Wraps
    1965   Athens   20.

MONTGOMERY, Horace   **Howell Cobb's Confederate Career.** Wraps
    1959   Tuscaloosa   Ltd.   25.

MURRAY, Alton J.   **South Georgia Rebels . . . True War Time Experiences of the 26th Regiment Georgia Volunteer Infantry, Lawton-Gordon-Evans Brigade, C.S.A. 1861-1865.**
    1976   Jacksonville, Florida   35.

Muster Roll of First Regiment Georgia Volunteers 1861. Wraps
    1890   Atlanta   100.

NICHOLS, G. W.   **A Soldier's Story of His Regiment.**
    1898   Jessup, Georgia   750.
    1961   Kennesaw   25.

NISBET, James Cooper   **Four Years on the Firing Line.**
    1914 (?)   Chattanooga   600.
    1963   Jackson, Tennessee   edited by Bell T. Wiley   40.

OLMSTEAD, Charles H.   **The Memoirs of _____** edited by Lilla Mills Hawes' Collections of Georgia Historical Society Vol. XIV.
    1964   Savannah   25.

OLMSTEAD, Charles H.   **Reminiscences of Services with the First Volunteer Regiment of Georgia, Charleston Harbor, in 1863.** Wraps
1879   Savannah   125.

PENDLETON, William Frederic   **Confederate Diary Capt. _____ January to April 1865.** Wraps
1957   Bryn Athyn, Pennsylvania   35.

PENDLETON, William Frederic   **Confederate Memoirs . . .** edited by Constance Pendleton.
1958   Pennsylvania   40.

WARREN, Kittrell J.   **Life and Public Services of an Army Straggler** edited by Floyd C. Watkins. Wraps
1961   Athens   20.

WILLIS, Edward   **Memorials of Gen _____ Commandant of the 12th Georgia Infantry.** Wraps
1890   Richmond   40.

ZETTLER, Berrien McPherson   **War Stories and School-Day Incidents for the Children.**
1912   New York   300.

ILLINOIS

GENERAL REFERENCES

Report of the Adjutant General of the State of Illinois. Vols. 1-8.
1900-02   Springfield   25. each

BALE, Florence Gratiot   **Galena's Yesterdays.** Wraps
1931   Waukegan   15.

BALE, Florence Gratiot (comp)   **Historic Galena, Yesterday and Today.**
1939   Galena   7.

BARNET, James (ed)   **The Martyrs and Heroes of Illinois in the Great Rebellion.**
1866   Chicago   75.

BURTON, William L.   **Descriptive Bibliography of Civil War Manuscripts in Illinois.**
1966   Illinois   20.

COLE, Arthur Charles   **The Era of the Civil War 1848-1870, Centennial History of Illinois.**
1919   Springfield   25.

COOK, Frederick Francis   **Bygone Days in Chicago, Recollections of the "Garden City" of the Sixties.**
1910   Chicago   30.

EDDY, Thomas M.   **The Patriotism of Illinois.** 2 vols.
1865-66   Chicago   100.

HAMAND, Lavern M. (ed)   **Coles County in the Civil War.** Wraps
1961   Charleston, Illinois   15.

HICKEN, Victor   **Illinois in the Civil War.**
1966   Urbana   20.

Illinois at Vicksburg.
1907   Chicago   50.

Illinois Military Units in the Civil War. Wraps
1962   Springfield   20.

Military Essays and Recollections, Papers Read Before the Commandery of Illinois, Mollus. 4 vols.
1891, 1894, 1899, 1907   Chicago   100.

Reminiscences of Chicago During the Civil War.
1914   Chicago   20.
1967   New York   15.

WOODRUFF, George H.   **Fifteen Years Ago: or, The Patriotism of Will County.**
1876   Joliet   75.

REGIMENTALS

ALLEN, Henry A.   **Sergeant Allen and Private Renick A Memoir of the Eleventh Illinois Cavalry.** Wraps
1971   Galesburg, Ill.   20.
AMBROSE, D. Leib   **History of the Seventh Regiment Illinois Volunteer Infantry.**
1868   Springfield   150.
ANDRUS, Onley   **Civil War Letters of . . .** edited by Fred A. Shannon.
1947   Urbana   40.
Annual Reunion 47th Regiment Illinois Volunteer Infantry.
1908   Peoria   35.
ATEN, Henry J. (comp)   **A History of the Eighty-Fifth Regiment Illinois Volunteer Infantry.**
1901   Hiawatha, Kansas   100.
AVERY, P. O.   **History of the Fourth Illinois Cavalry Regiment.**
1903   Humboldt, Nebraska   110.
AYERS, James T.   **The Diary of . . .** edited by John Hope Franklin.
1947   Springfield   20.
BARBER, Lucius W.   **Army Memoirs of _____ Company D, 15th Illinois Volunteer Infantry.**
1894   Chicago   125.
BARKER, Lorenzo A. ("Ren")   **Military History (Michigan Boys), Company "D" 66th Sharpshooters in the Civil War.**
1905   Reed City, Michigan   85.
BARTLESON, Frederick A.   **Letters from Libby Prison.** edited by Margaret W. Peelle.
1956   New York   30.
BEAR, Henry C.   **The Civil War Letters of Henry C. Bear, A Soldier in the 116th Illinois Volunteer Infantry** edited by Wayne C. Temple.
1961   Harrogate, Tennessee   25.
BENNETT, L. G. and **HAIGH,** Wm. M.   **History of the Thirty-Sixth Regiment Illinois Volunteers.**
1876   Aurora   80.
BENTLEY, William H.   **History of the 77th Illinois Volunteer Infantry.**
1883   Peoria   150.
BLACKMAN, William S.   **The Boy of Battle Ford and the Man.**
1906   Marion, Illinois   125.
BOGGS, Samuel S.   **Eighteen Months a Prisoner Under the Rebel Flag.**
1887   Lovington, Illinois   25.
1889   Lovington, Illinois   20.
BOUTON, Edward   **Events of the Civil War.** Wraps
1906   Los Angeles   90.
BROWN, Thaddeus C. S., **MURPHY,** Samuel J. and **PUTNEY,** Wm. G. (eds)   **Behind the Guns, The History of Battery I, Second Regiment Illinois Light Artillery.**
1965   Carbondale   Boxed   35.
BRYNER, Byron Cloyd   **Bugle Echoes, The Story of Illinois 47th.**
1905   Springfield   110.
BURDETTE, Robert J.   **The Drums of the 47th.**
1914   Indianapolis   40.
BURTON, Elijah P.   **Diary of _____, Surgeon 7th Reg. Illinois 3rd Brigade, 2nd Div.**
1939   Des Moines   40.
CALKINS, William Wirt   **The History of the One Hundred and Fourth Regiment of Illinois Volunteer Infantry.**
1895   Chicago   140.
CASTLE, Henry A.   **The Army Mule and Other War Sketches.**
1898   Indianapolis   35.

Catalogue of the Officers and Members of the Henry County Regiment, Being the 112th Regiment Illinois Volunteers. Wraps
    1862   Geneseo   100.

CHETLAIN, Augustus L.   **Recollections of Seventy Years.**
    1899   Galena   75.

CLUETT, William W.   **History of the 57th Regiment, Illinois Volunteer Infantry.**
    1886   Princeton   90.

Complete History of the 46th Illinois Veteran Infantry — 1861-1866.
    1866   Freeport   100.

CONNOLLY, James A.   **Three Years in the Army of the Cumberland The Letters and Diary of** _____ edited by Paul M. Angle.
    1959   Bloomington   25.

CORT, Charles Edwin   **"Dear Friends" The Civil War Letters and Diary of** _____ edited by Helyn W. Tomlinson.
    1962   n.p.   20.

CRIPPIN, Edward   **The Diary of** _____, **27th Illinois Volunteers 1861-1863.** edited by Robert J. Kerner.
    1909   Springfield   30.
    1910   Springfield   30.

CROWDER, James H.   **Before and After Vicksburg.** Wraps
    1924   Dayton   75.

DAVENPORT, Edward A. (ed)   **History of the Ninth Regiment Illinois Cavalry Volunteers.**
    1888   Chicago   135.

De ROSIER, Arthur H., Jr., (ed)   **Through the South with a Union Soldier.**
    1969   Johnson City, Tennessee   20.

DODGE, Wm. Sumner   **A Waif of the War: or, The History of the Seventy-Fifth Illinois Infantry.**
    1866   Chicago   125.

DONOVAN, William F.   **Membership Roll of the 36th Illinois Veteran Volunteer Infantry.** Wraps
    1903   Elgin (?)   40.

DRAKE, Julia A. (ed.)   **The Mail Goes Through, or The Civil War Letters of George Drake.**
    1964   San Angelo, Texas   20.

DUDLEY, Henry W.   **Autobiography of . . .**
    1914   Menasha, Wisconsin   150.

EBY, Henry Harrison   **Observations of an Illinois Boy in Battle, Camp and Prisons 1861-1865.**
    1910   Mendota   50.

EISENSCHIML, Otto   **The Fifty-Fifth Illinois at Shiloh.** Wraps
    1963 (?)   n.p.   20.

FIELD, Charles D.   **Three Years in the Saddle From 1861 to 1865, Memoirs of** _____. Wraps
    1898   Goldfield, Iowa   75.

FLEHARTY, Stephen F.   **Our Regiment, A History of the 102nd Illinois Infantry Volunteers.**
    1865   Chicago   175.

FLETCHER, Samuel H.   **The History of Company A, Second Illinois Cavalry.**
    1912   Chicago   150.

FORSYTH, George A.   **Thrilling Days in Army Life.**
    1900   New York   60.

FOX, Thomas Bailey   **Memorial of Henry Ware Hall, Adjutant 51st Regiment Infantry Volunteers, An Address.** Wraps
    1864   Boston   35.

FRANCIS, Charles L.   **Narrative of a Private Soldier in the Volunteer Army of the United States.**
    1879   Brooklyn   75.

GEORGE, G. Jasper   **William Newby, Alias "Dan Benton," Alias "Rickety Dan," Alias "Crazy Jack".**
    1893   Cincinnati   50.
GROSS, Luelja Zearing   **Sketch of the Life of Major James Roberts Zearing and Civil War Letters.**
    1922   Springfield, Illinois   30.
HARD, Abner   **History of the Eighth Cavalry Regiment, Illinois Volunteers.**
    1868   Aurora   200.
HAWES, Jesse   **Cahaba, A Story of Captive Boys in Blue.**
    1888   New York   125.
HAYNIE, J. Henry   **The Nineteenth Illinois, A Memoir of a Regiment.**
    1912   Chicago   85.
HEDLEY, F. Y.   **Marching Through Georgia.**
    1885   Chicago   30.
    1887   Chicago   30.
    1895   Chicago   25.
HEER, George W.   **Episodes of the Civil War, Nine Campaigns in Nine States.**
    1890   San Francisco   150.
Historical Sketch of the Chicago Board of Trade Battery, Horse Artillery, Illinois Volunteers.
    1902   Chicago   125.
HOBBS, Charles Albert   **Vicksburg, A Poem.**
    1880   Chicago   50.
HOWARD, Richard L.   **History of the 124th Regiment Illinois Infantry Volunteers.**
    1880   Springfield   75.
HUBERT, Charles F.   **History of the 50th Regiment Illinois Volunteer Infantry in War of the Union.**
    1894   Kansas City   200.
JOHNSON, Charles Beneulyn   **Muskets and Medicine.**
    1917   Philadelphia   65.
JONES, Thomas B.   **Complete History of the 46th Illinois Volunteer Infantry.**
    1907 (?)   Freeport   125.
JONES, Tilghman   **Five Days to Glory: Letters of _____** edited by Glenn W. Sunderland.
    1970   S. Brunswick/New York   20.
KIMBELL, Charles Bill   **History of Battery "A", First Illinois Light Artillery Volunteers.**
    1899   Chicago   125.
KINNEAR, John R.   **History of the Eighty-Sixth Regiment Illinois Volunteer Infantry.**
    1866   Chicago   125.
LATHROP, David   **The History of the Fifty-Ninth Regiment Illinois Volunteers.**
    1865   Indianapolis   175.
McCORD, William B.   **Battle of Corinth, The Campaigns Preceding and Leading Up to This Battle and Its Results.** Wraps
    n.d.   n.p.   20.
McELROY, John   **Andersonville, A Story of Rebel Military Prisons.**
    1879   Toledo   40.
    1899   Washington   2 vols.   Wraps   25.
McELROY, John   **Si Klegg: His Transformation from a Raw Recruit to a Veteran.** Wraps
    1910   Washington   25.
    1915   Washington   20.
McELROY, John   **This Was Andersonville.** edited by Roy Meredith.
    1957   New York   20.
    1958   New York   20.

MARSHALL, Albert O.   **Army Life from a Soldier's Journals.**
>   1883   Joliet   50.
>   1884   Joliet   50.

Military History and Reminiscences of the Thirteenth Regiment of Illinois Volunteer Infantry.
>   1892   Chicago   125.

Minutes of Proceedings of . . . Annual Reunion Survivors of Seventy-Third Illinois Volunteer Infantry. Wraps
>   1894   n.p.   15.
>   1904   Springfield   15.
>   1905   Farmer City   15.

MITCHELL, Frederick W.   **"A Conundrum of the Days of '64," D. C. Mollus War Paper 5.** Wraps
>   1890   n.p.   15.

MORRIS, William S.   **History 31st Regiment Illinois Volunteers.**
>   1902   Evansville, Ind.   100.

NEWLIN, William H.   **Account of the Escape of Six Federal Soldiers from Prison at Danville, Va.** Wraps
>   1886   Cincinnati   25.
>   1887   Cincinnati   25.
>   1889   Cincinnati   20.

NEWLIN, William H.   **A History of the Seventy-Third Regiment of Illinois Infantry Volunteers.**
>   1890   Springfield   85.

NEWSOME, Edmund   **Experience in the War of the Great Rebellion.**
>   1880   Carbondale   125.

Ninety-Second Illinois Volunteers.
>   1875   Freeport   125.

PARKS, George E.   **"The Long Winter" Being a Factual Narrative of One Story of the "Unusual" 109th Regiment Volunteer Infantry of State of Illinois.** Wraps
>   1963   n.p.   25.

PARTRIDGE, Charles A.   **History of the Ninety-Sixth Regiment Illinois Volunteer Infantry.**
>   1887   Chicago   150.

PAYNE, Edwin W.   **History of the Thirty-Fourth Regiment of Illinois Infantry, Sept. 7 1861 — July 12, 1865.**
>   1902   Clinton, Iowa   100.

POTTER, John   **Reminiscences of the Civil War in the United States.**
>   1897   Oskaloosa   100.

Proceedings of the Reunion . . . Association of Survivors of the Seventh Illinois Regiment. 2 vols. 1898-1911; 1912-1917
>   n.d.   n.p.   200.

Proceedings of Reunions of 55th Illinois Veteran Volunteer Infantry. Wraps
>   7th & 8th   25.
>   11th   25.
>   12th   25.
>   13th   25.
>   15th   25.
>   16th   25.

Reminiscences of the Civil War From Diaries of Members of 103d Illinois Volunteer Infantry
>   1904   Chicago   110.

Reunions of Taylor's Battery.
>   1890   Chicago   150.

Roster of the Living Members of the 102d Regt. Ill. Vols. Wraps
>   1911   Galesburg (?)   30.

Roster of the 115th Regiment Illinois Infantry Volunteers Issued by Regimental Reunion Assoc., Decatur, Illinois. Wraps
>   n.d.   n.p.   30.

ROYSE, Isaac Henry Clay   **History of the 115th Regiment Illinois Volunteer Infantry.**
1900   Terre Haute   Ltd.   125.
SANFORD, Washington L.   **History of Fourteenth Illinois Cavalry and the Brigades to Which It Belonged.**
1898   Chicago   175.
SHANK, John Daniel   **One Flag, One Country and Thirteen Greenbacks a Month, Letters from a Civil War Private and His Colonel.** compiled by Edna J. Shank Hunter.
1980   San Diego   Ltd.   25.
SIMMONS, Louis A.   **The History of the 84th Regiment Illinois Vols.**
1866   Macomb   200.
SMITH, Benj. T.   **Private Smith's Journal, Recollections of the Late War.** edited by Clyde C. Walton.
1963   Chicago   25.
SMITH, William B.   **On Wheels and How I Came There.**
1892   New York   30.
1893   New York   40.
SNETSINGER, Robert J. (ed)   **Kiss Clara for Me: The Story of Joseph Whitney and His Family, Early Days in the Midwest, and Soldiering in the American Civil War.**
1969   Pennsylvania   20.
Society of the 74th Volunteer Infantry, Reunion Proceedings and History of the Regiment.
1903   Rockford   125.
STEVENSON, Alexander F.   **The Battle of Stone's River Near Murfreesboro, Tennessee.**
1884   Boston   60.
1974   Gettysburg   20.
STILLWELL, Leander   **The Story of a Common Soldier of Army Life in the Civil War.**
1920   Erie, Kansas   60.
STOCKTON, Joseph   **War Diary (1862-5) of Brevet Brigadier General Joseph Stockton.** Wraps
1910   Chicago   75.
The Story of the Fifty-Fifth Regiment Illinois Volunteer Infantry.
1887   Clinton, Mass.   125.
STRONG, Robert Hale   **A Yankee Private's Civil War.** edited by Ashley Halsey.
1961   Chicago   20.
SURBY, Richard W.   **Grierson's Raids and Hatch's Sixty-Four Days' March.**
1865   Chicago   250.
THOMPSON, Bradford F.   **History of the 112th Regiment of Illinois Volunteer Infantry.**
1885   Toulon   75.
TRIMBLE, Harvey Marion   **History of the Ninety-Third Regiment Illinois Volunteer Infantry.**
1898   Chicago   75.
TYLER, William N.   **The Dispatch Carrier and Memoirs of Andersonville.** Wraps
1892   Port Byron, Illinois   50.
WARNER, Abraham J.   **The Private Journal of Abraham Joseph Warner.**
1973   San Diego   Ltd.   35.
WAY, Virgil G.   **History of the Thirty-third Regiment Illinois Veteran Volunteer Infantry**
1902   Gibson, Ill.   125.
WELLS, Seth J.   **The Siege of Vicksburg.**
1915   Detroit   60.
WILLS, Charles W.   **Army Life of an Illinois Soldier.**
1906   Washington   75.

WILSON, Ephraim A.   **Memoirs of the War.**
   1893   Cleveland   85.
WOOD, Wales W.   **A History of the Ninety-Fifth Regiment Illinois Infantry Volunteers.**
   1865   Chicago   150.
WOOLWORTH, Solomon   **Experiences in the Civil War.** Wraps
   1903   Newark   50.
   1904   Newark   50.
   1905   n.p.   40.
YOUNG, Jesse Bowman   **What a Boy Saw in the Army.**
   See same entry under Pennsylvania Regimentals.

INDIANA

GENERAL REFERENCES

Report of the Adjutant General of the State of Indiana. 8 vols.
   1865-69   Indianapolis   30. each
BARNHART, J.   **The Impact of the Civil War on Indiana.** Wraps
   1962   Indianapolis   10.
BEVERIDGE, Albert J.   **Address of _____ Dedication of Indiana's Monuments April 6, 1903.**
   1903   Indianapolis   15.
A Chronology of Indiana in the Civil War. Wraps
   1965   Indianapolis   10.
HANLY, J. Frank   **Dedication of the Indiana Monuments at Vicksburg, Mississippi, December 29, 1908.**
   1908   Cincinnati   20.
HAZZARD, George   **Hazzard's History of Henry County, Indiana 1822-1906 Military Edition.** Vols. I & II.
   1905-06   New Castle   150.
HOLLIDAY, John Hampden   **Indianapolis and the Civil War.** Wraps
   1972   Indianapolis   10.
Indiana at Antietam, Report of the Indiana Antietam Monument Commission and Ceremonies at the Dedication of the Monument.
   1911   Indianapolis   35.
Indiana at Chickamauga 1863-1900 Report of the Indiana Commissioners Chickamauga National Military Park.
   1900   Indianapolis   20.
Indiana at Shiloh, Report of the Commission.
   1904   Indianapolis   30.
Indiana at Vicksburg.
   1911   Indianapolis   30.
KEMPER, G. W. H.   **A Medical History of the State of Indiana.**
   1911   Chicago   40.
KERWOOD, A. L.   **Military History of Delaware County, Ind.**
   1909   n.p.   30.
LOVE, John   **Report of Major General Love, of the Indiana Legion.**
   1863   Indianapolis   40.
McCORMICK, David Isaac (comp)   **Indiana Battle Flags and Record of Indiana Organizations in the Mexican, Civil and Spanish-American Wars . . .** edited by Mrs. Mindwell C. Wilson.
   1928   Indianapolis   75.
MONTGOMERY, M. W.   **History of Jay County, Indiana.**
   1864 (?)   Chicago   75.

Proceedings of the Officers and Soldiers of the Indiana Regiments in the Army of the Cumberland.
1863   Indianapolis   50.
SCRIBNER, Theodore T.   **Indiana's Roll of Honor, Vol. II.**
1866   Indianapolis   50.
The Soldier of Indiana in the War for the Union.
1869   Indianapolis   100.
STEVENSON, David   **Indiana's Roll of Honor, Vol. I.**
1864   Indianapolis   35.
TERRELL, W. H. H.   **Indiana in the War of the Rebellion.**
1960   Indianapolis   25.
THORNBROUGH, Emma Lou   **Indiana in the Civil War Era, 1850-1880.** Wraps
1965   Indianapolis   15.
TURNER, Ann   **Guide to Indiana Civil War Manuscripts.** Wraps
1965   Indianapolis   25.
The War for the Union 1861-1865 A Record of Its Defenders, Living and Dead, from Steuben County, Ind.
1888-9   n.p.   75.
War Papers Read Before the Indiana Commandery, Mollus, Vol. 1 (all issued).
1898   Indianapolis   Ltd.   50.

REGIMENTALS

ANDERSON, Edward   **Camp Fire Stories, A Series of Sketches of the Union Army in the Southwest.**
1896   Chicago   35.
ANDREW, A. Piatt   **Some Civil War Letters of . . . III.**
1925   Gloucester, Massachusetts   50.
BAXTER, Nancy Niblack (ed)   **Hoosier Farm Boy in Lincoln's Army The Civil War Letters of Pvt. John R. McClure.**
1971   n.p.   20.
BRANT, Jefferson E.   **History of the Eighty-fifth Indiana Volunteer Infantry.**
1902   Bloomington   150.
BRIANT, Charles C.   **History of the 6th Regt. Indiana Volunteer Infantry.**
1891   Indianapolis   110.
BROWN, Edmund Randolph   **The Twenty-Seventh Indiana Volunteer Infantry in the War of the Rebellion.**
1899   Monticello   200.
BUTLER, Marvin Benjamin   **My Story of the Civil War and the Underground Railroad.**
1914   Huntington   75.
CLIFTON, William Baldwin   **Libby and Andersonville, A True Sketch.**
1910   Indianapolis   75.
COGLEY, Thomas S.   **History of the Seventh Indiana Cavalry Volunteers.**
1876   Laporte, Indiana   135.
DOLL, William H.   **History of the Sixth Regiment Indiana Volunteer Infantry.**
1903   Columbus, Indiana   125.
DUDLEY, William Wade   **The Iron Brigade at Gettysburg.** Wraps
1879   Cincinnati   Ltd.   85.
DUNN, Byron A.   **On General Thomas's Staff.**
1912   Chicago   30.
The Eighty-sixth Regiment Indiana Volunteer Infantry.
1895   Crawfordsville   125.
ELLIOTT, Joseph Taylor   **The Sultana Disaster.** Wraps
1913   Indianapolis   50.
FLOYD, David Bittle   **History of the 75th Regiment of Indiana Infantry Volunteers.**
1893   Philadelphia   125.

FOSTER, John W.   **War Stories for My Grandchildren.**
　　1918　　Washington　　50.
FOUT, Frederick W.   **The Dark Days of the Civil War, 1861 to 1865.**
　　1904　　St. Louis　　140.
GAGE, Moses D.   **From Vicksburg to Raleigh, or a Complete History of the 12th Regiment Indiana Volunteer Infantry.**
　　1865　　Chicago　　150.
GRAYSON, A. J.   **"The Spirit of 1861" History of the Sixth Indiana Regiment in the Three Months Campaign in Western Virginia.** Wraps
　　1875　　Madison, Indiana　　75.
GRECIAN, Joseph   **History of the Eighty-Third Regiment, Indiana Volunteer Infantry.**
　　1865　　Cincinnati　　175.
GRESHAM, Matilda   **Life of Walter Quinton Gresham 1832-1895.** 2 vols.
　　1919　　Chicago　　60.
GROSE, William   **The Story of the Marches, Battles and Incidents of the 36th Regiment Indiana Volunteer Infantry.**
　　1891　　New Castle　　110.
HADLEY, John V.   **An Indiana Soldier in Love and War: The Civil War Letters of** _____ edited by James I. Robertson, Jr.
　　1963　　Indianapolis　　25.
HADLEY, John V.   **Seven Months a Prisoner.** Wraps
　　1868　　Indianapolis　　150.
　　1898　　New York　　40.
HARTPENCE, William Ross   **History of the Fifty-First Indiana Veteran Volunteer Infantry.**
　　1894　　Cincinnati　　125.
HIGH, Edwin W.   **History of the Sixty-Eighth Regiment Indiana Volunteer Infantry 1862-1865.**
　　1902　　Metamora　　125.
History Eighty-Eighth Indiana Volunteers Infantry.
　　1895　　Fort Wayne　　125.
History of the Forty-Sixth Regiment Indiana Volunteer Infantry September 1861 to September 1865.
　　1888　　Logansport　　90.
History of the Seventy-ninth Regiment Indiana Volunteer Infantry in the Civil War of Eighteen Sixty-one.
　　1899　　Indianapolis　　100.
History of the Seventy-Third Indiana Volunteers in the War of 1861-65.
　　1909　　Washington　　125.
HORRALL, Spillard F.   **History of the Forty-second Indiana Volunteer Infantry**
　　1892　　Chicago　　125.
HOWE, Daniel Wait   **Civil War Times 1861-1865.**
　　1902　　Indianapolis　　40.
HUNTER, Alfred G.   **History of the Eighty-Second Indiana Volunteer Infantry.**
　　1893　　Indianapolis　　100.
KERWOOD, Asbury L.   **Annals of the Fifty-Seventh Regiment Indiana Volunteers, Marches, Battles, and Incidents of Army Life.**
　　1868　　Dayton　　200.
KIRKPATRICK, George Morgan   **42nd Indiana. The Experiences of a Private Soldier in the Civil War.** Wraps
　　1973　　Carmel　　20.
LONG, Lessel   **Twelve Months in Andersonville.**
　　1886　　Huntington, Indiana　　60.
LUCAS, Daniel R.   **New History of the 99th Indiana Infantry.**
　　1900　　Rockford, Ill.　　150.

McBRIDE, John Randolph   **History of the Thirty-Third Indiana Veteran Volunteer Infantry.**
1900   Indianapolis   100.

McCLURE, John R.   **Hoosier Farm Boy in Lincoln's Army, the Civil War Letters of _____** edited by Nancy N. Baxter.
1971   n.p.   15.

McGEE, Benjamin F.   **History of the 72nd Indiana Volunteer Infantry of the Mounted Lightning Brigade.**
1882   Lafayette   150.

McLEAN, William E.   **The Forty-third Regiment of Indiana Volunteers.**
1903   Terre Haute   100.

MAUZY, James H.   **Historical Sketch of the Sixty-Eighth Regiment Indiana Volunteers.**
1887   Rushville   125.

MERRILL, Samuel   **The Seventieth Indiana Volunteer Infantry in the War of the Rebellion.**
1900   Indianapolis   100.

MILLER, William Bluffton   **"I Soldiered for the Union" The Civil War Diary of William Bluffton Miller** edited by Robert J. Willey. Wraps
1982 (?)   n.p.   20.

MUNHALL, Leander W.   **The Chattanooga Campaign.** Wraps
1902   Philadelphia   25.

PERRY, Henry Fales   **History of the Thirty-Eighth Regiment Indiana Volunteer Infantry.**
1906   Palo Alto, California   75.

PICKERILL, William N.   **History of the Third Indiana Cavalry.**
1906   Indianapolis   125.

PUNTENNEY, George H.   **History of the Thirty-Seventh Regiment of Indiana Infantry Volunteers.**
1896   Rushville, Indiana   125.

RERICK, John H.   **The Forty-fourth Indiana Volunteer Infantry.**
1880   LaGrange   150.

Reunion of the 20th Regiment Indiana Veteran Volunteer Association. Wraps
Sept. 1, 1886   30.
Sept. 1, 1888   30.
Sept. 4, 5, 1889   30.

ROACH, Alva C.   **The Prisoner of War and How Treated.**
1865   Indianapolis   75.

ROWELL, John W.   **Yankee Artillerymen: Through the Civil War with Eli Lilly's Indiana Battery.**
1975   Knoxville   25.

SCRIBNER, Benjamin Franklin   **How Soldiers Were Made.**
1887   New Albany, Indiana   100.

SHAW, James Birney   **History of the Tenth Regiment Indiana Volunteer Infantry.**
1912   Lafayette   200.

SHERLOCK, Eli J.   **Memorabilia of the Marches and Battles in Which the 100th Regiment of Indiana Infantry Volunteers Took an Active Part.**
1896   Kansas City   100.

SIEVERS, Harry J.   **Benjamin Harrison, Hoosier Warrior 1833-1865.**
1952   Chicago   25.

SMITH, John Thomas   **A History of the Thirty-First Regiment of Indiana Volunteer Infantry in the War of the Rebellion.**
1900   Cincinnati   100.

STORMONT, Gilbert R.   **History of the Fifty-eighth Regiment of Indiana Volunteer Infantry.**
1895   Princeton   125.

SUNDERLAND, Glenn W.   **Lightning at Hoover's Gap, The Story of Wilder's Brigade.**
1969   New York   25.

THOMSON, Orville   **From Philippi to Appomattox, Narrative of the Service of the 7th Indiana Infantry.**
190?   n.p.   150.
UPSON, Theodore F.   **With Sherman to the Sea, The Civil War Letters, Diaries, and Reminiscences of** _____. edited by Oscar Osburn Winther.
1943   Baton Rouge   30.
1958   Bloomington   25.
VOORHIS, Jerry, Sr.   **The Life and Times of Aurelius Lyman Voorhis.**
1976   New York   25.
WALLACE, Lewis   **Lew Wallace: An Autobiography.** 2 vols.
1906   New York   50.
WILLEY, Robert   **The Iron 44th.**
n.d. (circa 1982)   n.p.   20.
WILLIAMS, Edward P.   **Extracts from Letters to A.B.T. from** _____ **During His Service in the Civil War 1862-64.**
1903   New York   50.

IOWA

GENERAL REFERENCES

Report of Adjutant General & Acting Quartermaster General of Iowa.
To Jan. 1, 1863   2 vols.   75.
To Jan.1, 1864   40.
To Jan. 1, 1865   40.
To Jan. 1, 1866   40.
To Jan. 1, 1867   25.
To Jan. 1, 1868   25.
ABERNETHY, Alonzo   **Dedication of Monuments Erected by the State of Iowa.**
1908   Des Moines   30.
BYERS, Samuel H. M.   **Iowa in War Times.**
1888   Des Moines   50.
INGERSOLL, Lurton Dunham   **Iowa and the Rebellion.**
1866   Philadelphia   60.
Iowa Commissioners' Report to Locate the Position of Iowa Troops in the Siege of Vicksburg. Wraps
1902   Des Moines   25.
Memorial to Civil War Soldiers, 1861 to 1866 . . . Kinsman Post. No. 7, G.A.R., Des Moines, Iowa. Wraps
1942   Des Moines   40.
ROBERTSON, James I., Jr.   **Iowa in the Civil War: A Reference Guide.** Wraps
n.d.   Iowa City   15.
ROSENBERG, Morton M.   **Iowa on the Eve of the Civil War.**
1972   Norman, Oklahoma   20.
Roster and Record of Iowa Soldiers in the War of the Rebellion, Vols. 1-6.
1908-11   Des Moines   35. each
SCHEE, George W. and **MONTZHEIMER,** O. H.   **Biographical Data and Army Record of Old Soldiers Who Have Lived in O'Brien County, Iowa.**
1909   Primghar, Iowa   75.
STUART, A. A.   **Iowa Colonels and Regiments.**
1865   Des Moines   75.
SWISHER, Jacob A. (comp)   **The Iowa Department of the Grand Army of the Republic.**
1936   Iowa City   20.
SWISHER, Jacob A.   **Iowa in Times of War.**
1943   Iowa City   30.

War Sketches and Incidents. Iowa Commandery, Mollus. 2 Vols.
  1893-1898   Des Moines   100.
WEED, Cora Chaplin (comp)   **Handbook for Iowa Soldiers' and Sailors'
Monument.**
  1898   n.p.   25.
WUBBEN, Hubert H.   **Civil War Iowa and the Copperhead Movement.**
  1980   Ames, Iowa   20.

REGIMENTALS

ALLEY, Charles   **Excerpts from the Civil War Diary of Lieutenant _____, Company "C" Fifth Iowa Cavalry.** edited by John S. Ezell. Wraps
  1951 (?)   Iowa City   25.
ARBUCKLE, John   **Civil War Experiences of a Foot-Soldier Who Marched with Sherman.**
  1930   Columbus   50.
BARNETT, Simeon   **History of the Twenty-Second Regiment Iowa Volunteer Infantry.** Wraps
  1865   Iowa City   125.
BARNEY, Chester   **Recollections of Field Service with the Twentieth Infantry Volunteers.**
  1865   Davenport   150.
BELKNAP, Wm. W.   **History of the Fifteenth Regiment, Iowa Veteran Volunteer Infantry.**
  1887   Keokuk   75.
BELL, John T.   **Tramps and Triumphs of the Second Iowa Infantry.** Wraps
  1886   Omaha   125.
  1961   Des Moines   25.
BOYD, Cyrus F.   **The Civil War Diary of _____ Fifteenth Iowa Infantry 1861-1863.** edited by Mildred Throne. Wraps
  1953   Iowa City   15.
BYERS, S. H. M.   **The March to the Sea: A Poem.**
  1896   Boston   20.
BYERS, S. H. M.   **What I Saw in Dixie: Or Sixteen Months in Rebel Prisons.** Wraps
  1868   Dansville, New York   75.
BYERS, S. H. M.   **With Fire and Sword.**
  1911   New York   60.
CATE, Wirt Armistead (ed)   **Two Soldiers, The Campaign Diaries of Thomas J. Key, C.S.A & Robert J. Campbell, U.S.A.**
  1938   Chapel Hill   50.
CLARK, James S.   **Life in the Middle West. Reminiscences of J. S. Clark**
  1916   Chicago   45.
COMPTON, James R.   **Andersonville. The Story of Man's Inhumanity to Man.**
  1887   Des Moines   50.
COX, Florence Marie Ankeny (ed.)   **Kiss Josey for Me.**
  1974   Santa Ana, Calif.   25.
CROOKE, George   **The Twenty-First Regiment of Iowa Volunteer Infantry.**
  1891   Milwaukee   100.
DODGE, Grenville M.   **Fiftieth Anniversary Fourth Iowa Veteran Volunteer Infantry, Dodge's Second Iowa Battery . . .** Wraps
  1911   Council Bluffs   40.
DOWNING, Alexander G.   **Downing's Civil War Diary.** edited by Olynthus B. Clark.
  1916   Des Moines   75.
FOSDICK, Charles   **Five Hundred Days in Rebel Prisons.**
  1887   Bethany, Missouri   60.
  1887   Chicago   50.

FOWLER, James A. and **MILLER,** Miles M.   **History of the Thirtieth Iowa Infantry.**
     1908   Mediapolis   125.

GULICK, William O.   **Journal and Letters of** _____
     1942   n.p.   40.

INGHAM, William H.   **Iowa Northern Border Brigade, Annals of Iowa, Vol V. No. 7.** Wraps
     1902   Des Moines   40.

JONES, Samuel Calvin   **Reminiscences of the Twenty-Second Iowa Volunteer Infantry.**
     1907   Iowa City   130.

KINER, Frederick F.   **One Year's Soldiering, Embracing the Battles of Fort Donelson and Shiloh.**
     1863   Lancaster, Pa.   85.

LOTHROP, Charles H.   **A History of the First Regiment Iowa Cavalry Veteran Volunteers.**
     1890   Lyons   200.

McARTHUR, Henry C.   **The Capture and Destruction of Columbia, South Carolina February 17, 1865.**
     1911   Washington   30.

MACY, Jesse   **Jesse Macy, An Autobiography.** edited by Katharine M. Noyes.
     1933   Springfield, Illinois   40.

MEAD, Homer   **The 8th Iowa Cavalry in the Civil War.**
     1927   Augusta, Illinois   75.

MICHAEL, William H.   **Cooperation Between General Grant and Commodore Foote and Between General Grant and Admiral Porter . . . Address.** Wraps
     1904   n.p.   50.

MYERS, Frank   **Soldiering in Dakota, Among the Indians in 1863-64-65.** Wraps
     1936   Pierre, South Dakota   25.

NOTT, Charles C.   **Sketches of the War: A Series of Letters to the North Moore Street School of New York.**
     1863   New York   40.
     1865   New York   35.
     1911   New York   25.

PIERCE, Lyman B.   **History of the 2nd Iowa Cavalry.**
     1865   Burlington   150.

REED, David W.   **Campaigns and Battles of the Twelfth Regiment Iowa Veteran Volunteer Infantry.**
     1903   Evanston, Illinois   100.

RICH, Joseph W.   **The Battle of Shiloh.**
     1911   Iowa City   35.

SCOTT, John (comp)   **Story of the Thirty-Second Iowa Infantry Volunteers.**
     1896   Nevada, Iowa   110.

SCOTT, William Forse   **Roster of the Fourth Iowa Cavalry Veteran Volunteers.**
     1902   New York   50.

SCOTT, William Forse   **The Story of a Cavalry Regiment. The Career of the Fourth Iowa Veteran Volunteers.**
     1893   New York   125.

SMITH, Henry I.   **History of the Seventh Iowa Veteran Volunteer Infantry During the Civil War.**
     1903   Mason City   200.

SPERRY, Andrew F.   **History of the 33d Iowa Infantry Volunteer Regiment.**
     1866   Des Moines   200.

STIBBS, John Howard   **Andersonville and the Trial of Henry Wirz.** Wraps
     1911   Iowa City   35.

SWIGGETT, S. A.   **The Bright Side of Prison Life.**
     1897   Baltimore   50.

THOMPSON, Seymour Dwight   **Recollections with the Third Iowa Regiment.**
     1864   Cincinnati   125.

VAUGHT, Elsa (ed)   **The Diary of an Unknown Soldier Sept 5, 1862 to December 7, 1862.** Wraps
    1959   Van Buren, Arkansas   20.
WARE, Eugene F.   **The Indian War of 1864.**
    1960   New York   30.
WARE, Eugene F.   **The Lyon Campaign in Missouri: Being a History of the First Iowa Infantry.**
    1907   Topeka   75.
WRIGHT, Henry H.   **A History of the Sixth Iowa Infantry.**
    1923   Iowa City   50.

KANSAS

GENERAL REFERENCES

Report of the Adjutant General of the State of Kansas 1861-1865. 2 vols.
    1896   Topeka   100.
BURKE, William S. (comp)   **Military History of Kansas Regiments During the War for the Suppression of the Great Rebellion.**
    1870   Leavenworth   450.
CASTEL, Albert   **A Frontier State at War: Kansas 1861-1865.**
    1958   Ithaca, New York   25.
CORY, C. E.   **Slavery in Kansas.** Wraps
    1902   n.p.   10.
CRAFTON, Allen   **Free States Fortress, The First Ten Years of the History of Lawrence, Kansas.**
    1954   Lawrence   25.
CRAWFORD, Samuel J.   **Kansas in the Sixties.**
    1911   Chicago   50.
DECKER, Eugene Donald   **Kansas in the Civil War.** Wraps
    1961   n.p.   10.
ELDRIDGE, Shalor Winchell   **Recollections of Early Days in Kansas — Contained in Pub. of Kansas State Historical Society.**
    1920   Topeka   25.
Roll of the Officers and Enlisted Men of the 3rd, 4th, 18th, and 19th Kansas Volunteers 1861.
    1902   Topeka   40.
War Talks in Kansas, A Series of Papers Read Before the Kansas Commandery, Mollus.
    1906   Kansas City   75.

REGIMENTALS

BAILEY, Mahlon   **Medical Sketch of the Nineteenth Regiment of Kansas Cavalry Volunteers.** Wraps
    1937   n.p.   10.
BRITTON, Wiley   **The Civil War on the Border . . . 1861-1862.**
    1890   New York   100.
    1891   New York   100.
    1899   New York   75.
BRITTON, Wiley   **Memoirs of the Rebellion on the Border 1863.**
    1882   Chicago   75.
BRITTON, Wiley   **The Union Indian Brigade in the Civil War.**
    1922   Kansas City   100.
CONNELLEY, William E.   **The Life of Preston B. Plumb.**
    1913   Chicago   40.

CORY, Charles E.   The Soldiers of Kansas, The 6th Kansas Cavalry and Its Commander. Wraps
    1910   n.p. (Topeka)   15.
FISHER, Hugh D.   The Gun and the Gospel.
    1896   Chicago   50.
    1902   Kansas City   40.
FOX, Simeon M.   The Early History of the Seventh Kansas Cavalry. Wraps
    1910   Topeka   15.
FOX, Simeon M.   The 7th Kansas Cavalry: Its Service in the Civil War. An Address. Wraps
    1908   Topeka   20.
FOX, Simeon M.   The Story of the Seventh Kansas. Wraps
    1902   Topeka   15.
HARVEY, A. M.   The Twenty-Second Kansas Volunteer Infantry. Wraps
    1935   Topeka   15.
MARTIN, John A.   Addresses . . . Delivered in Kansas.
    1888   Topeka   50.
STARR, Stephen Z.   Jennison's Jayhawkers.
    1973   Baton Rouge   30.
STEELE, James W.   The Battle of the Blue of the Second Regiment, K.S.M., Oct. 22 1864.
    1896   Chicago   75.

KENTUCKY

GENERAL REFERENCES

Report of the Adjutant General of the State of Kentucky 1861-1866. 2 vols.
    1866-67   Frankfort   200.
Report of the Adjutant General of the State of Kentucky for 1862.
    1863   Frankfort   40.
CHENAULT, John Cabell   Old Cane Springs: A Story of the War Between the States in Madison County, Kentucky. edited by Jonathan T. Dorris.
    1936   Louisville   50.
    1937   Louisville   50.
CLARK, Thomas D.   Pleasant Hill in the Civil War.
    1972   Lexington   15.
COLEMAN, J. Winston, Jr.   Lexington During the Civil War.
    1968   Lexington   Boxed   25.
COLEMAN, J. Winston   Slavery Times in Kentucky.
    1940   Chapel Hill   75.
COLLINS, Richard H.   Civil War Annals of Kentucky (1861-1865) edited by Hambleton Tapp (contained in Filson Club History Quarterly July 1961 Civil War Centennial Number). Wraps
    1961   Louisville   25.
Confederate Veteran Association of Kentucky, Constitution, By-Laws and Membership, With Name, Rank, Command and Residence.
    1891   n.p.   35.
COULTER, E. Merton   The Civil War and Readjustment in Kentucky.
    1926   Chapel Hill   75.
    1966   Gloucester   20.
EVANS, Clement A. (ed)   Confederate Military History Vol. IX — Kentucky and Missouri.
    1899   Atlanta   40.

GEORGE, Henry   **History of the Third, Seventh, Eighth, and Twelfth Kentucky, C.S.A.**
    1911   Louisville   200.
    1970   Lyndon   Ltd.   30.
HARRISON, Lowell H.   **The Civil War in Kentucky.**
    1975   Lexington   35.
KINCAID, Robert L.   **Kentucky in the Civil War.** Wraps
    1947   n.p.   20.
McDOWELL, Robert Emmett   **City of Conflict, Louisville in the Civil War 1861-65.**
    1962   Louisville   20.
RINGO, Willis L.   **Seventh Annual Reunion of the 1st Kentucky (Orphan) Brigade, CSA.** Wraps
    1889   Frankfort   45.
SPEED, Thomas;   **KELLY,** Robert M.; and   **PIRTLE,** Alfred.
    The Union Regiments of Kentucky.
    1897   Louisville   110.
THOMPSON, Edwin Porter   **History of the First Kentucky Brigade.**
    1868   Cincinnati   300.
THOMPSON, Edwin Porter   **History of the Orphan Brigade.**
    1898   Louisville   350.
    1973   Dayton   30.
TOWNSEND, William H.   **Lincoln and the Bluegrass.**
    1955   Lexington   25.

REGIMENTALS

Union

BLACKBURN, John   **A Hundred Miles A Hundred Heartbreaks.**
    1972   n.p.   15.
HAMILTON, Andrew G.   **Story of the Famous Tunnel Escape from Libby Prison.**
    Wraps
    1893   Chicago   25.
JOHNSTON, Isaac N.   **Four Months in Libby and the Campaign Against Atlanta.**
    Wraps
    1864   Cincinnati   100.
    1893   Cincinnati   75.
JOYCE, John A.   **A Checkered Life.**
    1883   Chicago   45.
JOYCE, John A.   **Jewels of Memory.**
    1895   Washington   40.
    1896   Washington   30.
STEVENSON, B. F.   **Letters from the Army.**
    1884   Cincinnati   125.
    1886   Cincinnati   100.
TARRANT, Eastham   **The Wild Riders of the First Kentucky Cavalry.**
    1894   Louisville   200.
    1969   Lexington   40.
VAUGHTER, John Bacon   **Prison Life in Dixie Giving a Short History of Inhuman and Barbarous Treatment of Our Soldiers by Rebel Authorities.** edited by Serg. Oats.
    1880   Chicago   50.
WRIGHT, Thomas J.   **History of the Eighth Regiment Kentucky Volunteer Infantry.**
    1880   St. Joseph, Missouri   250.

Confederate

AUSTIN, J. P.   **The Blue and the Gray.**
    1899   Atlanta   50.
BRECKINRIDGE, William C. P.   **The Ex-Confederate and What He Has Done in Peace, An Address.** Wraps
    1892   Richmond   40.
BRECKINRIDGE, William C. P.   **A Plea for a History of the Confederate War: An Address.** Wraps
    1887   Louisville   40.
BROWN, Dee Alexander   **The Bold Cavaliers, Morgan's 2nd Kentucky Cavalry Raiders.**
    1959   Philadelphia   35.
CASTLEMAN, John B.   **Active Service.**
    1917   Louisville   175.
CORN, James F.   **Jim Witherspoon, A Soldier of the South 1862-1865.** Wraps
    1962   Frankfort   20.
DYER, John Will   **Reminiscences or Four Years in the Confederate Army.**
    1898   Evansville   250.
GRAINGER, Gervis D.   **Company I, 6th Kentucky Infantry . . . . Four Years with the Boys in Gray.** Wraps
    1972   Dayton   10.
GREEN, John W.   **Johnny Green of the Orphan Brigade: The Journal of a Confederate Soldier.** edited by A. D. Kirwan.
    1956   Lexington   30.
JOHNSON, Adam Rankin   **The Partisan Rangers of the Confederate States Army.** edited by Wm. J. Davis.
    1904   Louisville   275.
MOSGROVE, George Dallas   **Kentucky Cavaliers in Dixie.**
    1895   Louisville   250.
    1957   Jackson, Tennessee   edited by Bell I. Wiley   40.
STONE, Henry Lane   **"Morgan's Men".** Wraps
    1919   Louisville   40.
YOUNG, Lot D.   **Reminiscences of a Soldier of the Orphan Brigade.** Wraps
    1918 (?)   Paris, Kentucky   30.

LOUISIANA

GENERAL REFERENCES

BARTLETT, Napier   **Military Record of Louisiana.**
    1875   New Orleans   500.
    1964   Baton Rouge   edited by T. H. Williams   35.
BARTLETT, Napier   **A Soldier's Story of the War, Including the Marches and Battles of the Washington Artillery, and of Other Louisiana Troops.**
    1874   New Orleans   400.
BOOTH, Andrew B. (comp)   **Records of Louisiana Confederate Soldiers and Louisiana Confederate Commands.** 3 vols. in 4.
    1920   New Orleans   1000.
BRAGG, Jefferson Davis   **Louisiana in the Confederacy.**
    1941   Baton Rouge   50.
CAPERS, Gerald M.   **Occupied City, New Orleans Under the Federals 1862-1865.**
    1965   Kentucky   25.
CASKEY, Willie Malvin   **Secession and Restoration of Louisiana.**
    1938   Louisiana   30.
EVANS, Clement A. (ed)   **Confederate Military History, Vol. X — Louisiana and Arkansas.**
    1899   Atlanta   40.

FICKLEN, John Rose   **History of Reconstruction in Louisiana.** Wraps
    1910   Baltimore   35.
FORTIER, James J. A. (ed.)   **Carpet-Bag Misrule in Louisiana.** Wraps
    1938   New Orleans   30.
GREER, James K.   **Louisiana Politics 1845-1861.**
    1930   Baton Rouge   25.
LONN, Ella   **Reconstruction in Louisiana After 1868.**
    1918   New York   50.
McCONNELL, Roland C.   **Negro Troops of Antebellum Louisiana.**
    1969   Baton Rouge   20.
McGINTY, Garnie W.   **Louisiana Redeemed: The Overthrow of Carpetbag Rule 1876-1880.**
    1941   New Orleans   30.
MARCHAND, S. A.   **Forgotten Fighters 1861-65 (From Ascension Parrish, Louisiana).**
    1966   Donaldsonville, Louisiana   30.
MOORE, Alison   **The Louisiana Tigers or The Two Louisiana Brigades of the Army of Northern Virginia 1861-1865.**
    1961   Baton Rouge   45.
RIPLEY, C. Peter   **Slaves and Freedmen in Civil War Louisiana.**
    1976   Baton Rouge   20.
ROLAND, Charles P.   **Louisiana Sugar Plantation During the American Civil War.**
    1957   Leiden, Netherlands   25.
TAYLOR, Joe Gray   **Louisiana Reconstructed 1863-1877.**
    1974   Baton Rouge   25.
WARMOTH, Henry Clay   **War, Politics and Reconstruction.**
    1930   New York   40.
WILMER, J. P. B.   **A Defense of Louisiana.** Wraps
    n.d. (circa 1868)   n.p.   30.
WINTERS, John D.   **The Civil War in Louisiana.**
    1963   Baton Rouge   35.

REGIMENTALS

BAKER, Henry H.   **A Reminiscent Story of the Great Civil War, Second Paper.** Wraps
    1911   New Orleans   200.
BEERS, Fannie A.   **Memories, A Record of Personal Experience and Adventure During Four Years of War.**
    1889   Philadelphia   30.
    1891   Philadelphia   30.
CARTER, Howell   **A Cavalryman's Reminiscences of the Civil War.**
    1900   New Orleans   200.
DORSEY, Sarah A.   **Recollections of Henry Watkins Allen.**
    1866   New York   75.
    1886   New Orleans   50.
DUFOUR, Charles L.   **Gentle Tiger: The Gallant Life of Roberdeau Wheat.**
    1957   Baton Rouge   45.
HANDERSON, Henry E.   **Yankee in Gray: The Civil War Memoirs of _____.**
    1962   Cleveland   30.
OWEN, William Miller   **In Camp and Battle with the Washington Artillery of New Orleans.**
    1885   Boston   200.
    1964   New Orleans   Ltd.   50.
PATRICK, Robert   **Reluctant Rebel. The Secret Diary of _____ 1861-65.** edited by F. Jay Taylor.
    1959   Baton Rouge   30.

POCHE, Felix Pierre   **A Louisiana Confederate, Diary of** _____ edited by Edwin C. Bearss.
>   1972   Natchitoches, Louisiana   30.

SHEERAN, James B.   **Confederate Chaplain, A War Journal of Rev.** _____ edited by Joseph Durkin.
>   1960   Milwaukee   25.

TUNNARD, W. H.   **A Southern Record: The History of the Third Regiment Louisiana Infantry.**
>   1866   Baton Rouge   800.
>   1970   Dayton   edited by Edwin C. Bearss   25.

WATSON, William   **Life in the Confederate Army.**
>   1887   London   275.
>   1888   New York   125.

MAINE

GENERAL REFERENCES

Annual Report of the Adjutant General of the State of Maine.
>   1862-1867   Augusta   25. each

Supplement to the Annual Reports of the Adjutant General of the State of Maine for the years 1861-1866. Alphabetical Index of Maine Volunteers.
>   1867   Augusta   50.

JORDAN, William B. (comp)   **Maine in the Civil War: Bibliographical Guide.** Wraps
>   1976   Portland   15.

Maine at Gettysburg. Report of the Maine Commissioners.
>   1898   Portland   30.

Portland Soldiers and Sailors in the War of the Rebellion. Wraps
>   1884   Portland   20.

STANLEY, R. H. and **HALL,** Geo. O.   **Eastern Maine and the Rebellion.**
>   1887   Bangor   40.

War Papers Read Before the Commandery of the State of Maine, Mollus. Vols. 1-4.
>   1898-1908   Portland   25. each

WHITMAN, William E. S. and **TRUE,** Charles H.   **Maine in the War for the Union: A History.**
>   1865   Lewiston   30.

REGIMENTALS

ADAMS, John R.   **Memorial & Letters of Rev.** _____ **Chaplain of the Fifth Maine and the One Hundred and Twenty-First New York Regiments.**
>   1890   Cambridge   75.

AMBLER, I. W.   **"Truth Is Stranger Than Fiction," The Life of Sergeant** _____
>   1873   Boston   30.
>   1883   Boston   25.
>   1886   Boston   25.

BOLTON, Horace Wilbert   **Personal Reminiscences of the Late War.**
>   1892   Chicago   25.

BRADY, Robert   **The Story of One Regiment, The Eleventh Maine Infantry Volunteers in the War of the Rebellion.**
>   1896   New York   75.

BURRAGE, Henry S.   **Thomas Hamlin Hubbard, Bvt. Brig.-Gen. U. S. Vols.**
>   1923   Portland   15.

CARVER, Willard   **Fourteenth Regt. Maine Infantry Roster of Survivors.**
>   1892   n.p.   30.

CHAMBERLAIN, Joshua L.   **The Passing of the Armies.**
 1915 New York 125.
 1974 Dayton 25.
CHASE, John F. **A Short Sketch of the Battle of Gettysburg.** Wraps
 n.d. n.p. 30.
First Maine Cavalry, Proceedings at Annual Reunions. Wraps
 1876-1882 20. each
GERRISH, Theodore **Army Life.**
 1882 Portland 35.
GERRISH, Theodore and **HUTCHINSON,** J. S. **The Blue and the Gray.**
 1884 Bangor 25.
GILMORE, Pascal P. **Civil War Memories.**
 1928 Bangor 40.
GOULD, Edward K. **Major General Hiram G. Berry.**
 1899 Rockland 60.
GOULD, John Mead **History of the First-Tenth-Twenty-Ninth Maine Regiment.**
 1871 Portland 75.
GOULD, John Mead **Joseph K. F. Mansfield, A Narrative of Events Connected with His Mortal Wounding at Antietam Sept. 17, 1862.**
 1895 Portland 25.
HOUGHTON, Edwin B. **The Campaigns of the Seventeenth Maine.**
 1866 Portland 125.
HOUSTON, Henry C. **The Thirty-Second Maine Regiment of Infantry Volunteers.**
 1903 Portland 75.
HOWARD, Oliver Otis **Autobiography of _____ Major General.** 2 vols.
 1907 New York 100.
JOHNSON, Hannibal A. **The Sword of Honor.**
 1903 Providence Wraps Ltd. 30.
 1906 Worcester 30.
 1906 Hallowell 30.
LAPHAM, William B. **My Recollections of the War of the Rebellion.**
 1892 Augusta 60.
LUFKIN, Edwin B. **History of the Thirteenth Maine Regiment.**
 1898 Brighton 100.
MADDOCKS, Elden B. **History of the Twenty-Sixth Maine Regiment.**
 1899 Bangor 75.
MAXFIELD, Albert and **BRADY,** Robert, Jr. **Roster and Statistical Record of Company D, of the Eleventh Regiment Maine Infantry Volunteers.** Wraps
 1890 New York 25.
MERRILL, Samuel H. **The Campaigns of the First Maine and First District of Columbia Cavalry.**
 1866 Portland 80.
NICHOLS, George W. **Major Soule, A Memorial of Alfred B. Soule.**
 1866 Salem 30.
PULLEN, John J. **A Shower of Stars. The Medal of Honor and the 27th Maine.**
 1966 Philadelphia/New York 20.
PULLEN, John J. **The Twentieth Maine.**
 1957 Philadelphia 30.
Roster of the 22nd Regiment Infantry Maine Vols. Mustered into U.S. Service at "Camp Pope" Bangor, Maine, October 10, 1862. Wraps
 1863 Bangor 30.
SHAW, Horace H. **The First Maine Heavy Artillery.**
 1903 Portland 100.
SHOREY, Henry A. **The Story of the Maine Fifteenth.**
 1890 Bridgton 125.
SMALL, Abner R. **The Road to Richmond, The Civil War Memoirs of _____ of the Sixteenth Maine Volunteers** edited by Henry A. Small.
 1939 Berkeley 40.
 1957 Berkeley 20.

SMALL, Abner R.   The Sixteenth Maine Regiment in the War of the Rebellion.
    1886   Portland   75.
SMITH, John Day   The History of the Nineteenth Regiment of Maine
    Volunteer Infantry, 1862-1865
    1909   Minneapolis   85.
STONE, James M.   The History of the Twenty-seventh Regiment
    Maine Volunteer Infantry.
    1895   Portland   40.
TOBIE, Edward   First Maine Cavalry Historical Sketch & Recollections. Wraps
    n.d.   n.p.   35.
TOBIE, Edward P.   History of the First Maine Cavalry.
    1887   Boston   100.
TOBIE, Edward P.   Personal Recollections of General Sherman. Wraps
    1889   Providence   Ltd.   25.
TOBIE, Edward P.   Service of the Cavalry in the Army of the Potomac. Wraps
    1882   Providence   Ltd.   25.
TOBIE, Edward P.   A Trip to Richmond as Prisoner of War. Wraps
    1879   Providence   Ltd.   25.
TWITCHELL, Albert Sobieski   Reunion Poems.
    1883   Gorham   15.
ULMER, George T.   Adventures and Reminiscences of a Volunteer. Wraps
    1892   Chicago   25.
Unveiling of Monument to the First Maine Cavalry at Gettysburg, Oct. 3, 1889.
    1889   Boston   20.
WALLACE, Willard M.   Soul of the Lion, A Biography of General Joshua L.
    Chamberlain.
    1960   New York   30.
    1960   Edinburgh   40.
WESTON, Edward P.   The Christian Soldier Boy . . . An Address. Wraps
    1862   Portland   15.
WING, Samuel B.   The Soldier's Story A Personal Narrative.
    1898   Phillips   50.
WOODWARD, Joseph T.   Historic Record and Complete Biographic Roster 21st
    Maine Volunteers.
    1907   Augusta   75.

MARYLAND

GENERAL REFERENCES

BOOTH, Geo. W. (comp)   Illustrated Souvenir, Maryland Line, Confederate
    Soldiers Home, Pikesville, Maryland.
    1894   Baltimore   75.
DAVIDSON, Laura Lee   The Services of the Women of Maryland to the Confed-
    erate States, A Prize Essay. Wraps
    1920   Baltimore   30.
DURST, Ross C.   Garrett County Maryland and the Civil War.
    1961   Oakland   15.
EVANS, Clement A. (ed)   Confederate Military History Vol. II — Maryland and
    West Virginia.
    1899   Atlanta   40.
GOLDSBOROUGH, William W.   The Maryland Line in the Confederate States
    Army.
    1869   Baltimore   250.
    1900   Baltimore   200.
    1972   Port Washington, New York   40.

GOLDSBOROUGH, William W.   **Index to the Maryland Line in the Confederate Army 1861-1865.** Wraps
    1944   Annapolis   30.
KLEIN, Frederic S.   **Just South of Gettysburg. Carroll County Maryland in the Civil War.**
    1963   Westminster   30.
974   Lancaster   20.
MANAKEE, Harold R.   **Maryland in the Civil War.**
    1961   n.p.   30.
    1969   Baltimore   35.
MAYER, Brantz   **The Emancipation Problem in Maryland.** Wraps
    1862   Baltimore   25.
MYERS, William Starr   **The Maryland Constitution of 1864.** Wraps
    1901   Baltimore   25.
MYERS, William Starr   **The Self-Reconstruction of Maryland.** Wraps
    1909   Baltimore   30.
SEABROOK, William L. W.   **Maryland's Great Part in Saving the Union.**
    1913   n.p.   100.
Secret Correspondence Illustrating the Condition of Affairs in Maryland. Wraps
    1863   Baltimore   125.
WILMER, L. Allison and **JARRETT,** J. H. and **VERNON,** Geo. W. F.   **History and Roster of Maryland Volunteers War of 1861-1865.** 2 vols.
    1898-99   Baltimore   150.

REGIMENTALS

Union

CAMPER, Chas. and **KIRKLEY,** J. W. (comps)   **Historical Record of the First Regiment Maryland Infantry.**
    1871   Washington   150.
GOLDSBOROUGH, Edward Yerbury   **Early's Great Raid.** Wraps
    1898   n.p.   85.
HINDS, Thomas   **Tales of War Times.**
    1904   Watertown, New York   125.
KING, John R.   **A Brief History of the Sixth Regiment Maryland Infantry Volunteers, Second Brigade, Third Division, Sixth Army Corps.** Wraps
    1915   Baltimore   60.
NEWCOMER, C. Armour   **Cole's Cavalry, or Three Years in the Saddle in the Shenandoah Valley.**
    1895   Baltimore   110.
    1970   New York   25.
RACINE, J. Polk   **Recollections of a Veteran; or, Four Years in Dixie.**
    1894   Elkton   150.
SHANE, John H.   **First Regiment Eastern Shore Maryland Infantry at Gettysburg July 1863.** Wraps
    1895   Baltimore   30.
WILD, Frederick W.   **Memoirs and History of Capt. F. W. Alexander's Baltimore Battery of Light Artillery, USV.**
    1912   Baltimore   100.

Confederate

ANDREWS, Richard S.   **Richard Snowden Andrews, Lt. Col. Commanding the First Maryland Artillery . . . A Memoir** edited by Tunstall Smith.
    1910   Baltimore   75.
BOOTH, George Wilson   **Personal Reminiscences of a Maryland Soldier in the War Between the States, 1861-1865.**
    1898   Baltimore   325.

GILL, John   **Reminiscences of Four Years as a Private Soldier in the Confederate Army.**
  1904   Baltimore   375.
GILMOR, Harry   **Four Years in the Saddle.**
  1866   New York   70.
  1866   London   75.
HOWARD, Jas. McHenry   **Recollections of a Maryland Confederate Soldier and Staff Officer Under Johnston, Jackson, and Lee.**
  1914   Baltimore   200.
  1975   Dayton   20.
JOHNSON, Bradley T.   **The First Maryland Campaign, An Address . . . at 4th Annual Re-union of Assoc. of Maryland Line.** Wraps
  1886   Baltimore   50.
McKIM, Randolph H.   **The Motives and Aims of the Soldiers of the South in the Civil War.** Wraps
  1904   n.p.   30.
McKIM, Randolph H.   **A Soldier's Recollections, Leaves from the Diary of a Young Confederate.**
  1910   New York   75.
  1911   New York   60.
  1921   New York   50.
RICH, Edward R.   **Comrades!**
  1898   Easton   200.
RICH, Edward R.   **Comrades Four.**
  1907   New York   350.
RITTER, William L.   **Biographical Memoir and Sketch of the Third Battery of Maryland Artillery.**
  1902   Baltimore   100.
STONEBRAKER, Joseph R.   **A Rebel of '61.**
  1899   New York   450.

MASSACHUSETTS

GENERAL REFERENCES

Annual Report of the Adjutant General of the State of Massachusetts. 5 vols.
  1862-1866   Boston   30. per vol..
BOWEN, James L.   **Massachusetts in the Civil War.**
  1889   Springfield   40.
BURR, Fearing and **LINCOLN,** George   **The Town of Hingham in the Late Civil War.**
  1876   Boston   30.
Ceremonies at the Dedication of the Soldiers' Monument in West Roxbury. Wraps
  1871   Boston   15.
Civil War Papers Read Before the Commandery of the State of Massachusetts, Mollus. 2 vols.
  1900   Boston   40.
CREASEY, George W.   **The City of Newburyport in the Civil War.**
  1903   Boston   20.
GARDNER, James B.   **Massachusetts Memorial to Her Soldiers and Sailors Who Died in the Department of North Carolina Dedicated at New Bern . . . 1908.**
  1909   Boston   35.
HEADLEY, P. C.   **Massachusetts in the Rebellion.**
  1866   Boston   25.
HIGGINSON, Thomas Wentworth   **Massachusetts in the Army and Navy During the War.** 2 vols.
  1896   Boston   50.

MARVIN, Abijah P.   **History of Worcester in the War of the Rebellion.**
    1870   Worcester   20.
    1870   Cleveland   20.
Massachusetts, Report of the Commission on Andersonville Monument.
    1902   Boston   15.
Massachusetts Soldiers, Sailors, and Marines in the Civil War. 8 vols. & index.
    1931-35   Norwood   200.
MOORE, George H.   **Notes on the History of Slavery in Massachusetts.**
    1866   New York   30.
NASON, George W.   **History and Complete Roster of the Massachusetts Regiments. Minute Men of '61.**
    1910   Boston   35.
RAYMOND, S.   **Memorial Volume. The Record of Andover During the Rebellion.**
    1875   Andover   20.
The Record of Athol, Massachusetts, in Suppressing the Great Rebellion.
    1866   Boston   25.
Record of Massachusetts Volunteers, 1861-65. 2 vols.
    1868-70   Boston   100.
The Record of the Procession and of the Exercises at the Dedication of the Monument . . . Erected by the People of Hanover, Mass. . . . In Grateful Memory of the Soldiers and Sailors . . . Who Died in the War for the Preservation of the Union. Wraps
    1878   Boston   15.
Register of the Commandery of the State of Massachusetts, Mollus.
    1912   Cambridge   25.
SCHOULER, William   **A History of Massachusetts in the Civil War.** 2 vols.
    1868   Boston   60.
The State of Sovereignty Record of Massachusetts by a Son of Norfolk. Wraps
    1872   Norfolk   15.
WARE, Edith Ellen   **Political Opinion in Massachusetts During Civil War and Reconstruction.** Wraps
    1916   New York   20.

REGIMENTALS

ADAMS, Herbert Lincoln   **Worcester Light Infantry 1803-1922 A History.**
    1924   Worcester   35.
ADAMS, John G. B.   **Reminiscences of the Nineteenth Massachusetts Regiment.**
    1899   Boston   50.
ALLEN, Stanton P.   **Down in Dixie.**
    1893   Boston   40.
AMORY, Charles B.   **A Brief Record of the Army Life of _____**
    1902   Boston (?)   25.
ANDERSON, John   **The Fifty-Seventh Regiment of Massachusetts Volunteers.**
    1896   Boston   50.
ARNOLD William B.   **The Fourth Massachusetts Cavalry in the Closing Scenes of the War for the Maintenance of the Union.**
    191__   Boston?   35.
BAKER, Levi W.   **History of the Ninth Mass. Battery.**
    1888   S. Framingham   85.
BARDEEN, Charles W.   **A Little Fifer's War Diary.**
    1910   Syracuse, N. Y.   75.
BARRETT, Edwin S.   **What I Saw at Bull Run: An Address.**
    1886   Boston   35.
BARTOL, Cyrus A.   **The Nation's Hour: A Tribute to Major Sidney Willard.** Wraps
    1862   Boston   15.

BEALE, James   **A Famous War Song, A Paper Read Before the United Service Club.**
1894   Philadelphia   Ltd.   40.
BEALE, James   **The Statements of Time on July 1, at Gettysburg, Pa. 1863.**
1897   Philadelphia   Ltd.   50.
BEALE, James   **Tabulated Roster of the Army of the Potomac at Gettysburg, Penna. July 1, 2, 3, 1863.** Wraps
1888   Philadelphia   30.
BENNETT, Andrew J.   **The Story of the First Massachusetts Light Battery.**
1886   Boston   75.
BENNETT, Edwin C.   **Musket and Sword; or The Camp, March and Firing Line in the Army of the Potomac.**
1900   Boston   40.
BIGELOW, John   **The Peach Orchard, Gettysburg, July 2, 1864.**
1910   Minneapolis   50.
BILLINGS, John D.   **Hard Tack and Coffee.**
1887   Boston   175.
1888   Boston   125.
1889   Boston   125.
1960   Chicago   edited by Richard Harwell   40.
1970   Glendale   25.
BILLINGS, John D.   **The History of the Tenth Massachusetts Battery of Light Artillery in the War of the Rebellion.**
1881   Boston   75.
1909   Boston   75.
BLAKE, Henry N.   **Three Years in the Army of the Potomac.**
1865   Boston   60.
BLANDING, Stephen F.   **In the Defences of Washington.**
1889   Providence   35.
BOIES, Andrew J.   **Record of the Thirty-Third Massachusetts Volunteer Infantry.**
1880   Fitchburg   30.
BOSSON, Charles P.   **History of the Forty-Second Regiment Infantry, Massachusetts Volunteers.**
1886   Boston   50.
BOWEN, James L.   **History of the Thirty-Seventh Regiment Mass. Volunteers in the Civil War.**
1884   Holyoke   50.
BRETT, David   **My Dear Wife, The Civil War Letters of _____, Union Cannoneer 9th Massachusetts Battery.**
1964   Little Rock   15.
BROWN, George William   **Baltimore and the Nineteenth of April, 1861.**
1887   Baltimore   25.
BRUCE, George   **The Twentieth Regiment of Massachusetts Volunteer Infantry.**
1906   Boston   50.
BURRAGE, Henry S.   **History of the Thirty-Sixth Regiment Mass. Volunteers.**
1884   Boston   55.
CARTER, Robert Goldthwaite   **Four Brothers in Blue.**
1913   Washington   300.
1978   Austin   17.
CLARK, Harvey   **My Experiences with Burnside's Expedition and 18th Army Corps.**
1914   Gardner   40.
CLARK, William H.   **Poems and Sketches with Reminiscences of the "Old 34th."** Wraps
1890   South Framingham   35.
CLARK, William H.   **Reminiscences of the Thirty-Fourth Regiment Mass. Vol. Infantry.** Wraps
1871   Holliston   45.

COOK, Benjamin F.   **History of the Twelfth Massachusetts Volunteers (Webster Regiment).**
1882   Boston   85.

CROWNINSHIELD, Benj. W. and **GLEASON,** D. H. L.   **A History of the First Regiment of Massachusetts Cavalry Volunteers.**
1891   Boston   100.

CUDWORTH, Warren H.   **History of the First Regiment Massachusetts Infantry.**
1866   Boston   50.

CUTLER, Frederick M.   **The Old First Massachusetts Coast Artillery in War and Peace.**
1917   Boston   50.

DAVIS, Charles E., Jr.   **Three Years in the Army. The Story of the Thirteenth Massachusetts Volunteers.**
1894   Boston   75.

DAY, David L.   **My Diary — Rambles with the 25th Mass. Volunteer Infantry.**
1884   Milford   40.

DENNY, J. Waldo   **Wearing the Blue in the Twenty-Fifth Mass. Volunteer Infantry with Burnside's Coast Division.**
1879   Worcester   75.

DERBY, William P.   **Bearing Arms in the Twenty-Seventh Massachusetts Regiment of Volunteer Infantry During the Civil War.**
1883   Boston   65.

DOLLARD, Robert   **Recollections of the Civil War, and Going West to Grow Up with the Country.**
1906   Scotland, South Dakota   75.

DRAPER, William F.   **Recollections of a Varied Career.**
1908   Boston   25.
1909   Boston   25.

DWIGHT, Wilder   **Life and Letters of _____ Lieut. Col. Second Mass. Inf. Vols.** edited by Elizabeth A. Dwight.
1868   Boston   35.

EARLE, David M.   **History of the Excursion of the Fifteenth Massachusetts Regiment and Its Friends to Battlefield of Gettysburg . . . 1886.**
1886   Worcester   25.

EATON, William   **History of the Richardson Light Guard, of Wakefield, Massachusetts 1851-1901.**
1901   Wakefield   20.

EMERSON, Edward W.   **Life and Letters of Charles Russell Lowell.**
1907   Boston   35.

EMILIO, Luis F.   **The Assault on Fort Wagner, July 18, 1863. The Memorable Charge of the 54th Massachusetts Vols.** Wraps
1887   Boston   25.

EMILIO, Luis F.   **History of the Fifty-Fourth Regiment of Massachusetts Volunteer Infantry 1863-1865.**
1891   Boston   75.
1894   Boston   65.

EMILIO, Luis F.   **Roanoke Island Its Occupation, Defense and Fall.** Wraps
1891   New York   30.

EMMERTON, James A.   **A Record of the Twenty-Third Regiment Mass Vol. Infantry.**
1886   Boston   75.

ESTABROOKS, Henry L.   **Adrift in Dixie: Or, A Yankee Officer Among the Rebels.**
1866   New York   35.

EWER, James K.   **The Third Massachusetts Cavalry in the War for the Union.**
1903   Maplewood   75.

Exercises at the Dedication of the Monument to Colonel Robert Gould Shaw, etc.
1897   Boston   20.

First Regiment of Infantry Massachusetts Volunteer Militia Col. Robert Cowdin, Commanding.
    1903   Boston   25.

FLINN, Frank M.   **Campaigning with Banks in Louisiana, '63 and '64 and with Sheridan in the Shenandoah Valley.**
    1887   Lynn   45.
    1889   Boston   40.

FLYNN, Frank J.   **The "Fighting Ninth" for Fifty Years and the Semi-Centennial Celebration.**
    1911   n.p.   25.

FORD, Andrew E.   **The Story of the Fifteenth Regiment Massachusetts Volunteer Infantry.**
    1898   Clinton   60.

FOWLE, George   **Letters to Eliza from a Union Soldier 1863-1865.** edited by Margery Greenleaf.
    1970   Chicago   15.

FOX, Charles B.   **Record of the Service of the Fifty-Fifth Regiment of Massachusetts Volunteer Infantry.**
    1868   Cambridge   Wraps   75.
    1971   Freeport, New York   20.

FULLER, Richard F.   **Chaplain Fuller.**
    1863   Boston   20.
    1864   Boston   15.

GAMMONS, John G.   **The Third Massachusetts Regiment Volunteer Militia in the War of the Rebellion 1861-1863.**
    1906   Providence   40.

GORDON, George H.   **Brook Farm to Cedar Mountain in the War of the Great Rebellion 1861-62.**
    1883   Boston   50.
    1885   Boston   40.

GORDON, George H.   **History of the Campaign of the Army of Virginia, Under John Pope.**
    1880   Boston   80.

GORDON, George H.   **History of the Second Massachusetts Regiment of Infantry.** Wraps
    1875   Boston   40.

GORE, Henry W.   **The Independent Corps of Cadets of Boston, Mass.**
    1888   Boston   Ltd.   75.

GOSS, Warren Lee   **Recollections of a Private A Story of the Army of the Potomac.**
    1890   New York   35.

GOSS, Warren Lee   **The Soldier's Story of His Captivity at Andersonville, Belle Isle, and Other Rebel Prisons.**
    1866   Boston   25.
    1867   Boston   25.
    Various Editions   20. each

GRISWOLD, Anna   **Colonel Griswold.**
    1866   Brookline   30.

HAINES, Zenas T.   **Letters from the Forty-Fourth Regiment, M.V.M. . . . in the Department of North Carolina in 1862-3.**
    1863   Boston   65.

HALLOWELL, Norwood Penrose   **The Negro as a Soldier in the War of the Rebellion: An Address Delivered on Memorial Day, May 30, 1896.**
    1896   Boston   100.

HANSON, John W.   **Historical Sketch of the Old Sixth Regiment of Massachusetts Volunteers.**
    1866   Boston   50.

HIGGINS, William C.   **Scaling the Eagle's Nest: Life of Russell H. Conwell.**
    1889   Springfield   25.

HILL, Alonzo   **In Memoriam A Discourse . . . on Lieut. Thomas Jefferson Spurr.** Wraps
    1862   Boston   25.
History of the Fifth Massachusetts Battery.
    1902   Boston   75.
History of the Thirty-Fifth Regiment Massachusetts Volunteers.
    1884   Boston   50.
HODGKINS, William H.   **The Battle of Fort Stedman (Petersburg, Virginia) Mar. 25, 1865.** Wraps
    1889   Boston   50.
HOLMES, Oliver Wendell, Jr.   **Touched with Fire. Civil War Letters and Diary.** edited by Mark deWolfe Howe.
    1946   Cambridge   20.
HOSMER, James Kendall   **The Color Guard: Being a Corporal's Notes of Military Service in the Nineteenth Army Corps.**
    1864   Boston   40.
HOSMER, James Kendall   **The Thinking Bayonet.**
    1865   Boston   20.
HOWE, Henry Warren   **Passages from the Life of _____ Consisting of Diary and Letters Written During the Civil War 1861-1865.**
    1899   Lowell   75.
HUBBARD, Charles Eustis   **The Campaign of the Forty-Fifth Regiment Massachusetts Volunteer Militia "The Cadet Regiment".**
    1882   Boston   75.
HUMPHREYS, Charles A.   **Field, Camp, Hospital and Prison in the Civil War 1863-1865.**
    1918   Boston   50.
    1971   Freeport, NY   20.
HUTCHINSON, Nelson V.   **History of the Seventh Massachusetts Volunteer Infantry in the War of the Rebellion.**
    1890   Taunton   125
JAMES, Henry B.   **Memories of the Civil War.**
    1898   New Bedford   30.
JOHNS, Henry T.   **Life with the Forty-Ninth Massachusetts Volunteers.**
    1864   Pittsfield   50.
    1890   Washington   40.
KINGSBURY, Allen A.   **The Hero of Medfield; Containing the Journal and Letters of . . .**
    1862   Boston   30.
KIRWAN, Thomas and **SPLAINE,** Henry   **Memorial History of the Seventeenth Regiment Massachusetts Volunteer Infantry . . . 1861-1865.**
    1911   Salem   45.
LENFEST, Solomon A.   **The Diary of _____ Co. G. Sixth Massachusetts Infantry While Stationed at Suffolk, Virginia August 29, 1862 to May 29, 1863.** Wraps
    1975   Suffolk   15.
Lt.-Col. Charles Lyon Chandler A Memorial.
    1864   Cambridge   25.
LINCOLN, Levi   **A Memorial of William Sever Lincoln.**
    1899   Worcester   30.
LINCOLN, William S.   **Life with the Thirty-Fourth Mass. Infantry.**
    1879   Worcester   75.
McKAY, Martha Nicholson   **When the Tide Turned in the Civil War.**
    1929   Indianapolis   20.
MacNAMARA, Daniel G.   **History of the Ninth Regiment Massachusetts Volunteer Infantry.**
    1899   Boston   65.
MacNAMARA, Michael H.   **The Irish Ninth in Bivouac and Battle.**
    1867   Boston   60.

MAGLATHLIN, Henry B.   **Company I, Fourth Massachusetts Regiment, Nine Months Volunteers in Service 1862-3.** Wraps
    1863   Boston   25.

MANN, Albert W.   **History of the Forty-Fifth Regiment Massachusetts Volunteer Militia.**
    1908   Boston   50.

MEACHAM, Henry H.   **The Empty Sleeve.** Wraps
    1869   Springfield   25.

A Memorial of Paul Joseph Revere and Edward H. R. Revere.
    1874   Boston   50.
    1913   Clinton   25.

MILLER, James Hervey   **My War Experiences.**
    n.d.   Gardner, Mass.   35.

MOORS, John F.   **History of the Fifty-Second Regiment Massachusetts Volunteers.**
    1893   Boston   55.

MORGAN, William H.   **A Narrative of the Service of Company D, First Massachusetts Heavy Artillery.**
    1907   Boston   50.

MORSE, Charles F.   **History of the Second Massachusetts, Regiment of Infantry, Gettysburg.** Wraps
    1882   Boston   25.

MORSE, Charles F.   **Letters Written During the Civil War 1861-1865.**
    1898   Boston   50.

NEWELL, Joseph Keith   **"Ours," Annals of the 10th Regiment Massachusetts Volunteers.**
    1875   Springfield   65.

NICHOLS, Samuel Edmund   **"Your Soldier Boy Samuel" Civil War Letters of Lt. _____.**
    1929   Buffalo   Ltd.   40.

OAKEY, Daniel   **History of the Second Massachusetts Regiment of Infantry, Beverly Ford.** Wraps
    1884   Boston   25.

OSBORNE, William H.   **The History of the Twenty-Ninth Regiment of Massachusetts Volunteer Infantry.**
    1877   Boston   65.

PALFREY, Francis Winthrop   **Memoir of William Francis Bartlett.**
    1878   Boston   30.
    1879   Boston   25.

PARKER, Francis J.   **The Story of the Thirty-Second Regiment Massachusetts Infantry.**
    1880   Boston   60.

PARKER, John L. and **CARTER,** Robert G.   **Henry Wilson's Regiment History of the Twenty-Second Massachusetts Infantry.**
    1887   Boston   100.

PEIRSON, Charles Lawrence   **A Monograph, Ball's Bluff: An Episode and Its Consequences to Some of us.**
    1913   Salem   35.

PERRY, Bliss   **Life and Letters of Henry Lee Higginson.** 2 vols.
    1921   Boston   Ltd.   25.
    1922   n.p.   25.

PERRY, John G.   **Letters from a Surgeon of the Civil War.** compiled by Martha D. Perry.
    1906   Boston   50.

PIERCE, Charles F.   **History and Camp Life of Company C, Fifty-First Regiment Mass. Vol. Militia.**
    1886   Worcester   75.

PLUMMER, Albert   **History of the Forty Eighth Regiment M.V.M.**
    1907   Boston   50.

POWERS, George W.   **The Story of the Thirty-Eighth Regiment of Massachusetts Volunteers.**
1866   Cambridge   100.

PUTNAM, Samuel H.   **The Story of Company A, Twenty-Fifth Regiment, Massachusetts Volunteers.**
1886   Worcester   Ltd.   125.

QUINCY, Samuel M.   **History of the Second Massachusetts Regiment of Infantry; A Prisoner's Diary.** Wraps
1882   Boston   25.

QUINT, Alonzo H.   **The Potomac and the Rapidan.**
1864   Boston   30.

QUINT, Alonzo H.   **The Record of the Second Massachusetts Infantry.**
1867   Boston   65.
1867   Boston   Ltd.   125.

Record of the Service of the Forty-Fourth Massachusetts Volunteer Militia in North Carolina.
1887   Boston   75.

ROBBINS, Gilbert   **The Christian Patriot: A Biography of James E. McClellan.**
1865   Worcester   15.

ROBINSON, Frank T.   **History of the Fifth Regiment, M.V.M.**
1879   Boston   65.

ROCKWELL, Francis Williams   **Address at the Unveiling of the Memorial Tablet of Col. Henry S. Briggs and the Tenth Mass. Infantry.**
1907   Pittsfield   15.

ROE, Alfred S.   **The Fifth Regiment Massachusetts Volunteer Infantry.**
1911   Boston   45.

ROE, Alfred S. and **NUTT**, Charles   **History of the First Regiment of Heavy Artillery Massachusetts Volunteers.**
1917   Worcester   75.

ROE, Alfred S.   **The Melvin Memorial, Sleepy Hollow Cemetery, Concord A Brother's Tribute, Exercises at Dedication June 16, 1909.**
1910   Cambridge   25.

ROE, Alfred S.   **The Tenth Regiment Massachusetts Volunteer Infantry.**
1909   Springfield   50.

ROE, Alfred S.   **The Thirty-Ninth Regiment Massachusetts Volunteers 1862-1865.**
1914   Worcester   50.

ROE, Alfred S.   **The Twenty-Fourth Regiment, Massachusetts Volunteers, 1861-66.**
1907   Worcester   60.

ROGERS, Edward H.   **Reminiscences of Military Service in the Forty-Third Regiment Massachusetts Infantry.**
1883   Boston   60.

RYDER, John J.   **Reminiscences of Three Years' Service in the Civil War. By a Cape Cod Boy.**
1928   New Bedford   35.

SMITH, Chas. M.   **From Andersonville to Freedom.** Wraps
1894   Providence   Ltd.   25.

STEARNS, Amos E.   **Narrative of _____ A Prisoner at Andersonville.** Wraps
1887   Worcester   40.

STEARNS, Austin C.   **Three Years with Company K, Sergt. Austin C. Stearns Company K, 13th Mass. Infantry (Deceased)** edited by Arthur A. Kent.
1976   Rutherford   25.

STEARNS, William Augustus   **A Memorial to Adjutant Stearns.**
1862   Boston   15.

STEVENS, William B.   **History of the Fiftieth Regiment of Infantry Massachusetts Volunteer Militia.**
1907   Boston   50.

STEVENSON, Joshua Thomas   **Memorial of Thomas Greely Stevenson 1836-1864.**
1864   Cambridge   30.

STONE, James M.   **Personal Recollections of the Civil War . . . As a Private Soldier in the 21st Vol. Regiment of Infantry.**
1918   Boston   60.

STURGIS, Thomas   **Prisoners of War 1861-1865.**
1912   New York   30.

SWIFT, George W.   **Experiences of a Falmouth Boy in Rebel Prisons.** Wraps
1899   Falmouth   40.

THAYER, George A.   **The Draft Riots of 1863, A Historical Study.** Wraps
1916 (?)   n.p.   25.

THAYER, George A.   **"Gettysburg," "As We Men on the Right Saw It." A Paper.** Wraps
1886   Cincinnati   25.

THAYER, George A.   **History of the Second Massachusetts Regiment of Infantry, Chancellorsville.** Wraps
1882   Boston   25.

TYLER, Mason Whiting   **Recollections of the Civil War.**
1912   New York   30.

UNDERWOOD, Adin B.   **The Three Years' Service of the Thirty-Third Mass. Infantry Regiment.**
1881   Boston   50.

VALENTINE, Herbert E. (ed)   **Dedication of the Boulder Commemorating the Service of the Twenty-Third Regiment Mass. Vol. Infantry.** Wraps
1905   Salem   15.

VALENTINE, Herbert E.   **Story of Company F, 23d Massachusetts Volunteers.**
1896   Boston   50.

WAITT, Ernest L. (comp)   **History of the Nineteenth Regiment Massachusetts Volunteer Infantry.**
1906   Salem   50.

WALCOTT, Charles F.   **History of the Twenty-First Regiment Massachusetts Volunteers.**
1882   Boston   65.

WARD, George W.   **History of the Excursion of the Fifteenth Massachusetts Regiment.**
1901   Worcester   25.

WATSON, Benjamin Frank   **An Oration Delivered at Huntington Hall, Lowell, Massachusetts April 19, 1886.**
1886   New York   35.

WELD, Stephen Minot   **War Diary and Letters of Stephen Minot Weld 1861-1865.**
1912   Cambridge   Ltd.   250.
1979   Boston   Ltd.   50.

WHIPPLE, George M.   **History of the Salem Light Infantry from 1805 to 1890.**
1890   Salem, Massachusetts   25.

WHITCOMB, Caroline E.   **History of the Second Massachusetts Battery (Nim's Battery) of Light Artillery.**
1912   Concord, New Hampshire   45.

WILLIAMS, Sidney S.   **From Spottsylvania to Wilmington, N. C. By Way of Andersonville and Florence.** Wraps
1899   Providence   Ltd.   25.

WILLIS, Henry A.   **The Fifty-Third Regiment Massachusetts Volunteers.**
1889   Fitchburg   60.

WYETH, John J.   **Leaves from a Diary Written While Serving in Co. E, 44th Massachusetts, Dept of N. C. Sept 1862 — June 1863.**
1878   Boston   55.

MICHIGAN

GENERAL REFERENCES

Adjutant General, Record of Service of Michigan Volunteers in the Civil War.
Vols. 1-46
1905   Kalamazoo   25. each
Annual Report of the Adjutant General of the State of Michigan, 1862-65.
1863-1866   Lansing   25. each
BELKNAP, Charles E.   **History of the Michigan Organizations at Chickamauga, Chattanooga and Missionary Ridge 1863.**
1899   Lansing   30.
ELLIS, Helen H.   **Michigan in the Civil War, A Guide to the Material in Detroit Newspapers 1861-1866.** Wraps
1965   Lansing   25.
FREITAG, Alfred J.   **Detroit in the Civil War.** Wraps
1951   Detroit   15.
KATZ, Irving I.   **The Jewish Soldier from Michigan in the Civil War.** Wraps
1962   Detroit   10.
LANMAN, Charles   **The Red Book of Michigan, A Civil, Military, and Biographical History.**
1862   New York   25.
1871   Detroit   30.
MAY, George S. (ed)   **Michigan Civil War History . . . An Annotated Bibliography.** Wraps
1961   Detroit   15.
Michigan at Gettysburg, July 1, 2, and 3, 1863, Proceedings Incident to the Dedication of the Michigan Monuments upon the Battlefield of Gettysburg.
1889   Detroit   50.
Michigan at Shiloh   Report of the Michigan Shiloh Soldiers' Monument Commission. Wraps
1920   Lansing   10.
Michigan Civil War Centennial Observance Commission.   During the Centennial, the Commission published 20 or more titles in blue wraps to sell for $2 - $5 each.
Michigan Women in the Civil War. Wraps
1963   Lansing   10.
MILLBROOK, Minnie Dubbs   **A Study in Valor   Michigan Medal of Honor Winners in the Civil War.** Wraps
1966   Lansing   10.
MILLBROOK, Minnie Dubbs (ed.)   **Twice Told Tales of Michigan and Her Soldiers in the Civil War.** Wraps
1966   Lansing   10.
NOLAN, A. T.   **The Iron Brigade.**
1975   Madison   40.
ROBERTSON, Jno.   **The Flags of Michigan.**
1877   Lansing   30.
ROBERTSON, Jno. (comp)   **Michigan in the War.**
1880   Lansing   50.
1882   Lansing   50.
SELBY, John   **The Iron Brigade.** Wraps
1973   New York   10.
War Papers Read Before the Michigan Commandery, Mollus. 2 vols.
1893-98   Detroit   150.
WOODFORD, Frank B.   **Father Abraham's Children, Michigan Episodes in the Civil War.**
1961   Detroit   25.

REGIMENTALS

ARNDT, Albert F. R.   **Reminiscences of an Artillery Officer.** Wraps
    1890   Detroit   25.

BACON, Edward   **Among the Cotton Thieves.**
    1867   Detroit   150.
    1962   n.p.   Ltd.   30.

BARRETT, Orvey S.   **Reminiscences, Incidents, Battles, Marches and Camp Life of the Old 4th Michigan Infantry in the War of the Rebellion.**
    1888   Detroit   50.
    n.d.   Detroit   Reprint   10.

BAUGHMAN, Theodore   **Baughman, The Oklahoma Scout: Personal Reminiscences of _____.**
    n.d.   Chicago   50.

BENNETT, Charles W.   **Historical Sketches of the Ninth Michigan Infantry (General Thomas' Headquarters Guards).**
    1913   Coldwater   200.

BERRY, Chester D.   **Loss of the Sultana and Reminiscences of Survivors.**
    1892   Lansing   75.

CLOWES, Walter F.   **The Detroit Light Guard.**
    1900   Detroit   75.

COOPER, David M.   **Obituary Discourse on Occasion of the Death of Noah Henry Ferry, Major of the 5th Michigan Cavalry, Killed at Gettysburg.** Wraps
    1863   New York   35.

CROTTY, Daniel G.   **Four Years Campaigning in the Army of the Potomac.**
    1874   Grand Rapids   125.

CUMMINGS, Charles L.   **The Great War Relic, Valuable as a Curiosity of the Rebellion, Together with a Sketch of My Life, Service in the Army, and How I Lost My Feet in the War.** Wraps
    188?   Harrisburg   25.

CURTIS, Orson B.   **History of the Twenty-Fourth Michigan of the Iron Brigade.**
    1891   Detroit   150.

CUTCHEON, Byron M.   **The Story of the Twentieth Michigan Infantry July 15th, 1862 to May 30th, 1865.**
    1904   Lansing   175.

DANNETT, Sylvia G.   **She Rode with the Generals. The True and Incredible Story of Sarah Emma Seelye, Alias Franklin Thompson.**
    1960   New York   25.

DICKINSON, Julian G.   **The Capture of Jeff. Davis.** Wraps
    1888   Detroit   25.

DOWLING, Morgan E.   **Southern Prisons or, Josie the Heroine of Florence.**
    1870   Detroit   125.

DUFFIELD, Henry M.   **Chickamauga.** Wraps
    1888   Detroit   25.

EDMONDS, Sara Emma E.   **Nurse and Spy in the Union Army.**
    1865   Hartford   25.

EDMONDS, S. Emma E.   **Unsexed; or, The Female Soldier.**
    1864   Philadelphia   30.

ELDERKIN, James D.   **Biographical Sketches and Anecdotes of a Soldier of Three Wars.**
    1899   Detroit   75.

ELY, Ralph   **Diary of Capt._____ of the 8th Michigan Infantry.** edited by Geo. M. Blackburn. Wraps
    1965   Mt. Pleasant   10.

FOOTE, Corydon Edward and **HORMEL,** Olive Deane   **With Sherman to the Sea, A Drummer's Story of the Civil War.**
    1960   New York   20.

FOX, Wells B.   **What I Remember of the Great Rebellion.**
    1892   Lansing   80.

GILLASPIE, Ira   **From Michigan to Murfreesboro: The Diary of the _____ of the Eleventh Michigan Infantry.** edited by Daniel B. Weber. Wraps
   1965   Mt. Pleasant, Michigan   10.

GRAHAM, Ziba B.   **On to Gettysburg   Ten Days from My Diary of 1863.** Wraps
   1893   Detroit   25.

GUNN, Jane Augusta   **Memorial Sketches of Doctor Moses Gunn.**
   1889   Chicago   75.

HARRIS, Samuel   **Personal Reminiscences.**
   1897   Chicago   100.

HOPPER, George C.   **The Battle of Groveton, or, Second Bull Run.** Wraps
   1893   Detroit   25.

ISHAM, Asa B.   **An Historical Sketch of the Seventh Regiment Michigan Volunteer Cavalry.**
   1893   New York   150.

ISHAM, Asa B.   **Experience in Rebel Prisons.**
   1890   Cincinnati   60.

JOHNSON, Ben C.   **A Soldier's Life: The Civil War Experiences of _____ , Originally Entitled "Sketches of the Sixth Regiment Michigan Infantry".** edited by Alan S. Brown. Wraps
   1962   Kalamazoo   10.

JOHNSON, George Kinney   **The Battle of Kernstown, March 23, 1862.** Wraps
   1890   Detroit   30.

KEEN, Joseph S.   **Experiences in Rebel Military Prisons at Richmond, Danville, Andersonville, and Escape from Andersonville.**
   1890   Detroit   75.

KIDD, James H.   **Address of _____ at the Dedication of Michigan Monuments upon the Battlefield of Gettysburg Jun 12, 1889.**
   n.d.   n.p.   35.

KIDD, James H.   **The Michigan Cavalry Brigade in the Wilderness.** Wraps
   1889   Detroit   35.

KIDD, James H.   **Personal Recollections of a Cavalryman.**
   1908   Ionia   175.
   1969   Grand Rapids   40.

LEE, William O. (comp)   **Personal and Historical Sketches and Facial History of and by Members of the Seventh Regiment Michigan Volunteer Cavalry.**
   1901   Detroit   250.
   (Not having had a copy of this book, we presume upon the bibliographical expertise of Charles Dornbusch as regards the word, "facial." Should the word in fact be "factual" no doubt Charles will lose face.)

LESTER, Frank A.   **Society of the Ninth Michigan Infantry Veteran Volunteers Semi-Centennial Roster.** Wraps
   1911   Lansing   50.

LINCOLN, Charles P.   **"Engagement at Thompson Station, Tenn."** Wraps
   1893   n.p.   20.

LYSTER, Henry Francis LeHunte   **Recollections of the Bull Run Campaign.** Wraps
   1888   Detroit   25

MAILE, John Levi   **"Prison Life in Andersonville."**
   1912   Los Angeles   Ltd.   40.

MAYO, Perry   **The Civil War Letters of Perry Mayo.** edited by Robert W. Hodge. Wraps
   1967   East Lansing   20.

PAGE, James Madison   **The True Story of Andersonville Prison.**
   1908   New York & Washington   75.

PARKHURST, John G.   **Recollections of Stone's River.** Wraps
   1890   Detroit   25.

PITTMAN, Samuel Emlen   **The Operations of Gen. Alpheus S. Williams and His Command in the Chancellorsville Campaign.** Wraps
   1888   Detroit   25.

RANSOM, John L.   **Andersonville Diary, Escape, and List of the Dead.**
   1881   Auburn, New York   50.
   1883   Philadelphia   40.
   1963   New York   entitled: **John Ransom's Diary.**   30.
SMITH, Donald L.   **The Twenty-Fourth Michigan of the Iron Brigade.**
   1962   Harrisburg   50.
SWIFT, Frederick W.   **My Experiences as a Prisoner of War.** Wraps
   1888   Detroit   25.
TAYLOR, John C.   **Lights and Shadows in the Recollections of a Youthful Volunteer in the Civil War.** Wraps
   n.d.   Ionia   100.
THATCHER, Marshall P.   **A Hundred Battles in the West, St. Louis to Atlanta 1861-1865.**
   1884   Detroit   125.
TIVY, Joseph A.   **Souvenir of the Seventh Containing a Brief History of It.**
   190?   Detroit   150.
TRAVIS, Benjamin F.   **The Story of the Twenty-Fifth Michigan.**
   1897   Kalamazoo   175.
TROWBRIDGE, Luther S.   **A Brief History of the Tenth Michigan Cavalry.**
   1905   Detroit   100.
TROWBRIDGE, Luther S.   **The Stoneman Raid of 1865, a Paper.** Wraps
   1888   Detroit   25.
TUTHILL, Richard S.   **With Sherman's Artillery at the Battle of Atlanta.** Wraps
   n.d.   Chicago   25.
WELLS, James M.   **"With Touch of Elbow" or Death Before Dishonor.**
   1909   Philadelphia   75.
   1909   Chicago   60.
WOOD, Edward A., II   **Dr. Eugene V. N. Hall, Veteran of the Civil War.** Wraps
   1956   Chicago   10.
WOOD, Helen Everett (ed)   **Delevan Arnold, A Kalamazoo Volunteer in the Civil War.** Wraps
   1962   Kalamazoo   10.
WITHINGTON, William Herbert   **Michigan in the Opening of the War.** Wraps
   1889   Detroit   20.

MINNESOTA

GENERAL REFERENCES

Annual Report of the Adjutant General of the State of Minnesota for the Year Ending Dec. 1 1866, and **Of Military Forces of the State from 1861-1866.**
   1866   St. Paul   40.
CARLEY, Kenneth   **Minnesota in the Civil War.**
   1961   Minneapolis   20.
Report of Minnesota Commission, Report of . . . National Military Cemeteries at Little Rock, Memphis and Andersonville.
   1916   St. Paul   20.
Minnesota in the Civil War and Indian Wars 1861-1865. 2 vols.
   1890-93   St. Paul   100.
Glimpses of the Nation's Struggle, Papers Read Before the Minnesota Commandery, Mollus. 6 vols.
   1887-1909   St. Paul   25. each.

REGIMENTALS

ANDREWS, Christopher C.   **Christopher C. Andrews . . . General in the Civil War. Recollections 1829-1922.** edited by Alice E. Andrews.
   1928   Cleveland   30.

BASSETT, M. H.   **From Bull Run to Bristow Station, Civil War Letters of a Soldier with the First Minnesota.**
   1962   St. Paul   20.

BIRCHER, William   **A Drummer Boy's Diary: Comprising Four Years of Service with the Second Regiment Minnesota Vet. Vols.**
   1889   St. Paul   50.

BISHOP, Judson W.   **The Story of a Regiment, Being a Narrative of the Service of the Second Regiment Minnesota Veteran Vol. Infantry.**
   1890   St. Paul   150.

BISHOP, Judson W.   **Van Derveer's Brigade at Chickamauga.** Wraps
   1903   St. Paul (?)   25.

BROWN, Alonzo L.   **History of the Fourth Regiment of Minnesota Infantry Volunteers.**
   1892   St. Paul   100.

HILL, Alfred J.   **History of Company E of the Sixth Minnesota Regiment of Volunteer Infantry.** Wraps
   1899   St. Paul   125.

IMHOLTE, John Q.   **The First Minnesota Volunteers.**
   1963   Minneapolis   25.
   1969   Minneapolis   20.

KELLEY, Duren F.   **The War Letters of _____ 1862-1865.** edited by R. S. Offenberg and R. R. Parsonage.
   1967   New York   20.

KING, Josias Ridgate   **The Battle of Bull Run, A Confederate Victory Obtained, but not Achieved.** Wraps
   1907   n.p.   25.

SAYNER, Donald B.   **The Orders of Col. Samuel McPhail 1863 Minnesota Mounted Rangers.** Wraps
   1973   Tucson, Ariz.   20.

TAYLOR, Isaac L.   **Campaigning with the First Minnesota A Civil War Diary.** edited by Hazel Wolf.
   1944   St. Paul   35.

MISSISSIPPI

GENERAL REFERENCES

BEARSS, Edwin C.   **Decision in Mississippi.**
   1962   Jackson   30.
   1962   Little Rock   30.

BETTERSWORTH, John K.   **Confederate Mississippi.**
   1943   Baton Rouge   40.
   1970   New York   30.

BETTERSWORTH, John K. and **SILVER,** James W. (eds)   **Mississippi in the Confederacy.** 2 vols.
   1961   Baton Rouge   Boxed   60.

BLACK, Patti C. and **GRIMES,** Maxyne M. (comps)   **Guide to Civil War Source Material in the Dept. of Archives and History, State of Mississippi.** Wraps
   1962   Jackson   10.

CONERLY, Luke Ward   **Pike County, Mississippi 1698-1876.**
   1909   Nashville   75.

Constitution and Ordinances of the State of Mississippi. 41st Cong. 1st Sess. Ho. of Reps. Misc. Doc. 14. Wraps
    1869   Washington   35.

DAVIS, Reuben   **Recollections of Mississippi and Mississippians.**
    1890   Boston   40.

EVANS, Clement A. (ed)   **Confederate Military History, Vol. VII-Alabama and Mississippi.**
    1899   Atlanta   40.

GARNER, James Wilford   **Reconstruction in Mississippi.**
    1901   New York   100.
    1968   Baton Rouge   Wraps   15.

LEWIS, William T.   **The Centennial History of Winston County, Mississippi.** Wraps
    1972   Pasadena, Texas   20.

LYON, James A.   **A Lecture on Christianity and the Civil Laws.** Wraps
    1859   Columbus, Mississippi   30.

The Mississippi Historical Society, Publications of. Vols. 1-11
    1898-1910   Oxford   40. each
    1916-1921   Centenary Series Vols. 1-4   40. each

MULVIHILL, M. J.   **Vicksburg and Warren County, Mississippi . . . Civil War Veterans.**
    1931   Vicksburg   30.

RAINWATER, Percy Lee   **Mississippi, Storm Center of Secession 1856-1861.**
    1938   Baton Rouge   Ltd.   125.

Resolutions Adopted by Convention of Republican Party of Mississippi . . . in Favor of Readmission of That State Into the Union. 40th Cong. 3d Sess. Senate Doc. 8. Wraps
    1868   Washington   30.

RIETTI, John C. (comp)   **Military Annals of Mississippi.**
    1976   Spartanburg   15.

ROWLAND, Dunbar   **Military History of Mississippi, The Official and Statistical Register of the State of Mississippi.**
    1908   Nashville   150.

SYKES, Edward T.   **Walthall's Brigade.**
    1905   Columbus, Mississippi   100.
    1906   n.p.   75.

WALKER, Peter F.   **Vicksburg: A People at War.**
    1960   Chapel Hill   30.

REGIMENTALS

BANKS, Robert W.   **Battle of Franklin Nov. 30, 1864.**
    1908   New York   200.

BECKETT, Richard C.   **A Sketch of the Career of Company B, Armistead's Cavalry Regiment.**
    1904   Oxford   30.

BROWN, Maud Morrow   **The University Greys, Company A, Eleventh Mississippi Regiment.**
    1940   Richmond   30.

FONTAINE, Lamar   **My Life and My Lectures.**
    1908   New Yorek   175.

HOLMES, Robert M.   **Kemper County Rebel. The Civil War Diary of _____ Co. I, 24th Miss. Vols., C.S.A.** edited by Frank A. Dennis
    1973   Jackson   25.

HOWELL, H. Grady, Jr.   **Going to Meet the Yankees, a History of the "Bloody Sixth" Mississippi Infantry, C.S.A.**
    1981   Jackson   50.

MONTGOMERY, Franklin A.   **Reminiscences of a Mississippian in Peace and War.**
    1901   Cincinnati   100.

MOORE, Robert A.   **A Life for the Confederacy . . . Diaries of _____ Co. G, 17th Mississippi Regiment.** edited by James N. Silver.
    1959   Jackson   35.
MULVIHILL, M. J., Sr.   **First Mississippi Regiment — Its Foundation, Organization and Record.** Wraps
    1931 (?)   Vicksburg   35.
ROBUCK, J. E.   **My Own Personal Experience and Observation as a Soldier in the Confederate Army.**
    n.d.   Memphis   Reprint   14.
WILSON, LeGrand J.   **The Confederate Soldier.** edited by James W. Silver.
    1973   Memphis   15.

MISSOURI

GENERAL REFERENCES

Annual Report of the Adjutant General of Missouri for 1864.
    1865   Jefferson City   35.
    For the Year 1865.
    1866   Jefferson City   50.
Annual Report of the Quartermaster General of Missouri for the Year 1863.
    1864   St. Louis   100.
ADAMSON, Hans Christian   **Rebellion in Missouri 1861.**
    1961   Philadelphia   25.
ANDERSON, Ephraim M.   **Memoirs Historical and Personal Including the Campaigns of the 1st Missouri Confederate Brigade.**
    1868   St. Louis   300.
    1972   Dayton   35.
BENECKE, Louis   **Some Light Upon a Chariton County (Missouri) Episode of '64.**
    1895   Brunswick   50.
BEVIER, Robert S.   **History of the First and Second Missouri Confederate Brigades 1861-1865.**
    1879   St. Louis   200.
CARR, Lucien   **Missouri: A Bone of Contention.**
    n.d.   Boston   15.
DENSLOW, Ray V.   **Civil War and Masonry in Missouri.**
    1930   n.p.   25.
EVANS, Clement A. (ed)   **Confederate Military History, Vol. IX — Kentucky and Missouri.**
    1899   Atlanta   40.
History of Greene County, Missouri.
    1883   St. Louis   125.
History of Henry and St. Clair Counties, Missouri.
    1968   Clinton   25.
Journal and Proceedings of the Missouri State Convention, Held at Jefferson City, and St. Louis, March 1861.
    1861   St. Louis   35.
Letter from the Secretary of War . . . Missouri Troops in Service During the Civil War. 57th Cong. 1st Sess. Senate Doc. 412.
    1902   Washington   60.
Letter from Secretary of War . . . Relative to Military Service Rendered by the Missouri Militia. 38th Cong. 1st Sess. Ho. of Reps. Doc. 59. Wraps
    1864   Washington   20.
MILLER, George   **Missouri's Memorable Decade 1860-1870.**
    1898   Missouri   40.

Organization and Status of Missouri Troops (Union and Confederate) in Service During the Civil War.
>1902   Washington   60.

PARRISH, William E.   **Turbulent Partnership, Missouri and the Union 1861-1865.**
>1963   Columbia   20.

PORTER, Valentine M.   **History of Battery "A" of St. Louis.**
>1905   St. Louis   75.

Reminiscences of the Women of Missouri During the Sixties.
>n.d.   Jefferson City   60.

ROMBAUER, Robert J.   **The Union Cause in St. Louis in 1861.**
>1909   St. Louis   75.

SCHRANTZ, Ward L.   **Jasper County, Missouri, in the Civil War.**
>1923   Carthage   100.

TREXLER, Harrison Anthony   **Slavery in Missouri 1804-1865.** Wraps
>1914   Baltimore   25.

War Papers and Personal Reminiscences, 1861-1865 Read Before the Commandery of the State of Missouri, Mollus. Vol. 1 (all pub).
>1892   St. Louis   60.

WEBB, W. L.   **Battles and Biographies of Missourians, or The Civil War Period of Our State.**
>1900   Kansas City   50.

REGIMENTALS

Union

ANDERS, Leslie   **The Eighteenth Missouri.**
>1968   Indianapolis   30.

ANDERS, Leslie   **The 21st Missouri From Home Guard to Union Regiment.**
>1975   Westport   25.

BAILEY, George W.   **A Private Chapter of the War.**
>1880   St. Louis   75.

FREMONT, Jessie Benton   **The Story of the Guard: A Chronicle of the War.**
>1863   Boston   35.

GOODMAN, Thomas M.   **Sergeant Thomas M. Goodman's "Thrilling Record."** Wraps
>1960   Maryville   10.

NEAL, W. A. (ed)   **An Illustrated History of the Missouri Engineer & the 25th Infantry Regiments.**
>1889   Chicago   150.

PETERSON, Cyrus A.   **Narrative of the Capture and Murder of Major James Wilson.** Wraps
>1906   St. Louis   85.

POMPEY, Sherman Lee   **Keep the Home Fires Burning: A History of the 7th Regt. Missouri State Militia Cavalry in the Civil War.** Wraps
>1962   Warrensburg, Missouri   20.

ROGERS, William H.   **William H. Rogers's Personal Experiences.** Wraps
>n.d.   n.p.   30.

WARING, George E., Jr.   **Whip and Spur.**
>1875   Boston   40.
>1886   Boston   Ltd.   75.
>1897   New York   35.

WARMOTH, Henry C.   **War, Politics and Reconstruction.**
>1930   New York   40.

WOODRUFF, Matthew   **A Union Soldier in the Land of the Vanquished, Diary of Sgt. Matthew Woodruff in Louisiana Jun. — Dec. 1865.** edited by F. N. Boney.
>1969   University, Alabama   15.

Confederate

MUDD, Joseph A.   **With Porter in North Missouri: A Chapter in the History of the War Between the States.**
1909   Washington   100.

NEBRASKA

GENERAL REFERENCES

Civil War Sketches and Incidents, Nebraska Commandery, Mollus. Vol. 1 (all published).
1902   Omaha   75.

DUDLEY, Edgar S. (comp.)   **Roster of Nebraska Volunteers From 1861 to 1869.**
1888   Hastings   65.

Roster of Soldiers, Sailors and Marines of the War of 1812, the Mexican War, and the War of the Rebellion Residing in Nebraska June 1, 1891.
1892   Lincoln   30.

Roster of Soldiers, Sailors, and Marines of the War of 1812, the Mexican War and the War of the Rebellion Residing in Nebraska, 1895.
1895   York   30.

Roster of Soldiers, Sailors and Marines, Who Served in the War of the Rebellion, World War . . .(and Residing in Nebraska).
1925   Omaha   25.

NEW HAMPSHIRE

GENERAL REFERENCES

Adjutant General Revised Register of the Soldiers and Sailors of New Hampshire . . . 1861-65.
1895   Concord   75.

Report of the Adjutant General of the State of New Hampshire.
For Year 1863   20.
For Year 1865   2 vols.   50.
For Year 1866   2 vols.   50.
For Year 1868   25.

BATCHELLOR, A. S.   **Historical and Bibliographical Notes on the Military Annals of New Hampshire with Special Reference to Regimental Histories.**
1898   Concord   25.

CLEVELAND, Dr. Mather   **New Hampshire Fights the Civil War.**
1969   New London   25.

CONN, Granville   **History of the New Hampshire Surgeons in the War of Rebellion.**
1906   Concord   65.

GILMORE, George C.   **Manchester Men: Soldiers and Sailors in the Civil War 1861-1866.**
1898   Concord   15.

REDINGTON, E. D., and **HODGKINS,** W. H.   **Military Record of the Sons of Dartmouth.**
1907   Boston   20.

ROBINSON, H. L.   **Pittsfield, N. H. in the Great Rebellion.**
1893   Pittsfield   15.

WAITE, Otis F. R.   **Claremont War History: April 1861 to April 1865 New Hampshire Regiments.**
1868   Concord   30.

WAITE, Otis F. R.   **New Hampshire in the Great Rebellion . . .**
1870   Claremont   30.

REGIMENTALS

AARON, Fletcher Stevens'   **Aug. 9, 1819, May 10, 1887.**
190?   Nashua   30.
ABBOTT, Stephen G.   **The First Regiment New Hampshire Volunteers.**
1890   Keene   30.
BARTLETT, Asa W.   **History of the Twelfth Regiment, New Hampshire Volunteers in the War of the Rebellion.**
1897   Concord   85.
BOUTON, John Bell   **A Memoir of General Louis Bell.**
1865   New York   30.
BRUCE, George A.   **The Capture and Occupation of Richmond.**
n.d.   n.p.   40.
BUFFUM, Francis H.   **A Memorial of the Great Rebellion, Being a History of the Fourteenth Regiment, N. H. Volunteers.**
1882   Boston   75.
BUFFUM, Francis H.   **Sheridan's Veterans, A Souvenir of Their Two Campaigns in the Shenandoah Valley.** Wraps
1883   Boston   40.
BUFFUM, Francis H.   **Sheridan's Veterans, No. II A Souvenir of Their Third Campaign in the Shenandoah Valley.** Wraps
1886   Boston   30.
CANFIELD, William A.   **A History of William A. Canfield's Experience in the Army.** Wraps
1869   Manchester   25.
CASE, Ervin T.   **Battle of the Mine.** Wraps
1879   Providence   Ltd.   25.
CHILD, William   **History of the Fifth Regiment New Hampshire Volunteers.**
1893   Bristol   75.
COGSWELL, Leander W.   **History of the Eleventh New Hampshire Regiment Volunteer Infantry.**
1891   Concord   60.
Complete Roster of the Eighth Regiment, New Hampshire Volunteers
189?   Concord   25.
COPP, Elbridge J.   **Reminiscences of the War of the Rebellion.**
1911   Nashua   45.
ELDREDGE, Daniel   **The Third New Hampshire and All About It.**
1893   Boston   75.
HADLEY, Amos   **Life of Walter Harriman.**
1888   Boston   25.
HAYNES, Martin A.   **History of the Second Regiment, New Hampshire Volunteers. Its Camps, Marches and Battles.**
1865   Manchester   60.
HAYNES, Martin A.   **A History of the Second Regiment, New Hampshire Volunteer Infantry in the War of the Rebellion.**
1896   Lakeport   75.
HAYNES, Martin A. (comp)   **Muster Out Roll of the Second New Hampshire Regiment in the War of the Rebellion.**
1917   Lakeport   Ltd.   25.
HUTCHINSON, John G.   **Roster Fourth Regiment New Hampshire Volunteers.**
1896   Manchester   50.
JEWETT, Albert Henry Clay   **A Boy Goes to War.**
1944   Bloomington   25.
KENT, Charles N.   **History of the Seventeenth Regiment, New Hampshire Volunteer Infantry.**
1898   Concord   40.
LITTLE, Henry F. W.   **The Seventh Regiment New Hampshire Volunteers in the War of the Rebellion.**
1896   Concord   65.

LIVERMORE, Thomas L.   **Days and Events 1860-1866.**
    1920   Boston   60.
LIVERMORE, Thomas L.   **History of the Eighteenth New Hampshire Volunteers.**
    1904   Boston   50.
LORD, Edward O. (ed)   **History of the Ninth Regiment New Hampshire Volunteers.**
    1895   Concord   65.
McGREGOR, Charles   **History of the Fifteenth New Hampshire Volunteers 1862-1863.**
    1900   Concord   60.
NASON, W. A.   **With the Ninth Army Corps in East Tennessee.** Wraps
    1891   Providence   Ltd.   25.
STANYAN, John Minot   **History of the Eighth Regiment, New Hampshire Volunteers.**
    1892   Concord   75.
THOMPSON, S. Millett   **Thirteenth Regiment of New Hampshire Volunteer Infantry in the War of the Rebellion 1861-1865.**
    1888   Boston   75.
TOWNSEND, Luther T.   **History of the Sixteenth Regiment, New Hampshire Volunteers.**
    1897   Washington   45.

NEW JERSEY

GENERAL REFERENCES

BAQUET, Camille   **History of the First Brigade, New Jersey Volunteers From 1861 to 1865.**
    1910   Trenton   110.
FOSTER, John Y.   **New Jersey and the Rebellion.**
    1868   Newark   50.
MIERS, Earl Schenck   **New Jersey and the Civil War.**
    1964   New Brunswick   15.
Record of Officers and Men of New Jersey in the Civil War, 2 vols.
    1876   Trenton   150.
Register of the Commissioned Officers and Privates of the New Jersey Volunteers in the Service of the United States.
    1863   Jersey City   60.
SINCLAIR, Donald A.   **The Civil War and New Jersey: A Bibliography.**
    1968   New Brunswick   20.
TOOMBS, Samuel   **New Jersey Troops in the Gettysburg Campaign from June 5 to July 31, 1863.**
    1888   Orange   40.

REGIMENTALS

BELLARD, Alfred   **Gone for a Soldier, The Civil War Memoirs of _____.** edited by David Herbert Donald.
    1975   Boston   30.
BORTON, Benjamin   **Awhile with the Blue; or Memories of War Days.**
    1898   Passaic, N. J.   75.
BORTON, Benjamin   **On the Parallels; or, Chapters of Inner History.**
    1903   Woodstown   60.
CROWELL, Joseph E.   **The Young Volunteer, Everyday Experiences of a Soldier Boy in the Civil War.**
    1906   New York   35.
DODD, Ira S.   **Song of the Rappahannock, Sketches of the Civil War.**
    1898   New York   35.
DRAKE, James Madison   **Fast and Loose in Dixie.**
    1880   New York   85.

DRAKE, James Madison   **Historical Sketches of the Revolutionary and Civil Wars.**
1908   New York   50.

DRAKE, James Madison   **The History of the Ninth New Jersey Veteran Volunteers.**
1889   Elizabeth   100.

FERGUSON, Joseph   **life-struggles in rebel PRISONS.**
1865   Philadelphia   50.

FRANCINE, Albert Philip   **Louis Raymond Francine, Brevet Brigadier-General U. S. Volunteers 1837-1863.**
1910   n.p.   Ltd.   40.

GODFREY, Carlos E.   **Sketch of Major Henry Washington Sawyer, First Regiment Cavalry, New Jersey Volunteers.** Wraps
1907   Trenton   35.

HAINES, Alanson A.   **History of the Fifteenth Regiment, New Jersey Volunteers.**
1883   New York   100.

HAINES, William P.   **History of the Men of Co-F, with Description of the Marches and Battles of the 12th New Jersey Vols.**
1897   Mickleton   110.

HANIFEN, Michael   **History of Battery B, First New Jersey Artillery.**
1905   Ottawa, Ill.   100.

History of the Reunion Society of the 23rd Regiment N. J. Volunteers.
1890   Philadelphia   60.

HOPKINS, Charles A.   **The March to the Sea.** Wraps.
1885   Providence   Ltd.   25.

JAGO, Frederick West   **The Twelfth New Jersey Volunteers 1862-1865.** Wraps
1967   Gloucester   15.

LINDSLEY, J. Frank   **Pilgrimage of the Fifteenth Regiment New Jersey Volunteers' Veteran Assoc. to White Oak Church Camp Grounds and Battlefields of Fredericksburg, Va. & Vicinity May 22 to 26, 1906.**
1906   Newark   60.

MARBAKER, Thomas D.   **History of the Eleventh New Jersey Volunteers.**
1898   Trenton   125.

PYNE, Henry R.   **The History of the First New Jersey Cavalry.**
1871   Trenton   100.

PYNE, Henry R.   **Ride to War, The History of the First New Jersey Cavalry.** edited by Earl S. Miers.
1961   New Brunswick   20.

Report of State Commission for Erection of Monument to Ninth New Jersey Volunteers at New Berne, N. C. . . .
1906   Philadelphia   30.

Reunion, First Annual _____ **of the Ninth New Jersey Veteran Volunteers.**
1887   Elizabeth   25.

REVERE, Joseph W.   **Keel and Saddle.**
1872   Boston   45.
1873   Boston   30.

ROBBINS, Walter R.   **War Record and Personal Experiences of . . .** edited by Lilian Rea. Wraps
1923   Chicago(?)   85.

TERRILL, John Newton   **Campaign of the Fourteenth Regiment New Jersey Volunteers.**
1884   New Brunswick   110.

TOOMBS, Samuel   **Reminiscences of the War, Comprising a Detailed Account of the Experiences of the Thirteenth New Jersey Volunteers.**
1878   Orange   85.

WEISER, George   **Nine Months in Rebel Prisons.**
1890   Philadelphia   50.

WORLOCK, Wilbur W.   **Poetic War Record of Drake's Veteran Zouaves of Elizabeth, N. J.** Wraps
1885   Elizabeth   30.

NEW MEXICO

GENERAL REFERENCES

KELEHER, William A.   **Turmoil in New Mexico.**
  See: California Regimentals
NORVELL, Stevens T.   **New Mexico in the Civil War.** Wraps
  1903   Washington(?)   30.
RITTENHOUSE, Jack D.   **New Mexico Civil War Bibliography.**
  1961   Houston   Ltd.   50.
STANLEY, F.   **The Civil War in New Mexico.**
  1960   New York   35.
  1960   Denver   25.

NEW YORK

GENERAL REFERENCES

Annual Report, Adjutant General, State of New York, Albany.
  1863-1900   20. per vol.
  Some years were issued in multiple volumes
BARLOW, F. C.   **Albany Zouave Cadets to the Rochester Union Blues.**
  1866   Albany   30.
BURT, Silas W.   **My Memoirs of the Military History of the State of New York During The War for the Union 1861-65.** Wraps
  1902   Albany   25.
CLARK, Rufus W.   **The Heroes of Albany.**
  1866   Albany   40.
  1867   Albany   30.
DORNBUSCH, Charles E.   **The Communities of New York and the Civil War.**
  1962   New York   15.
DOTY, Lockwood L.   **Presentation of Flags of the New York Volunteer Regiments . . . To Gov. Fenton.**
  1865   Albany   30.
GRAHAM, M. J.   **Concerning the Battle of Antietam, Letter of Lt. M. J. Graham to Col. Rush C. Hawkins, 9th New York Volunteers.** Wraps
  1894   New York   20.
JONES, Paul   **The Irish Brigade.**
  1969   Washington/New York   30.
McKELVEY, Blake (ed)   **Rochester in the Civil War.**
  1944   New York   30.
The Manual of the . . . National Guard N. Y.
  1868   New York   20.
NAYLOR, Colin T., Jr.   **Civil War Days in a Country Village.**
  1961   Peekskill, New York   20.
New York at Andersonville, Dedication of Monument Erected by the State of New York at Andersonville, Georgia 1914.
  1916   Albany   30.
New York at Antietam, Dedication of the New York State Monument on the Battlefield of Antietam.
  1923   Albany   30.
New York at Chattanooga.
  1928   New York   30.
New York at Gettysburg, N. Y. Monuments Commission. . . 3 vols.
  1900   Albany   75.
New York, Monuments Commission Fiftieth Anniversary of the Battle of Gettysburg.
  1916   Albany   25.

New York Monument Commission — Major Gen. Francis C. Barlow at Gettysburg and Other Battlefields.
    1923   Albany   30.
New York State and the Civil War. Wraps
    1961-1963   24 numbers   50.
New York State Soldier's Depot, Report of the Board of Managers. Wraps
    1864   Albany   35.
Personal Recollections of the War of the Rebellion: Addresses Delivered Before the New York Commandery, Mollus. 4 vols.
    1891-1912   30. per vol.
PHISTERER, Frederick (comp)   **New York in the War of the Rebellion 1861-1865.**
    1890   Albany   50 .
PHISTERER, Frederick (comp)   **New York in the War of the Rebellion 1861-1865.**
    5 vols. & index.
    1912   Albany   160.
PLANK, W.   **Banners and Bugles: A Record of Ulster County in the Civil War.**
    Wraps
    1963   Marlborough   25.
    1972   Marlborough   15.
Presentation of Regimental Colors to the Legislature, State of New York. Wraps
    1863   n.p.   30.
Proceedings of the Albany Bar on the Occasion of the Death of Col. Lewis Benedict of Albany.
    1864   Albany   15.
Record of the Commissioned Officers, Non-Commissioned Officers and Privates of the Regiments . . . New York. 8 vols.
    1864-68   Albany   200.
REED, I. Richard   **100 Years Ago Today: Niagara County in the Civil War as Reported in the Pages of "the Niagara Falls Gazette."** Wraps
    1966   Lockport   20.
Register of Officers Commissioned in the Volunteer Regiments from the State of New York 1861-1865.
    1868   New York   30.
Special Committee on Volunteering . . . In Filling the Quota of the County of N. Y. 1864 for 500,000 Men.
    1864   New York   40.
WOLCOTT, Walter   **The Military History of Yates County, N. Y.**
    1895   Penn Yan   35.

REGIMENTALS

ABBOTT, Allen O.   **Prison Life in the South.**
    1865   New York   25.
ADAMS, Francis Colburn   **The Story of a Trooper.**
    1865   New York   50.
ADAMS, Francis Colburn   **A Trooper's Adventures in the War for the Union.**
    n.d.   New York   25.
Album of the Second Battalion Duryee Zouaves, 165th Regt. New York Volunteer Infantry.
    1906   New York (?)   100.
AMES, Nelson   **History of Battery G, First Regiment New York Light Artillery.**
    1900   Marshalltown, Iowa   75.
Anniversary and Reunion of the 10th New York Cavalry Association.
    37th   1898   Wraps   25.
    57th   1913   25.
APPLEGATE, John S.   **Reminiscences and Letters of George Arrowsmith of New Jersey.**
    1893   Red Bank, New Jersey   60.

ARMES, George A.   **Ups and Downs of an Army Officer.**
1900   Washington   65.
ARMSTRONG, Nelson   **Nuggets of Experience.**
1906   Los Angeles   35.
ATKINS, Thomas A. and **OLIVER,** John W.   **Yonkers in the Rebellion of 1861-1865.**
1892   New York   35.
AVERY, William B.   **The Marine Artillery with the Burnside Expedition and the Battle of Camden, N. C.** Wraps
1880   Providence   Ltd.   20.
BABCOCK, Willoughby M., Jr.   **Selections from the Letters and Diaries of Brevet-Brigadier General Willoughby Babcock of the 75th New York Volunteers.** Wraps
1922   Albany   50.
BACON, William Johnson   **Memorial of William Kirkland Bacon, Late Adjutant of the Twenty-Sixth Regiment of New York State Volunteers.**
1863   Utica   20.
n.d.   Boston   20.
BARLOW, Albert R.   **Company G. A Record of the Services of One Company of the 157th New York Volunteers.**
1899   Syracuse   80.
BEACH, William H.   **The First New York (Lincoln) Cavalry.**
1902   New York   90.
BEAUDRY (BOUDRY), Louis N.   **Historic Records of the Fifth New York Cavalry, First Ira Harris Guard.**
1865   Albany   70.
1868   Albany   60.
BEECHER, Harris H.   **Record of the 114th Regiment, N.Y.S.V.**
1866   Norwich   75.
BENTON, Charles E.   **As Seen from the Ranks.**
1902   New York   35.
BEST, Isaac O.   **History of the 121st New York State Infantry.**
1921   Chicago   75.
BIDWELL, Frederick D.   **History of the Forty-Ninth New York Volunteers.**
1916   Albany   60.
BOUDRY, Louis N.   see: **BEAUDRY,** Louis N.
BOWEN, James R.   **Regimental History of the First New York Dragoons.**
1900   Lyons, Michigan   85.
BOYCE, Charles W.   **A Brief History of the Twenty-Eighth Regiment New York State Volunteers.**
1896   Buffalo   75.
BRAINARD, Mary G.   **Campaign of the 146th Regiment of New York State Volunteers.**
1915   New York   90.
BROWN, Augustus C.   **The Diary of a Line Officer.**
1906   New York   75.
BROWN, Henri LeFevre (comp)   **History of the Third Regiment, Excelsior Brigade 72d New York Volunteer Infantry.**
1902   Jamestown   70.
BUDINGTON, William Ives   **A Memorial of Giles F. Ward, Jr. Late First Lieut. Twelfth N. Y. Cavalry.**
1866   New York   25.
BUTTERFIELD, Julia Lorrilard (ed)   **A Biographical Memorial of General Daniel Butterfield.**
1896   New York   Wraps   40.
1903   New York   Ltd.   100.
1904   New York   40.
CALVERT, Henry Murray   **Reminiscences of a Boy in Blue.**
1920   New York   50.

CARROLL, John F.   **A Brief History of New York's Famous Seventh Regiment.**
1961   New York   25.

CAVANAGH, Michael   **Memoirs of Gen. Thomas Francis Meagher.**
1892   Worcester   40.

CHAPIN, Louis N.   **A Brief History of the Thirty-Fourth Regiment, N.Y.S.V.**
1903   New York   75.

CHENEY, Newel   **History of the Ninth Regiment, New York Volunteer Cavalry.**
1901   Jamestown   90.

CLARK, Emmons   **History of the Second Company of the Seventh Regiment N.Y.S. Militia. Vol. 1** (all published).
1864   New York   30.

CLARK, Emmons   **History of the Seventh Regiment of New York 1806-1889.** 2 vols.
1890   New York   75.

CLARK, James H.   **The Iron Hearted Regiment.**
1865   Albany   50.

CLARK, Orton S.   **The One Hundred and Sixteenth Regiment of New York State Volunteers.**
1868   Buffalo   90.

COLE, Jacob Henry   **Under Five Commanders: or, A Boy's Experiences with the Army of the Potomac.**
1906   Paterson   75.

COLLINS, George K.   **An Abbreviated Account of Certain Men of Onondaga County Who Did Service in the War of 1861-65 in the 149th New York Volunteer Regiment Infantry.** Wraps
1928   Syracuse   40.

COLLINS, George K.   **Memoirs of the 149th Regiment, N. Y. Vol. Infantry.**
1891   Syracuse   90.

CONYNGHAM, David P.   **The Irish Brigade and Its Campaigns.**
1867   New York   100.
1869   Boston   75.

COOK, S. G. and **BENTON,** Charles E. (eds)   **The "Dutchess County Regiment" (150th Regiment of New York State Volunteer Infantry) in the Civil War.**
1907   Danbury   80.

COOPER, Alonzo   **In and Out of Rebel Prisons.**
1888   Oswego   40.

CORBY, William   **Memoirs of Chaplain Life.**
1894   Notre Dame   50.

CORELL, Philip   **History of the Naval Brigade, 99th N. Y. Volunteers, Union Coast Guard, 1861-1865.**
1905   New York   Ltd.   250.

CORY, Eugene A.   **A Private's Recollections of Fredericksburg.** Wraps
1884   Providence   Ltd.   20.

COWTAN, Charles W.   **Services of the Tenth New York Volunteers.**
1882   New York   75.

CRIBBEN, Henry   **The Military Memoirs of Captain _____ of the 140th New York Volunteers.** edited by J. Clayton Youker.
1911   Chicago   75.

CRONIN, David E.   **The Evolution of a Life Described in the Memoirs of Major Seth Eyland, Late of the Mounted Rifles.**
1884   New York   50.

CUNNINGHAM, John L.   **Three Years with the Adirondack Regiment 118th N. Y. Volunteers Infantry.**
1920   Norwood, Massachusetts   75.

CURTIS, Newton Martin   **From Bull Run to Chancellorsville, The Story of the Sixteenth New York Infantry.**
1906   New York   35.

DAUCHY, George K.   **The Battle of Ream's Station.** Wraps
1899   Chicago   20.

DAVENPORT, Alfred   **Camp and Field Life of the Fifth New York Volunteer Infantry (Duryee Zouaves).**
1879   New York   100.
Dedicatory Ceremonies Held on the Battlefield of Manassas or 2nd Bull Run, Virginia, . . . The 5th Regt. NY Vol. Inf. "Duryee Zouaves".
1907   Brooklyn   25.
DeFOREST, Bartholomew S.   **Random Sketches and Wandering Thoughts.**
1866   Albany   50.
DePEYSTER, J. Watts   **Address . . . Inauguration of a Monument Erected by . . . Tivoli-Madalin to Her Defenders Who Lost Their Lives.** Wraps
1867   New York   Ltd.   35.
DILL, Samuel P.   **Journal of the Escape and Re-capture of Captain _____.** Wraps
1886   Brooklyn   50.
DOWLEY, Morris Francis   **History and Honorary Roll of the Twelfth Regiment Infantry N.G. S. N. Y.**
1869   New York   60.
DUGANNE, Augustine J. H.   **Camps and Prisons, Twenty Months in the Department of the Gulf.**
1865   New York   75.
DUGANNE, Augustine J. H.   **The Fighting Quakers, A True Story of the War for Our Union.**
1866   New York   35.
DUGANNE, Augustine J. H.   **The Quaker Soldiers — A True Story of the War for Our Union.**
1869   New York   35.
EDDY, Richard   **History of the Sixtieth Regiment New York State Volunteers.**
1864   Philadelphia   65.
Exercises Connected with the Unveiling of the Ellsworth Monument at Mechanicville, May 27, 1874.
1875   Albany   25.
FAIRCHILD, Charles B.   **History of the 27th Regiment N. Y. Vols.**
1888   Binghamton   60.
FAVILL, Josiah M.   **The Diary of a Young Officer.**
1909   Chicago   85.
The First Hundred Years of Company I, Seventh Regiment N.G.N.Y. 1838-1938.
n.d. (circa 1938)   n.p.   30.
FISK, Joel C. and **BLAKE,** William H. D.   **A Condensed History of the 56th Regiment New York Veteran Volunteer Infantry.**
1906   Newburgh   65.
FLETCHER, Daniel C.   **Reminiscences of California and the Civil War.**
1894   Ayer, Massachusetts   75.
FLOYD, Fred C.   **History of the Fortieth (Mozart) Regiment New York Volunteers.**
1909   Boston   75.
FOSTER, Alonzo   **Reminiscences and Record of the 6th New York V.V. Cavalry.**
1892   Brooklyn   75.
FRANCIS, Augustus T.   **History of the 71st Regiment N.G.N.Y.**
1919   New York   40.
FREDERICK, Gilbert   **The Story of a Regiment Being a Record of the Military Services of the 57th New York State Volunteer Infantry.**
1895   Chicago   100.
GATES, Theodore B.   **The "Ulster Guard" (20th N. Y. State Militia) and the War of the Rebellion.**
1879   New York   75.
GATES, Theodore B.   **War of the Rebellion.**
1884   New York   85.
GLAZIER, Willard   **Battles for the Union.**
1875   Hartford   20.
1878   Hartford   20.

GLAZIER, Willard   **The Capture, The Prison Pen and the Escape.**
1866-1870   Various Editions   20. each
GLAZIER, Willard   **Three Years in the Federal Cavalry.**
1870   New York   30.
1873   New York   20.
1874   New York   20.
GRAHAM, Matthew J.   **The Ninth Regiment New York Volunteers (Hawkins' Zouaves).**
1900   New York   80.
GREENE, Albert R.   **From Bridgeport to Ringgold by Way of Lookout Mountain.** Wraps
1890   Providence   Ltd.   20.
HAERRER, William   **With Drum and Gun in '61.** Wraps
1908   Greenville, Pa.   75.
HALL, Isaac   **History of the Ninety-Seventh Regiment, New York Volunteers (Conkling Rifles).**
1890   Utica   90.
HALPINE, Charles G.   **Baked Meats of the Funeral, Collection of Essays, Poems, Speeches Histories** by Miles O'Reilly.
1866   New York   25.
HALPINE, Charles G.   **The Life and Adventures Songs, Services and Speeches of Private Miles O'Reilly.**
1864   New York   30.
HAMBLIN, Deborah   **Brevet Major General Joseph Eldridge Hamblin, 1861-1865.**
1902   Boston   50.
HANABURGH, David H.   **History of the One Hundred and Twenty-Eighth Regiment, New York Volunteers.**
1894   Poughkeepsie   85.
HAVENS, Lewis C.   **Historical Sketch of the 136th New York Infantry, 1862-1865.** Wraps
1934   Dalton   40.
Historical Sketch: Dedication of Monument . . . 150th New York Volunteer Infantry, Gettysburg, Sept. 17, 18, 1889.
1889   New York   30.
History of the DeWitt Guard Co. A 50th Regiment, NG NY.
1866   Ithaca   35.
History of the 2nd Battalion, Duryee Zouaves, 165th Regiment New York Volunteer Infantry.
1905   New York   75.
History of the Sixth New York Cavalry (Second Ira Harris Guard).
1908   Worcester   125.
HOADLEY, John C. (ed)   **Memorial of Henry Sanford Gansevoort, Captain Fifth Artillery.**
1875   Boston   40.
HOLLIS, John J.   **Reminiscences of John J. Hollis.** Wraps
1913   Sandy Creek, N. Y.   25.
HOUGH, Franklin   **History of Duryee's Brigade, During the Campaign in Virginia Under Gen. Pope, and in Maryland Under Gen. McClellan.**
1864   Albany   Ltd.   125.
HOWE, Thomas H.   **Adventures of an Escaped Union Prisoner from Andersonville.** Wraps
1886   San Francisco   45.
HOWELL, Helena A.   **Chronicles of the One Hundred Fifty-First Regiment New York State Volunteer Infantry.**
1911   Albion   75.
HUDSON, Henry N.   **A Chaplain's Campaign with General Butler.** Wraps
1865   New York   25.

HUSSEY, George A. and **TODD,** William   **History of the Ninth Regiment NYSM, NGSNY (Eighty-Third N. Y. Volunteers).**
1889   New York   60.

In Memoriam Alexander Stewart Webb 1835-1911.
1916   Albany   30.

INGRAHAM, Charles A.   **Elmer E. Ellsworth and the Zouaves of '61.** Wraps
1925   Chicago   30.

JOHNSON, Charles F.   **The Long Roll.**
1911   New York   Ltd.   125.

JUDD, David W.   **The Story of the Thirty-Third N.Y.S. Vols.**
1864   Rochester   60.

KELLEY, Daniel G.   **What I Saw and Suffered in Rebel Prisons.** Wraps
1866   Buffalo   25.
1868   Buffalo   25.

KENNEDY, Elijah R.   **John B. Woodward, A Biographical Memoir.**
1897   New York   30.

KIMBALL, Orville S.   **History and Personal Sketches of Company I, 103 N.Y.S.V., 1862-1864**
1900   Elmira   60.

KING, David H. (comp)   **History of the Ninety-Third Regiment, New York Volunteer Infantry 1861-1865.**
1895   Milwaukee   100.

KIRK, Hyland C.   **Heavy Guns and Light: History of the 4th New York Heavy Artillery.**
1890   New York   100.

KITCHING, J. Howard   **More Than Conqueror or Memorials of Col. J. Howard Kitching.** edited by Theodore Irving.
1873   New York   30.

KITTINGER, Joseph   **Diary 1861-1865, 23rd New York Independent Battery.** Wraps
n.d.   New York   25.

KREUTZER, William   **Notes and Observations Made During Four Years Service with Ninety-Eighth New York Volunteers.**
1878   Philadelphia   65.

LANGWORTHY, Daniel Avery   **Reminiscences of a Prisoner of War and His Escape.**
1915   Minneapolis   35.

LEWIS, Charles Edward   **War Sketches.**
1897   London   75.

LOCKWOOD, James D.   **Life and Adventures of a Drummer-Boy.**
1893   Albany   60.

LOCKWOOD, John   **Our Campaign Around Gettysburg.**
1864   Brooklyn   55.

LORD, George A.   **A Short Narrative and Military Experience of Corp.** _____
Wraps
1864   Troy   50.

LUSK, William Thompson   **War Letters of** _____
1911   New York   50.

M'CANN, Thomas H.   **The Campaigns of the Civil War.**
1915   New York   35.

McCOWAN, Archibald   **The Prisoners of War.**
1901   New York   40.

McGRATH, Franklin   **The History of the 127th New York Volunteers.**
1898 (?)   n.p.   90.

McKEE, James H.   **Back "In War Times" History of the 144th Regiment New York Volunteer Infantry.**
1903   Unadilla, New York   60.

McKINNEY, E. P.   **Life in Tent and Field 1861-1865.**
1922   Boston   50.

MANDEVILLE, James de (comp)   **History of the 13th Regiment, N.G., S.N.Y.**
1894   New York   60.

MARTIN, C. S.   **Seventy Five Years with the 10th Regiment, Infantry N.Y. N.G. (177th New York Volunteer Infantry 1860-1935).**
n.d.   n.p.   30.

MAXSON, William P.   **Camp Fires of the Twenty-Third.** By Pound Sterling
1863   New York   50.

MERRELL, William H.   **Five Months in Rebeldom: or Notes from the Diary of Bull Run Prisoner at Richmond.** Wraps
1862   Rochester   50.

MERRILL, Julian W.   **Records of the 24th Independent Battery, New York Light Artillery.**
1870   New York   65.

MERWIN, John W.   **Roster and Monograph, 161st Regt. N.Y.S. Volunteer Infantry**
1902   Elmira   50.

MEYER, Henry C.   **Civil War Experiences Under Bayard, Gregg, Kilpatrick, Custer Raulston, and Newberry.**
1911   New York   85.

MICHIE, Peter S.   **Life and Letters of Emory Upton.**
1885   New York   35.

MILLER, Delevan S.   **Drum Taps in Dixie, Memories of a Drummer Boy 1861-1865.**
1905   Watertown   40.

MILLS, J. Harrison   **Chronicles of the Twenty-First Regiment, N. Y. State Vols.**
1867   Buffalo   150.
1887   Buffalo   60.

MORAN, Frank E.   **Bastiles of the Confederacy.**
1890   Baltimore   25.

MORHOUS, Henry C.   **Reminiscences of the 123rd Regiment, N.Y.S.V.**
1879   Greenwich   85.

MORRIS, Gouverneur   **The History of a Volunteer Regiment . . . Known as Wilson's Zouaves.**
1891   New York   75.

MORSE, Francis W.   **Personal Experiences in the War of the Great Rebellion.**
1866   Albany   60.

MOWRIS, James A.   **History of the 117th Regiment N. Y. Volunteers (4th Oneida).**
1866   Hartford   45.
n.d.   n.p.   40.

NASH, Eugene A.   **History of the 44th Regiment New York Volunteer Infantry.**
1911   Chicago   90.

NICHOLS, James M.   **Perry's Saints or The Fighting Parson's Regiment.**
1886   Boston   60.

NORTHROP, John Worrell   **Chronicles from the Diary of a War Prisoner in Andersonville and Other Military Prisons of the South in 1864.**
1904   Wichita   50.

NORTON, Henry   **Deeds of Daring: or History of the Eighth N. Y. Volunteer Cavalry.**
1889   Norwich   125.

NOTT, Charles C.   **Sketches in Prison Camps. A Continuation of Sketches of the War.**
1865   New York   45.

OWENS, John Algernon   **Sword and Pen, or Ventures & Adventures of Willard Glazier.**
    1880   Philadelphia   20.
    1881   Philadelphia   20.
    1882   Philadelphia   20.
    1883   Philadelphia   20.
    1889   Philadelphia   20.
PALMER, Abraham J.   **The History of the Forty-Eighth Regiment, New York State Volunteers.**
    1885   New York   65.
PARKER, David B.   **A Chautauqua Boy in '61 and Afterward.** edited by Torrance Parker.
    1912   Boston   40.
PEET, Frederick Tomlinson   **Civil War Letters and Documents of _____ with the 7th New York.**
    1917   Newport   Ltd.   250.
PEET, Frederick Tomlinson   **Personal Experiences in the Civil War.**
    1905   New York   Ltd.   250.
PELLET, Elias P.   **History of the 114th Regiment New York State Volunteers.**
    1866   Norwich   85.
PETTY, A. Milburn   **History of the 37th Regiment, New York Volunteers.**
    1937   New York   30.
PORTER, Burton B.   **One of the People, His Own Story.**
    1907   Colton, California   35.
POST, Marie Caroline   **The Life and Memoirs of Comte Regis de Trobriand.**
    1910   New York   50.
POTTER, Orlando B.   **Oration of Hon. _____ on the Dedication of the Monument Erected by the 9th Regiment, N.G.S.NY.**
    1888   n.p.   25.
PRESTON, Noble D.   **History of the Tenth Regiment of Cavalry New York State Volunteers.**
    1892   New York   150.
PUTNAM, George Haven   **Memories of My Youth 1844-1865.**
    1914   New York   25.
PUTNAM, George Haven   **A Prisoner of War in Virginia 1864-5.**
    1912   New York   30.
    1914   New York   30.
RANDALL, Ruth Painter   **Colonel Elmer Ellsworth.**
    1960   Boston   25.
Recollections of the Early Days of the National Guard . . . of the Famous Seventh Regiment New York Militia.
    1868   New York   25.
Record of the Proceedings at the Dedication of the Monument . . . Gettysburg by the Survivors of the Tammany Regiment. Wraps
    1892   New York   25.
REMINGTON, Cyrus Kingsbury   **A Record of Battery I, First NY Light Artillery Vols. Otherwise Known as Wiedrich's Battery.**
    1891   Buffalo   90.
REMINISCO, Don Pedro Q. (pseud)   **Life in the Union Army . . . A History, in Verse, of the 15th Regiment New York Engineers.** Wraps
    1864   New York   40.
Report, Annual Reunion & Dinner of the Old Guard Association, 12th Regiment, N.G.S.N.Y. Sat. April 32st, 1894. Wraps
    1894   New York   35.
Report of Annual Reunions of 64th Regiment N. Y. Vol. Infantry.
    1894-97   Wraps   20. each
RIX, Guy S. (comp)   **Roster of the Known Living Members of Col. Peter A. Porter's Regiment, 8th N.Y. Heavy Artillery.**
    1892   Concord   45.

ROBACK, Henry   **The Veteran Volunteers of Herkimer and Otsego Counties in the War of the Rebellion.**
1888   Little Falls   85.

ROBERTSON, Robert S.   **Diary of the War by Rob't S. Robertson, 93rd Regt. N.Y. Vols. & A.D.C. to Gen. N. A. Miles, Commanding 1st Brigade, 1st Division, 2nd Army Corps.** edited by Charles N. & Rosemary Walker.
1965   n.p.   35.

ROBERTSON, Robert S.   **Personal Recollections of the War. A Record of Service with the Ninety-Third New York Vol. Infantry.**
1895   Milwaukee   60.

ROBERTSON, Robert Stoddart   **From the Wilderness to Spottsylvania, A Paper Read Before the Ohio Commandery of the Mollus.** Wraps
1884   Cincinnati   30.

ROBINSON, Chas. S.   **A Memorial Discourse Occasioned by the Death of Lieut. Col. James M. Green, Forty-Eighth N.Y.S.V.** Wraps
1864   Troy, New York   25.

ROE, Alfred S.   **From Monocacy To Danville.** Wraps
1889   Providence   Ltd.   30.

ROE, Alfred S.   **In a Rebel Prison; or, Experiences in Danville, Va.** Wraps
1891   Providence   Ltd.   30.

ROE, Alfred S.   **The Ninth New York Heavy Artillery.**
1899   Worcester   100.

ROE, Alfred S.   **Recollections of Monocacy.** Wraps
1885   Providence   Ltd.   30.

ROE, Alfred S.   **Richmond, Annapolis, and Home.**
1892   Providence   Wraps   Ltd.   30.

ROEHRENBECK, William J.   **The Regiment That Saved the Capital.**
1961   New York   25.

ROEMER, Jacob   **Reminiscences of the War of the Rebellion 1861-1865.**
1897   Flushing   60.

ROGERS, William H.   **History of the One Hundred and Eighty-Ninth Regiment of New York Volunteers.**
1865   New York   65.
1866   New York   65.

SCRYMSER, James A.   **Personal Reminiscences of _____ in Times of Peace and War.**
1915   New York   30.

SHAW, Albert D.   **A Full Report of the First Reunion and Banquet of the Thirty-Fifth N.Y. Vols.**
1888   Watertown   75.

SIMONS, Ezra D.   **A Regimental History, The One Hundred and Twenty-Fifth New York State Volunteers.**
1888   New York   60.

SMITH, Abram P.   **History of the Seventy-Sixth Regiment, New York Volunteers.**
1867   Syracuse   90.

SMITH, Henry B.   **Between the Lines. Secret Service Stories Told Fifty Years After.**
1911   New York   75.

SMITH, James E.   **A Famous Battery and Its Campaigns . . . The Career of Corporal James Tanner.**
1892   Washington   50.

SMITH, Thomas West   **The Story of a Cavalry Regiment: "Scott's 900" Eleventh New York Cavalry.**
1897   Chicago   110.

SOUTHWICK, Thomas P.   **A Duryee Zouave.**
1930   Washington   50.

STARR, Frederick, Jr.   **The Loyal Soldier, A Discourse . . . at the Funeral of Major John Barnet Sloan.** Wraps
1864   Penn Yan   30.

STEARNS, Albert   **Reminiscences of the Late War.**
  1881   Brooklyn   50.
STEVENS, George T.   **Three Years in the Sixth Corps.**
  1866   Albany   60.
  1870   New York   55.
STOWITS, George H.   **History of the One Hundredth Regiment of New York Volunteers.**
  1870   Buffalo   85.
Sullivan County and the Civil War, Brass Buttons and Leather Boots.
  1963   n.p.   Ltd.   30.
SWINTON, William   **History of the Seventh Regiment, National Guard, State of New York, During the War of the Rebellion.**
  1870   New York   35.
  1876   New York   30.
  1886   New York   30.
TELFER, William D.   **Reminiscence of the First Battle of Manassas: A Camp-Fire Story of the 71st Regiment.**
  1864   New York   35.
Testimonial to Col. Rush C. Hawkins, 9th Regiment N.Y.V., "Hawkins Zouaves." Wraps
  1863   New York   30.
TEVIS, C. V.   **The History of the Fighting Fourteenth.**
  1911   New York   75.
THOMAS, Howard   **Boys in Blue from the Adirondack Foothills.**
  1960   Prospect   25.
THOMPSON, Joseph Parrish   **The Sergeant's Memorial by His Father.**
  1863   New York   20.
TIEBOUT, Samuel   **The Civil War Diary of Samuel Tiebout, 5th N. Y. Vol. Infantry.** edited by Bruce T. McCully. Wraps
  1943   Cooperstown   15.
TIEMANN, William F. (comp)   **The 159th Regiment Infantry, New York State Volunteers.**
  1891   Brooklyn   65.
TILNEY, Robert   **My Life in the Army Three Years and a Half with the Fifth Army Corps.**
  1912   Philadelphia   75.
TODD, William   **The Seventy-Ninth Highlanders, New York Volunteers in the War of the Rebellion.**
  1886   Albany   75.
TROBRIAND, Philippe Regis de   **Four Years with the Army of the Potomac.**
  1889   Boston   50.
TROBRIAND, Phillippe Regis de   **Quatre Ans de Campagnes a L'Armee du Potomac.** 2 vols.
  1867-8   Paris   75.
The Uniformed Battalion of the Veterans of the 7th Regiment, N. G., N. Y. 1861-1892.
  1893   New York   20.
VAIL, Enos B.   **Reminiscences of a Boy in the Civil War.**
  1915   Brooklyn   60.
VAN ALSTYNE, Lawrence   **Diary of an Enlisted Man.**
  1910   New Haven   60.
VAN SANTVOORD, Cornelius   **The One Hundred and Twentieth Regiment New York State Volunteers.**
  1894   Rondout   75.
VINTER, Thomas H.   **Memoirs of _____**
  1926   Philadelphia   50.
WASHBURN, Geo. H.   **A Complete History of the 108th Regiment N. Y. Vols. Together with Roster, Letters, Rebel Oaths of Allegiance, Rebel Passes, Reminiscences.** Wraps
  1887   New York   50.

WASHBURN, Geo. H.　　**A Complete Military History and Record of the 108th Regiment NY Vols. from 1862 to 1894.**
　　1894　　Rochester　　125.
WATSON, Winslow C.　　**Eulogium Commemorative of Gorton T. Thomas.** Wraps
　　1862　　Burlington　　20.
WEISS, Francis　　**Reminiscences of Chevalier Karl De Unter-Schill, Later Known as Colonel Francis Weiss.**
　　1903　　Troy, N.Y.　　25.
WELLER, Edwin　　**A Civil War Courtship, the Letters of Edwin Weller from Antietam to Atlanta.** edited by William Walton.
　　1980　　Garden City　　10.
WESTERVELT, William B.　　**Lights and Shadows of Army Life as Seen by a Private Soldier.**
　　1886　　Marlboro　　50.
WEYGANT, Charles H.　　**History of the One Hundred and Twenty-Fourth Regiment N.Y.S.V.**
　　1877　　Newburgh　　110.
WHEELER, William　　**In Memoriam . . . Letters of _____ of the Class of 1855 Y. C.**
　　1875　　Cambridge　　60.
WHITMAN, George Washington　　**Civil War Letters of _____** edited by Jerome M. Loving.
　　1975　　Durham, North Carolina　　15.
WHITNEY, John H.　　**The Hawkins Zouaves: (Ninth N.Y.V.) Their Battles and Marches.**
　　1866　　New York　　125.
WILKESON, Frank　　**Recollections of a Private Soldier in the Army of the Potomac.**
　　1887　　New York　　30.
　　1972　　Freeport　　20.
WILLIAMS, George F.　　**Bullet and Shell.**
　　1882　　New York　　30.
　　1883　　New York　　25.
WILLSON, Arabella M.　　**Disaster, Struggle, Triumph; Adventures of 1,000 "Boys in Blue".**
　　1870　　Albany　　60.
WINGATE, George W.　　**History of the Twenty-Second Regiment of N.G.S.N.Y.**
　　1896　　New York　　50.
WINGATE, George W.　　**Last Campaign of the Twenty-Second Regiment N.G.S.N.Y.** Wraps
　　1864　　New York　　30.

NORTH CAROLINA

GENERAL REFERENCES

ANDERSON, Mrs. John Huske　　**North Carolina Women of the Confederacy.** Wraps
　　1926　　Fayetteville　　75.
　　n.d.　　n.p.　　reprint　　30.
BARRETT, John G.　　**The Civil War in North Carolina.**
　　1963　　Chapel Hill　　12.50
BIRDSONG, James Cook　　**Brief Sketches of the North Carolina State Troops in the War Between the States.** Wraps
　　1894　　Raleigh　　350.
Ceremonies Attending the Presentation and Unveiling of the North Carolina Memorial on the Battlefield of Gettysburg, Wednesday, July 3, 1929. Wraps
　　1929 (?)　　n.p.　　20.

CLARK, Walter   **Histories of the Several Regiments and Battalions from North Carolina in the Great War 1861-1865.** 5 vols.
  1901   Goldsboro, North Carolina   750.
  1982   Wendell   250.
CLARK, Walter   **North Carolina at Gettysburg & Pickett's Charge A Misnomer.** Wraps
  1921   Raleigh   35.
Confederate Memoirs, Alamance County Troops of the War Between the States 1861-1865.
  n.d. (circa 1965)   n.p.   35.
The Confederate Reveille Memorial Edition. Wraps
  1898   Raleigh   100.
CONNOR, R. D. W. (comp)   **Addresses at the Unveiling of the Memorial to the North Carolina Women of the Confederacy.** Wraps
  1914   Raleigh   30.
EVANS, Clement A. (ed)   **Confederate Military History, Vol. IV — North Carolina.**
  1899   Atlanta   40.
Five Points in the Record of North Carolina in the Great War of 1861-65. Wraps
  1904   Goldsboro   40.
Guide to Civil War Records in the North Carolina State Archives. Wraps
  1966   Raleigh   15.
HAHN, Geo. W. (ed)   **The Catawba Soldier of the Civil War, A Sketch of Every Soldier from Catawba County.**
  1911   Hickory   300.
HAMILTON, J. G. de R.   **Reconstruction in North Carolina.**
  1914   New York   150.
  1964   Gloucester   50.
HILL, Daniel Harvey   **Bethel to Sharpsburg.** 2 vols.
  1926   Raleigh   150.
HOLLOWELL, J. M.   **War-Time Reminiscences and Other Selections.** Wraps
  1939   Goldsboro   75.
McCORMICK, John Gilchrist   **Personnel of the Convention of 1861 and Legislation of the Convention of 1861** by Kemp P. Battle. Wraps
  1900   Chapel Hill   25.
MANARIN, Louis H.   **A Guide to Military Organizations and Installations North Carolina 1861-1865.** Wraps
  1961   Raleigh   20.
MANARIN, Louis H. (comp)   **North Carolina Troops 1861-1865 A Roster.**
  1966-1981   Raleigh
  Vols. 1-3   175. each
  Vol. 4   100.
  Vols. 5-8   25. each
MITCHELL, Memory F.   **Legal Aspects of Conscription and Exemption in North Carolina 1861-1865.** Wraps
  1965   Chapel Hill   20.
MONTGOMERY, Walter A.   **Address and Poem Delivered at the Unveiling of the Monument Erected to the Memory of the Confederate Dead of Warren County, N. C.** Wraps
  1906   Raleigh   20.
MOORE, John W.   **Roster of North Carolina Troops in the War Between the States.** 4 vols.
  1882   Raleigh   750.
MORROW, D. F.   **Then and Now, Reminiscences and Historical Romance 1856-1865.**
  1926   Macon, Georgia   25.
NEAL, Lois (comp)   **Genealogical Index to North Carolina Volume of Confederate Military History.** Expanded portion of N. C. Volume. Wraps
  1975   Raleigh   10.

PEARCE, Thilbert H.   **They Fought, The Story of Franklin County N. C. Men in the Years 1861-65.**
n.d.   n.p.   15.

SITTERSON, Joseph C.   **The Secession Movement in North Carolina.** Wraps
1939   Chapel Hill   20.

SLOAN, John A.   **North Carolina in the War Between the States.** Wraps
1883   Washington   125.

SMITH, Mrs. S. L. (comp)   **North Carolina's Confederate Monuments and Memorials.**
1941   Raleigh   50.

SPENCER, Cornelia Phillips   **The Last Ninety Days of the War in North Carolina.**
1866   New York   125.

THORPE, John H.   **Roster of Nash County Confederate Soldiers.**
1925   Raleigh   150.

TUCKER, Glenn   **Front Rank.**
1962   Raleigh   50.

WAGSTAFF, Henry McGilbert   **State Rights and Political Parties in North Carolina, 1776-1861.**
1906   Baltimore   25.

War Days in Fayetteville, North Carolina, Reminiscences of 1861 to 1865. Wraps
1910   n.p.   50.

WRIGHT, Stuart T.   **Historical Sketch of Person County.**
1974   Danville   15.

YEARNS, W. Buck and **BARRETT,** John G. (eds)   **North Carolina Civil War Documentary.**
1980   Chapel Hill   17.95

REGIMENTALS

BAHNSON, Henry T.   **The Last Days of the War.** Wraps
1903   Hamlet, North Carolina   30.

BETTS, Alexander Davis   **Experiences of a Confederate Chaplain 1861-1865.** Wraps
n.d.   n.p.   reprint   30.

CARPENTER, Kinchen Jahu   **War Diary of _____ Company I, Fiftieth North Carolina Regiment War Between the States 1861-65** prepared by Mrs. Julie Carpenter Williams. Wraps
1955   Rutherfordton, North Carolina   30.

COLTRANE, Daniel Branson   **The Memoirs of Daniel Branson Coltrane, Co. I, 63rd Reg., N. C. Cavalry C.S.A.**
1956   Raleigh   50.

ELLIOTT, James Carson   **The Southern Soldier Boy.** Wraps
1907   Raleigh   75.

FREEMAN, Benjamin H.   **The Confederate Letters of _____** edited by Stuart Wright.
1974   New York   10.

GRAHAM, James A.   **The James A. Graham Papers 1861-1864.** edited by H. M. Wagstaff. Wraps
1928   Chapel Hill   25.

GREEN, Wharton J.   **Recollections and Reflections.**
1906   Raleigh   75.

GRIMES, Bryan   **Extracts of Letters of Major-General Grimes to His Wife Written While in Active Service in the Army of Northern Virginia . . .** comp. by Pulaski Cowper. Wraps
1883   Raleigh   200.
1884   Raleigh   125.

HALL, Harry H.   **A Johnny Reb Band from Salem: The Pride of Tarheelia.** Wraps
1963   Raleigh   25.

HARRELL, Lawson   **Reminiscences of 1861-1865.** Wraps
1910   Statesville   200.

IOBST, Richard W. et al   **The Bloody Sixth   The Sixth N. C. Regt. C.S.A.** Wraps
    1965   Raleigh   35.
LEDFORD, Preston L.   **Reminiscences of the Civil War 1861-1865.** Wraps
    1909   Thomasville   75.
LEE, Laura Elizabeth   **Forget-Me-Nots of the Civil War.**
    1909   St. Louis   125.
LEON, Louis   **Diary of a Tar Heel Confederate Soldier.**
    1913   Charlotte   100.
MALONE, Bartlett Yancey   **Whipt 'em Everytime, The Diary of _____ Co. H, 6th N. C. Regiment.** edited by Wm. Whatley Pierson, Jr.
    1960   Jackson   25.
NORMAN, William M.   **A Portion of My Life, Being a Short and Imperfect History Written While a Prisoner of War on Johnson's Island   1864.**
    1959   Winston-Salem   10.
PARRAMORE, T. C., **JOHNSON,** F. R. and **STEPHENSON,** E. F. (eds)   **Before the Rebel Flag Fell.**
    1968   Murfreesboro   10.
PUTNAM, Mildred Patterson (ed)   **Day Book of I. Frank Patterson, July 22, 1864 to April 30, 1865.** Wraps
    1962   n.p.   Ltd.   26.
SLOAN, John A.   **Reminiscences of the Guilford Grays, Co. B 27th N.C. Regiment.**
    1883   Washington   200.
    1978   Wendell   15.
SMITH, William Alexander   **The Anson Guards, Co. C, 14th Regt N.C. Vols. 1861-1865.**
    1914   Charlotte   300.
    1978   Wendell   20.
UNDERWOOD, George C.   **History of the 26th Regiment of North Carolina Troops.**
    1901   Goldsboro   250.
    1978   Wendell   15.
WELLMAN, Manly Wade   **Rebel Boast: First at Bethel — Last at Appomattox.**
    1956   New York   25.

OHIO

GENERAL REFERENCES

Annual Report of the Adjutant General to the Governor of the State of Ohio.
    1862-1863   Wraps   30. per vol.
Annual Report of Quartermaster General, Ohio.
    1863-1864   Wraps   30. per volume
Brief Historical Sketch of the Cuyahoga County Soldiers and Sailors Monument. Wraps
    1896   Cleveland   15.
A Brief Historical Sketch of the "Fighting McCooks." Wraps
    n.d.   New York   40.
CARRINGTON, Henry B.   **General Regulations for the Military Forces of Ohio with the Laws Pertinent Thereto.**
    1861   Columbus   25.
CLARK, Peter H.   **The Black Brigade of Cincinnati; Being a Report of Its Labors and a Muster Roll of Its Members, etc.** Wraps
    1864   Cincinnati   100.
Complete History of Fairfield County, Ohio 1795-1876.
    1877   Columbus   80.

EVANS, N. W.   **In Memoriam: A Tribute of Respect to the Memory of the Deceased Soldiers of Adams County, Ohio.** Wraps
    1902   Portsmouth   25.
GLEASON, William J.   **History of the Cuyahoga County Soldiers' and Sailor's Monument.**
    1894   Cleveland   35.
GREEN, Charles R.   **A Historical Pamphlet, Wakeman, Ohio, Lives of the Volunteers in the Civil War.**
    1914   Olathe, Kansas   40.
KEESY, William Allen   **Roster of Richmond Soldiers and History of Richmond Township, Tiffin Ohio.**
    1908   n.p.   35.
Licking County's Gallant Soldiers, Who Died in Defence of Our Glorious Union. Wraps
    1874   Newark   25.
A Memorial: Soldier Spirit of Waterville, Ohio, A Souvenir.
    1899   n.p.   40.
Military History of Ohio.
    1886   Toledo Montgomery County ed.   50.
    1886   Toledo Stark Co. ed.   50.
    1887   Toledo Franklin County ed.   50.
    1888   Toledo Morgan County ed.   50.
    1889   Toledo Mahoning County ed.   50.
MILLER, Charles D.   **Report of the Great Re-Union of the Veteran Soldiers and Sailors of Ohio Held at Newark July 22, 1878.**
    1879   Newark   35.
Official Roster of the Soldiers of the State of Ohio in the War of the Rebellion and in the War with Mexico. 12 vols.
    1886-1895   Akron, Cincinnati, Norwalk   250.
    Individual Vols.   20. each
Ohio at Antietam, Report of the Ohio Antietam Battlefield Commission.
    1904   Springfield   30.
Ohio at Shiloh, Report of the Commission.
    1903   Cincinnati   25.
Ohio at Vicksburg, Report of Ohio Vicksburg Battlefield Commission.
    1906   Columbus   25.
POLAND, Charles A.   **Army Register of Ohio Volunteers in the Service of the United States, April 1862.** Wraps
    1862   Columbus   40.
REID, Whitelaw   **Ohio in the War: Her Statesmen Her Generals, and Soldiers.** 2 vols.
    1868   Cincinnati   125.
    1868   New York   125.
    1893   Columbus   100.
ROBINSON, George F.   **After Thirty Years, A Complete Roster by Townships of Greene County, Ohio Soldiers.**
    1895   Xenia   35.
Roll of Honor, The Soldiers of Champaign County, Ohio Who Died for the Union.
    n.d.   n.p.   50.
RYAN, Daniel J.   **The Civil War Literature of Ohio.**
    1911   Cleveland   75.
Sketches of War History 1861-1865 Papers Read Before Ohio Commandery, Mollus. 6 vols.
    1888-1908   Cincinnati   200.
    Individual Vols. 35. each
Special Military History of Ohio, Hardesty's Historical and Geographical Encyclopedia.
    1885   New York   125.

VAN CLEAF, Aaron R. (comp)   History of Pickaway County, Ohio and Representative Citizens.
1906   Chicago   100.
WHEELER, Kenneth W. (ed)   For the Union, Ohio Leaders in the Civil War.
1968   Columbus   15.

REGIMENTALS

ABBOTT, Horace R.   My Escape from Belle Isle. Wraps
1889   Detroit   30.
ADAMS, Jacob   Diary of _____, Private in Company F, 21st OVI.
1930   Columbus   30.
ANDERSON, Edward L.   Colonel Archibald Gracie's The Truth About Chickamauga. Wraps
n.d.   n.p.   25.
ANDERSON, Nicholas Longworth   Letters and Journals of General _____ edited
by Isabel Anderson.
1942   New York   25.
ASHBURN, Joseph Nelson   History of the Eighty-Sixth Regiment Ohio Volunteer
Infantry.
1909   Cleveland   75.
ASTON, Howard   History and Roster of the Fourth and Fifth Independent Battalions and Thirteenth Regiment Ohio Cavalry Volunteers. Wraps
1902   Columbus   100.
BARTLETT, Robert F. (comp)   Roster of the Ninety-Sixth Regiment, Ohio Volunteer Infantry 1862 to 1865.
1895   Columbus   60.
BATES, Ralph O. (Billy)   Billy and Dick. From Andersonville Prison to the
White House.
1910   Santa Cruz, California   35.
BEACH, John N.   History of the Fortieth Ohio Volunteer Infantry.
1884   London   125.
BEATTY, John   The Citizen-Soldier: or Memories of a Volunteer.
1879   Cincinnati   65.
1946   New York   entitled: Memoirs of a Volunteer edited by Harvey S.
Ford.   25.
BERING, John A. and MONTGOMERY, Thomas   History of the Forty-Eighth
Ohio Vet. Vol. Inf.
1880   Hillsboro   90.
BIGGER, David Dwight   Ohio's Silver-Tongued Orator, Life and Speeches of
General William H. Gibson.
1901   Dayton   35.
BOYNTON, Henry V.   Was General Thomas Slow at Nashville?
1896   New York   Ltd.   50.
BRISTOL, Frank Milton   The Life of Chaplain McCabe, Bishop of the Metho-
dist Episcopal Church.
1908   New York   20.
BURSON, William   A Race for Liberty: or, My Capture, Imprisonment and
Escape.
1867   Wellsville   100.
CALDWELL, David S.   Incidents of War; or Southern Prison Life. Wraps
1864   Dayton   125.
CANFIELD, Silas S.   History of the 21st Regiment Ohio Volunteer Infantry in the
War of the Rebellion.
1893   Toledo   75.
CHAMBERLAIN, W. P.   Memorandum Book of _____, 2nd Lt. CO. A, 23rd
Ohio Volunteer Infantry July 9 1863 to July 25, 1863.
n.d.   n.p.   250.

CHAMBERLIN, William Henry   History of the Eighty-First Regiment Ohio Infantry Volunteers During the War of the Rebellion.
1865   Cincinnati   125.

CHASE, John A.   History of the Fourteenth Ohio Regiment O.V.V.I.
1881   Toledo   100.

CLARK, Charles T.   Opdycke Tigers 125th O.V.I. a History of the Regiment.
1895   Columbus   150.

CONNELLY, Thomas W.   History of the Seventieth Regiment from Its Organization to Its Mustering Out. Wraps
1902   Cincinnati   150.

Constitution, By-Laws, Roster and History of the 97th O.V.I. Regimental Association. Wraps
n.d.   n.p.   75.

CONWELL, Russell H.   Life and Public Services of Gov. Rutherford B. Hayes.
1876   Boston   20.

COPE, Alexis   The Fifteenth Ohio Volunteers and Its Campaigns.
1916   Columbus   125.

CROFTS, Thomas   History of the Service of the Third Ohio Veteran Cavalry in the War for Preservation of the Union from 1861-1865.
1910   Toledo   125.

CROSS, Frederick C.   Nobly They Served the Union. Wraps
1976   Walnut Creek, Calif.   20.

CULP, Edward C.   The 25th Ohio Vet. Vol. Infantry in the War for the Union.
1885   Topeka   150.

CURRY, William Leontes   Four Years in the Saddle, History of the First Regiment Ohio Vol. Cavalry.
1898   Columbus   175.

CUTTER, Orlando Phelps   Our Battery: or, The Journal of Company B, 1st O.V.A. Wraps
1864   Cleveland   90.

DALZELL, James McCormick   Private Dalzell, His Autobiography, Poems and Comic War Papers.
1888   Cincinnati   25.

DAVIDSON, Henry M.   Fourteen Months in Southern Prisons.
1865   Milwaukee   100.

DAVIDSON, Henry M.   History of Battery A, 1st Regiment Ohio Vol. Light Artillery.
1865   Milwaukee   125.

DAY, Lewis W.   Story of the One Hundred and First Ohio Infantry.
1894   Cleveland   75.

DEMORET, Alfred   A Brief History of the Ninety-Third Regiment Ohio Volunteer Infantry. Wraps
1898   Ross   80.

DEVELLING, Charles Theodore (comp)   History of the 17th Regiment, 1st Brigade, 3rd Division, 14th Corps, Army of the Cumberland.
1889   Zanesville   150.

DOAN, Isaac C.   Reminiscences of the Chattanooga Campaign. Wraps
1894   Richmond   40.

DOWNS, Edward C.   Four Years a Scout & Spy.
1866   Zanesville   60.

DOWNS, Edward C.   The Great American Scout and Spy, "General Bunker."
1868   New York   25.
1870   New York   25.

DOWNS, Edward C.   Perils of Scout Life. by C. L. Ruggles
1875   New York   30.

DUKE, John K.   History of the Fifty-Third Regiment Ohio Volunteer Infantry.
1900   Portsmouth   125.

EMPSON, W. H.   **A Story of Rebel Military Prisons.** Wraps
   n.d.   Lockport, New York   350.
Eulogy on Comrade H. G. Palmer, CO "G" 15th O.V.V.I. Wraps
   1910   n.p.   15.
EWING, Elmore Ellis   **Bugles and Bells; or Stories Told Again.**
   1899   Cincinnati   75.
FLEISCHMANN, S. M.   **The Memorial Tablet Published Under the Auspices of Buckley Post 12, GAR.**
   1883   Akron   15.
GALWEY, Thomas Francis   **The Valiant Hours.** edited by W. S. Nye.
   1961   Harrisburg   30.
GASKILL, Joseph W.   **Footprints Through Dixie.**
   1919   Alliance   45.
GAUSE, Isaac   **Four Years with Five Armies.**
   1908   New York   100.
GEER, John J.   **Beyond the Lines.**
   1863   Philadelphia   35.
   1864   Philadelphia   25.
GILBERT, Alfred W.   **Col. A. W. Gilbert, Citizen Soldier of Cincinnati.** edited by W. E. Smith and O. D. Smith.
   1934   Cincinnati   25.
GILLESPIE, Samuel L.   **A History of Co. A, First Ohio Cavalry 1861-1865 A Memorial Volume.**
   1898   Washington Courthouse   175.
GILSON, John H. (comp)   **Concise History of the 126th Regiment Ohio Volunteer Infantry.**
   1883   Salem   150.
GRANGER, Moses Moorhead   **The Official War Record of the 122nd Regiment of Ohio Infantry from Oct. 8, 1862 to June 26, 1865.** Wraps
   1912   Zanesville   75.
HAMILTON, William Douglas   **Recollections of a Cavalryman of the Civil War After Fifty Years 1861-1865.**
   1915   Columbus   110.
HANNAFORD, Ebenezer   **The Story of a Regiment: A History of the Campaigns and Associations in the Field of the Sixth Regiment Ohio Volunteer Infantry.**
   1868   Cincinnati   100.
HARDEN, Henry O.   **History of the 90th Ohio Volunteer Infantry in the War of the Rebellion.**
   1902   Stoutsville   125.
HAWKINS, M. L.   **Sketch of the Battle of Winchester, September 19, 1864, a Paper.** Wraps
   1884   Cincinnati   25.
HAYES, Rutherford B.   **Remarks of Gen._____ at the Annual Reunion of the 23rd Regiment, Ohio Vet. Vol. Inf. at Youngstown, Ohio Sept 17, 1879.**
   1879 (?)   n.p.   25.
HAYES, Rutherford B.   **Remarks of General _____ at the Reunion of the 23rd Ohio Veterans, Canton, Sept 1, 1880.**
   n.d.   n.p.   25.
HAYS, Ebenezer Z. (ed)   **History of the Thirty-Second Regiment Ohio Veteran Volunteer Infantry.**
   1896   Columbus   100.
HAZEN, William B.   **A Narrative of Military Service.**
   1885   Boston   75.
HINMAN, Wilbur F.   **Corporal Si Klegg and His "Pard."**
   1887   Cleveland   25.
   1888   Cleveland   25.
   1889   Cleveland   25.
   1892   Cleveland   25.

HINMAN, Wilbur F.   **The Story of the Sherman Brigade.**
1897   Alliance   150.
HOPKINS, Owen J.   **Under the Flag of the Nation.** edited by Otto F. Bond.
1961   Columbus   15.
HORTON, Joshua H.   **A History of the Eleventh Regiment (Ohio).**
1866   Dayton   125.
HOWBERT, Abraham R.   **Reminiscences of the War.**
1888   Springfield   35.
HUNTINGTON, James Freeman   **The Battle of Chancellorsville.** Wraps
1897   n.p.   20.
HURST, Samuel H.   **Journal-History of the Seventy-Third Ohio Volunteer Infantry.**
1866   Chillicothe   125.
HYDE, Solon   **A Captive of War.**
1900   New York   50.
JACKSON, Isaac   **Some of the Boys . . . Civil War Letters of** _____. edited by
Joseph O. Jackson.
1960   Carbondale   25.
JACKSON, Oscar L.   **The Colonel's Diary: Journals Kept Before and During the
Civil War.**
1922   Sharon, Pennsylvania   100.
JOHNSON, Lewis Warren   **First Independent Battery, Ohio Light Artillery, The
Thornless Rose.**
1910   n.p.   50.
JONES, Frank J.   **Personal Recollections of Some of the Generals in Our Army
During the Civil War.** Wraps
1913 (?)   n.p.   25.
JONES, John Sills   **History of the 174th O.V.I.** Wraps
1894   Marysville   100.
KEESY, William Allen   **War as Viewed From the Ranks.**
1898   Norwalk   75.
KEIFER, Joseph Warren.   **Slavery and Four Years of War.** 2 vols.
1900   New York   75.
KEPLER, William   **History of the Three Months' and Three Years' Service . . .
Fourth Regiment Ohio Volunteer Infantry.**
1886   Cleveland   150.
KERN, Albert (comp)   **History of the First Regiment Ohio Vol. Infantry in the
Civil War.**
1918   Dayton   75.
KEYES, Charles M. (ed)   **Military History of the 123rd Regiment of Ohio Vol. Inf.**
1874   Sandusky   100.
KIMBERLY, Robert L. and **HOLLOWAY,** E. S.   **The 41st Ohio Veteran Volunteer
Infantry in the War of the Rebellion 1861-1865.**
1897   Cleveland   150.
LEWIS, George W.   **The Campaigns of the 124th Regiment Ohio Volunteer
Infantry.**
1894   Akron   125.
LOWERY, Roland   **The Story of Battery I First Regiment Ohio Volunteer Light
Artillery 1861-1865.** Wraps
1971   Cincinnati   10.
1972   Cincinnati   10.
LYLE, William W.   **Lights and Shadows of Army Life.**
1865   Cincinnati   35.
McADAMS, Francis Marion   **Every-Day Soldier LIfe: or, A History of the 113th
Ohio Volunteer Infantry.**
1884   Columbus   125.
McBRIDE, Robert W.   **Lincoln's Body Guard, The Union Light Guard of Ohio.**
Wraps
1911   Indianapolis   45.

McCORD, Simeon   **Letters Home 1861-1865. Camp and Campaign Life of a Union Artilleryman.**
   n.d.   n.p.   40.

McFARLAND, Robert White   **The Surrender of Cumberland Gap, September 9, 1863.** Wraps
   1898   Columbus   40.

MANDERSON, Charles F.   **The Twin Seven-Shooters.**
   1902   New York   30.

MARSHALL, Thomas B.   **History of the 83rd Ohio Volunteer Infantry, The Greyhound Regiment.**
   1912   Cincinnati   125.

MASON, Frank Holcomb   **The Forty-Second Ohio Infantry.**
   1876   Cleveland   150.

A Military Record of Battery D, First Ohio Veteran Volunteer Light Artillery.
   1908   Oil City, Pennsylvania   100.

MONTFORT, Elias R.   **From Grafton to McDowell Through Tygart's Valley.** Wraps
   1886   Cincinnati   25.

MUNK, Joseph A.   **Activities of a Lifetime.**
   1924   Los Angeles   60.

NEIL, Henry M.   **A Battery at Close Quarters: A Paper Read Before the Ohio Commandery of the Loyal Legion, Oct 6, 1909.**
   n.d.   n.p.   35.

Ninth Reunion of the 37th OVVI, St. Marys, Ohio Sept. 10 and 11, 1889.
   1890   Toledo   75.

Oldroyd, Osborn H.   **A Soldier's Story of the Siege of Vicksburg, from the Diary of _____.**
   1885   Springfield   85.

OSBORN, Hartwell   **The Eleventh Army Corps, Western Reserve Bulletin.** Wraps
   1913   n.p.   25.

OSBORN, Hartwell   **Trials and Triumphs: The Record of the Fifty-Fifth Ohio Volunteer Infantry.**
   1904   Chicago   100.

OVERHOLSER, James F.   **Diary of _____ Co. D, 81st Ohio Infantry. Three Years with the Union Army.** Wraps
   n.d. (1937?)   n.p.   125.

OWENS, Ira S.   **Greene County Soldiers in the Late War . . .**
   1884   Dayton   75.

PALMER, Jewett   **Historical Sketch of Company B, 18th Regiment Ohio Infantry.** Wraps
   1911   Marietta   50.

PATTON, Joseph T.   **Personal Recollections of Four Years in Dixie.**
   1892   Detroit   30.

PAVER, John M.   **What I Saw from 1861 to 1864 Personal Recollections of _____** Wraps
   1906   Indianapolis   100.

PEPPER, George W.   **Personal Recollections of Sherman's Campaigns in Georgia and the Carolinas.**
   1866   Zanesville   110.

PEPPER, George W.   **Under Three Flags, or The Story of My Life.**
   1899   Cincinnati   30.

PERKINS, George   **A Summer in Maryland and Virginia, or Campaigning with the 149th Ohio Volunteer Infantry.**
   1911   Chillicothe   60.

Personal Reminiscences and Experiences by Members of the 103rd Ohio Volunteer Infantry.
   1900   Oberlin   75.

PIKE, James   **The Scout and Ranger.**
    1865   Cincinnati   400.

Proceedings of the 48th Annual Reunion of the 15th Ohio Regimental Assoc. Held at Mansfield, Ohio Sept. 26 and 27, 1912. Wraps
    n.d.   Mansfield   30.

RANKIN, Richard C.   **History of the Seventh Ohio Volunteer Cavalry.** Wraps
    1881   Ripley   100.

Record of the Ninety-Fourth Regiment Ohio Volunteer Infantry.
    189?   Cincinnati   100.

Reminiscences of the Cleveland Light Artillery.
    1906   Cleveland   60.

RICHARDS, Henry   **Letters of Captain Henry Richards of the Ninety-Third Ohio Infantry.** Wraps
    1883   Cincinnati   50.

ROBERTS, John N.   **Reminiscences of the Civil War.** Wraps
    1925   n.p.   35.

ROCKWELL, Alphonso David   **Rambling Recollections.**
    1920   New York   40.

Roster and Historical Sketch of the 101st Regiment Ohio Volunteer Infantry.
    1897   Tiffin   50.

Roster of the 147th Regiment Ohio Volunteer Infantry with Age at Enlistment. Wraps
    1913   West Milton   60.

Roster of the 134th Regiment O.V.I. Wraps
    1898   Ohio   40.

Roster of Surviving Members of the 41st Regiment, Ohio Veteran Volunteer Infantry in the War of the Rebellion 1861-1865. Wraps
    1899   Cleveland   25.

RUDOLPH, Joseph   **Pickups from the "American Way", Early Life and Civil War Reminiscences of Capt. Joseph Rudolph.** Wraps
    1941   Hiram   30.

SAUNIER, Joseph A. (ed)   **A History of the Forty-Seventh Ohio Veteran Volunteer Infantry.**
    1903   Hillsboro   150.

SAWYER, Franklin   **A Military History of the 8th Regiment Ohio Vol. Infantry, Its Battles, Marches and Army Movements.**
    1881   Cleveland   125.

SCOFIELD, Levi T.   **Retreat from Pulaski to Nashville, Tenn.**
    1909   Cleveland   50.

SCOTT, William Forse   **Philander P. Lane, Colonel of Volunteers in the Civil War 11th Ohio Infantry.**
    1920   New York   100.

SeCHEVERALL, John Hamilton   **Journal History of the Twenty-Ninth Ohio Veteran Volunteers 1861-1865.**
    1883   Cleveland   75.

SHELLENBERGER, John K.   **The Battle of Spring Hill, Tenn. November 29, 1864.** Wraps
    1913   Cleveland   60.

SHERMAN, Sylvester M.   **History of the 133rd Regiment O.V.I.**
    1896   Columbus   100.

SHERWOOD, Isaac R.   **Memories of the War.**
    1923   Toledo   30.

SMITH, Charles H.   **The History of Fuller's Ohio Brigade, 1861-1865.**
    1909   Cleveland   150.

SMITH, Walter George   **Life & Letters of Thomas Kilby Smith.**
    1898   New York   75.

STERLING, James T.   **Personal Experiences of the Early Days of 1861.** Wraps
    1892   Detroit   25.

STEVENSON, Thomas M.   **History of the 78th Regiment Ohio Veteran Volunteer Infantry.**
1865   Zanesville   150.
STEWART, Nixon B.   **Dan McCook's Regiment, 52nd O.V.I.**
1900   Alliance   125.
STIPP, Joseph A.   **The History and Service of the 154th Ohio Volunteer Infantry.**
1896   Toledo   100.
n.d.   n.p.   10.
THEAKER, James G.   **Through One Man's Eyes: Letters of _____,** Belmont County, Ohio Volunteer. edited by Paul E. Rieger.
1974   Mt. Vernon   20.
THOBURN, Thomas C.   **My Experiences During the Civil War.** compiled by Lyle Thoburn.
1963   Cleveland   30.
THURSTON, W. S.   **History of the 111th Regiment O.V.I.**
1894   Toledo   150.
TIBBETTS, George W.   **A Brief Sketch of the Cleveland Grays.**
n.d.   n.p.   45.
TOURGEE, Albion W.   **The Story of a Thousand.**
1896   Buffalo   75.
TRACIE, Theodore C.   **Annals of the Nineteenth Ohio Battery Volunteer Artillery.**
1878   Cleveland   100.
WHITTLESEY, Charles   **War Memoranda, Cheat River to the Tennessee 1861-1862.**
1884   Cleveland   50.
WILDER, Theodore   **The History of Company C, Seventh Regiment, O.V.I.**
1866   Oberlin   100.
WILDES, Thomas Francis   **Record of the One Hundred and Sixteenth Regiment, Ohio Infantry Volunteers in the War of the Rebellion.**
1884   Sandusky   125.
WILLIAMS, T. Harry   **Hayes of the Twenty Third.**
1965   New York   30.
WILSON, Lawrence   **Itinerary of the Seventh Ohio Volunteer Infantry 1861-1865.**
1907   New York   175.
2 vol. edition   200.
WINTERS, Erastus   **Serving Uncle Sam in the 50th Ohio.** Wraps
1905   East Walnut Hills   100.
WISE, George M.   **Marching Through South Carolina: Another Civil War Letter of Lieutenant _____.** edited by Wilfred W. Black. Wraps
1957   n.p.   10.
WOOD, David W. (comp)   **History of the 20th Ohio Veteran Volunteer Infantry Regiment.** Wraps
1876   Columbus   100.
WOOD, George L.   **The Seventh Regiment: A Record.**
1865   New York   75.
1865   New York   entitled: **Famous Deeds By American Heroes: A Record of Events from Sumter to Lookout Mountain. . .**   50.
WOODS, Joseph Thatcher   **Services of the 96th Ohio Volunteers.**
1874   Toledo   125.
WOODS, Joseph Thatcher   **Steedman and His Men at Chickamauga.**
1876   Toledo   50.
WOOLSON, Alvin M.   **First O.V.H.A., Company M.**
1914   Toledo   90.
WORTHINGTON, Thomas   **A Correct History . . . Gen Grant at Shiloh.** Wraps
1880   Washington   35.
WORTHINGTON, Thomas   **Shiloh, or The Tennessee Campaign of 1862.** Wraps
1872   Washington   35.
WRIGHT, Charles   **A Corporal's Story, Experiences in the Ranks of Company C, 81st Ohio Vol. Infantry.**
1887   Philadelphia   Ltd.   100.

WULSIN, Lucien   Roster of Surviving Members of the 4th Regiment Ohio Volunteer Cavalry with a Brief Historical Sketch of the Regiment.
    1891   Cincinnati   75.
WULSIN, Lucien   The Story of the 4th Regiment Ohio Vet. Vol. Cavalry.
    1912   Cincinnati   125.

OREGON

GENERAL REFERENCES

Report of the Adjutant General of the State of Oregon. Wraps
    For 1863   35.
    For 1865   35.
HILLEARY, William M.   The Diary of 1864-1866 A Webfoot Volunteer edited by H. B. Nelson and P. E. Onstad.
    1965   Corvallis   20.

PENNSYLVANIA

GENERAL REFERENCES

Annual Report of Adjutant General of Pennsylvania.
    1863-1866   Harrisburg   25. each
Annual Report of the Board of Military Claims of the State of Pennsylvania, for the Year 1863.
    1864   Harrisburg   30.
BATES, Samuel P.   History of Pennsylvania Volunteers. 5 vols.
    1869   Harrisburg   250.
BATES, Samuel P.   Martial Deeds of Pennsylvania.
    1875   Philadelphia   50.
    1876   Philadelphia   35.
BOOK, Janet Mae   Northern Rendezvous, Harrisburg During the Civil War.
    1951   Harrisburg   20.
Eleven Days in the Militia During the War of the Rebellion: Being a Journal of the Emergency Campaign of 1862.
    1883   Philadelphia   30.
EVANS, Samuel M.   Allegheny County, Penna in the War . . . Roll of Honor.
    1924   Pittsburgh   40.
FRAZIER, John W.   Gettysburg, Reunion of the Blue and Gray Philadelphia Brigade and Pickett's Division. Wraps
    1906   Philadelphia   30.
GRAY, John Gordon   Lieut.-Colonel Robert Burns Beath, Memoir. Wraps
    1915 (?)   Philadelphia   25.
KOEHLER, Leroy Jennings   The History of Monroe County, Penna. During the Civil War.
    1950   Monroe County   30.
LACIAR, J. D.   Patriotism of Carbon County.
    1867   Mauch Chunk   45.
LANARD, Thomas S.   One Hundred Years with the State Fencibles: A History of the First Company.
    1913   Philadelphia   30.
NICHOLAS, Alexander F. (ed)   Second Brigade of the Pennsylvania Reserves at Antietam . . . Reports & Ceremonies at Dedication of the Monuments.
    1908   Harrisburg   25.

OVERMILLER, Howard   **York, Pennsylvania in the Hands of the Confederates June 28-30 1863.** Wraps
    n.d.   n.p.   15.
Pennsylvania at Andersonville, Ga., Ceremonies at the Dedication of the Memorial.
    1905   n.p.   20.
    1909   Harrisburg   20.
Pennsylvania at Antietam, Reports and Ceremonies at the Dedication of the Monuments.
    1906   Harrisburg   20.
Pennsylvania at Chickamauga and Chattanooga.
    1897   Harrisburg   25.
    1900   Harrisburg   20.
    1901   Harrisburg   20.
Pennsylvania at Cold Harbor Dedication of the Monument.
    1912   Harrisburg   15.
Pennsylvania at Culpeper Report of the Culpeper Monument Commission.
    1914   Harrisburg   15.
Pennsylvania at Gettysburg, Battlefield Commission. 4 vols.
    1893-1939   25. per vol.
Pennsylvania at Salisbury, N. C., Ceremonies at the Dedication of the Memorial.
    1910   Harrisburg   15.
Register of the Commandery of the State of Pennsylvania, Mollus.
    1902   Philadelphia   25.
TAYLOR, Frank H.   **Philadelphia in the Civil War 1861-1865.**
    1913   Philadelphia   25.
TUBBS, Charles   **Osceola in the War of the Rebellion.**
    1885   Wellsboro   35.
WALLACE, Francis B.   **Memorial of the Patriotism of Schuylkill County.**
    1865   Pottsville   45.

REGIMENTALS

ALBERT, Allen D.   **A Grandfather's Oft Told Tales of the Civil War.** Wraps
    1913   Williamsport   25.
ALBERT, Allen D. (ed)   **History of the 45th Regiment, Pennsylvania Veteran Volunteer Infantry.**
    1912   Williamsport   65.
ARMSTRONG, William H.   **Red-Tape and Pigeon-Hole Generals.**
    1864   New York   35.
BALTZ, John D.   **Hon. Edward D. Baker . . . Colonel E. D. Baker's Defense in the Battle of Ball's Bluff.**
    1888   Lancaster   65.
BANES, Charles H.   **History of the Philadelphia Brigade 69th, 71st, 72nd, and 106th Pennsylvania Infantries.**
    1876   Philadelphia   100.
BATES, Samuel P.   **A Brief History of the One Hundredth (sic) Regiment (Roundheads).**
    1884   New Castle   125.
BAYARD, Samuel J.   **The Life of George Dashiell Bayard.**
    1874   New York   50.
BLOODGOOD, John D.   **Personal Reminiscences of the War.**
    1893   New York   45.
BOSBYSHELL, Oliver C.   **The 48th in the War.**
    1895   Philadelphia   75.
BOYLE, John Richards   **Soldiers True, The Story of the One Hundred and Eleventh Regiment Pennsylvania Veteran Volunteers.**
    1903   New York   65.

BREWER, Abraham T.   **History Sixty-First Regiment Pennsylvania Volunteers 1861-1865.**
  1911   Pittsburgh   45.
BRIGHT, Adam S. and **BRIGHT,** Michael S.   **Respects to All: Letters of Two Pennsylvania Boys in the War.** edited by A. C. Truxall.
  1962   Pittsburgh   20.
BURR, Frank A.   **Life and Achievements of James Addams Beaver.**
  1882   Philadelphia   30.
CAVADA, Frederick F.   **Libby Life.**
  1864   Philadelphia   35.
  1865   Philadelphia   35.
CHAMBERLIN, Thomas   **History of the 150th Regiment Pennsylvania Volunteers . . . Bucktail Brigade.**
  1895   Philadelphia   100.
  1905   Philadelphia   85.
CHARLES, Edwin F. and **CHARLES,** John E. (comps.)   **Henry Fitzgerald Charles Civil War Record 1862-1865.** Wraps
  1969   Middleburg, Pa.   20.
Charter, Constitution and By-Laws of the Veteran Corps, of the First Regiment Infantry, N.G. of Pa. Wraps
  1881   Philadelphia   30.
CLARK, William   **History of Hampton Battery F, Independent Pennsylvania Light Artillery.**
  1909   Akron   40.
COLLIS, Charles H. T.   **Letters and Testimony Presented by Mr. Collis Defending Himself Against Accusation Made to the Mollus as to His Military Record.** Wraps
  1891   New York   45.
COLLIS, Septima M.   **A Woman's War Record 1861-1865.**
  1889   New York   40.
  1892   New York   35.
COLTON, Matthias Baldwin   **Civil War Journal and Correspondence of** _____ edited by Jessie S. Colton.
  1931   Philadelphia   Ltd.   75.
COX, Robert C.   **Memories of the War.** Wraps
  1893   Wellsboro, Pa.   40.
CRAFT, David   **History of the 141st Regiment Pennsylvania Volunteers.**
  1885   Towanda   90.
CRUIKSHANK, George L.   **Back in the Sixties. Reminiscences of the Service of Co. A, 11th Pennsylvania Regiment.** Wraps
  1893   Fort Dodge, Iowa   75.
CUFFEL, Charles A.   **Durell's Battery . . . Independent Battery D, Pennsylvania Volunteer Artillery.**
  1900   Philadelphia   40.
  1903   Philadelphia   entitled: **History of Durell's Battery.**   40.
CUTLER, Elbridge Jefferson   **Fitzhugh Birney, A Memoir.** Wraps
  1866   Cambridge   30.
DARBY, Geo. W.   **Incidents and Adventures in Rebeldom, Libby, Belle-Isle, Salisbury.**
  1899   Pittsburgh   40.
DAVIS, William W. H.   **History of the Doylestown Guards.**
  1887   Doylestown   50.
DAVIS, William W. H.   **History of the 104th Pennsylvania Regiment.**
  1866   Philadelphia   75.
Dedication of the Monument of the 6th Penna. Cavalry "Lancers" on the Battlefield of Gettysburg. Wraps
  1889   Philadelphia   30.

DICKEY, Luther S.   **History of the 85th Regiment Pennsylvania Volunteer Infantry 1861-1864.**
1915   New York   50.

DICKEY, Luther S.   **History of the 103d Regiment Pennsylvania Veteran Volunteer Infantry 1861-1865.**
1910   Chicago   45.

DONAGHY, John   **Army Experiences of Captain _____, 103rd Pennsylvania Volunteers 1861-1864.**
1926   Deland   60.

DORNBLASER, Thomas Franklin   **My Life-Story for Young and Old.**
1930   Chicago   25.

DORNBLASER, Thomas Franklin   **Sabre Strokes of the Pennsylvania Dragoons, in the War of 1861-1865.**
1884   Philadelphia   75.

EDMONDS, Howard O.   **Owen-Edmonds, Incidents of the American Civil War 1861-1865.**
1928   Chicago   40.

ELWOOD, John William   **Elwood's Stories of the Old Ringgold Cavalry.**
1914   Coal Center   100.

FALLER, Leo W. and John I.   **Dear Folks at Home, The Civil War Letters of _____.** edited by Milton E. Flower. Wraps
1963   Carlisle   20.

FARRAR, Samuel Clark   **The Twenty-Second Pennsylvania Cavalry and the Ringgold Battalion 1861-1865.**
1911   Pittsburgh   65.

FEATHERSTON, John C.   **Battle of the Crater, an Address.** Wraps
1906 (?)   n.p.   50.

FLEMING, George Thornton (ed)   **Life and Letters of Alexander Hays.**
1919   Pittsburgh   150.

FOERING, John O.   **Register of the Members of the "Artillery Corps Washington Grays" of the City of Philadelphia Who Served in the War of the Rebellion 1861-1865.**
1912   Philadelphia   25.

GALLOWAY, G. Norton   **The Ninety-Fifth Pennsylvania Volunteers in the Sixth Corps.** Wraps
1884   Philadelphia   75.

GHERST, M. A.   **A History of a Trip Across the Plains Made by Company A, 14th Pennsylvania Cavalry.** Wraps
1893   Pittsburgh   20.

GIBBS, James M.   **History of the First Battalion Pennsylvania Six Months Volunteers and 187th Regiment Pennsylvania Volunteer Infantry.**
1905   Harrisburg   50.

GIBSON, Joseph T. (ed)   **History of the 78th Pennsylvania Volunteer Infantry.**
1905   Pittsburgh   40.

GLOVER, Edwin A.   **Bucktailed Wildcats.**
1960   New York   30.

GORDON, Marquis Lafayette   **M. L. Gordon's Experiences in the Civil War.** edited by Donald Gordon.
1922   Boston   100.

GOULD, Joseph   **The Story of the Forty-Eighth.**
1908   Philadelphia   65.

GRACEY, Samuel L.   **Annals of the Sixth Pennsylvania Cavalry.**
1868   Philadelphia   100.

GREEN, Robert M.   **History of the One Hundred and Twenty-Fourth Regiment Pennsylvania Volunteers 1862-1863.**
1907   Philadelphia   50.

GREGG, John Chandler   **Life in the Army in the Departments of Virginia and the Gulf.**
1868   Philadelphia   30.

HARDIN, Martin D.   **History of the 12th Regiment Penna. Reserve Volunteer Corps.**
  1890   New York   90.
HARRIS, Wm. C.   **Prison Life in the Tobacco Warehouse at Richmond.**
  1862   Philadelphia   40.
HARROLD, John   **Libby, Andersonville, Florence, The Capture, Imprisonment, Escape and Rescue of** _____.
  1870   Philadelphia   50.
  1892   Atlantic City, New Jersey   40.
HASSON, B. F.   **Escape from the Confederacy.**
  1900   Bryant, Ohio   35.
HAYS, Alexander   **General Alexander Hays at the Battle of Gettysburg.** Wraps
  1913   Pittsburgh   20.
HAYS, Gilbert Adams (comp)   **Under the Red Patch: Story of the 63rd Regiment Pennsylvania Volunteers 1861-1865.**
  1908   Pittsburgh   75.
HILL, Archibald F.   **Our Boys.**
  1864   Philadelphia   30.
  1865   Philadelphia   25.
  1890   Philadelphia   25.
History and Roster of the Seventh Pa. Cavalry. Wraps
  1904   Pottsville   90.
History of the 18th Regiment of Cavalry, Pennsylvania Volunteers (163rd Regiment of the Line).
  1909   New York   75.
History of the 11th Pennsylvania Volunteer Cavalry.
  1902   Philadelphia   100.
History of the Fifty-Seventh Regiment, Pennsylvania Veteran Volunteer Infantry.
  1904   Meadville   125.
History of the 125th Regiment, Pa. Vols. 1862-1863.
  1906   Philadelphia   50.
  1907   Philadelphia   50.
History of the One Hundred Twenty-First Regiment Penn. Vols.
  1893   Philadelphia   50.
  1906   Philadelphia   50.
History of the 127th Regiment Pennsylvania Volunteers Familiarly Known as the "Dauphin County Regiment".
  1902   Lebanon   65.
History of the Third Pennsylvania Cavalry, 60th Regiment Pennsylvania Volunteers.
  1905   Philadelphia   90.
HITCHCOCK, Frederick L.   **War from the Inside; Story of the 132nd Pennsylvania Volunteer Infantry.**
  1904   Philadelphia   60.
HOFMANN, J. William   **Remarks on the Battle of Gettysburg.** Wraps
  1880   Philadelphia   20.
HUEY, Pennock   **A True History of the Charge of the Eighth Pennsylvania Cavalry at Chancellorsville.**
  1883   Philadelphia   50.
  1885   Philadelphia   40.
  1888   Philadelphia   40.
HUIDEKOPER, Henry S.   **Oration by General** _____ **at the Reunion of the Survivors of the 150th Regiment Pa. Vols. (Bucktails) at Gettysburg.** Wraps
  1894   n.p.   15.
HUYETTE, Miles Clayton   **The Maryland Campaign and the Battle of Antietam.**
  1915   Buffalo   35.
HYNDMAN, William   **History of a Cavalry Company, a Complete Record of Company A, 4th Penna. Cavalry.**
  1872   Philadelphia   85.

JACKSON, Samuel M.   **Diary of General _____ for the Year 1862.** Wraps
   1925   Apollo   50.
JOHNSTON, Adam S.   **The Soldier Boy's Diary Book.**
   1867   Pittsburgh   60.
JUDSON, Amos M.   **History of the 83rd Regiment Pennsylvania Volunteers.**
   1865   Erie   125.
KIEFER, William R.   **History of the 153rd Regiment Pennsylvania Volunteer . . . Infantry Northampton County.**
   1909   Easton   60.
KIEFFER, Henry M.   **The Recollections of a Drummer-Boy.**
   1883   Boston   25.
   1888   Boston   20.
   1889   Boston   20.
   1911   Boston   20.
KIRK, Charles H. (comp)   **History of the 15th Pennsylvania Volunteer Cavalry.**
   1906   Philadelphia   65.
LATTA, James W.   **History of the 1st Regiment Infantry National Guard . . . (Gray Reserves).**
   1912   Philadelphia   35.
LEONARD, Albert C.   **The Boys in Blue of 1861-65.**
   1904   Lancaster   20.
LEWIS, Osceola   **History of the 138th Regiment, Pennsylvania Volunteer Infantry.**
   1866   Norristown   50.
LLOYD, William P.   **History of the First Regiment Pennsylvania Reserve Cavalry.**
   1864   Philadelphia   65.
LOCKE, William H.   **The Story of the Regiment.**
   1868   Philadelphia   85.
McBRIDE, Robert E.   **In the Ranks; From the Wilderness to Appomattox Courthouse.**
   1881   Cincinnati   75.
McCALMONT, Alfred B.   **Extracts from Letters Written by Alfred B. McCalmont, Late Lt. Col., 142nd Regt.**
   1908   Franklin, Pa.   75.
MacCAULEY, Clay   **Through Chancellorsville Into and Out of Libby Prison.** Wraps
   1904   n.p.   30.
McDERMOTT, Anthony Wayne   **A Brief History of the 69th Regiment Pennsylvania Veteran Volunteers.**
   1889   Philadelphia   85.
MARK, Penrose G.   **Red, White and Blue Badge Pennsylvania Veteran Volunteers.**
   1911   Harrisburg   60.
MARKS, James Junius   **The Peninsular Campaign in Virginia.**
   1874   Philadelphia   35.
MARSHALL, D. Porter   **Company K, 155th Pa. Volunteer Zouaves.**
   1888   n.p.   125.
MERCHANT, Thomas E.   **Eighty-Fourth Regiment, Pennsylvania Volunteers.**
   1890   Philadelphia   60.
MOORE, James   **Kilpatrick and Our Cavalry.**
   1865   New York   30.
MOORE, John Hampton   **Baker at Ball's Bluff, An Address of _____ . . . Oct. 21, 1911.** Wraps
   n.d.   n.p.   40.
MOTT, Smith B.   **The Campaigns of the 52nd Regiment Penn. Volunteer Infantry, First Known as "The Luzerne Regiment".**
   1911   Philadelphia   55.
MOWRER, George H. (comp)   **History of the Organization and Service of Co. A, 14th Pennsylvania Cavalry.**
   189?   n.p.   85.

MOYER, Henry P. (comp) **History of the 17th Regt. Penna. Volunteer Cavalry.**
1911 Lebanon 65.

MUFFLY, Joseph W. (ed) **Story of Our Regiment; History of the 148th Pennsylvania Volunteers.**
1904 Des Moines 100.

MULHOLLAND, St. Clair A. **The American Volunteer.**
1909 Philadelphia 30.

MULHOLLAND, St. Clair A. **The Story of the 116th Regiment Pennsylvania Infantry.**
1903 Philadelphia 75.

MYERS, John C. **A Daily Journal of the 192nd Regiment Pennsylvania Volunteers.**
1864 Philadelphia 60.

NELSON, Alanson H. **The Battles of Chancellorsville and Gettysburg.**
1899 Minneapolis 40.

NESBIT, John W. **General History of Company D, 149th Pennsylvania Volunteers.**
1908 Oakdale, Calif. 110.

NEWHALL, Frederic C. **With General Sheridan in Lee's Last Campaign.**
1866 Philadelphia 50.

NEWHALL, Walter S. **A Memoir.**
1864 Philadelphia 40.

NIEBAUM, John H. **History of the Pittsburgh Washington Infantry. 102nd (Old 13th) Regiment Pennsylvania Veteran Volunteers.**
1931 Pittsburgh 65.

NORTON, Oliver Willcox **Army Letters 1861-1865 Being Extracts from Private Letters.**
1903 Chicago 100.

NORTON, Oliver Willcox **The Attack and Defense of Little Round Top.**
1913 New York 60.

NORTON, Oliver Willcox **Strong Vincent and His Brigade at Gettysburg July 2, 1863.**
1909 Chicago 30.

OBREITER, John **The 77th Pennsylvania at Shiloh.**
1905 Harrisburg 35.
1908 Harrisburg 35.

ORWIG, Joseph R. **History of the 131st Pennsylvania Volunteers.**
1902 Williamsport 65.

PALMER, William J. **Letters, 1853-1868.** Compiled by Isaac H. Clothier.
1906 Philadelphia 75.

PARKER, Thomas H. **History of the 51st Regiment of Pennsylvania Volunteers and Veteran Volunteers.**
1869 Philadelphia 90.

PAXTON, John R. **Sword and Gown.** edited by Calvin D. Wilson.
1926 New York 25.

PHILLIPS, John Wilson **The Civil War Diary of _____.** edited by Robert G. Athearn. Wraps
1954 Virginia 15.

PLEASANTS, Henry, Jr. and **STRALEY,** George H. **Inferno at Petersburg.**
1961 Philadelphia 20.

PLEASANTS, Henry **The Tragedy of the Crater.**
1938 Boston 30.

PRICE, Isaiah **History of the Ninety-Seventh Regiment, Pennsylvania Volunteer Infantry, During the War of the Rebellion 1861-65.**
1875 Philadelphia 75.

PRICE, Isaiah **Reunion of the 97th Regiment Pa. Vols. Oct. 29th, 1884 . . . West Chester, Pa.**
1884 Philadelphia 25.

PROWELL, George R.   **History of the 87th Regiment Pennsylvania Volunteers.**
  1901   York   85.

RAUCH, William H. (comp)   **Pennsylvania Reserve Volunteer Corps: "Round-Up".**
  1903   Philadelphia   15.

RAUSCHER, Frank   **Music on the March 1862-65 With the Army of the Potomac 114th Regt. P.V. Collis' Zouaves.**
  1892   Philadelphia   85.

RAWLE, William Brooke   **Gregg's Cavalry Fight at Gettysburg . . . Address.** Wraps
  1884   Philadelphia   40.

RAWLE, William Brooke   **The Right Flank at Gettysburg, An Account of the Operations of General Gregg's Cavalry Command.** Wraps
  1878   Philadelphia   35.

RAWLE, William Brooke   **With Gregg in the Gettysburg Campaign.** Wraps
  1884   Philadelphia   40.

REED, John A and **DICKEY,** L. S.   **History of the 101st Regiment Pennsylvania Veteran Volunteer Infantry 1861-1865.**
  1910   Chicago   45.

RICHARDS, Henry M. M.   **Pennsylvania's Emergency Men at Gettysburg. A Touch of Bushwhacking.** Wraps
  1895   Reading   35.

ROBERTS, A. L.   **As They Remembered: The Story of the 45th Penna. Vet. Vol. Inf. Regt. 1861-65.** Wraps
  1964   New York   15.

ROSE, Thomas Ellwood   **Col. Rose's Story of the Famous Tunnel Escape from Libby Prison.** Wraps
  n.d.   n.p.   25.

ROWE, David W.   **A Sketch of the 126th Regiment Pennsylvania Volunteers.**
  Wraps
  1869   Chambersburg   60.

ROWELL, John W.   **Yankee Cavalrymen: Through the Civil War with the Ninth Pennsylvania Cavalry.**
  1971   Knoxville   35.

ROY, Andrew   **Recollections of a Prisoner of War.**
  1905   Columbus   60.
  1909   Columbus   45.

RUDISILL, James J.   **The Day of Our Abraham, 1811-1899.**
  1936   York, Pa.   Ltd.   40.

SCOTT, James K. P.   **The Story of the Battles at Gettysburg.**
  1927   Harrisburg   25.

SCOTT, Kate M.   **History of the 105th Regiment of Pennsylvania Volunteers.**
  1877   Philadelphia   110.

SELLERS, Alfred J.   **Reunions of the Survivors of the 90th Pa. Vol. Inf. on the Battlefield of Gettysburg Sept. 2 & 3, 1888 and Sept. 1 & 2, 1889.** Wraps
  1889   Philadelphia   50.

SETTLE, William S.   **History of the Third Pennsylvania Heavy Artillery and One Hundred and Eighty-eighth Pa. Vol. Infantry.** Wraps
  1886   Lewistown   100.

SIPES, William B.   **The 7th Pennsylvania Veteran Volunteer Cavalry.**
  1906   Pottsville   85.

The Sixty-Second Pennsylvania Volunteers in the War for the Union. Wraps
  1889   Pittsburgh   60.

SMITH, John L.   **Antietam to Appomattox with the 118th Pa. Volunteers.**
  1892   Philadelphia   60.

SMITH, John L. (comp)   **History of the Corn Exchange Regiment, 118th Pennsylvania Volunteers.**
  1888   Philadelphia   60.

SMITH, John L.   **History of the 118th Pennsylvania Volunteers — the Corn Exchange Regiment.**
  1905   Philadelphia   40.

SPANGLER, Edward W.   **My Little War Experience with Historical Sketches and Memorabilia.**
  1904   York   40.
SPEESE, Andrew J.   **Story of Companies H, A, and C, 3rd Pa. Cavalry at Gettysburg, July 3, 1863.**
  1906   Germantown   50.
SPRENGER, George F.   **Concise History of the Camp and Field Life of the 122nd Regiment Penna. Volunteers.**
  1885   Lancaster   85.
STAFFORD, David W.   **In Defense of the Flag, A True War Story.** Wraps
  1912   Warren   30.
  1915   Warren   25.
STEWART, Alexander M.   **Camp, March and Battlefield.**
  1865   Philadelphia   60.
STEWART, Robert L.   **History of the 140th Regiment, Pennsylvania Volunteers.**
  1912   Philadelphia   65.
STRANG, Edgar B.   **General Stoneman's Raid, or The Amusing Side of Army Life.** Wraps
  1911   Philadelphia   30.
SYPHER, Josiah R. (comp)   **History of the Pennsylvania Reserve Corps.**
  1865   Lancaster   65.
THOMAS, Hampton S.   **Some Personal Reminiscences of Service in the Cavalry of the Army of the Potomac.** Wraps
  1889   Philadelphia   60.
THOMPSON, Heber S.   **Diary of _____ 7th Penna Cavalry.** Wraps
  191?   Pottsville   40.
THOMPSON, Heber S.   **The First Defenders.**
  1910   n.p.   65.
THOMSON, O. R. and **RAUCH,** W. H.   **History of the "Bucktails" Kane Rifle Regiment of the Pennsylvania Reserve Corps.**
  1906   Philadelphia   75.
Under the Maltese Cross, Antietam to Appomattox, The Loyal Uprising in Western Pennsylvania.
  1910   Pittsburgh   125.
URBAN, John W.   **Battle Field and Prison Pen.**
  1882   Philadelphia   40.
URBAN, John W.   **In Defense of the Union: or Through Shot and Shell and Prison Pen.**
  1887   n.p.   20.
VALE, Joseph G.   **Minty and the Cavalry.**
  1886   Harrisburg   110.
VANDERSLICE, Catherine H.   **The Civil War Letters of George Washington Beidelman**
  1978   New York   15.
VANSCOTEN, M. H.   **The Conception, Organization and Campaigns of Company "H" 4th Penn. Reserves.** compiled by Mrs. M. H. France.
  1883   Tunkhannock   90.
  1885   Tunkhannock   90.
VAUTIER, John D.   **History of the 88th Pennsylvania Volunteers.**
  1894   Philadelphia   110.
WARD, George W.   **History of the 2nd Pennsylvania Veteran Heavy Artillery.**
  1904   Philadelphia   60.
WARD, Joseph R. C.   **History of the 106th Regiment Pennsylvania Volunteers, 2nd Brigade, 2nd Division, 2nd Corps.**
  1883   Philadelphia   75.
  1906   Philadelphia   70.
WARD, Lester F.   **Young Ward's Diary.** edited by B. J. Stern.
  1935   New York   45.

WARREN, H. N.   **Declaration of Independence and War History, Bull Run to Appomattox.**
    1894   Buffalo, New York   55.
WARREN, Horatio N.   **Two Reunions of the 142nd Regiment Penna. Vols.**
    1890   Buffalo   50.
WEAVER, Ethan Allen   **Owen Rice, Christian, Scholar and Patriot, A Genealogical and Historical Memoir.** Wraps
    1911   Germantown   30.
WEBB, Alexander S.   **An Address Delivered at Gettysburg . . .At the Dedication of the Monument, 72nd Pa. Vols.** Wraps
    1883   Philadelphia   30.
WESTBROOK, Robert S.   **History of the 49th Pennsylvania Volunteers.**
    1898   Altoona   90.
WHISTLER, French and Kirk   **130th Regiment, Penna. Vol. Inf. at Antietam Dedication of the Monument to the Regiment on the Antietam Battlefield on Sept 17, 1904.** Wraps
    n.d.   n.p.   20.
WILLIAMS, John A. B.   **Leaves from a Trooper's Diary.**
    1869   Philadelphia   35.
WILSON, Suzanne Colton (comp)   **Column South with the 15th Penn. Cavalry.**
    1960   Flagstaff   45.
WISTAR, Isaac Jones   **Autobiography of _____ 1827-1905.**
    1937   New York   30.
WOODWARD, Evan M.   **History of the 198th Pennsylvania Volunteers.**
    1884   Trenton   60.
WOODWARD, Evan M.   **History of the 3rd Pennsylvania Reserve.**
    1883   Trenton   70.
WOODWARD, Evan M.   **Our Campaigns.**
    1865   Philadelphia   30.
WRAY, William J.   **History of the 23rd Pennsylvania Volunteer Infantry, Birney's Zouaves.**
    1904   Philadelphia   85.
YOUNG, Jesse Bowman   **The Battle of Gettysburg.**
    1913   New York   30.
    1976   Dayton   17.50
YOUNG, Jesse Bowman   **What a Boy Saw in the Army.**
    1894   New York   30.

RHODE ISLAND

GENERAL REFERENCES

Annual Report of Adjutant General of Rhode Island.
    1862   Wraps   20.
    1863   Wraps   20.
    1865   2 vols.   30.
BARKER, Harold R.   **History of the Rhode Island Combat Units in the Civil War.** edited by A. Gurney.
    1964   n.p.   35.
BARTLETT, John R.   **Memoirs of Rhode Island Officers Who Were Engaged in the Service of Their Country During the Great Rebellion.**
    1867   Providence   45.
DYER, Elisha   **Official Register of Rhode Island Officers and Men Who Served in the U. S. Army & Navy from 1861 to 1866.** 2 vols.
    1893-1895   Providence   100.
Rhode Island, Report of the Joint Special Comm. on Erection of Monument at Andersonville, Ga.
    1903   Providence   20.

REGIMENTALS

ALDRICH, Thomas M.   **The History of Battery A, First Regiment Rhode Island Light Artillery.**
1904   Providence   55.

ALLEN, George H.   **Forty-Six Months with the 4th Rhode Island Volunteers.**
1887   Providence   75.

BURLINGAME, John K.   **History of the Fifth Regiment of Rhode Island Heavy Artillery During 3½ Years of Service in North Carolina.**
1892   Providence   60.

CHASE, Philip S.   **Battery F, First Regiment Rhode Island Light Artillery in the Civil War, 1861-1865.**
1892   Providence   Ltd.   90.

CHENERY, William H.   **The Fourteenth Regiment Rhode Island Heavy Artillery (Colored) in the War to Preserve the Union.**
1898   Providence   60.
1969   New York   20.

DENISON, Frederic   **Sabres and Spurs, The First Regiment Rhode Island Cavalry.**
1876   Central Falls   85.

DENISON, Frederic   **Shot and Shell, The Third Rhode Island Heavy Artillery in the Rebellion, 1861-1865.**
1879   Providence   65.

FENNER, Earl   **The History of Battery H, First Regiment Rhode Island Light Artillery.**
1894   Providence   50.

GRANT, Joseph W.   **The Flying Regiment. Journal of the Campaign of the 12th Regiment Rhode Island Volunteers.**
1865   Providence   60.

GRANT, Joseph W.   **My First Campaign**
1863   Boston   50.

HEYSINGER, Isaac W.   **Antietam and the Maryland and Virginia Campaigns of 1862.**
1912   New York   75.

History of the Organization of the First Light Infantry Veteran Association of Providence, R.I. with a Roster of the Association. Vol. I. (all pub.)
1870   Providence (?)   25.

HOPKINS, William P.   **The Seventh Regiment, Rhode Island Volunteers.**
1903   Providence   65.

LEWIS, George   **The History of Battery E, First Regiment Rhode Island Light Artillery.**
1892   Providence   65.

Memorial of Colonel John Stanton Slocum, First Colonel of the 2nd Rhode Island Vols. Who Fell in the Battle of Bull Run, Va. July 21, 1861.
1886   Providence   25.

MOWRY, William A.   **Camp Life in the Civil War Eleventh R. I. Infantry.** Wraps
1914   Boston   35.

NICKERSON, Ansel D.   **A Raw Recruit's War Experiences.**
1888   Providence   Ltd.   30.

PETTENGILL, Samuel B.   **The College Cavaliers.**
1883   Chicago   25.

POORE, Ben Perley   **The Life and Public Services of Ambrose E. Burnside.**
1882   Providence   25.

REICHARDT, Theodore   **Diary of Battery A, First Regiment Rhode Island Light Artillery.**
1865   Providence   75.

RHODES, John H.   **The History of Battery B, First Regiment Rhode Island Light Artillery.**
1894   Providence   75.

SABRE, Gilbert E.   **Nineteen Months a Prisoner of War.**
    1865   New York   35.
SPICER, William A.   **History of the 9th and 10th Regiments Rhode Island Volunteers and the 10th Rhode Island Battery.**
    1892   Providence   45.
STONE, Edwin M.   **Rhode Island in the Rebellion, Battery C, First R.I. Light Artillery.**
    1864   Providence   35.
SUMNER, George C.   **Battery D, First Rhode Island Light Artillery in the Civil War, 1861-1865.**
    1897   Providence   45
THOMPSON, John C.   **History of the Eleventh Regiment Rhode Island Volunteers by R. W. Rock.**
    1881   Providence   55.
TILLINGHAST, Pardon Elisha   **History of the Twelfth Regiment Rhode Island Volunteers in the Civil War 1862-1865.**
    1904   Providence   60.
WOODBURY, Augustus   **Ambrose Everett Burnside.**
    1867   Providence   25.
WOODBURY, Augustus   **A Narrative of the Campaign of the 1st Rhode Island Regiment in the Spring and Summer in 1861.**
    1862   Providence   35.
WOODBURY, Augustus   **The Second Rhode Island Regiment. A Narrative of Military Operations.**
    1875   Providence   50.
WYMAN, Lillie B. C.   **A Grand Army Man (Augustine A. Mann) of Rhode Island.**
    1925   Newton   Ltd.   25.

SOUTH CAROLINA

GENERAL REFERENCES

ABBOTT, Martin   **The Freedmen's Bureau in South Carolina 1865-1872.**
    1967   Chapel Hill   20.
The Address of the People of South Carolina Assembled in Convention to the People of the Slaveholding States of the United States. Wraps
    1860   Charleston   50.
ALLEN, Walter   **Governor Chamberlain's Administration in South Carolina.**
    1888   New York   50.
BALL, William Watts   **The State that Forgot. South Carolina's Surrender to Democracy.**
    1932   Indianapolis   20.
CALDWELL, J. F. J.   **History of a Brigade of South Carolinians, Known First as "Gregg's" and Subsequently as "McGowan's Brigade".**
    1866   Philadelphia   500.
    1951   Marietta   35.
CAUTHEN, Charles E. (ed)   **Journals of the South Carolina Executive Councils of 1861 and 1862.**
    1956   Columbia   30.
CAUTHEN, Charles E.   **South Carolina Goes to War 1860-1865.** Wraps
    1950   Chapel Hill   30.
Ceremonies at the Unveiling of the South Carolina Monument on the Chickamauga Battlefield, May 27, 1901. Wraps
    n.d.   n.p.   25.
CHANNING, Steven A.   **Crisis of Fear, Secession in South Carolina.**
    1970   New York   20.
COXE, Elizabeth Allen   **Memories of a South Carolina Plantation During the War.**
    1912   n.p.   80.

DAVIS, Nora M. (comp)   **Military and Naval Operations in South Carolina 1860-1865.** Wraps
 1959   Columbia   10.
DICKERT, D. Augustus   History of Kershaw's Brigade.
 1899   Newberry   750.
 1973   Dayton   25.
Hampton Legion Survivors, Minutes of the Proceedings of the Reunion, Held in Columbia, S. C. Wraps
 1875   Charleston   35.
HOLLIS, John Porter   **The Early Period of Reconstruction in South Carolina.** Wraps
 1905   Baltimore   25.
JERVEY, Theodore D.   **Charleston During the Civil War.** Wraps
 1915   Washington   15.
LANDRUM, J. B. O.   **History of Spartanburg County.**
 1954   Spartanburg   30.
MAY, John Amasa and **FAUNT,** Joan Reynolds   **South Carolina Secedes.**
 1960   Columbia   30.
PIKE, James S.   **The Prostrate State. South Carolina Under Negro Government.**
 1935   New York   30.
REYNOLDS, John S.   **Reconstruction in South Carolina 1865-1877.**
 1905   Columbia   80.
 1969   New York   20.
SALLEY, Alexander S., Jr.   **South Carolina Troops in Confederate Service.** 3 vols.
 1913-1930   Columbia   350.
 Vol. I only   60.
 Vol. II only   200.
 Vol. III only   60.
SIMKINS, Francis B. and **WOODY,** Robert Hilliard   **South Carolina During Reconstruction.**
 1932   Chapel Hill   40.
SMYTHE, POPPENHEIM & TAYLOR (eds)   **South Carolina Women in the Confederacy.** 2 vols.
 1903 & 1907   150.
Suggestions as to Arming the State. Wraps
 1860   Charleston   100.
THOMPSON, Henry T.   **Ousting the Carpetbagger from South Carolina.**
 1926   Columbia   100.
 1926   Columbia   100.
War Records, South Carolina College Cadets in the War. Wraps
 1908   Columbia   25.
WILLIAMSON, Joel   **After Slavery, The Negro in South Carolina During Reconstruction 1861-1877.**
 1967   Chapel Hill   25.

REGIMENTALS

Andrews, Robert W.   **The Life and Adventures of Capt. Robert W. Andrews, of Sumter, South Carolina.** Wraps
 1887   Boston   50.
ANDREWS, W. J.   **Sketch of Co. K, 23rd South Carolina Volunteers.** Wraps
 n.d.   n.p.   Reprint   15.
BLACK, John Logan   **Crumbling Defenses, or Memoirs and Reminiscences of** _____
 1960   Macon   50.
BOYKIN, E. M.   **The Falling Flag.**
 1874   New York   225.

BOYKIN, Richard Manning   **Captain Alexander Hamilton Boykin One of South Carolina's Distinguished Citizens.**
1942   New York   Ltd.   50.
BROWN, Varina Davis   **A Colonel at Gettysburg and Spotsylvania.**
1931   Columbia   50.
Carolina Rifle Club, The Presentation of the Battle Flag of the Tenth Regiment, S.C.V., C.S.A. June 12,, 1875. Wraps
1875   Charleston   40.
COKER, James Lide   **History of Company G., Ninth S. C. Regiment, Infantry S.C. Army and Company E, Sixth S. C. Regiment, Infantry, S. C. Army.**
n.d.   n.p.   reprint   15.
DALY, Louise H.   **Alexander Cheves Haskell, The Portrait of a Man.**
1934   Norwood   Ltd.   250.
EMANUEL, S.   **Historical Sketch of the Georgetown Rifle Guards.** Wraps
1909   Georgetown   100.
FORD, Arthur P.   **Life in the Confederate Army, Being Personal Experiences of a Private Soldier in the Confederate Army. Published and bound with FORD,** Marion Johnstone   **Some Experiences and Sketches of Southern Life.**
1905   New York   150.
GASTON, John Thomas   **Confederate War Diary of** _____ edited by Allifaire (Allie) Gaston Walden. Wraps
1960   Columbia   30.
HUDSON, Joshua Hilary   **Sketches and Reminiscences.**
1903   Columbia   50.
IZLAR, William Valmore   **A Sketch of the War Record of the Edisto Rifles 1861-1865.**
1914   Columbia   125.
This title is usually quite stained, probably due to a mishap in storage after printing.
KERSHAW, Miss C. D. (comp)   **Richard Kirkland, C.S.A.** Wraps
1910   Camden   75.
McCRADY, Edward, Jr.   **Formation, Organization, Discipline and Characteristics of the Army of Northern Virginia: An Address.** Wraps
1886   Richmond   40.
McCRADY, Edward   **Gregg's Brigade of South Carolinians in the Second Battle of Manassas, An Address.** Wraps
1885   Richmond   80.
MIXSON, Frank M.   **Reminiscences of a Private.**
1910   Columbia   350.
PLOWDEN, John Covert   **The Letters of Private** _____ **1862-1865.** edited by Henry B. Rollins. Wraps
1970   Sumter   30.
PORTER, A. Toomer   **Led on: Step by Step.**
1898   New York   40.
Public Ceremonies in Connection with the War Memorials of the Washington Light Infantry with the Orations of Hampton, Simonton, and Porter. Wraps
1894   Charleston   30.
REID, Jesse W.   **History of the 4th Regiment of South Carolina Volunteers.**
1892   Greenville   Wraps   200.
1975   Dayton   12.50
Rolls of the Washington Light Infantry in Confederate Service. Wraps
1888   Charleston   50.
TAYLOR, John S.   **Sixteenth South Carolina Regiment CSA from Greenville County, S.C.** Wraps
1964   n.p.   25.
Tentative Roster of the Third Regiment, South Carolina Volunteers, Confederate States Provisional Army. edited by A. S. Salley, Jr. Wraps
1908   Columbia   40.

WALKER, C. Irvine   **Rolls and Historical Sketch of the Tenth Regiment, So. Ca. Volunteers.**
1881   Charleston   350.
WELCH, Spencer Glasgow   **A Confederate Surgeon's Letters to His Wife.**
1954   Marietta   30.
WELLS, Edward L.   **A Sketch of the Charleston Light Dragoons.** Wraps
1888   Charleston   75.

TENNESSEE

GENERAL REFERENCES

ALEXANDER, Thomas B.   **Political Reconstruction in Tennessee.**
1950   Nashville   25.
ALLEN, V. C.   **Rhea and Meigs Counties (Tennessee) in the Confederate War.**
1908   n.p.   75.
Biographical Sketches and Pictures of Company B, Confederate Veterans of Nashville, Tenn. Wraps
1902   Nashville   15.
BLANKENSHIP, Lela McDowell   **When Yesterday Was Today.**
1966   Nashville   20.
CAMPBELL, Mary Emily Robertson   **The Attitude of Tennesseans Toward the Union.**
1961   New York   20.
EVANS, Clement A. (ed)   **Confederate Military History, Vol. VIII — Tennessee.**
1899   Atlanta   40.
FERGUSON, Edwin L.   **Sumner County, Tennessee in the Civil War.**
1972   Tompkinsville   25.
FORRESTER, Rebel C.   **Glory and Tears, Obion County, Tennessee 1860-1870.**
1966   Union City   20.
GARRETT, Jill K. (ed)   **Confederate Soldiers and Patriots of Maury County Tenn.**
1970   Columbia   25.
GOVAN, Gilbert E. and **LIVINGOOD,** James W.   **Chattanooga Under Military Occupation 1863-1865.** Wraps
1951   n.p.   10.
HALE, Will T.   **History of DeKalb County Tennessee.**
1969   McMinnville   20.
HORN, Stanley F. (comp & ed)   **Tennessee's War 1861-65 Described by Participants.**
1965   Nashville   30.
HUDDLESTON, Ed   **The Civil War in Middle Tennessee.**
1965   Nashville   25.
HUMES, Thomas William   **The Loyal Mountaineers of Tennessee.**
1888   Knoxville   100.
LINDSLEY, John B.   **Military Annals of Tennessee, Confederate.**
1886   Nashville   150.
MATHES, J. Harvey   **The Old Guard in Gray.**
1897   Memphis   125.
RENNOLDS, Edwin H.   **A History of the Henry County Commands Which Served in the Confederate States Army.**
1904   Jacksonville   500.
1961   Kennesaw   30.
TEMPLE, Oliver P.   **East Tennessee and the Civil War.**
1899   Cincinnati   100.
1972   Knoxville   Ltd.   25.
Tennesseans in the Civil War, A Military History of Confederate and Union Units with Available Rosters of Personnel. 2 parts
1964-5   Nashville   100.

WILLIAMS, Emma Inman   **Historic Madison, The Story of Jackson County, Tenn.**
    1946   Jackson   50.
WRIGHT, Marcus J.   **Tennessee in the War.**
    1908   New York   40.

REGIMENTALS

Union

CARTER, William Randolph   **History of the 1st Regiment of Tennessee Volunteer Cavalry.**
    1902   Knoxville   150.
RAGAN, Robert A.   **Escape from East Tennessee to the Federal Lines.**
    1910   Washington   50.
RULE, William   **The Loyalists of Tennessee in the Late War: A Paper . . .1887.** Wraps
    1887   Cincinnati   25.
SCOTT, Samuel W. and **ANGEL,** Samuel P.   **History of the Thirteenth Regiment, Tenn. Volunteer Cavalry, U.S.A.**
    1903   Philadelphia   100.
    1973   Blountville   35.

Confederate

CAMPBELL, Andrew Jackson   **The Civil War Diary of _____ .** edited by Jill Knight Garrett. Wraps
    1965   Columbia   25.
CANNON, Newton   **The Reminiscences of Sergeant _____ .** edited by Campbell H. Brown. Wraps
    1963   Franklin   15.
CLARK, C. W., Jr.   **My Grandfather's Diary of the War, Carrol H. Clark, Co. I, 16th Regiment, Tenn. Vols. C.S.A.** Wraps
    1963   n.p.   30.
COPLEY, John M.   **A Sketch of the Battle of Franklin, Tenn.**
    1893   Austin   100.
FAY, Edwin H.   **"This Infernal War" The Confederate Letters of Sgt. _____ .** edited by Bell Wiley & Lucy Fay.
    1958   Austin   35.
GUILD, George B.   **A Brief Narrative of the Fourth Tennessee Cavalry Regiment.**
    1913   Nashville   250.
HANCOCK, Richard R.   **Hancock's Diary; or, A History of the 2nd Tennessee Cavalry.** 2 vols. in 1.
    1887   Nashville   175.
HEAD, Thomas A.   **Campaigns and Battles of the 16th Regiment Tennessee Volunteers.**
    1885   Nashville   85.
    1961   McMinnville   45.
HUBBARD, John M.   **Notes of a Private.**
    1909   Memphis   100.
    1911   St. Louis   75.
    1913   St. Louis   60.
    1973   n.p.   20.
McLEARY, A. C.   **Humorous Incidents of the Civil War.** Wraps
    1903 (?)   n.p.   75.
McMURRAY, William Josiah   **History of the 20th Tennessee Regiment Volunteer Infantry, C.S.A.**
    1904   Nashville   100.
    1976   Nashville   20.
MALONE, Thomas H.   **Memoir of _____ .**
    1928   Nashville   150.

QUINTARD, Charles T.   **Doctor Quintard, Chaplain C.S.A.** edited by Arthur H. Noll.
    1905   Sewanee   250.
SULLINS, David   **Recollections of an Old Man Seventy Years in Dixie 1827-1897.**
    1910   Bristol   75.
TONEY, Marcus B.   **The Privations of a Private.**
    1905   Nashville   125.
    1907   Nashville   100.
VAUGHAN, Alfred J.   **Personal Record of the Thirteenth Regiment, Tenn. Infantry C.S.A. by Its Old Commander.**
    1897   Memphis   150.
    1975   Brentwood   Ltd.   20.
WATKINS, Sam R.   **"Co. Aytch" Maury Grays First Tennessee Regiment.**
    1882   Nashville   500.
    1900   Chattanooga   300.
    1952   Jackson   edited by Bell I. Wiley   30.
    1982   Dayton   20.
WOMACK, James J.   **Civil War Diary of Capt _____, Co. E 16th Tenn. C.S.A.** Wraps
    1961   McMinnville   25.
WORSHAM, William J.   **The Old Nineteenth Tennessee Regiment,**
    1902   Knoxville   300.
    1973   Blountville   35.
YOUNG, John P.   **The Seventh Tennessee Cavalry (Confederate) A History.**
    1890   Nashville   275.
    1976   Dayton   17.50

TEXAS

GENERAL REFERENCES

ASHCRAFT, Allan C.   **Texas in the Civil War: A Resume History.** Wraps
    1962   Austin   10.
ASKEW, H. G.   **2nd Texas Brigade, United Confederate Veterans.**
    1916   Austin   25.
BARR, Alwyn   **Polignac's Texas Brigade.** Wraps
    1964   Houston   15.
BEARSS, Edwin C.   **Texas at Vicksburg.** Wraps
    1971   Austin   10.
A Brief and Condensed History of Parsons Texas Cavalry Brigade.
    1962   Waco   Ltd.   35.
EVANS, Clement A. (ed)   **Confederate Military History, Vol XI — Texas and Florida.**
    1899   Atlanta   40.
FARBER, James   **Fort Worth in the Civil War.**
    1960   Belton   15.
FARBER, James   **Texas, C.S.A. A Spotlight on Disaster.**
    1947   New York   30.
A Few Historic Records of the Church in the Diocese of Texas During the Rebellion, Together with a Correspondence Between Rt. Rev. Alexander Gregg and the Rev. Charles Gillette. Wraps
    1865   New York   40.
FITZHUGH, Lester N. (comp)   **Texas Batteries, Battalions, Regiments, Commanders and Field Officers, C.S.A. 1861-1865.** Wraps
    1959   Midlothian   20.

GALLOWAY, B. P. (ed)   **Dark Corner of the Confederacy, Accounts of Civil War Texas.** Wraps
    1968   Dubuque   10.
HALL, Martin Hardwick   **The Confederate Army of New Mexico.**
    1978   Austin   30.
HAMILTON, A. J.   **Speech . . . at the War Meeting at Faneuil Hall, April 1863.** Wraps
    1863   Boston   75.
HAMILTON, A. J.   **Address . . .to the People of Texas.** Wraps
    1864   New Orleans   250.
HENDERSON, Harry McCorry   **Texas in the Confederacy.**
    1955   San Antonio   30.
JOHNSON, Sidney Smith   **Texans Who Wore the Gray. Vol. I** (all published)
    1907   Tyler   275.
Journal of the Secession Convention of Texass 1861. Wraps
    1912   Austin   30.
KELLEY, Dayton   **The Texas Brigade at the Wilderness, May 6, 1864.**
    n.d.   Gatesville   Ltd.   25.
KERR, Homer   **Fighting with Ross' Texas Cavalry Brigade, C.S.A.**
    1976   Hillsboro   15.
NORTH, Thomas   **Five Years in Texas.**
    1870   Cincinnati   200.
    1871   Cincinnati   125.
PIERCE, Gerald S.   **Texas Under Arms.**
    1969   Austin   Ltd.   40.
POLLEY, J. B.   **Hood's Texas Brigade.**
    1910   New York/Washington   800.
    1976   Dayton   22.50
RAMSDELL, Charles W.   **Reconstruction in Texas.** Wraps
    1910   New York   125.
RAMSEY, Grover C.   **Confederate Postmasters in Texas.** Wraps
    1963   Waco   Ltd.   25.
RICHARDSON, Rupert N.   **The Frontier of Northwest Texas 1846 to 1876.**
    1963   Glendale   25.
ROBERTSON, Jerome B.   **Touched with Valor, Civil War Papers and Casualty Reports of Hood's Texas Brigade.** edited by Harold B. Simpson.
    1964   Hillsboro   25.
ROSE, Victor M.   **Ross' Texas Brigade.**
    1881   Louisville   1400.
    1960   Kennesaw   30.
SIMPSON, Harold B.   **Hood's Texas Brigade: A Compendium.**
    1977   Hillsboro   16.
    Ltd. edition   125.
SIMPSON, Harold B. (ed)   **Hood's Texas Brigade In Poetry and Song.**
    1968   Hillsboro   20.
SIMPSON, Harold B.   **Hood's Texas Brigade in Reunion and Memory.**
    1974   Hillsboro   25.
    1974   Hillsboro   Ltd. Edition of 25 copies   125.
SIMPSON, Harold B.   **Hood's Texas Brigade: Lee's Grenadier Guard.**
    1970   Waco   40.
SIMPSON, Harold B.   **Red Granite for Gray Heroes.**
    1969   Hillsboro   Ltd.   Boxed   35.
WINKLER, Angelina V.   **The Confederate Capital and Hood's Texas Brigade.**
    1894   Austin   300.
WINSOR, Bill   **Texas in the Confederacy.**
    1978   Hillsboro   15.
WOOD, W. D.   **A Partial Roster of the Officers and Man Raised in Leon County, Texas, for the Service of the Confederate States.**
    1963   Waco   Ltd.   25.

WRIGHT, Marcus J.   **Texas in the Civil War 1861-1865.** edited by Harold B. Simpson.
1965   Hillsboro   25.
YEARY, Mamie (comp)   **Reminiscences of the Boys in Gray 1861-1865.**
1912   Dallas   325.

REGIMENTALS

ANDERSON, John Q. (ed)   **Campaigning with Parsons' Texas Cavalry, C.S.A. The War Journal and Letters of the Four Orr Brothers 12th Texas Cavalry Regiment.**
1967   Hillsboro   15.
BARRON, Samuel B.   **The Lone Star Defenders, A Chronicle of the 3rd Texas Cavalry, Ross' Brigade.**
1908   New York   1400.
1964   Waco   25.
BARZIZA, Decimus et Ultimus   **Adventures of a Prisoner of War.**
1865   Houston   3500.
1964   Austin   25.
BATCHELOR, Benjamin F.   **Batchelor-Turner Letters 1861-1864 Written by Two of Terry's Texas Rangers.** annotated by H. J. H. Rugeley. Wraps
1961   Austin   25.
BITTON, Davis (ed)   **The Reminiscences and Civil War Letters of Levi Lamoni Wight.**
1970   Salt Lake City   30.
BLACKBURN, James K. P.   **Reminiscences of the Terry Rangers.** Wraps
1919   Austin   70.
1979   Austin   10.
BLESSINGTON, Joseph P.   **The Campaigns of Walker's Texas Division by a Private Soldier.**
1875   New York   300.
1968   Austin   30.
COLLINS, R. M.   **Chapters from the Unwritten History of the War Between the States.**
1893   St. Louis   250.
1982   Dayton   30.
DAVIS, Nicholas A.   **The Campaign from Texas to Maryland, with The Battle of Fredericksburg.**
1863   Richmond   See: **Confederate Imprints**
1961   Austin   Boxed   30.
DAVIS, Nicholas A.   **Chaplain Davis & Hood's Texas Brigade.** edited by Donald E. Everett.
1962   San Antonio   25.
DEBRAY, Xavier B.   **A Sketch of the History of Debray's 26th Regiment of Texas Cavalry.** Wraps
1961   Waco   25.
D'HAMEL, Enrique B.   **The Adventures of a Tenderfoot.** Wraps
1965   Waco   Ltd.   10.
DODD, Ephraim Shelby   **Diary of _____ .** Wraps
1914   Austin   125.
1979   Austin   10.
DOUGLAS, Lucia Rutherford (ed)   **Douglas' Texas Battery, C.S.A.**
1966   Tyler   30 .
DUAINE, Carl L.   **The Dead Men Wore Boots: An Account of the 32nd Texas Volunteer Cavalry.**
1966   Austin   20.
FITZHUGH, Lester N.   **Terry's Texas Rangers, 8th Texas Cavalry, C.S.A.** Wraps
1958   Dallas   15.

FLETCHER, William Andrew   **Rebel Private Front and Rear: Experiences and Observations.**
  1908   Beaumont   1400.
  Most of the edition was destroyed by fire. Surviving copies are usually smoked.
  1954   Austin   30.
FOSTER, Samuel T.   **One of Cleburne's Command, the Civil War Reminiscences and Diary of Capt. _____ , Granbury's Texas Brigade.** edited by Norman D. Brown.
  1980   Austin   15.
GARRETT, David R.   **The Civil War Letters of _____ , Detailing the Adventures of the 6th Texas Cavalry.** edited by Max Lale & Hobart Key, Jr. Wraps
  1964   Marshall   Ltd.   20.
GASTON, Robert H & William H.   **"Tyler to Sharpsburg" The War Letters of _____ .** edited by Robert Glover. Wraps
  1960   Waco   15.
GILES, Leonidas B.   **Terry's Texas Rangers.**
  1911   Austin   1000.
  1967   Austin   15.
GILES, Val C.   **Rags and Hope: The Memoirs of _____ , Four Years with Hood's Brigade, Fourth Texas Infantry 1861-1865.** edited by Mary Lasswell.
  1961   New York   25.
GOOD, John J.   **Cannon Smoke: Letters of Captain John J. Good, Good-Douglas Texas Battery, C.S.A.** edited by Lester N. Fitzhugh.
  1971   Hillsboro   30.
GRABER, William Henry   **The Life Record of H. W. Graber, A Terry Texas Ranger.**
  1961   n.p.   750.
GRADY, John C. and **FELMLY,** Bradford K.   **Suffering to Silence, 29th Texas Cavalry, CSA.**
  1975   Quanah   30.
GUESS, George W.   **Civil War Letters of Colonel _____ to Mrs. Sarah Horton Cockrell.**
  1946   n.p.   Ltd.   100.
HAMILTON, D. H.   **History of Company M, First Texas Volunteer Infantry, Hood's Brigade.**
  1962   Waco   Ltd.   40.
HEARTSILL, William W.   **Fourteen Hundred and 91 Days in the Confederate Army.** edited by Bell I. Wiley.
  1954   Jackson   40.
JEFFRIES, Charlie C.   **Terry's Rangers.**
  1961   New York   25.
LANE, Walter P.   **Adventures and Recollections of . . .**
  1928   Marshall   50.
  1970   Austin   20.
NOEL, Theophilus   **Autobiography and Reminiscences of _____ .**
  1904   Chicago   125.
NOEL, Theophilus   **A Campaign from Santa Fe to the Mississippi.** edited by Martin Hall & Edwin Davis.
  1961   Houston   35.
PETTY, Elijah P.   **Journey to Pleasant Hill, the Civil War Letters of _____ , Walker's Texas Division.** edited by Norman D. Brown.
  1982   San Antonio   35.
  Collector's edition   Ltd.   Boxed   75.
POLK, J. M.   **Memories of the Lost Cause, Stories and Adventures of a Confederate Soldier.** Wraps
  1905   Austin   50.
POLK, J. M.   **The North and South American Review.** Wraps
  1912   Austin   40.

POLLEY, Joseph B.   **A Soldier's Letters to Charming Nellie.**
  1908   New York   375.
SCOTT, Joe M.   **Four Years in the Southern Army.**
  1897   Mulberry   2000.
  1958   Fayetteville   Wraps   30.
SEATON, Benjamin M.   **The Bugle Softly Blows, The Confederate Diary of** _____.
  edited by Harold B. Simpson.
  1965   Waco   25.
SIMPSON, Harold B.   **Gaines Mill to Appomattox.**
  1963   Waco   25.
SIMPSON, Harold B.   **The Recruiting, Training, and Camp Life of a Company of Hood's Brigade in Texas, 1861.** Wraps
  1962   Waco   Ltd.   30.
SMITH, Ralph J.   **Co. K. 2nd Texas Infantry: Reminiscences of the Civil War and Other Sketches.**
  1962   Waco   Ltd.   30.
SMITH, Thomas C.   **Here's Yer Mule, The Diary of** _____ .
  1958   Waco   Ltd.   35.
SPARKS, A. W.   **The War Between the States as I Saw It.**
  1901   Tyler   350.
SPURLIN, Charles   **West of the Mississippi with Waller's 13th Texas Cavalry Battalion.** Wraps
  1971   Hillsboro   20.
STEVENS, John W.   **Reminiscences of the Civil War.**
  1902   Hillsboro   650.
  1982   Powhatan   19.
TODD, George T.   **First Texas Regiment.**
  1963   Waco   Ltd.   40.
WALTON, William Martin   **An Epitome of My Life: Civil War Reminiscences.**
  1965   Austin   30.
WEDDLE, Robert S.   **Plow Horse Cavalry, The Caney Creek Boys of the 34th Texas.**
  1974   Austin   15.
WEST, John C.   **A Texan in Search of a Fight.**
  1901   Waco   250.
  1969   Waco   25.

UTAH

GENERAL REFERENCES

FISHER, Margaret M.   **Utah and the Civil War.**
  1929   Salt Lake City   60.
LONG, E. B.   **The Saints and the Union, Utah Territory During the Civil War.**
  1981   Urbana   20.

VERMONT

GENERAL REFERENCES

Report of the Adjutant & Inspector General of the State of Vermont. Wraps
  1862-1865   Montpelier   20. each
BENEDICT, George G.   **Vermont in the Civil War.** 2 vols.
  1886-1888   Burlington   50.
FOLSOM, William R.   **Vermonters in Battle and Other Papers.**
  1953   Burlington   20.

PECK, Theodore S. (comp)   **Revised Roster of Vermont Volunteers . . . During the War of the Rebellion.**
1892   Montpelier   75.
All copies we have seen (15+) were waterstained.
Proceedings of the Reunion Society of Vermont Officers.
1885   Burlington   25.
Register of Commissioned Officers of the Vermont Volunteers in the Service of the United States. Wraps
1863   Woodstock   20.
RIPLEY, Wm. Y. W.   **Vermont Riflemen in the War for the Union 1861-1865 A History of Company F, First United States Sharp Shooters.**
1883   Rutland   150.
1981   Rochester   20.
WAITE, Otis F. R.   **Vermont in the Great Rebellion.**
1869   Claremont   15.

REGIMENTALS

ABBOTT, Lemuel A.   **Personal Recollections and Civil War Diary, 1864.**
1908   Burlington   75.
BENEDICT, George Grenville   **Army Life in Virginia: Letters from the Twelfth Vermont Regiment.**
1895   Burlington   50.
BENEDICT, George Grenville   **A Short History of the 14th Vermont Regiment.** Wraps
1887   Bennington   40.
CARPENTER, George N.   **History of the 8th Regiment Vermont Volunteers 1861-1865.**
1886   Boston   65.
CHAMBERLIN, George E.   **Letters of George E. Chamberlin.**
1883   Springfield, Ill.   50.
CHASE, Peter S.   **A Reunion Greeting, Together with an Historical Sketch . . . of Co. I, 2nd Regiment Vermont Volunteers.**
1891   Brattleboro   40.
DUFUR, Simon M.   **Over the Dead Line, or Tracked by Blood-Hounds.**
1902   Burlington   35.
HAYNES, Edwin M.   **A History of the 10th Regiment Vermont Vols.**
1894   Rutland   65.
1870   Lewiston   40.
HILL, Herbert E.   **Campaign in the Shenandoah Valley 1864, A Paper.** Wraps
1886   Boston   25.
HOLBROOK, Wm. C.   **A Narrative of the Officers & Enlisted Men of 7th Regiment Vermont Volunteers.**
1882   New York   50.
JACKSON, Horatio N.   **Dedication of the Statue to Brevet Major General William Wells and the Officers and Men of the 1st Regiment Vermont Cavalry.**
1914   Burlington (?)   40.
KIMBALL, Moses   **A Discourse Commemorative of Major Charles Jarvis of the 9th Vermont Volunteers.** Wraps
1864   New York   15.
McKEEN, Silas   **Heroic Patriotism Sermon Delivered . . . in the Presence of the Bradford Guards . . . 1st Regt. of Vermont Vols.** Wraps
1861   Windsor   20.
PALMER, Edwin Franklin   **The Second Brigade, or Camp Life by a Volunteer.**
1864   Montpelier   40.
PRINGLE, Cyrus   **The Record of a Quaker Conscience, Cyrus Pringle's Diary.**
1918   New York   30.
Proceedings of the 1st and 2nd Reunions of the 7th Vermont Veteran Volunteers.
1883   New York   30.

RIPLEY, Edward Hastings **Vermont General, The Unusual War Experiences of**
 _____ . edited by Otto Eisenschiml.
 1960 New York 20.
STURTEVANT, Ralph O. **Pictorial History Thirteenth Regiment**
Vermont Volunteers War of 1861-1865.
 1910 n.p. 85.
WALKER, Aldace F. **The Vermont Brigade in the Shenandoah Valley 1864.**
 1869 Burlington 35.
WILLIAMS, John C. **Life in Camp, A History of the Nine Months' Service of the**
14th Vermont Regiment.
 1864 Claremont 40.

VIRGINIA

GENERAL REFERENCES

BAILEY, James H. **Henrico Home Front 1861-1865.** Wraps
 1963 Richmond 30.
BOHANNAN, Willis W. **Surry County at War 1861-1865.** Wraps
 1963 (?) n.p. 10.
BRICE, M. M. **The Stonewall Brigade Band.**
 1967 Verona 20.
CALFEE, Mrs. B. G. **Confederate History of Culpeper County.** Wraps
 n.d. n.p. 15.
Constitution of the State of Virginia and Ordinances Adopted by Convention . . . 13th
Day of Feb., 1864. Wraps
 1864 Alexandria 100.
COPLAND, Mary Ruffin **Confederate History of Charles City County, Virginia.**
Wraps
 1957 n.p. 15.
Craig's Share in the War Between the States 1861-1865, Craig Chapter No. 121,
U.D.C. Wraps
 n.d. Roanoake 25.
DANDRIDGE, Danske **Historic Shepherdstown.**
 1910 Charlottesville 35.
Diaries, Letters, and Recollections of the War Between the States, Va. Soldiers in the
Civil War. Wraps
 1955 Winchester 25.
DIVINE, John **Loudoun County and the Civil War.** Wraps
 1961 Leesburg 10.
ECKENRODE, H. J. **The Political History of Virginia During the Reconstruction.**
 1904 Baltimore 30.
EVANS, Clement A. (ed) **Confederate Military History, Vol. III — Virginia.**
 1889 Atlanta 40.
 1975 Dayton Expanded Volume 32.50
Fairfax County and the War Between the States. Wraps
 1961 Vienna 10.
GAINES, William H., Jr. **Biographical Register of Members Virginia State**
Convention of 1861, 1st Sess. Wraps
 1969 Richmond 10.
GOLD, Thomas D. **History of Clarke County, Virginia and Its Connections with**
the War Between the States.
 1914 Berryville 100.
 1962 Berryville 30.
GOODHART, Briscoe **History of the Independent Loudoun Virginia Rangers,**
U.S. Volunteer Cavalry (Scouts).
 1896 Washington 125.

HALSEY, Don P.   **Historic and Heroic Lynchburg.**
  1935   Lynchburg   40.
HEADSPETH, W. Carroll   **Halifax Volunteers in the Confederate Army.** Wraps
  1939 (?)   n.p.   50.
JONES, B. W.   **Battle Roll of Surry County, Virginia in the War Between the States.**
  1913   Richmond   300.
KIMBALL, William J. (ed)   **Richmond in Time of War.** Wraps
  1960   Boston   25.
McDONALD, William N.   **A History of the Laurel Brigade.**
  1907   Baltimore   300.
  1969   Arlington   32.
Magazine of Albemarle County History, Civil War Issue. Wraps
  1964   Charlottesville   20.
MANARIN, Louis H. and **WALLACE,** Lee A., Jr.   **Richmond Volunteers.**
  1969   Richmond   30.
Memorial to Confederate Soldiers Elmwood Cemetery, Shepherdstown, W. Va. Unveiled September 18, 1937. Wraps
  n.d.   n.p.   35.
Military Operations in Jefferson County . . . 1861-1865.
  1911   Charles Town   80.
MONTAGUE, Ludwell Lee   **Gloucester County in the Civil War.** Wraps
  1965   Gloucester   15.
MUNFORD, Beverley B.   **Virginia's Attitude Toward Slavery and Secession.**
  1909   New York   25.
  1914   Richmond   25.
  1915   Richmond   25.
  1969   New York   20.
MUNFORD, Robert B., Jr.   **Richmond Homes and Memories.**
  1936   Richmond   35.
Northumberland Historical Society, Bulletin of . . . Civil War Centennial Issue, Vol. 1, No. 1. Wraps
  1965   n.p.   10.
POINDEXTER, C.   **Richmond, an Illustrated Hand-Book and Guide with Notices of the Battle-fields.** Wraps
  1896   Richmond   25.
PORTER, John W. H.   **A Record of Events in Norfolk County, Virginia, from April 19th 1861 to May 10th 1862.**
  1892   Portsmouth   90.
RAMEY, Emily and **GOTT,** John (comps)   **The Years of Anguish: Fauquier County, Virginia 1861-1865.**
  1965   Warrenton   20.
The Returned Battleflags of the Virginia Regiments in the War Between the States. Wraps
  n.d.   Richmond   15.
RICHEY, Homer and **LINNEY,** C. B.   **Memorial History of the John Bowie Strange Camp, United Confederate Veterans.**
  1920   Charlottesville   40.
ROBERTSON, James I., Jr.   **The Stonewall Brigade.**
  1963   Baton Rouge   20.
ROBERTSON, James I., Jr.   **Virginia, 1861-1865, Iron Gate to the Confederacy.** Wraps
  1961   Richmond   20.
Roster and Historical Sketch of A. P. Hill Camp C. V. No. 6, Va. Wraps
  n.d. (circa 1915)   n.p.   30.
Roster of R. E. Lee Camp, No. 2, Confederate Veterans of Alexandria, Va. Wraps
  n.d.   n.p.   30.

SELBY, John   **The Stonewall Brigade.**
   1971   Norwich   15.
   1973   New York   10.
SHANKS, Henry T.   **The Secession Movement in Virginia.**
   1934   Richmond   25.
SMITH, Mrs. Cabell   **Forty Years with the Virginia Division U.D.C.** Wraps
   n.d. (circa 1935)   n.p.   20.
SQUIRES, W. H. T.   **The Land of Decision.**
   1931   Portsmouth   Ltd.   100.
SQUIRES, W. H. T.   **Unleashed at Long Last, Reconstruction in Virginia April
   9, 1865 — Jan 26, 1870.**
   1939   Portsmouth   Ltd.   50.
STUART, Alex. H. H.   **A Narrative of the Leading Incidents of the Organization of
   the First Popular Movement in Virginia in 1865 . . . to Secure Restoration of
   Virginia to the Union.**
   1888   Richmond   50.
STUART, Meriwether   **The Record of the Virginia Forces, A Study in the Compilation of Civil War Records.** Wraps
   1960   Virginia   30.
**Three Rebels Write Home: Edgar Allan Jackson, James Fenton Bryant, Irvin Cross
   Wills and Miscellaneous Items.** Wraps
   1955   Franklin   Ltd.   30.
WADDELL, Jos. A.   **Annals of Augusta County, Virginia . . . with a Diary of the
   War 1861-5 and A Chapter on Reconstruction.**
   1886   Richmond   75.
WALLACE, Lee A., Jr.   **Guide to Virginia Military Organizations 1861-1865.** Wraps
   1964   Richmond   80.
WAYLAND, John W.   **Twenty-Five Chapters on the Shenandoah Valley.**
   1957   Strasburg   35.

REGIMENTALS

ALEXANDER, John H.   **Mosby's Men.**
   1907   New York   225.
   This volume usually has badly spotted covers.
ANDREWS, Andrew J.   **A Sketch of the Boyhood Days of _____ of Gloucester
   County, Virginia.**
   1905   Richmond   175.
Annual Reunion of Pegram Battalion. Wraps
   1886   Richmond   150.
BARCLAY, Alexander T.   **The Liberty Hall Volunteers from Lexington to
   Manassas.** Wraps
   1904   Lynchburg   50.
BAYLOR, George   **Bull Run to Bull Run, or Four Years in the Army of Northern
   Virginia.**
   1900   Richmond   75.
BEALE, George William   **A Lieutenant of Cavalry in Lee's Army.**
   1918   Boston   1000.
BEALE, Richard Lee Turberville   **History of the Ninth Virginia Cavalry in the War
   Between the States.**
   1899   Richmond   1000.
   n.d.   n.p.   Reprint   Ltd.   28.50
BEAN, William G.   **The Liberty Hall Volunteers, Stonewall's College Boys.**
   1964   Charlottesville   20.
BELL, John W.   **Memoirs of Governor William Smith of Virginia.**
   1891   New York   125.

BERNARD, George S.   **The Battle of the Crater in Front of Petersburg July 30, 1864 An Address.** Wraps
    1890   Petersburg   50.
    1892   Petersburg   50.
    1937   n.p.   20.

BLACKFORD, Charles M., Jr.   **Annals of the Lynchburg Home Guard.**
    1891   Lynchburg   750.

BLACKFORD, Susan L. (comp)   **Letters from Lee's Army.**
    1947   New York   30.

BLACKFORD, Susan Leigh   **Memoir.** Wraps
    1959   Madison Heights   30.

BLACKFORD, William W.   **War Years with Jeb Stuart.**
    1945   New York   30.
    1946   New York   30.

BOSANG, James N.   **Memoirs of a Pulaski Veteran.** Wraps
    1930   Pulaski   50.

BROWN, Philip Francis   **Reminiscences of the War of 1861-1865.** Wraps
    1912   Roanoke   225.
    1917   Richmond   175.

BROWN, R..Shepard   **Stringfellow of the Fourth.**
    1960   New York   25.

BRYAN, John Stewart   **Joseph Bryan, His Times, His Family, His Friends A Memoir.**
    1935   Richmond   1--.

CASADA, James A.   **History of the 48th Virginia Infantry, Hist. Soc. of Washington Co.** Wraps
    1969   Abingdon   10.

CASLER, John O.   **Four Years in the Stonewall Brigade.**
    1893   Guthrie, Oklahoma   400.
    1906   Girard, Kansas   350.
    1951   Marietta   30.
    1971   Dayton   edited by James I. Robertson, Jr.   15.

CHAMBERLAINE, William W.   **Memoirs of the Civil War.**
    1912   Washington   650.

CHAMBERLAYNE, E. H., Jr. (comp)   **Record of the Richmond City and Henrico County Virginia Troops, Confederate States Army.** Series 1-10. Wraps
    1879   Richmond   600.

CHAMBERLAYNE, Edwin H.   **War History and Roll of the Richmond Fayette Artillery, 38th Virginia Battalion Artillery.** Wraps
    1883   Richmond   250.

Contributions to a History of the Richmond Howitzer Battalion. Wraps
    1883-1886   Richmond   400.
    No. 1   50.
    No. 2   100.
    No. 3   100.
    No. 4   50.

CRAWFORD, J. Marshall   **Mosby and His Men.**
    1867   New York   150.

CROCKER, James F.   **My Personal Experiences in Taking up Arms and in the Battle of Malvern Hill, Address.** Wraps
    1905   Portsmouth   50.

CUTCHINS, John A.   **A Famous Command, The Richmond Light Infantry Blues.**
    1934   Richmond   50.

CUTCHINS, John A.   **Richmond Light Infantry Blues, A Sketch.** Wraps
    1910   Richmond   20.

DAME, William M.   **From the Rapidan to Richmond & the Spottsylvania Campaign.**
    1920   Baltimore   75.

DANIEL, Frederick S.   **Richmond Howitzers in the War.** Wraps
    1891   Richmond   300.
DAWSON, Francis W.   **Our Women in the War.** Wraps
    1887   Charleston   50.
DAWSON, Francis W.   **Reminiscences of Confederate Service 1861-1865.**
    1882   Charleston   Ltd.   3500.
DELANEY, Wayne Richard, and **BOWERY,** Marie E. (eds)   **The Seventeenth Virginia Volunteer Infantry Regiment CSA.** Wraps
    1961   Washington   20.
DeNOON, Charles E.   **Charlie's Letters: the Correspondence of Charles E. DeNoon.** edited by Richard T. Couture. Wraps
    1982   n.p.   20.
DICKINSON, Henry Clay   **Diary of Capt. Henry Dickinson, C.S.A.**
    191?   Denver   Ltd.   400.
DOOLEY, John   **John Dooley, Confederate Soldier: His War Journal.** edited by Joseph T. Durkin.
    1945   Washington   40.
DOUGLAS, Henry Kyd   **I Rode with Stonewall.**
    1940   Chapel Hill   25.
    1943   Chapel Hill   20.
DUNAWAY, Wayland Fuller   **Reminiscences of a Rebel.**
    1913   New York   100.
EDWARDS, John Ellis   **The Confederate Soldier, Being a Memorial Sketch of George N. and Bushrod W. Harris.**
    1868   New York   250.
EGGLESTON, George Cary   **A Rebel's Recollections.**
    1875   New York   75.
    1889   New York   75.
    1897   New York   75.
    1959   Bloomington   25.
FIGG, Royall W.   **"Where Men Only Dare to Go!" or The Story of a Boy Company (C.S.A.)**
    1885   Richmond   150.
FONERDEN, Clarence A.   **Brief History of the Military Career of Carpenter's Battery.**
    1911   New Market   500.
GALLAHER, De Witt Clinton   **A Diary Depicting the Experiences of DeWitt Clinton Gallaher in the War Between the States.** Wraps
    1945   Charleston   30.
GORDON, Armistead C.   **Memories and Memorials of William Gordon McCabe.** 2 vols.
    1925   Richmond   75.
GRAVES, Joseph A.   **The History of the Bedford Light Artillery.** Wraps
    1903   Bedford City   250.
GRIMSLEY, Daniel A.   **Battles in Culpeper County, Virginia.** Wraps
    1900   Culpeper   75.
HACKLEY, Woodford B.   **The Little Fork Rangers A Sketch of Company "D" Fourth Virginia Cavalry.**
    1927   Richmond   75.
HALE, Laura Virginia and **PHILLIPS,** Stanley S.   **History of the Forty-Ninth Virginia Infantry C.S.A. "Extra Billy Smith's Boys."**
    1981   Lanham   20.
HALL, James E.   **Diary of a Confederate Soldier.** edited by Ruth W. Dayton.
    1961   Charleston   25.
HARRIS, Nathaniel E.   **Autobiography: The Story of an Old Man's Life, With Reminiscences of Seventy Five Years.**
    1925   Macon   25.

HOPKINS, Luther W.   **From Bull Run to Appomattox, A Boy's View.**
    1908   Baltimore   75.
    1911   n.p.   60.
    1914   Baltimore   50.
HUFFMAN, James   **Ups and Downs of a Confederate Soldier.**
    1940   New York   Ltd.   50.
HUNTER, Alexander   **Johnny Reb and Billy Yank.**
    1905   New York   250.
IRBY, Richard   **The Captain Remembers: The Papers of Captain Richard Irby.**
    edited by V. F. Jordan. Wraps
    1975   n.p.   15.
IRBY, Richard   **Historical Sketches of the Nottoway Grays.**
    1878   Richmond   150.
    Usually lacks frontis and illustrations.
JOHNSTON, David E.   **The Story of a Confederate Boy in the Civil War.**
    1914   Portland   100,
JONES, Benjamin Washington   **Under the Stars and Bars.**
    1909   Richmond   450.
    1975   Dayton   20.
JONES, C. W.   **In Prison at Point Lookout.** Wraps
    n.d. (circa 1890)   Martinsville   30.
JONES, Virgil Carrington   **Ranger Mosby.**
    1944   Chapel Hill   25.
    Many Later Editions.
KRICK, Robert K.   **Parker's Virginia Battery, C.S.A.**
    1975   Berryville   30.
LEWIS, John Howard   **Recollections from 1860 to 1865.** Wraps
    1895   Washington   750.
LOEHR, Charles T.   **War History of the Old First Virginia Infantry Regiment.**
    Wraps
    1884   Richmond   600.
    1970   Dayton   10.
LONG, Walter E.   **Andrew Davidson Long, Stonewall's Foot Cavalryman.**
    1965   Austin   30.
McALLISTER, J. Gray   **Sketch of Captain Thompson McAllister, Citizen, Soldier, Christian.** Wraps
    1896   Petersburg   75.
McCABE, William Gordon   **Speech of Capt. _____** Wraps
    1900   Nashville   40.
McCARTHY, Carlton   **Detailed Minutiae of Soldier Life in the Army of Northern Virginia.**
    1882   Richmond   100.
    1884   Richmond   80.
    1888   Richmond   80.
    1899   Richmond   35.
MACON, Thomas J. (comp)   **Life Gleanings.**
    1913   Richmond   60.
MACON, Thomas J.   **Reminiscences of the First Company of Richmond Howitzers.**
    190?   Richmond   125.
    1913   Richmond   100.
MAURY, Richard L.   **The Battle of Williamsburg and the Charge of the 24th Virginia, of Early's Brigade.** Wraps
    1880   Richmond   250.
    1960   Williamsburg   10.
MONTEIRO, Aristides   **War Reminiscences by the Surgeon of Mosby's Command.**
    1890   Richmond   Wraps   150.

MOORE, Edward A.　　**The Story of a Cannoneer Under Stonewall Jackson.**
　　1907　　New York/Washington　　150.
　　In all of the untrimmed copies we have seen, the first few pages vary in size from the rest of the book.
　　1910　　Lynchburg　　75.
　　1971　　Freeport　　20.
MORGAN, William H.　　**Personal Reminiscences of the War of 1861-5.**
　　1911　　Lynchburg, Virginia　　75.
　　n.d.　　n.p.　　Reprint　　15.
MOSBY, John S.　　**The Memoirs of** _____. edited by Charles W. Russell.
　　1917　　Boston　　175.
　　1959　　Bloomington　　30.
　　1975　　New York　　22.
MOSBY, John S.　　**Mosby's War Reminiscences & Stuart's Cavalry Campaigns.**
　　1887　　New York　　Wraps　　100.
　　1887　　Boston　　75.
　　1898　　New York　　75.
　　1958　　New York　　25.
MOSBY, John S.　　**Stuart's Cavalry in the Gettysburg Campaign.**
　　1908　　New York　　75.
MUNSON, John W.　　**Reminiscences of a Mosby Guerrilla.**
　　1906　　New York　　75.
MURRAY, John Ogden　　**The Immortal Six Hundred.**
　　1905　　Winchester　　150.
　　1911　　Roanoke　　80.
MURRAY, John Ogden　　**Three Stories in One.**
　　1911　　Roanoke　　75.
　　1915　　n.p.　　560.
MYERS, Frank M.　　**The Comanches: A History of White's Battalion.**
　　1871　　Baltimore　　1000.
　　1956　　Marietta　　50.
NEALE, Walter　　**The Sovereignty of the States.**
　　1910　　New York　　100.
NEESE, George M.　　**Three Years in the Confederate Horse Artillery.**
　　1911　　New York　　300.
O'FERRALL, Charles Triplett　　**Forty Years of Active Service.**
　　New York　　1904　　60.
OPIE, John N.　　**A Rebel Cavalryman with Lee, Stuart, and Jackson.**
　　1899　　Chicago　　200.
　　All copies we have seen lack the second page of the table of contents.
　　1972　　Dayton　　25.
PEAVEY, James Dudley (comp & ed)　　**Confederate Scout: Virginia's Frank String-fellow.** Wraps
　　1956　　Onacock　　25.
ROBSON, John S.　　**How a One-Legged Rebel Lives.** Wraps
　　1891　　Charlottesville　　100.
　　1898　　Durham　　100.
ROYALL, William L.　　**Some Reminiscences.**
　　1909　　New York　　140.
SCOTT, John　　**Partisan Life with Colonel John S. Mosby.**
　　1867　　New York　　150.
SCOTT, W. W. (ed)　　**Two Confederate Items, Diary of Capt. H. W. Wingfield and Reminiscences of the Civil War by Judge E. C. Moncure.** VSL Bulletin. Wraps
　　1927　　Richmond　　20.
SHOTWELL, Randolph Abbott　　**The Papers of Randolph Abbott Shotwell.** edited J. G. Hamilton. 3 vols.
　　1929　　Raleigh　　125.
SLAUGHTER, Philip　　**A Sketch of the Life of Randolph Fairfax.**
　　1878　　Baltimore　　150.

A Souvenir of the Unveiling of the Richmond Howitzer Monument of Richmond, Va.,
Dec. 13, 1892. Wraps
  1893   Richmond   75.
SPENCER, Carrie Esther (ed)   **A Civil War Marriage in Virginia; Reminiscences**
and Letters.
  1956   Boyce   25.
STEWART, William H.   **A Pair of Blankets.**
  1911   New York   200.
STILES, Robert   **Four Years Under Marse Robert.**
  1903   New York   75.
  1977   Dayton   17.50
STRIDER, Robert Edward Lee   **The Life and Work of George W. Peterkin.**
  1929   Philadelphia   30.
TINSLEY, Henry C.   **Observations of a Retired Veteran.**
  1904   Staunton   100.
TOWNSEND, Harry C.   **Townsend's Diary, Last Months of the War.**
  1907   Richmond   100.
WARFIELD, Edgar   **A Confederate Soldier's Memoirs.**
  1936   Richmond   Ltd.   200.
WILLIAMSON, James J.   **Mosby's Rangers, A Record of the Operations of the**
Forty-Third Battalion of Virginia Cavalry.
  1896   New York   200.
  1909   New York   125.
  1982   n.p.   22.50
WILLIAMSON, James J.   **Prison Life in the Old Capitol and Reminiscences of the**
Civil War.
  1911   West Orange   90.
WILSON, William L.   **A Borderland Confederate, Civil War Letters and Diaries of**
_____ edited by Festus P. Summers.
  1962   Pittsburgh   30.
WISE, George   **History of the Seventeenth Virginia Infantry, C.S.A.**
  1870   Baltimore   200.
  1969   Arlington   20.
WOOD, James H.   **The War: Stonewall Jackson, His Campaigns and Battles**
The Regiment as I Saw Them.
  1910   Cumberland   150.
WOOD, William Nathaniel   **Reminiscences of Big I.**
  1909   Charlottesville   700.
  1956   Jackson   edited by Bell I. Wiley   35.
WORSHAM, John H.   **One of Jackson's Foot Cavalry.**
  1912   New York   150.
  1964   Jackson   edited by James I. Robertson   35.
YOUNG, Charles P.   **History of Crenshaw Battery, Pegram's Battalion.** Wraps
  1904   Richmond   100.

WEST VIRGINIA

GENERAL REFERENCES

Annual Report of the Adjutant General of the State of West Virginia for the Year
Ending Dec. 31, 1865.
  1866   Wheeling   50.
BUSHONG, Millard Kessler   **A History of Jefferson County, West Virginia.**
  1941   Charles Town   50.
COHEN, Stan   **The Civil War in West Virginia, A Pictorial History.** Wraps
  1976   Missoula   10.
COOK, Roy Bird   **Lewis County in the Civil War.**
  1924   Charleston   125.

EVANS, Clement A. (ed)   **Confederate Military History, Vol. II — Maryland and West Virginia.**
   1899   Atlanta   40.
LANG, Theodore F.   **Loyal West Virginia from 1861 to 1865.**
   1895   Baltimore   150.
LEWIS, Virgil A.   **How West Virginia was made, proceedings of the First Convention of the People of Northwestern Virginia at Wheeling.**
   1909   Charleston   30.
MOORE, George Ellis   **A Banner in the Hills, West Virginia's Statehood.**
   1963   New York   20.
SHETLER, Charles   **West Virginia Civil War Literature.** Wraps
   1963   Morgantown   30.
SIVITER, Anna Pierpont   **Recollections of War and Peace 1861-1868.** edited by Charles H. Ambler.
   1938   New York   30.
STUTLER, Boyd B.   **West Virginia in the Civil War.**
   1963   Charleston   30.
   1966   Charleston   25.
WILLEY, William P.   **An Inside View of the Formation of the State of West Virginia.**
   1901   Wheeling   40.

REGIMENTALS

Union

BARTON, Thomas H.   **Autobiography of _____ . . . . Including a History of the 4th West Virginia Inf. Vol.**
   1890   Charleston   75.
EGAN, Michael.   **The Flying Gray-Haired Yank.**
   1888   Philadelphia   75.
   n.d.   n.p.   60.
HEWITT, William   **History of the Twelfth West Virginia Volunteer Infantry.** Wraps
   1892   Steubenville   100.
McDOUGAL, Henry Clay   **Recollections 1844-1909.**
   1910   Kansas City   50.
MATHENY, Herman E.   **Major General Thomas Maley Harris.**
   1963   Parsons   20.
MILLER, James N.   **The Story of Andersonville and Florence.** Wraps
   1900   Des Moines   40.
RAWLING, Charles J.   **History of the First Regiment Virginia Infantry.**
   1887   Philadelphia   125.
READER, Frank S.   **History of the Fifth West Virginia Cavalry.**
   1890   New Brighton   85.
SENSENEY, Charles H.   **Address Delivered . . . To his Comrades . . . Fiftieth Anniversary . . . of Battery D, First West Virginia Light Artillery.** Wraps
   1912   Wheeling   25.
SUTTON, J. J.   **History of the Second Regiment, West Virginia Cavalry Volunteers.**
   1892   Portsmouth   100.

WISCONSIN

GENERAL REFERENCES

Annual Report of the Adjutant General of the State of Wisconsin. 1861-1865
   1861-1865   25. each
BRADLEY, Isaac Samuel (Comp)   **A Bibliography of Wisconsin's Participation in the War Between the States.**
   1911   Madison   25.

ESTABROOK, Charles E. (ed)   **Records and Sketches of Military Organizations.**
      1914   Milwaukee   40.
HURN, Ethel Alice   **Wisconsin Women in the War Between the States.**
      1911   Madison   30.
LEACH, Eugene Walter   **Racine County Militant, an Illustrated Narrative of War Times and a Soldier's Roster.**
      1915   Racine   50.
LOVE, William DeLoss   **Wisconsin in the War of the Rebellion.**
      1866   Chicago   60.
PAUL, William G. (comp)   **Wisconsin's Civil War Archives.** Wraps
      1965   Madison   10.
QUINER, Edwin B.   **The Military History of Wisconsin.**
      1866   Chicago   80.
Roster of Wisconsin Volunteers, War of the Rebellion 1861-1865. 2 vols.
      1886   Madison   125.
Soldiers' and Citizens' Album of Biographical Record Containing Personal Sketches of Army Men and Citizens Prominent in Loyalty to the Union. 2 vols.
      1888-1890   Chicago   100.
THWAITES, Reuben Gold (ed)   **Civil War Messages and Proclamations of Wisconsin War Governors.**
      1912   Madison   30.
War Papers read before the Commandery of the State of Wisconsin, Mollus. 4 vols.
      1891-1914   Milwaukee   25. each
Wisconsin at Andersonville, Report of the Wisconsin Monument Commission Appointed to Erect a Monument at Andersonville, Georgia.
      1911   Madison   25.
Wisconsin at Vicksburg, Report of the Wisconsin-Vicksburg Monument Commission Including the Story of the Campaign and Siege of Vicksburg in 1863.
      1914   Madison   40.
Wisconsin Volunteers, War of the Rebellion 1861-1865.
      1914   Madison   75.

REGIMENTALS

ACKER, Henry J.   **Gulf Spy, Sgt. Henry J. Acker 23rd Wisconsin Vol. Inf.** Wraps
      1961   Tall Timbers, Md.   20.
AUBERY, James M.   **The 36th Wisconsin Volunteer Infantry.**
      1900   Milwaukee   100.
BARRETT, Joseph O.   **"Old Abe" the Soldier Bird.** Wraps
      1876   Madison   30.
BEECHAM, Robert K.   **Gettysburg, The Pivotal Battle of the Civil War.**
      1911   Chicago   45.
BRADLEY, George S.   **The Star Corps.**
      1865   Milwaukee   85.
BROBST, John F.   **Well Mary: Civil War Letters of a Wisconsin Volunteer,** edited by Margaret B. Roth.
      1960   Madison   20.
BRYANT, Edwin E.   **History of the 3rd Regiment of Wisconsin Veteran Volunteer Infantry 1861-1865.**
      1891   Madison   85.
BUSLETT, Ole Amundson   **Det Femtende Regiment Wisconsin Frivillige, Samlet Og Bearbeidet Af O. A. Buslett.**
      1894   Decorah   75.
CASTLEMAN, Alfred L.   **The Army of the Potomac, Behind the Scenes.**
      1863   Milwaukee   80.
CHEEK, Philip and **POINTON,** Mair   **History of the Sauk County Riflemen known as Company "A" Sixth Wisconsin Veteran Volunteer Infantry 1861-1865.**
      1909   Madison   150.

CLARK, John   **The True Story of the Capture of Jeff. Davis.** Wraps
    1910   n.p.   40.
DAMON, Herbert C.   **History of the Milwaukee Light Guard.**
    1875   Milwaukee   75.
DAWES, Rufus R.   **Service with the Sixth Wisconsin Volunteers.**
    1890   Marietta   125.
    1936   Marietta   100.
    1962   Madison   30.
A Diary of the 30th Regiment, Wisconsin Volunteers. A History of the Regiment since its Organization.
    1864   Madison   125.
DODGE, James H.   **Across the Plains with the Ninth Wisconsin Battery in 1862, D. C. MOLLUS War Paper 23.** Wraps
    1896   n.p.   25.
DRIGGS, George W.   **Opening of the Mississippi, or Two Years' Campaigning in the Southwest.**
    1864   Madison   125.
EDEN, Robert C.   **The Sword and Gun. A History of the 37th Wisconsin Volunteer Infantry.**
    1865   Madison   75.
FITCH, Michael H.   **The Chattanooga Campaign.**
    1911   Madison   30.
FITCH, Michael H.   **Echoes of the Civil War as I Hear Them.**
    1905   New York   75.
FLOWER, Frank Abial   **Old Abe, The Eighth Wisconsin War Eagle.**
    1885   Madison   40.
GRIGSBY, Melvin   **The Smoked Yank.**
    1888   Sioux Falls   40.
    1911 Sioux Falls   35.
HARNDEN, Henry   **The Capture of Jefferson Davis.**
    1898   Madison   50.
HASKELL, Frank A.   **The Battle of Gettysburg.**
    1908   Boston   35.
    1908   Madison   35.
    1910   Madison   30.
    1958   Cambridge edited by Bruce Catton   20.
HEG, E. Biddle   **Stephen O. Himoe, Civil War Physician. Norwegian-American Studies and Records,** Vol. XI.
    1940   Northfield   20.
HEG, Hans Christian   **The Civil War Letters of Colonel** _____ edited by T. C. Blegen.
    1936   Northfield   25.
HINKLEY, Julian Wisner   **A Narrative of Service with the Third Wisconsin Infantry.**
    1912   Madison   30.
HINKLEY, Julian Wisner   **Some Experiences of a Veteran in the Rear.** Wraps
    1893   Minneapolis   25.
HODGES, William R.   **Lest We Forget.** Wraps
    1912   St. Louis   15.
HOLMES, Mead   **A Soldier of the Cumberland: Memoir of** _____. Wraps
    1864   Boston   35.
JONES, Adoniram J.   **A Private of the Cumberland, Memoirs and Reminiscences of the Civil War.**
    190?   n.p.   60.
JONES, Evan R.   **Four Years in the Army of the Potomac.**
    1881   London   75.
JONES, Jenkin Lloyd   **An Artilleryman's Diary.**
    1914   Madison   65.
KAKUSKE, Herbert P.   **A Civil War Drama. The Adventures of a Union Soldier in Southern Imprisonment.**
    1970   New York   15.

KEENE, Harry S.   **History of the Sixth Wisconsin Battery with Roster of Officers and Members.** Wraps
   1879   Lancaster   90.
KELLOGG, John A. and SPENCER, R. H.   **Capture and Escape.**
   Wraps
   1896   Algona, Iowa   40.
KELLOGG, John Azor   **Capture and Escape a Narrative of Army and Prison Life.**
   1908   Madison   40.
KEYES, Dwight W.   **The First Wisconsin Infantry U.S. Vols. Its Organization, and Move to the Front.**
   1896   Milwaukee   30.
LYON, William Penn   **Reminiscences of the Civil War Compiled from the War Correspondence of Col.** _____ edited by Wm. P. Lyon, Jr.
   1907   San Jose, Ca.   100.
MILLER, Alonzo   **Diaries and Letters Written by Pvt. Alonzo Miller, Co. A, 12th Wisconsin Infantry.**
   1958   Marietta, Ga.   35.
MILLER, Charles D.   **"Old Abe" the War Eagle in Report of the Great Re-Union of the Veteran Soldiers and Sailors of Ohio.**
   1878   Newark   35.
MILLER, Edward G.   **Captain Edward Gee Miller of the 20th Wisconsin, His War 1861-1865.** edited by W. J. Lemke. Wraps
   1960   Fayetteville   25.
NELSON, C. P.   **Abe The War Eagle.** Wraps
   1903   Lynn   25.
NEWTON, James K.   **A Wisconsin Boy in Dixie, The Selected Letters of . . . .** edited by Stephen Ambrose.
   1961   Madison   20.
NOLAN, Alan T.   **The Iron Brigade.**
   1961   New York   40.
PEARSALL, Uri B.   **Official Reports of Building the "Red River Dam" at Alexandria, LA.**
   1896   Lansing   30.
PIERCE, Solon W.   **Battle Fields and Camp Fires of the Thirty-Eighth.**
   1866   Milwaukee   150.
PRUTSMAN, Christian Miller   **A Soldier's Experience in Southern Prisons.**
   1901   New York   40.
REID, Harvey   **The View from Headquarters, Civil War Letters of Harvey Reid.** edited by Frank L. Byrne.
   1965   Madison   20.
Reunion . . . 12th Wisconsin Infantry. Wraps
   1904-1924   15. each
ROBINSON, Arthur J.   **Memorandum and Anecdotes of the Civil War 1862 to 1865.** Wraps
   1912   n.p.   35.
ROBINSON, Oliver S.   **The Diary and Letters of Oliver S. Robinson.** Wraps
   1968   Kensington, Md.   35.
ROGERS, James B.   **War Pictures Experiences and Observations of a Chaplain in the U.S. Army in the War of the Southern Rebellion.**
   1863   Chicago   85.
ROOD, Hosea W.   **The Story of the Service of Company E, and of the Twelfth Wisconsin Regiment Veteran Volunteer Infantry.**
   1893   Milwaukee   150.
STELLE, Abel Clarkson   **1861 to 1865 Memoirs of the Civil War, the 31st Regiment Wisconsin Volunteer Infantry.** Wraps
   1904   New Albany   90.

STOCKWELL, Elisha	**Private Elisha Stockwell, Jr. Sees the Civil War.** edited by
Byron Abernethy.
1958	Norman	25.
VILAS, William F.	**A View of the Vicksburg Campaign.**
1908	Madison	25.
WEBSTER, Dan and **CAMERON,** Don C.	**History of the First Wisconsin Battery
Light Artillery.**
1907	Washington	125.
WESCOTT, M. Ebenezer	**Civil War Letters 1861 to 1865 Written to
My Mother.** Wraps
1909	Mora, Minn.	35.
WILLIAMS, John M.	**The Eagle Regiment, 8th Wis. Inf'try Vols.**
1890	Belleville	100.
WINKLER, Frederick C.	**Letters of Frederick C. Winkler — 1862 to 1865.**
1963	Milwaukee	Ltd.	40.

CONFEDERATE

IMPRINTS

CONFEDERATE IMPRINTS
Official Publications
CONSTITUTION

6   Constitution of the Confederate States of America. Adopted unanimously by the Congress of the Confederate States of America, March 11, 1861. Milledgeville, 1861. $400.

CONGRESS

15   Acts and Resolutions of the first session of the Provisional Congress of the Confederate States. 1861. Montgomery, Ala., 1861. $150.

18   Acts and resolutions of the fourth session of the Provisional Congress of the Confederate States, held at Richmond, Va. Richmond, 1862. $100.

19   The statutes at large of the Provisional Government of the Confederate States . . . from . . . February 8, 1861, to . . . February 18, 1862 . . . Edited by James M. Matthews. Richmond, 1864. $250.

20   The statutes at large of the Confederate States of America . . . first session . . . first Congress; 1862 . . . Edited by James M. Matthews. Richmond, 1862. $40.

21   The statutes at large of the Confederate States of America . . . second session . . . first Congress; 1862 . . . Richmond, 1862. $50.

22   The statutes at large of the Confederate States of America . . . third session . . . first Congress; 1863 . . . Richmond, 1863. $60.

23   The statutes at large of the Confederate States of America . . . fourth session . . . first Congress; 1863-64 . . . Richmond, 1864. $75.

24   The statutes at large of the Confederate States of America . . . first session . . . second Congress; 1864 . . . Richmond, 1864. $75.

36   Laws of the Provisional Congress of the Confederate States in relation to the War Department. Richmond, 1861. $250.

41   Tariff of the Confederate States of America approved by Congress, May 21, 1861 . . . Charleston, 1861. "Treasury Circular, no. 10." $50.

42   An act recognizing the existence of war between the United States and the Confederate States . . . Montgomery, Ala., 1861. $300.

43   An act relative to prisoners of war . . . Approved May 21, 1861. Montgomery, Ala., 1861. $60.

44   An act to amend an act entitled "An act recognizing the existence of war . . . , and concerning letters of marque, prizes and prize goods . . . Montgomery, Ala., 1861. $100.

50   An act to perpetuate testimony in cases of slaves abducted or harbored by the enemy, and of other property seized, wasted, or destroyed by them. No. 270 . . . , Richmond, 1861. $100.

62   An act to reduce the currency, and to authorize a new issue of treasury notes. —An act to levy additional taxes for the common defence and support of the government. —An act to organize forces to serve during the war. Richmond, 1864. $50.

66   An act to amend the tax laws. Richmond, 1864. $20.

73   Address of Congress to the people of the Confederate States. Richmond, 1864. $100.

77   Proceedings of the Congress on the announcement of the death of Col. Francis S. Bartow . . . Richmond, 1861. $150.

78   Proceedings on the announcement of the death of Hon. John Tyler . . . Richmond, 1862. $100.

87   Report of the Joint select committee appointed to investigate the condition and treatment of prisoners of war. Richmond, 1865. $125.

88   Report of the Joint select committee appointed to investigate the condition and treatment of prisoners of war. Richmond, 1865. $100.

SENATE

110   (Senate, no. 13). A bill to be entitled An act in relation to the public printing. Richmond, 1863. $30.

130   Letter from Gen. Wise . . . to Hon. Jas. Lyons . . . endorsing and enclosing the memorial of Generals Hardee, Stevenson and other officers . . . Richmond, 1863. $40.

171   (Senate bill, no. 121). A bill declaring the mode of ascertaining the value of the tithe deliverable to the government under existing laws. Richmond, 1864. $20.

180   Amendment to Senate bill (S. 129) to provide for the employment of free negroes and slaves to work upon fortifications, and to perform other labor connected with the defenses of the country. Richmond, 1864. $50.

191   (Senate engrossed bill, no. 121). A bill declaring the mode of ascertaining the value of the tithe deliverable to the government under the true construction of existing laws. Richmond, 1865? $20.

203   Amendment proposed by the Committee on Finance, to the bill (H.R. 229) to provide more effectually for the reduction and redemption of the currency. Richmond, 1865. $20.

204   Resolution of the Legislature of the State of North Carolina in relation to the pay of disabled soldiers. Richmond, 1865. $25.

227   Directory of the Confederate States Senate, for the second session of the second Congress, commencing November 7, 1864. Richmond, 1864. $50.

HOUSE OF REPRESENTATIVES

265   (House bill no. 4) A bill to regulate the navigation of the Confederate States and to establish direct trade with foreign nations. Richmond, 1862. $30.

274   (House bill, no. 4). A bill to be entitled An act making appropriations for the executive, legislative and judicial expenses of the government . . . Richmond, 1862. $20.

298   (House bill, no. 8). Preamble and resolutions on the subject of taxes. Richmond, 1863. $20.

315   A bill to be entitled An act to provide for holding elections for representatives in the Congress of the Confederate States, in the states occupied by the forces of the enemy. Richmond, 1863. $40.

316   Amendment proposed by Mr. Kenner, from Committee on Ways and Means, to bill "to lay taxes for the common defense, and carry on the government of the Confederate States." Richmond, 1863. $20.

318   A bill to establish a Nitre and Mining Bureau. Richmond, 1863. $30.

319   Communication of G. Tochman, touching his memorial now before Congress. Richmond, 1863. $30.

320   (House, no. 1) Joint resolutions on the subject of the war, and in regard to the free navigation of the Mississippi River. Richmond, 1863. $25.

321   (House bill no. 27). A bill to be entitled An act to provide for the payment of officers acting under temporary appointment from the commander of any department, corps, division or brigade. Richmond, 1863. $20.

322   (House bill, no. 1). A bill to be entitled An act to provide for keeping in repair the railroads of the Confederate States necessary for the transportation of troops and government supplies. Richmond, 1863. $35.

334   A bill to raise a tax for the support of the government. Richmond, 1863. $30.

339   (House of Representatives no. 9). Resolution on finance. Richmond, 1863. $20.

350   (House of Representatives no. 3.). . . Suggestions for financial relief. Richmond, 1863. $30.

354   A bill to be entitled An act to allow commissioned officers of the army rations and the privilege of purchasing clothing from the Quartermaster's Department. Richmond, 1863. $25.

355   A bill to be entitled An act to grant a special copyright to W. J. Hardee and S. H. Goetzel, for Hardee's Rifle and infantry tactics. Richmond, 1863. $60.

360   A bill to be entitled An act to provide for wounded and disabled officers and soldiers an asylum to be called "The Veteran Soldiers Home." Richmond, 1863. $35.

366   (House of Representatives - Secret session). A bill to be entitled "An act to tax, fund, and limit the currency." Richmond, 1863. $20.

370   (House of Representatives - Secret session). Amendment by Mr. Swan. Richmond, 1864. $20.

379   (House of Representatives - Secret session). Finance proposition. Richmond, 1864. $20.

380   (House of Representatives - Secret session). Resolutions of instructions. Richmond, 1864. $20.

382   . . . Resolutions expressive of the determination of Georgia to prosecute the present war with the utmost vigor and energy. Richmond, 1864. $40.

384   (House of Representatives - Secret session). Mr. Chilton's amendments to the bill of the committee. Richmond, 1864. $20.

385   Proposition of finance. Richmond, 1864. $20.

388   (House of Representatives - Secret session). A bill to regulate the currency. Richmond, 1864. $25.

389   Gen. Tochman's case. Richmond, 1864. $60.

391   (House bill.) . . . A bill to be entitled An act to suppress abuses in the Quartermaster and Commissary Departments of the army. Richmond, 1864. $45.

393   A bill to be entitled An act extending the privilege of purchasing clothing at government cost, to all persons in its employment, who have been discharged [sic] the army on account of wounds received or disease contracted whilst in the service. Richmond, 1864. $25.

398   A bill to be entitled An act to authorize the impressment of meat for the use of the army, under certain circumstances. Richmond, 1864. $25.

409   (House of Representatives, no. 366.) . . . A bill to be entitled "An act to provide means to carry on the government." Richmond, 1864. $25.

412   A bill supplemental to the several acts in relation to public printing. Richmond, 1864. $20.

413   Joint resolutions in reference to the treatment of colored troops. Richmond, 1864. $75.

414   (House bill no. 7). A bill to amend an act entitled "An act to lay additional taxes for the common defense and support of the government." Richmond, 1864. $25.

415   (House bill no. 9). A bill to organize a corps of scouts and signal guards, to facilitate communications with the Trans-Mississippi Department. Richmond, 1864. $30.

416   (House bill, no. 10). A bill to amend an act entitled An act to allow commissioned officers of the army rations and the privilege of purchasing clothing from the Quartermaster's Department . . . Richmond, 1864. $30.

418   (House bill, no. 25). A bill to be entitled An act to establish a Bureau of Foreign Supplies in the War Department, with an agency in the Trans-Mississippi Department. Richmond, 1864. $30.

419   (House bill, no. 26). A bill to be entitled An act to provide a fund to be employed for the relief of disabled soldiers and seamen, after the termination of the existing war. Richmond, 1864. $25.

421   (House of Representatives, no. 30). Joint resolutions of the State of Texas. Richmond, 1864. $40.

423   (House bill, no. 48). A bill to be entitled An act to amend an act entitled "An act to regulate impressments," . . . Richmond, 1864. $20.

424   (House bill, no. 49). A bill to be entitled An act to amend an act entitled An act to increase the efficiency of the army, by the employment of free negroes and slaves in certain capacities . . . and to repeal an act for the enlistment of cooks in the army, . . . Richmond, 1864. $30.

426   (House bill, no. 11). A bill to provide for the settlement of claims for property illegally impressed in the Trans-Mississippi Department. Richmond, 1864. $25.

427   (House bill, no. 28). A bill to be entitled An act to establish a Bureau of Foreign Supplies in the War Department, with an agency in the Trans-Mississippi Department. Richmond, 1864. $35.

428   (House bill, no 82). A bill to be entitled "An act to provide for the appointment of commissioners in the several states of the Confederacy to inquire into and report upon the claims against the government of the Confederate States for property taken, used, injured or destroyed by the Army, or any part of it, of the Confederate States, and to provide for the punishment of perjury, subordination of perjury and for presenting fraudulent claims. Richmond, 1864. $25.

429   Resolutions of the Legislature of the State of Mississippi in relation to the recent act . . . suspending the privilege of the writ of *habeas corpus*. Richmond, 1864. $25.

435   (House bill, no. 93). A bill to be entitled an Act for the organization of the Bureau of Conscription, and the appointment of officers in said Bureau. Richmond, 1864. $25.

436   (House bill, no. 120). A bill to be entitled An act to compensate Charles E. Stuart, Israel C. Owings and J. H. Taylor for the use of an improvement in instruments for sighting cannon. Richmond, 1864. $30.

440   (House bill, no. 124). A bill to be entitled An act making appropriations for the support of the government of the Confederate States of America from July 1 to December 31, 1864, and to supply a deficiency. Richmond, 1864. $25.

441   Joint resolutions requiring the settlement of the accounts of the Post-Office Department prior to the first day of July, 1863. Richmond, 1864. $20.

453   (House bill, no. 191) . . . A bill to be entitled "An act to facilitate the settlement of claims of deceased officers and soldiers." Richmond, 1864. $35.

454   (House bill, no. 203.) . . . A bill to be entitled "An act to protect the Confederate States against frauds and to provide remedies against officers and employees of the government committing them." Richmond, 1864. $30.

455   A bill to be entitled An act to define and punish conspiracy against the Confederate States. Richmond, 1864. $30.

458   (House bill, no. 230). A bill to be entitled "An act to amend An act to provide revenue from commodities imported from foreign countries" . . . Richmond, 1864. $20.

459   (House bill, no. 231). A bill to be entitled "An act to exempt from taxation loans made on hypothecation of nontaxable bonds. Richmond, 1864. $20.

460   (House bill, no. 232). A bill to be entitled "An act to exempt from taxation the capital of bonds and certificates issued by the Confederate States." Richmond, 1864. $20.

461   (House bill, no. 233). A bill to be entitled An act to consolidate and amend the laws relative to impressments. Richmond, 1864. $25.

462   (House bill, no. 239). A bill to be entitled An act to organize the Supreme Court. Richmond, 1864. $25.

463   (House bill, no. 240 - Secret session). A bill to provide for the establishment of a bureau of special and secret service. Richmond, 1864. $20.

467   (House bill, no. 267 - Secret). A bill to suspend the privilege of writ of *habeas corpus,* in certain cases, for a limited time. Richmond, 1864. $30.

472   A bill to authorize the employment of instructors for the acting midshipmen of the navy, and to regulate their rank and pay. Richmond, 1864. $30.

473   (House bill, no. 276). A bill making an appropriation to erect additional quarters for acting midshipmen at Drewry's Bluff. Richmond, 1864. $30.

474   (House of Representatives, no. 277). A bill making appropriation for the removal of the naval rope walk and erection of the same. Richmond, 1864. $25.

475   (House of Representatives, no. 278). A bill to increase the number of midshipmen in the navy, and to prescribe the manner of appointment. Richmond, 1864. $25.

476   (House of Representatives, no. 279). A bill to provide for the transfer of certain mechanics, artisans, and other persons, from the army to the navy. Richmond, 1864. $25.

477   (House of Representatives, no. 280). A bill to be entitled "An act to impose a duty on tobacco and an additional duty on cotton exported from the Confederate States. Richmond, 1864. $20.

487   (House of Representatives, no. 285). A bill to lay a tax for revenue to provide for the common defense and carrying on the government of the Confederate States. Richmond, 1864. $20.

490   A bill to be entitled An act to provide for organizing, arming and disciplining the militia of the Confederate States . . . Richmond, 1864. $50.

493   (House bill no. 303). A bill to be entitled An act for the further organization of the field artillery of the Confederate States. Richmond, 1864. $75.

496   (House bill, no. 311.) . . . A bill to provide additional clothing and privileges to troops in the field. Richmond, 1864. $25.

497   . . . Substitute for the bill (H. R. 203) to protect the Confederate States against frauds, and to provide remedies against officers and employees of the government committing them. Richmond, 1864. $35.

506   (House of Representatives, no. 322). A bill to be entitled An act repealing certain abatements from the property tax and income tax, and amending the said tax laws. Richmond, 1865. $20.

512   Joint resolution of confidence in and thanks to President Jefferson Davis. Richmond, 1865. $25.

515   (House of Representatives, no. 183). A bill to be entitled An act to consolidate the public debt. Richmond, 1865. $25.

522   (House of Representatives, no. 344). A bill to be entitled An act to provide for auditing and paying for horses and equipments taken from dismounted cavalrymen for the use of the government. Richmond, 1865. $30.

523   (House of Representatives, no. 349.) . . . A bill to amend An act to organize forces to serve during the war. Richmond, 1865. $30.

525   (House of Representatives, no. 282). A bill to be entitled An act for the prevention of frauds on the revenues of the Post Office Department, and prohibiting the transportation of mailable matter over the post routes of the Confederate States by unauthorized persons. Richmond, 1865. $20.

526   Amendments proposed by Mr. Baldwin to the impressment bill reported from the Judiciary Committee. Richmond, 1865. $25.

538   Resolutions adopted by McGowan's Brigade, South Carolina Volunteers. Richmond, 1865. $100.

542   (Secret session). (House bill no. 370). A bill to amend An act to organize forces to serve during the war. Richmond, 1865. $20.

543   A bill making appropriations to supply a deficiency in the appropriations for the Department of Justice . . . Richmond, 1865. $20.

545   (House of Representatives, no. 378). A bill to provide for the immediate payment of arrears due to the army and navy. Richmond, 1865. $20.

547   Joint resolutions expressing the sense of Congress on the subject of the late peace commission. Richmond, 1865. $50.

548   A bill to increase the efficiency of the cavalry of the Confederate States. Richmond, 1865. $30.

549   (House of Representatives, no. 385). A bill making additional appropriations for the support of the government of the Confederate States . . . Richmond, 1865. $20.

550   (House of Representatives, no. 386). A bill making further regulations for the taxation of banks and bank notes, and for the confiscation of such notes held by alien enemies. Richmond, 1865. $20.

551   (House bill no. 391). A bill to provide means to pay the army and navy, and carry on the war. Richmond, 1865. $20.

553   (House of Representatives, no. 341). A bill requiring suit to be brought against persons connected with the Cotton Bureau and Cotton Office in Texas. Richmond, 1865. $25.

557   Amendment proposed by the Senate to the bill (H.R. 379) to levy additional taxes for the year eighteen hundred and sixty-five, for the support of the government. Richmond, 1865. $20.

562   Calendar of the House of Representatives. Richmond, 1864. January 25, 1864. $25.

570   Report of Committee on Claims. In the case of Mary Clark . . . December 29, 1863. Richmond, 1863. $50.

577   Majority report of the Committee on Foreign Affairs. Richmond, 1862. $35.

583   Report of Committee on Quartermaster and Commissary Departments on case of Major Frank G. Ruffin. Richmond, 1863. $20.

586   Report of the Committee on Rules of the House of Representatives. Richmond, 1865? $30.

589   Report of the Committee on the Judiciary upon martial law. Richmond, 1862. $25.

591   Minority report of the Committee of Ways and Means on the tax bill. Richmond, 1864. $20.

598   Report of the Special Committee on the Charge of Corruption made in the Richmond Examiner, Jan. 7, 1864. Richmond, 1864. $40.

600   Report of the Special Committee on the Pay and Clothing of the Army. Richmond, 1865. $20.

PRESIDENT

612   President's Message. Richmond, November 18, 1861. $30.

624   Message of the President [transmitting a copy of an act of the Legislature of South Carolina, offering a guaranty by that state of the bonds of the Confederate States]. Richmond, 1863. $25.

626   Message of the President. Richmond, April 16, 1863. $20.

627   President's message. Richmond, December 7, 1863. $40.

629   President's message. Richmond, May 2, 1864. $25.

631   President's Message. Richmond, May 28, 1864. $25.

632   Message of the President. Richmond, May 30, 1864. $25.

633   Message of the President. Richmond, November 7th, 1864. $25.

634   Message of the President [transmitting the reports made by the Treasury and War Departments, relative to "A bill to impose regulations upon the foreign commerce of the Confederate States, to provide for the public defense."]. Richmond, December 20, 1864. $30.

637   Message of the President [submitting the report of the commissioners to confer with the President of the United States with a view to the restoration of peace]. Richmond, 1865. $50.

ARMY

669   Resolutions of the Texas Brigade. n.p., 1865. $60.

697   Resolutions of Forsberg's Brigade, Wharton's Division. n.p., 1865. $60.

774R
(H222)   General orders. Houston, 1865. Nos. 1-31; January 1-May 20, 1865. No. 19 issued at Galveston. Each $60.

797-2   General orders. Head Quarters Trans.-Miss. Dept. Shreveport, 1863. Nos. 1-61;
(H236)   March 7-December 10, 1863. Each $40.

BUREAU OF PUBLIC PRINTING

816   Report of the Superintendent of Public Printing . . . April 26, 1864. Richmond,
1864. $20.

DEPARTMENT OF JUSTICE

827   Communication from Attorney General . . . Dec. 15, 1863. Richmond, 1863. $20.

828   Communication from Attorney General . . . January 9, 1864. Richmond, 1864.
$20.

829   Communication from Attorney General . . . May 17, 1864. Richmond, 1864. $20.

835   Report of the Attorney General . . . April 25, 1864. Richmond, 1864. $35.

836   Report of the Attorney General . . . 1st November, 1864. Richmond, 1864. $35.

DEPARTMENT OF STATE

839   Correspondence of the Department of State, in relation to the British consuls
resident in the Confederate States. Richmond, 1863. $75.

DISTRICT COURTS

848   Decisions of Hon. James D. Halyburton, judge of the Confederate States District
Court for the Eastern District of Virginia, in the cases of John B. Lane and John H.
Leftwich, in relation to their exemption, as mail contractors, from the performance
of military service. Richmond, 1864. $75.

NAVY DEPARTMENT

861   Communication from Secretary of Navy . . . Transmitted with Message of the
President . . . March 10, 1863. $25.

862   Communication from the Secretary of the Navy . . . [relative to "a flour and grist
mill and baker," established by the Department, at Albany, Georgia]. Richmond,
1865. $20.

863   Communication of Secretary of the Navy . . . [conveying the information that "no
coals were taken from the steamer 'Advance,' in October last, or at any other time,
for the naval service"]. Richmond, 1865. $50.

881   Register of the commissioned and warrant officers of the Navy of the Confederate
States . . . Richmond, 1863. $200.

888   Report of the Secretary of the Navy . . . November 5, 1864. Richmond, 1864. $125.

PATENT OFFICE

896   Annual report of the Commissioner of Patents . . . Richmond, 1865. $45.

897   Report of the Commissioner of Patents, January, 1862. Richmond, 1862. $45.

898   Report of the Commissioner of Patents . . . January, 1863. Richmond, 1863. $45.

899   Report of the Commissioner of Patents . . . Jan. 1864. Richmond, 1864. $45.

POST-OFFICE DEPARTMENT

923   Report of the Postmaster General . . . December 7, 1863. Richmond, 1863. $35.

SURGEON-GENERAL'S OFFICE

1042   Guide for inspection of hospitals and inspector's report. Richmond, 186-. $75.

1057   A manual of military surgery. Prepared for the use of the Confederate States Army
        . . . By order of the Surgeon-General. Richmond, 1863. $750.

TREASURY DEPARTMENT

1066   Abstracts of drafts of members of the C.S. House of Representatives . . . Richmond,
        1863. $20.

1067   Additional estimates for the support of the government. Richmond, 1864. $20.

1083   Communication accompanying copies of circulars issued in respect to the produce
        loan. Richmond, 1862. $20.

1090   . . . Communication from Secretary of Treasury . . . Feb. 19, 1863, relative to the
        settlement of the claims of deceased soldiers. Richmond, 1863. $60.

1091   . . . Communication from Secretary of Treasury . . . Feb. 25, 1863, in reference to the
        amount of funds paid into the Treasury under the operation of the sequestration
        act. Richmond, 1863. $25.

1093   . . . Communication from Secretary of Treasury . . . December 31, 1863, enclosing
        an estimate of appropriation necessary for the payment of interest on the removal
        and subsistence fund due the Cherokee Indians in North Carolina. Richmond,
        1864. $75.

1096   Communications from Secretary of Treasury . . . May 10, 1864 . . . Richmond, 1864.
        $25.

1098   Communication from the Secretary of the Treasury, recommending certain
        changes in the impressment laws . . . May 20th, 1864. Richmond, 1864. $20.

1100   Communication from Secretary of Treasury . . . May 25, 1864 . . . Richmond, 1864.
        $20.

1103   Communication of Secretary of Treasury . . . November 28, 1864 . . . Richmond,
        1864. $20.

1107   Communication of Secretary of Treasury . . . December 28th, 1864 . . . Richmond,
        1865. $20.

1109   Communication of Secretary of Treasury . . . January 5th, 1865 . . . Richmond,
        1865. $20.

1111   . . . Communication from Secretary of Treasury . . . Feb. 1st, 1865. Richmond,
        1865. $25.

1112   Communication from Secretary of Treasury . . . February 1, 1865 . . . Richmond,
        1865. $20.

1113   Communication of Secretary of Treasury . . . February 8th, 1865 . . . Richmond,
        1865. $20.

1114   Communication of Secretary of Treasury . . . February 11th, 1865 . . . Richmond,
        1865. $20.

1116   Communication of Secretary of Treasury . . . February 20th, 1865 . . . Richmond,
        1865. $20.

1126   Estimate of an additional appropriation required for the service of the government. Richmond, 1862. $25.

1128   Estimate of an additional appropriation required for the service of government, for the year ending February 18th, 1862. Richmond, 1862. $25.

1130   Estimate of an appropriation required for the redemption of such treasury notes as have been, or may be, rendered unfit for circulation by the holders. Richmond, 1862. $25.

1132   Estimates of additional appropriations required for the service of the Navy Department . . . Richmond, 1861. $25.

1140   Instructions for collectors of taxes . . . May 15, 1863. Richmond, 1863. $20.

1147   Letter to the commissioners appointed to receive subscriptions to the produce loan . . . October 15th, 1861. Richmond, 1861. $25.

1150   Letter of the Secretary of the Treasury . . . Jan. 12, 1863 . . . Richmond, 1863. $20.

1151   Letter of the Secretary of the Treasury . . . December 10, 1863 [covering estimates of sums needed for the public service among the Indian tribes]. Richmond, 1863. $50.

1153   Letter of Secretary of Treasury . . . December 12, 1864 . . . Richmond, 1864. $20.

1157   Open letter to the banks concerning the act of Congress to reduce the currency. Richmond, 1864. $20.

1161   Regulations as to certificates of indebtedness . . . May 5th, 1864. Richmond, 1864. $20.

1163   Regulations established for the disposal at private sale of the six per cent. non-taxable bonds of the Confederate States. Richmond, 1864. $20.

1165   Regulations . . . established in relation to the receipt of four per cent. bonds and certificates offered in payment for taxes. Richmond, 1864. $25.

1168   Regulations in relation to the issue of certificates for bonds and registered stock . . . February 25, 1863. Richmond, 1863. $20.

1174   Regulations to authorize the depositaries of the Treasury to receive balances in the hands of post-masters in the Confederate States. Richmond, 1864. $20.

1186   Report of the Secretary of Treasury . . . Nov. 7, 1864. Richmond, 1864. $40.

1187   Report on the condition of government cotton, contiguous to the Mississippi and its tributaries . . . May 16, 1864. Richmond, 1864. $40.

1191   A schedule of all the articles and subjects of taxation, under the provisions of the act of Congress "to lay taxes for the common defense . . . ." Richmond, 1863. $25.

1197   Special report of the Secretary of the Treasury on the subject of the finances . . . January 9th, 1865. Richmond, 1865. $20.

1205   Treasury Circular, no. 1-25. Montgomery and Richmond, 1861-'64. Each $20.

WAR DEPARTMENT

1208   Army regulations, adopted for the use of the Army of the Confederate States . . . New Orleans, 1861. $150.

1210   Army regulations, adopted for the use of the Army of the Confederate States . . . Raleigh, 1861. $200.

1211   Army regulations, adopted for the use of the Army of the Confederate States . . . Richmond, 1861. $175.

1214   Articles of war, for the government of the armies of hte [*sic*] Confederate States. Charleston, 1861. $300.

1215   Articles of war, for the government of the Army of the Confederate States. Montgomery, 1861. $300.

1220   Quartermaster General's Circular (listing those entitled or not entitled to transportation). Richmond, 1861. $20.

1264   Communication of the Secretary of War . . . January 27, 1863 . . . Richmond, 1863. $20.

1271   Communication from the Secretary of War . . . Feb. 5, 1863 . . . Richmond, 1863. $20.

1275   Communication from Secretary of War . . . Feb. 17, 1863 . . . Richmond, 1863. $20.

1279   Communication from the Secretary of War . . . March 3, 1863 . . . Richmond, 1863. $20.

1287   Communication from Secretary of War . . . Dec. 19, 1863 . . . Richmond, 1863. $20.

1296   . . . Communication from the Secretary of War, January 28, 1864 . . . Richmond, 1864. $25.

1300   Communication of the Secretary of War . . . Feb. 4, 1864 . . . Richmond, 1864. $25.

1305   Communication from the Secretary of War . . . November 14, 1864 [submitting an estimate for the steamer *Phoenix*]. Richmond, 1864. $25.

1306   Communication from Secretary of War . . . Nov. 17, 1864 [relative to the act of June 14, 1864, to provide and organize a General Staff]. Richmond, 1864. $25.

1311   Communication from Secretary of War . . . Dec. 6, 1864 . . . Richmond, 1864. $20.

1312   Communication from Secretary of War . . . December 7, 1864 . . . [submitting an estimate of funds required to meet our treaty obligations to the Indian nations . . .]. Richmond, 1864. $50.

1313   Communication from Secretary of War . . . Dec. 16, 1864 . . . Transmitted with Message of the President . . . Jan. 5, 1865. Richmond, 1865. $20.

1314   Communication from Secretary of War . . . Dec. 20, 1864 . . . [conveying information relative to the impressment of slaves]. Richmond, 1865. $30.

1315   Communication from Secretary of War . . . Dec. 21, 1864 . . . [transmitting an estimate by the Chief of the Engineer Bureau, for the schooner *Isabel*]. Richmond, 1865. $30.

1318   Communication of Secretary of War . . . January 6, 1865 . . . Richmond 1865. $20.

1321   Communication of Secretary of War . . . Feb. 7, 1864 [*i.e.,* 1865] . . . Richmond, 1865. $20.

1323   Communication from the Secretary of War . . . Feb. 15th, 1865 . . . Richmond, 1865. $20.

1327   Communication of Secretary of War . . . Feb. 22, 1865 [relative to the number of able-bodied men between the ages of eighteen and forty-five, claimed to be exempt from conscription by the Governor, laws and resolutions of the State of Georgia]. Richmond, 1865. $30.

1330   Correspondence between the Secretaries of War and the Treasury, on the subject of a deficiency of funds. Richmond, 1864. $25.

1343   General Orders from Adjutant and Inspector-General's Office, . . . from January, 1862, to December, 1863 . . . Columbia, 1864. $200.

1344   General orders from the Adjutant and Inspector-General's Office, Confederate States Army, for the year 1863, with a full index. Richmond, 1864. $400.

1345   General Orders from the Adjutant and Inspector-General's Office, Confederate States Army, from January 1, 1864, to July 1, 1864, inclusive . . . Columbia, 1864. $200.
          Variant copy, front wrap and title page information differ. $200.

1348   General Orders. Adjutant and Inspector-General's Office. Richmond, 1862.
          Nos. 1-112; January 1-December 30, 1862. Each $30.

1349   General orders. Adjutant and Inspector-General's Office. Richmond, 1863.
          Nos. 1-164, January 3-December 30, 1863. Each $30.

1358   Letter from the Secretary of War . . . March 31, 1862, communicating copies of the oficial reports, on file in this department, of the battle of Bethel, on the 10th of June, 1861. Richmond, 1862. $50.

1377   Official reports of battles. Richmond, 1864. $300.

1393   Regulations for the Army of the Confederate States, 1863. Richmond, Va. 1863. $225.

1401   Regulations for the Army of the Confederate States, and for the Quartermaster's Department and Pay Department. Richmond, 1861. $100.

1415   Report of Brig. Gen. John S. Williams of operations in East Tennessee, from 27th September to 15th October, 1863. Richmond, 1864. $150.

1422   Report of Major General Hindman, of his operations in the Trans-Mississippi District . . . Richmond, 1864. $300.

1431   Report of the Secretary of War . . . April 28, 1864. Richmond, 1864. $50.

1432   Report of the Secretary of War . . . November 3, 1864. Richmond, 1864. $50.

1435   Reports of the operations of the Army of Northern Virginia, from June 1862, to and including the battle of Fredericksburg, Dec. 13, 1862 . . . Richmond, 1864. Two volumes. $300.

1436   Response of Secretary of War, to the resolutions of the Senate, adopted December 5th, 1864 . . . Richmond, 1864. $35.

1448-3   Uniform and dress of the Army. Richmond, 1861. $825.
(H 398)

ALABAMA

1455-2   Report and resolutions, from the Committee of Thirteen, upon the formation of a
(H 405)   provisional and permanent government between the seceding states. Montgomery, 1861. $250.

ARKANSAS

1485   Ordinances of the State Convention, which convened in Little Rock, May 6, 1861. Little Rock, 1861. $175.

GEORGIA

1518   Journal of the public and secret proceedings of the Convention of the people of Georgia, held in Milledgeville, and in Savannah in 1861 . . . with the ordinances adopted. Milledgeville, 1861. $200.

1521   Acts of the General Assembly of the State of Georgia, passed . . . at an annual session in November and December, 1861. Milledgeville, 1861. $80.

1522   Acts of the General Assembly . . . passed . . . at an annual session in November and December, 1862; also extra session of 1863. Milledgeville, 1863. $100.

1523   Acts of the General Assembly . . . passed . . . at an annual session in November and December, 1863; also, extra session of 1864. Milledgeville, 1863. $80.

1531   The code of the State of Georgia . . . Atlanta, 1861. $100.

1538   Papers relative to the mission of Hon. T. Butler King, to Europe. Milledgeville, Ga. 1863. $100.

MISSISSIPPI

1655   Journal of the State Convention, and ordinances and resolutions adopted in March, 1861. Jackson, 1861. $35.

1659   Laws . . . passed at a called session . . . July 1861. Jackson, 1861. $30.

1660   Laws . . . passed at the regular session . . . November & December 1861, and January, 1862. Jackson, 1862. $30.

1661   Laws . . . passed at a called and regular session . . . Dec. 1862 and Nov. 1863. Selma, Ala., 1864. $30.

1664   Laws . . . passed at a called session . . . February and March, 1865. Meridian, Miss., 1865. $40.

NORTH CAROLINA

1756   Ordinances and resolutions passed by the State Convention of North Carolina, at its several sessions in 1861-'62. Raleigh, 1862. $250.

1757   Ordinances of the State Convention, published in pursuance of a resolution of the General Assembly, (ratified 11th Feb., 1863.) Raleigh, 1863. Bound with Crandall 1796, 1797, 1799, 1804, 1805, 1806. $200.

1789   Executive and legislative documents. Session 1862-'63. Raleigh, 1863. Documents 1-24. Each $50.

1791   Executive and legislative documents. Extra sessions 1863-'64. Raleigh, 1864. $125.

1792   Executive and legislative documents. Session of 1864-'65. Raleigh, 1865. $30.

1795   Private laws of the State of North Carolina, passed by the General Assembly at its session of 1860-'61. Raleigh, 1861. Private laws of the State of North Carolina, passed by the General Assembly, at its first extra session, 1861. Bound with Crandall, 1802. $100.

1796   Private laws of the State of North Carolina, passed by the General Assembly at its session of 1862-'63. Raleigh, 1863. See Crandall 1757.

1797   Private laws of the State of North Carolina, passed by the General Assembly at its adjourned session of 1862-'63. Raleigh, 1863. See Crandall 1757.

1799   Private laws of the State of North Carolina, passed by the General Assembly at its called session of 1863. Raleigh, 1863. See Crandall 1757.

1800   Private laws of the State of North Carolina, passed by the General Assembly at its adjourned session of 1863. Bound with Crandall 1801, 1807 and 1808. $30.

1801   Private laws of the State of North Carolina, passed by the General Assembly at its adjourned session of 1864. Raleigh, 1864. See Crandall 1800.

1802   Public laws of the State of North Carolina, passed by the General Assembly, at its session of 1860-'61; together with the Comptroller's statement of public revenue and expenditure. Raleigh, 1861. Public laws of the State of North Carolina, passed by the General Assembly, at its first extra session of 1861. See Crandall 1795.

1803   Public laws of the State of North Carolina, passed by the General Assembly, at its second extra session, 1861. Raleigh, 1861. $75.

1804   Public laws of the State of North Carolina, passed by the General Assembly, at its session of 1862-'63. Raleigh, 1863. See Crandall 1757.

1805   Public laws of the State of North-Carolina, passed by the General Assembly, at its adjourned session of 1862-'63: Raleigh, 1863. See Crandall 1757.

1806   Public laws of the State of North Carolina, passed by the General Assembly at its called session of 1863. Raleigh, 1863. See Crandall 1757.

1807   Public laws of the State of North Carolina, passed by the General Assembly at its adjourned session of 1863. Raleigh, 1863. See Crandall 1800.

1808   Public laws of the State of North Carolina, passed by the General Assembly at its adjourned session of 1864. Raleigh, 1864. See Crandall 1800.

1816   Journal of the Senate of the General Assembly of the State of North Carolina, at its extra session, 1861. Raleigh, 1861. Bound with Crandall 1844. $35.

1817   Journal of the Senate of the General Assembly of the State of North Carolina, at its first session, 1862. Raleigh, 1862. Bound with Crandall 1818 and 1845. $150.

1818   Journal of the Senate of the General Assembly of the State of North Carolina, at its second session, 1863. Raleigh, 1863. See Crandall 1817.

1844   Journal of the House of Commons of the General Assembly of the State of North Carolina, at its second extra session, 1861. Raleigh, N.C., 1862. See Crandall 1816.

1845   Journal of the House of Commons of North Carolina, at its session 1862-'63. Raleigh, 1862. Journal of the House of Commons of North Carolina at its adjourned session 1862-'63. Raleigh, 1863. See Crandall 1817.

1861-2   Statements of the Comptroller of Public Accounts for the two fiscal years ending
(H 744)   Sept. 30, 1861 and 1862. Raleigh, 1862. $100.

1861-9   Cases at law, argued and determined in the Supreme Court of North Carolina, at
(H 751)   Raleigh, June term, 1863. Raleigh? 1863. $150.

1863-4   List of the wounded from the State of North Carolina. In the battle of Richmond,
(H 760)   from June 26th to July 1st, 1862 . . . n.p., 1862. $100.

SOUTH CAROLINA

1871   Convention documents. Report of the Special Committee of Twenty-one, on the communication of His Excellency Governor Pickens, together with the reports of heads of departments, and other papers. Columbia, 1862. $100.

1873   Declaration of the immediate causes which induce and justify the secession of South Carolina from the federal union; and the ordinance of secession. Charleston, 1860. $400.

1900 Acts of the General Assembly . . . passed in December, 1862, and February and April, 1863 . . . Columbia, 1863. $30.

2104 Message no. 1 of His Excellency, F. W. Pickens, to the Legislature, at the regular session of November, 1862. Columbia, S. C., 1862. $50.

2122 The correspondence between the commissioners of the State of So. Ca. to the government at Washington and the President of the United States . . . Charleston, 1861. $80.

2135 Census of the city of Charleston, South Carolina, for the year 1861 . . . by Frederick A. Ford. $50.

TENNESSEE

2139 Public acts . . . passed at the extra session of the thirty-third General Assembly, April, 1861. Nashville, 1861. $60.

TEXAS

2150 The constitution of the State of Texas, as amended in 1861. The constitution of the Confederate States of America. The ordinances of the Texas Convention: and an address to the people of Texas . . . Austin, 1861. $350.

2152 A declaration of the causes which impel the State of Texas to secede from the federal union. Austin, 1861. $750.

2171 General laws of the ninth Legislature of the State of Texas. Houston, 1862. $200.

VIRGINIA

2256 The new constitution of Virginia, with the amended bill of rights, as adopted by the Reform Convention of 1850-51, and amended by the Convention of 1860-61. Richmond?, 1861? Bound with Crandall 2273 and 2274. $60.

2257 Addresses delivered before the Virginia State Convention by Hon. Fulton Anderson, commissioner from Mississippi, Hon. Henry L. Benning, commissioner from Georgia, and Hon. John S. Preston, commissioner from South Carolina, February 1861. Richmond, 1861. $150.

2258 Documents. Richmond, 1861. Nos. 1-54 (lacking no. 39 which apparently was not printed). $300.

2271 Acts of the General Assembly . . . passed in 1861 . . . Richmond, 1861. $60.

2272 Acts of the General Assembly . . . passed in 1861-62 . . . Richmond, 1862. $60.

2273 Acts of the General Assembly . . . passed at called session, 1862 . . . Richmond, 1862. See Crandall 2256.

2274 Acts of the General Assembly . . . passed at adjourned session, 1863 . . . Richmond, 1863. See Crandall 2256.

2275 Acts of the General Assembly . . . passed at called session, 1863 . . . Richmond, 1863. Bound with Crandall 2276. $50.

2276 Acts of the General Assembly . . . passed at session of 1863-64 . . . Richmond, 1864. See Crandall 2275.

2279 Documents. 1861-62. Richmond, 1862. Nos. 1-68. Each $15.

2295 Journal of the Senate of the Commonwealth of the Virginia: begun and held at the Capitol in the city of Richmond, on Monday, the second day of December, in the year one thousand eight hundred and sixty-one—being the eighty-fifth year of the Commonwealth. Richmond, 1861. $300.

2357 Journal of the House of Delegates of the State of Virginia, for the session of 1861-62. Richmond, 1861. Bound with Crandall 2358. $75.

2358 Journal of the House of Delegates of the State of Virginia, for the extra session, 1862. Richmond, 1862. See Crandall 2357.

2359 Journal of the House of Delegates of the State of Virginia, for the called session of 1862. Richmond, 1862. Bound with Crandall 2360. $150.

2360 Journal of the House of Delegates of the State of Virginia, for the adjourned session, 1863. Richmond, 1863. See Crandall 2359.

2361 Journal of the House of Delegates of the State of Virginia, for the called session of 1863. Richmond, 1863. Bound with Crandall 2362. $75.

2362 Journal of the House of Delegates of the State of Virginia, for the session of 1863-64. Richmond, 1863. See Crandall 2361.

2377 Resolutions of Wise's Brigade. *n.p.*, 1865. $75.

Unofficial Publications

MILITARY TEXTS AND MANUALS

2400 **BUCKHOLTZ,** Louis von. Tactics for officers of infantry, cavalry and artillery . . . Richmond, 1861. $200.

2401 **BUGEAUD DE LA PICONNERIE,** Thomas Robert, *duc d'Isly* The practice of war. By C. F. Pardigon. Richmond, 1863. $200.

2409 **DAVIS,** James Lucius. The trooper's manual: or, Tactics for light dragoons and mounted riflemen . . . Richmond, 1861. 284 pgs. $200.

2410 **DAVIS** James Lucius. The trooper's manual: or, Tactics for light dragoons and mounted riflemen . . . Richmond, 1861. 303 pgs. $250.

2418 **GILHAM,** William. Manual of instruction for the volunteers and militia of the Confederate States . . . Richmond, 1861. $200.

2419 **GILHAM,** William. Manual of instruction for the volunteers and militia of the Confederate States. Richmond, 1862. $250.

2421 **HARDEE,** William Joseph . . . Rifle and infantry tactics . . . (First edition). Mobile, 1861. Two volumes. $250.

2425 **HARDEE,** William Joseph. Rifle and infantry tactics . . . (Third edition). Mobile, 1861. Two volumes. $250.

2429 **HARDEE,** William Joseph . . . Rifle and infantry tactics . . . (Ninth edition) . . . Mobile, 1863. Two volumes. $600.

2430 **HARDEE,** William Joseph . . . Rifle and infantry tactics . . . Raleigh, 1862. $200.

2433 **HARDEE,** William Joseph . . . Rifle and light infantry tactics . . . Memphis, 1861. Two volumes in one. $250.

2436 **HARDEE,** William Joseph . . . Rifle and light infantry tactics . . . Richmond, Va., 1861. Two volumes in one. $600.
ANOTHER COPY, Printed without plates. Crandall notes at 2436: "Emory University has another issue of this edition printed without plates." $400.

2441 **LEE,** Charles Henry. The judge advocates vade mecum: Embracing a general view of military law and the practice before courts martial . . . Richmond, 1863. $150.

2448 **LEE,** James Kendall . . . The volunteer's hand book . . . (Third edition) Richmond, Va., 1861. $250.

2449 **[LeGAL,** Eugene]. The school for guides, for the use of the Army of the Confederate States . . . Savannah, 1861. $300.

2459 **MAHAN,** Dennis Hart A treatise on field fortifications . . . Richmond, 1862. $250.

2462 **MARMONT,** Auguste F. L. Viesse De. The spirit of military institutions . . . Columbia, 1864. $400.

2464 **NOLAN,** Lewis Edward. Cavalry; its history and tactics . . . Columbia, 1864. $250.

2469 **RICHARDSON,** John H. Infantry tactics, or, rules for the exercise and manoeuvres of the Confederate States infantry . . . Richmond, Va., 1862. $400.

2470 **RICHARDSON,** John H. Infantry tactics, or, rules for the exercise and manoeuvres of the Confederate States infantry . . . Shreveport, La., 1864. $250.

2471 **RICHARDSON,** William H. A manual of infantry and rifle tactics . . . Richmond, Va., 1861. $200.

2479 **SCOTT,** Winfield. Infantry-tactics; or rules of the exercise and manoeuvres of infantry . . . Raleigh, 1862. $200.

2482 **STARK,** Alexander W. Instruction for field artillery . . . Richmond, 1864. $500.

2485 Instruction for heavy artillery; prepared by a board of officers for use of the Army of the United States. Charleston, 1861. $350.

2486 Instruction for heavy artillery . . . Richmond, 1862. $350.

2487 The ordinance manual for the use of the officers of the United States Army. Second edition. Charleston, 1861. $250.

2488 The ordinance manual for the use of the officers of the United States Army. Second edition. Richmond, 1861. $250.

2490 **VIELE,** Egvert Ludovikus. Hand-book of field fortifications and artillery . . . Richmond, 1861. $250.

2491 **WHEELER,** Joseph. A revised system of cavalry tactics, for the use of the cavalry and mounted infantry, C.S.A. Mobile, 1863. $300.

MILITARY MISCELLANIES

2544 **SIMONS,** James. Address to the officers of the Fourth Brigade, giving the grounds for his resignation . . . Charleston, 1861. $125.

BIOGRAPHY

2563 **COOKE,** John Esten. The life of Stonewall Jackson. By a Virginian . . . Richmond, 1863. $450.

2573 **EDWARDS,** Weldon Nathaniel. Memoir of Nathaniel Macon, of North Carolina. Raleigh, 1862. $150.

2576 **FURMAN,** James Clement. Sermon on the death of Rev. James M. Chiles, preached at Horeb Church, Abbeville District, S.C., on Sunday, 29th of March, 1863. Greenville, S.C., 1863. $100.

2583 **HOWE,** George. Discourse in commemoration of the life and labors of Rev. George Cooper Gregg . . . Columbia, 1862. $75.

2587 **JAMISON,** David Flavel. The life and times of Bertrand Du Guesclin: a history of the fourteenth century. Charleston, 1864. Two volumes. $200.

2593 **McCABE,** James Dabney. The life of Thomas J. Jackson. By an ex-cadet. Second edition. Richmond, 1864. $350.

2600 **RAMSEY,** James Beverlin. True eminence founded on holiness. A discourse occasioned by the death of Lieut. Gen. T. J. Jackson . . . May 24th, 1863. Lynchburg, Va., 1863. $125.

HISTORY

2615 The battle of Fort Sumter . . . Charleston, 1861. $200.

2621 **DAVIS,** Nicholas A. The campaign from Texas to Maryland. Richmond, 1863. $2500.

2623 [**DeFONTAINE,** Felix Gregory]. Marginalia; or, Gleanings from an army note-book. By "Personne" . . . Columbia, 1864. $200.

2628 **HARRIS,** W. A. The record of Fort Sumter, from its occupation by Major Anderson . . . Columbia, S.C., 1862. $250.

2636 **JONES,** Charles Colcock, Jr. Monumental remains of Georgia. Part first. Savannah, 1861. $175.

2641 A Narrative of the battles of Bull Run and Manassas Junction, July 18th and 21st, 1861 . . . Charleston, 1861. $350.

2643 **POLLARD,** Edward Alfred. The first year of the war. Richmond, 1862. $150.

2645 **POLLARD,** Edward Alfred. The first year of the war . . . Richmond, 1862. $175.

2647 **POLLARD,** Edward Alfred. Observations in the North: eight months in prison and on parole. Richmond, 1865. $300.

2654 **POLLARD,** Edward Alfred. The seven days' battles in front of Richmond. Richmond, 1862. $200.

2658 **REA,** D. B. Sketches from Hampton's cavalry . . . Columbia, S. C., 1864. $500.

2662 **WARDER,** T. B., and **CATLETT,** James M. Battle of Young's Branch; or, Manassas Plain, fought July 21, 1861 . . . Richmond, 1862. $600.

2664 **WEST,** Beckwith. Experience of a Confederate States prisoner . . . Richmond, 1862. $350.

DESCRIPTION AND TRAVEL

2670 **FREMANTLE,** Sir Arthur James Lyon. Three months in the Southern States: April, June, 1863. Mobile, 1864. $650.

2675 **PETTIGREW,** James Johnston. Notes on Spain and the Spaniards, in the summer of 1859, with a glance at Sardinia. Charleston, 1861. $450.

2676 The Stranger's guide and official directory for the city of Richmond . . . Richmond, 1863. $250.

2679 **WIGGS,** A. R. Hal's travels in Europe, Egypt, and the Holy Land . . . Nashville, Tenn., 1861. $150.

POLITICS, FINANCE AND ECONOMICS

2716   THE CONFEDERATE. By a South Carolinian. Mobile, 1863. $500.

2728   DE JARNETTE, Daniel C. The Monroe Doctrine . . . Richmond?, 1865. $75.

2735   ELECTION, Wednesday, November 6th, 1861. For President, Jefferson Davis . . . Richmond? 1861. *Broadside.* $200.

2744   FOR PRESIDENT, Jefferson Davis, of Mississippi. For Vice President, A. H. Stephens, of Georgia . . . *n.p.,* 1861. *Broadside.* Four variant printings and sizes. $200.

2784   **MacMAHON,** T. W. Cause and contrast: an essay on the American crisis. Richmond, 1862. $150.

2824   **POLLARD,** Edward Alfred. The Southern spy. Letters on the policy and inauguration of the Lincoln war . . . Richmond, 1861. Second edition. $150.

2831   **RICHARDSON,** George W. Speech . . . in Committee of the Whole, on the report of the Committee on Federal Relations, in the Convention of Virginia, April 4, 1861. Richmond, 1862. $40.

2845   **SMITH,** William Russell. The history and debates of the Convention of the people of Alabama . . . in which is preserved the speeches of the secret sessions and many valuable state papers. Montgomery, 1861. $400.

2861   **THORNWELL,** James Henley. The state of the country . . . Columbia, 1861. $75.

2879   **YANCEY,** William Lowndes. Speeches . . . made in the Senate of the Confederate States during the session commencing on the eighteenth day of August, A.D., 1862. Montgomery, 1862. $200.

SLAVERY AND THE NEGRO

2882   **BERRY,** Harrison. Slavery and abolitionism, as viewed by a Georgia slave. Atlanta, 1861. $500.

2886   **DE BOW,** James Dunwoody Brownson. The interest in slavery of the Southern non-slaveholder. Charleston, 1860. $200.

2888   **JONES,** Charles Colcock, Sr. Religious instruction of the negroes . . . Richmond, 1862? $175.

BUSINESS AND AGRICULTURE

2903   **CHAMPOMIER,** P. A. Statement of the sugar crop of Louisiana, of 1861-62. New Orleans, 1862. $100.

2918   **JONES,** Joseph. Agricultural resources of Georgia. Address before the Cotton Planters Convention of Georgia at Macon, December 13, 1860. Augusta, Ga., 1861. $60.

RAILROADS, STEAMBOATS AND CANALS

2992   Proceedings of the fourteenth annual meeting of the stockholders of the Raleigh and Gaston Rail Road Company . . . Raleigh, 1864. $40.

MEDICINE

3026   **CHISOLM,** John Julian. A manual of military surgery, for the use of surgeons in the Confederate Army . . . Charleston, 1861. $800.

3028   **CHISOLM,** John Julian. A manual of military surgery, for the use of surgeons in the Confederate Army . . . Richmond, 1862. $600.

3041   **PORCHER,** Francis Peyre. Resources of the Southern fields and forests, medical, economical and agricultural. Being a medical botany of the Confederate States . . . Charleston, 1863. $1200.

3042   **PORCHER,** Francis Peyre. Resources of the Southern fields and forests, medical, economical, and agricultural. Being also a medical botany of the Confederate States . . . Richmond, 1863. $1500.

3044   **WARREN,** Edward. An epitome of practical surgery, for field and hospital. Richmond, Va., 1863. $1200.

MAPS

3056   **McRAE,** A. T. Map of the battle ground of Greenbrier River . . . Richmond, 1861? $500.

3057   **MANOUVRIER,** J., & Co. Map of the present seat of war in Missouri. N. O. 1861? $500.

3060   **MITCHELL,** Samuel P. Sketch of the country occupied by the Federal & Confederate armies on the 18th & 21st July 1861. Richmond, 1861? $500.

3065   TOPOGRAPHICAL sketch of the battle of Bethel, June 10th, 1861. *n.p.* 1861? $500.

3066   **WEST & JOHNSTON.** Map of the State of Virginia containing the counties, principal towns, railroads, rivers, canals & all other internal improvements. Richmond, Va., 1862. $600.

3067   **WEST & JOHNSTON.** Map of the State of Virginia containing the counties, principal towns, rail-roads, rivers, canals & all other internal improvements. Richmond, 1862. $750.

FICTION

3072   **BRADDON,** Mary Elizabeth. Aurora Floyd. Richmond, 1863. $350.

3082   **DAVIS,** Mrs. Mary Elizabeth (Moragne). The British partizan: a tale of the olden time. By a lady of South Carolina. Macon, Ga., 1864. $200.

3088   **EDGEVILLE,** Edward. Castine . . . Raleigh, 1865. $100.

3095   **DERRINGTON,** W. D. The deserter's daughter. Raleigh, 1865. $200.

3096   **HUGO,** Victor Marie. Les miserables . . . Richmond, 1863-64. Issued in five parts. $800.

3104   **McCABE,** James Dabney. The aid-de-camp; a romance of the war. Richmond, 1863. $225.

3105   **MUNDT,** *Frau* Clara. Henry VIII, and his court, or Catherine Parr. A historical novel, By L. Muhlbach. Mobile, 1865. Two volumes. $275.

3106   **MUNDT,** *Frau* Clara. Joseph II. and his court . . . by L. Muehlbach . . . Mobile, 1864. Four volumes. $1000.

3111   **THACKERAY,** William Makepeace. The adventures of Philip on his way through the world . . . Columbia, S.C., 1864. $1000.

3112   **TUCKER,** Nathaniel Beverley. The partisan leader . . . Richmond, 1862. $600.

3114 **WILSON,** *Mrs.* Augusta Jane (Evans). Macaria; or, Altars of sacrifice. Richmond, 1864. $450.

3115 **WILSON,** *Mrs.* Augusta Jane (Evans). Macaria; or Altars of Sacrifice. Second edition. Richmond, 1864. $450.

POETRY

3138 **FANE,** Julian Henry Charles, and **BULWER-LYTTON,** Edward. Tannhaeuser; or, The battle of the bards . . . By Neville Temple and Edward Trevor. Mobile, 1863. $150.

3141 **HILL,** Theophilus Hunter. Hesper, and other poems . . . Raleigh, 1861. $100.

3149 **PRESTON,** *Mrs.* Margaret (Junkin). Beechenbrook; a rhyme of the war. Richmond, 1865. $225.

3154 **SHEPPERSON,** William G., Ed. War Songs of the South. Edited by "Bohemian" . . . Richmond, 1862. $200.

BROADSIDE VERSE

3157-5 Battle Hymn of a Virginia Soldier. n.p., 186-? $100.
(H 1221)

3165 The Confederate Soldier's wife parting from her husband! n.p. 1861? $100.

3166 Country, home and liberty. n.p., 1861? $50.

3167-1 The dying Confederate's last words. n.p., 186-? $100.
(H 1227)

3170 The Georgia Volunteer. Savannah, 1861? $100.

3170-1 God and Liberty! n.p., 186-? $100.
(H 1230)

3171-1 Hark! O'er the Southern hills . . . n.p., 186-? $100.
(H 1232)

3176 Hurrah for Dixie! n.p., 1861? $175

3180-1 L.R. Dear liberty, or Maryland will be free. Richmond, 186-? $100.
(H 1239)

3181 **LAMB,** Robert. Rally around the stars and bars! n.p., 1861? $125.

3185 Lines on the death of the Confederate Gen. Albert Sidney Johnston, of Ky. . . . n.p., 1862? $150.

3192 North Carolina. A call to arms!!! Raleigh, 1861. $100.

3199 Prison Bill of fare, by a prisoner of war, composed, written and spoken at the exhibition of the "Prisoners of War Dramatic Association" . . . Richmond?, 1861. $250.

3210 South Carolina. Charleston, 1861. $150.

3213 **STANTON,** Henry Thompson. Awake in Dixie . . . [by] H.T.S. Winchester, Va., Feb. 24, 1862. $150.

3215 Tennessee! Fire away! n.p., 1861? $150.

3217 **TIMROD,** Henry. Ode on the meeting of the Southern Congress. n.p., 1861? $225.

3219-1   **TUCKER,** Henry St. George. The Southern Cross . . . Selma, Ala., 1861. $150.
(H 1255)

3224   **WHITAKER,** D. K. Maryland in chains . . . Richmond Examiner, May 14, 1861.
          $150.

PLAY-BILLS AND ENTERTAINMENTS

3239   Grand Military ball. The pleasure of your company is respectfully solicited at a ball
          to be given at Camp Carondelet, near Manassas, Tuesday evening, February 25th,
          1862. $250.

SONGSTERS AND MUSICAL INSTRUCTION

3254   The bold soldier boy's song book. Richmond, n.d. $125.

3256   **BRANSON,** Thomas A. The Jack Morgan songster. Raleigh, N. C., 1864. $300.

3265   The Punch songster . . . Richmond, 1864. $150.

3271   Songs of the South. Richmond, 1864. $150.

BOOKS AND PUBLISHING

3279   **HARDEE,** William Joseph, and **GOETZEL,** S. H. Memorial to the Congress of
          the Confederate States. Mobile, 1863. $60.

SHEET MUSIC

3292   Ah! I have sigh'd to rest me . . . Macon, Ga., 186-. $50.

3298   "All quiet along the Potomac to-night" . . . Columbia, 1863. $50.

3301   Angel of dreams . . . Augusta, Ga., c. 1864. $50.

3302   Annie Lawrie [*sic*] . . . Augusta, Ga., 186-. $50.

3304   Annie of the vale . . . Richmond and Columbia, 186-. $50.

3310   Aura Lea . . . Richmond, c. 1864. $50.

3314   Battery Wagner . . . Columbia, 1863. $75.

3320   The Beauregard Manassas quick-step. Augusta, c. 1861. $50.

3325   "Bessie Bell" Waltz . . . Richmond, c. 1864. $50.

3331   The bonnie blue flag . . . Augusta, Ga., c. 1861. $50.

3338   The bonnie blue flag . . . New Orleans, c. 1861. $50.

3339   The bonnie blue flag . . . New Orleans, c. 1861. $50.

3341   . . . Bonny Eloise, the belle of the Mohawk vale. Augusta, 1861. $50.

3346   Bonny Jean . . . Augusta and New Orleans, 186-. $50.

3348   Boys keep your powder dry . . . Augusta, c. 1863. $50.

3349   Brave boys are they . . . Augusta, c. 1864. $50.

3351   Brightest eyes, Macon, 186-. $50.

3352   The brightest eyes galop . . . Augusta, c. 1861. $50.

3357   "Call me not back from the echoless shore . . . Columbia, 186-. $50.

3358   Camp-fire song . . . Augusta, c. 1864. $50.

3368   Carrie Bell . . . Augusta, c. 1861. $50.

3372   The child of the regiment . . . Macon, 186-. $50.

3375   Christmas and New Year musical souvenir; "Fairies have broken their wands" . . . Richmond and Columbia, c. 1863. $125.

3383   Come where my love lies dreaming . . . Macon and Savannah, c. 1863. $50.

3391   Confederate's grand march. New Orleans, c. 1861. $50.

3396   Confederates' polka march . . . Augusta, c. 1864. $50.

3407   Darling little blue-eyed Nell . . . New Orleans, 186-. $50.

3412   Dearest mother I've come home to die . . . Richmond and Columbia, 186-. $50.

3413   The dearest spot of earth to me is home . . . Augusta and New Orleans, 186-. $50.

3431   Dreams . . . Macon, 186-. $50.

3432   The drummer boy of Shiloh . . . Augusta, c. 1863. $60.

3438   Empire State grand march . . . Macon & Savannah, c. 1864. $50.

3439   Ever of thee . . . Augusta, 186-. $50.

3449   Fairy-belle . . . New Orleans, 186-. $50.

3452   "Farewell enchanting hope;" . . . Richmond and Columbia, c. 1863. $50.

3457   First love waltz . . . Richmond, c. 1864. $50.

3468   Freedom's muster-drum . . . Macon and Savannah, c. 1864. $50.

3476   Gen. Beauregard's grand march . . . Macon, 186-. $50.

3489   Gen'l Morgan's grand march . . . Richmond and Columbia, c. 1864. $50.

3492   Gen'l Robert E. Lee's quick march . . . New Orleans and Augusta, c. 1863. $75.

3499   . . . God and our rights . . . New Orleans, 1861. $50.

3502   God save the South! . . . Augusta, 186-. $75.

3510   God save the Southern land . . . Richmond, c. 1864. $75.

3511   God will defend the right . . . Richmond and Augusta, c. 1861. $50.

3515   The good bye at the door . . . Augusta, 186-. $50.

3517   "Good bye sweetheart, good bye" . . . Richmond and Columbia, c. 1863. $50.

3521   Harp of the South awake! . . . Richmond and Columbia, c. 1863. $50.

3525   "Her bright smile haunts me still;" . . . Macon, 186-. $50.

3528   "Her bright smile haunts me still" . . . Richmond, c. 1864. $50.

3532   Home sweet home . . . Macon & Savannah, 186-. $50.

3533   How can I leave thee. Augusta, 186-. $50.

3541   I cannot forget thee . . . Augusta, c. 1864. $50.

3543   I dream of thee . . . Augusta, c. 1864. $75.

3546   . . . I remember the hour when sadly we parted . . . Mobile, c. 1864. $50.

3547   I see her still in my dreams . . . Augusta, 186-. $50.

3548   I see her still in my dreams . . . Macon, 186-. $50.

3552   I will meet thee . . . Macon & Savannah, c. 1863. $50.

3557   I would like to change my name . . . New Orleans, c. 1862. $50.

3559   I'd be a star . . . Augusta and New Orleans, 186-. $50.

3571   Improvisation on the Bonnie blue flag . . . New Orleans, c. 1862. $50.

3582   Juanita . . . Augusta, c. 186-. $50.

3583   Juanita . . . Macon, 186-. $50.

3588   Kathleen Mavourneen . . . Richmond. Columbia, 186-. $50.

3590   Keep me awake, mother . . . Columbia, c. 1863. $50.

3591   Keep me awake, mother . . . Macon, c. 1863. $50.

3592   Kentucky, once so proud and free . . . Macon, 1863. $100.

3594   Kiss me before I die mother . . . Augusta, 186-. $50.

3600   Let me kiss him for his mother . . . Augusta, 186-. $50.

3601   Let me kiss him for his mother . . . Macon, 186-. $50.

3609   Lorena . . . Augusta, 186-. $50.

3621   Love me! . . . Richmond, 186-. $50.

3627   The maiden's prayer. Macon, 186-. $50.

3628   The maiden's prayer. Macon & Savannah, 186-. $50.

3634   The March of the Southern men. Richmond and Columbia, c. 1863. $50.

3638   Mary of Argyle . . . Augusta, 186-. $50.

3641   Maryland! my Maryland! . . . Augusta and New Orleans, c. 1862. $75.

3642   Maryland! my Maryland! . . . Augusta and New Orleans, c. 1862. $75.

3644   Maryland! my Maryland! . . . New Orleans, c. 1862. $75.

3645   Maryland! my Maryland! . . . New Orleans, c. 1862. $75.

3658   The mocking bird quickstep . . . Richmond, c. 1864. $50.

3659   Mollie's dream waltz. Augusta, 186-. $50.

3666   Mother, is the battle over [?] . . . Columbia, c. 1863. $50.

3669   Mother, oh! sing me to rest . . . Richmond and Columbia, 186-. $50.

3670   Mother would comfort me! . . . Augusta, 186-. $50.

3671   The murmur of the shell . . . Richmond, c. 1864. $50.

3676   My wife and child . . . Richmond and Columbia, c. 1863. $50.

3681   Never surrender quick step . . . Augusta, c. 1863. $75.

3686   No one to love; Macon and Savannah, 186-. $50.

3687   "No one to love;" . . . Richmond and Columbia, 186-. $50.

3693   Not for gold or precious stones. Macon and Savannah, 186-. $50.

3703   The officer's funeral . . . Macon, 186-. $50.

3707   "Oh, whisper what thou feelest!" . . . Macon and Savannah, c. 1864. $50.

3710   Old Dominion march . . . Richmond, c. 1863. $50.

3712   On guard; . . . Richmond and Columbia, c. 1864. $50.

3713   On the mountain's airy summit; Macon, 186-. $50.

3737   Patty mazurka; . . . Danville, [Va.] and Richmond, c. 1863. $50.

3738   Paul Vane . . . Augusta, 186-. $50.

3739   Paul Vane . . . Macon 186-. $50.

3753   Pray, maiden, pray! . . . Richmond, c. 1864. $50.

3757   The prisoner's lament. Augusta, c. 1863. $50.

3760   Rest, darling, rest . . . Augusta, c. 1864. $50.

3773   Rochester schottish . . . Macon and Savannah, 186-. $50.

3779   Rock me to sleep, mother . . . Columbia, 1862. $50.

3781   Rock me to sleep, mother . . . Macon, 186-. $50.

3793   "See at your feet a suppliant one;" . . . Richmond and Columbia, 186-. $50.

3816   The soldier's suit of grey; . . . Augusta, c. 1864. $75.

3819   "Something to love me;" . . . Richmond and Columbia, 186-. $50.

3829   The Southern cross; Richmond, and Columbia, c. 1863. $75.

3832   The Southern Marseillaise; . . . Augusta, c. 1862. $50.

3839   The Southern soldier boy; . . . Richmond and Columbia, c. 1863. $50.

3850   Spring time polka. Richmond, c. 1864. $50.

3851   The standard bearer . . . Richmond, c. 1864. $50.

3856   The stars of our banner . . . Augusta, c. 1861. $50.

3863   Stonewall Jackson's grand march. Macon, c. 1863? $75.

3864   Stonewall Jackson's grand march. Macon and Savannah, c. 1863. $75.

3867   Stonewall Jackson's grand march. New Orleans and Augusta, c. 1863. $75.

3873   The Switzer's farewell; . . . Augusta, 186-. $50.

3878   Take me home . . . Macon and Savannah, c. 1864. $50.

3882   Then you'll remember me . . . Macon, 186-. $50.

3888   There's life in the old land yet . . . Augusta, 186-. $50.

3893   They said my love would change with time . . . Macon and Savannah, 186-. $50.

3898   Three cheers for our Jack Morgan! . . . Augusta, 186-. $50.

3909   The unknown dead . . . Macon and Savannah, c. 1863. $50.

3910   Up with the flag . . . Richmond and Columbia, c. 1863. $50.

3914   The vale of rest. Macon, 186-. $50.

3917   Violetta (or, I'm thinking of a flower) . . . Augusta, c. 1862. $50.

3922   Virginian Marseillaise . . . Richmond and Columbia, c. 1863. $75.

3924   The volunteer. New Orleans, c. 1861. $75.

3925   The volunteer . . . Augusta and New Orleans, c. 1861. $50.

3927   The volunteer . . . Augusta, 1864. $50.

3930   The volunteer . . . New Orleans, c. 1861. $50.

3933   Wait till the war, love, is over . . . Augusta, c. 1864. $50.

3934   Wait till the war, love, is over . . . Richmond, c. 1864. $50.

3942   Washington Artillery polka march . . . Augusta, c. 1864. $75.

3944   We conquer or die. Macon, c. 1861. $75.

3945   We conquer, or die! . . . Macon, c. 1861. $50.

3947   "We have parted." Richmond, and Columbia, c. 1863. $50.

3948   We may be happy yet . . . Augusta, 186-. $50.

3954   When I saw sweet Nellie home . . . Macon and Savannah, 186-. $50.

3956   When the boys come home! . . . Augusta, 186-. $50.

3961   When this cruel war is over . . . Richmond and Columbia. 186-. $50.

3962   When this cruel war is over . . . Richmond and Columbia, c. 1864. $50.

3967   Who will care for mother now . . . Richmond and Columbia, c. 1863. $50.

3968   Who will care for mother now . . . Richmond, c. 1864. $50.

3972   Why no one to love? . . . Richmond and Columbia, 186-. $50.

3983   The young volunteer: . . . Macon and Savannah, c. 1863. $50.

EDUCATION AND EDUCATIONAL INSTITUTIONS

3984   Address to the people of North Carolina. Raleigh? 1861? $100.

4006   NORTH CAROLINA UNIVERSITY, *Chapel Hill* Catalogue of the trustees, faculty and students of the University of North Carolina, 1861-'62. Raleigh, 1862. $40.

4013   SOUTH CAROLINA COLLEGE Catalogue of the trustees, faculty and students, of the South Carolina College, January, MDCCCLXI. Columbia, S. C., 1861. $40.

4015   South Carolina Institution for the Education of the Deaf and Dumb, and the Blind. Fourteenth annual report, 1862. Columbia, 1862. $40.

4019   Virginia Military Institute. Register of the officers and cadets of the Virginia Military Institute, Lexington, Virginia, July 1863. Richmond, 1863. $250.

4022   VIRGINIA UNIVERSITY, *Charlottesville* University of Virginia. List of the distinguished, proficients & graduates, session 1860-61 . . . Charlottesville, 1861 *Broadside*. $300.

4025   **WILEY,** Calvin Henderson. Circular, to the authorities and People of North Carolina. Greensboro, N. C., 1863. $150.

TEXT BOOKS

4036   **CAMPBELL,** William A. The child's first book. Richmond, 1864. $250.

4039   **CHAUDRON,** Adelaide De Vendel. Chaudron's spelling book . . . Mobile, 1865. Fourth edition - thirtieth thousand. $200.

4040   **CHAUDRON,** Adelaide De Vendel. Chaudron's spelling book . . . Mobile, 1865. Fifth edition - fortieth thousand. $200.

4059   **JOHNSON,** L. An elementary arithmetic, designed for beginners . . . Raleigh, 1864. $200.

4061   **LANDER,** S. Our own school arithmetic. Richmond, Va., 1863. $300.

4068   **MOORE,** *Mrs.* Marinda Branson. The first Dixie reader; designed to follow the Dixie primer. Raleigh, 1863. $350.

4070   **MOORE,** Marinda Branson. The geographical reader, for the Dixie children. Raleigh, 1863. Issued with 6 double page maps. Occurs with maps colored and uncolored. $1500.

4074-1   **CUSHING,** E. H. (ed.). The New Texas Reader. Designed for the use of schools in
(H 1375) Texas. Houston, 1864. $1500.

4086   **SMITH,** Richard McAllister. The Confederate spelling book . . . Richmond, 1865. $100.

4088   **SMITH,** Richard McAllister. Smith's English grammar, on the productive system . . . Richmond, 1863. $350.

4097   **STERLING,** Richard. Our own first reader . . . Greensboro, 1862. $125.

4105   **STERLING,** Richard. Our own third reader: for the use of schools and families. Greensboro, N.C., and Richmond, Va., 1863? $250.

4107   **STEWART,** Kensey Johns. A geography for beginners. Richmond, 1864. $100.

4121   **YORK,** Brantley. York's English grammar revised and adapted to Southern schools. Raleigh, 1864. $150.

SERMONS

4136   **DOGGETT,** David Seth. A nation's Ebenezer . . . Richmond, 1862. $40.

4144   **ELLIOTT,** Stephen. God's presence with our army at Manassas! . . . Savannah, 1861. $200.

4161   **JONES,** John. The Southern soldier's duty; . . . Rome, 1861. $300.

4175   **PALMER,** Benjamin Morgan. A discourse before the General Assembly of South Carolina, on December 10, 1863 . . . Columbia, 1864. $50.

4194   **STILES,** Joseph Clay. National rectitude the only true basis of national prosperity . . . Petersburg, 1863. $50.

BIBLES

4215   The New Testament of our Lord and Savior Jesus Christ . . . Atlanta, 1862. $300.

4216   The New Testament of our Lord and Saviour Jesus Christ . . . Atlanta, Ga., 1862. $400.

DEVOTIONALS

4221-1   Patriotic Prayer for the Southern cause. n.p., 186-? $200.
(H 1420)

4222   Prayers and other devotions for the use of the soldiers of the Army of the Confederate States. Charleston, 186-. $50.

4232   The army and navy prayer book. Richmond, 1865. $300.

4233   Prayer book for the camp. Richmond, 1863. $200.

HYMN BOOKS

4241   A collection of Sabbath School hymns . . . Raleigh, 1863. $125.

4246   HYMNS for the camp . . . Raleigh, 1864. $300.

4247   Hymns for the camp. Second edition . . . Raleigh, 1862. $200.

4248   Hymns for the camp. Third edition . . . Raleigh, 186-. $200.

4250   THE SOLDIER'S hymn book . . . Charleston, 1863. $300.

CATECHISMS AND BIBLE STUDY

4261   **ROOT,** Sidney. Primary Bible questions for young children. Third edition . . . Atlanta, 1864. $70.

MISCELLANEOUS RELIGIOUS WRITINGS

4275   **McGILL,** John. Faith, the victory . . . Richmond, 1865. $125.

4286   **TUCKER,** John Randolph. The bible or atheism. Richmond?, 186-. $175.

CHURCH PUBLICATIONS

4385   Minutes of the forty-second anniversary of the State Convention of the Baptist Denomination in S. C., held at Greenville, July 25th-28th, 1862. Columbia, S.C., 1862. $75.

4468   Minutes of the seventy-fourth annual session of the South Carolina Conference of the Methodist Episcopal Church, South, held in Chester, S.C., commencing Thursday, December 12th, 1861. Charleston, 1862. $50.

4478   Minutes of the General Assembly of the Presbyterian Church in the Confederate States . . . Augusta, 1861. $60.

TRACTS

4578-1   BETHEL. *n.p.,* 186-?. $100.
(H 1631)

4579   BIBLE . . . The soldier's pocket Bible. Issued for the use of the army of Oliver Cromwell. (Original title page.) The soldier's pocket Bible . . . Charleston, S.C. 186-. $150.

4674   **GRASTY,** John Sharshall. A Noble Testimony. Raleigh, 186-. $50.

4689   **HEBER,** Reginald. Noah's carpenters. Raleigh, 186-. $50.

4716-1   It is I! Richmond?, 1861? $50.
(H 1664)

SOCIETIES AND CHARITIES

4967   By-laws of the Orphan House of Charleston . . . Charleston, 1861. $40.

4972   Proceedings of the State Bible Convention of South Carolina . . . Columbia, 1862. $50.

ALMANACS

4988   The Confederate States almanac . . . Second edition. Vicksburg, 1861. $250.

4990   . . . THE CONFEDERATE States almanac, and repository of useful knowledge. For the year 1864 . . . Mobile, Ala., 1863. $250.

4995   Confederate States almanac for the year of our Lord 1864 . . . Mobile, 1863. $250.

4996   Confederate States almanac for the year of our Lord 1864 . . . Macon, 1863. $250.

5026   Miller's planters' & merchants' state rights almanac, for the year of our Lord 1862 . . . Charleston, 1861. $100.

5034   Richardson's Virginia & North Carolina almanac, for the year of our Lord 1862. Richmond, 1861. $100.

FRATERNAL ORGANIZATIONS

5072   Proceedings of the annual communication of the Grand Lodge of Alabama . . . Montgomery, 1861. $50.

5073   Proceedings of the annual communication of the Grand Lodge of Alabama . . . Montgomery, 1862. $50.

5093   Proceedings of the Grand Lodge of Free and Accepted Masons of North Carolina . . . Raleigh, 1865. $100.

5102   Free masonry and the war. Report of the committee under the resolutions of 1862, Grand Lodge of Virginia . . . Richmond, 1865. $40.

5112   By-laws and list of members of Richmond Lodge, No. 10 . . . Richmond, 1864. $60.

NEWSPAPERS AND PERIODICALS

5135   *The Charleston Daily Courier.* Charleston, 1861-65. Per issue $50.

5136   *The Charleston Mercury.* Charleston, 1861-65. Per issue $25.

5265   *The Southern Illustrated News.* Richmond, 1862-64. Vol. I-III. 2000 per volume. Individual issues range from $50 - $200 each.

5266   *The Southern Literary Messenger.* Richmond, 1861-64. Per issue $20.

UNRECORDED IMPRINTS

OFFICIAL

- - - -   Charleston Mercury Extra: . . . An ordinance to dissolve the Union . . . [Charleston, 1860]. Broadside. $2500.

- - - -   The Constitution of the Confederate States of America Adopted March 11, 1861. n.p., n.d. $400.

- - - -   The Courier Extra. Charleston, Feb. 18, 1861. Broadside. Jefferson Davis' inaugural address, printed in two sections. $300.

- - - - Evidence taken before the committee of the House of Representatives appointed to enquire into the treatment of prisoners at Castle Thunder. Richmond, 1863. $150.

- - - - Georgia. Militia. General orders . . . Milledgeville, 1862. No. 24, Dec. 27, 1862. Small broadside measuring 23½ x 11 cm. $150.

- - - - The ordinance of secession: a poll to take the sense of the qualified voters of this commonwealth upon the ratification or rejection of 'An Ordinance to repeal the ratification of the Constitution of the United States of America, by the State of Virginia . . . , adopted in convention . . . on the 17th day of April, 1861 . . . n.p., 1861. $450.

- - - - Rules of the House and joint rules of both houses of the legislature of Texas. Austin, 1863. $250.

- - - - Tax in kind: Instructions on various procedures for taxing in kind. Richmond, 1863. $20.

UNOFFICIAL

- - - - BIBLE. New Testament. The New Testament of our Lord and Savior Jesus Christ . . . Nashville, 1861. $175.

- - - - **HORNADY,** Henry Carr. How to be saved. Macon, Ga., 186-. $150.

- - - - **McCARTHY,** Henry. The bonnie blue flag. n.p., n.d. Broadside. $175.

- - - - **MOORE,** William D. . . . The new Confederate flag song book. Mobile, Ala., 1864. $300.

- - - - **RANDALL,** James Ryder. Maryland. Air—"My Normandy!" n.p., n.d. Broadside. 2 cols. $225.

- - - - **SHERWOOD,** A. Conversation in a text. Macon, [Ga.], n.d. Ga. Bib. & Col. Society . . . No. 13. $60.

- - - - A song of the Trinity. Air—'Rock of Ages.' Augusta, Dec. 30, 1864. Broadside. $250.

- - - - State Journal Extra. n.p., 1864. Broadside. $200.

- - - - **STERLING,** Richard. Our own first reader: for the use of schools and families. Greensboro, N.C., Richmond, Va., 1862. $275.

- - - - To Churchmen: Memorial to the General Council of the Protestant Episcopal Church in the Confederate States . . . Montgomery, 1862. $50.

- - - - The Westminster shorter catechism . . . Richmond, 1862. $75.